Building Web Services with Java: Making Sense of XML, SOAP, WSDL, and UDDI

Steve Graham, Simeon Simeonov, Toufic Boubez,
Doug Davis, Glen Daniels, Yuichi Nakamura, Ryo Neyama

201 West 103rd St., Indianapolis, Indiana, 46290 USA

Building Web Services with Java: Making Sense of XML, SOAP, WSDL, and UDDI

Copyright © 2002 by Sams Publishing

International Standard Book Number: 0-672-32181-5

Library of Congress Catalog Card Number: 2001090920

Printed in the United States of America

First Printing: December 2001

04   03   02   4   3

Trademarks

All terms mentioned in this book that are known to be trademarks or service marks have been appropriately capitalized. Sams Publishing cannot attest to the accuracy of this information. Use of a term in this book should not be regarded as affecting the validity of any trademark or service mark.

Warning and Disclaimer

Every effort has been made to make this book as complete and as accurate as possible, but no warranty or fitness is implied. The information provided is on an "as is" basis. The authors and the publisher shall have neither liability nor responsibility to any person or entity with respect to any loss or damages arising from the information contained in this book.

EXECUTIVE EDITOR
Michael Stephens

ACQUISITIONS EDITOR
Michael Stephens

DEVELOPMENT EDITOR
Tiffany Taylor

MANAGING EDITOR
Matt Purcell

PROJECT EDITOR
Christina Smith

COPY EDITOR
Tiffany Taylor

INDEXER
Eric Schroeder

PROOFREADER
Plan-It Publishing

TECHNICAL EDITOR
Chad Fowler
Craig Pfiefer

TEAM COORDINATOR
Pamalee Nelson

MEDIA DEVELOPER
Dan Scherf

INTERIOR DESIGNER
Anne Jones

COVER DESIGNER
Aren Howell

PAGE LAYOUT
Heather Stephenson

Contents at a Glance

Table of Contents

About the Authors

Steve Graham is an architect in the Emerging Technologies division of IBM Software Group. He has spent the last several years working on service-oriented architectures, most recently as part of the IBM Web Services Initiative. Prior to this, Steve worked as a technologist and consultant on various emerging technologies such as Java and XML, and before that he was an architect and consultant with the IBM Smalltalk consulting organization.

Before joining IBM, Steve was a developer with Sybase, a consultant, and a faculty member in the Department of Computer Science at the University of Waterloo. Steve holds a BMath and MMAth in computer science from the University of Waterloo. You can reach him at `sggraham@us.ibm.com`.

Simeon (Sim) Simeonov has been developing software for more than 15 years. Sim's areas of expertise encompass object-oriented technology, compiler theory, Internet tools, enterprise computing, and the broad spectrum of XML technologies. As chief architect at Macromedia Inc., Sim provides direction for the evolution of the company's technology and product strategy as well as the architecture of its server-side platform products. Previously, Sim was chief architect at Allaire Corporation, where his initiatives brought about numerous innovations to the core product lines.

Sim is currently working on service-oriented architectures for the next generation of distributed XInternet applications. He is actively involved with the Java Community Process in the areas of Internet applications, XML, and Web Services. Sim also represents Macromedia on the W3C working group on XML Protocol. He is a regular speaker at conferences and a monthly columnist for *XML Journal*. Sim holds a B.A. in Computer Science, Economics, and Mathematics and a MSc in Computer Science.

Toufic Boubez is the chief technology officer of Saffron Technology. Prior to joining Saffron, he was a senior technologist in IBM's Emerging Technologies group, and lead architect of IBM's Web services initiative. He was IBM's technical representative to the UDDI Web Services Consortium with Microsoft and Ariba and co-authored the UDDI API specification. He was also the IBM technical lead on the UN/CEFACT/OASIS ebXML initiative and helped drive IBM's early XML and Web services strategies.

Dr. Boubez has more than 15 years of experience in IT and has published and presented on Web services, XML, object technology, distributed computing, intelligent agents, B2B, business modeling, simulation, neural networks, and wavelet analysis. He holds a doctorate in Biomedical Engineering from Rutgers University.

Doug Davis works in the Emerging Technology organization of IBM, working on IBM's Web Services Toolkit, and he is one of IBM's representatives in the W3C XML Protocol working group. Previous projects include WebSphere's Machine Translation project, TeamConnection, and IBM's FORTRAN 90 compiler. Doug has a Bachelor of Science degree from the University of California at Davis and a Master's degree in Computer Science from Michigan State University.

Glen Daniels, in his 13 years in the software industry, has run the gamut from device drivers and network stacks up through user interface and Web site work, in everything from assembly language to C++ to Lisp. Distributed computing has always been a passion, and as such he is currently technical lead for the JRun Web Services team at Macromedia. Glen is an active member of the W3C XML Protocol group as well as one of the lead developers of Axis. When not coding, he can often be found playing bass or harmonica, hanging out with his many crazy friends in the Boston area, or relaxing with his cats.

Yuichi Nakamura is an advisory researcher at the IBM Tokyo Research Laboratory. His research interests are Web services including SOAP and XML security, object-oriented systems, J2EE, multiagent systems, B2B e-commerce, and knowledge engineering. He received an MSc and a PhD in Applied Physics from Osaka University in 1987 and 1990, respectively.

Ryo Neyama is a researcher at the IBM Tokyo Research Laboratory. His research interests are distributed object systems including Web services, object request brokers, and security. He received an MSc in Information and Computer Science from Waseda University in 1999.

Acknowledgments

To Karen, Erin and Jessie, my family, my inspiration. For all the moments sacrificed to create this book, my most heartfelt thanks for your understanding.

My thanks to my coworkers at IBM, and in particular the WSTK team for doing such an outstanding job. My thanks also to Rod Smith for fostering an excellent environment for creative work.

My thanks also to the staff at Sams, particularly Tiffany Taylor and Michael Stephens, for the hard work that went into making this project a reality.

Romans 12:2.

—Steve Graham

It is much easier to write a book when others believe you can. My deepest thanks to Pyrra: my true love and a constant source of inspiration. Thanks also to all my friends and co-workers who never stopped being interested in Web services and the progress of the book. See? It's done.

—Sim Simeonov

To Lucy and Yasmine: Thank you for your patience, love, and understanding. This was a major undertaking for a new dad with another full-time job. To my old IBM team, Sam Adams, Steve Burbeck, Jay Casler, Steve Graham, Maryann Hondo, and Rod Smith, thank you for the great, challenging, and receptive work environment. I seriously don't think the concept of Web services would have evolved to where it is today in a different environment. To my new team at Saffron, thank you for replicating that environment!

—Toufic Boubez

Lin—I owe so many things to your patience, support, and most of all your sense of humor. I can never say it enough, but thank you.

—Doug Davis

For all my friends and family who so patiently continue to be there for me through even the busiest times—love and thanks to all of you.

—Glen Daniels

To Michiyo: Thank you for your understanding and patience during this work. Thanks to my kids, Arisa and Ryotaro: You always made me happy with your lovely smiles.

My thanks to all XML and Security team members at IBM Tokyo Research Laboratory.

—Yuichi Nakamura

My thanks to my parents, Jun and Sachie, for bringing me up and always supporting me. My thanks also to Takako and my friends for their encouragement and understanding.

My thanks to my coworkers at IBM Tokyo Research Laboratory for their deep insights on Web services and related technologies.

—Ryo Neyama

Tell Us What You Think!

As the reader of this book, *you* are our most important critic and commentator. We value your opinion and want to know what we're doing right, what we could do better, what areas you'd like to see us publish in, and any other words of wisdom you're willing to pass our way.

As an Executive Editor for Sams Publishing, I welcome your comments. You can fax, e-mail, or write me directly to let me know what you did or didn't like about this book—as well as what we can do to make our books stronger.

Please note that I cannot help you with technical problems related to the topic of this book, and that due to the high volume of mail I receive, I might not be able to reply to every message.

When you write, please be sure to include this book's title and authors' names as well as your name and phone or fax number. I will carefully review your comments and share them with the authors and editors who worked on the book.

Fax: 317-581-4770

E-mail: feedback@samspublishing.com

Mail: Michael Stephens
          Executive Editor
          Sams Publishing
          201 West 103rd Street
          Indianapolis, IN 46290 USA

Introduction

Welcome to the world of Web services! This is a rapidly evolving set of standards and implementation technologies that have great promise for the world of application integration and distributed computing.

Before we get going, we need to clarify some things about the purpose and structure of the book. Let's talk about them now.

Goals of this Book

The overall goal of this book is to familiarize you with the concept of Web services and what it will take to incorporate Web services as part of your business.

We will introduce the concept of Web services and give you a framework that describes how you can position the various emerging standards that are associated with Web services, such as Simple Object Access Protocol (SOAP), Web Services Description Language (WSDL), and Universal Description Discovery and Integration (UDDI).

We will help position Web services from a business and technical perspective, explaining and demonstrating how Web services can be used to address various business problems, particularly related to application integration.

Another goal of this book is to help developers understand the issues and details related to building Web services using the techniques covered by this book. What pieces are required when you're planning a Web services strategy? What things do you need to take care of when developing Web services? We provide lots of examples and running code to demonstrate these approaches. We also review in detail the Apache Axis Web services infrastructure with our running examples. Other tools and Web services infrastructures are discussed as well, but not in the same detail as Axis.

Assumed Background

This book is meant for computing technical professionals with some experience building Web applications and distributed computing systems. You don't need to be a seasoned veteran of the distributed object wars to appreciate this book, but some familiarity with Web-based architectures and techniques such as HTTP and HTML is assumed. If you do not have any experience with these techniques, some of the material could be a little confusing—particularly some of the code examples—but you should still be able to get a lot out of this book.

We assume you are familiar with Java, and in particular the Java Server Pages (JSP) and Java servlet technologies. We also briefly discuss the relationship between Enterprise Java Beans (EJBs) and Web services, so some familiarity with EJBs is helpful as well. If you need to supplement your understanding of these techniques, many, many good books on programming with Java, JSP, servlets, and EJB are available on the market.

You will also discover that the Extensible Markup Language (XML) is at the core of all things dealing with Web service. Although we devote an entire chapter to explaining the core pieces of XML needed to build Web services, the more understanding of XML you have, the more successful you will be in building Web services.

Philosophy

It is difficult to structure a book on Web services. The concepts and standards are very much interdependent. It is hard to cover each topic in isolation, because it is the combination of these concepts and standards that make Web services important to distributed computing.

The philosophy of this book can be summarized by four points: pragmatics, progressive disclosure, a running example, and a service-oriented architecture framework.

Pragmatics

In this book, we try to get to programming examples and running code as quickly as possible. In particular, we focus on building and consuming SOAP-based Web services using the Apache Axis Web services infrastructure. This is a Java-centric approach to building Web services. Whereas we emphasize that Web services are fundamentally programming language neutral, ultimately, any given Web service is implemented in some programming language technology. In the case of this book, we have chosen Java. Where issues of interoperability with Web services written in other programming languages might appear, we note them. Detailed coverage of other Web services implementation approaches, such as Microsoft's .NET, is beyond the scope of this book, although we do give some basic examples of .NET and other environments in Chapter 8, "Interoperability, Tools, and Middleware Products."

Progressive Disclosure

After the overview of Web services, we start with the fundamentals of XML, and then layer on new concepts, motivated by a business computing problem. These layers produce a series of Web services technology "stacks." For each of the technologies and standards in the Web services arena, we focus on understanding the technology from the perspective of what problems it solves, balancing the explanation of the technology itself.

Running Example

The technologies and standards that make up the Web services concept are each examined in the context of a running example (which we discuss later in this introduction). The use of the running example adds insight to the explanation of the concept in the text of the book and supports the progressive disclosure approach as we follow the example, adding the layers of Web services technology to the solution. This approach helps position various best-practices approaches to Web service development and deployment. You can download the source code for these running examples from `www.samspublishing.com`. When you reach that page, enter this book's ISBN number (0672321815) in the search box to access information about the book and a Source Code link.

Service-Oriented Architecture

The examples and Web services concepts are discussed in the context of a service-oriented architecture (SOA) that we introduce in Chapter 1, "Web Services Overview." We use the SOA framework to help position the various Web services concepts back into a bigger picture.

Overview of the Book's Composition

Chapter 1 begins the book with an explanation of what the Web services approach is all about. We describe what a Web service is, what standards and technologies are associated with Web services, and what problems can be solved using Web services. We use this chapter to introduce the SOA conceptual framework and begin to explain how the various Web services standards such as SOAP, WSDL, and UDDI fit together. This chapter will give you a solid conceptual basis for the rest of the book.

Before we can get into the core Web services standards, we take a brief side trip to explain XML in Chapter 2, "XML Primer." Because XML is at the heart of all the Web services standards and techniques, it is important you understand it well. XML is a huge topic, but we focus our examination of XML on what you will need to know in order to understand the rest of the Web services topics.

After the review of XML, Chapter 3, "Simple Object Access Protocol (SOAP)," dives in to the core problem of invoking a Web service. We review the topic of XML messaging in a distributed computing environment, focusing on the SOAP message enveloping standard. SOAP forms the core basis of communication between a service requestor and a service provider in a Web services environment.

Chapter 4, "Creating Web Services," refines your understanding of SOAP in the context of a particular SOAP infrastructure: the Apache Axis project. Chapter 4 dives into the details of how Axis works and how you can use it to make it easy to deploy Web services and have your applications consume Web services.

At this point, you will have a great background understanding of SOAP and at least one way to make SOAP real: Axis. But SOAP alone is not enough to do more than very simple Web services. Chapter 5, "Using SOAP for e-Business," adds detail to the concepts introduced in Chapters 3 and 4 by explaining how you can build Web services for complete business computing problems. Chapter 5 discusses how Web services addresses many distributed computing problems including security, performance, quality of service, reliability, and so on.

Chapter 6, "Describing Web Services," introduces the important notion of service description, which is key to making Web services the great application integration technology for building loosely coupled systems. Chapter 6 discusses how Web services uses service description to address the problem of communicating what details the service requestor needs to know about the Web service in order to properly understand how (and why) to invoke it.

Now, you need to understand how the service requestor got the service description in the first place. Chapter 7, "Discovering Web Services," picks up where Chapter 6 left off, discussing the various techniques for Web service discovery. This chapter examines the standards related to finding what Web services are provided by businesses with which a company might want to collaborate.

Chapter 8, "Interoperability, Tools, and Middleware Products," fills out your understanding of best practices in the Web services arena by examining various other Web services infrastructure and tooling environments.

The book concludes with a forward-looking Chapter 9, "Future Concepts," which speculates on some possible future uses of Web services technologies to address other problems in distributed computing.

> **NOTE**
>
> This book introduces quite a few terms with which you might not be familiar. We have included a glossary at the back of this book that acts as a great reference guide to the terminology used in the book. We will annotate the first use of each term appearing in the glossary using the 📖 symbol.

So, before we get started, let's introduce the fictional company we'll use for our examples throughout this book: SkatesTown. We will follow SkatesTown as the company exploits Web services to improve its business.

Introducing SkatesTown

SkatesTown is a small but growing business in New York founded by three mechanically inclined friends with a passion for cars and skateboards. They started by designing and selling custom pre-built boards out of Dean Carroll's garage, and word soon spread about the quality of their work. They came up with some innovative new construction techniques, and within months they had orders piling up. Now SkatesTown has a small manufacturing operation in Brooklyn, and the company is selling boards, clothing, and equipment to stores around the city. Dean, Frank Stemkowski, and Chad Washington couldn't be happier about how their business has grown.

Of the three, Chad is the real gearhead, and he has been responsible for most of the daring construction and design choices that have helped SkatesTown get where it is today. He's the president and head of the team. Frank, gregarious and a smooth talker ever since childhood, now handles marketing and sales. Dean has tightly tracked the computer revolution over the years, and is chief technical officer for the company.

A few years back, Dean realized that networking technology was going to be big, and he wanted to make sure that SkatesTown could catch the wave and utilize distributed computing to leverage its business. This focus turned out to be a great move.

Dean set up a Web presence so SkatesTown could help its customers stay up-to-date without requiring a large staff to answer phones and questions. He also built an online order-processing system to help streamline the actual flow of the business with network-enabled clients. In recent months, more and more stores who carry SkatesTown products have been using the system to great effect.

Our Story Begins...

At present, Dean is pretty happy with the way things are working with SkatesTown's electronic commerce systems. But there have been a few problems, and Dean is sure that things could be even better. He realizes that as the business grows, the manual tasks associated with order gathering and inventory resupply will limit the company's success. Always one to watch the horizon, Dean has heard the buzz about Web services, and wants to know more. At the urging of a friend, he got in touch with Al Rosen, a contractor for Silver Bullet Consulting. Silver Bullet specializes in Web services solutions, and after a couple of meetings with Al, Dean was convinced—he hired SBC to come in, evaluate SkatesTown's systems, and help the company grow into a Web service–enabled business.

As we move through the rest of the book, we'll keep an eye on how SkatesTown uses technologies like XML and, later, SOAP, WSDL, and UDDI to increase efficiency, productivity, and establish new and valuable relationships with its customers and business partners. Silver Bullet, as we'll see, usually lives up to its name.

Web Services Overview

IN THIS CHAPTER

In this chapter, we will provide the basic terminology and set of concepts that put the remainder of the book into context. We will define what we mean by a *Web service* 📖 and describe situations in which Web services will play an important role. We will describe a simple framework, called *service-oriented architecture* 📖, that helps structure the application of Web services technologies. We will also provide a framework, in the form of three "interoperability" stacks that position how the various Web services technologies such as *Simple Object Access Protocol (SOAP)* 📖, *Web Services Description Language (WSDL)* 📖, and *Universal Description Discovery and Integration (UDDI)* 📖 relate.

The rest of the book, then, is an elaboration of the basic concepts presented here.

What Is a Web Service?

This is a book about building Web services. We cannot describe how to build a Web service without first clarifying what we mean by a Web service.

The term *Web services* has gained a lot of momentum in the last year. Many software vendors (large and small) are announcing Web services initiatives and adoption (see the sidebar "Web Services Market Dynamics"). Many organizations are involved in the refinement of Web services standards. Although there seems to be a slow convergence towards a common understanding of what the term means, there is no single, universally adopted definition of what is meant by the term *Web service*. This situation is reminiscent of the early days of object-oriented programming: Not until the concepts of inheritance, encapsulation, and polymorphism were well defined did object-oriented programming become accepted into the mainstream of development methodologies.

Several major Web services infrastructure providers have published their definitions for a Web service:

IBM offers this definition at `http://www4.ibm.com/software/solutions/Webservices/` `pdf/WSCA.pdf`:

> "A Web service is an interface that describes a collection of operations that are network accessible through standardized XML messaging. Web services fulfill a specific task or a set of tasks. A Web service is described using a standard, formal XML notion, called its service description, that provides all of the details necessary to interact with the service, including message formats (that detail the operations), transport protocols, and location.
>
> The nature of the interface hides the implementation details of the service so that it can be used independently of the hardware or software platform on which it is implemented and independently of the programming language in which it is written. This allows and encourages Web services based applications to be loosely coupled, component-oriented, cross-technology implementations. Web services can be used alone or in conjunction with other Web services to carry out a complex aggregation or a business transaction."

Microsoft has a couple of definitions for Web service. The first is at `http://msdn.microsoft.com/library/default.asp?url=/nhp/Default.asp?contentid=28000442`:

> "A Web service is a unit of application logic providing data and services to other applications. Applications access Web services via ubiquitous Web protocols and data formats such as HTTP, XML, and SOAP, with no need to worry about how each Web service is implemented. Web services combine the best aspects of component-based development and the Web, and are a cornerstone of the Microsoft .NET programming model."

The other Microsoft definition is at `http://msdn.microsoft.com/library/default.asp?url=/library/en-us/dnWebsrv/html/Websvcs_platform.asp`:

> "A Web service is programmable application logic accessible using standard Internet protocols. Web services combine the best aspects of component-based development and the Web. Like components, Web services represent black-box functionality that can be reused without worrying about how the service is implemented. Unlike current component technologies, Web services are not accessed via object-model-specific protocols, such as the distributed Component Object Model (DCOM), Remote Method Invocation (RMI), or Internet Inter-ORB Protocol (IIOP). Instead, Web services are accessed via ubiquitous Web protocols and data formats, such as Hypertext Transfer Protocol (HTTP) and Extensible Markup Language (XML). Furthermore, a Web service interface is defined strictly in terms of the messages the Web service accepts and generates. Consumers of the Web service can be implemented on any platform in any programming language, as long as they can create and consume the messages defined for the Web service interface."

Sun provides the following definition at `http://www.sun.com/software/sunone/faq.html#2`:

> "Web services are software components that can be spontaneously discovered, combined, and recombined to provide a solution to the user's problem/request. The Java™ language and XML are the prominent technologies for Web services."

As you can see, there is broad agreement on what a Web service might be, but no single agreed-upon definition. Many developers will claim they cannot define what a Web service is, but they know one when they see one.

From the perspective of this book, a Web service is a *platform and implementation independent* software component that can be:

- *Described* using a service description language
- *Published* to a registry of services
- *Discovered* through a standard mechanism (at runtime or design time)
- *Invoked* through a declared API, usually over a network
- *Composed* with other services

One important point is that a Web service need not necessarily exist on the World Wide Web. This is an unfortunate historical naming issue. A Web service can live anywhere on the network, Inter- or intranet; some Web services can be invoked by a simple method invocation in the same operating system process, or perhaps using shared memory between tightly coupled processes running on the same machine. In fact, Web services have little to do with the browser-centric, HTML-focused World Wide Web. Sometimes, the names we choose in the information technology (IT) industry don't make a lot of sense; they simply take on a life of their own.

Another important point is that a Web service's implementation and deployment platform details are not relevant to a program that is invoking the service. A Web service is available through its declared API and invocation mechanism (network protocol, data encoding schemes, and so on). This is analogous to the relationship between a Web browser and a Web application server: Very little shared understanding exists between the two components. The Web browser doesn't particularly care if the Web application server is Apache Tomcat, Microsoft IIS, or IBM Websphere. The shared understanding is that they both speak HTTP and converse in HTML or a very limited set of MIME types. Similarly, the Web application server really doesn't care what kind of client is using it—various brands of Web browsers or even non-browser clients. This minimal shared understanding between components allows Web services to form a system of loosely coupled components.

Business Perspective

To a business person, the Web services approach is all about integration: integrating application functionality within an organization or integrating applications between business partners (in a supply chain, for example). The scenario in this book illustrates this approach, particularly in Chapter 7, "Discovering Web Services." This application integration allows time and cost efficiencies for receiving purchase orders, answering status inquiries, processing shipment requests, and so on. The important point is that application integration is enabled without tight lock-in to any particular business partner. If another supplier has a better price, shipping terms, or quality assurance, then a company's reorder systems can be easily repositioned to use that supplier; doing so is as easy as pointing a Web browser at a different Web site. With a broader adoption of Web services and XML document format standards, this style of dynamic business partner integration will become more broadly used.

When systems are this easy to integrate, an organization's reach to suppliers, customers, and other business partners is extended, yielding cost savings, flexible business models, better customer service, higher customer retention, and so on. Just as IT is fundamental to the efficient operations of an organization, Web services-based systems integration will be fundamental to flexible, lightweight systems integration—for internal application integration within an organization over an intranet and external partner integration over the Intranet or extended virtual private network.

So, from a business perspective, a Web service is a business process or step within a business process that is made available over a network to internal and/or external business partners to achieve some business goal.

Technical Perspective

From a technical perspective, a Web service is nothing more than a collection of one or more related operations that are accessible over a network and are described by a service description. At this level, the Web services concept is not new. With Web services, the IT industry is trying to address the fundamental challenge of distributed computing that has been around for decades—locating and accessing remote systems. The big difference is that now the industry is approaching this problem using open technology (XML and Internet protocols) and open standards managed by broad consortia such as the *World Wide Web Consortium* 📖 (W3C, which manages the evolution of the SOAP and WSDL specifications). Further, the approach often taken with Web services uses *capabilities-based lookup* 📖, where the kind of service is searched for, as opposed to a service of a particular name or object identifier.

The Web Service Opportunity

The Web services approach is an application integration concept; it is a set of technologies that provides access to business functionality, such as purchase order processing. Often, the business functionality already exists in the form of legacy transaction processing systems, existing Web applications, Enterprise Java Beans, and so on. Web services technology is about access and application integration; it is not an implementation technology.

Organizations use Web services technology in two broad categories: *Enterprise Application Integration (EAI)* 📖 and *business-to-business (B2B)* 📖 partner integration over the Internet. In either of these categories, Web services can range in sophistication from simple request response functions such as a credit card check to very complicated multi-party, multi-stage long-running business transactions such as a supply configuration and order system. Web services can be invoked by PC-based programs, mainframe systems, Web browsers, or even small mobile devices such as cell phones or personal digital assistants (PDAs).

Regardless of the application, Web services will be used for systems integration: flexible, loosely-coupled systems integration yielding systems that can be decomposed and recomposed to reflect changes in the business.

Enterprise Application Integration

Enterprise Application Integration is still a field where large consulting companies command multimillion dollar contracts to help their clients deal with a mess of applications that were never meant to interoperate.

The state of the art within many enterprise systems remains that of large, monolithic application "silos." These systems are often extremely difficult to change, let alone integrate with other systems. These applications often define unique data formats, and sometimes (for historical, often performance-related reasons) even define their own communications protocols. Furthermore, many systems, particularly in large organizations, can exist on multiple different platform technologies. Interoperability between systems is a significant challenge. In many organizations, particularly organizations that result from a merger of two previously independent companies, IT integration costs can seriously impact the financial health of the company.

The Web services approach offers an attractive set of technologies by which existing legacy systems can be wrapped as Web services and made available for integration with other systems within the organization. Applications exposed as Web services are accessible by other applications running on different hardware platforms and written in different programming languages. Using this approach, the complexity of these systems can be encapsulated behind industry-standard XML protocols. Pair-wise system integration projects can be replaced with one-to-many systems interactions based on Web services. The promise of higher-level interoperability initiatives is that over time we will be able to develop the set of standards, technologies, and tools that will enable small and large businesses all over the world to easily integrate systems internally, and then mix and match the implementation of various activities within a business process, maintaining the option to, at any time, choose to outsource any or all of these activities if doing so makes business sense.

For many organizations, their first implementations using Web services technology will be internal application integration, because that is the biggest problem for them to address with IT. Flexible systems will yield flexible business models. Flexible business models will yield organizations better able to adapt to changes in the business environment.

B2B

Another key driver behind the rise of Web services is the continuing evolution of B2B computing. B2B computing is about integrating the business systems of two or more companies to support cross-enterprise business processes such as supply chain management. Some industry pundits claim that supply chain integration will be the killer application of Web services, particularly as a result of the standardization of common industry formats for XML and Web services related to supply chain business processes. B2B applications can be as simple as automated credit card validation or as complex as the full automation of the multi-billion-dollar supply chain of a Fortune 100 company. The challenges of building B2B applications combined with their huge market potential drove rapid innovation that has taken the industry from simple *business-to-consumer (B2C)* applications to SOAP-enabled Web services in a matter of five years.

B2C, B2B, and Web services

Online HTML-based applications are consumer-oriented. The classic example of a B2C Web application is the Amazon book search. To access this functionality, a human being needs to use a Web browser to navigate the company's site through multiple page transitions, input information using Web forms, submit them, and get the results back in human-readable form. The only way to automate this process is to simulate how a human uses the system. Doing so involves reverse-engineering the Web application to see how it moves data between pages, passing the data automatically from page to page, and, finally, parsing any data contained in the response HTML of pages. This screen-scraping approach was popular in the early years of the Web (1995–97). It is very error prone. Any changes in the Web application—even changes that are completely UI-centric and do not change the data being passed back and forth—can break screen-scraping applications. These problems are compounded because most of these applications do not properly separate presentation from application processing logic. The only true way to integrate applications on the Web is to use a B2B-focused solution.

Because B2B applications are designed to have other applications as their clients, they are fundamentally different from B2C applications. Table 1.1 summarizes some of these differences for Java applications. Both types of application are unrestricted as to the type of backend they can use—typically, Java classes or Enterprise Java Beans (EJBs). (We discuss how Web services work with EJBs in more detail in Chapter 5, "Using SOAP for e-Business.") This is where the similarities end, however. To customize backend logic, B2C applications use servlets or Java Server Pages (JSPs) that are hosted in a servlet engine. B2B applications customize their backends using straight Java code (often EJBs) that is hosted inside a Web service engine. B2C applications communicate with a browser over HTTP. B2B applications can use any of the open Internet protocols such as HTTP, SMTP, or FTP, or proprietary networks such as EDI. B2C applications handle data over the straight HTTP protocol. Input comes as GET parameters (on the URL/query string) or as POST parameters from Web forms. Only strings can be exchanged. Any other datatypes, even numbers, need to be encoded as strings. For output, data is mixed together with formatting rules inside HTML pages. This is in marked contrast with B2B applications that use XML for both data input and output. XML is perfect for B2B computing because it is programming language- and platform-neutral, it can represent arbitrary data structures, it is easy to process, and it can be validated independently of its processing. B2C applications need to have some UI (typically HTML, although some have used Java applets) because their clients are humans. B2B applications have no UI because their clients are other applications.

TABLE 1.1   Comparing B2C and B2B Java Applications

Area	B2C application	B2B application
Backend logic	Java classes and EJBs	Java classes and EJBs
Custom logic	Servlets and JSPs	Web service engine
Communication protocol	HTTP	HTTP, SMTP, FTP, TCP/IP, EDI, JMS, RMI/IIOP…
Data input	HTTP GET/POST parameters	XML
Data output	HTML	XML
UI	HTML + script	N/A
Client	Human behind a browser	Software application

Trends in e-business

It is clear that the network economy is currently driving the evolution of business. Businesses must respond to increasingly dynamic marketplaces. Within corporate departments, application integration has been a major issue in the last few years. Traditional architectures are brittle, and this brittleness is being exposed as the scale, demand level, transaction volume, and rate of change of transaction volume increases.

Interoperability, particularly between heterogeneous distributed systems components, has been one of the major themes in software engineering in general, and EAI in particular, for the last decade. It's unfortunate that the seamless interoperability vision is still a dream. Brittleness in all current architectures is preventing software from achieving this vision. Brittleness comes from tightly coupled systems that generate dependencies at every level in the system. One of the most important lessons we learned as developers and architects is that systems need to be able to find resources (software or otherwise) automatically, when and as needed, without human intervention. This ability frees business people to concentrate on their business and customers rather than worry about IT complexities. At the same time, it frees system developers to concentrate on enabling their business and their customers rather than deal with interoperability headaches by writing glue code and patching systems together. More than any technical consideration, this concept of implicit, seamless integration as a major business benefit is one of the main drivers for service orientation. In other words, the time has come for "just in time" integration!

Trends in application design are moving from rigid structures to flexible architectures. Trends in business partner interactions are moving from static agreements to more dynamic agreements. Trends in B2B integration are moving from technology-based integration to business process-based integration. There is a corresponding shift in programming and architecture models to enable these trends: from tightly coupled applications to loosely coupled services.

On the technical side, major shifts have occurred toward flexibility and interoperability, through open and widely accepted standards. The first major shift happened two decades ago with the advent of TCP/IP as an open platform for networking. This step enabled such important and pervasive architectures as client-server computing. It took the advent of the World Wide Web for the next major shift, with HTML and HTTP providing the first truly universal open and portable user interface. Next, Java gave us truly open portable programming, and finally XML brought with it open portable data exchange. The next step in this evolution of open standards is the integration step. How do all these ingredients come together to facilitate the next evolution of e-business? Web services.

One aspect of more loosely coupled systems is reflected in the move from Remote Procedure Call (RPC) interfaces towards a messaging or *document-centric* 📖 model of distributed computing interface. With a document-centric approach, the interface to the Web service becomes much more simple and flexible. An RPC interface presenting a fixed set of parameters in a fixed order is quite brittle. Small changes to information required—for example, a new requirement for an expiration date on a credit card—require a new interface to be created, published, and understood by the service requestor. With a document-centric approach, the new information can be added to the document schema defined in the Web service interface. Programs that use the older schema don't necessarily break when the new XML element is added (this is a property of XML namespaces that you will see in Chapter 2, "XML Primer"). This approach yields Web services interfaces that are much more flexible, resulting in systems that are much more adaptive.

Web Services Market Dynamics

Most major software companies and many smaller software vendors have embraced the concept of Web services in one form or another. Some might just be giving it lip service, hedging on whether it's just another fad, or using it as a buzzword to generate marketing fodder. Others have staked their future on it. Here is a brief examination of the Web services initiatives from a few major players:

- IBM: Dynamic e-business—IBM provides a broad collection of Web services technology, including a SOAP stack as part of WebSphere (derived from Apache SOAP 2.2), WSDL tooling in the Web Services Toolkit, and a UDDI implementation. Many major products within IBM are incorporating the Web services approach in some fashion.

- Microsoft: .NET—It can be argued that Microsoft is "betting the business" on the success of .NET. Although .NET is based on Web services technologies, the

.NET initiative is much broader than Web services, including a new programming language, C#, and a common runtime layer upon which implementations of multiple programming languages can be built. We will look at .NET in more detail in Chapter 8, "Interoperability, Tools, and Middleware Products."

- *Sun: SunOne (Open Net Environment)*—Sun declared the notion of *smart Web services* that can somehow understand the context in which they were deployed or invoked (such as user identity, type of client device and privacy policy, and so on). Smart Web services includes a standard for sharing this notion of "context" and an infrastructure SunONE upon which to deploy it.

  Sun's approach to Web services is fairly similar to the approach taken by the other major IT vendors, in that Sun bases its Web services technology on the core XML, SOAP, WSDL, UDDI technology set. Sun also augments these technologies with technologies derived from ebXML. The details are not clear as to how these technologies merge together.

  Sun's sponsorship of the Java Community Process and its definition of Java specifications related to Web services is also a major component of the company's Web services initiative.

- *Oracle: Oracle 9i Web Services Broker*—The Oracle approach to Web services also follows the traditional SOAP, WSDL, UDDI perspective. Oracle emphasizes the role of its database technology as a service registry (broker) providing security and other value added services as an intermediary between service requestor and service provider.

- *Macromedia: Macromedia platform*—Macromedia has embraced Web services throughout its mass-enterprise platform. Its rich clients can display information retrieved through Web services, its application servers make building Web services possible for developers at all skill levels, and its tools provide high-level support for building applications that leverage Web services.

It is exciting to see so many software vendors active in Web services. With multiple vendors, there is a risk of incompatibility of implementations. Unless Web services from different vendors can interoperate, Web services will fail to attain critical mass of adoption. Happily, there is significant focus among the various Web services implementations to develop and maintain interoperability.

Chapter 8 will look at a collection of Web services implementations in the industry, from large software vendors to smaller boutique Web services infrastructure providers.

Why Do We Need a Web Services Approach?

The beginning of this chapter explained the motivation for application-to-application communication over the Internet to address the current challenges of distributed computing and B2B integration in particular. Since 1999, the software industry has been rapidly evolving XML-based Web services technologies as the approach to these problems. In the maelstrom of press hype, product releases, and standards announcements, many people have been left wondering whether this is a good in which direction to go. After all, we already have many different mechanisms for distributed computing. Surely, some of them would be able to rise to meet the challenges of e-business. Why build a completely new distributed computing stack based on Web services?

This is a very good question and one that is hard to give a short answer to. "Because Web services use XML" is not the right answer. It is a correct observation, but it doesn't answer the crucial question as to why using XML makes such a big difference. At a basic level, there are three key reasons why existing distributed computing approaches are inferior to Web services for solving the problems of e-business:

- The scope of problems they try to address
- The choice of available technology
- Industry dynamics around standards control and innovation

Scoping the Problem

Traditional distributed computing mechanisms have typically evolved around technical architectures rather than broader problems of application integration. For example, CORBA evolved as a solution to the problem of implementing rich distributed object architectures. At the time, it was implicitly assumed that this was the right approach to getting applications to communicate with one another. As we discussed earlier, experience has shown that RPCs are not always the best architecture for this requirement. The need for loosely coupled applications and business process automation has clearly shown the benefits of simply exchanging messages containing data (typically a business document) between the participants of e-business interactions, a so-called document-centric approach. Distributed computing specifications address messaging as a computing architecture; however, there has been no unifying approach that brings RPCs and messaging to the same level of importance—until Web services, that is.

Web services have evolved not around pre-defined architectures but around the problem of application integration. This is a very important distinction. The choice of problem scope defines the focus of a technology initiative. Web services technologies have been designed from the ground up to focus on the problems of application integration. As a result, we are able to do things outside the scope of traditional distributed computing approaches:

- Support both document-centric messaging and RPCs
- Transport encoded data from both applications and business documents
- Work over open Internet protocols such as HTTP and SMTP

In other words, Web services are better suited for the task than what we have so far because we have specifically built them with this in mind. COM/CORBA/RMI are still great technologies for tying together distributed objects on the corporate network. However, the e-business application integration problem is best tackled by Web services.

Core Technologies

Because Web services address a much more broadly scoped problem, they use much more flexible technologies than traditional distributed computing approaches. Further, with Web services we can leverage all that we have learned about connecting and integrating applications since we first started doing distributed computing. These two factors put Web services on a better technology foundation for solving the problems of e-business than traditional distributed computing approaches.

Later, in the "Web Services Interoperability Stacks" section, we introduce the notion of Web services interoperability stacks. These interoperability stacks organize a layering of technologies that define the capabilities of Web services. It is possible to compare the Web services approach to traditional distributed computing approaches level-by-level to see why the technical foundation of Web services is more appropriate for the problems it needs to solve. Rather than going through this lengthy process, let's focus on two key capabilities: the ability to represent data structures and the ability to describe these data structures.

Data encoding is a key weakness for traditional distributed computing approaches, particularly those that are programming language independent. Sure, they typically have a mechanism to represent simple data (numbers, strings, booleans, date-time values, and so on), basic arrays, and structures with properties. However, mapping existing complex datatypes in applications to the underlying data encoding mechanisms was very difficult. Adding new native datatypes was practically impossible (doing so required a complete update of specifications). The fact that data was encoded in binary formats further complicated matters. For example, processing code had to worry about little- vs. big-endian issues when reading and writing numbers.

Web services address these issues by using XML to represent information. XML's text-based form eliminates byte ordering concerns. The wide availability of XML processing tools makes participation in the world of Web services relatively easy. XML's hierarchical structure (achieved by the nesting of XML elements) allows changes at some level of nesting in an XML document to be made with ease without worrying about the effect on other parts of the document. Also, the expressive nature of attributes and nested elements makes it considerably easier to represent complex data structures in XML than in the pure binary formats tradition-ally used by COM and CORBA, for example. In short, XML makes working with arbitrary data easier.

The choice of XML brought another advantage to Web services—the ability to describe datatypes and validate whether data coming on the wire complies with its specification. This happens through the use of XML meta-languages such as XML Schema. Binary data encod-ings typically used for distributed computing offered no such mechanism and thus pushed data validation into application logic, considerably complicating applications dealing with non-trivial data.

Industry Dynamics

Momentum is a very important aspect of the dynamics of software innovation. Great problems gate great opportunities. The desire to capitalize on the opportunities generates momentum around a set of initiatives targeted at solving the problem. This momentum is the binding force of our industry. This is how major innovation takes place on a broad scale. The challenge of e-business application integration is great; this is why all the key players in the industry are focused on it (see the sidebar "Web Services Market Dynamics"). Customer need, market pres-sure, and the desire to be part of the frontier-defining elite have pushed many companies to become deeply engaged with Web services. Good things are bound to happen. Consider this: The last time every one of the key infrastructure vendors was focused on the same set of issues was during the early days of e-business when the industry was trying to address the challenges of building Web applications. The net result was a new model for application development that leveraged the Web browser as a universal client and the Web application server as a universal backend. In short, trust that some of the very best minds in the industry working together under the aegis of organizations such as the W3C and OASIS will be able to come up with a good solution to the problems of e-business integration.

To the veterans of the software industry, momentum sometimes equals hype. So, are we trying to say that Web services will succeed because there is so much hype around them? Absolutely not! The momentum around Web services is real and different from what we have experienced so far with other distributed computing fads. The fundamental difference is around the ability of many industry players to engage in complementary standardization *in parallel*.

Parallelism is key to building real momentum and increasing the bandwidth of innovation. Traditional distributed computing efforts could not achieve this kind of parallelism because they were either driven by a single vendor—Microsoft promoting COM, for example—or they were driven by a large, slow organization such as the Object Management Group (OMG), which owns the CORBA standards. In both cases, the key barrier to fast progress was the cen-tralized management of standards. Any change had to be approved by the body owning the standard. And Microsoft and OMG owned all of COM and CORBA, respectively. This is no way to gain real momentum, regardless of the size of the marketing budgets to promote any given technology. Vendors that feel they have very little control over the evolution of a technology will likely spend very little time investing in its evolution. In other words, you might use COM, but if you think you have no chance of influencing Microsoft's direction on COM you will probably not spend much time thinking about and prototyping ways to improve COM. Open-source efforts such as the Linux operating system and projects of the Apache Software Foundation fundamentally generate momentum because people working on them can have a direct influence on the end product. The momentum of Web services is real because standardization work is going on in parallel at the W3C, OASIS, UDDI, and many other horizontal and vertical industry standards organizations. Further, the major players so far have shown a commitment to do a lot of innovation out in the open.

The interesting thing from a technical perspective is that XML actually has something to do with the ability of Web service standardization to be parallelized. XML has facilities (namespaces and schema) that enable the decentralized evolution of XML-based standards without preventing the later composition of these standards in the context of a single solution. For example, if group A owns some standard and group B is trying to build an extension to the standard, then with some careful use of XML, group B can design the extensions such that:

- Its extension can be published independently of the standard.
- Its extension can be present in cases where the standard is used.
- Applications that do not understand the extension will not break if the extension is present.
- Applications that need the extension will only work if the extension is present.

The industry's focus on Web services combines the right scope (e-business application integration) with the right technologies (XML-based standards) with the potential for significant parallelism and high-bandwidth innovation. This is why Web services will be successful.

Distributed Computing History

Historically, distributed computing has been focused on the problem of distributing computation between several systems that are jointly working on a problem. The most often used distributed computing abstraction is the RPC. RPCs allow a remote function to be invoked as if it were a local one. Distributed object-oriented systems require object-based RPCs (ORPCs). ORPCs need some additional context to be able to invoke methods on specific object instances. The history of RPC-style distributed computing and distributed objects is fairly complicated. The following timeline illustrates some of the key events:

- 1987
  - Sun Microsystems developed the Open Network Computing (ONC) RPC system as the basic communication mechanism for its Network File System (NFS).
  - Apollo Computer developed the Network Computing System (NCS) RPC system for its Domain operating system.
- 1989
  - The Open Software Foundation (OSF, now The Open Group) issued a Request for Technology (RFT) for an RPC system. OSF received two key submissions. The first submission came from HP/DEC based on NCS (HP had acquired Apollo). The other submission came from Sun based on ONC. OSF selected NCS as the RPC mechanism for its Distributed Computing Environment (DCE).
  - The Object Management Group (OMG) was formed to deliver language- and platform-neutral specifications for distributed computing. (The consortium includes about 650 members as of the time of this writing.) The OMG began development of specifications for Common Object Request Broker Architecture (CORBA), a distributed objects platform.
- 1990
  - Microsoft based its RPC initiatives on a modified version of DCE/RPC.
- 1991
  - DCE 1.0 was released by OSF.
  - CORBA 1.0 shipped with a single language mapping for the C language. The term Object Request Broker (ORB) gained popularity to denote the infrastructure software that enables distributed objects.
- 1996
  - Microsoft shipped the Distributed Component Object Model (DCOM), which was closely tied to previous Microsoft component efforts such as Object Linking and Embedding (OLE), non-distributed COM (a.k.a. OLE2), and ActiveX (lightweight components for Web applications). The core DCOM capabilities are based on Microsoft's RPC technologies. DCOM is an ORPC protocol.
  - CORBA 2.0 shipped with major enhancements in the core distributed computing model as well as higher-level services that distributed objects could use. The Internet Inter-ORB Protocol (IIOP) was part of the specification. IIOP allows multiple ORBs to interoperate in a vendor-agnostic manner. IIOP is an ORPC protocol.

- 1997
  - Sun shipped JDK 1.1, which included Remote Method Invocation (RMI). RMI defines a model for distributed computing using Java objects. RMI is similar to CORBA and DCOM but works only with Java objects. RMI has an ORPC protocol called Java Remote Method Protocol (JRMP).
  - Microsoft announced the first iteration of COM+, the successor of DCOM. The capabilities of COM+ brought it much closer to the CORBA model for distributed computing.
- 1999
  - Sun shipped J2EE (Java 2 Platform Enterprise Edition). The Java 2 platform integrated RMI with IIOP, making it easy to interoperate between Java and CORBA systems.
  - Simple Object Access Protocol (SOAP) appeared for the first time. The era of Web services was born.

Although RPCs and distributed objects have been the traditional approaches for building distributed systems, they are by no means the only ones. Another very important approach is that of *data-oriented* or *document-centric* messaging. Rather than being focused on distributing computation by specifically invoking remote code, messaging takes a different approach. Applications that communicate via messaging run their own independent computations and communicate via messages that contain pure data. Messaging was popularized via the efforts of system integrators who were trying to get highly heterogeneous systems to interoperate. In most cases, the systems were so different that the requirement to perform fine-grain integration via RPCs was impossible to satisfy. Instead, system integrators were happy to be able to reliably move pure data between the systems. Commercially, the importance of messaging applications has been steadily growing since IBM released its messaging product MQSeries in 1993. Microsoft's messaging product is the Microsoft Message Queuing Server (MSMQ). J2EE defines a set of APIs for messaging through the Java Messaging Service (JMS). There has been no attempt to define a standard interoperability protocol for messaging servers.

One of the key benefits of Web services is that the core Web service protocols can support RPCs and messaging with equal ease. Chapter 3, "Simple Object Access Protocol (SOAP)," has a section that addresses this topic in detail.

Service-Oriented Architectures

Early on in the Web services technology evolution, we noticed a pattern. Each time we applied Web services technologies to an application integration problem, a pattern emerged. We called this pattern *service-oriented architecture (SOA)*. SOA is a simple concept, which makes it applicable to a wide variety of Web services situations. Figure 1.1 depicts the main roles and operations in an SOA.

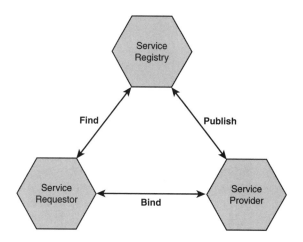

Figure 1.1
Service-oriented architecture.

Any service-oriented architecture contains three roles: a *service requestor* 📖, a *service provider* 📖, and a *service registry* 📖:

- A service provider is responsible for creating a *service description* 📖, publishing that service description to one or more service registries, and receiving Web service invocation messages from one or more service requestors. A service provider, then, can be any company that hosts a Web service made available on some network. You can think of a service provider as the "server side" of a client-server relationship between the service requestor and the service provider.

- A service requestor is responsible for finding a service description published to one or more service registries and is responsible for using service descriptions to bind to or invoke Web services hosted by service providers. Any consumer of a Web service can be considered a service requestor. You can think of a service requestor as the "client side" of a client-server relationship between the service requestor and the service provider.

- The service registry is responsible for advertising Web service descriptions published to it by service providers and for allowing service requestors to search the collection of service descriptions contained within the service registry. The service registry role is simple: be a match-maker between service requestor and service provider. Once the service registry makes the match, it is no longer needed in the picture; the rest of the interaction is directly between the service requestor and the service provider for the Web service invocation.

Each of these roles can be played by any program or network node. In some circumstances, a single program might fulfill multiple roles; for example, a program can be a service provider, providing a Web service to downstream consumers as well as a service requestor, itself consuming Web services provided by others.

An SOA also includes three operations: *publish* 📖, *find* 📖, and *bind* 📖. These operations define the contracts between the SOA roles:

- The publish operation is an act of service registration or service advertisement. It acts as the contract between the service registry and the service provider. When a service provider publishes its Web service description to a service registry, it is advertising the details of that Web service to a community of service requestors. The actual details of the publish API depend on how the service registry is implemented. In certain simple or "direct publish" scenarios, the service registry role is played by the network itself, with publish being simply an act of moving the service description into a Web application server's directory structure. Other services registry implementations, such as UDDI, define a very sophisticated implementation of the publish operation.

- The find operation is the logical dual of the publish operation. The find operation is the contract between a service requestor and a service registry. With the find operation, the service requestor states a search criteria, such as type of service, various other aspects of the service such as quality of service guarantees, and so on. The service registry matches the find criteria against its collection of published Web service descriptions. The result of the find operation is a list of service descriptions that match the find criteria. Of course, the sophistication of the find operation varies with the implementation of the service registry role. Simple service registries can provide a find operation with nothing more sophisticated than an unparameterized HTTP GET. This means the find operation always returns all Web services published to the service registry and it is the service requestor's job to figure out which Web service description matches its needs. UDDI, of course, provides extremely powerful find capabilities.

- The bind operation embodies the client-server relationship between the service requestor and the service provider. The bind operation can be quite sophisticated and dynamic, such as on-the-fly generation of a client-side proxy based on the service description used to invoke the Web service; or it can be a very static model, where a developer hand-codes the way a client application invokes a Web service.

The key to SOA is the service description. It is the service description that is published by the service provider to the service registry. It is the service description that is retrieved by the service requestor as a result of the find operation. It is a service description that tells the service requestor everything it needs to know in order to bind to or invoke the Web service provided by the service provider. The service description also indicates what information (if any) is returned to the service requestor as a result of the Web service invocation.

Each time a service-oriented architecture is deployed, there might be different technologies to fulfill each role. Chapter 7, "Discovering Web Services," discusses various options for implementing a service registry and goes into great detail on the UDDI service registry technology. Chapter 6, "Describing Web Services," discusses service description and how a service description can be used to automate the task of building a client-side proxy to the Web service and a server-side skeleton to dispatch the Web service invocation to the target Web service implementation. Chapters 3 and 4, "Simple Object Access Protocol (SOAP)" and "Creating Web Services," focus on the use of SOAP to fulfill the bind operation; Chapter 5, "Using SOAP for e-Business," details how the bind can be made ready for e-business.

Web Services Interoperability Stacks

An alphabet soup of technologies is swimming around the Web services space. We have XML, SOAP, WSDL, UDDI, WSEL, WSFL, and more. How can anyone make sense of what these technologies are and how they fit together? Well, that is one of the purposes of this book.

To help put a framework around these technologies, we refer to a trio of Web services interoperability stacks, first proposed to the W3C by IBM and Microsoft in March 2001 (`http://www.w3.org/2001/03/WSWS-popa/paper51`). This proposal factored Web services technologies into three stacks:

- The wire stack
- The description stack
- The discovery stack

The contents of the stacks presented in this book reflect a different factoring than originally proposed to the W3C, due in part to the additional standards efforts that have come into play since March 2001.

The Wire Stack

Figure 1.2 shows the wire stack as we define it.

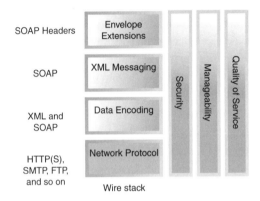

FIGURE 1.2

The wire stack.

The wire stack represents the technologies that determine how a message is sent from the service requestor to the service provider. The base of the wire stack is a network protocol. Web services can be based on a variety of standard, Internet wire protocols such as HTTP or HTTPS, SMTP, FTP, and so on, as well as sophisticated enterprise-level protocols such as RMI/IIOP and MQSeries.

For data encoding, Web services use XML. In addition, non-XML content can be referenced from a Web service invocation message, allowing full flexibility in the kinds of data used in the message. For data specification, Web services use XML Schema. This includes both custom schemas in the case of XML messaging or schemas conforming to a set of pre-defined rules, such as the SOAP encoding rules discussed in Chapter 3.

Built on top of the networking protocol and data-encoding layers are the XML messaging layers. For XML messaging, Web services use SOAP in all its data encoding, interaction style, and protocol binding variations. SOAP is used as a simple approach to wrapper an XML message in an envelope. The result is a solid, standards-based foundation for Web services.

Conceptually layered on top of the SOAP enveloping mechanism is a mechanism for envelope extensions called SOAP *headers* 📖. With SOAP headers, orthogonal extensions such as a digital signature can be associated with the body of the message contained within the SOAP envelope. Chapter 3 will give details on the SOAP enveloping mechanism and the SOAP header facility.

The layers of this stack are well defined, either as standard networking protocols or as the SOAP specification itself. This stack is the most accepted and most widely deployed set of technologies for Web services.

At right in Figure 1.2 are three vertical columns representing associated technologies that impact multiple levels of the wire stack. Security, for example, can appear at each level—SSL at the network protocol level and digital signatures at the envelope extensions level, for instance. It is doubtful there will ever be a single standard that fits all aspects of Web services security needs. Chapter 5 goes into more detail on the current Web services–related security technologies like XML digital signatures and XML cryptography. Other vertical towers listed include Quality of Service and Manageability. These are just a handful of facets of Web services that can appear at several levels of the wire stack. There is no well-accepted standard for these facets, but work is underway in these areas.

The Description Stack

The wire stack is only where the capabilities of Web services begin. Even the simplest example of Web service use shows the need for a higher level of interoperability.

Consider the following situation (we'll see this example in greater detail in Chapter 3). A company has provided an inventory checking service, allowing customers to determine whether a particular number of items are in stock for a given product code (as represented as a stock keeping unit [SKU]). The Web service takes as parameters a string representing the SKU and an integer representing the number of units needed. If the company has on hand the requested number of units, the Web service responds with a Boolean true value; otherwise, the response is a Boolean false.

From a pure SOAP perspective, the interaction with this Web service is trivial. However, things get much more complicated when we consider how much common understanding must exist between the service requestor and the service provider. For the interaction to succeed, at a minimum, the service requestor needs to know the following:

- The address of the Web service.
- It should make requests and receive responses over HTTP.
- It should use SOAP 1.1.
- Requests and responses should use the SOAP data encoding.
- Requests will be RPC requests containing as parameters a string SKU and an integer indicating the desired quantity.
- Responses will be RPC responses containing a Boolean indicating the inventory check outcome.

Throw in security, payments, error handling, and other capabilities required to build enterprise-grade Web services, and the need for shared knowledge expands even further.... How can the service requestor acquire this information? Well, traditionally Web services have advertised their capabilities in some human readable form. Developers have read the description of these capabilities and configured user applications to be able to communicate with particular Web services.

While this approach works in principle, it is not scalable for many reasons:

- It requires costly (in terms of both time and money) manual configuration by highly skilled, and therefore scarce, personnel.
- It is error prone because it does not utilize formalized service specifications.
- It precludes automatic discovery and engagement of Web services; *a priori* knowledge is required for configuration of the user application.
- No built-in mechanism exists for change notifications and/or failure recovery; every time a Web service evolves, there is a risk that existing user applications will fail.

These are some of the reasons why industry leaders are developing the standards described in a service description stack. Figure 1.3 shows the service description stack.

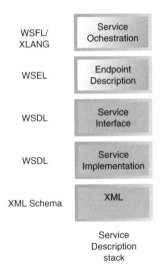

FIGURE 1.3

The service description stack.

Key to the entire service-oriented architecture approach is the service description itself. Many aspects of a Web service need to be communicated, and therefore the description stack has multiple levels. The focus on service description is to communicate those aspects of a service that might be important to the service requestor. Chapter 6 goes into detail on each of the technologies used for service description.

In Web services, XML is the basis of service description. XML schema is the base data type mechanism in the service description and all of the service description technologies in the stack are expressed using XML. Much of the power of Web services is derived from the power of XML.

The next two levels of the stack, service implementation and service interface, are described using the Web Services Description Language (WSDL). WSDL is a note to the W3C, and there is active work to refine this language into a standard. WSDL is the interface definition language for Web services; it is the key to understanding Web services. With WSDL, a developer describes the set of operations supported by a Web service, including the kinds of objects that are expected as input and output of the operations, the various bindings to concrete network and data encoding schemes. This level constitutes the core definition of the service's interface. The service implementation defines the network address where the service itself can be invoked. WSDL allows for automatic code-generation of Web service clients based on this information.

But IDL is not enough for Web services. Other aspects of the Web service could affect whether a service requestor would choose to bind to a Web service. For example, if two different service providers host implementations of the same service interface, perhaps a stock quote service, then from the IDL perspective, the services are almost indistinguishable: The network address is the only difference. However, the service providers might differ widely in their privacy policy, cost to use, timeliness of response, and so on. These non-operational characteristics might be critical to the service requestor. The role of the endpoint definition is to layer on top of the WSDL description information about characteristics of the Web service that are impacted by its implementation environment. Work in this area is at its very beginnings. The notion of a *Web Services Endpoint Language (WSEL)* has only been hinted at publicly. Other examples of this sort of description include the ebXML Collaboration-Protocol Profile and Agreement Specification (CPP).

At the top of the service description stack is the elusive promise of seamless, automatic service integration: the service orchestration layer. With *service orchestration*, the developer describes how a collection of Web services is combined to produce a more sophisticated Web service. For example, you would use service orchestration to model how a purchase order submission Web service could be combined with a notification service and a returns-processing service to produce a richer overall purchasing Web service. At this level, several alternative approaches exist. IBM has proposed the Web Services Flow Language, and Microsoft has Xlang. A single standard has not emerged in this space.

The orchestration of Web services poses significant challenges from both a technical and a business perspective. On the technical side, seamless service integration requires a significant technological foundation. Most important is the description of service behavior, defined by the rules for sequencing operation invocations and for sending and receiving messages. Next is the problem of composing services into process-based interactions. The problem is made harder by the requirement that some composition bindings must happen at runtime. Without this capability, it is difficult to map the technology to well-established business processes such as representation, referral, and brokering. On the business side, the problems are no less significant. From a business perspective, service integration is a workflow problem and as such could introduce dependencies on aspects of companies' core business models. Particularly difficult in this perspective is potentially the most valuable type of service integration—the one that spans enterprise boundaries.

The Discovery Stack

Given the ability to describe Web services, we are better off than we were, but we still have solved only part of the Web service integration problem. Service descriptions tell us how to bind to Web services, but how did the service requestor get the service description in the first place? Clearly, we need some form of a Web service discovery mechanism. The requirement here is for a directory or search engine for Web services. Service providers will need a publication mechanism so that they can provide information about the Web services they offer and make changes as their Web services evolve. Service requestors will need well-defined find APIs. This is the SOA service registry role we described earlier.

Figure 1.4 shows the third interoperability stack, the discovery stack. The discovery stack organizes technologies associated with Web service discovery.

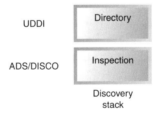

FIGURE 1.4
The discovery stack.

The first level of the stack represents a simple inspection level. *Inspection* 📖 is a technique of discovering the service description given that the details about the service (a service identifier or URL, for example) are already known. Once again, no single standard exists in this space. IBM has *ADS* 📖 and Microsoft has *DISCO* 📖.

The directory level represents the capability of discovering Web services and business partners using a capabilities-based lookup. Unlike previous distributed computing techniques that relied on well known names as the basis for remote discovery of services, Web services can use find techniques based on the kind of service or service capabilities. The UDDI standard is the proposed technology for Web services directory.

Chapter 7 is dedicated to explaining service discovery in much more detail, and in particular reviewing the UDDI standard.

Putting the Interoperability Stacks Together

Does any given Web service require *all* of these technologies in order to be considered a Web service? Certainly not.

Looking at the wire stack, no single network protocol—not even HTTP—is a required part of a Web service; any number of networking protocols can be used. Some Web services don't even need to use a network protocol. Techniques such as the Web Services Invocation Framework (WSIF) (`http://www.alphaworks.ibm.com/tech/wsif`) discuss the possibility of a Web service being a simple Java method invocation, where the service requestor and service provider are in the same Java Virtual Machine. Moving up the stack, we can discover that even SOAP is not a necessary technology for Web services. It is possible that a component accessed through a simple HTTP POST can be considered a Web service. In these cases, the commonality that makes these components Web services is the use of WSDL to describe the service.

So, is a service description required in order for a component to be considered a Web service? Again, not necessarily. Many Web services, particularly older Web services developed when SOAP was first introduced, do not have a corresponding service description. These components are considered Web services, but it is worth noting that without a service description, the Web service cannot be a part of the publish, find, bind operations in a service-oriented architecture. As the WSDL standard is adopted, you will see fewer Web services provided that do not have a corresponding WSDL description. Many developers have concluded that a Web service is simply "anything that can be described using WSDL."

Does a Web service have to appear in a UDDI registry in order to be considered a Web service? Clearly not. Many Web services advertised on the Web do not appear in UDDI and do not support the ADS or DISCO simple service discovery conventions.

So you will agree that any given Web service doesn't need *all* of these technologies to be considered a Web service. But are *any* of these technologies found in *each and every* Web service? If you follow the arguments above, clearly not. Is SOAP required in all Web services? No. Is WSDL? No. UDDI? No. There is no single Web services technology whose use determines that a component is a Web service. For this reason, defining what is a Web service remains difficult.

In addition to writing great specifications, the Web services industry has been busy building software that makes the standards come to life and solve meaningful business problems. This book uses Apache Axis at the heart of our Web services examples. Axis is an advanced Web services engine with a highly scalable and extensible architecture. We will examine Axis in great depth in Chapter 4.

There are, however, other great Web services implementations from multiple vendors. Chapter 8 looks at the currently available best-of-breed Web services tooling, its capabilities and its interoperability record.

Interoperability is key for Web services. In the World Wide Web, does my browser care about which Web server you are running? No. The same thing is true in Web services. Any service requestor should be able to consume any standard (no custom extensions) Web service provided via any Web services engine. We might be some distance from this holy grail, but the industry is working hard at it because everyone knows this is the only way to make Web services (and dynamic application integration) successful.

Summary

In this chapter, we provided you with a definition for Web services and helped position where these technologies will benefit businesses. We also provided a conceptual framework—service-oriented architecture—you can use to think about problems related to Web services. We introduced the alphabet soup of Web services technologies and illustrated an organizational framework around three related interoperability stacks.

The rest of this book builds upon what we introduced here. Chapter 2 explores the root of all Web services technologies: XML. Chapter 3 builds upon that discussion by examining the wire stack and, in particular, the SOAP technology as the access mechanism of choice for many Web services. Chapter 4 shows how SOAP is implemented in the Apache Axis project. Chapter 5 expands upon SOAP and Axis, describing how other e-business aspects such as security can be layered into a Web service. Chapter 6 explores the service description stack, focusing on how the service requestor knows what kind of message to send and where to send it. Chapter 7 examines the discovery stack and in particular the UDDI standard. Chapter 8 explores other Web services infrastructures. We close with Chapter 9, "Future Concepts," which discusses some future trends for Web services.

XML Primer

IN THIS CHAPTER

Since its introduction in 1998, Extensible Markup Language (XML) has revolutionized the way in which we think about structuring, describing, and exchanging information. The ways in which XML is used in the software industry are many and growing. Certainly for Web services the importance of XML is paramount; all key Web service technologies are based on it.

One great thing about XML is that it is constantly changing and evolving. However, this can also be its downside. New problems require new approaches and uses of XML that drive aggressive technological innovation. The net result is a maelstrom of invention—a pace of change so rapid that it leaves most people confused. To say that you are using XML is meaningless. Are you using DTDs or XML Schema and, if so, then whose? How about XML Namespaces, XPointer, XLink, XPath, XSLT, XQuery, RDF, SOAP, WSDL, UDDI, XAML, WSFL, WSCL, or WS-I? Does your software use SAX, DOM, JAXB, JAXP, JAXM, JAXR, or JAX-RPC? It is easy to get lost, to drown in the acronym soup. You are interested in Web services (you bought this book, remember?). How much do you really need to know about XML?

The truth is pleasantly surprising. First, many XML technologies you might have heard about are not relevant to Web services. You can safely forget half the acronyms you wish you knew more about. Second, even with relevant technologies, you need to know only a few core concepts. (The 80/20 rule does not disappoint.) Third, this chapter is all you need to read and understand to be able to handle the rest of the book and make the most of it. This chapter will cover, in sufficient detail:

- The origins of XML and the fundamental difference between document- and data-centric XML applications
- The syntax and rules governing XML documents
- XML Namespaces, the key specification enabling the distributed evolution of XML technologies
- XML Schema, the *de facto* standard for describing document structure and XML datatypes for data-oriented applications
- The key mechanisms for creating and processing XML with Java software

This chapter will develop a set of examples around SkatesTown's purchase order submission and invoice generation process. The examples will cover all the technologies we've listed here.

If you are an old hand at XML who understands the XML namespace mechanism and feels at home with schema extensibility and the use of `xsi:type`, you should go straight to Chapter 3, "Simple Object Access Protocol (SOAP)" and dive into Web services. If you can parse and process a significant portion of the previous sentence, you should skim this chapter to get a quick refresher of some core XML technologies. If you are someone with more limited XML experience, do not worry—by the end of this chapter, you will be able to hold your own.

Origins of XML

World Wide Web Consortium (W3C) began work on Extensible Markup Language (XML) in the middle of 1996. XML 1.0, released on February 10, 1998, resulted from the computer industry's need to develop a simple yet extensible mechanism for the textual representation of structured and semi-structured information. The design inspiration for XML came from two main sources: Standard Generalized Markup Language (SGML) and HTML.

The concept of generalized markup (GM) has been around for decades. It involves using *tags* to identify pieces of information. Simply put, tags are names surrounded by pointy brackets (< and >). For example, `<title>` is a tag. The innovative thing about GM is that it requires information to be surrounded by both start and end tags. End tags look like start tags with the addition of a forward slash (/) before the tag name, as in `</title>`. The notion of start and end tags allows for nesting, which, in turn, lets you structure information in a hierarchical manner.

Consider the following example, which uses markup to indicate that a book has a title and several authors:

```
<book>
    <title>Building Web Services with Java</title>
    <authors>
        <author>Steve Graham</author>
        <author>Simeon Simeonov</author>
        <author>Toufic Boubez</author>
        <author>Doug Davis</author>
        <author>Glen Daniels</author>
        <author>Yuichi Nakamura</author>
        <author>Ryo Neyama</author>
    </authors>
</book>
```

Using markup to represent information about books has many benefits. The information is readily readable by humans. It is also quite easy to process with software because start and end tags clearly delineate where certain pieces of information start and where they end. Further, this way to represent information is inherently extensible. For example, you can easily imagine how to add more authors or other information (such as the book's ISBN) to the book description. Markup is appealing because of its simplicity combined with the potential for extensibility. Not all markup is simple, though. In fact, our industry's first attempt to formally define generalized markup yielded a very complex specification. SGML was ratified by ISO in 1986. It defined everything you could ever want to know about markup and more. SGML-enabled software was expensive; typically, only large companies could afford it. The software also tended to be full of defects. Over time, a growing community of SGML experts began to voice opinions that, perhaps, the core ideas of SGML could be organized in a much simpler fashion. All that was needed was a catalyst to force the change and an organization that could lead the standardization effort. The catalyst was the combination of HTML and the Web. The organization was the W3C.

By its nature, SGML is a *meta-language* 📖. It does not prescribe any particular markup; instead, it defines how any given markup language can be formally specified. For better or worse, the term for these markup languages is *SGML applications* 📖. Because the term is confusing (a markup language specification is not a piece of software), it is rarely used nowadays, but you still might encounter it in some of the reference materials pointed out at the end of the chapter.

The most popular SGML application is HTML, the markup language that rules the Web. HTML combines markup from several different categories to provide a rich hypertext experience:

- Text structuring tags: <H1>, <H2>, <P>,
- Formatting tags: <B>, <I>
- Linking and embedding tags: <IMG>, <A>
- Data input tags: <FORM>, <INPUT>, <SELECT>

The HTML specification is owned by W3C. Unfortunately, due to the rapid growth of the Internet and the market pressure caused by the browser wars, the leading browser vendors introduced a number of incompatible tags to HTML completely outside the scope of the HTML specification. These tags created problems for Internet software vendors and HTML document authors—they had to be careful what markup they used, based on the type of browser that would display the HTML document. Yet at the same time, they themselves were not able to extend HTML with markup that could have been useful to them.

The need to simplify SGML coincided with the need to control the evolution of HTML and create a simple generalized markup language for use on the Web. SGML was too heavy for this purpose—it simply took too much effort to support and process. XML became that lightweight language. After about one-and-a-half-years of work, the XML working group at the W3C produced a final specification. XML is similar to SGML in that it preserves the notion of GM. However, the specification is much simpler. There are very few optional features, and most SGML features that were deemed difficult to implement were abandoned.

XML is here to stay. The XML industry is experiencing a boom. XML has become the *de facto* standard for representing structured and semi-structured information in textual form. Many specifications are built on top of XML to extend its capabilities and enable its use in a broader range of scenarios. One of the most exciting areas of use for XML is Web services.

The rest of this chapter will introduce the set of XML technologies and standards that are the foundation of Web services:

- *XML instances*—The rules for creating syntactically correct XML documents
- *XML Schema*—A recent standard that enables detailed validation of XML documents as well as the specification of XML datatypes
- *XML Namespaces*—Definitions of the mechanisms for combining XML from multiple sources in a single document
- *XML processing*—The core architecture and mechanisms for creating, parsing, and manipulating XML documents from programming languages

Document- Versus Data-Centric XML

Generally speaking, there are two broad application areas of XML technologies. The first relates to document-centric applications, and the second to data-centric applications. Because XML can be used in so many different ways, it is important to understand the difference between these two categories.

Document-Centric XML

Because of its SGML origins, in the early days of its existence XML gained rapid adoption within publishing systems as a mechanism for representing semi-structured documents such as technical manuals, legal documents, and product catalogs. The content in these documents is typically meant for human consumption, although it could be processed by any number of applications before it is presented to humans. The key element of these documents is semi-structured marked-up text.

The following markup is a perfect example of XML used in a document-centric manner. The content is directed towards human consumption—it's part of the FastGlide skateboard user guide. The content is semi-structured. The usage rules for tags such as <B>, <I> and <LINK> are very loosely defined; they could appear pretty much anywhere in the document:

```
<H1>Skateboard Usage Requirements</H1>
<P>In order to use the <B>FastGlide</B> skateboard you have to
have:</P>
<LIST>
<ITEM>A strong pair of legs.</ITEM>
<ITEM>A reasonably long stretch of smooth road surface.</ITEM>
<ITEM>The impulse to impress others.</ITEM>
</LIST>
<P>If you have all of the above, you can proceed to <LINK
HREF="Chapter2.xml">Getting on the Board</LINK>.</P>
```

Data-Centric XML

By contrast, data-centric XML is used to mark up highly structured information such as the textual representation of relational data from databases, financial transaction information, and programming language data structures. Data-centric XML is typically generated by machines and is meant for machine consumption. It is XML's natural ability to nest and repeat markup that makes it the perfect choice for representing these types of data.

Consider the purchase order example in Listing 2.1. It is a purchase order from the Skateboard Warehouse, retailer of skateboards to SkatesTown. The order is for 5 backpacks, 12 skateboards, and 1,000 SkatesTown promotional stickers (this is what the stock keeping unit [SKU] of 008-PR stands for).

LISTING 2.1 Purchase Order in XML

```
<po id="43871" submitted="2001-10-05">
   <billTo>
      <company>The Skateboard Warehouse</company>
      <street>One Warehouse Park</street>
      <street>Building 17</street>
      <city>Boston</city>
      <state>MA</state>
      <postalCode>01775</postalCode>
   </billTo>
   <shipTo>
      <company>The Skateboard Warehouse</company>
      <street>One Warehouse Park</street>
      <street>Building 17</street>
      <city>Boston</city>
      <state>MA</state>
      <postalCode>01775</postalCode>
   </shipTo>
   <order>
      <item sku="318-BP" quantity="5">
         <description>Skateboard backpack; five pockets</description>
      </item>
      <item sku="947-TI" quantity="12">
         <description>Street-style titanium skateboard.</description>
      </item>
      <item sku="008-PR" quantity="1000">
      </item>
   </order>
</po>
```

The use of XML is very different from the previous user guide example:

- The ratio of markup to content is high. The XML includes many different types of tags. There is no long-running text.

- The XML includes machine-generated information; for example, the submission date of the purchase order uses a date-time format of year-month-day. A human authoring an XML document is unlikely to enter a date-time value in this format.

- The tags are organized in a highly structured manner. Order and positioning matter, relative to other tags. For example, <description> must be under <item>, which must be under <order>, which must be under <po>. The <order> tag can be used only once in the document.

- Markup is used to describe what a piece of information *means* rather than how it should be presented to a human.

In short, if you can easily imagine the XML as a data structure in your favorite programming language, you are probably looking at a data-centric use of XML. An example Java class that could, with a bit more work, be used to represent the purchase order data is shown here:

```
class PO
{
    int id;
    Date submitted;
    Address billTo;
    Address shipTo;
    Item order[];
}
```

Document Lifetime

Document- and data-centric uses of XML can differ in one other very significant aspect—the lifetime of the XML document. Typically, XML documents for human consumption (such as technical manuals and research papers) live a long time because the information contained in them can be used for a long time. On the other hand, some data-centric XML could live for only a few milliseconds. Consider the example of a database that is returning the results of a query in XML format. The whole operation takes several milliseconds. After the query is used, the data is discarded. Further, no real XML document exists. The XML is just bits on a wire or bits in an application's data structure. Still, for convenience purposes, we will use the term *XML document* to refer to any particular whole piece of XML being used. As a general identification of parts of a whole XML document, this book uses the highly technical term *chunk*.

Web services are about data-centric uses of XML. Through the rest of this chapter and the rest of this book, we will purposefully ignore discussing document-centric XML.

XML Instances

The structure and formatting of XML in an XML document must follow the rules of the XML instance syntax. The term *instance* 📖 is used to explicitly distinguish the difference between the use of some particular type of XML and its specification. This usage parallels the difference in object-oriented terminology between an object instance and an object type.

Document Prolog

XML documents contain an optional *prolog* 📖 followed by a *root element* 📖 that contains the contents of the document.

Typically the prolog serves up to three roles:

- Identifies the document as an XML document
- Includes any comments about the document
- Includes any meta-information about the content of the document

A document can be identified as an XML document through the use of a *processing instruction* 📖. Processing instructions (PIs) are special directives to the application that will process the XML document. They have the following syntax:

```
<?PITarget ...?>
```

PIs are enclosed in `<? ... ?>`. The PI target is a keyword meaningful to the processing application. Everything between the PI target and the `?>` marker is considered the contents of the PI.

In general, data-oriented XML applications do not use application-specific processing instructions. Instead, they tend to put all information in elements and attributes. However, you should use one standard processing instruction—the *XML declaration* 📖—in the XML document prolog to determine two very important pieces of information: the version of XML in the document and the character encoding:

```
<?xml version="1.0" encoding="UTF-8"?>
```

The `version` parameter of the `xml` PI tells the processing application the version of the XML specification to which the document conforms. Currently, there is only one version: `"1.0"`. The `encoding` parameter is optional. It identifies the character set of the document. The default value is `"UTF-8"`.

> **NOTE**
>
> UTF-8 is a variable-length character encoding standard that generates 7-bit safe output. This type of output makes it easy to move XML on the Internet using standard communication protocols such as HTTP, SMTP, and FTP. Keep in mind that XML is internationalized by design and can support other character encodings such as Unicode and ISO/IEC 10646. However, for simplicity and readability purposes, this book will use UTF-8 encoding for all samples.

If you omit the XML declaration, the XML version is assumed to be 1.0, and the processing application will try to guess the encoding of the document based on clues such as the raw byte order of the data stream. This approach has problems, and whenever interoperability is of high importance—such as for Web services—applications should always provide an explicit XML declaration and use UTF-8 encoding.

XML document prologs can also include comments that pertain to the whole document. Comments use the following syntax:

```
<!-- Sample comment and more ... -->
```

Comments can span multiple lines but cannot be nested (comments cannot enclose other comments). Everything inside the comment markers will be ignored by the processing application. Some of the XML samples in this book will use comments to provide you with useful context about the examples in question.

With what you have learned so far, you can extend the purchase order example from Listing 2.1 to include an XML declaration and a comment about the document (see Listing 2.2).

LISTING 2.2 XML Declaration and Comment for the Purchase Order

```
<?xml version="1.0" encoding="UTF-8"?>
<!-- Created by Bob Dister, approved by Mary Jones -->
<po id="43871" submitted="2001-10-05">
   <!-- The rest of the purchase order will be the same as before -->
   ...
</po>
```

In this case, po is the root element of the XML document.

Elements

The term *element* 📖 is a technical name for the pairing of a start and end tag in an XML document. In the previous example, the po element has the start tag <po> and the end tag </po>. Every start tag must have a matching end tag and vice versa. Everything between these two tags is the *content* of the element. This includes any nested elements, text, comments, and so on.

Element names can include all standard programming language identifier characters ([0-9A-Za-z]) as well as underscore (_), hyphen (-), and colon (:), but they must start with a letter. customer-name is a valid XML element name. However, because XML is case-sensitive, customer-name is not the same element as Customer-Name.

According to the XML Specification, elements can have three different *content types*. They can have *element-only* content, *mixed* content, or *empty* content. Element-only content consists entirely of nested elements. Any whitespace separating elements is not considered significant in this case. Mixed content refers to any combination of nested elements and text. All elements in the purchase order example, with the exception of description, have element content. Most elements in the skateboard user guide example earlier in the chapter had mixed content.

Note that the XML Specification does not define a text-only content model. Outside the letter of the specification, an element that contains only text is often referred to as having *data* content; but, technically speaking, it has mixed content. This awkwardness comes as a result of XML's roots in SGML and document-oriented applications. However, in most data-oriented applications, you will never see elements whose contents are both nested elements and text. It will typically be one or the other, because limiting the content to be either elements or text makes processing XML much easier.

The syntax for elements with empty content is a start tag immediately followed by an end tag, as in <emptyElement></emptyElement>. Because this is simply too much text, the XML Specification also allows the shorthand form <emptyElement/>. For example, because the last item in our purchase order does not have a nested description element, it has empty content. Therefore, we could have written it as follows:

```
<item sku="008-PR" quantity="1000"/>
```

XML elements must be strictly nested. They cannot overlap, as shown here:

```
<!-- This is correct nesting -->
<P><B><I>Bold, italicized text in a paragraph</I></B></P>

<!--Bad syntax: overlapping I and B tags -->
<P><I><B>Bold, italicized text in a paragraph</I></B></P>
```

```
<!-- Bad syntax: overlapping P and B tags -->
<B><P><I>Bold, italicized text in a paragraph</I></B></P>
```

The notion of an XML document root implies that there can be only one element at the very top level of a document. For example, the following would not be a valid XML document:

```
<first>I am the first element</first>
<second>I am the second element</second>
```

It is easy to think of nested XML elements as a hierarchy. For example, Figure 2.1 shows a hierarchical tree representation of the XML elements in the purchase order example together with the data (text) associated with them.

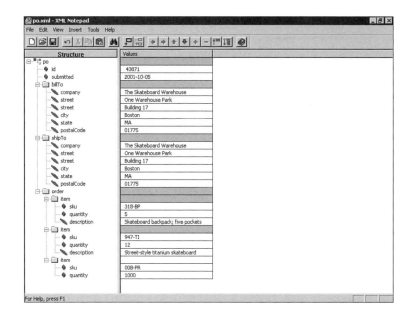

FIGURE 2.1

Tree representation of XML elements in a purchase order.

Unfortunately, it is often difficult to identify XML elements precisely in the hierarchy. To aid this task, the XML community has taken to using genealogy terms such as parent, child, sibling, ancestor, and descendant. Figure 2.2 illustrates the terminology as it applies to the order element of the purchase order:

- Its parent is po.
- Its ancestor is po.
- Its siblings are billTo and shipTo.

- Its children are three item elements.
- Its descendants are three item elements and two description elements.

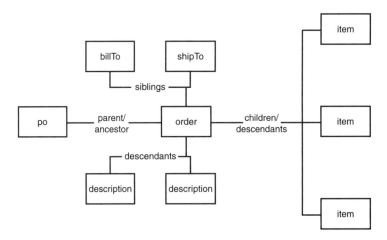

FIGURE 2.2
Common terminology for XML element relationships.

Attributes

The start tags for XML elements can have zero or more *attributes*. An attribute is a name-value pair. The syntax for an attribute is a name (which uses the same character set as an XML element name) followed by an equal sign (=), followed by a quoted value. The XML Specification requires the quoting of values; both single and double quotes can be used, provided they are correctly matched. For example, the po element of our purchase order has two attributes, id and submitted:

```
<po id="43871" submitted="2001-10-05"> ... </po>
```

A family of attributes whose names begin with xml: is reserved for use by the XML Specification. Probably the best example is xml:lang, which is used to identify the language of the text that is the content of the element with that attribute. For example, we could have written the description elements in our purchase order example to identify the description text as English:

```
<description xml:lang="en">Skateboard backpack; five pockets</description>
```

Note that applications processing XML are not required to recognize, process, and act based on the values of these attributes. The key reason why the XML Specification identified these attributes is that they address common use-cases; standardizing them would aid interoperability between applications.

Without any meta-information about an XML document, attribute values are considered to be pieces of text. In the previous example, the id might look like a number and the submission date might look like a date, but to an XML processor they will both be just strings. This obviously causes some headaches when processing data-oriented XML, and it is one of the primary reasons most data-oriented XML documents have associated meta-information described in XML Schema (introduced later in this chapter).

At the same time, XML applications are free to attach any semantics they choose to XML markup. A common use-case is leveraging attributes to create a basic linking mechanism within an XML document. The typical scenario involves a document having duplicate information in multiple locations. The goal is to eliminate information duplication. The process has three steps:

1. Put the information in the document only once.

2. Mark the information with a unique identifier.

3. Refer to this identifier every time you need to refer to the information.

The purchase order example offers the opportunity to try this out (see Listing 2.3). As shown in the example, in most cases, the bill-to and ship-to addresses will be the same.

LISTING 2.3   Duplicate Address Information in a Purchase Order

```
<po id="43871" submitted="2001-10-05">
   <billTo>
      <company>The Skateboard Warehouse</company>
      <street>One Warehouse Park</street>
      <street>Building 17</street>
      <city>Boston</city>
      <state>MA</state>
      <postalCode>01775</postalCode>
   </billTo>
   <shipTo>
      <company>The Skateboard Warehouse</company>
      <street>One Warehouse Park</street>
      <street>Building 17</street>
      <city>Boston</city>
      <state>MA</state>
      <postalCode>01775</postalCode>
   </shipTo>
   ...
</po>
```

There is no reason to duplicate this information. Instead, we can use the markup shown in Listing 2.4.

LISTING 2.4   Using ID/IDREF Attributes to Eliminate Redundancy

```
<po id="43871" submitted="2001-10-05">
   <billTo id="addr-1">
      <company>The Skateboard Warehouse</company>
      <street>One Warehouse Park</street>
      <street>Building 17</street>
      <city>Boston</city>
      <state>MA</state>
      <postalCode>01775</postalCode>
   </billTo>
   <shipTo href="addr-1"/>
   ...
</po>
```

We followed the three steps described previously:

1. We put the address information in the document only once, under the `billTo` element.

2. We uniquely identified the address as `"addr-1"` and stored that information in the `id` attribute of the `billTo` element. We only need to worry about the uniqueness of the identifier within the XML document.

3. To refer to the address from the `shipTo` element we use another attribute, `href`, whose value is the unique address identifier `"addr-1"`.

The attribute names `id` and `href` are not required but nevertheless are commonly used by convention.

You might have noticed that now both the `po` and `billTo` elements have an attribute called `id`. This is fine, because attributes are always associated with an element.

Elements Versus Attributes

Given that information can be stored in both element content and attribute values, sooner or later the question of whether to use an element or an attribute arises. This debate has erupted a few times in the XML community and has claimed many casualties.

One common rule is to represent structured information using markup. For example, you should use an `address` element with nested `company`, `street`, `city`, `state`, `postalCode`, and `country` elements instead of including a whole address as a chunk of text.

Even this simple rule is subject to interpretation and the choice of application domain. For example, the choice between

```
    <work number="617.219.2000">
```
and
```
    <work>
       <area>617</area>
       <number>219.2000</number>
       <ext/>
    </work>
```
really depends on whether your application needs to have phone number information in granular form (for example, to perform searches based on the area code only).

In other cases, only personal preference and stylistic choice apply. We might ask if SkatesTown should have used
```
    <po>
       <id>43871</id>
       <submitted>2001-10-05</submitted>
       ...
    </po>
```
instead of
```
    <po id="43871" submitted="2001-10-05">
       ...
    </pol>
```
There really isn't a good way to answer this question without adding all sorts of stretchy assumptions about extensibility needs, and so on.

In general, whenever humans design XML documents, you will see more frequent use of attributes. This is true even in data-oriented applications. On the other hand, when XML documents are automatically "designed" and generated by applications, you might see a more prevalent use of elements. The reasons are somewhat complex; Chapter 3 will address some of them.

Character Data

Attribute values as well as the text and whitespace between tags must follow precisely a small but strict set of rules. Most XML developers tend to think of these as mapping to the string data type in their programming language of choice. Unfortunately, things are not that simple.

Encoding

First, and most important, all character data in an XML document must comply with the document's encoding. Any characters outside the range of characters that can be included in the document must be escaped and identified as *character references* 📖. The escape sequence used throughout XML uses the ampersand (&) as its start and the semi-colon (;) as its end. The syntax for character references is an ampersand, followed by a pound/hash sign (#), followed by either a decimal character code or lowercase *x* followed by a hexadecimal character code, followed by the semicolon. Therefore, the 8-bit character code 128 will be encoded in a UTF-8 XML document as €.

Unfortunately, for obscure document-oriented reasons, there is no way to include character codes 0 through 7, 9, 11, 12, or 14 through 31 (typically known as *non-whitespace control characters* in ASCII) in XML documents. Even a correctly escaped character reference will not do. This situation can cause unexpected problems for programmers whose string data types can sometimes end up with these values.

Whitespace

Another legacy from the document-centric world that XML came from is the rules for white-space handling. It is not important to completely define these rules here, but a couple of them are worth mentioning:

- An XML processor is required to convert any carriage return (CR) character, as well as the sequence of a carriage return and a line feed (LF) character, it sees in the XML document into a single line feed character.
- Whitespace can be treated as either significant or insignificant. The set of rules for how applications are notified about either of these has erupted more than one debate in the XML community.

Luckily, most data-oriented XML applications care little about whitespace.

Entities

In addition to character references, XML documents can define *entities* as well as references to them (*entity references*). Entities are typically not important for data-oriented applications and we will not discuss them in detail here. However, all XML processors must recognize several pre-defined entities that map to characters that can be confused with markup delimiters. These characters are less than (<); greater than (>); ampersand (&); apostrophe, a.k.a. single quote ('); and quote, a.k.a. double quote ("). Table 2.1 shows the syntax for escaping these characters.

TABLE 2.1 Pre-defined XML Character Escape Sequences

Character	Escape sequence
<	&lt;
>	&gt;
&	&amp;
'	&apos;
"	&quot;

For example, to include a chunk of XML as text, not markup, inside an XML document, all special characters should be escaped:

```
<example-to-show>
    &lt;?xml version=&quot;1.0&quot;?&gt;
    &lt;rootElement&gt;
        &lt;childElement id=&quot;1&quot;&gt;
            The man said: &quot;Hello, there!&quot;.
        &lt;/childElement&gt;
    &lt;/rootElement&gt;
</example-to-show>
```

The result is not only reduced readability but also a significant increase in the size of the document, because single characters are mapped to character escape sequences whose length is at least four characters.

To address this problem, the XML Specification has a special multi-character escape construct. The name of the construct, *CDATA section* 📖, refers to the section holding character data. The syntax is `<![CDATA[`, followed by any sequences of characters allowed by the document encoding that does not include `]]>`, followed by `]]>`. Therefore, you can write the previous example much more simply as follows:

```
<example-to-show><![CDATA[
    <?xml version="1.0"?>
    <rootElement>
        <childElement id="1">
            The man said: "Hello, there!".
        </childElement>
    </rootElement>
]]></example-to-show>
```

A Simpler Purchase Order

Based on the information in this section, we can re-write the purchase order document as shown in Listing 2.4.

LISTING 2.4   Improved Purchase Order Document

```
<?xml version="1.0" encoding="UTF-8"?>
<!-- Created by Bob Dister, approved by Mary Jones -->
<po id="43871" submitted="2001-10-05">
    <billTo id="addr-1">
        <company>The Skateboard Warehouse</company>
        <street>One Warehouse Park</street>
        <street>Building 17</street>
```

LISTING 2.4 Continued

```
      <city>Boston</city>
      <state>MA</state>
      <postalCode>01775</postalCode>
   </billTo>
   <shipTo href="addr-1"/>
   <order>
      <item sku="318-BP" quantity="5">
         <description>Skateboard backpack; five pockets</description>
      </item>
      <item sku="947-TI" quantity="12">
         <description>Street-style titanium skateboard.</description>
      </item>
      <item sku="008-PR" quantity="1000"/>
   </order>
</po>
```

XML Namespaces

An important property of XML documents is that they can be composed to create new documents. This is the most basic mechanism for reusing XML. Unfortunately, simple composition creates the problems of recognition and collision.

To illustrate these problems, consider a scenario where SkatesTown wants to receive its purchase orders via the XML messaging system of XCommerce Messaging, Inc. The format of the messages is simple:

```
<message from="..." to="..." sent="...">
   <text>
      This is the text of the message.
   </text>
   <!-- A message can have attachments -->
   <attachment>
      <description>Brief description of the attachment.</description>
      <item>
         <!-- XML of attachment goes here -->
      </item>
   </attachment>
</message>
```

Listing 2.5 shows a complete message with a purchase order attachment.

LISTING 2.5 Message with Purchase Order Attachment

```xml
<message from="bj@bjskates.com" to="orders@skatestown.com"
    sent="2001-10-05">
    <text>
        Hi, here is what I need this time. Thx, BJ.
    </text>
    <attachment>
        <description>The PO</description>
        <item>
            <po id="43871" submitted="2001-10-05">
                <billTo id="addr-1">
                    <company>The Skateboard Warehouse</company>
                    <street>One Warehouse Park</street>
                    <street>Building 17</street>
                    <city>Boston</city>
                    <state>MA</state>
                    <postalCode>01775</postalCode>
                </billTo>
                <shipTo href="addr-1"/>
                <order>
                    <item sku="318-BP" quantity="5">
                        <description>
                            Skateboard backpack; five pockets
                        </description>
                    </item>
                    <item sku="947-TI" quantity="12">
                        <description>
                            Street-style titanium skateboard.
                        </description>
                    </item>
                    <item sku="008-PR" quantity="1000"/>
                </order>
            </po>
        </item>
    </attachment>
</message>
```

2

XML PRIMER

It is relatively easy to identify the two problems mentioned earlier in the composed document:

- *Recognition*—How does an XML processing application distinguish between the XML elements that describe the message and the XML elements that are part of the purchase order?

- *Collision*—Does the element `description` refer to attachment descriptions in messages or order item descriptions? Does the `item` element refer to an item of attachment or an order item?

Very simple applications might not be bothered by these problems. After all, the knowledge of what an element means can reside in the application logic. However, as application complexity increases and the number of applications that need to work with some particular composed document type grows, the need to clearly distinguish between the XML elements becomes paramount. The XML Namespaces specification brings order to the chaos.

Namespace Mechanism

The problem of collision in composed XML documents arises because of the likelihood of elements with common names (description, item, and so on) to be reused in different document types. This problem can be addressed by *qualifying* an XML element name with an additional *identifier* that is much more likely to be unique within the composed document. In other words:

Qualified name (a.k.a. QName) = Namespace identifier + Local name

This approach is similar to how namespaces are used in languages such as C++ and C# and to how package names are used in the Java programming language.

The problem of recognition in composed XML documents arises because no good mechanism exists to identify all elements belonging to the same document type. Given namespace qualifiers, the problem is addressed in a simple way—all elements that have the same namespace identifier are considered together.

For identifiers, XML Namespaces uses *Uniform Resource Identifiers* (URIs). URIs are described in RFC 2396. URIs are nothing fancy, but they are very useful. They can be locators, names, or both. URI locators are known as *Uniform Resource Locators* (URLs), a term familiar to all using the Web. URLs are strings such as `http://www.skatestown.com/services/POSubmission` and `mailto:orders@skatestown.com`.

Uniform Resource Names (URNs) are URIs that are globally unique and persistent. *Universally Unique Identifiers* (UUIDs) are perfect for use as URNs. UUIDs are 128-bit identifiers that are designed to be globally unique. Typically, they combine network card (Ethernet) addresses with a high-precision timestamp and an increment counter. An example URN using a UUID is `urn:uuid:2FAC1234-31F8-11B4-A222-08002B34C003`. UUIDs are used as unique identifiers in Universal Description Discovery and Integration (UDDI) as detailed in Chapter 7, "Discovering Web Services."

Namespace Syntax

Because URIs can be rather long and typically contain characters that are not allowed in XML element names, the syntax of including namespaces in XML documents involves two steps:

1. A namespace identifier is associated with a *prefix*, a name that contains only legal XML element name characters with the exception of the colon (:).

2. Qualified names are obtained as a combination of the prefix, the colon character, and the local element name, as in myPrefix:myElementName.

Listing 2.6 shows an example of the composed XML document using namespaces.

LISTING 2.6   Message with Namespaces

```
<msg:message from="bj@bjskates.com" to="orders@skatestown.com"
   sent="2001-10-05" xmlns:msg="http://www.xcommercemsg.com/ns/message"
   xmlns:po="http://www.skatestown.com/ns/po">
<msg:text>
   Hi, here is what I need this time. Thx, BJ.
</msg:text>
<msg:attachment>
   <msg:description>The PO</msg:description>
   <msg:item>
      <po:po id="43871" submitted="2001-10-05">
         <po:billTo id="addr-1">
            <po:company>The Skateboard Warehouse</po:company>
            <po:street>One Warehouse Park</po:street>
            <po:street>Building 17</po:street>
            <po:city>Boston</po:city>
            <po:state>MA</po:state>
            <po:postalCode>01775</po:postalCode>
         </po:billTo>
         <po:shipTo href="addr-1"/>
         <po:order>
            <po:item sku="318-BP" quantity="5">
               <po:description>
                  Skateboard backpack; five pockets
               </po:description>
            </po:item>
            <po:item sku="947-TI" quantity="12">
               <po:description>
                  Street-style titanium skateboard.
               </po:description>
            </po:item>
            <po:item sku="008-PR" quantity="1000"/>
```

LISTING 2.6   Continued

```
            </po:order>
          </po:po>
        </msg:item>
      </msg:attachment>
</msg:message>
```

In this example, the elements prefixed with msg are associated with a namespace whose identifier is http://www.xcommercemsg.com/ns/message, and those prefixed with po are associated with a namespace whose identifier is http://www.skatestown.com/ns/po. The prefixes are linked to the complete namespace identifiers by the attributes on the top message element beginning with xmlns: (xmlns:msg and xmlns:po). XML processing software will have access to both the prefixed name and to the mapping of prefixes to complete namespace identifiers.

Adding a prefix to every single element in the document somewhat decreases readability and increases document size. Therefore, XML Namespaces let you use a default namespace in a document. Elements belonging to the default namespace do not require prefixes. Listing 2.7 makes the msg namespace the default.

LISTING 2.7   Using Default Namespaces

```
<message from="bj@bjskates.com" to="orders@skatestown.com"
    sent="2001-10-05" xmlns ="http://www.xcommercemsg.com/ns/message"
    xmlns:po="http://www.skatestown.com/ns/po">
    <text>
       Hi, here is what I need this time. Thx, BJ.
    </text>
    <attachment>
       <description>The PO</description>
       <item>
          <po:po id="43871" submitted="2001-10-05">
             ...
          </po:po>
       </item>
    </attachment>
</message>
```

Default namespaces work because the content of any namespace-prefixed element is considered to belong to the namespace of its parent element unless, of course, the element is explicitly defined to be in another namespace with its own xmlns-type attribute. We can use this to further clean up the composed XML document by moving the PO namespace declaration to the po element (see Listing 2.8).

LISTING 2.8   Using Nested Namespace Defaulting

```
<message from="bj@bjskates.com" to="orders@skatestown.com"
    sent="2001-10-05" xmlns="http://www.xcommercemsg.com/ns/message">
    <text>
        Hi, here is what I need this time. Thx, BJ.
    </text>
    <attachment>
        <description>The PO</description>
        <item>
            <po:po id="43871" submitted="2001-10-05"
                xmlns:po="http://www.skatestown.com/ns/po">
                <billTo id="addr-1">
                    ...
                </billTo>
                <shipTo href="addr-1"/>
                <order>
                    ...
                </order>
            </po:po>
        </item>
    </attachment>
</message>
```

This example shows an efficient, readable syntax that completely eliminates the recognition and collision problems. XML processors can identify the namespace of any element in the document.

Namespace-Prefixed Attributes

Attributes can also have namespaces associated with them. Initially, it might be hard to imagine why a capability like this would be useful for XML applications. The common use-case scenario is the desire to extend the information provided by an XML element without having to make changes directly to its document type.

A concrete example might involve SkatesTown wanting to have an indication of the priority of certain items in purchase orders. High-priority items could be shipped immediately, without waiting for any back-ordered items to become available and complete the whole order. Item priorities are not something that SkatesTown's automatic order processing software understands. They are just a hint for the fulfillment system on how it should react in case of back-ordered items.

A simple implementation could involve extending the item element with an optional priority attribute. However, this could cause a problem for the order processing software that does not expect to see such an attribute. A better solution is to attach priority information to items using a namespace-prefixed `priority` attribute. Because the attribute will be in a namespace different from that of the `item` element, the order processing software will simply ignore it.

The example in Listing 2.9 uses this mechanism to make the backpacks high priority and the promotional materials low priority. By default, any items without a `priority` attribute, such as the skateboards, are presumed to be of medium priority.

LISTING 2.9   Adding Priority to Order Items

```
<message from="bj@bjskates.com" to="orders@skatestown.com"
   sent="2001-10-05" xmlns="http://www.xcommercemsg.com/ns/message">
   <text>
      Hi, here is what I need this time. Thx, BJ.
   </text>
   <attachment>
      <description>The PO</description>
      <item>
         <po:po id="43871" submitted="2001-10-05"
            xmlns:po="http://www.skatestown.com/ns/po">
            xmlns:p="http://www.skatestown.com/ns/priority">
            ...
            <po:order>
               <po:item sku="318-BP" quantity="5" p:priority="high">
                  <po:description>
                     Skateboard backpack; five pockets
                  </po:description>
               </po:item>
               <po:item sku="947-TI" quantity="12">
                  <po:description>
                     Street-style titanium skateboard.
                  </po:description>
               </po:item>
               <po:item sku="008-PR" quantity="1000" p:priority="low"/>
            </po:order>
         </po:po>
      </item>
   </attachment>
</message>
```

Dereferencing URIs

All the examples in this section have used namespace URIs that are URLs. A natural question arises: What is the resource at that URL? The answer is that it doesn't matter. XML Namespaces does not require that a resource be there. The URI is used entirely for identification purposes.

This could cause problems for applications that see an unknown namespace in an XML document and have no way to obtain more information about the elements and attributes that belong to that namespace. Later in this chapter, in the section on XML Schemas, you will see a mechanism that addresses this issue.

Document Type Definitions

Document Type Definitions (DTDs) are an optional feature of XML documents. A document associated with a DTD has a set of rules regarding what elements and attributes can be part of the document and where can they appear. DTDs originate from SGML, although XML's DTDs are greatly simplified. The presence of DTDs in XML documents allows us to distinguish the concepts of *well-formedness* 📖 and *validity* 📖.

Well-Formedness and Validity

If a document subscribes to the rules of XML syntax (as described in the section "XML Instances") it is considered well-formed. Well-formedness implies that XML processing software can read the document without any basic errors associated with parsing such as invalid character data, mismatched start and end tags, multiple attributes with the same name, and so on. The XML Specification mandates that if any well-formedness constraint is not met, the XML parser must immediately generate a non-recoverable error. This rigid mandate makes it easy to separate the doings of the software focused on the *logical structure* 📖 of an XML document (what the markup means) from the mundane details of the *physical structure* 📖 of the document (the markup syntax).

However, well-formedness is not sufficient for most applications. Consider, for example, the SkatesTown order processing application. When an XML document is submitted to it, it cares not that it is well-formed XML but that it is indeed a purchase order in the specific XML format it requires. The notion of *format* applies to the set of rules describing SkatesTown's purchase orders: "The document must begin with a po element that has two attributes (id and submitted) which will be followed by a billTo element..." and so on. In other words, before a submitted document is processed, it must be identified as a valid purchase order.

This is how the notion of validity comes in. DTDs offer an automated, declarative mechanism for validating the contents of XML documents as they are parsed. Therefore, XML applications can limit the amount of validation they need to perform. If the SkatesTown purchase order processing application could not delegate validation to the XML processor, it would have had to express all validation rules directly in code. Code is procedural in nature and much harder to maintain than DTDs, which are declarative and have a reasonably readable syntax.

To handle validity checks, DTDs must enable the following:

- Identification of the elements that can be in a document
- Identification of the order and relation between elements
- Identification of the attributes of every element and whether they are optional or required

Last but not least, there needs to be a mechanism to associate DTDs with XML documents.

Document Structure

DTDs are a mechanism to express the valid structure of a document. One way to visualize the structure of a document is as a tree of possible element and attribute combinations. For example, Figure 2.3 shows the document structure for purchase orders as expressed by a popular XML processing tool. The image uses some syntax from regular expressions to visualize the multiplicity of elements: question mark (?) stands for optional (zero or one), asterisk (*) stands for any (zero or more) , and plus (+) stands for at least some (one or more).

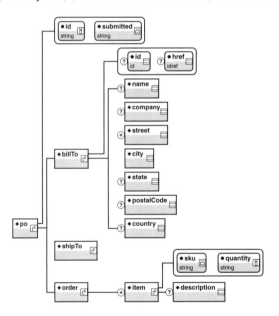

FIGURE 2.3
Document structure defined by the purchase order DTD.

Every element in the document structure tree has an associated *model group*. Model groups identify the *sequencing* and *multiplicity* of element content. There are two types of sequences: *sequence* and *choice*. Sequence defines the exact order in which child elements must appear. In

DTDs, the sequence operator in model groups is the comma (,). The model group (A, B, C) defines a content model where the first child element will be A, followed by B, followed by C. Choice defines the possible elements that can appear at any given position in the content model. The choice operator in model groups is the pipe character (|). The model group (A | B | C) defines a content model where there will be only one child element that can be A or B or C. Sequences and choices can be nested, as in ((A | (X, Y, Z)), B, (C | D)). This content model defines the following possible combinations of child elements:

- A, B, C
- A, B, D
- X, Y, Z, B, C
- X, Y, Z, B, D

The multiplicity of elements is defined using the same regular expression syntax used in document structure trees. The absence of a suffix stands for exactly one, question mark (?) stands for optional (zero or one), asterisk (*) stands for any (zero or more), and plus (+) stands for at least some (one or more). For example, the model group (A, B?, C*, D+) allows for the following combinations of child elements (… stands for "potentially many more of the same element"):

- A, D…
- A, B, D…
- A, B, C…, D…
- A, C…, D…

Are DTDs Enough?

Documents associated with DTDs are a huge step forward from basic XML markup. DTDs allow for validating document structure (element content, allowed attributes, and their value types), which significantly reduces the amount of custom validation code that needs to be written in XML applications. However, DTDs have some notable deficiencies:

- Although they express structured information, they do not use XML markup. DTD syntax is not as easy to process and manipulate as XML.

- DTDs were designed before namespaces came into existence and don't have good facilities for dealing with them. This is a problem for data-oriented applications that rely heavily on namespaces.

- DTDs do not offer sufficient reusability and extensibility capabilities. No mechanism exists for associating more than one DTD with an XML document. It is easy to reach the limit of what DTDs allow for even basic applications.

- DTDs model groups are sometimes too restrictive, in particular with respect to the order of child elements. No convenient DTD mechanism exists for declaring, for example, that the content of some element could include two child elements A and five child elements B, regardless of the order in which they appear.

- DTDs have no notion of data types. This hurts data-oriented applications where XML is eventually bound to some application-level data structure in a programming language. For example, DTDs offer no mechanism to enforce the simple rule that the values of the `quantity` attribute of the `item` element should be positive integers.

- For these reasons and others, one of the main Web service protocols—Simple Object Access Protocol (SOAP), which we'll discuss in Chapter 3—explicitly forbids the use of DTDs for defining document structure.

For these reasons, this chapter will not discuss DTDs in any further detail. We won't even introduce the basic DTD syntax here because data-oriented XML applications have moved away from DTDs; these applications use another mechanism to validate XML documents and to enforce document structure and datatype rules. To address the problems inherent in DTDs, the XML community developed XML Schema, a much richer meta-language for XML documents expressed natively in XML.

XML Schemas

XML provides a flexible set of structures that can represent many different types of document- and data-oriented information. As part of XML 1.0, DTDs offered the basic mechanism for defining a *vocabulary* specifying the structure of XML documents in an attempt to establish a contract (how an XML document will be structured) between multiple parties working with the same type of XML. DTDs came into existence because people and applications wanted to be able to treat XML at a higher level than a collection of elements and attributes. Well-designed DTDs attach semantics (meaning) to the XML syntax in documents.

At the same time, DTDs fail to address the common needs of namespace integration, modular vocabulary design, flexible content models, and tight integration with data-oriented applications. This failure comes as a direct result of XML's SGML origins and the predominantly document-centric nature of SGML applications. To address these issues, the XML community, under the leadership of the W3C, took up the task of creating a meta-language for describing both the structure of XML document and the mapping of XML syntax to data types. After long deliberation, the effort produced the final version of the XML Schema specification in March, 2001. In a nutshell, XML Schema can be described as powerful but complex. It is powerful because it allows for much more expressive and precise specification of the content of XML documents. It is complex for the same reason. The specification is broken into three parts:

- *XML Schema Part 0: Primer* is a non-normative document that tries to make sense of XML Schema by parceling complexity into small chunks and using many examples.
- *XML Schema Part 1: Structures* focuses primarily on serving the needs of document-oriented applications by laying out the rules for defining the structure of XML documents.
- *XML Schema Part 2: Datatypes* builds upon the structures specification with additional capabilities that address the needs of data-oriented applications such as defining reusable datatypes, associating XML syntax with schema datatypes, and mapping these to application-level data.

Part 0 is meant for general consumption, whereas Parts 1 and 2 are deeply technical and require a skilled and determined reader. The rest of this section will attempt to provide an introduction to XML Schema that is very much biased towards schema usage in data-oriented applications. You should be able to gain sufficient understanding of structure and datatype specifications to comprehend and use common Web service schemas. Still, because XML Schema is fundamental to Web services, we highly recommend that you go through the primer document of the XML Schema specification.

XML Schema Basics

Listing 2.10 shows the basic structure of the SkatesTown purchase order schema.

LISTING 2.10 Basic XML Schema Structure

```
<?xml version="1.0" encoding="UTF-8"?>
<xsd:schema xmlns="http://www.skatestown.com/ns/po"
            xmlns:xsd="http://www.w3.org/2001/XMLSchema"
            targetNamespace="http://www.skatestown.com/ns/po">

   <xsd:annotation>
      <xsd:documentation xml:lang="en">
         Purchase order schema for SkatesTown.
      </xsd:documentation>
   </xsd:annotation>

   ...

</xsd:schema>
```

The most striking difference between schemas (that is how the book will informally refer to XML Schemas) and DTDs is that schemas are expressed in XML. This was done to eliminate the need for XML parsers to know another syntax (that of DTDs) and also to gain the power of expressive XML syntax. Of course, the XML Schema vocabulary is itself defined using schema as an ultimate proof of the power of the schema meta-language.

The second very important feature of schema is that they are designed with namespaces in mind from the ground up. In this particular schema document, all elements belonging to the schema specification are prefixed with xsd:. The prefix's name is not important, but xsd: (which comes from XML Schema Definition) is the convention. The prefix is associated with the http://www.w3.org/2001/XMLSchema namespace that identifies the W3C Recommendation of the XML Schema specification. The default namespace of the document is set to be http://www.skatestown.com/ns/po, the namespace of the SkatesTown purchase order. The schema document needs both namespaces to distinguish between XML elements that belong to the schema specification versus XML elements that belong to purchase orders. Finally, the targetNamespace attribute of the schema element identifies the namespace of the documents that will conform to this schema. This is set to the purchase order schema namespace.

The schema is enclosed by the xsd:schema element. The content of this element will be other schema elements that are used for element, attribute, and datatype definitions. The annotation and documentation elements can be used liberally to attach auxiliary information to the schema.

Associating Schemas with Documents

Schemas do not have to be associated with XML documents. For example, applications can be pre-configured to use a particular schema when processing documents. Alternatively, there is a powerful mechanism for associating schemas with documents. Listing 2.11 shows how to associate the previous schema with a purchase order document.

LISTING 2.11   Associating Schema with Documents

```
<?xml version="1.0" encoding="UTF-8"?>
<po:po xmlns:po="http://www.skatestown.com/ns/po"
       xmlns:xsi="http://www.w3.org/2001/XMLSchema-instance"
       xsi:schemaLocation="http://www.skatestown.com/ns/po
                           http://www.skatestown.com/schema/po.xsd"
       id="43871" submitted="2001-10-05">

    ...

</po:po>
```

First, because the purchase order schema identified a target namespace, purchase order documents are required to use namespaces to identify their elements. The purchase order document uses the po prefix for this task.

Next, the document uses another namespace—http://www.w3.org/2001/ XMLSchema-instance—that has a special meaning. It defines a number of attributes that are part of the schema specification. These attributes can be applied to elements in instance documents to provide additional information to a schema-aware XML processor. By convention, most documents use the namespace prefix `xsi:` (for XML Schema: Instance).

The binding between the purchase order document and its schema is established via the `xsi:schemaLocation` attribute. This attribute contains a pair of values. The first value is the namespace identifier whose schema's location is identified by the second value. Typically, the second value will be a URL, but specialized applications can use other types of values, such as an identifier in a schema repository or a well-known schema name. If the document used more than one namespace, the `xsi:schemaLocation` attribute would contain multiple pairs of values.

Simple Types

One of the biggest problems of DTDs is that they have no notion of datatypes, even for simple values such as the character data content of an element or an attribute value. Because of this, prior to the arrival of XML schema, XML applications included a large amount of validation code. For example, even a simple purchase order requires the following validation rules that are outside the scope of DTDs:

- Attribute `id` of the `po` element must be a positive integer.
- Attribute `submitted` of the `po` element must be a date in the format *yyyy-mm-dd*.
- Attribute `quantity` of the `item` element must be a positive integer.
- Attribute `sku` (stock keeping unit) of the `item` element must be a string with the format three digits followed by a dash followed by two uppercase letters.

XML schemas address these issues in two ways. First, the specification comes with a large set of pre-defined basic datatypes such as string, positive integer, and date. These can be used directly. For custom data types, such as the values of the `sku` attribute, the specification defines a powerful mechanism for defining new types. Table 2.2 shows some of the commonly used pre-defined schema types with some examples of their use.

TABLE 2.2 Pre-defined XML Schema Simple Types

Simple Type	Examples (delimited by commas)	Notes
string	Confirm this is electric	
base64Binary	GpM7	
hexBinary	0FB7	
integer	-126789, -1, 0, 1, 126789	
positiveInteger	1, 126789	
negativeInteger	-126789, -1	

TABLE 2.2 Continued

Simple Type	Examples (delimited by commas)	Notes
nonNegativeInteger	0, 1, 126789	
nonPositiveInteger	-126789, -1, 0	
decimal	-1.23, 0, 123.4, 1000.00	
boolean	true, false 1, 0	
time	13:20:00.000, 13:20:00.000-05:00	
dateTime	1999-05-31T13:20:00.000-05:00	May 31st 1999 at 1.20pm Eastern Standard Time, which is 5 hours behind Coordinated Universal Time
duration	P1Y2M3DT10H30M12.3S	1 year, 2 months, 3 days, 10 hours, 30 minutes, and 12.3 seconds
date	1999-05-31	
Name	shipTo	XML 1.0 Name type
QName	po:USAddress	XML Namespace QName
anyURI	http://www.example.com/, http://www.example.com/doc.html#ID5	
ID		XML 1.0 ID attribute type
IDREF		XML 1.0 IDREF attribute type

The information in this table comes from the XML Schema Primer.

A note on ID/IDREF attributes: An XML processor is required to generate an error if a document contains two ID attributes with the same value or an IDREF with a value that has no matching ID value. This makes ID/IDREF attributes perfect for handling attributes such as the id/href ones in SkatesTown's purchase order address element.

The process for creating new simple datatypes is straightforward. The new type must be derived from a *base type*: a pre-defined schema type or another already defined simple type. The base type is *restricted* along a number of *facets* to obtain the new type. The facets identify various characteristics of the types such as:

- `length`, `minLength` and `maxLength`—the exact, minimum and maximum character length of the value
- `pattern`—a regular expression pattern for the value
- `enumeration`—a list of all possible values
- `whiteSpace`—the rules for handling whitespace in the value
- `minExclusive`, `minInclusive`, `maxInclusive` and `maxExclusive`—the range of numeric values that are allowed
- `totalDigits`—the number of decimal digits in numeric values
- `fractionDigits`—the number of decimal digits after the decimal point

Of course, not all facets apply to all types. For example, the notion of fraction digits makes no sense for a date or a name. Tables 2.3 and 2.4 cross-link the pre-defined types and the facets that are applicable for them.

TABLE 2.3   XML Schema Facets for Simple Types

Simple Types	*Facets*					
	length	minLength	maxLength	pattern	enumeration	whiteSpace
string	✓	✓	✓	✓	✓	✓
base64Binary	✓	✓	✓	✓	✓	✓
hexBinary	✓	✓	✓	✓	✓	✓
integer				✓	✓	✓
positiveInteger				✓	✓	✓
negativeInteger				✓	✓	✓
nonNegativeInteger				✓	✓	✓
nonPositiveInteger				✓	✓	✓
decimal				✓	✓	✓
boolean				✓		✓
time				✓	✓	✓
dateTime				✓	✓	✓
duration				✓	✓	✓

TABLE 2.3 Continued

Simple Types				Facets		
	length	minLength	maxLength	pattern	enumeration	whiteSpace
date				✓	✓	✓
Name	✓	✓	✓	✓	✓	✓
QName	✓	✓	✓	✓	✓	✓
anyURI	✓	✓	✓	✓	✓	✓
ID	✓	✓	✓	✓	✓	✓
IDREF	✓	✓	✓	✓	✓	✓

The information in this table comes from the XML Schema Primer.

The facets listed in Table 2.4 apply only to simple types that have an implicit order.

TABLE 2.4   XML Schema Facets for Ordered Simple Types

Simple Types	Facets					
	Max Inclusive	Max Exclusive	Min Inclusive	Min Exclusive	Total Digits	Fraction Digits
integer	✓	✓	✓	✓	✓	✓
positiveInteger	✓	✓	✓	✓	✓	✓
negativeInteger	✓	✓	✓	✓	✓	✓
nonNegativeInteger	✓	✓	✓	✓	✓	✓
nonPositiveInteger	✓	✓	✓	✓	✓	✓
decimal	✓	✓	✓	✓	✓	✓
time	✓	✓	✓	✓		
dateTime	✓	✓	✓	✓		
duration	✓	✓	✓	✓		
date	✓	✓	✓	✓		

The information in this table comes from the XML Schema Primer.

The syntax for creating new types is simple. For example, the schema snippet in Listing 2.12 defines a simple type for purchase order SKUs. The name of the type is skuType. It is based on a string and it restricts it to have the pattern of three digits followed by dash followed by two uppercase letters.

LISTING 2.12 Using Patterns to Define String Format

```
<xsd:simpleType name="skuType">
   <xsd:restriction base="xsd:string">
      <xsd:pattern value="\d{3}-[A-Z]{2}"/>
   </xsd:restriction>
</xsd:simpleType>
```

Listing 2.13 shows how to force purchase order ids to be greater than 10,000 but less than 100,000 and define an enumeration of all U.S. states.

LISTING 2.13 Using Ranges and Enumerations

```
<xsd:simpleType name="poIdType">
   <xsd:restriction base="xsd:integer">
      <xsd:minExclusive value="10000"/>
      <xsd:maxExclusive value="100000"/>
   </xsd:restriction>
</xsd:simpleType>

<xsd:simpleType name="stateType">
   <xsd:restriction base="xsd:string">
      <xsd:enumeration value="AK"/>
      <xsd:enumeration value="AL"/>
      <xsd:enumeration value="AR"/>
      ...
   </xsd:restriction>
</xsd:simpleType>
```

Complex types

In XML Schema, simple types define the valid choices for character-based content such as attribute values and elements with character content. *Complex types*, on the other hand, define complex content models, such as those of elements that can have attributes and nested children. Complex type definitions do address both the sequencing and multiplicity of child elements as well as the names of associated attributes and whether they are required or optional. The main difference with respect to DTDs is that the schema syntax is much more expressive and the schema capabilities are much more powerful.

The syntax for defining complex types is straightforward:

```
<xsd:complexType name="typeName">
   <xsd:someTopLevelModelGroup>
      <!-- Sequencing and multiplicity constraints for
           child elements defined using xsd:element -->
   </xsd:someTopLevelModelGroup>
```

```
<!-- Attribute declarations using xsd:attribute -->
</xsd:complexType>
```

The element `xsd:complexType` identifies the type definition. There are many different ways to specify the model group of the complex type. The most commonly used top-level model group elements you will see are:

- `xsd:sequence`—A sequence of elements
- `xsd:choice`—Allows one out of a number of elements
- `xsd:all`—Allows a certain set of elements to appear once or not at all but in any order
- `xsd:group`—References a model group that is defined someplace else

These could be further nested to create more complex model groups. The `xsd:group` model group element is covered later in this chapter in the section "Content Model Groups."

Inside the model group specification, child elements are defined using `xsd:element`. The model group specification is followed by any number of attribute definitions using `xsd:attribute`.

For example, one possible way to define the content model of the purchase order address used in the `billTo` and `shipTo` elements is shown in Listing 2.14. The name of the complex type is `addressType`. Using `xsd:sequence` and `xsd:element`, it defines a sequence of the elements `name`, `company`, `street`, `city`, `state`, `postalCode`, and `country`.

LISTING 2.14 Schema Fragment for the Address Complex Type

```
<xsd:complexType name="addressType">
   <xsd:sequence>
      <xsd:element name="name" type="xsd:string" minOccurs="0"/>
      <xsd:element name="company" type="xsd:string" minOccurs="0"/>
      <xsd:element name="street" type="xsd:string"
                   maxOccurs="unbounded"/>
      <xsd:element name="city" type="xsd:string"/>
      <xsd:element name="state" type="xsd:string" minOccurs="0"/>
      <xsd:element name="postalCode" type="xsd:string"
                   minOccurs="0"/>
      <xsd:element name="country" type="xsd:string" minOccurs="0"/>
   </xsd:sequence>
   <xsd:attribute name="id" type="xsd:ID"/>
   <xsd:attribute name="href" type="xsd:IDREF"/>
</xsd:complexType>
```

The multiplicities of these elements' occurrences are defined using the `minOccurs` and `maxOccurs` attributes of `xsd:element`. The value of zero for `minOccurs` renders an element's presence optional ("?" in the document structure diagrams). The default value for `minOccurs` is 1. The special value for `maxOccurs` of `"unbounded"` is used for the street element to indicate that there must be at least one present ("+" in the document structure diagrams).

Every element is associated with a type using the type attribute `xsd:element`. In this example, all elements have simple character content of type string, identified by the `xsd:string` type. It might seem unusual to you that the namespace prefix is used inside an attribute value. It is true, the XML Namespaces specification does not explicitly address this use of namespace prefixes. However, the idea is simple. A schema can define any number of types. Some of them are built into the specification, and others are user-defined. The only way to know for sure which type is being referred to is to associate the type name with the namespace from which it is coming. What better way to do this than to prefix all references to the type with a namespace prefix?

After the model group definition come the attribute definitions. In this example, `xsd:attribute` is used to define attributes `id` and `href` of types `ID` and `IDREF`, respectively. Both attributes are optional by default.

Now, consider a slightly more complex example of a complex type definition—the `po` element's type (see Listing 2.15).

LISTING 2.15 Schema Fragment for the Purchase Order Complex Type

```
<xsd:complexType name="poType">
   <xsd:sequence>
      <xsd:element name="billTo" type="addressType"/>
      <xsd:element name="shipTo" type="addressType"/>
      <xsd:element name="order">
         <xsd:complexType>
            <xsd:sequence>
               <xsd:element name="item" type="itemType"
                            maxOccurs="unbounded"/>
            </xsd:sequence>
         </xsd:complexType>
      </xsd:element>
   </xsd:sequence>
   <xsd:attribute name="id" use="required"
                  type="xsd:positiveInteger"/>
   <xsd:attribute name="submitted" use="required"
                  type="xsd:date"/>
</xsd:complexType>
```

The `poType` introduces three interesting aspects of schema:

- It shows how easy it is to achieve basic reusability of types. Both the `billTo` and `shipTo` elements refer to the `addressType` defined previously. Note that because this is a user-defined complex type, a namespace prefix is not necessary in this case.

- It shows that the association between elements and their types can be implicit. The `order` element's type is defined inline as a sequence of one or more item elements of type `itemType`. This is convenient because it keeps the schema more readable and it prevents the need to define a global type that is used in only one place.

- It shows that the presence of attributes can be required through the `use="required"` attribute-value pair of the `xsd:attribute` element. To give default and fixed values to attributes, you can also use the aptly named `default` and `fixed` attributes of `xsd:attribute`.

The Purchase Order Schema

With the information gathered so far, we can completely define the SkatesTown purchase order schema. The document structure tree in Figure 2.4 looks very similar to that from the section on DTDs. The main difference is the presence of more detailed datatype information. Listing 2.16 shows the complete schema.

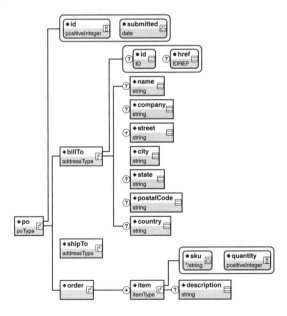

FIGURE 2.4

Document structure defined by purchase order schema.

LISTING 2.16   The Complete SkatesTown Purchase Order Schema (po.xsd)

```xml
<?xml version="1.0" encoding="UTF-8"?>
<xsd:schema xmlns="http://www.skatestown.com/ns/po"
            xmlns:xsd="http://www.w3.org/2001/XMLSchema"
            targetNamespace="http://www.skatestown.com/ns/po">

   <xsd:annotation>
      <xsd:documentation xml:lang="en">
         Purchase order schema for SkatesTown.
      </xsd:documentation>
   </xsd:annotation>


   <xsd:element name="po" type="poType"/>


   <xsd:complexType name="poType">
      <xsd:sequence>
         <xsd:element name="billTo" type="addressType"/>
         <xsd:element name="shipTo" type="addressType"/>
         <xsd:element name="order">
            <xsd:complexType>
               <xsd:sequence>
                  <xsd:element name="item" type="itemType"
                               maxOccurs="unbounded"/>
               </xsd:sequence>
            </xsd:complexType>
         </xsd:element>
      </xsd:sequence>
      <xsd:attribute name="id" use="required"
                     type="xsd:positiveInteger"/>
      <xsd:attribute name="submitted" use="required"
                     type="xsd:date"/>
   </xsd:complexType>


   <xsd:complexType name="addressType">
      <xsd:sequence>
         <xsd:element name="name" type="xsd:string" minOccurs="0"/>
         <xsd:element name="company" type="xsd:string" minOccurs="0"/>
         <xsd:element name="street" type="xsd:string"
                     maxOccurs="unbounded"/>
         <xsd:element name="city" type="xsd:string"/>
         <xsd:element name="state" type="xsd:string" minOccurs="0"/>
         <xsd:element name="postalCode" type="xsd:string"
                     minOccurs="0"/>
         <xsd:element name="country" type="xsd:string" minOccurs="0"/>
      </xsd:sequence>
      <xsd:attribute name="id" type="xsd:ID"/>
      <xsd:attribute name="href" type="xsd:IDREF"/>
```

LISTING 2.16   Continued

```
    </xsd:complexType>

    <xsd:complexType name="itemType">
        <xsd:sequence>
            <xsd:element name="description" type="xsd:string"
                        minOccurs="0"/>
        </xsd:sequence>
        <xsd:attribute name="sku" use="required">
            <xsd:simpleType>
                <xsd:restriction base="xsd:string">
                    <xsd:pattern value="\d{3}-[A-Z]{2}"/>
                </xsd:restriction>
            </xsd:simpleType>
        </xsd:attribute>
        <xsd:attribute name="quantity" use="required"
                        type="xsd:positiveInteger"/>
    </xsd:complexType>
</xsd:schema>
```

Everything should look familiar except perhaps for the standalone definition of the po element right after the schema annotation. This brings us to the important topic of local versus global elements and attributes. Any element or attribute defined inside a complex type definition is considered local to that definition. Conversely, any element or attribute defined at the top level (as a child of xsd:schema) is considered global.

All global elements can be document roots. That is the main reason why most schemas define a single global element. In the case of the SkatesTown purchase order, the po element must be the root of the purchase order document and is hence defined as a global element.

The notion of global attributes might not make much sense at first, but they are very convenient. You can use global attributes (in namespace-prefixed form) on any element in a document that allows them. The item priority attribute discussed in the section "XML Namespaces" can be defined with the short schema in Listing 2.17.

LISTING 2.17   Defining the Priority Global Attribute Using Schema

```
<?xml version="1.0" encoding="UTF-8"?>
<xsd:schema xmlns="http://www.skatestown.com/ns/priority"
            targetNamespace="http://www.skatestown.com/ns/priority"
            xmlns:xsd="http://www.w3.org/2001/XMLSchema">
```

Listing 2.17 Continued

```
   <xsd:attribute name="priority" use="optional" default="medium">
      <xsd:simpleType>
         <xsd:restriction base="xsd:string">
            <xsd:enumeration value="low"/>
            <xsd:enumeration value="medium"/>
            <xsd:enumeration value="high"/>
         </xsd:restriction>
      </xsd:simpleType>
   </xsd:attribute>
</xsd:schema>
```

Basic Schema Reusability

The concept of reusability is important for XML Schema. Reusability deals with the question of how to best leverage any already created assets in new projects. In schema, the assets include element and attribute definitions, content model definitions, simple and complex datatypes, and whole schemas. We can roughly break down reusability mechanisms into two kinds: basic and advanced. The basic reusability mechanisms address the problems of using existing assets in multiple places. Advanced reusability mechanisms address the problems of modifying existing assets to serve needs that are perhaps different from what they were originally designed for.

This section will address the following basic reusability mechanisms:

- Element references
- Content model groups
- Attribute groups
- Schema includes
- Schema imports

Element References

In XML Schema, you can define elements using a name and a type. Alternatively, element declarations can refer to pre-existing elements using the `ref` attribute of `xsd:element` as follows, where a globally defined comment element is being reused for both a person and a task complex type:

```
<xsd:element name="comment" type="xsd:string"/>

<xsd:complexType name="personType">
   <xsd:sequence>
```

```
      <xsd:element name="name" type="xsd:string"/>
      <xsd:element ref="comment" minOccurs="0"/>
   </xsd:sequence>
</xsd:complexType>

<xsd:complexType name="taskType">
   <xsd:sequence>
      <xsd:element name="toDo" type="xsd:string"/>
      <xsd:element ref="comment" minOccurs="0"/>
   </xsd:sequence>
</xsd:complexType>
```

Content Model Groups

Element references are perfect for reusing the definition of a single element. However, if your goal is to reuse whole or part of a content model, then element groups are the way to go. Element groups are defined using xsd:group and are referred to using the same mechanism used for elements. The following schema fragment illustrates the concept. It extends the previous example so that instead of a single comment element, public and private comment elements are reused as a group:

```
<xsd:group name="comments">
   <xsd:sequence>
      <xsd:element name="publicComment" type="xsd:string"
                   minOccurs="0"/>
      <xsd:element name="privateComment" type="xsd:string"
                   minOccurs="0"/>
   </xsd:sequence>
</xsd:group>

<xsd:complexType name="personType">
   <xsd:sequence>
      <xsd:element name="name" type="xsd:string"/>
      <xsd:group ref="comments"/>
   </xsd:sequence>
</xsd:complexType>

<xsd:complexType name="taskType">
   <xsd:sequence>
      <xsd:element name="toDo" type="xsd:string"/>
      <xsd:group ref="comments"/>
   </xsd:sequence>
</xsd:complexType>
```

Attribute Groups

The same reusability mechanism can be applied to commonly used attribute groups. The following example defines the ID/IDREF combination of an id and href attribute as a referenceable attribute group. It is then applied to both the person and the task type:

```
<xsd:attributeGroup name="referenceable">
    <xsd:attribute name="id" type="xsd:ID"/>
    <xsd:attribute name="href" type="xsd:IDREF"/>
</xsd:attributeGroup>

<xsd:complexType name="personType">
    <xsd:sequence>
        <xsd:element name="name" type="xsd:string"/>
    </xsd:sequence>
    <xsd:attributeGroup ref="referenceable"/>
</xsd:complexType>

<xsd:complexType name="taskType">
    <xsd:sequence>
        <xsd:element name="toDo" type="xsd:string"/>
    </xsd:sequence>
    <xsd:attributeGroup ref="referenceable"/>
</xsd:complexType>
```

Schema Includes and Imports

Element references and groups as well as attribute groups provide reusability within the same schema document. However, when you're dealing with very complex schema or trying to achieve maximum reusability, you'll often need to split a schema into several documents. The schema *include* and *import* mechanisms allow these documents to reference one another.

Consider the scenario where SkatesTown is intent on reusing the schema definition for its address type for a mailing list schema. SkatesTown must solve three small problems:

- Put the address type definition in its own schema document
- Reference this schema document from the purchase order schema document
- Reference this schema document from the mailing list schema document

Pulling the address definition into its own schema is as easy as a simple cut-and-paste operation (see Listing 2.18). Even though this is a different document than the main purchase order schema, they both define portions of the SkatesTown purchase order namespace. The binding between schema documents and the namespaces they define is not one-to-one. It is explicitly identified by the targetNamespace attribute of the xsd:schema element.

LISTING 2.18   Standalone Address Type Schema

```
<?xml version="1.0" encoding="UTF-8"?>
<xsd:schema xmlns="http://www.skatestown.com/ns/po"
            xmlns:xsd="http://www.w3.org/2001/XMLSchema"
            targetNamespace="http://www.skatestown.com/ns/po">

   <xsd:annotation>
      <xsd:documentation xml:lang="en">
         Address type schema for SkatesTown.
      </xsd:documentation>
   </xsd:annotation>

   <xsd:complexType name="addressType">
      <xsd:sequence>
         <xsd:element name="name" type="xsd:string" minOccurs="0"/>
         <xsd:element name="company" type="xsd:string" minOccurs="0"/>
         <xsd:element name="street" type="xsd:string"
                      maxOccurs="unbounded"/>
         <xsd:element name="city" type="xsd:string"/>
         <xsd:element name="state" type="xsd:string" minOccurs="0"/>
         <xsd:element name="postalCode" type="xsd:string"
                      minOccurs="0"/>
         <xsd:element name="country" type="xsd:string" minOccurs="0"/>
      </xsd:sequence>
      <xsd:attribute name="id" type="xsd:ID"/>
      <xsd:attribute name="href" type="xsd:IDREF"/>
   </xsd:complexType>

</xsd:schema>
```

Referring to this schema is also very easy. Instead of having the address type definition inline, the purchase order schema needs to include the address schema using the `xsd:include` element. During the processing of the purchase order schema, the address schema will be retrieved and the address type definition will become available (see Listing 2.19).

LISTING 2.19   Referring to the Address Type Schema

```
<?xml version="1.0" encoding="UTF-8"?>
<xsd:schema xmlns="http://www.skatestown.com/ns/po"
            xmlns:xsd="http://www.w3.org/2001/XMLSchema"
            targetNamespace="http://www.skatestown.com/ns/po">

   <xsd:include
```

LISTING 2.19   Continued

```
          schemaLocation="http://www.skatestown.com/schema/address.xsd"/>


   ...
</xsd:schema>
```

The mailing list schema is very simple. It defines a single `mailingList` element that contains any number of contact elements whose type is `address`. Being an altogether different schema than purchase orders, the mailing list schema uses a new namespace, `http://www.skatestown.com/ns/mailingList`. Listing 2.20 shows one possible way to define this schema.

LISTING 2.20   Mailing List Schema

```
<?xml version="1.0" encoding="UTF-8"?>
<xsd:schema xmlns="http://www.skatestown.com/ns/po"
            xmlns:xsd="http://www.w3.org/2001/XMLSchema"
            targetNamespace="http://www.skatestown.com/ns/mailingList">

   <xsd:include
      schemaLocation="http://www.skatestown.com/schema/address.xsd"/>

   <xsd:annotation>
      <xsd:documentation xml:lang="en">
         Mailing list schema for SkatesTown.
      </xsd:documentation>
   </xsd:annotation>

   <xsd:element name="mailingList">
      <xsd:sequence>
         <xsd:element name="contact" type="addressType"
                      minOccurs="0" maxOccurs="unbounded"/>
      </xsd:sequence>
   </xsd:element>

</xsd:schema>
```

This example uses `xsd:include` to bring in the schema fragment defining the address type. There is no problem with that approach. However, there might be a problem with authoring mailing list documents. The root of the problem is that the `mailingList` and `contact` elements are defined in one namespace (`http://www.skatestown.com/ns/mailingList`), whereas the elements belonging to the address type—name, `company`, `street`, `city`, `state`, `postalCode`, `country`—are defined in another (`http://www.skatestown.com/ns/po`). Therefore, the mailing list document must reference both namespaces (see Listing 2.21).

LISTING 2.21   Mailing List that References Two Namespaces

```xml
<?xml version="1.0" encoding="UTF-8"?>
<list:mailingList xmlns:list="http://www.skatestown.com/ns/mailingList"
    xmlns:addr="http://www.skatestown.com/ns/po"
    xmlns:xsi="http://www.w3.org/2001/XMLSchema-instance"
    xsi:schemaLocation="http://www.skatestown.com/ns/mailingList
                        http://www.skatestown.com/schema/mailingList.xsd
                        http://www.skatestown.com/ns/po
                        http://www.skatestown.com/schema/address.xsd">
    <contact>
        <addr:company>The Skateboard Warehouse</addr:company>
        <addr:street>One Warehouse Park</addr:street>
        <addr:street>Building 17</addr:street>
        <addr:city>Boston</addr:city>
        <addr:state>MA</addr:state>
        <addr:postalCode>01775</addr:postalCode>
    </contact>
</list:mailingList>
```

Ideally, when reusing the address type definition in the mailing list schema, we want to hide the fact that it originates from a different namespace and treat it as a true part of the mailing list schema. Therefore, the xsd:include mechanism is not the right one to use, because it makes no namespace changes. The reuse mechanism that will allow the merging of schema fragments from multiple namespaces into a single schema is the import mechanism. Listing 2.22 shows the new mailing list schema.

LISTING 2.22   Importing Rather Than Including the Address Type Schema

```xml
<?xml version="1.0" encoding="UTF-8"?>
<xsd:schema xmlns="http://www.skatestown.com/ns/po"
            xmlns:xsd="http://www.w3.org/2001/XMLSchema"
            xmlns:addr="http://www.skatestown.com/ns/po"
            xmlns:xsi="http://www.w3.org/2001/XMLSchema-instance"
            xsi:schemaLocation="http://www.skatestown.com/ns/po
                http://www.skatestown.com/schema/address.xsd"
            targetNamespace="http://www.skatestown.com/ns/mailingList">

    <xsd:import namespace="http://www.skatestown.com/ns/po"/>

    <xsd:annotation>
        <xsd:documentation xml:lang="en">
            Mailing list schema for SkatesTown.
        </xsd:documentation>
    </xsd:annotation>
```

LISTING 2.22   Continued

```
<xsd:element name="mailingList">
  <xsd:sequence>
    <xsd:element name="contact" type="addr:addressType"
                 minOccurs="0" maxOccurs="unbounded"/>
  </xsd:sequence>
</xsd:element>

</xsd:schema>
```

Although the mechanism is simple to describe, it takes several steps to execute:

1. We declare the namespace of the address type definition and assign it the prefix `addr`.

2. We use the standard `xsi:schemaLocation` mechanism to point to the location of the address schema.

3. We use `xsd:import` instead of `xsd:include`. We import just the namespace; we already know the schema location.

4. When referring to the address type, we use its fully qualified name `addr:addressType`.

The net result is that the mailing list instance document has been simplified (see Listing 2.23).

LISTING 2.23   Simplified Instance Document that Requires a Single Namespace

```
<?xml version="1.0" encoding="UTF-8"?>
<list:mailingList xmlns:list="http://www.skatestown.com/ns/mailingList"
   xmlns:xsi="http://www.w3.org/2001/XMLSchema-instance"
   xsi:schemaLocation="http://www.skatestown.com/ns/mailingList
                       http://www.skatestown.com/schema/mailingList.xsd">
  <contact>
     <company>The Skateboard Warehouse</company>
     <street>One Warehouse Park</street>
     <street>Building 17</street>
     <city>Boston</city>
     <state>MA</state>
     <postalCode>01775</postalCode>
  </contact>
</list:mailingList>
```

Advanced Schema Reusability

The previous section demonstrated how you can reuse types and elements "as is" from the same or a different namespace. This capability can go a long way in some cases, but many real-world scenarios require more sophisticated reuse capabilities. Consider, for example, the format of the invoice that SkatesTown will send to The Skateboard Warehouse based on its purchase order (see Listing 2.24).

LISTING 2.24   SkatesTown Invoice Document

```xml
<?xml version="1.0" encoding="UTF-8"?>
<invoice:invoice xmlns:invoice="http://www.skatestown.com/ns/invoice"
   xmlns:xsi="http://www.w3.org/2001/XMLSchema-instance"
   xsi:schemaLocation="http://www.skatestown.com/ns/invoice
                       http://www.skatestown.com/schema/invoice.xsd"
   id="43871" submitted="2001-10-05">
   <billTo id="addr-1">
      <company>The Skateboard Warehouse</company>
      <street>One Warehouse Park</street>
      <street>Building 17</street>
      <city>Boston</city>
      <state>MA</state>
      <postalCode>01775</postalCode>
   </billTo>
   <shipTo href="addr-1"/>
   <order>
      <item sku="318-BP" quantity="5" unitPrice="49.95">
         <description>Skateboard backpack; five pockets</description>
      </item>
      <item sku="947-TI" quantity="12" unitPrice="129.00">
         <description>Street-style titanium skateboard.</description>
      </item>
      <item sku="008-PR" quantity="1000" unitPrice="0.00">
         <description>Promotional: SkatesTown stickers</description>
      </item>
   </order>
   <tax>89.89</tax>
   <shippingAndHandling>200</shippingAndHandling>
   <totalCost>2087.64</totalCost>
</invoice:invoice>
```

The invoice document has many of the features of a purchase order document, with a few important changes:

- Invoices use a different namespace, http://www.skatestown.com/ns/invoice.
- The root element of the document is invoice and not po.
- The invoice element has three additional children: tax, shippingAndHandling, and totalCost.
- The item element has an additional attribute, unitPrice.

How can we leverage the work done to define the purchase order schema in defining the invoice schema? This section will introduce the advanced schema reusability mechanisms that make this possible.

Design Principles

Imagine that purchase orders, addresses, and items were represented as classes in an object-oriented programming language such as Java. We could create an invoice object by sub-classing item to invoiceItem (which adds unitPrice) and po to invoice (which adds tax, shippingAndHandling, and totalCost). The benefit of this approach is that any changes to related classes such as address will be automatically picked up by both purchase orders and invoices. Further, any changes in base types such as item will be automatically picked up by derived types such as invoiceItem.

The following pseudo-code shows how this approach might work:

```
class Address { ... }

class Item
{
    String sku;
    int quantity;
}

class InvoiceItem extends Item
{
    float unitPrice;
}

class PO
{
    int id;
    Date submitted;
    Address billTo;
    Address shipTo;
    Item order[];
}

class Invoice extends PO
{
    float tax;
    float shippingAndHandling;
    float totalCost;
}
```

Everything looks good except for one important detail. You might have noticed that Invoice probably shouldn't subclass PO. The reason is that the order array inside an invoice object must hold InvoiceItems and not just Item. The subclassing relationship will force you to work with Items instead of InvoiceItems. Doing so will weaken static type-checking and will require constant downcasting, which is generally a bad thing in well-designed object-oriented systems. A better design for the Invoice class, unfortunately, requires some duplication of PO's data members:

```
class Invoice
{
    int id;
    Date submitted;
    Address billTo;
    Address shipTo;
    InvoiceItem order[];
    float tax;
    float shippingAndHandling;
    float totalCost;
}
```

Note that subclassing Item to get InvoiceItem is a good decision because InvoiceItem is a pure extension of Item. It adds new data members; it does not in any way require modifications to Item's data members, nor does it change the way they are used.

Extensions and Restrictions

The analysis from object-oriented systems can be directly applied to the design of SkatesTown's invoice schema. The schema will define the invoice element in terms of pre-existing types such as addressType, and the invoice's item type will reuse the already defined purchase order item type via *extension* (see Listing 2.25).

LISTING 2.25   SkatesTown Invoice Schema

```
<?xml version="1.0" encoding="UTF-8"?>
<xsd:schema xmlns="http://www.skatestown.com/ns/invoice"
    targetNamespace="http://www.skatestown.com/ns/invoice"
    xmlns:xsd="http://www.w3.org/2001/XMLSchema"
    xmlns:po="http://www.skatestown.com/ns/po">

  <xsd:import namespace="http://www.skatestown.com/ns/po"
      schemaLocation="http://www.skatestown.cm/schema/po.xsd"/>

  <xsd:annotation>
    <xsd:documentation xml:lang="en">
```

LISTING 2.25   Continued

```xsd
          Invoice schema for SkatesTown.
      </xsd:documentation>
   </xsd:annotation>

   <xsd:element name="invoice" type="invoiceType"/>

   <xsd:complexType name="invoiceType">
      <xsd:sequence>
         <xsd:element name="billTo" type="po:addressType"/>
         <xsd:element name="shipTo" type="po:addressType"/>
         <xsd:element name="order">
            <xsd:complexType>
               <xsd:sequence>
                  <xsd:element name="item" type="itemType"
                               maxOccurs="unbounded"/>
               </xsd:sequence>
            </xsd:complexType>
         </xsd:element>
         <xsd:element name="tax" type="priceType"/>
         <xsd:element name="shippingAndHandling" type="priceType"/>
         <xsd:element name="totalCost" type="priceType"/>
      </xsd:sequence>
      <xsd:attribute name="id" use="required"
                     type="xsd:positiveInteger"/>
      <xsd:attribute name="submitted" use="required" type="xsd:date"/>
   </xsd:complexType>

   <xsd:complexType name="itemType">
      <xsd:complexContent>
         <xsd:extension base="po:itemType">
            <xsd:attribute name="unitPrice" use="required"
                           type="priceType"/>
         </xsd:extension>
      </xsd:complexContent>
   </xsd:complexType>

   <xsd:simpleType name="priceType">
      <xsd:restriction base="xsd:decimal">
         <xsd:minInclusive value="0"/>
      </xsd:restriction>
   </xsd:simpleType>

</xsd:schema>
```

By now the schema mechanics should be familiar. The beginning of the schema declares the purchase order and invoice namespaces. The purchase order schema has to be imported because it does not reside in the same namespace as the invoice schema.

The `invoiceType` schema address type is defined in terms of `po:addressType`, but the `order` element's content is of type `itemType` and not `po:itemType`. That's because the invoice's `itemType` needs to extend `po:itemType` and add the `unitPrice` attribute. This happens at the next complex type definition. In general, the schema extension syntax, although somewhat verbose, is easy to use:

```
<xsd:complexType name="...">
   <xsd:complexContent>
      <xsd:extension base="...">
         <!-- Optional extension content model -->
         <!-- Optional extension attributes -->
      </xsd:extension>
   </xsd:complexContent>
</xsd:complexType>
```

The content model of extended types contains all the child elements of the base type plus any additional elements added by the extension. Any attributes in the extension are added to the attribute set of the base type.

Last but not least, the invoice schema defines a simple price type as a non-negative decimal number. The definition happens via restriction of the lower bound of the decimal type using the same mechanism introduced in the section on simple types.

The restriction mechanism in schema applies not only to simple types but also to complex types. The syntax is similar to that of extension:

```
<xsd:complexType name="...">
   <xsd:complexContent>
      <xsd:restriction base="...">
         <!-- Content model and attributes -->
      </xsd:restriction>
   </xsd:complexContent>
</xsd:complexType>
```

The concept of restriction has a very precise meaning in XML Schema. The declarations of the type derived by restriction are very close to those of the base type but more limited. There are several possible types of restrictions:

- Multiplicity restrictions
- Deletion of optional element

- Tighter limits on occurrence constraints
- Providing default values
- Providing types where there were none, or narrowing types

For example, you can extend the address type by restriction to create a corporate address that does not include a name:

```xsd
<xsd:complexType name="corporateAddressType">
    <xsd:complexContent>
        <xsd:restriction base="addressType">
            <xsd:sequence>
                <!-- Add maxOccurs="0" to delete optional name element -->
                <xsd:element name="name" type="xsd:string"
                             minOccurs="0" maxOccurs="0"/>
                <!-- The rest is the same as in addressType -->
                <xsd:element name="company" type="xsd:string"
                             minOccurs="0"/>
                <xsd:element name="street" type="xsd:string"
                             maxOccurs="unbounded"/>
                <xsd:element name="city" type="xsd:string"/>
                <xsd:element name="state" type="xsd:string"
                             minOccurs="0"/>
                <xsd:element name="postalCode" type="xsd:string"
                             minOccurs="0"/>
                <xsd:element name="country" type="xsd:string"
                             minOccurs="0"/>
            </xsd:sequence>
            <xsd:attribute name="id" type="xsd:ID"/>
            <xsd:attribute name="href" type="xsd:IDREF"/>
        </xsd:restriction>
    </xsd:complexContent>
</xsd:complexType>
```

The Importance of `xsi:type`

The nature of restriction is such that an application that is prepared to deal with the base type can certainly accept the derived type. In other words, you can use a corporate address type directly inside the billTo and shipTo elements of purchase orders and invoices without a problem. There are times, however, when it might be convenient to identify the actual schema type that is used in an instance document. XML Schema allows this through the use of the global xsi:type attribute. This attribute can be applied to any element to signal its actual schema type, as Listing 2.26 shows.

LISTING 2.26   Using xsi:type

```xml
<?xml version="1.0" encoding="UTF-8"?>
<po:po xmlns:po="http://www.skatestown.com/ns/po"
       xmlns:xsi="http://www.w3.org/2001/XMLSchema-instance"
       xsi:schemaLocation="http://www.skatestown.com/ns/po
                           http://www.skatestown.com/schema/po.xsd"
       id="43871" submitted="2001-10-05">
  <billTo xsi:type="po:corporateAddressType">
      <company>The Skateboard Warehouse</company>
      <street>One Warehouse Park</street>
      <street>Building 17</street>
      <city>Boston</city>
      <state>MA</state>
      <postalCode>01775</postalCode>
  </billTo>
  ...
</po:po>
```

Although derivation by restriction does not require the use of xsi:type, derivation by extension often does. The reason is that an application prepared for the base schema type is unlikely to be able to process the derived type (it adds information) without a hint. But, why would such a scenario ever occur? Why would an instance document contain data from a type derived by extension in a place where a base type is expected by the schema?

One reason is that XML Schema allows derivation by extension to be used in cases where it really should not be used, as in the case of the invoice and purchase order datatypes. In these cases, xsi:type must be used in the instance document to ensure successful validation. Consider a scenario where the invoice type was derived by extension from the purchase order type:

```xml
<xsd:complexType name="invoiceType">
   <xsd:complexContent>
      <xsd:extension base="po:poType">
         <xsd:element name="tax" type="priceType"/>
         <xsd:element name="shippingAndHandling" type="priceType"/>
         <xsd:element name="totalCost" type="priceType"/>
      </xsd:extension>
   </xsd:complexContent>
</xsd:complexType>
```

Remember, extension does not change the content model of the base type; it can only add to it. Therefore, this definition will make the item element inside invoices of type po:itemType, not invoice:itemType. The use of xsi:type (see Listing 2.27) is the only way to add unit prices to items without violating the validity constraints of the document imposed by the schema. An imperfect analogy from programming languages is that xsi:type provides the true type to downcast to when you are holding a reference to a base type.

LISTING 2.27   Using xsi:type to Correctly Identify Invoice Item Elements

```
<order>
   <item sku="318-BP" quantity="5" unitPrice="49.95"
        xsi:type="invoice:itemType">
      <description>Skateboard backpack; five pockets</description>
   </item>
   <item sku="947-TI" quantity="12" unitPrice="129.00"
        xsi:type="invoice:itemType">
      <description>Street-style titanium skateboard.</description>
   </item>
   <item sku="008-PR" quantity="1000" unitPrice="0.00"
        xsi:type="invoice:itemType">
      <description>Promotional: SkatesTown stickers</description>
   </item>
</order>
```

This example shows a use of xsi:type that comes as a result of poor schema design. If, instead of extending purchase order, the invoice type is defined on its own, the need for xsi:type disappears. However, sometimes even good schema design does not prevent the need to identify actual types in instance documents.

Imagine that, due to constant typos in shipping and billing address postal codes, SkatesTown decides to become more restrictive in its document validation. The company defines three types of addresses that can be used in purchase orders and schema. The types have the following constraints:

- Address—Same as always
- USAddress—Country is not allowed, and the Zip code pattern "\d{5}(-\d{4})?" is enforced
- UKAddress—Country is fixed to UK and the postal code pattern "[0-9A-Z]{3} [0-9A-Z]{3}" is enforced

To get the best possible validation, SkatesTown's applications need to know the exact type of address that is being used in a document. Without using xsi:type, the purchase order and invoice schema will each have to define nine (three squared) possible combinations of billTo and shipTo elements: billTo/shipTo, billTo/shipToUS, billTo/shipToUK, billToUS/shipTo, and so on. It is better to stick with billTo and shipTo and use xsi:type to get exact schema type information.

There's More

This completes the whirlwind tour of XML Schema. Fortunately or unfortunately, much material useful for data-oriented applications falls outside the scope of what can be addressed in this chapter. Some further material will be introduced throughout the rest of the book as needed.

Processing XML

So far, this chapter has introduced the key XML standards and explained how they are expressed in XML documents. The final section of the chapter focuses on processing XML with a quick tour of the specifications and APIs you need to know to be able to generate, parse, and process XML documents in your Java applications.

Basic Operations

The basic XML processing architecture shown in Figure 2.5 consists of three key layers. At far left are the XML documents an application needs to work with. At far right is the application. In the middle is the infrastructure layer for working with XML documents, which is the topic of this section.

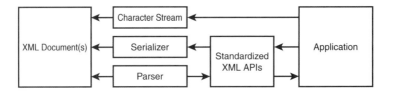

FIGURE 2.5

Basic XML processing architecture.

For an application to be able to work with an XML document, it must first be able to parse it. *Parsing* is a process that involves breaking up the text of an XML document into small identifiable pieces (*nodes*). Parsers will break documents into pieces such as start tags, end tags, attribute value pairs, chunks of text content, processing instructions, comments, and so on. These pieces are fed into the application using a well-defined API implementing a particular parsing model. Four parsing models are commonly in use:

- *Pull parsing* 📖 involves the application always having to ask the parser to give it the next piece of information about the document. It is as if the application has to "pull" the information out of the parser and hence the name of the model. The XML community has not yet defined standard APIs for pull parsing. However, because pull parsing is becoming popular, this could happen soon.

- *Push parsing* 📖—The parser sends notifications to the application about the types of XML document pieces it encounters during the parsing process. The notifications are sent in "reading" order, as they appear in the text of the document. Notifications are typically implemented as event callbacks in the application code, and thus push parsing is also commonly known as *event-based parsing*. The XML community created a *de facto* standard for push parsing called *Simple API for XML (SAX)* 📖. SAX is currently released in version 2.0.

- *One-step parsing* 📖—The parser reads the whole XML document and generates a data structure (a *parse tree*) describing its entire contents (elements, attributes, PIs, comments, and so on). The data structure is typically deeply nested; its hierarchy mimics the nesting of elements in the parsed XML document. The W3C has defined a *Document Object Model (DOM)* 📖 for XML. The XML DOM specifies the types of objects that will be included in the parse tree, their properties, and their operations. The DOM is so popular that one-step parsing is typically referred to as *DOM parsing*. The DOM is a language- and platform-independent API. It offers many obvious benefits but also some hidden costs. The biggest problem with the DOM APIs is that they often do not map well to the native data structures of particular programming languages. To address this issue for Java, the Java community has started working on a Java DOM (JDOM) specification whose goal is to simplify the manipulation of document trees in Java by using object APIs tuned to the common patterns of Java programming.

- *Hybrid parsing* 📖—This approach tries to combine different characteristics of the other two parsing models to create efficient parsers for special scenarios. For example, one common pattern combines pull parsing with one-step parsing. In this model, the application thinks it is working with a one-step parser that has processed the whole XML document from start to end. In reality, the parsing process has just begun. As the application keeps accessing more objects on the DOM (or JDOM) tree, the parsing continues incrementally so that just enough of the document is parsed at any given point to give the application the objects it wants to see.

The reasons there are so many different models for parsing XML have to do with trade-offs between memory efficiency, computational efficiency, and ease of programming. Table 2.6 identifies some of the characteristics of the different parsing models. Control of parsing refers to who has to manage the step-by-step parsing process. Pull parsing requires that the application does that. In all other models, the parser will take care of this process. Control of context refers to who has to manage context information such as the level of nesting of elements and their location relative to one another. Both push and pull parsing delegate this control to the application. All other models build a tree of nodes that makes maintaining context much easier. This approach makes programming with DOM or JDOM generally easier than working with SAX. The price is memory and computational efficiency, because instantiating all these objects

takes up both time and memory. Hybrid parsers attempt to offer the best of both worlds by presenting a tree view of the document but doing incremental parsing behind the scenes.

TABLE 2.6   XML Parsing Models and Their Trade-offs

Model	Control of Parsing	Control of context	Memory efficiency	Computational efficiency	Ease of programming
Pull	Application	Application	High	Highest	Low
Push (SAX)	Parser	Application	High	High	Low
One-step (DOM)	Parser	Parser	Lowest	Lowest	High
One-step (JDOM)	Parser	Parser	Low	Low	Highest
Hybrid (DOM)	Parser	Parser	Medium	Medium	High
Hybrid (JDOM)	Parser	Parser	Medium	Medium	Highest

In the Java world, a standardized API—*Java API for XML Processing (JAXP)* 📖—exists for
instantiating XML parsers and parsing documents using either SAX or DOM. Without JAXP,
Java applications were not completely portable across XML parsers because different parsers,
despite following SAX and DOM, had different APIs for creation, configuration, and parsing
of documents. JAXP is currently released in version 1.1. It does not support JDOM yet because
the JDOM specification is not complete at this point.

Although XML parsing addresses the problem of feeding data from XML documents into
applications, XML output addresses the reverse problem—applications generating XML documents. At the most basic level, an application can directly output XML markup. In Figure 2.5,
this is indicated by the application working with a character stream. This is not very difficult to
do, but handling all the basic syntax rules (attributes quoting, special character escaping, and
so on) can become cumbersome. In many cases, it might be easier for the application to construct a data structure (DOM or JDOM tree) describing the XML document that should be generated. Then, the application can use a *serialization* 📖 process to traverse the document tree
and emit XML markup corresponding to its elements. This capability is not directly defined in
the DOM and JDOM APIs, but most XML toolkits make it very easy to do just that.

Data-Oriented XML Processing

When you're thinking about applications working with XML, it is important to note that all the
mechanisms for parsing and generating XML described so far are *syntax-oriented*. They force
the application to work with concepts such as elements, attributes, and pieces of text. This is
similar to applications that use text files for storage being forced to work with characters, lines,
carriage returns (CR), and line feeds (LF). Typically, applications want a higher-level view of
their data. They are not concerned with the *physical structure* of the data, be it characters and
lines in the case of text files or elements and attributes in the case of XML documents. They

want to abstract this away and expose the *meaning* or semantics of the data. In other words, applications do not want to work with syntax-oriented APIs, they want to work with *data-oriented* APIs. Therefore, typical data-oriented XML applications introduce a data abstraction layer between the syntax-oriented parsing and output APIs and application logic (see Figure 2.6).

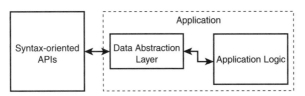

FIGURE 2.6
Data abstraction layer in XML applications.

When working with XML in a data-oriented manner, you'll typically use one of two approaches: *operation-centric* and *data-centric*. The operation-centric approach works in terms of custom-built APIs for certain operations on the XML document. The implementation of these APIs hides the details of XML processing. Only non-XML types are passed through the APIs.

Consider for example, the task of SkatesTown trying to independently check the total amount on the invoices it is sending to its customers. From a Java application perspective, a good way to implement an operation like this would be through the interface shown in Listing 2.28.

LISTING 2.28 InvoiceChecker Interface

```java
package com.skatestown.invoice;

import java.io.InputStream;

/**
 * SkatesTown invoice checker
 */
public interface InvoiceChecker {
    /**
     * Check invoice totals.
     *
     * @param       invoiceXML Invoice XML document
     * @exception   Exception  Any exception returned during checking
     */
    void checkInvoice(InputStream invoiceXML) throws Exception;
}
```

The actual implementation of `checkInvoice` will have to do the following:

1. Obtain an XML parser.
2. Parse the XML from the input stream.
3. Initialize a running total to zero.
4. Find all order items and calculate item subtotals by multiplying quantities and unit prices. Add item subtotals to the running total.
5. Add tax to the running total.
6. Add shipping and handling to the running total.
7. Compare the running total to the total on invoice.
8. If there is a difference, throw an exception.
9. Otherwise, return.

The most important aspect to this approach is that any XML processing details will be hidden from the application. It can happily work with the `InvoiceChecker` interface, never knowing or caring about how `checkInvoice` does its work.

An alternative is the data-centric approach. Data-centric XML computing reduces the problem of working with XML documents to that of mapping the XML to and from application data and then working with the data entirely independent of its XML origins. Application data covers the common datatypes developers work with every day: boolean values, numbers, strings, date-time values, arrays, associative arrays (dictionaries, maps, hash tables), database record-sets, and complex object types. Note that in this context, DOM tree objects will not be considered "true" application data because they are tied to XML syntax. The process of converting application data to XML is called *serialization*. The XML is a serialized representation of the application data. The process of generating application data from XML is called *deserialization* 📖.

For example, the XML invoice markup could be mapped to the set of Java classes introduced in the schema section (see Listing 2.29).

LISTING 2.29 Java Classes Representing Invoice Data

```
class Address { ... }

class Item { ... }

class InvoiceItem extends Item { ... }
```

LISTING 2.29 Continued

```
class Invoice
{
    int id;
    Date submitted;
    Address billTo;
    Address shipTo;
    InvoiceItem order[];
    float tax;
    float shippingAndHandling;
    float totalCost;
}
```

The traditional approach for generating XML from application data has been to sit down and custom-code how data values become elements, attributes, and element content. The traditional approach of working with XML to produce application data has been to parse it using a SAX or a DOM parser. Data structures are built from the SAX events or the DOM tree using custom code. There are, however, better ways to map data to and from XML using technologies specifically built for serializing and deserializing data to and from XML. Enter schema compilation tools. Schema compilers are tools that analyze XML schema and code-generate serialization and deserialization modules specific to the schema. These modules will work with data structures tuned to the schema. Figure 2.7 shows the basic process for working with schema compilers. The schema compiler needs to be invoked only once. Then the application can use the code-generated modules just like any other API. For example, a schema compiler working on the SkatesTown invoice schema could have generated the helper class shown in Listing 2.30 to wrap serialization and deserialization.

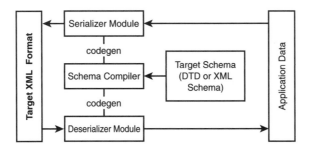

FIGURE 2.7
Using a schema compiler.

LISTING 2.30   Serialization/Deserialization Helper

```
class InvoiceXMLHelper
{
   // All exception signatures removed for readability
   public static InvoiceXMLHelper create();
   public serialize(Invoice inv, OutputStream xml);
   public Invoice deserialize(InputStream xml);
}
```

Chapters 3 ("Simple Object Access Protocol (SOAP)") and 4 ("Creating Web Services") will introduce some advanced data mapping concepts specific to Web services as well as some more sophisticated mechanisms for working with XML. The rest of this section will offer a taste of XML processing by implementing the checkInvoice() API described earlier using both a SAX and a DOM parser.

SAX-based checkInvoice

The basic architecture of the JAXP SAX parsing APIs is shown in Figure 2.8. It uses the common abstract factory design pattern. First, you must create an instance of SAXParserFactory that is used to create an instance of SAXParser. Internally, the parser wraps a SAXReader object that is defined by the SAX API. JAXP developers typically do not have to work directly with SAXReader. When the parser's parse() method is invoked, the reader starts firing events to the application by invoking certain registered callbacks.

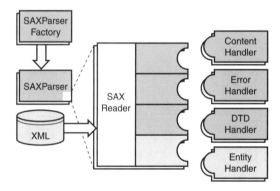

FIGURE 2.8
SAX parsing architecture.

Working with JAXP and SAX involves four important Java packages:

Package	Description
org.xml.sax	Defines the SAX interfaces
org.xml.sax.ext	Defines advanced SAX extensions for DTD processing and detailed syntax information
org.xml.sax.helpers	Defines helper classes such as DefaultHandler
javax.xml.parsers	Defines the SAXParserFactory and SAXParser classes

Here is a summary of the key SAX-related objects:

SAXParserFactory	A SAXParserFactory object creates an instance of the parser determined by the system property, javax.xml.parsers.SAXParserFactory.
SAXParser	The SAXParser interface defines several kinds of parse() methods. In general, you pass an XML data source and a DefaultHandler object to the parser, which processes the XML and invokes the appropriate methods in the handler object.
DefaultHandler	Not shown in Figure 2.8, DefaultHandler implements all SAX callback interfaces with null methods. Custom handlers subclass DefaultHandler and override the methods they are interested in receiving.

The following list contains the callback interfaces and some of their important methods:

- ContentHandler—Contains methods for all basic XML parsing events:

  Void startDocument()

  Receive notification of the beginning of a document.

  Void endDocument()

  Receive notification of the end of a document.

  Void startElement(String namespaceURI, String localName, String qName, Attributes atts)

  Receive notification of the beginning of an element.

  Void characters(char[] ch, int start, int length)

  Receive notification of character data.

- ErrorHandler—Contains methods for receiving error notification. The default implementation in DefaultHandler throws errors for fatal errors but does nothing for non-fatal errors, including validation errors:

  Void error(SAXParseException exception)

Receive notification of a recoverable error. An example of a recoverable error is a validation error.

```
Void fatalError(SAXParseException exception)
```

Receive notification of a non-recoverable error. An example of a non-recoverable error is a well-formedness error.

- DTDHandler—Contains methods for dealing with XML entities.
- EntityResolver—Contains methods for resolving the location of external entities.

SAX defines an event-based parsing model. A SAX parser will invoke the callbacks from these interfaces as it is working through the document. Consider the following sample document:

```
<?xml version="1.0" encoding="UTF-8"?>
<sampleDoc>
    <greeting>Hello, world!</greeting>
</sampleDoc>
```

An event-based parser will make the series of callbacks to the application as follows:

```
start document
start element: sampleDoc
start element: greeting
characters: Hello, world!
end element: greeting
end element: sampleDoc
end document
```

Because of the simplicity of the parsing model, the parser does not need to keep much state information in memory. This is why SAX-based parsers are very fast and highly efficient. The flip side to this benefit is that the application has to manage any context associated with the parsing process. For example, for the application to know that the string "Hello, world!" is associated with the greeting element, it needs to maintain a flag that is raised in the start element event for greeting and lowered in the end element event. More complex applications typically maintain a stack of elements that are in the process of being parsed. Here are the SAX events with an added context stack:

```
start document            ()
start element: sampleDoc  (sampleDoc)
start element: greeting    (sampleDoc, greeting)
characters: Hello, world!  (sampleDoc, greeting)
end element: greeting      (sampleDoc, greeting)
end element: sampleDoc     (sampleDoc)
end document              ()
```

With this information in mind, building a class to check invoice totals becomes relatively simple (see Listing 2.31).

LISTING 2.31   SAX-based Invoice Checker (InvoiceCheckerSAX.java)

```java
package com.skatestown.invoice;

import java.io.InputStream;
import org.xml.sax.Attributes;
import org.xml.sax.SAXException;
import javax.xml.parsers.SAXParser;
import javax.xml.parsers.SAXParserFactory;
import org.xml.sax.helpers.DefaultHandler;

/**
 * Check SkatesTown invoice totals using a SAX parser.
 */
public class InvoiceCheckerSAX
    extends DefaultHandler
    implements InvoiceChecker
{
    // Class-level data
    // invoice running total
    double runningTotal = 0.0;
    // invoice total
    double total = 0.0;

    // Utility data for extracting money amounts from content
    boolean isMoneyContent = false;
    double amount = 0.0;

    /**
     * Check invoice totals.
     * @param       invoiceXML       Invoice XML document
     * @exception Exception        Any exception returned during checking
     */
    public void checkInvoice(InputStream invoiceXML) throws Exception {
        // Use the default (non-validating) parser
        SAXParserFactory factory = SAXParserFactory.newInstance();
        SAXParser saxParser = factory.newSAXParser();

        // Parse the input; we are the handler of SAX events
        saxParser.parse(invoiceXML, this);
    }

    // SAX DocumentHandler methods
    public void startDocument() throws SAXException {
        runningTotal = 0.0;
        total = 0.0;
```

LISTING 2.31 Continued

```java
        isMoneyContent = false;
    }

    public void endDocument() throws SAXException {
        // Use delta equality check to prevent cumulative
        // binary arithmetic errors. In this case, the delta
        // is one half of one cent
        if (Math.abs(runningTotal - total) >= 0.005) {
            throw new SAXException(
                "Invoice error: total is " + Double.toString(total) +
                " while our calculation shows a total of " +
                Double.toString(Math.round(runningTotal * 100) / 100.0));
        }
    }

    public void startElement(String namespaceURI,
                             String localName,
                             String qualifiedName,
                             Attributes attrs) throws SAXException {
        if (localName.equals("item")) {
            // Find item subtotal; add it to running total
            runningTotal +=
                Integer.valueOf(attrs.getValue(namespaceURI,
                    "quantity")).intValue() *
                Double.valueOf(attrs.getValue(namespaceURI,
                    "unitPrice")).doubleValue();
        } else if (localName.equals("tax") ||
                   localName.equals("shippingAndHandling") ||
                   localName.equals("totalCost")) {
            // Prepare to extract money amount
            isMoneyContent = true;
        }
    }

    public void endElement(String namespaceURI,
                           String localName,
                           String qualifiedName) throws SAXException {
        if (isMoneyContent) {
            if (localName.equals("totalCost")) {
                total = amount;
            } else {
                // It must be tax or shippingAndHandling
                runningTotal += amount;
            }
```

LISTING 2.31 Continued

```
            isMoneyContent = false;
        }
    }

    public void characters(char buf[], int offset, int len)
        throws SAXException {
        if (isMoneyContent) {
            String value = new String(buf, offset, len);
            amount = Double.valueOf(value).doubleValue();
        }
    }
}
```

InvoiceCheckerSAX must implement the InvoiceChecker interface in order to provide the checkInvoice functionality. It also subclasses DefaultHandler to obtain default implementations for all SAX callbacks. In this way the implementation can focus on overriding only the relevant callbacks.

The class members runningTotal and total maintain state information about the invoice during the parsing process. The class members isMoneyContent and amount are necessary in order to maintain parsing context. Because events about character data are independent of events about elements, we need a flag to indicate whether we should attempt to parse character data as a dollar amount for the tax, shippingAndHandling, and totalCost elements. This is what isMoneyContent does. After we parse the text into a dollar figure, we save it into the amount member variable and wait until the endElement() callback to determine what to do with it.

The checkInvoice() method implementation shows how easy it is to use JAXP for XML parsing. Parsing an XML document with SAX only takes three lines of code.

At the beginning of the document, we have to initialize all member variables. At the end of the document, we check whether there is a difference between the running total and the total cost listed on the invoice. If there is a problem, we throw an exception with a descriptive message. Note that we cannot use an equality check because no exact mapping exists between decimal numbers and their binary representation. During the many additions to runningTotal, a very tiny error will be introduced in the calculation. So, instead of checking for equality, we need to check whether the difference between the listed and the calculated totals is significant. *Significant* in this case would be any amount greater than half a cent, because a half-cent difference can affect the rounding of a final value to a cent.

The parser pushes events about the new elements to the startElement() method. If the element we get a notification about is an item element, we can immediately extract the values of the quantity and unitPrice attributes from its attributes collection. Multiplying them together creates an item subtotal, which we add to the running total. Alternatively, if the element is one of `tax`, `shippingAndHandling`, or `totalCost`, we prepare to extract a money amount from its text content. All other elements are simply ignored.

We only care to process end element notifications if we were expecting to extract a money amount from their content. Based on the name of the element, we decide whether to save the amount as the total cost of the invoice or whether to add it to the running total.

When we process character data and we are expecting a dollar value, we extract the element content, convert it to a double value, and save it in the `amount` class member for use by the `endElement()` callback.

Note that we could have skipped implementing `endElement()` altogether if we had also stored the element name as a string member of the class or used an enumerated value. Then, we would have decided how to use the dollar amount right inside `characters()`.

That's all there is to it. Of course, this is a very simple example. A real application would have done at least two things differently:

- It would have used namespace information and prefixed element names instead of simply using local names.
- It would have defined its own exception type to communicate invoice validation information. It would have also overridden the default callbacks for `error()` and `fatalError()` and used these to collect better exception information.

Unfortunately, these extensions fall outside the scope of this chapter. The rest of the book has several examples of building robust XML processing software.

DOM-based `checkInvoice`

The basic architecture of the JAXP DOM parsing APIs is shown in Figure 2.9. It uses the same factory design pattern as the SAX API. An application will use the `javax.xml.parsers.DocumentBuilderFactory` class to get a `DocumentBuilder` object instance, and use that to produce a document that conforms to the DOM specification. The value of the system property `javax.xml.parsers.DocumentBuilderFactory` determines which factory implementation will produce the builder. This is how JAXP enables applications to work with different DOM parsers.

The important packages for working with JAXP and DOM are as follows:

Package	Description
`org.w3c.dom`	Defines the DOM programming interfaces for XML (and, optionally, HTML) documents, as specified by the W3C
`javax.xml.parsers`	Defines `DocumentBuilder` and `DocumentBuilderFactory` classes

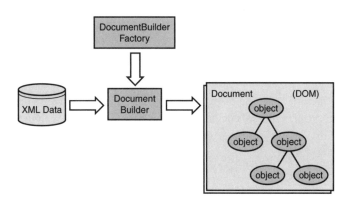

FIGURE 2.9

DOM parsing architecture.

The DOM defines APIs that allow applications to navigate XML documents and to manipulate their content and structure. The DOM defines interfaces, not a particular implementation. These interfaces are specified using the Interface Description Language (IDL) so that any language can define bindings for them. Separate Java bindings are provided to make working with the DOM in Java very easy.

The DOM has several levels and various facets within a level. In the fall of 1998, DOM Level 1 was released. It provided the basic functionality to navigate and manipulate XML and HTML documents. DOM Level 2 builds upon Level 1 with more and better-segmented functionality:

- The DOM Level 2 Core API builds upon Level 1, fixes some problem spots, and defines additional ways to navigate and manipulate the content and structure of documents. These APIs also provide full support for namespaces.

- The DOM Level 2 Views API specifies interfaces that provide programmers with the ability to view alternate presentations of the XML or HTML document.

- The DOM Level 2 Style API specifies interfaces that provide programmers with the ability to dynamically access and manipulate style sheets.

- The DOM Level 2 Events API specifies interfaces that provide programmers with a generic event system.

- The DOM Level 2 Traversal-Range API specifies interfaces that provide programmers with the ability to traverse a representation of the XML document.

- The DOM Level 2 HTML API specifies interfaces that provide programmers with the ability to work with HTML documents.

All interfaces apart from the core ones are optional. This is the main reason why most applications choose to rely entirely on the DOM Core. You can expect more of the DOM to be supported by parsers soon. In fact, the W3C is currently working on DOM Level 3.

The DOM originated as an API for XML processing at a time when the majority of XML applications were document-centric. As a result, the interfaces in the DOM describe fairly low-level syntax constructs in XML documents. This makes working with the DOM for data-oriented applications somewhat cumbersome, and is one of the reasons the Java community is working on the JDOM APIs.

To better understand the XML DOM, you need to understand the core interfaces and the most significant methods in them. Figure 2.10 shows a Universal Modeling Language (UML) diagram describing some of these.

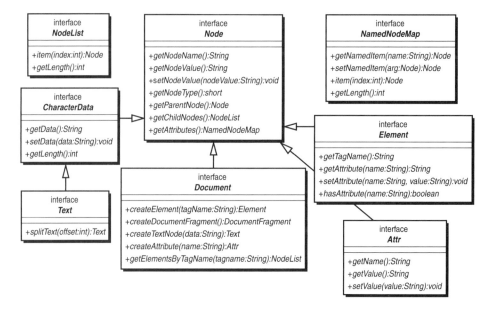

FIGURE 2.10
Key DOM interfaces and operations.

The root interface is Node. It contains methods for working with the node name (getNodeName()), type (getNodeType()), and attributes (getNodeAttributes()). Node types cover various possible XML syntax elements: document, element, attributes, character data, text node, comment, processing instruction, and so on. All of these are shown in subclass Node but not all are shown in Figure 2.10. To traverse the document hierarchy, nodes can access their parent (getParentNode()) as well as their children (getChildNodes()). Node also has several convenience methods for retrieving the first and last child as well as the previous and following sibling.

The most important operations in Document involve creating nodes (at least one for every node type), assembling these nodes into the tree (not shown), and locating elements by name, regardless of their location in the DOM (getElementsByTagName()). This last API is very convenient because it can save you from having to traverse the tree to get to a particular node.

The rest of the interfaces on the figure are very simple. Elements, attributes, and character data offer a few methods each for getting and setting their data members. NodeList and NamedNodeMap are convenience interfaces for dealing with collections of nodes and attributes, respectively. What Figure 2.10 does not show is that DOM Level 2 is fully namespace aware and all DOM APIs have versions that take in namespace URIs. Typically, their name is the same as the name of the original API with *NS* appended, such as Element's getAttributeNS(String nsURI, String localName).

With this information in mind, building a class to check invoice totals becomes relatively simple. The DOM implementation of InvoiceChecker is shown in Listing 2.32.

LISTING 2.32   DOM-based Invoice Checker (InvoiceCheckerDOM.java)

```java
package com.skatestown.invoice;

import java.io.InputStream;
import org.w3c.dom.Node;
import org.w3c.dom.NodeList;
import org.w3c.dom.Document;
import org.w3c.dom.Element;
import org.w3c.dom.CharacterData;
import javax.xml.parsers.DocumentBuilder;
import javax.xml.parsers.DocumentBuilderFactory;

/**
 * Check SkatesTown invoice totals using a DOM parser.
 */
public class InvoiceCheckerDOM implements InvoiceChecker {
    /**
     * Check invoice totals.
     *
     * @param       invoiceXML Invoice XML document
     * @exception   Exception  Any exception returned during checking
     */
    public void checkInvoice(InputStream invoiceXML)
        throws Exception
    {
        // Invoice running total
        double runningTotal = 0.0;
```

LISTING 2.32   Continued

```java
// Obtain parser instance and parse the document
DocumentBuilderFactory factory =
    DocumentBuilderFactory.newInstance();
DocumentBuilder builder = factory.newDocumentBuilder();
Document doc = builder.parse(invoiceXML);

// Calculate order subtotal
NodeList itemList = doc.getElementsByTagName("item");
for (int i = 0; i < itemList.getLength(); i++) {
    // Extract quantity and price
    Element item = (Element)itemList.item(i);
    Integer qty = Integer.valueOf(
        item.getAttribute("quantity"));
    Double price = Double.valueOf(
        item.getAttribute("unitPrice"));

    // Add subtotal to running total
    runningTotal += qty.intValue() * price.doubleValue();
}

// Add tax
Node nodeTax = doc.getElementsByTagName("tax").item(0);
runningTotal += doubleValue(nodeTax);

// Add shipping and handling
Node nodeShippingAndHandling =
    doc.getElementsByTagName("shippingAndHandling").item(0);
runningTotal += doubleValue(nodeShippingAndHandling);

// Get invoice total
Node nodeTotalCost =
    doc.getElementsByTagName("totalCost").item(0);
double total = doubleValue(nodeTotalCost);

// Use delta equality check to prevent cumulative
// binary arithmetic errors. In this case, the delta
// is one half of one cent
if (Math.abs(runningTotal - total) >= 0.005)
{
    throw new Exception(
        "Invoice error: total is " + Double.toString(total) +
        " while our calculation shows a total of " +
        Double.toString(Math.round(runningTotal * 100) / 100.0));
}
}
```

Listing 2.32   Continued

```
/**
 * Extract a double from the text content of a DOM node.
 *
 * @param        node A DOM node with character content.
 * @return       The double representation of the node's content.
 * @exception    Exception Could be the result of either a node
 *               that does not have text content being passed in
 *               or a node whose text content is not a number.
 */
private double doubleValue(Node node) throws Exception {
    // Get the character data from the node and parse it
    String value = ((CharacterData)node.getFirstChild()).getData();
    return Double.valueOf(value).doubleValue();
}
}
```

InvoiceCheckerDOM must implement the InvoiceChecker interface in order to provide the checkInvoice functionality. Apart from this, it is a standalone class. Also, note that the class has no member data, because there is no need to maintain parsing context. The context is implicit in the hierarchy of the DOM tree that will be the result of the parsing process.

The factory pattern used here to parse the invoice is the same as the one from the SAX implementation; it just uses DocumentBuilderFactory and DocumentBuilder instead. Although the SAX parse method returns no data (it starts firing events instead), the DOM parse() method returns a Document object that holds the complete parse tree of the invoice document.

Within the parse tree, the call to getElementsByTagName("item") retrieves a node list of all order items. The loop iterates over the list, extracting the quantity and unitPrice attributes for every item, obtaining an item subtotal, and adding this to the running total.

The same getElementsByTagName() API combined with the utility function doubleValue() extracts the amounts of tax, the shipping and handling, and the invoice total cost.

Just as in the SAX example, the code has to use a difference check instead of a direct equality check to guard against inexact decimal-to-binary conversions.

The class also defines a convenient utility function that takes in a DOM node that should have only character content and returns the numeric representation of that content as a double. Any non-trivial DOM processing will typically require these types of utility functions. It goes to prove that the DOM is very syntax-oriented and not at all concerned about data.

That's all there is to it. Of course, this is a very simple example and, just as in the SAX example, a real application would have done at least three things differently:

- It would have used namespace information and prefixed element names instead of simply using local names.

- It would have defined its own exception type to communicate invoice validation information. It would have implemented try-catch logic inside the `checkInvoice` method in order to report more meaningful errors.

- It would have either explicitly turned on validation of the incoming XML document or traversed the DOM tree step-by-step from the document root to all the elements of interest. Using `getElementsByTagName()` presumes that the structure of the document (relative positions of elements) has already been validated. If this is the case, it is OK to ask for all item elements regardless of where they are in the document. The example implementation took this approach for code readability purposes.

These changes are not complex, but they would have increased the size and complexity of the example beyond its goals as a basic introduction to DOM processing.

Testing the Code

Rather than forcing you to set up the Java Runtime Environment (JRE), modify CLASSPATH environment variables, and run examples from the command line, this book has taken a novel, Web-centric approach. All examples are accessible from the book's example Web site.

The actual example code is written using Java Server Pages (JSP). JSP allows Java code to be mixed in with HTML for building Web applications. JSP builds on top of the Java servlet standard for building Web components. Java application servers compile JSPs down to servlets.

The example code that drives `InvoiceCheckerSAX` and `InvoiceCheckerDOM` appears in Listing 2.33.

LISTING 2.33   JSP Page for Checking Invoices (`/ch2/ex1/index.jsp`)

```
<%@ page import="java.io.*,bws.BookUtil,com.skatestown.invoice.*" %>
<HTML>
<HEAD><TITLE>Invoice Checker</TITLE></HEAD>
<h1>Invoice Checker</h1>

<p>This example implements a web form driver for SkatesTowns's invoice
checker. You can modify the invoice on the form if you wish (the
default one is from Chapter 2), select a DOM or SAX parser and perform
 a check on the invoice total.</p>

<FORM action="index.jsp" method="POST">
<%
    String xml = request.getParameter("xml");
    if (xml == null) {
        xml = BookUtil.readResource(application,
                       "/resources/sampleInvoice.xml");
    }
```

LISTING 2.33   Continued

```
%>
    <TEXTAREA NAME="xml" ROWS="20" COLS="90"><%= xml%></TEXTAREA>
    <P></P>
    Select parser type:
    <INPUT type="RADIO" name="parserType" value="SAX" CHECKED> SAX
    <INPUT type="RADIO" name="parserType" value="DOM"> DOM
    <P></P>
    <INPUT type="SUBMIT" value=" Check Invoice ">
</FORM>

<%
    // Check for form submission
    if (request.getParameter("xml") != null) {
        out.println("<HR>");

        // Instantiate appropriate parser type
        InvoiceChecker ic;
        if (request.getParameter("parserType").equals("SAX")) {
            out.print("Using SAX parser...<br>");
            ic = new InvoiceCheckerSAX();
        } else {
            out.print("Using DOM parser...<br>");
            ic = new InvoiceCheckerDOM();
        }

        // Check the invoice
        try {
            ic.checkInvoice(new StringBufferInputStream(xml));
            out.print("Invoice checks OK.");
        } catch(Exception e) {
            out.print(e.getMessage());
        }
    }
%>

</BODY>
</HTML>
```

JSP uses the <%@ ... %> syntax for compile-time directives. The page import="..." directive accomplishes the equivalent of a Java import statement.

The HTML code sets up a simple Web form that will post back to the same page. The form contains a text area with the name xml that will contain the XML of the invoice to be validated.

In JSP, you can use the construct <% ... %> to surround arbitrary Java code embedded in the JSP page. The request object is an implicit object on the page associated with the Web request.

Implicit objects in JSP are set up by the JSP compiler. They can be used without requiring any type of declaration or setup. One of the most useful methods of the request object is `getParameter()`, which retrieves the value of a parameter passed from the Web such as a form field or returns null if this parameter did not come with the request. The code uses `getParameter("xml")` to check whether the form is being displayed (return is null) versus submitted (return is non-null). If the form is displayed for the first time, the page loads the invoice XML from a sample file in `/resources/sampleInvoice.xml`.

The rest of the Java code runs only if the form has been submitted. It uses the implicit `out` object to send output to the resulting Web page. It uses the value of the `parserType` field in the Web page to determine whether to instantiate a SAX or a DOM parser. It then checks the invoice by passing the value of the `xml` text area on the page to the `checkInvoice()` method. If the call is successful, the invoice checks OK, and an appropriate message is displayed. If an exception is thrown by `checkInvoice()`, an invoice total discrepancy (or an XML processing error) has been detected, which will be output to the browser.

That's all there is to creating a Web test client for the invoice checker. Figure 2.11 shows the Web page ready for submission.

FIGURE 2.11
Invoice checker Web page.

Summary

This chapter has focused on explaining some of the core features of XML and related technologies. The goal was to prepare you for the Web service–related material in the rest of the book, which relies heavily on the concepts presented here. To this end, we covered, in some detail:

- The origins of XML and the fundamental difference between document- and data-centric XML applications. Web services are an extreme example of data-centric XML use. The material in this chapter purposefully ignored some aspects of XML that are more document-oriented.

- The syntax and rules governing the physical structure of XML documents: document prologs, elements, attributes, character content, CDATA sections, and so on. We omitted document-oriented features of XML such as entities and notations due to their infrequent use in the context of Web services. The SkatesTown purchase order document format made its initial appearance.

- XML Namespaces, the key tool for resolving the problems of name recognition and name collision in XML applications. Namespaces are fundamental to mixing information from multiple schemas into a single document, something that all core Web service technologies rely upon. SkatesTown's purchase order inside an XML message wrapper is an example of a common pattern for XML use that will be explored in depth in the next chapter. The namespace mechanism is simple and beautiful; however, people often try to read more into it than is really there, as demonstrated by the debate over whether namespace URIs should point to meaningful resources. One of the slightly more complex aspects of the specification is the multiple namespace defaulting mechanisms that simplify document markup while preserving namespace information.

- The concepts of well-formedness and validity and Document Type Definitions (DTDs) as a mechanism to validate XML document structure. DTDs are powerful, but they also have great limitations such as non-XML syntax, no ties to namespaces, and poor support for even basic data types such as numbers and dates.

- XML Schema, the *de facto* standard for describing document structure and XML datatypes for data-oriented applications. Although XML Schema is a recent standard, the XML community had defined specifications based on draft versions of the standard for nearly two years. The flexible content models, the large number of pre-defined datatypes and the powerful extensibility and reuse features make this one of the most important developments in the XML space since XML 1.0. All Web service specifications are described using schema. Through the definition of SkatesTown's purchase order and invoice schemas, this chapter introduced enough of the key capabilities of the technology to prepare you for what is to come in the rest of the book.

- The key mechanisms for creating and processing XML with software. Starting with the basic syntax-oriented XML processing architecture, the chapter progressed to define a data-oriented XML processing architecture together with the key concepts of XML data mapping and XML parsing. In the context of SkatesTown's desire to independently validate invoice totals sent to its customers, we used the Java APIs for XML Processing (JAXP), the Simple APIs for XML (SAX), and the XML Document Object Model (DOM) to build two separate implementations of an invoice checker. A simple Web-based front end served as the test bed for the code.

This chapter explicitly did not focus on other important but not very relevant XML technologies such as XPointer/XLink, Resource Definition Framework (RDF), XPath, Extensible Stylesheet Language Transformations (XSLT), or XQuery. They are important in their own domains and useful to be familiar with in general but are not commonly used in the context of Web services. Other more technical XML specification such as XML Digital Signatures will be introduced later in the book as part of meaningful Web service usage scenarios.

Right now, you know enough about XML to go deep into the exciting world of Web services. Chapter 3 introduces the core Web service messaging technologies: Simple Object Access Protocol (SOAP) and XML Protocol (XMLP).

Resources

- *DOM Level 1*—DOM Level 1 Specification (W3C, October 1998). Available at `http://www.w3.org/TR/REC-DOM-Level-1`.
- *DOM Level 2 Core*—W3C (World Wide Web Consortium) Document Object Model Level 2 Core (W3C, November 2000). Available at `http://www.w3.org/TR/2000/REC-DOM-Level-2-Core-20001113`.
- *JAXP*—Java API for XML Processing 1.1 (Sun Microsystems, Inc., February 2001). Available at `http://java.sun.com/xml/xml_jaxp.html`.
- *JDOM*—Java Document Object Model. Available at `http://www.jdom.org/docs/apidocs`.
- *JSP*—Java Server Pages 1.2 (Sun Microsystems, Inc., April 2001). Available at `http://java.sun.com/products/jsp`.
- *RFC2396*—RFC 2396, "Uniform Resource Identifiers (URI): Generic Syntax" (IETF, August 1998). Available at `http://www.ietf.org/rfc/rfc2396.txt`.
- *SAX*—Simple API for XML (SAX) 2.0 (May 2000). Available at `http://www.megginson.com/SAX/Java/index.html`.
- *XML*—Extensible Markup Language (XML) 1.0, 2nd ed. (W3C, August 2000). Available at `http://www.w3.org/TR/2000/WD-xml-2e-20000814`.

- *XML Namespaces*—"Namespaces in XML" (W3C, January 1999). Available at `http://www.w3.org/TR/1999/REC-xml-names-19990114`.

- *XML Schema Part 0: Primer*—"XML Schema Part 0: Primer" (W3C, May 2001). Available at `http://www.w3.org/TR/2001/REC-xmlschema-0-20010502`.

- *XML Schema Part 1: Structures*—"XML Schema Part 1: Structures" (W3C, May 2001). Available at `http://www.w3.org/TR/2001/REC-xmlschema-1-20010502`.

- *XML Schema Part 2: Datatypes*—"XML Schema Part 2: Datatypes" (W3C, May 2001). Available at `http://www.w3.org/TR/2001/REC-xmlschema-2-20010502`..

Simple Object Access Protocol (SOAP)

IN THIS CHAPTER

There is a lot more to Web services than Simple Object Access Protocol (SOAP). Chapter 1, "Web Services Overview," introduced the Web services interoperability stack that went several levels higher than SOAP. SOAP is synonymous with Web services, however, because since its introduction in late 1999, it has become the *de facto* standard for Web services messaging and invocation. With competitive and market pressures driving the Web services industry in a hard race to provide meaningful solutions to cross-enterprise integration problems, SOAP is the go-to-market technology of choice.

What is SOAP all about, you ask? Will it save you from failure (and keep you clean) while you toil 80-hour work weeks on a business-to-business (B2B) integration project from hell? Will it support your extensibility needs as requirements change, and provide you with interoperability across multi-vendor offerings? Will it be the keyword on your resume that will guarantee you a big raise as you switch jobs? In short, is it the *new new* thing? Well, maybe.

SOAP is so simple and so flexible that it can be used in many different ways to fit the needs of different Web service scenarios. This is both a blessing and a curse. It is a blessing because chances are that SOAP can fit your needs. It is a curse because you probably won't know how to make it do that. This is where this chapter comes in. When you are through with it, you will know not only how to use SOAP straight out of the box, but also how to extend SOAP in multiple ways to support your diverse and changing needs. You will also have applied design best practices to build several meaningful e-commerce Web services for our favorite company, SkatesTown. Last but not least, you will be ready to handle the rest of the book and climb still higher toward the top of the Web services interoperability stack. To this end, the chapter will discuss the following topics:

- The evolution of XML protocols and the history and motivation behind SOAP's creation
- The SOAP envelope framework, complete with discussions of versioning, header-based vertical extensibility, intermediary-based horizontal extensibility, error handling, and bindings to multiple transport protocols
- The various mechanisms for packaging information in SOAP messages, including SOAP's own data-encoding rules and a number of heuristics for putting just about any kind of data in SOAP messages
- The use of SOAP within multiple distributed system architectures such as RPC- and messaging-based systems in all their flavors
- Building and consuming Web services using the Java-based Apache Axis Web services engine

One final note before we begin. The SOAP 1.1 specification is slightly over 40 pages long. This chapter is noticeably longer, because the purpose of this book is to be something more than an annotated spec or a tutorial for building Web services. We've tried hard to create a thorough treatment of Web services for people who want answers to questions that begin not only with "what" and "how" but also with "why." To become an expert at Web services, you need to be comfortable dealing with the latter type of questions. We are here to help.

So, why SOAP? As this chapter will show, SOAP is simple, flexible, and highly extensible. Because it is XML based, SOAP is programming language, platform, and hardware neutral. What better choice for the XML protocol that is the foundation of Web services? To prove this point, let's start the chapter by looking at some of the earlier work that inspired SOAP.

Evolution of XML Protocols

The enabling technology behind Web services is built around *XML protocols* 📖. XML protocols govern how communication happens and how data is represented in XML format on the wire. XML protocols can be broadly classified into two generations. First-generation protocols are based purely on XML 1.0. Second-generation protocols take advantage of both XML Namespaces and XML Schema. SOAP is a second-generation XML protocol.

First-Generation XML Protocols

There were many interesting first-generation XML protocol efforts. They informed the community of important protocol requirements and particular approaches to satisfying these requirements. Unfortunately, very few of the first-generation XML protocols achieved multi-vendor support and broad adoption. Two are worth mentioning: Web Distributed Data Exchange (WDDX) and XML-RPC.

WDDX

WDDX 📖 provides a language- and platform-neutral mechanism for data exchange between applications. WDDX is perfect for data syndication and remote B2B integration APIs because it is all about representing data as XML. For example, Moreover Technologies, the Web feed company, exposes all its content through a WDDX-based remote API. Access `http://moreover.com/cgi-local/page?index+wddx` with an XML-aware browser such as Internet Explorer and you will get a WDDX packet with current headline news. A simplified version of the packet is shown in the following example. You can see from it that the data format is a recordset (tabular data) with three fields containing the URL to the full article, its headline text, and the publishing source:

```
<wddxPacket version="1.0">
    <header/>
    <data>
        <recordset rowCount="2" fieldNames="url,headline_text,source">
            <field name="url">
                <string>http://c.moreover.com/click/here.pl?x22535276</string>
```

```
            <string>http://c.moreover.com/click/here.pl?x22532205</string>
        </field>
        <field name="headline_text">
            <string>Firefighters hold line in Wyoming</string>
            <string>US upbeat as China tensions ease</string>
        </field>
        <field name="source">
            <string>CNN</string>
            <string>BBC</string>
        </field>
    </recordset>
  </data>
</wddxPacket>
```

Allaire Corporation (now Macromedia, Inc.) created WDDX in 1998. WDDX is currently supported in many environments and is flexible enough to handle most useful datatypes (strings, numbers, booleans, date/time, binary, arrays, structures, and recordsets), but it cannot represent arbitrary data in XML. It is an epitome of the 80/20 rule: flexible enough to be useful yet simple enough to be broadly supported. Because WDDX is not bound to any particular transport, applications can exchange WDDX packets via HTTP, over e-mail, or by any other means. Many applications persist data as XML in a relational database using WDDX.

XML-RPC

XML-RPC 📖 is an RPC protocol introduced in the market in 1998 by Userland. XML-RPC supports a set of datatypes similar to that supported by WDDX and uses HTTP as the underlying transport protocol. Because of its simplicity, XML-RPC enjoyed good multi-vendor support. Here's an example XML-RPC method call and response:

```
<methodCall>
    <methodName>NumberToText</methodName>
    <params>
        <param>
            <value><i4>28</i4></value>
        </param>
    </params>
</methodCall>
...
<methodResponse>
    <params>
        <param>
            <value><string>twenty-eight</string></value>
        </param>
    </params>
</methodResponse>
```

First-Generation Problems

Although first-generation XML protocols have been and still are very useful, their simplicity and reliance on XML 1.0 alone causes some problems.

First-generation protocols are not very extensible. The protocol architects had to reach agreement before any changes were implemented, and the protocol version had to be revved up in order to let tools distinguish new protocol versions from old ones and handle the XML appropriately. For example, when XML-RPC and WDDX added support for binary data, both protocols had to update their specifications, and the protocol implementations on all different languages and platforms supporting the protocols had to be updated. The overhead of constantly revising specifications and deploying updated tools for handling the latest versions of the protocols imposed limits on the speed and scope of adoption of first-generation protocols. Second-generation protocols address the issue of extensibility with XML namespaces.

The second problem with first-generation protocols had to do with datatyping. First-generation XML protocols stuck to a single Document Type Definition (DTD) to describe the representation of serialized data in XML. In general, they used just a few XML elements. This approach made building tools supporting these protocols relatively easy. The trouble with such an approach is that the XML describing the data in protocol messages expressed datatype information and not semantic information. In other words, to gain the ability to represent data in XML, first-generation XML protocols went without the ability to preserve information about the meaning of the data. Second-generation XML protocols use XML schema as a mechanism to combine descriptive syntax with datatype information.

To sum things up, the need to provide broad extensibility without centralized standardization and the need to combine datatype information with semantic information were the driving forces behind the effort to improve upon first-generation efforts and to create SOAP, the *de facto* standard XML protocol for modern Web services and B2B applications.

Simple Object Access Protocol (SOAP)

This section looks at the history, design center, and core capabilities of SOAP as a means for establishing the base on which to build our understanding of Web services.

The Making of SOAP

Microsoft started thinking about XML-based distributed computing in 1997. The goal was to enable applications to communicate via Remote Procedure Calls (RPCs) on top of HTTP. DevelopMentor and Userland joined the discussions. The name *SOAP* was coined in early 1998. Things moved forward, but as the group tried to involve wider circles at Microsoft, politics stepped in and the process was stalled. The DCOM camp at the company disliked the idea of SOAP and believed that Microsoft should use its dominant position in the market to push the DCOM wire protocol via some form of HTTP tunneling instead of pursuing XML. Some XML-focused folks at Microsoft believed that the SOAP idea was good but that it had come too early. Perhaps they were looking for some of the advanced facilities that could be provided by XML Schema and Namespaces. Frustrated by the deadlock, Userland went public with a cut of the spec published as XML-RPC in the summer of 1998.

In 1999, as Microsoft was working on its version of XML Schema (XML Data) and adding support for namespaces in its XML products, the idea of SOAP gained additional momentum. It was still an XML-based RPC mechanism, however. That's why it met with resistance from the BizTalk (`http://www.biztalk.org`) team. The BizTalk model was based more on messaging than RPCs. It took people a few months to resolve their differences. SOAP 0.9 appeared for public review on September 13, 1999. It was submitted to the IETF as an Internet public draft. With few changes, in December 1999, SOAP 1.0 came to life.

On May 8, 2000 SOAP 1.1 was submitted as a Note to the World Wide Web Consortium (W3C) with IBM as a co-author—an unexpected and refreshing change. In addition, the SOAP 1.1 spec was much more extensible, eliminating concerns that backing SOAP implied backing some Microsoft proprietary technology. This change, and the fact that IBM immediately released a Java SOAP implementation that was subsequently donated to the Apache XML Project (`http://xml.apache.org`) for open-source development, convinced even the greatest skeptics that SOAP is something to pay attention to. Sun voiced support for SOAP and started work on integrating Web services into the J2EE platform. Not long after, many vendors and open-source projects were working on Web service implementations.

Right before the XTech 2000 Conference, the W3C made an announcement that it was looking into starting an activity in the area of XML protocols: "We've been under pressure from many sources, including the advisory board, to address the threat of fragmentation of and investigate the exciting opportunities in the area of XML protocols. It makes sense to address this now because the technology is still early in its evolution…" (`http://lists.w3.org/Archives/Public/xml-dist-app/2000Feb/0006.html`). On September 13, 2000 the XML Protocol working group at the W3C was formed to design the XML protocol that was to become the core of XML-based distributed computing in the years to come. The group started with SOAP 1.1 as a foundation and produced the first working draft of SOAP 1.2 on July 9, 2001.

What Should SOAP Do?

SOAP claims to be a specification for a *ubiquitous XML distributed computing infrastructure*. It's a nice buzzword-compliant phrase, but what does it mean? Let's parse it bit by bit to find out what SOAP should do.

XML means that, as a second-generation XML protocol, SOAP is based on XML 1.0, XML Schema, and XML Namespaces.

Distributed computing implies that SOAP can be used to enable the interoperability of remote applications (in a very broad sense of the phrase). Distributed computing is a fuzzy term and it means different things to different people and in different situations. Here are some "facets" you can use to think about a particular distributed computing scenario: the protocol stack used for communication, connection management, security, transaction support, marshalling and unmarshalling of data, protocol evolution and version management, error handling, audit trails, and so on. The requirements for different facets will vary between scenarios. For example, a stock ticker service that continuously distributes stock prices to a number of subscribers will have different needs than an e-commerce payment-processing service. The stock ticker service will probably need no support for transactions and only minimal, if any, security or audit trails (it distributes publicly available data). The e-commerce payment-processing service will require Cerberean security, heavy-duty transaction support, and full audit trails.

Infrastructure implies that SOAP is aimed at low-level distributed systems developers, not developers of application/business logic or business users. Infrastructure products such as application servers become "SOAP enabled" by including a Web service engine that understands SOAP. SOAP works behind the scenes making sure your applications can interoperate without your having to worry too much about it.

Ubiquitous means omnipresent, universal. On first look, it seems to be a meaningless term, thrown into the phrase to make it sound grander. It turns out, however, that this is the most important part. The ubiquity goal of SOAP is a blessing because, if SOAP-enabled systems are everywhere on the Internet, it should be easier to do distributed computing. After all, that's what SOAP is all about. However, the ubiquity of SOAP is also a curse, because one technology specification should be able to support many different types of distributed computing scenarios, from the stock ticker service to the e-commerce payment-processing service. To meet this goal, SOAP needs to be a highly abstract and flexible technology. However, the more abstract SOAP becomes, the less support it will provide for specific distributed computing scenarios. Furthermore, greater abstraction means more risk that different SOAP implementations will fail to interoperate. This is the eternal tug-of-war between generality and specificity.

What Is SOAP, Really?

Like most new technologies that change the rules of how applications are being developed, Web services and SOAP have sometimes been over-hyped. Despite the hype, however, SOAP is still of great importance because it is the industry's best effort to date to standardize on the infrastructure technology for cross-platform XML distributed computing.

Above all, SOAP is relatively simple. Historically, simplicity is a key feature of most successful architectures that have achieved mass adoption. The Web with HTTP and HTML at its core is a prime example. Simple systems are easier to describe, understand, implement, test, maintain, and evolve. At its heart, SOAP is a specification for a simple yet flexible second-generation XML protocol. SOAP 1.0 printed at about 40 pages. The text of the specification has grown since then (the authors have to make sure the specification is clear and has no holes), but the core concepts remain simple.

Because SOAP is focused on the common aspects of all distributed computing scenarios, it provides the following:

- A mechanism for defining the unit of communication. In SOAP, all information is packaged in a clearly identifiable SOAP *message*. This is done via a SOAP *envelope* that encloses all other information. A message can have a *body* in which potentially arbitrary XML can be used. It can also have any number of *headers* that encapsulate information outside the body of the message.

- A mechanism for error handling that can identify the source and cause of the error and allows for error-diagnostic information to be exchanged between participants in an interaction. This is done via the notion of a SOAP *fault*.

- An extensibility mechanism so that evolution is not hindered and there is no lock-in. XML, schemas, and namespaces really shine here. The two key requirements on extensions are that they can be orthogonal to other extensions and they can be introduced and used without the need for centralized registration or coordination. Typically, extensions are introduced via SOAP headers. They can be used to build more complex protocols on top of SOAP.

- A flexible mechanism for data representation that allows for the exchange of data already serialized in some format (text, XML, and so on) as well as a convention for representing abstract data structures such as programming language datatypes in an XML format.

- A convention for representing Remote Procedure Calls (RPCs) and responses as SOAP messages, because RPCs are the most common type of distributed computing interaction and because they map so well to procedural programming language constructs.

- A document-centric approach to reflect more natural document exchange models for business interactions. This is needed to support the cases in which RPCs result in interfaces that are too fine grained and, therefore, brittle.

- A binding mechanism for SOAP messages to HTTP, because HTTP is the most common communication protocol on the Internet.

Although solid consensus exists in the industry about the core capabilities of SOAP, there is considerably less agreement on how higher-level issues such as security and transaction-management should be addressed. Nearly everyone agrees that to tackle the broad spectrum of interesting problems we are faced with, we need to work in parallel on a set of layered specifications for XML distributed computing. Indeed, many loosely coupled industry initiatives are developing standards and technologies around SOAP. Tracking these efforts is like trying to shoot at many moving targets. The authors of this book have tried our best to address the relevant efforts in this space and to provide you with up-to-date information. Chapter 1 showed how many of these efforts layered around the notion of the Web services interoperability stack. Chapter 5, "Using SOAP for e-Business," goes into more detail about the set of standards surrounding SOAP that enable secure, robust, and scalable enterprise-grade Web services.

Now, let's take a look at how SkatesTown is planning to use SOAP and Web services.

Doing Business with SkatesTown

When Al Rosen of Silver Bullet Consulting first began his engagement with SkatesTown, he focused on understanding the e-commerce practices of the company and its customers. After a series of conversations with SkatesTown's CTO Dean Caroll, he concluded the following:

- SkatesTown's manufacturing, inventory management, and supply chain automation systems are in good order. These systems are easily accessible by SkatesTown's Web-centric applications.

- SkatesTown has solid consumer-oriented online presence. Product and inventory information is fed into the online catalog that is accessible to both direct consumers and SkatesTown's reseller partners via two different sites.

- Although SkatesTown's order processing system is sophisticated, it is poorly connected to online applications. This is a pain point for the company because SkatesTown's partners are demanding better integration with their supply chain automation systems.

- SkatesTown's purchase order system is solid. It accepts purchase orders in XML format and uses XML Schema-based validation to guarantee their correctness. Purchase order item stock keeping units (SKUs) and quantities are checked against the inventory management system. If all items are available, an invoice is created. SkatesTown charges a uniform 5% tax on purchases and the highest of 5% of the total purchase or $20 for shipping and handling.

Digging deeper into the order processing part of the business, Al discovered that it uses a low-tech approach that has a high labor cost and is not suitable for automation. He noticed one area that badly needed automation: the process of purchase order submission. Purchase orders are sent to SkatesTown by e-mail. All e-mails arrive in a single manager's account in operations. The manager manually distributes the orders to several subordinates. They have to open the e-mail, copy only the XML over to the purchase order system, and enter the order there. The system writes an invoice file in XML format. This file must be opened, and the XML must be copied and pasted into a reply e-mail message. Simple misspellings of e-mail addresses and cut-and-paste errors are common. They cost SkatesTown and its partners both money and time.

Another area that needs automation is the inventory checking process. SkatesTown's partners used to submit purchase orders without having a clear idea whether all the items were in stock. This often caused delayed order processing. Further, purchasing personnel from the partner companies would engage in long e-mail dialogs with operations people at SkatesTown. This situation was not very efficient. To improve it, SkatesTown built a simple online application that communicates with the company's inventory management system. Partners could log in, browse SkatesTown's products, and check whether certain items were in stock. The application interface is shown in Figure 3.1. (You can access this application as Example 1 under Chapter 3 in the example application on this book's Web site.) This application was a good start, but now SkatesTown's partners are demanding the ability to have their purchasing applications directly inquire about order availability.

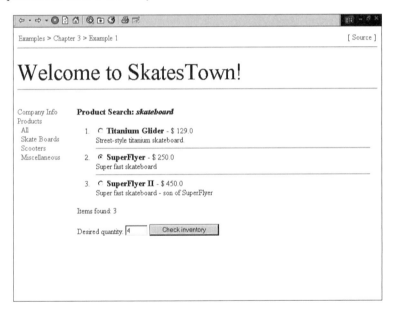

FIGURE 3.1
SkatesTown's online inventory check application.

Looking at the two areas that most needed to be improved, Al Rosen chose to focus on the inventory checking process because the business logic was already present. He just had to enable better automation. To do this, he had to better understand how the application worked.

Interacting with the Inventory System

The logic for interacting with the inventory system is very simple. Looking through the Java Server Pages (JSPs) that made up the online application, Al easily extracted the key business logic operations from /ch3/ex1/inventoryCheck.jsp. Here is the process for checking SkatesTown's inventory:

```
import bws.BookUtil;
import com.skatestown.data.Product;
import com.skatestown.backend.ProductDB;

String sku = ...;
int quantity = ...;

ProductDB db = BookUtil.getProductDB(...);
Product   p = db.getBySKU(sku);

boolean isInStock = (p != null && p.getNumInStock() >= quantity);
```

Given a SKU and a desired product quantity, an application needs to get an instance of the SkatesTown product database and locate a product with a matching SKU. If such a product is available and if the number of items in stock is greater than or equal to the desired quantity, the inventory check succeeds. Because most of the examples in this chapter talk to the inventory system, it is good to take a deeper look at its implementation.

> **NOTE**
>
> A note of caution: this book's sample applications demonstrate realistic uses of Java technology and Web services to solve real business problems while, at the same time, remaining simple enough to fit in the book's scope and size limitations. Further, all the examples are directly accessible in many environments and on all platforms that have a JSP and servlet engine without any sophisticated installation. To meet these somewhat conflicting criteria, something has to give. For example:
>
> - To keep the code simple, we do as little data validation and error checking as possible without allowing applications to break. You won't find us defining custom exception types or producing long, readable error messages.
>
> - To get away from the complexities of external system access, we use simple XML files to store data.
>
> - To make deployment easier, we use the BookUtil class as a place to go for all operations that depend on file locations or URLs. You can tune the deployment options for the example applications by modifying some of the constants defined in BookUtil.
>
> - All file paths are relative to the installation directory of the example application.

SkatesTown's inventory is represented by a simple XML file stored in /resources/
products.xml (see Listing 3.1). By modifying this file, you can change the behavior of many
examples. The Java representation of products in SkatesTown's systems is the
com.skatestown.data.Product class. It is a simple bean that has one property for every
element under product.

LISTING 3.1   SkatesTown Inventory Database

```xml
<?xml version="1.0" encoding="UTF-8"?>
<products>
   <product>
      <sku>947-TI</sku>
      <name>Titanium Glider</name>
      <type>skateboard</type>
      <desc>Street-style titanium skateboard.</desc>
      <price>129.00</price>
      <inStock>36</inStock>
   </product>
   ...
</products>
```

SkatesTown's inventory system is accessible via the ProductDB (for product database) class in
package com.skatestown.backend. Listing 3.2 shows the key operations it supports. To construct an instance of the class, you pass an XML DOM Document object representation of
products.xml. (BookUtil.getProductDB() does this automatically.) After that, you can get a
listing of all products or you can search for a product by its SKU.

LISTING 3.2   SkatesTown's Product Database Class

```java
public class ProductDB
{
    private Product[] products;

    public ProductDB(Document doc) throws Exception
    {
        // Load product information
    }

    public Product getBySKU(String sku)
    {
        Product[] list = getProducts();
        for ( int i = 0 ; i < list.length ; i++ )
```

LISTING 3.2   Continued

```
            if ( sku.equals( list[i].getSKU() ) ) return( list[i] );
        return( null );
    }

    public Product[] getProducts()
    {
        return  products;
    }
}
```

This was all Al Rosen needed to know to move forward with the task of automating the inventory checking process.

Inventory Check Web Service

SkatesTown's inventory check Web service is very simple. The interaction model is that of an RPC. There are two input parameters: the product SKU (a string) and the quantity desired (an integer). The result is a simple boolean value—true if more than the desired quantity of the product are in stock and false otherwise.

Choosing a Web Service Engine

Al Rosen decided to host all of SkatesTown's Web services on the Apache Axis Web service engine for a number of reasons:

- The open-source implementation guaranteed that SkatesTown will not experience vendor lock-in in the future. Further, if any serious problems were discovered, you could always look at the code to see what is going on.

- Axis is one of the best Java-based Web services engines. It is better architected and much faster than its Apache SOAP predecessor. The core Axis team includes some of the great Web service gurus from companies such as HP, IBM, and Macromedia.

- Axis is also probably the most extensible Web service engine. It can be tuned to support new versions of SOAP as well as the many types of extensions current versions of SOAP allow.

- Axis can run on top of a simple servlet engine or a full-blown J2EE application server. SkatesTown could keep its current J2EE application server without having to switch.

This combination of factors leads to an easy sell. SkatesTown's CTO agreed to have all Web services developed on top of Axis. Al spent some time on http://xml.apache.org/axis learning more about the technology and its capabilities. He learned how to install Axis on top of SkatesTown's J2EE server by reading the Axis installation instructions.

Service Provider View

To expose the Web service, Al Rosen had to do two things: implement the service backend and deploy it into the Web service engine.

Building the backend for the inventory check Web service was simple because the logic was already available in SkatesTown's JSP pages (see Listing 3.3).

LISTING 3.3   Inventory Check Web Service Implementation

```
import org.apache.axis.MessageContext;
import bws.BookUtil;
import com.skatestown.data.Product;
import com.skatestown.backend.ProductDB;

/**
 * Inventory check Web service
 */
public class InventoryCheck
{
    /**
     * Checks inventory availability given a product SKU and
     * a desired product quantity.
     *
     * @param msgContext    This is the Axis message processing context
     *                      BookUtil needs this to extract deployment
     *                      information to load the product database.
     * @param sku           product SKU
     * @param quantity      quantity desired
     * @return              true|false based on product availability
     * @exception Exception most likely a problem accessing the DB
     */
    public static boolean doCheck(MessageContext msgContext,
                                  String sku, int quantity)
    throws Exception
    {
        ProductDB db = BookUtil.getProductDB(msgContext);
        Product prod = db.getBySKU(sku);
        return (prod != null && prod.getNumInStock() >= quantity);
    }
}
```

One Axis-specific feature of the implementation is that the first argument to the doCheck() method is an Axis message context object. You need the Axis context so that you can get to the product database using the BookUtil class. From inside the Axis message context, you can get access to the servlet context of the example Web application. (Axis details such as message context are covered in Chapter 4, "Creating Web Services.") Then you can use this context to load the product database from resources/products.xml. Note that this parameter will not be "visible" to the requestor of a Web service. It is something Axis will provide you with if it notices it (using Java reflection) to be the first parameter in your method. The message context parameter would not be necessary in a real-world situation where the product database would most likely be obtained via JNDI.

Deploying the Web service into Axis is trivial because Axis has the concept of a Java Web Service (JWS) file. A JWS file is a Java file stored with the .jws extension somewhere in the externally accessible Web applications directory structure (anywhere other than under /WEB-INF). JWSs are to Web services somewhat as JSPs are to servlets. When a request is made to a JWS file, Axis will automatically compile the file and invoke the Web service it provides. This is a great convenience for development and maintenance.

In this case, the code from Listing 3.3 is stored as /ch3/ex2/InventoryCheck.jws. This automatically makes the Web service available at the application URL appRoot/ch3/ex2/InventoryCheck.jws. For the example application deployed on top of Tomcat, this URL is http://localhost:8080/bws/ch3/ex2/InventoryCheck.jws.

Service Requestor View

Because SOAP is language and platform neutral, the inventory check Web service can be accessed from any programming environment that is Web services enabled. There are two different ways to access Web services, depending on whether service descriptions are available. Service descriptions use the Web Services Description Language (WSDL) to specify in detail information about Web services such as the type of data they require, the type of data they produce, where they are located, and so on. WSDL is to Web services what IDL is to COM and CORBA and what Java reflection is to Java classes. Web services that have WSDL descriptions can be accessed in the simplest possible manner. Chapter 6, "Describing Web Services," introduces WSDL, its capabilities, and the tools that use WSDL to make Web service development and usage simpler and easier. In this chapter, we will have to do without WSDL.

Listing 3.4 shows the prototypical model for building Web service clients in the absence of a formal service description. The basic class structure is simple:

- A private member stores the URL where the service can be accessed. Of course, this property can have optional getter/setter methods.

- A simple constructor sets the target URL for the service. If the URL is well known, it can be set in a default constructor.

- There is one method for every operation exposed by the Web service. The method signature is exactly the same as the signature of the Web service operation.

LISTING 3.4 Inventory Check Web Service Client

```
package ch3.ex2;

import org.apache.axis.client.ServiceClient;

/*
 * Inventory check web service client
 */
public class InventoryCheckClient
{
    /**
     * Service URL
     */
    private String url;

    /**
     * Point a client at a given service URL
     */
    public InventoryCheckClient(String targetUrl)
    {
        url = targetUrl;
    }

    /**
     * Invoke the inventory check web service
     */
    public boolean doCheck(String sku, int quantity) throws Exception
    {
        ServiceClient call = new ServiceClient(url);
        Boolean result = (Boolean) call.invoke(
            "",
            "doCheck",
            new Object[] { sku, new Integer(quantity) } );
        return result.booleanValue();
    }
}
```

This approach for building Web service clients by hand insulates developers from the details of XML, the SOAP message format and protocol, and the APIs for invoking Web services using some particular client library. For example, users of InventoryCheckClient will never know that you have implemented the class using Axis. This is a good thing.

Chapter 4 will go into the details of the Axis API. Here we'll briefly look at what needs to happen to access the Web service. First, you need to create a ServiceClient object using the service URL. The service client is the abstraction used to make a Web service call. Then, you call the `invoke()` method of the `ServiceClient`, passing in the name of the operation you are trying to invoke and an object array of the two operation parameters: a `String` for the SKU and an `Integer` for the quantity. The result will be a `Boolean` object.

That's all there is to invoking a Web service using Axis.

Putting the Service to the Test

Figure 3.2 shows a simple JSP page (`/ch3/ex2/index.jsp`) that uses `InventoryCheckClient` to access SkatesTown's Web service. You can experiment with different SKU and quantity combinations and see how SkatesTown's SW responds. You can check the responses against the contents of the product database in `/resources/products.xml`.

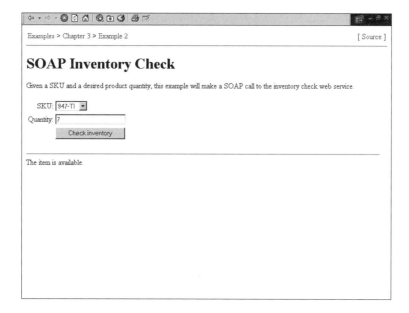

FIGURE 3.2
Putting the SkatesTown inventory check Web service to the test.

The inventory check example demonstrates one of the promises of Web services—you don't have to know XML to build them or to consume them. This finding validates SOAP's claim as an infrastructure technology. The mechanism that allows this to happen involves multiple abstraction layers (see Figure 3.3). Providers and requestors view services as Java APIs. Invoking a Web service requires one or more Java method invocations. Implementing a Web service requires implementing a Java backend (a class or an EJB, for example). The Web service view is one of SOAP messages being exchanged between the requestor and the provider.

These are both logical views in that this is not how the requestor and provider communicate. The only "real" view is the wire-level view where HTTP packets containing SOAP messages are exchanged between the requestor's application and the provider's Web server. The miracle of software abstraction has come to our aid once again.

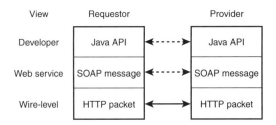

FIGURE 3.3
Layering of views in Web service invocation.

SOAP on the Wire

The powers of abstraction aside, really understanding Web services does require some knowledge of XML. Just as a highly skilled Java developer has an idea about what the JVM is doing and can use this knowledge to write higher performance applications, so must a Web service guru understand the SOAP specification and how SOAP messages are moved around between requestors and providers. This does not mean that to build or consume sophisticated or high-performance Web services you have to work with raw XML—layers can be applied to abstract your application from SOAP. However, knowledge of SOAP and the way in which a Web service engine translates Java API calls into SOAP messages and vice versa allows you to make educated decisions about how to define and implement Web services.

TCPMon

Luckily, the Apache Axis distribution comes with an awesome tool that can monitor the exchange of SOAP messages on the wire. The aptly named *TCPMon* 📖 tool will monitor all traffic on a given port. You can learn how to use TCPMon by looking at the examples installation section in /readme.html.

TCPMon will redirect all traffic to another host and port. This ability makes TCPMon great not only for monitoring SOAP traffic but also for testing the book's examples with a backend other than Tomcat. Figure 3.4 shows TCPMon in action on the inventory check Web service. In this case, the backend is running on the Macromedia JRun J2EE application server. By default, JRun's servlet engine listens on port 8100, not on 8080 as Tomcat does. In the figure, TCPMon is set up to listen on 8080 but to redirect all traffic to 8100. Essentially, with TCPMon you can make JRun (or IBM WebSphere or BEA Weblogic) appear to listen on the same port as Tomcat and run the book's examples without any changes.

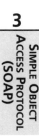

FIGURE 3.4
TCPMon in action.

The SOAP Request

Here is the information that passed on the wire as a result of the inventory check Web service request. Some irrelevant HTTP headers have been removed and the XML has been formatted for better readability but, apart from that, no substantial changes have been made:

```
POST /bws/inventory/InventoryCheck.jws HTTP/1.0
Host: localhost
Content-Type: text/xml; charset=utf-8
Content-Length: 426
SOAPAction: ""

<?xml version="1.0" encoding="UTF-8"?>
<SOAP-ENV:Envelope
   SOAP-ENV:encodingStyle="http://schemas.xmlsoap.org/soap/encoding/"
   xmlns:xsd="http://www.w3.org/2001/XMLSchema"
   xmlns:SOAP-ENV="http://schemas.xmlsoap.org/soap/envelope/"
   xmlns:xsi="http://www.w3.org/2001/XMLSchema-instance">
   <SOAP-ENV:Body>
      <doCheck>
         <arg0 xsi:type="xsd:string">947-TI</arg0>
         <arg1 xsi:type="xsd:int">1</arg1>
      </doCheck>
   </SOAP-ENV:Body>
</SOAP-ENV:Envelope>
```

3
SIMPLE OBJECT
ACCESS PROTOCOL
(SOAP)

Later in the chapter, we will look in detail at all parts of SOAP. For now, a quick introduction will suffice.

The HTTP packet begins with the operation, a POST, and the target URL of the Web service (/bws/inventory/InventoryCheck.jws). This is how the requestor identifies the service to be invoked. The host is localhost (127.0.0.1) because you are accessing the example Web service that comes with the book from your local machine. The content MIME type of the request is text/xml. This is how SOAP must be invoked over HTTP. The content length header is automatically calculated based on the SOAP message that is part of the HTTP packet's body. The SOAPAction header pertains to the binding of SOAP to the HTTP protocol. In some cases it might contain meaningful information. JWS-based Web service providers don't require it, however, and that's why it is empty.

The body of the HTTP packet contains the SOAP message describing the inventory check Web service request. The message is identified by the SOAP-ENV:Envelope element. The element has three xmlns: attributes that define three different namespaces and their associated prefixes: SOAP-ENV for the SOAP envelope namespace, xsd for XML Schema, and xsi for XML Schema instances. One other attribute, encodingStyle, specifies how data in the SOAP message will be encoded.

Inside the SOAP-ENV:Envelope element is a SOAP-ENV:Body element. The body of the SOAP message contains the real information about the Web service request. In this case, this element has the same name as the method on the Web service that you want to invoke—doCheck(). You can see that the Axis ServiceClient object auto-generated element names—arg0 and arg1—to hold the parameters passed to the method. This is fine, because no external schema or service description specifies how requests to the inventory check service should be made. In lieu of anything like that, Axis has to do its best in an attempt to make the call. Both parameter elements contain self-describing data. Axis introspected the Java types for the parameters and emitted xsi:type attributes, mapping these to XML Schema types. The SKU is a java.lang.String and is therefore mapped to xsd:string, and the quantity is a java.lang.Integer and is therefore mapped to xsd:int. The net result is that, even without a detailed schema or service description, the SOAP message contains enough information to guarantee successful invocation.

The SOAP Response

Here is the HTTP response that came back from Axis:

```
HTTP/1.0 200 OK
Content-Type: text/xml; charset=utf-8
Content-Length: 426

<?xml version="1.0" encoding="UTF-8"?>
<SOAP-ENV:Envelope
```

```
SOAP-ENV:encodingStyle="http://schemas.xmlsoap.org/soap/encoding/"
xmlns:xsd="http://www.w3.org/2001/XMLSchema"
xmlns:SOAP-ENV="http://schemas.xmlsoap.org/soap/envelope/"
xmlns:xsi="http://www.w3.org/2001/XMLSchema-instance">
<SOAP-ENV:Body>
   <doCheckResponse>
      <doCheckResult xsi:type="xsd:boolean">true</doCheckResult>
   </doCheckResponse>
</SOAP-ENV:Body>
</SOAP-ENV:Envelope>
```

The HTTP response code is 200 OK because the service invocation completed successfully. The content type is also text/xml. The SOAP message for the response is structured in an identical manner to the one for the request. Inside the SOAP body is the element doCheckResponse. Axis has taken the element name of the operation to invoke and added *Response* to it. The element contained within uses the same pattern but with *Result* appended to indicate that the content of the element is the result of the operation. Again, Axis uses xsi:type to make the message's data self-describing. This is how the service client knows that the result is a boolean. Otherwise, you couldn't have cast the result of call.invoke() to a java.lang.Boolean in Listing 3.4.

If the messages seem relatively simple, it is because SOAP is designed with simplicity in mind. Of course, as always, some complexity lurks in the details. The next several sections will take an in-depth look at SOAP in an attempt to uncover and explain all that you need to know about SOAP to become a skilled and successful Web service developer and user.

SOAP Envelope Framework

The most important part that SOAP specifies is the envelope framework. Although it consists of just a few XML elements, it provides the structure and extensibility mechanisms that make SOAP so well suited as the foundation for all XML-based distributed computing. The SOAP envelope framework defines a mechanism for identifying *what* information is in a message, *who* should deal with the information, and whether this is *optional* or *mandatory*. A SOAP message consists of a mandatory *envelope* 📖 wrapping any number of optional *headers* 📖 and a mandatory *body* 📖. These concepts are discussed in turn in the following sections.

SOAP Envelope

SOAP messages are XML documents that define a unit of communication in a distributed environment. The root element of the SOAP message is the Envelope element. In SOAP 1.1, this element falls under the http://schemas.xmlsoap.org/soap/envelope/ namespace. Because the Envelope element is uniquely identified by its namespace, it allows processing tools to immediately determine whether a given XML document is a SOAP message.

This certainly is convenient, but what do you trade off for this capability? The biggest thing you have to sacrifice is the ability to send arbitrary XML documents and perform simple schema validation on them. True, you can embed arbitrary XML inside the SOAP Body element, but naïve validation will fail when it encounters the Envelope element at the top of the document instead of the top document element of your schema. The lesson is that for seamless validation of arbitrary XML inside SOAP messages, you must integrate XML validation with the Web services engine. In most cases, the Web services engine will have to separate SOAP-specific from application-specific XML before validation can take place.

The SOAP envelope can contain an optional Header element and a mandatory Body element. Any number of other XML elements can follow the Body element. This extensibility feature helps with the encoding of data in SOAP messages. We'll discuss it later in this chapter in the section "SOAP Data Encoding Rules."

SOAP Versioning

One interesting note about SOAP is that the Envelope element does not expose any explicit protocol version, in the style of other protocols such as HTTP (HTTP/1.0 vs. HTTP/1.1) or WDDX (<wddxPacket version="1.0"> ... </wddxPacket>). The designers of SOAP explicitly made this choice because experience had shown simple number-based versioning to be fragile. Further, across protocols, there were no consistent rules for determining what changes in major versus minor version numbers truly mean. Instead of going this way, SOAP leverages the capabilities of XML namespaces and defines the protocol version to be the URI of the SOAP envelope namespace. As a result, the only meaningful statement that you can make about SOAP versions is that they are the same or different. It is no longer possible to talk about compatible versus incompatible changes to the protocol.

What does this mean for Web service engines? It gives them a choice of how to treat SOAP messages that have a version other than the one the engine is best suited for processing. Because an engine supporting a later version of SOAP will know about all previous versions of the specification, it has a range of options based on the namespace of the incoming SOAP message:

- If the message version is the same as any version the engine knows how to process, the engine can just process the message.
- If the message version is older than any version the engine knows how to process, the engine can do one of two things: generate a version mismatch error and/or attempt to negotiate the protocol version with the client by sending some information regarding the versions that it can accept.

- If the message version is newer than any version the engine knows how to process, the engine can choose to attempt processing the message anyway (typically not a good choice) or it can go the way of a version mismatch error combined with some information about the versions it understands.

All in all, the simple versioning based on the namespace URI results in the fairly flexible and accommodating behavior of Web service engines.

SOAP Headers

Headers are the primary extensibility mechanism in SOAP. They provide the means by which additional facets can be added to SOAP-based protocols. Headers define a very elegant yet simple mechanism to extend SOAP messages in a decentralized manner. Typical areas where headers get involved are authentication and authorization, transaction management, payment processing, tracing and auditing, and so on. Another way to think about this is that you would pass via headers any information orthogonal to the specific information needed to execute a request.

For example, a transfer payment service only really needs from and to account numbers and a transfer amount to execute. In real-world scenarios, however, a service request is likely to contain much more information, such as the identity of the person making the request, account/payment information, and so on. This additional information is usually handled by infrastructure services (login and security, transaction coordination, billing) outside the main transfer payment service. Encoding this information as part of the body of a SOAP message will only complicate matters. That is why it will be passed in as headers.

A SOAP message can include any number of header *entries* (simply referred to as *headers*). If any headers are present, they will all be children of the SOAP Header element, which, if present, must appear as the first child of the SOAP Envelope element. The following example shows a SOAP message with two headers, Transaction and Priority. Both headers are uniquely identified by the combination of their element name and their namespace URI:

```
<SOAP-ENV:Envelope
  xmlns:SOAP-ENV="http://schemas.xmlsoap.org/soap/envelope/"
  SOAP-ENV:encodingStyle="http://schemas.xmlsoap.org/soap/encoding/"/>
  <SOAP-ENV:Header>
     <t:Transaction xmlns:t="some-URI" SOAP-ENV:mustUnderstand="1">
            12345
     </t:Transaction>
     <p:Priority xmlns:p="some-Other-URI">
            <ReallyVeryHigh/>
     </p:Priority>
  </SOAP-ENV:Header>
  <SOAP-ENV:Body>
     ...
```

```
    </SOAP-ENV:Body>
</SOAP-ENV:Envelope>
```

The contents of a header (sometimes referred to as the header *value*) are determined by the schema of the header element. This allows headers to contain arbitrary XML, another example of the benefits of SOAP being an XML-based protocol. Compare it to protocols such as HTTP where header values must be simple strings, thus forcing any structured information to be somehow encoded to become a string. For example, cookie values come in a semicolon delimited format, such as `cookie1=value1;cookie2=value2`. It is easy to reach the limits of these simple encodings. XML is a much better way to represent this type of structured information.

Also, notice the SOAP `mustUnderstand` attribute with value 1 that decorates the `Transaction` element. This attribute indicates that the recipient of the SOAP message must process the `Transaction` header entry. If a recipient does not know how to process a header tagged with `mustUnderstand="1"`, it must abort processing with a well-defined error. This rule allows for robust evolution of SOAP-based protocols. It ensures that a recipient that might be unaware of certain important protocol extensions does not ignore them.

Note that because the `Priority` header is not tagged with `mustUnderstand="1"`, it can be ignored during processing. Presumably, this will be OK because a server that does not know how to process message priorities will assume normal priority.

You might have noticed that the SOAP body can be treated as a well-specified SOAP header flagged with `mustUnderstand="1"`. Although this is certainly true, the SOAP designers thought that having a separation between the headers and body of a message does not complicate the protocol and is convenient for readability.

Before leaving the topic of headers, it is important to point out that, despite the obvious need for header extensions to support such basic distributed computing concepts such as authentication credentials or transaction information, there hasn't been a broad standardization effort in this area, with the exception of some security extensions that we'll review in Chapter 5. Some of the leading Web service vendors are doing interesting work, but the industry as a whole is some way away from agreeing on core extensions to SOAP. Two primary forces maintain this unsatisfactory status quo:

- Most current Web service engines do not have a solid extensibility architecture. Therefore, header processing is relatively difficult right now. At the time of this writing, Apache Axis is a notable exception to this rule.

- Market pressure is pushing Web service vendors to innovate in isolation and to prefer shipping software over coordinating extensions with partners and competitors.

Wider Web service adoption will undoubtedly put pressure on the Web services community to think more about interoperability and begin broad standardization in some of these key areas.

SOAP Body

The SOAP Body element immediately surrounds the information that is core to the SOAP message. All immediate children of the Body element are body *entries* (typically referred to simply as *bodies*). Bodies can contain arbitrary XML. Sometimes, based on the intent of the SOAP message, certain conventions will govern the format of the SOAP body. The conventions for representing RPCs are discussed later in the section "SOAP-based RPCs." The conventions for communicating error information are discussed in the section "Error Handling in SOAP."

Taking Advantage of SOAP Extensibility

Let's take a look at how SkatesTown can use SOAP extensibility to its benefit. It turns out that SkatesTown's partners are demanding some type of proof that certain items are in SkatesTown's inventory. In particular, partners would like to have an e-mail record of any inventory checks they have performed.

Al Rosen got the idea to use SOAP extensibility in a way that allows the existing inventory check service implementation to be reused with no changes. SOAP inventory check requests will include a header whose element name is EMail belonging to the http://www.skatestown.com/ns/email namespace. The value of the header will be a simple string containing the e-mail address to which the inventory check confirmation should be sent.

Service Requestor View

Service requestors will have to modify their clients to build a custom SOAP envelope that includes the EMail header. Listing 3.5 shows the necessary changes. The e-mail to send confirmations to is provided in the constructor.

LISTING 3.5   Updated Inventory Check Client

```
package ch3.ex3;

import org.apache.axis.client.ServiceClient;
import org.apache.axis.message.SOAPEnvelope;
import org.apache.axis.message.SOAPHeader;
import org.apache.axis.message.RPCElement;
import org.apache.axis.message.RPCParam;
import javax.xml.parsers.DocumentBuilder;
import javax.xml.parsers.DocumentBuilderFactory;
import org.w3c.dom.Document;
import org.w3c.dom.Element;

/*
```

LISTING 3.5 Continued

```
 * Inventory check web service client
 */
public class InventoryCheckClient {
    /**
     * Service URL
     */
    String url;

    /**
     * Email address to send confirmations to
     */
    String email;

    /**
     * Point a client at a given service URL
     */
    public InventoryCheckClient(String url, String email) {
        this.url = url;
        this.email = email;
    }

    /**
     * Invoke the inventory check web service
     */
    public boolean doCheck(String sku, int quantity) throws Exception {
        // Build the email header DOM element
        DocumentBuilderFactory factory =
            DocumentBuilderFactory.newInstance();
        DocumentBuilder builder = factory.newDocumentBuilder();
        Document doc = builder.newDocument();
        Element emailElem = doc.createElementNS(
            "http://www.skatestown.com/", "EMail");
        emailElem.appendChild(doc.createTextNode(email));

        // Build the RPC request SOAP message
        SOAPEnvelope reqEnv = new SOAPEnvelope();
        reqEnv.addHeader(new SOAPHeader(emailElem));
        Object[] params = new Object[]{ sku, new Integer(quantity), };
        reqEnv.addBodyElement(new RPCElement("", "doCheck", params));

        // Invoke the inventory check web service
        ServiceClient call = new ServiceClient(url);
        SOAPEnvelope respEnv = call.invoke(reqEnv);

        // Retrieve the response
```

LISTING 3.5 Continued

```
        RPCElement respRPC = (RPCElement)respEnv.getFirstBody();
        RPCParam result = (RPCParam)respRPC.getParams().get(0);
        return ((Boolean)result.getValue()).booleanValue();
    }
}
```

To set a header in Axis, you first need to build the DOM representation for the header. The code in the beginning of doCheck() does this. Then you need to manually construct the SOAP message that will be sent. This involves starting with a new SOAPEnvelope object, adding a SOAPHeader with the DOM element constructed earlier, and, finally, adding an RPCElement as the body of the message. At this point, you can use ServiceClient.invoke() to send the message.

When the call is made with a custom-built SOAP envelope, the return value of invoke() is also a SOAPEnvelope object. You need to pull the relevant data out of that envelope by getting the body of the response, which will be an RPCElement. The result of the operation will be the first RPCParam inside the RPC response. Knowing that doCheck() returns a boolean, you can get the value of the parameter and safely cast it to Boolean.

As you can see, the code is not trivial, but Axis does provide a number of convenience objects that make working with custom-built SOAP messages straightforward. Figure 3.5 shows a UML diagram with some of the key Axis objects related to SOAP messages.

3

SIMPLE OBJECT
ACCESS PROTOCOL
(SOAP)

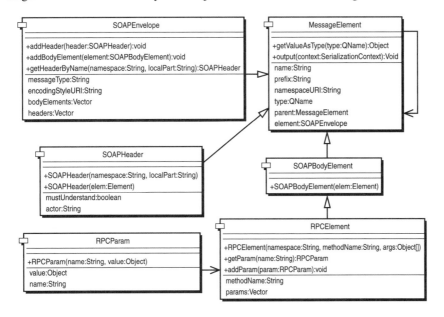

FIGURE 3.5

Axis SOAP message objects.

Service Provider View

The situation on the side of the Axis-based service provider is a little more complicated because we can no longer use a simple JWS file for the service. JWS files are best used for simple and straightforward service implementations. Currently, it is not possible to indicate from a JWS file that a certain header (in this case the e-mail header) should be processed. Al Rosen implements three changes to enable this more sophisticated type of service:

- He moves the service implementation from the JWS file to a simple Java class.
- He writes a handler for the `EMail` header.
- He extends the Axis service deployment descriptor with information about the service implementation and the header handler.

Moving the service implementation is as simple as saving `InventoryCheck.jws` as `InventoryCheck.java` in `/WEB-INF/classes/com/skatestown/services`. No further changes to the service implementation are necessary.

Building a handler for the `EMail` header is relatively simple, as Listing 3.6 shows. When the handler is invoked by Axis, it needs to find the SOAP message and lookup the `EMail` header using its namespace and name. If the header is present in the request message, the handler sends a confirmation e-mail of the inventory check. The implementation is complex because to produce a meaningful e-mail confirmation, the handler needs to see both the request data (SKU and quantity) and the result of the inventory check. The basic process involves the following steps:

1. Get the request or the response message using `getRequestMessage()` or `getResponseMessage()` on the Axis `MessageContext` object.
2. Get the SOAP envelope by calling `getAsSOAPEnvelope()`.
3. Retrieve the first body of the envelope and cast it to an `RPCElement` because the body represents either an RPC request or an RPC response.
4. Get the parameters of the RPC element using `getParams()`.
5. Extract parameters by their position and cast them to their appropriate type. As seen earlier in Listing 3.5, the response of an RPC is the first parameter in the response message body.

LISTING 3.6   E-mail Header Handler

```
package com.skatestown.services;

import java.util.Vector;
import org.apache.axis.* ;
import org.apache.axis.message.*;
```

LISTING 3.6   Continued

```java
import org.apache.axis.handlers.BasicHandler;
import org.apache.axis.encoding.SOAPTypeMappingRegistry;
import bws.BookUtil;
import com.skatestown.backend.EmailConfirmation;

/**
 * EMail header handler
 */
public class EMailHandler extends BasicHandler
{
    /**
     * Utility method to retrieve RPC parameters
     * from a SOAP message.
     */
    private Object getParam(Vector params, int index)
    {
        return ((RPCParam)params.get(index)).getValue();
    }

    /**
     * Looks for the EMail header and sends an email
     * confirmation message based on the inventory check
     * request and the result of the inventory check
     */
    public void invoke(MessageContext msgContext) throws AxisFault
    {
        try
        {
            // Attempt to retrieve EMail header
            Message       reqMsg = msgContext.getRequestMessage();
            SOAPEnvelope  reqEnv = reqMsg.getAsSOAPEnvelope();
            SOAPHeader    header = reqEnv.getHeaderByName(
                "http://www.skatestown.com/",
                "EMail" );

            if (header != null)
            {
                // Mark the header as having been processed
                header.setProcessed(true);

                // Get email address in header
                String email = (String)header.getValueAsType(
                    SOAPTypeMappingRegistry.XSD_STRING);

                // Retrieve request parameters: SKU & quantity
                RPCElement reqRPC = (RPCElement)reqEnv.getFirstBody();
```

LISTING 3.6   Continued

```
                Vector params = reqRPC.getParams();
                String sku = (String)getParam(params, 0);
                Integer quantity = (Integer)getParam(params, 0);

                // Retrieve inventory check result
                Message respMsg = msgContext.getResponseMessage();
                SOAPEnvelope respEnv = respMsg.getAsSOAPEnvelope();
                RPCElement respRPC = (RPCElement)respEnv.getFirstBody();
                Boolean result = (Boolean)getParam(
                                                respRPC.getParams(), 0);

                // Send confirmation email
                EmailConfirmation ec = new EmailConfirmation(
                    BookUtil.getResourcePath(msgContext,
                                        "/resources/email.log"));
                ec.send(email, sku,
                        quantity.intValue(), result.booleanValue());
            }
        }
        catch(Exception e)
        {
            throw new AxisFault(e);
        }
    }

    /**
     * Required method of handlers. No-op in this case
     */
    public void undo(MessageContext msgContext)
    {
    }
}
```

It's simple code, but it does take a few lines because several layers need to be unwrapped to get to the RPC parameters. When all data has been retrieved, the handler calls the e-mail confirmation backend, which, in this example, logs e-mails "sent" to /resources/email.log.

Finally, adding deployment information about the new header handler and the inventory check service involves making a small change to the Axis Web services deployment descriptor. The book example deployment descriptor is in /resources/deploy.xml. Working with Axis deployment descriptors will be described in detail in Chapter 4.

Listing 3.7 shows the five lines of XML that need to be added. First, the e-mail handler is registered by associating a handler name with its Java class name. Following that is the description of the inventory check service. The service options identify the Java class name for the service and the method that implements the service functionality. The service element has two attributes. Pivot is an Axis term that specifies the type of service. In this case, the value is RPCDispatcher, which implies that InventoryCheck is an RPC service. The response attribute specifies the name of a handler that will be called after the service is invoked. Because the book examples don't rely on an e-mail server being present, instead of sending confirmation this class writes messages to a log file in /resources/email.log.

LISTING 3.7   Deployment Descriptor for Inventory Check Service

```
<!-- Chapter 3 example 3 services -->
<handler name="Email" class="com.skatestown.services.EMailHandler"/>
<service name="InventoryCheck" pivot="RPCDispatcher" response="Email">
    <option name="className" value="com.skatestown.services.InventoryCheck"/>
    <option name="methodName" value="doCheck"/>
</service>
```

Putting the Service to the Test

With all these changes in place, we are ready to test the improved inventory check service. There is a simple JSP test harness in ch3/ex3/index.jsp that is modeled after the JSP test harness we used for the JWS-based inventory check service (see Figure 3.6).

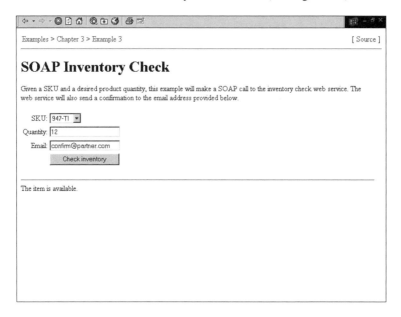

FIGURE 3.6

Putting the enhanced inventory check Web service to the test.

SOAP on the Wire

With the help of TCPMon, we can see what SOAP messages are passing between the client and the Axis engine. We are only interested in seeing the request message because the response message will be identical to the one before the EMail header was added.

Here is the SOAP request message with the EMail header present:

```
POST /bws/services/InventoryCheck HTTP/1.0
Content-Length: 482
Host: localhost
Content-Type: text/xml; charset=utf-8
SOAPAction: "/doCheck"

<?xml version="1.0" encoding="UTF-8"?>
<SOAP-ENV:Envelope
    SOAP-ENV:encodingStyle="http://schemas.xmlsoap.org/soap/encoding/"
    xmlns:xsd="http://www.w3.org/2001/XMLSchema"
    xmlns:SOAP-ENV="http://schemas.xmlsoap.org/soap/envelope/"
    xmlns:xsi="http://www.w3.org/2001/XMLSchema-instance">
    <SOAP-ENV:Header>
        <e:EMail xmlns:e="http://www.skatestown.com/ns/email">
            confirm@partners.com
        </e:EMail>
    </SOAP-ENV:Header>
    <SOAP-ENV:Body>
        <ns1:doCheck xmlns:ns1="AvailabilityCheck">
            <arg0 xsi:type="xsd:string">947-TI</arg0>
            <arg1 xsi:type="xsd:int">1</arg1>
        </ns1:doCheck>
    </SOAP-ENV:Body>
</SOAP-ENV:Envelope>
```

There are no surprises in the SOAP message. However, a couple of things have changed in the HTTP message. First, the target URL is /bws/services/InventoryCheck. This is a combination of two parts: the URL of the Axis servlet that listens for SOAP requests over HTTP (/bws/services) and the name of the service we want to invoke (InventoryCheck). Also, the SOAPAction header, which was previously empty, now contains the name of the method we want to invoke. The service name on the URL and the method name in SOAPAction are both hints to Axis about the service we want to invoke.

That's all there is to taking advantage of SOAP custom headers. The key message is one of simple yet flexible extensibility. Remember, the inventory check service implementation did not change at all!

SOAP Intermediaries

So far, we have addressed SOAP headers as a means for *vertical extensibility* 📖 within SOAP messages. There is another related notion, however: *horizontal extensibility* 📖. Vertical extensibility is about the ability to introduce new pieces of information within a SOAP message, and horizontal extensibility is about targeting different parts of the same SOAP message to different recipients. Horizontal extensibility is provided by SOAP *intermediaries* 📖.

The Need for Intermediaries

SOAP intermediaries are applications that can process parts of a SOAP message as it travels from its origination point to its final destination point (see Figure 3.7). Intermediaries can both accept and forward SOAP messages. Three key use-cases define the need for SOAP intermediaries: crossing trust domains, ensuring scalability, and providing value-added services along the SOAP message path.

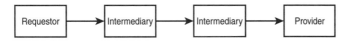

FIGURE 3.7
Intermediaries on the SOAP message path.

Crossing trust domains is a common issue faced while implementing security in distributed systems. Consider the relation between a corporate or departmental network and the Internet. For small organizations, it is likely that the IT department has put most computers on the network within a single trusted security domain. Employees can see their co-workers computers as well as the IT servers and they can freely exchange information between them without the need for separate logons. On the other hand, the corporate network probably treats all computers on the Internet as part of a separate security domain that is not trusted. Before an Internet request reaches the network, it needs to cross from its untrustworthy domain to the trusted domain of the network. Corporate firewalls and virtual private network (VPN) gateways are the Cerberean guards of the gates to the network's riches. Their job is to let some requests cross the trust domain boundary and deny access to others.

Another important need for intermediaries arises because of the scalability requirements of distributed systems. A simplistic view of distributed systems could identify two types of entities: those that request some work to be done (clients) and those that do the work (servers). Clients send messages directly to the servers with which they want to communicate. Servers, in turn, get some work done and respond. In this naïve universe, there is little need for distributed computing infrastructure. Alas, you cannot use this model to build highly scalable distributed systems.

Take basic e-mail as an example—the service we've grown to depend on so much in the Net era. When `someone@company.com` sends an e-mail message to `myfriend@london.co.uk`, it is definitely not the case that their e-mail client locates the mail server `london.co.uk` and sends the message to it. Instead, the client sends the message to its e-mail server at `company.com`. Based on the priority of the message and how busy the mail server is, the message will leave either by itself or in a batch of other messages. Messages are often batched to improve performance. It is likely that the message will make a few hops through different nodes on the Internet before it gets to the mail server in London.

The lesson from this example is that highly scalable distributed systems (such as e-mail) require flexible buffering of messages and routing based not only on message parameters such as origin, destination, and priority but also on the state of the system measured by parameters such as the availability and load of its nodes as well as network traffic information. Intermediaries hidden from the eyes of the originators and final recipients of messages perform all this work behind the scenes.

Last but not least, you need intermediaries so that you can provide value-added services in a distributed system. The type of services can vary significantly. Here are a couple of common examples:

- Securing message exchanges, particularly when transmitting messages through untrustworthy domains, such as using HTTP/SMTP on the Internet. You could secure SOAP messages by passing them through an intermediary that first encrypts them and then digitally signs them. On the receiving side, an intermediary will perform the inverse operations—checking the digital signature and, if it is valid, decrypting the message.

- Providing message-tracing facilities. Tracing allows the recipient of messages to find out the exact path that the message went through complete with detailed timings of arrivals and departures to and from intermediaries along the way. This information is indispensable for tasks such as measuring quality of service (QoS), auditing systems, and identifying scalability bottlenecks.

Intermediaries in SOAP

As the previous section has shown, intermediaries are an extremely important concept in distributed systems. SOAP is specifically designed with intermediaries in mind. It has simple yet flexible facilities that address the three key aspects of an intermediary-enabled architecture:

- How do you pass information to intermediaries?
- How do you identify who should process what?
- What happens to information that is processed by intermediaries?

From the discussion of intermediaries, you can see that most of the information that intermediaries require is completely orthogonal to the information contained in SOAP message bodies. For example, whether logging of inventory check requests is enabled or not is irrelevant to the inventory check service. Therefore, only information in SOAP headers can be explicitly targeted at intermediaries. The question then becomes one of deciding how to target the recipient of a particular header. This does not mean that an intermediary cannot look at, process, or change the SOAP message body; it certainly can do that. However, SOAP itself defines no mechanism to instruct an intermediary to do that. Contrast this to a SOAP message explicitly targeting a piece of information contained in a SOAP header at an intermediary with the understanding that it must at least attempt to process it.

All header elements can optionally have the `SOAP-ENV:actor` attribute. The value of the attribute is a URI that identifies who should handle the header entry. Essentially, that URI is the "name" of the intermediary. The special value `http://schemas.xmlsoap.org/soap/actor/next` indicates that the header entry's recipient is the next SOAP application that processes the message. This is useful for hop-by-hop processing required, for example, by message tracing. Of course, omitting the actor attribute implies that the final recipient of the SOAP message should process the header entry. The message body is intended for the final recipient of the SOAP message.

The issue of what happens to a header that is processed by an intermediary is a little trickier. The SOAP specification states, "the role of a recipient of a header element is similar to that of accepting a contract in that it cannot be extended beyond the recipient." This means that the intermediary should remove any header targeted for it that it has processed. The intermediary is free to introduce a new header in the message that looks the same but then this constitutes a contract between the intermediary and the next application. The goal here is to reduce system complexity by requiring that contracts about the presence, absence, and content of information in SOAP messages be very narrow in scope—from the originator of that information to the first SOAP application that handles it and not beyond.

Putting It All Together

To get a better sense of how you might use intermediaries in the real world, let's consider the potentially realistic albeit contrived example of SkatesTown's overall B2B integration architecture. Please keep in mind that all XML in the example is purely fictional—currently there isn't a standardized way to handle security and routing of SOAP messages.

SkatesTown needs to integrate various applications in several of its departments with some of its partners' applications (see Figure 3.8). Silver Bullet Consulting started working with the purchasing department building Web services to automate business functions such as checking inventory. Following the success of this engagement, Silver Bullet Consulting has been asked to use Web services to automate processes in other departments such as customer service. SkatesTown's corporate IT department is demanding centralized control over the entry point of all Web service requests to the company. They also require that all SOAP messages be transmitted over HTTPS for security reasons.

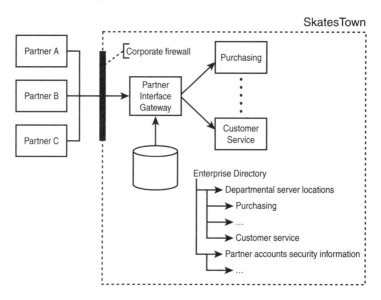

FIGURE 3.8

SkatesTown's system integration architecture.

At the same time, individual departments demand that their own IT units control the servers that run their own Web services. These servers have their own trust domains and are sitting deep inside the corporate network, invisible to the outside world. To address this issue, Silver Bullet Consulting develops a partner interface gateway SOAP application that acts as an intermediary between the partner applications sending SOAP messages and the department-level applications that are handling them. The gateway application is hosted on an application server that is visible to the partner applications. This server is managed by the corporate IT department. A firewall is configured to allow access to the gateway application from the partner networks only.

The gateway application has the responsibility to validate partners' security credentials and to route messages to the appropriate departmental SOAP applications. Security information and department server locations are available from SkatesTown's enterprise directory.

Here is an example message the gateway application might receive:

```
POST /bws/inventory/InventoryCheck HTTP/1.0
Host: partnergateway.skatestown.com
Content-Type: text/xml; charset="utf-8"
Content-Length: nnnn
SOAPAction: "/doCheck"

<?xml version="1.0" encoding="UTF-8"?>
<SOAP-ENV:Envelope
    SOAP-ENV:encodingStyle="http://schemas.xmlsoap.org/soap/encoding/"
    xmlns:xsd="http://www.w3.org/2001/XMLSchema"
    xmlns:SOAP-ENV="http://schemas.xmlsoap.org/soap/envelope/"
    xmlns:xsi="http://www.w3.org/2001/XMLSchema-instance">
    <SOAP-ENV:Header>
        <td:TargetDepartment
            xmlns:td="http://www.skatestown.com/ns/partnergateway"
            SOAP-ENV:actor="urn:X-SkatesTown:PartnerGateway"
            SOAP-ENV:mustUnderstand="1">
            Purchasing
        </td:TargetDepartment>
        <ai:AuthenticationInformation
            xmlns:ai="http://www.skatestown.com/ns/security"
            SOAP-ENV:actor="urn:X-SkatesTown:PartnerGateway"
            SOAP-ENV:mustUnderstand="1">
            <username>PartnerA</username>
            <password>LongLiveSOAP</password>
        </ai:AuthenticationInformation>
    </SOAP-ENV:Header>
    <SOAP-ENV:Body>
        <doCheck>
            <arg0 xsi:type="xsd:string">947-TI</arg0>
            <arg1 xsi:type="xsd:int">1</arg1>
        </doCheck>
    </SOAP-ENV:Body>
</SOAP-ENV:Envelope>
```

There are two header entries. The first identifies the target department as purchasing, and the second passes the authentication information of the message originator, partner A in this case. Both header entries are marked with mustUnderstand="1" because they are critical to the successful processing of the message. The partner gateway application is identified by the actor attribute as the place to process these.

After processing the message, the partner gateway application might forward the following message:

```
POST /bws/services/InventoryCheck HTTP/1.0
Host: purchasing.skatestown.com
Content-Type: text/xml; charset="utf-8"
Content-Length: nnnn
SOAPAction: "/doCheck"

<?xml version="1.0" encoding="UTF-8"?>
<SOAP-ENV:Envelope
    SOAP-ENV:encodingStyle="http://schemas.xmlsoap.org/soap/encoding/"
    xmlns:xsd="http://www.w3.org/2001/XMLSchema"
    xmlns:SOAP-ENV="http://schemas.xmlsoap.org/soap/envelope/"
    xmlns:xsi="http://www.w3.org/2001/XMLSchema-instance">
    <SOAP-ENV:Header>
        <cc:ClientCredentials
            xmlns:cc="http://schemas.security.org/soap/security"
            SOAP-ENV:mustUnderstand="1">
            <ClientID>/External/Partners/PartnerA</ClientID>
        </cc:ClientCredentials>
    </SOAP-ENV:Header>
    <SOAP-ENV:Body>
        <doCheck>
            <arg0 xsi:type="xsd:string">947-TI</arg0>
            <arg1 xsi:type="xsd:int">1</arg1>
        </doCheck>
    </SOAP-ENV:Body>
</SOAP-ENV:Envelope>
```

Note how the previous two header entries have disappeared. They were meant for the gateway application only. Having extracted the purchasing department's location from the enterprise directory, the gateway application forwards the message to purchasing.skatestown.com. A new header entry is meant for the final recipient of the message. The entry specifies the security identity of the message originator as /External/Partners/PartnerA. This identity was presumably obtained from SkatesTown's security system following the successful authentication of partner A. The applications in the purchasing department will use this identity to check whether partner A is authorized to perform the operation requested in the SOAP message body.

This example scenario shows that intermediaries bring significant capabilities to SOAP-enabled applications and can be introduced and implemented at a fairly low cost. The inventory check service implementation does not need to change. The partner gateway does not need to know anything about inventory checking; it only understands the target department and authentication headers. Inventory check clients only need to add a couple of headers to the messages they are sending to fit in the new architecture.

Error Handling in SOAP

So far in our examples everything has gone according to plan. Murphy's Law guarantees that this is not how things work out in the real world. What would happen, for example, if partner A failed to authenticate with the partner gateway application? How will this exceptional condition be communicated via SOAP? The answer lies in the semantics of the SOAP `Fault` element.

Consider the following possible reply message caused by the authentication failure:

```
HTTP/1.0 500 Internal Server Error
Content-Type: text/xml; charset="utf-8"
Content-Length: nnnn

<SOAP-ENV:Envelope
  xmlns:SOAP-ENV="http://schemas.xmlsoap.org/soap/envelope/"
  SOAP-ENV:encodingStyle="http://schemas.xmlsoap.org/soap/encoding/">
  <SOAP-ENV:Body>
    <SOAP-ENV:Fault>
      <faultcode>Client.AuthenticationFailure</faultcode>
      <faultstring>Failed to authenticate client</faultstring>
      <faultactor>urn:X-SkatesTown:PartnerGateway</faultactor>
    </SOAP-ENV:Fault>
  </SOAP-ENV:Body>
</SOAP-ENV:Envelope>
```

Before we look at the XML, note that the HTTP response code is `500 Internal Server Error`. This is a required response in the case of any SOAP-related error by the HTTP transport binding as presented in the SOAP specification. Other protocols will have their own way to report errors. The HTTP SOAP binding is discussed in detail in the section "SOAP Protocol Bindings."

The body of the response contains a single `Fault` element in the SOAP envelope namespace. SOAP uses this mechanism to indicate that an error has occurred and to provide some diagnostic information. There are three child elements.

The `faultcode` element must be present in all cases. It provides information that can be used to identify the specific error that occurred. It is not meant for human consumption. The content of the element is a string prefixed by one of the four `faultcode` values specified by SOAP:

- `VersionMismatch` indicates that the namespace of the `Envelope` element is invalid.
- `MustUnderstand` indicates that a required header entry was not understood.
- `Client` indicates that likely cause of the error lies in the content or formatting of the SOAP message. In other words, the client should probably not re-send the message without making some changes to it.

- `Server` indicates that the message failed due to reasons other than its content or its format. This leaves the door open for the same message to perhaps succeed at a later time.

A hierarchical namespace of values can be obtained by separating fault values with the dot (.) character. In our example, `Client.AuthenticationFailure` is a more specific fault code than `Client`.

The `faultstring` element contains a human-readable message identifying the cause of the fault. It must always be present. Here we simply state that the client has failed to authenticate.

The `faultactor` element provides information about where in the message path the fault occurred. It must be present if the failure occurred somewhere other than at the final destination of the SOAP message. The content of the element is the URI of the actor where the error occurred. In our example, we identify the partner gateway application as the failure point.

What is not shown in this example is how application-specific error diagnostic information can be exchanged. SOAP provides a simple mechanism for this, as well. If the fault occurred during the processing of the message body, an optional `detail` element can be added after `faultactor`. There are no restrictions on its contents. This rule has one important exception: If the fault occurred during the processing of a header entry, a `detail` element cannot be returned. Instead, the header entry should be returned with detailed error information contained therein. This is the mechanism SOAP uses to determine whether a fault was the result of header versus body processing.

SOAP Message Processing

Now that we have covered headers with `mustUnderstand` behavior, intermediaries, and error handling, we can completely define the rules for SOAP message processing. Upon receiving a message, a SOAP application must:

1. Determine whether it understands the version of SOAP that the message uses by inspecting the namespace value of the SOAP `Envelope` element. If the version is unknown, it must discard the message with a `VersionMismatch` error. Otherwise, it has to move to the next step.

2. Identify all parts of the message intended for the application. Typically this is done considering the application's role in the message path (intermediary or final recipient) and the values of the actor global attribute, but other information can be taken into account as well.

3. Verify that all mandatory parts of the message identified in Step 2 are supported by the application. These include `mustUnderstand` headers and, in the case of a final recipient, the body. If any mandatory part cannot be supported, the message is discarded with a

MustUnderstand error in the case of headers and an application-specific error in the case of bodies. Otherwise, the application will move to Step 4.

4. Process all mandatory parts identified in Step 2 plus any optional parts that it knows about.

5. If the application is not the final recipient of the message, it must remove all headers that it has processed before passing the message forward along its path.

Having covered the SOAP envelope framework, intermediaries, and error handling, it is now time to move to other areas of the SOAP specification.

SOAP Data Encoding

Another important area of SOAP has to do with the rules and mechanisms for encoding data in SOAP messages. So far, our Web service example, the inventory check, has dealt only with very simple datatypes: strings, integers, and booleans. All these types have direct representation in XML Schema so it was easy, through the use of the xsi:type attribute, to describe the type of data being passed in a message. What would happen if our Web services needed to exchange more complex types, such as arrays and arbitrary objects? What algorithm should be used to determine their representation in XML format? In addition, given SOAP's extensibility requirements, how can a SOAP message specify different encoding algorithms? This section addresses such questions.

Specifying Different Encodings

SOAP provides an elegant mechanism for specifying the encoding rules that apply to the message as a whole or any portion of it. This is done via the encodingStyle attribute in the SOAP envelope namespace. The attribute is defined as global in the SOAP schema; it can appear with any element, allowing different encoding styles to be mixed and matched in a SOAP message. An encodingStyle attribute applies to the element it decorates and its content, excluding any children that might have their own encodingStyle attribute. Therefore, any element in a SOAP message can have either no encoding style specified or exactly one encoding style. The rules for determining the encoding style of an element are simple:

1. If an element has the encodingStyle attribute, then its encoding style is equal to the value of that attribute.

2. Otherwise, the encoding style is equal to the encoding style of the closest ancestor element that has the encodingStyle attribute...

3. ...Unless there is no such ancestor, which implies that the element has no specified encoding style.

SOAP defines one particular set of data encoding rules. They are identified by `SOAP-ENV:encodingStyle="http://schemas.xmlsoap.org/soap/encoding"` in SOAP messages. You will often see this attribute applied directly to the `Envelope` element in a SOAP message. There is no notion of default encoding in a SOAP message. Encoding style must be explicitly specified.

Despite the fact that the SOAP specification defines these encoding rules, it does not mandate them. SOAP implementations are free to choose their own encoding styles. There are costs and benefits to making this choice. A benefit could be that the implementations can choose a more optimized data encoding mechanism than the one defined by the SOAP specification. For example, some SOAP engines already on the market detect whether they are exchanging SOAP messages with the same type of engine and, if so, switch to a highly optimized binary data encoding format. Because this switch happens only when both ends of a communication channel agree to it, interoperability is not hindered. At the same time, however, supporting these different encodings does have an associated maintenance cost, and it is difficult for other vendors to take advantage of the benefits of an optimized data encoding.

SOAP Data Encoding Rules

The SOAP data encoding rules exist to provide a well-defined mapping between abstract data models (ADMs) and XML syntax. ADMs can be mapped to directed labeled graphs (DLGs)—collections of named nodes and named directed edges connecting two nodes. For Web services, ADMs typically represent programming language and database data structures. The SOAP encoding rules define algorithms for executing the following three tasks:

- Given meta-data about an ADM, construct an XML schema from it.
- Given an instance graph of the data model, we can generate XML that conforms to the schema. This is the serialization operation.
- Given XML that conforms to the schema, we can create an instance graph that conforms to the abstract data model's schema. This is the deserialization operation. Further, if we follow serialization by deserialization, we should obtain an identical instance graph to the one we started with.

Although the purpose of the SOAP data encoding is so simple to describe, the actual rules can be somewhat complicated. This section is only meant to provide an overview of topic. Interested readers should pursue the data encoding section of the SOAP Specification.

Basic Rules

The SOAP encoding uses a type system based on XML Schema. *Types* are schema types. *Simple types* 📖 (often known as *scalar* types in programming languages) map to the built-in types in XML Schema. Examples include `float`, `positiveInteger`, `string`, `date`, and any restrictions of these, such as an enumeration of RGB colors derived by restricting xsd:string to only "red", "green", and "blue". *Compound types* 📖 are composed of several parts, each of which has an associated type. The parts of a compound type are distinguished by an *accessor* 📖. An accessor can use the name of a part or its position relative to other parts in the XML representation of values. *Structs* 📖 are compound types whose parts are distinguished only by their name. *Arrays* 📖 are compound types whose parts are distinguished only by their ordinal position.

Values are instances of types, much in the same way that a string object in Java is an instance of the java.lang.String class. Values are represented as XML elements whose type is the value type. *Simple values* are encoded as the content of elements that have a simple type. In other words, the elements that represent simple values have no child elements. *Compound values* are encoded as the content of elements that have a compound type. The parts of the compound value are encoded as child elements whose names and/or positions are those of the part accessors. Note that values can never be encoded as attributes. The use of attributes is reserved for the SOAP encoding itself, as you will see a bit later.

Values whose elements appear at the top level of the serialization are considered *independent* 📖, whereas all other values are *embedded* 📖 (their parent is a value element).

The following snippet shows an example XML schema fragment describing a person with a name and an address. It also shows the associated XML encoding of that schema according to the SOAP encoding rules:

```
<!-- This is an example schema fragment -->

<xsd:element name="Person" type="Person"/>
<xsd:complexType name="Person">
   <xsd:sequence>
      <xsd:element name="name" type="xsd:string"/>
      <xsd:element name="address" type="Address"/>
   </xsd:sequence>
   <!-- This is needed for SOAP encoding use; there may be a need
        to specify some encoding parameters, e.g., encodingStyle,
        through the use of attributes -->
   <xsd:anyAttribute namespace="##other" processContents="strict"/>
</xsd:complexType>

<xsd:element name="Address" type="Address"/>
<xsd:complexType name="Address">
   <xsd:sequence>
      <xsd:element name="street" type="xsd:string"/>
      <xsd:element name="city" type="xsd:string"/>
      <xsd:element name="state" type="USState"/>
```

```
   </xsd:sequence>
   <!-- Same as above in Person -->
   <xsd:anyAttribute namespace="##other" processContents="strict"/>
</xsd:complexType>

<xsd:simpleType name="USState">
   <xsd:restriction base="xsd:string">
      <xsd:enumeration value="AK"/>
      <xsd:enumeration value="AL"/>
      <xsd:enumeration value="AR"/>
      <!-- ... -->
   </xsd:restriction>
</xsd:simpleType>

<!-- This is an example encoding fragment using this schema -->

<!-- This value is of compound type Person (a struct) -->
<p:Person>
   <!-- Simple value with accessor "name" is of type xsd:string -->
   <name>Bob Smith</name>
   <!-- Nested compound value address -->
   <address>
      <street>1200 Rolling Lane</street>
      <city>Boston</city>
      <!-- Actual state type is a restriction of xsd:string -->
      <state>MA</state>
   </address>
</p:Person>
```

One thing should be apparent: The SOAP encoding rules are designed to fit well with traditional uses of XML for data-oriented applications. The example encoding has no mention of any SOAP-specific markup. This is a good thing.

Identifying Value Types

When full schema information is available, it is easy to associate values with their types. In some cases, however, this is hard to do. Sometimes, a schema will not be available. In these cases, Web service interaction participants should do their best to make messages as self-describing as possible by using `xsi:type` attributes to tag the type of at least all simple values. Further, they can do some guessing by inspecting the markup to determine how to deserialize the XML. Of course, this is difficult. The only other alternative is to establish agreement in the Web services industry about the encoding of certain generic abstract data types. The SOAP encoding does this for arrays.

Other times, schema information might be available, but the content model of the schema element will not allow you to sufficiently narrow the type of contained values. For example, if the schema content type is "any", it again makes sense to use xsi:type as much as possible to specify the exact type of value that is being transferred.

The same considerations apply when you're dealing with type inheritance, which is allowed by both XML Schema and all object-oriented programming languages. The SOAP encoding allows a sub-type to appear in any place where a super-type can appear. Without the use of xsi:type, it will be impossible to perform good deserialization of the data in a SOAP message.

Sometimes you won't know the names of the value accessors in advance. Remember how Axis auto-generates element names for the parameters of RPC calls? Another example would be the names of values in an array—the names really don't matter; only their position does. For these cases, xsi:type could be used together with auto-generated element names. Alternatively, the SOAP encoding defines elements with names that match the basic XML Schema types, such as SOAP-ENC:int or SOAP-ENC:string. These elements could be used directly as a way to combine name and type information in one. Of course, this pattern cannot be used for compound types.

SOAP Arrays

Arrays are one of the fundamental data structures in programming languages. (Can you think of a useful application that does not use arrays?) Therefore, it is no surprise that the SOAP data encoding has detailed rules for representing arrays. The key requirement is that array types must be represented by a SOAP-ENC:Array or a type derived from it. These types have the SOAP-ENC:arrayType attribute, which contains information about the type of the contained items as well as the size and number of dimensions of the array. This is one example where the SOAP encoding introduces an attribute and another reason why values in SOAP are encoded using only element content or child elements.

Table 3.1 shows several examples of possible arrayType values. The format of the attribute is simple. The first portion specifies the contained element type. This is expressed as a fully qualified XML type name (QName). Compound types can be freely used as array elements. If the contained elements are themselves arrays, the QName is followed by an indication of the array dimensions, such as [] and [,] for one- and two- dimensional arrays, respectively. The second portion of arrayType specifies the size and dimensions of the array, such as [5] or [2,3]. There is no limit to the number of array dimensions and their size. All position indexes are zero-based, and multidimensional arrays are encoded such that the rightmost position index changes the quickest.

TABLE 3.1   Example SOAP-ENC:arrayType Values

arrayType Value	*Description*
xsd:int[5]	An array of five integers
xsd:int[][5]	An array of five integer arrays
xsd:int[,][5]	An array of five two-dimensional arrays of integers
p:Person[5]	An array of five people
xsd:string[2,3]	A 2x3, two-dimensional array of strings

If schema information is present, arrays will typically be represented as XML elements whose type is or derives from SOAP-ENC:Array. Further, the array elements will have meaningful XML element names and associated schema types. Otherwise, the array representation would most likely use the pre-defined element names associated with schema types from the SOAP encoding namespace. Here is an example:

```
<!-- Schema fragment for array of numbers -->
<element name="arrayOfNumbers">
  <complexType base="SOAP-ENC:Array">
    <element name="number" type="xsd:int" maxOccurs="unbounded"/>
  </complexType>
    <xsd:anyAttribute namespace="##other" processContents="strict"/>
</element>

<!-- Encoding example using the array of numbers -->
<arrayOfNumbers SOAP-ENC:arrayType="xsd:int[2]">
    <number>11</number>
    <number>22</number>
</arrayOfNumbers>

<!-- Array encoding w/o schema information -->
<SOAP-ENC:Array SOAP-ENC:arrayType="xsd:int[2]">
    <SOAP-ENC:int>11</SOAP-ENC:int>
    <SOAP-ENC:int>22</SOAP-ENC:int>
</SOAP-ENC:Array>
```

Referencing Data

Abstract data models allow a single value to be referred to from multiple locations. Given any particular data structure, a value that is referred to by only one accessor is considered *single-reference* 📖, whereas a value that has more than one accessor referring to it is considered *multi-reference* 📖. The examples shown so far have assumed single-reference values. The rules for encoding multi-reference values are relatively simple, however:

- Multi-reference values are represented as independent elements at the top of the serialization. This makes them easy to locate in the SOAP message.

- They all have an unqualified attribute named id of type ID per the XML Schema specification. The ID value provides a unique name for the value within the SOAP message.

- Each accessor to the value is an unqualified href attribute of type uri-reference per the XML Schema specification. The href values contain URI fragments pointing to the multi-reference value.

Here is an example that brings together simple and compound types, and single- and multi-reference values and arrays:

```
<!-- Person type w/ multi-ref attributes added -->
<xsd:complexType name="Person">
   <xsd:sequence>
      <xsd:element name="name" type="xsd:string"/>
      <xsd:element name="address" type="Address"/>
   </xsd:sequence>
   <xsd:attribute name="href" type="uriReference"/>
   <xsd:attribute name="id" type="ID"/>
   <xsd:anyAttribute namespace="##other" processContents="strict"/>
</xsd:complexType>

<!-- Address type w/ multi-ref attributes added -->
<xsd:complexType name="Address">
   <xsd:sequence>
      <xsd:element name="street" type="xsd:string"/>
      <xsd:element name="city" type="xsd:string"/>
      <xsd:element name="state" type="USState"/>
   </xsd:sequence>
   <xsd:attribute name="href" type="uriReference"/>
   <xsd:attribute name="id" type="ID"/>
   <xsd:anyAttribute namespace="##other" processContents="strict"/>
</xsd:complexType>

<!-- Example array of two people sharing an address -->
<SOAP-ENC:Array SOAP-ENC:arrayType="p:Person[2]">
   <p:Person>
      <name>Bob Smith</name>
      <address href="#addr-1"/>
   </p:Person>
   <p:Person>
      <name>Joan Smith</name>
      <address href="#addr-1"/>
   </p:Person>
</SOAP-ENC:Array>
```

3

SIMPLE OBJECT
ACCESS PROTOCOL
(SOAP)

```
<p:address id="addr-1">
   <street>1200 Rolling Lane</street>
   <city>Boston</city>
   <state>MA</state>
</p:address>
```

The schema fragments for the compound types had to be extended to support the `id` and `href` attributes required for multi-reference access.

Odds and Ends

The SOAP encoding rules offer many more details that we have glossed over in the interest of keeping this chapter focused on the core uses of SOAP. Three data encoding mechanisms are worth a brief mention:

- Null values of a specific type are represented in the traditional XML Schema manner, by tagging the value element with `xsi:null="1"`.

- The notion of "any" type is also represented in the traditional XML Schema manner via the `xsd:ur-type` type. This type is the base for all schema datatypes and therefore any schema type can appear in its place.

- The SOAP encoding allows for the transmission of partial arrays by specifying the starting offset for elements using the `SOAP-ENC:offset` attribute. Sparse arrays are also supported by tagging array elements with the `SOAP-ENC:position` attribute. Both of these mechanisms are provided to minimize the size of the SOAP message required to transmit a certain array-based data structure.

Having covered the SOAP data encoding rules, it is now time to look at the more general problem of encoding different types of data in SOAP messages.

Choosing a Data Encoding

Because data encoding needs vary a lot, there are many different ways to approach the problem of representing data for Web services. To add some structure to the discussion, think of the decision space as a choice tree. A choice tree has yes/no questions at its nodes and outcomes at its leaves (see Figure 3.9).

XML Data

Probably the most common choice has to do with whether the data already is in (or can easily be converted to) an XML format. If you can represent the data as XML, you only need to decide how to include it in the XML instance document that will represent a message in the protocol. Ideally, you could just mix it in amidst the protocol-specific XML but under a different namespace. This approach offers several benefits. The message is easy to construct and easy to process using standard XML tools. However, there is a catch.

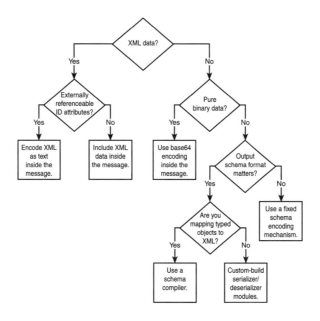

FIGURE 3.9

Possible choice tree for data encoding.

The problem has to do with a little-considered but very important aspect of XML: the uniqueness rule for ID attributes. The values of attributes of type ID must be unique in an XML instance so that the elements with these attributes can be conveniently referred to using attributes of type IDREF, as shown here:

```
<Target id="mainTarget"/>
<Reference href="#mainTarget"/>
```

The problem with including a chunk of XML inline (textually) within an XML document is that the uniqueness of IDs can be violated. For example, in the following code both message elements have the same ID. This makes the document invalid XML:

```
<message id="msg-1">
  A message with an attached <a href="#msg-1">message</a>.
  <attachment id="attachment-1">
    <!-- ID conflict right here -->
    <message id="msg-1">
      This is a textually included message.
    </message>
  </attachment>
</message>
```

And no, namespaces do not address the issue. In fact, the problems are so serious that nothing short of a change in the core XML specification and in most XML processing tools can change the status quo. Don't wait for this to happen.

You can work around the problem two ways. If no one will ever externally reference specific IDs within the protocol message data, then your XML protocol toolset can automatically re-write the IDs and references to them as you include the XML inside the message, as follows:

```
<message id="msg-1">
  A message with an attached <a href="#id-9137">message</a>.
  <attachment id="attachment-1">
    <!-- ID has been changed -->
    <message id="id-9137">
      This is a textually included message.
    </message>
  </attachment>
</message>
```

This approach will give you the benefits described earlier at the cost of some extra processing and a slight deterioration in readability due to the machine-generated IDs.

If you cannot do this, however, you will have to include the XML as an opaque chunk of text inside your protocol message:

```
<message id="msg-1">
  A message with an attached message that
  we can no longer refer to directly.
  <attachment id="attachment-1">
    <!-- Message included as text -->
    &ltmessage id="id-9137"&gt;
      This is a textually included message.
    &lt;/message&gt;
  </attachment>
</message>
```

In this case, we have escaped all pointy brackets, but we also could have included the whole message in a CDATA section. The benefit of this approach is that it is easy and it works for any XML content. However, you don't get any of the benefits of XML. You cannot validate, query, or transform the data directly, and you cannot reference pieces of it from other parts of the message.

Binary Data

So far, we have discussed encoding options for pre-existing XML data. However, what if you are not dealing with XML data? What if you want to transport binary data as part of your message, instead? The commonly used solution is good old base64 encoding:

```
<SOAP-ENV:Envelope
  xmlns:SOAP-ENV="http://schemas.xmlsoap.org/soap/envelope/"
  SOAP-ENV:encodingStyle="http://schemas.xmlsoap.org/soap/encoding/">
  <SOAP-ENV:Body>
    <x:StorePicture xmlns:x="Some URI">
        <Picture xsi:type="SOAP-ENC:base64">
          aG93IG5vDyBicm73biBjb3cNCg==
        </Picture>
    </x:StorePicture>
  </SOAP-ENV:Body>
</SOAP-ENV:Envelope>
```

On the positive side, base64 data is easy to encode and decode, and the character set of base64-encoded data is valid XML element content. On the negative side, base64 encoding takes up nearly 33% more memory than pure binary representation. If you need to move much binary data and space/time efficiency is a concern, you might have to look for alternatives. (More on this in a bit.)

You might want to consider using base64 encoding even when you want to move some plain text as part of a message, because XML's document-centric SGML origin led to several awkward restrictions on the textual content of XML instances. For example, an XML document cannot include any control characters (ASCII codes 0 through 31) except tabs, carriage returns, and line feeds. This limitation includes both the straight occurrences of the characters and their encoded form as character references, such as &#x04;. Further, carriage returns are always converted to line feeds by XML processors. It is important to keep in mind that not all characters you can put in a string variable in a programming language can be represented in XML documents. If you are not careful, this situation can lead to unexpected runtime errors.

Abstract Data Models

If you are not dealing with plain text, XML, or binary data, you probably have some form of structured data represented via an abstract data model.

The key question when dealing with abstract data models and XML is whether the output XML format matters. For example, if you have to generate SkatesTown purchase orders, then the output format is clearly important. If, on the other hand, you just want to make an RPC call over SOAP to pass some data to a Web service, then the exact format of the XML representing your RPC parameters does not matter. All that matters is that the Web service engine can decode the XML and reconstruct a similar data structure with which to invoke the backend.

In the latter case, it is safe to use pre-built automatic "data to XML and back" encoding systems (see Figure 3.10). For example, Web service engines have data serialization/deserialization modules that support the rules of SOAP encoding. These rules are flexible enough to represent most application-level data types. Suffice to say, in many cases you will never have to worry about the mechanics of the serialization/deserialization processes.

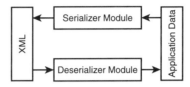

FIGURE 3.10
Generic XML serialization/deserialization.

The SOAP encoding is a flexible schema model for representing data—element names in the instance document often depend on the type and format of data that is being encoded. This model allows for a link between the data and its type, which enables validation. It is one of the core reasons why XML protocols such as SOAP moved to this encoding model, as discussed earlier in the chapter when we considered the evolution of XML protocols.

In the cases where the XML output format does not matter (typically RPC scenarios), you can rely on the default rules provided by various XML data encoding systems. In many cases, however, the XML format is fixed based on the specification of a service. A SkatesTown purchase order submission service is a perfect example. From a requestor's perspective, the input format must be a PO document and the output format must be an invoice document. Requestors are responsible for mapping whatever data structures they might be using to represent POs in their order systems to the SkatesTown PO format. Also, SkatesTown is responsible for always outputting responses in its invoice XML format.

There are two typical approaches to handling this scenario. The simplest one is to completely delegate XML processing to the application. In other words, the Web service engine is responsible only for delivering a chunk of XML to the Web service implementation. Another approach involves building and registering custom serializers/deserializers (datatype mappers) with the Web service engine. The serializers manipulate application data to produce XML. The deserializers manipulate the XML to generate application data. You can build these serializer/deserializer modules two ways: by hand, using the APIs of the Web service engine; or using a tool for mapping data to and from XML given a pre-existing schema. These tools are known as *schema compilers* (see Figure 3.11).

Schema compilers are tools that analyze XML schema and code-generate serialization and deserialization modules specific to the schema. These modules will work with data structures tuned to the schema.

Schema compilation is a difficult problem, and this is one reason there aren't many excellent tools in this space. The Java Architecture for XML Binding (JAXB) is one of the projects that is trying to address this problem in the context of the Java programming language (`http://java.sun.com/xml/jaxb/`). Unfortunately, at the time of this writing, JAXB only supports DTDs and does not support XML Schema. Chapter 8, "Interoperability, Tools, and Middleware Products," focuses on the current Web service tooling for the Java platform. It provides more details on these and other important implementation efforts in the space.

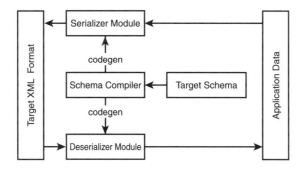

FIGURE 3.11
Serialization/deserialization process with a schema compiler.

Linking Data

So far, we have only considered scenarios where the encoded data is part of the XML document describing a protocol message. This can create some problems for including pre-existing XML content and can waste space in the case of base64-encoded binary objects. The alternative would be keeping the data outside of the message and somehow bringing it in at the right time. For example, an auto insurance claim might carry along several accident pictures that come into play only when the insurance claim needs to be displayed in a browser or printed.

You can use two general mechanisms in such cases. The first comes straight out of XML 1.0. It involves external entity references, which allow content external to an XML document to be brought in during processing. Many people in the industry prefer pure markup and therefore favor a second approach that uses explicit link elements that comply with the XLink specification. Both methods could work. Both require extensions to the core Web services toolsets that are available now. In addition, purely application-based methods are available for linking; you could just pass a URI known to mean "get the actual content here." However, this approach does not scale to generic data encoding mechanisms because it requires application-level knowledge.

External content can be kept on a separate server to be delivered on demand. It can also be packaged together with the protocol message in a MIME envelope. The SOAP Messages with

Attachments Note to the W3C (`http://www.w3.org/TR/2000/NOTE-SOAP-attachments-20001211`) defines a mechanism for doing this. An example SOAP message with an attachment is shown later in the chapter in the section "SOAP Protocol Bindings."

There are many, many ways to encode data in XML, and well-designed XML protocols will let you plug any encoding style you choose. How should you make this important decision? First, of course, keep it simple. If possible, choose standards-based and well-deployed technology. Then, consider your needs and match them against some of the important facets of XML data encoding described here.

Architecting Distributed Systems with Web Services

Although SOAP is typically demoed with simple RPC-based Web services, such as SkatesTown's inventory check service, the SOAP specification does not mandate any particular communication mechanism or interaction pattern between the participants of a Web-service–enabled distributed system. System designers basically have complete control over the system architecture, choice of communication protocols, message routing, intermediary configuration, and so on. The hard part about having so much flexibility is that without solid experience with distributed systems and good judgment, it is easy to make sub-optimal choices.

The most commonly asked questions about distributed systems based on Web services center around a long-running debate in distributed computing circles regarding the rules and regulations for using RPC and messaging (often identified as Message Oriented Middleware—MOM) to solve problems. Typically, the debate takes the unnecessarily polarized form of "MOM vs. RPC." The fact of the matter is that both messaging and RPC play significant, albeit different, roles in distributed computing. Both approaches continue to be very relevant in the era of Web services.

Unfortunately, a lot of confusion exists about the meaning of the terms, the capabilities of messaging and RPC systems, and the scenarios in which they are best applied. Service-oriented architectures fundamentally can support both models. Therefore, to best take advantage of Web services, it helps to have a good understanding of both. What follows is a brief analysis of the two approaches and their relation to SOAP and Web services. Given that people are generally more familiar with RPCs, we start with a discussion of messaging in its many forms.

Messaging

As a model for distributed computing, *messaging* 📖 refers to a mechanism for getting systems to interact via the passing of messages. A message is a single unit of communication encapsulating some information. (A SOAP message is a great example.) This is where the differences begin. Messaging models can vary significantly based on the following criteria:

- Number of participants and their organization
- Interaction patterns
- Synchronicity of message exchanges
- Direct versus queued messaging
- Quality of service (QoS)
- Message format

Message Participants

There are three different ways to organize messaging participants (see Figure 3.12). The simplest case is 1-to-1 (point-to-point) messaging, which involves only two systems. An example could be an e-commerce scenario where the client application submits a purchase order to a digital marketplace. In this case, the sender needs to know where to send the message.

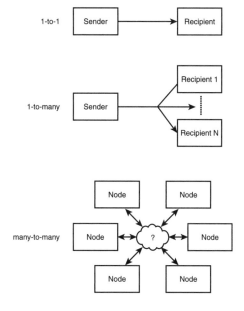

FIGURE 3.12

Messaging patterns.

A slightly more complicated organization is 1-to-many messaging, where the sender sends a single message but copies of it go to multiple recipients. This is often referred to as *publish/subscribe* 📖 or *topic-based messaging* 📖. The idea is that the sender is a publisher that sends a message to a "topic" and that the recipients are all the systems that have subscribed to receive notifications on this topic. E-mail distribution lists are a good example of this type of messaging. The name of the distribution list is the topic, and the subscribers are all the e-mail addresses on the list.

Finally, many-to-many messaging involves a pattern of message exchange among any number of participants. Clearly, in this case, some system in the middle (typically some type of a workflow engine supporting business processes) needs to direct message traffic. This is described by the cloud in Figure 3.12.

Interaction Patterns

There are four common messaging interaction patterns (see Figure 3.13). One-way (*fire-and-forget*) messaging involves the simple sending of a message from one system to another. No response is generated at the application level. Of course, depending on the transport (such as HTTP), a response might be generated at the network level. In the case of request-response messaging, a response message is generated for every request message. The response message is sent from the target of the request message to its source. Chapter 6 describes how requests and responses can be correlated and how multiple request-response pairs can be organized into logical "conversations."

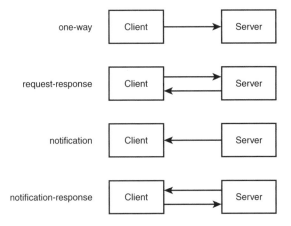

FIGURE 3.13
Interaction patterns.

The other two interaction patterns, notification and notification-response, are mirror images of one-way and request-response. They are callback patterns. Rather than a client system pushing messages to a server system, the server system is pushing messages to the client. The stock ticker application you might have on your desktop is a perfect example of notification combined with publish-subscribe messaging. Chapter 6 gets into more detail about Web service interaction patterns.

Synchronicity

Messaging can be either synchronous or asynchronous. In synchronous messaging, a send operation does not complete until the target of the message has finished processing the message. Asynchronous messaging is harder to define. Typically, the send operation will return immediately (or very quickly), before the target has processed the message. Response messages, if any, typically arrive via callbacks.

Direct vs. Queued Messaging

The synchronicity of messaging is controlled by the presence of messaging middleware, particularly queuing systems. *Direct messaging* 📖 works without any middleware present. For messages to be exchanged, a direct connection between the source and the target(s) must be available. This is why it is sometimes referred to as *connection-oriented messaging* 📖. You can get some amount of asynchronicity in direct messaging by using threads to manage the sending and receiving of messages.

Indirect messaging involves some type of message queuing. Queues provide message buffering and dispatch capabilities. Consider the e-mail server example from earlier in the chapter. An e-mail server is a perfect example of a message queuing system. When you send an e-mail message, your e-mail client does not contact the e-mail client of the person you are trying to reach. Instead, your e-mail client sends the message to a local e-mail server. The server saves the message in some safe place and waits for a good moment to send it out. Typically, many messages are sent at once. This is the buffering function. The dispatch function has to do with the e-mail server inspecting the target e-mail addresses and deciding where to forward the e-mail message. In some cases, an e-mail message will make several hops between e-mail servers before it arrives at the destination e-mail server where your mail client can read it. This configuration is so powerful because it works even in the cases where mail clients and even some mail servers are offline for long periods of time. A mail server will keep trying to send e-mail for several days and will store received messages potentially indefinitely.

Figure 3.14 contrasts direct messaging (the topmost configuration) with a number of possible queuing configurations. In the second and third configurations, the queuing system acts primarily as a message buffer. For example, if the receiver is not on the network, the message will still be safely stored in the queue. The last configuration is the most interesting, in that the message can be moved from the local to the remote system without either the sender or the receiver being online—the message queuing systems can do the job by themselves. In addition, the presence of more than one queuing system allows for flexible message dispatch.

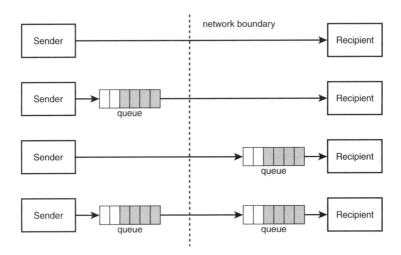

FIGURE 3.14
Variations of queuing configurations.

Quality of Service

Another important aspect of messaging is *quality of service* 📖 (QoS). Direct messaging exhibits the QoS parameters with which we are most familiar, such as security and transaction management. When queuing is in use, other types of QoS become available. For example, messages can be stored in the queuing server in various ways: in memory (the fastest queuing mechanism but one that does not guarantee against system failure) or in some persistent store, such as a DBMS.

Further, transactions can guarantee that the message is sent to the receiver once and only once or not at all. In the case of message delivery failure, QoS policy might dictate that a failure notification is sent to the message sender. In addition, it is common QoS policy to send acknowledgement notifications that the message has been successfully delivered to the receiver. These types of QoS considerations are very relevant to Web services. Chapter 5 looks in more detail at some QoS aspects.

Message Format

The last but not least important aspect of messaging is the format of message data. Most messaging systems allow the transfer of text and binary data, which enables the easy transfer of XML. Some newer messaging systems treat XML messages specially and try to use an optimized XML encoding format. There is also the notion of queues that can automatically allow only XML messages that comply with certain schema. Some platform-focused messaging systems, such as Java Messaging Service (JMS) middleware and Microsoft's .NET messaging server, also allow for the automatic serialization of application data (Java objects in the case of JMS and Common Language Runtime [CLR] data structures in the case of Microsoft).

Messaging Versus RPC

If messaging is all about possibilities and variations, RPCs are much more constrained. As the name suggests, the goal of RPCs is to make the invocation of remote code seem like a local procedure call (LPC). To make an RPC call, you need the following information:

- A target to invoke
- An operation name
- Optionally, parameters to pass to the operation

Therefore, whereas messaging is primarily about data (which can be in any conceivable format), RPCs are about combining specific application-level data with remote code. This is the one fundamental difference between messaging and RPC. A nice side-effect is that programmers using RPC do not have to worry about manually performing data encoding and decoding—something that typically has to happen when using messaging systems, especially across programming languages and platforms.

Another way to state the main difference between messaging and RPC is to note that messaging deals with generic APIs such as `sendMessage()`, `getMessage()`, and `registerMessageResponseCallback()`, whereas RPCs deal with special-purpose APIs that vary based on the interface of the target that is being invoked. For example, if you are trying to invoke a remote EJB that has a `processOrder()` method, you will most likely call the `processOrder()` method of a local object that acts like a proxy to the remote EJB. Chapter 6 discusses this topic in much more detail.

Another key difference between RPCs and messaging is that RPCs are direct invocations. There is no queuing mechanism; the backend must be running and it must be directly accessible at a well-known location. This limits the dispatch capabilities of RPC middleware. MOM message dispatch can be much more flexible.

Finally, extensive use of RPCs tends to result in somewhat brittle distributed systems. Because the APIs are fine-grained, even small changes in the data being passed around can break the system. Messaging uses much rougher-grain data exchanges and is therefore more likely to sustain small changes in the data being exchanged without failure.

Apart from these key differences, RPCs and messaging have many similarities:

- RPCs can be implemented on top of a request-response messaging pattern.
- Contrary to popular belief, however, RPCs do not have to have a request-response messaging pattern. Some systems support one-way RPCs.

- In addition, RPCs do not have to be synchronous. Some systems automatically spawn threads to wait in the background for RPC responses.
- RPCs and messaging share many of the same QoS requirements such as security and transaction management.
- Direct, synchronous, 1-to-1 messaging can be simulated via a simple RPC, e.g., `void sendMessage(data)`.

It should become clear by now that the real issue isn't which of the two approaches to distributed computing is better (the simple interpretation of "messaging vs. RPC") but when each approach should be used in the world of Web services. To answer this question, after we have mentioned so many possible variations of both messaging and RPC, it helps to establish some stereotypes. When working with Web services, it will generally be the case that:

- RPCs will be direct, synchronous, request-response invocations that pass encoded application-level data structures from a client to a target backend that implements the RPC functionality.
- Messages will carry XML data. The interaction pattern is most likely to be one-way or request-response. Simple architectures will use direct messaging. The organization of participants will likely be 1-to-1. More advanced architectures will be queued and therefore asynchronous.

In both cases, messages will be represented on the wire using SOAP. QoS-related information that is part of the message will be represented as message headers. A good example would be an authentication header that carries a username and password; Chapter 5 shows an example.

Table 3.2 presents a number of benefits and concerns about using messaging and RPC. Based on these and the current state-of-the-art in Web service middleware and tooling, we would recommend that you go with a simple RPC-based solution or a direct messaging solution unless disconnected operation will be of benefit, the system requires 1-to-many interactions, or synchronous operation is causing performance problems.

TABLE 3.2 Pros and Cons of Messaging and RPC for Web Services

	Pros	*Cons*
Direct messaging	• The basic messaging APIs are very simple. • Any data can be passed. • Separates data from the code that operates on it.	• Applications must perform manual data encoding/decoding.

TABLE 3.2   Continued

	Pros	*Cons*
Queued messaging	• Same as above, plus...	• Same as above plus...
	• Asynchronicity spreads the load and improves performance.	• Most useful forms of messaging require a queuing infrastructure.
	• Allows for disconnected operation.	• Current message queuing products do not interoperate well.
	• Allows for 1-to-many and many-to-many interactions.	• Asynchronicity makes programming more difficult.
RPC	• Local APIs match backend APIs.	• Synchronicity can cause bottlenecks.
	• Synchronicity makes programming easy.	• Backend must be running for RPCs to succeed.
	• Application data is automatically encoded/decoded.	• Only 1-to-1 interactions are supported.
	• Exceptions provide a good error-handling mechanism.	
	• RPC products interoperate reasonably well.	

We would expect that as messaging middleware vendors embrace Web services to a greater extent and as more Web services become increasingly used in the context of complex business process workflows, the importance of Web service messaging will grow. Broad standardization efforts such as ebXML (http://www.ebxml.org) and Java API for XML Messaging (JAXM, http://java.sun.com/xml/jaxm/index.html) will help speed up the process.

SOAP-based RPCs

So far in this chapter we have presented several examples of SOAP-based RPC without ever mentioning the details of representing RPCs in SOAP messages as described by the SOAP specification. The rules are very simple.

Recall that to invoke an RPC, you need a target URI, an operation name, some parameters, and any amount of context information (such as security context). Any such context information is modeled as SOAP headers.

SOAP's RPC binding does not specify how the target URI is going to be provided. In other words, it leaves it up to the SOAP processor to determine how to dispatch a SOAP RPC request to a target backend. There are three common ways to do this dispatch. Two of these are HTTP-specific, and the other is based on the contents of the SOAP message:

- In the case of HTTP, the SOAP processor can dispatch based on the target URL (as in the inventory check example).
- Alternatively, it may dispatch based on the value of the SOAPAction HTTP header that comes as part of the HTTP request.
- Alternatively, it can use the value of the namespace URI for the first element inside the SOAP body.

Most Web services engines do not support any combination of these dispatch mechanisms. Axis can be configured to work with any combination.

In the language of the SOAP encoding, the actual RPC invocation is modeled as a struct. The name of the struct (that is, the name of the first element inside the SOAP body) is identical to the name of the method/procedure. This is not a problem, because the character set of XML elements is a superset of the character set of valid identifier names in programming languages. Every in and in-out parameter of the RPC is modeled as an accessor with a name identical to the name of the RPC parameter and type identical to the type of the RPC parameter mapped to XML according to the rules of the active encoding style. The accessors appear in the same order, as do the parameters in the operation signature.

The RPC response is also modeled as a struct. By convention, the name of the struct is the same as the name of the operation, with *Response* appended to it. There are accessors for the operation result and all in-out and out parameters. The result is the first accessor, followed by the parameters in the order they appear in the operation signature. By convention, the result element's name is the same as the name of the operation, with *Result* appended to it.

Java developers are not used to the concept of in-out or out parameters because, typically, in Java all objects are automatically passed by reference. When using RMI, simple objects can be passed by value, but other objects are still passed by reference. In this sense, any mutable objects (ones whose state can be modified) are automatically treated as in-out parameters.

In Web services, the situation is different. All parameters are passed by value. SOAP has no notion of passing values by reference. This design decision was made in order to keep SOAP and its data encoding simple. Passing values by reference in a distributed system requires distributed garbage collection. This not only complicates the design of the system but also imposes restrictions on some possible system architectures and interaction patterns. For example, how can you do distributed garbage collection in a queued messaging architecture when the requestor and the provider of a service can both be offline at the same time?

Therefore, for Web services, the notion of in-out and out parameters does not involve passing objects by reference and letting the target backend modify their state. Instead, copies of the data are exchanged. It is then up to the service client code to create the perception that the actual state of the object that has been passed in to the client method has been modified. Different Web service clients might have different ways to do this.

Consider the following operation signature:

```
boolean doCheck(in String sku, in int quantity, out int numInStock)
```

Some possible SOAP RPC request and response bodies are:

```
<!-- RPC request body -->
<SOAP-ENV:Body>
   <doCheck>
      <sku xsi:type="xsd:string">947-TI</sku>
      <quantity xsi:type="xsd:int">1</quantity>
   </doCheck>
</SOAP-ENV:Body>

<!-- RPC response body -->
<SOAP-ENV:Body>
   <doCheckResponse>
      <doCheckResult xsi:type="xsd:boolean">true</doCheckResult>
      <numInStock xsi:type="xsd:int">150</numInStock>
   </doCheckResponse>
</SOAP-ENV:Body>
```

Of course, if a description of the operation is available, you can generate a schema for all the elements in the SOAP body. Doing so would eliminate the need to use xsi:type everywhere in the SOAP message. Chapter 6 looks in more detail at the mechanisms for doing this.

SOAP-based Messaging

The technical term for non-RPC SOAP messaging is *document-centric* 📖 messaging. The name comes from the fact that the data sent over SOAP is represented as an XML document embedded inside the SOAP envelope. Although the RPC binding for SOAP has a number of rules governing the representation and encoding of operation names and parameters, simple SOAP messages have absolutely no restrictions as to the information that can be stored in their bodies. In short, any XML can be included in the SOAP message. The next section of this chapter shows an example of SOAP-based messaging.

Purchase Order Submission Web Service

Recall that when Al Rosen of Silver Bullet Consulting was investigating SkatesTown's e-business processes, he noticed that one area that badly needed automation was purchase order submission. Purchase orders and invoices were being exchanged over e-mail, and they were manually input into the company's purchase order system.

Because SkatesTown already has defined an XML schema for its purchase orders and invoices, Al thinks it makes sense to build a purchase order Web service that accepts a purchase order as an XML document and returns an XML invoice. This service would be an example of 1-to-1 direct messaging using a request-response interaction pattern.

Purchase Order and Invoice Schemas

The schemas for SkatesTown's purchase orders and invoices are explained in detail in Chapter 2. Listings 3.8 and 3.9 show example XML document instances for both.

LISTING 3.8   Example SkatesTown Purchase Order

```
<po xmlns="http://www.skatestown.com/ns/po"
    id="50383" submitted="2001-12-06">
   <billTo>
      <company>The Skateboard Warehouse</company>
      <street>One Warehouse Park</street>
      <street>Building 17</street>
      <city>Boston</city>
      <state>MA</state>
      <postalCode>01775</postalCode>
   </billTo>
   <shipTo>
      <company>The Skateboard Warehouse</company>
      <street>One Warehouse Park</street>
      <street>Building 17</street>
      <city>Boston</city>
      <state>MA</state>
      <postalCode>01775</postalCode>
   </shipTo>
   <order>
      <item sku="318-BP" quantity="5">
         <description>Skateboard backpack; five pockets</description>
      </item>
      <item sku="947-TI" quantity="12">
         <description>Street-style titanium skateboard.</description>
      </item>
      <item sku="008-PR" quantity="1000"/>
   </order>
</po>
```

LISTING 3.9   Example SkatesTown Invoice

```
<invoice inv="http://www.skatestown.com/ns/invoice"
         id="50383" submitted="2001-12-06">
   <billTo>
      <company>The Skateboard Warehouse</company>
      <street>One Warehouse Park</street>
      <street>Building 17</street>
      <city>Boston</city>
      <state>MA</state>
      <postalCode>01775</postalCode>
   </billTo>
   <shipTo>
      <company>The Skateboard Warehouse</company>
      <street>One Warehouse Park</street>
      <street>Building 17</street>
      <city>Boston</city>
      <state>MA</state>
      <postalCode>01775</postalCode>
   </shipTo>
   <order>
      <item sku="318-BP" quantity="5" unitPrice="49.95">
         <description>Skateboard backpack; five pockets</description>
      </item>
      <item sku="947-TI" quantity="12" unitPrice="129.00">
         <description>Street-style titanium skateboard.</description>
      </item>
      <item sku="008-PR" quantity="1000" unitPrice="0.00">
         <description>Promotional: SkatesTown stickers</description>
      </item>
   </order>
   <tax>89.89</tax>
   <shippingAndHandling>89.89</shippingAndHandling>
   <totalCost>1977.52</totalCost>
</invoice>
```

XML-Java Data Mapping

Unfortunately, Al Rosen finds out that the actual SkatesTown purchase order system does not know how to deal with XML. The XML capabilities were added as an extension to the system by a developer who has since left the company. To make matters worse, much of the source code pertaining to XML processing seems to have been lost during an upgrade of the source control management (SCM) system at the company.

The PO system's APIs work in terms of a set of Java beans representing concepts such as product, purchase order, invoice, address, and so on. Figure 3.15 shows a UML diagram.

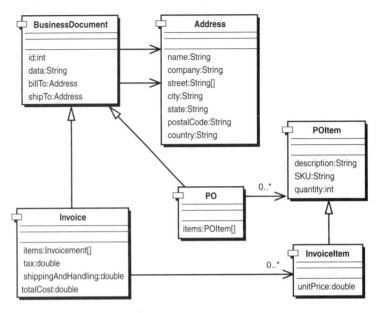

FIGURE 3.15
UML model for the PO system's data objects.

Al knows that because he is using SOAP-based messaging, the task of mapping the purchase order XML to Java objects and the invoice Java objects back to XML is left entirely up to him. Therefore, he implements a serializer and a deserializer that know how to encode and decode objects from the com.skatestown.data package to and from XML. Because the schemas for purchase orders and invoices are relatively simple, he decides to do this by hand rather than to rely on available schema compiler tools; he has had no experience with these. The two classes that he builds are `Serializer` and `Deserializer` in the com.skatestown.xml package. The combined code size is slightly over 300 lines of Java code.

Listing 3.10 shows the key purchase order deserialization methods. They use a number of simple utility methods such as `getValue()` and `getElements()` to traverse the DOM representation of a purchase order and construct a purchase order and all its contained objects. Reusable functionality, such as reading the common properties of POItem and InvoiceItem or creating addresses, is put in separate methods (`readItem()` and `createAddress()`, respectively). This pattern for XML to Java data mapping is very simple and readable yet flexible to handle a large variety of input XML formats.

LISTING 3.10 Core Purchase Deserialization Methods

```
protected void readDocument(BusinessDocument doc, Element elem)
{
    doc.setId(Integer.parseInt(elem.getAttribute( "id" )));
    doc.setDate(elem.getAttribute("submitted"));

    doc.setBillTo(createAddress(getElement(elem, "billTo")));
    doc.setShipTo(createAddress(getElement(elem, "shipTo")));
}

protected void readItem(POItem item, Element elem)
{
    item.setSKU(elem.getAttribute("sku"));
    item.setQuantity(Integer.parseInt(elem.getAttribute("quantity")));
    item.setDescription( getValue( elem, "description" ) );
}

protected Address createAddress(Element elem)
{
    Address addr  = new Address();
    addr.setName( getValue( elem, "name" ) );
    addr.setCompany( getValue( elem, "company" ) );
    addr.setStreet( getValues( elem, "street" ) );
    addr.setCity( getValue( elem, "city" ) );
    addr.setState( getValue( elem, "state" ) );
    addr.setPostalCode( getValue( elem, "postalCode" ) );
    addr.setCountry( getValue( elem, "country" ) );
    return addr;
}

protected PO _createPO(Element elem)
{
    PO po = new PO();

    readDocument(po, elem);

    Element[] orderItems = getElements(elem, "item");
    POItem[] items = new POItem[orderItems.length];
    for (int i = 0 ; i < items.length; ++i)
    {
        POItem item = new POItem();
        readItem(item, elem);
        items[i] = item;
```

LISTING 3.10   Continued

```
    }
    po.setItems(items);

    return po;
}
```

Listing 3.11 shows the key invoice serialization methods. In this case, they traverse the Java data structures describing an invoice and use utility methods such as addChild() to construct a DOM tree representing an invoice document. Again, shared functionality such as serializing an address is separated in methods that are called from multiple locations.

LISTING 3.11   Core Invoice Serialization Methods

```
protected void writeDocument(BusinessDocument bdoc, Element elem)
{
    elem.setAttribute("id", ""+bdoc.getId());
    elem.setAttribute("submitted", bdoc.getDate());
    writeAddress(bdoc.getBillTo(), addChild(elem, "billTo"));
    writeAddress(bdoc.getShipTo(), addChild(elem, "shipTo"));
}

protected void writeAddress(Address addr, Element elem)
{
    addChild(elem, "name", addr.getName());
    addChild(elem, "company", addr.getCompany());
    addChildren(elem, "street", addr.getStreet());
    addChild(elem, "city", addr.getCity());
    addChild(elem, "state", addr.getState());
    addChild(elem, "postalCode", addr.getPostalCode());
    addChild(elem, "country", addr.getCountry());
}

protected void writePOItem(POItem item, Element elem)
{
    elem.setAttribute("sku", item.getSKU());
    elem.setAttribute("quantity", ""+item.getQuantity());
    addChild(elem, "description", item.getDescription());
}

protected void writeInvoiceItem(InvoiceItem item, Element elem)
{
    writePOItem(item, elem);
    elem.setAttribute("unitPrice", nf.format(item.getUnitPrice()));
```

LISTING 3.11   Continued

```
}

protected void writeInvoice(Invoice invoice, Element elem)
{
    writeDocument(invoice, elem);
    Element order = addChild(elem, "order");
    InvoiceItem[] items = invoice.getItems();
    for (int i = 0; i < items.length; ++i)
    {
        writeInvoiceItem(items[i], addChild(order, "item"));
    }

    addChild(elem, "tax", nf.format(invoice.getTax()));
    addChild(elem, "shippingAndHandling",
        nf.format(invoice.getShippingAndHandling()));
    addChild(elem, "totalCost", nf.format(invoice.getTotalCost()));
}
```

Service Requestor View

The PO Web service client implementation follows the same pattern as the invoice checker clients (see Listing 3.12). The goal of its API is to hide the details of Axis-specific APIs from the service requestor. Therefore, the invoke() method takes an InputStream for the purchase order XML and returns the generated invoice as a string. Alternatively, the invoke() method might have been written to take in and return DOM documents.

LISTING 3.12   PO Submission Web Service Client

```
package ch3.ex4;

import java.io.*;
import org.apache.axis.encoding.SerializationContext;
import org.apache.axis.message.SOAPEnvelope;
import org.apache.axis.message.SOAPBodyElement;
import org.apache.axis.client.ServiceClient;
import org.apache.axis.Message;
import org.apache.axis.MessageContext;

/**
 * Purchase order submission client
 */
public class POSubmissionClient
{
    /**
```

LISTING 3.12   Continued

```java
     * Target service URL
     */
    private String url;

    /**
     * Create a client with a target URL
     */
    public POSubmissionClient(String targetUrl)
    {
        url = targetUrl;
    }

    /**
     * Invoke the PO submission web service
     *
     * @param po Purchase order document
     * @return Invoice document
     * @exception Exception I/O error or Axis error
     */
    public String invoke(InputStream po) throws Exception
    {
        // Send the message
        ServiceClient client = new ServiceClient(url);
        client.setRequestMessage(new Message(po, true));
        client.invoke();

        // Retrieve the response body
        MessageContext ctx = client.getMessageContext();
        Message outMsg = ctx.getResponseMessage();
        SOAPEnvelope envelope = outMsg.getAsSOAPEnvelope();
        SOAPBodyElement body = envelope.getFirstBody();

        // Get the XML from the body
        StringWriter w = new StringWriter();
        SerializationContext sc = new SerializationContext(w, ctx);
        body.output(sc);
        return w.toString();
    }
}
```

Sending the request message is simple. We have to create a `ServiceClient` from the target URL and set its request message to a message constructed from the purchase order input stream. The second parameter to the `Message` constructor, the boolean `true`, is an indication that the input stream represents the message body as opposed to the whole message. Calling `invoke()` sends the message to the Web service.

The second part of the method has to do with retrieving the body of the response message. This code should be familiar from the implementation of the `E-mail` header handler.

Finally, we use an Axis serialization context to write the XML in the response body into a `StringWriter`. We could have easily gotten the body as a DOM element by calling is `getAsDOM()` method. The trouble is, there is no standard way in DOM Level 2 to convert a DOM element into a string! Java API for XML Processing (JAXP) defines such a mechanism in its transformation API (`javax.xml.transform` package), but the method is fairly cumbersome. It is easiest to use an Axis `SerializationContext` object.

Service Provider View

The implementation of the purchase order submission service is very simple (see Listing 3.13). Because this is not an RPC-based service, the input and output are both XML documents (represented via DOM `Document` objects). The input document is deserialized to produce a purchase order object. It is passed to the actual PO processing backend. Its implementation is not shown here because it has nothing to do with Web services. It looks up item prices by their SKU, calculates totals based on item quantities, and adds tax and shipping and handling. The resulting invoice object is serialized to produce the result of the purchase order submission service.

LISTING 3.13   Purchase Order Submission Web Service

```
package com.skatestown.services;

import javax.xml.parsers.*;
import org.w3c.dom.*;
import org.apache.axis.MessageContext;
import com.skatestown.backend.*;
import com.skatestown.data.*;
import com.skatestown.xml.*;
import bws.BookUtil;

/**
 * Purchase order submission service
 */
public class POSubmission
{
    /**
```

LISTING 3.13   Continued

```
    * Submit a purchase order and generate an invoice
    */
    public Document submitPO(MessageContext msgContext, Document inDoc)
    throws Exception
    {
        // Create a PO from the XML document
        DocumentBuilderFactory factory = DocumentBuilderFactory.newInstance();
        DocumentBuilder builder = factory.newDocumentBuilder();
        PO po = Deserializer.createPO(inDoc.getDocumentElement());

        // Get the product database
        ProductDB db = BookUtil.getProductDB(msgContext);

        // Create an invoice from the PO
        POProcessor processor = new POProcessor(db);
        Invoice invoice = processor.processPO(po);

        // Serialize the invoice to XML
        Document newDoc = Serializer.writeInvoice(builder, invoice);

        return newDoc;
    }
}
```

Finally, adding deployment information about the new service involves making a small change to the Axis Web services deployment descriptor (see Listing 3.14). Again, Chapter 4 will go into the details of Axis deployment descriptors.

LISTING 3.14   Deployment Descriptor for Purchase Order Submission Service

```
<!-- Chapter 3 example 4 services -->
<service name="POSubmission" pivot="MsgDispatcher">
  <option name="className" value="com.skatestown.services.POSubmission"/>
  <option name="methodName" value="doSubmission"/>
</service>
```

Putting the Service to the Test

A simple JSP test harness in ch3/ex4/index.jsp (see Figure 3.16) tests the purchase order submission service. By default, it loads /resources/samplePO.xml, but you can modify the purchase order on the page and see how the invoice you get back changes.

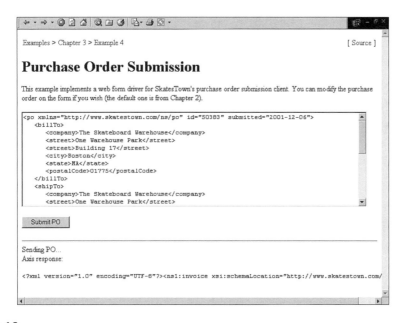

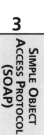

FIGURE 3.16

Putting the PO submission Web service to the test.

SOAP on the Wire

With the help of TCPMon, we can see what SOAP messages are passing between the client and the Axis engine:

```
POST /bws/services/POSubmission HTTP/1.0
Host: localhost
Content-Length: 1169
Content-Type: text/xml; charset=utf-8
SOAPAction: ""

<?xml version="1.0" encoding="UTF-8"?>
<SOAP-ENV:Envelope
   SOAP-ENV:encodingStyle="http://schemas.xmlsoap.org/soap/encoding/"
   xmlns:xsd="http://www.w3.org/2001/XMLSchema"
   xmlns:SOAP-ENV="http://schemas.xmlsoap.org/soap/envelope/"
   xmlns:xsi="http://www.w3.org/2001/XMLSchema-instance">
   <SOAP-ENV:Body>
      <po xmlns="http://www.skatestown.com/ns/po"
         id="50383" submitted="2001-12-06">
         ...
      </po>
   </SOAP-ENV:Body>
</SOAP-ENV:Envelope>
```

The target URL is `/bws/services/POSubmission`. The response message simply carries an invoice inside it, much in the same way that the request message carries a purchase order. As a result, there is no need to show it here.

That's all there is to taking advantage of SOAP-based messaging. Axis makes it very easy to define and invoke services that consume and produce arbitrary XML messages.

Figure 3.17 shows one way to think about the interaction of abstraction layers in SOAP messaging. It is modeled after Figure 3.3 earlier in the chapter but includes the additional role of a service developer. As before, the only "real" on-the-wire communication happens between the HTTP client and the Web server that dispatches a service request to Axis.

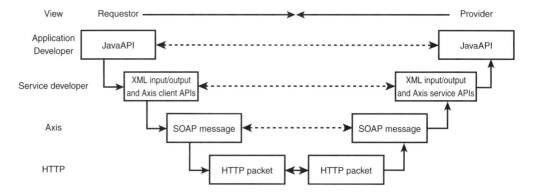

FIGURE 3.17

Layering of abstraction for SOAP messaging.

The abstractions at this level are HTTP packets. At the Axis level, the abstractions are SOAP messages with some additional context. For example, on the provider side, the target service is determined by the target URL of the HTTP packet. This piece of context information is "attached" to the actual SOAP message by the Axis servlet that listens for HTTP-based Web service requests. The job of a service-level developer is to create an abstraction layer that maps Java APIs to and from SOAP messages. During SOAP messaging, a little more work needs to happen at this level than when doing RPCs. The reason is that data must be manually encoded and decoded by both the Web service client and the Web service backend. Finally, at the top of the stack on both the requestor and provider sides sits the application developer who is happily insulated from the fact that Web services are being used and that Axis is the Web service engine. The application developer needs only to understand the concepts pertaining to his application domain—in this case, purchase orders and invoices.

SOAP Protocol Bindings

So far in this chapter, we have only shown SOAP being transmitted over HTTP. SOAP, however, is transport-independent and can be bound to any protocol type. This section looks at some of the issues involved in building Web services and transporting SOAP messages over various protocols.

General Considerations

The key issue in deciding how to bind SOAP to a particular protocol has to do with identifying how the requirements for a Web service (RPC or not, interaction pattern, synchronicity, and so on) map to the capabilities of the underlying transport protocol. In particular, the task at hand is to determine how much of the total information needed to successfully execute the Web service needs to go in the SOAP message versus somewhere else.

As Figure 3.18 shows with an HTTP example, many protocols have a packaging notion. If SOAP is to be transmitted over such protocols, a distinction needs to be made between physical (transport-level) and logical (SOAP) messages. Context information can be passed in both. In the case of HTTP, context information is passed via the target URI and the SOAPAction header. Security information might come as HTTP username and password headers. In the case of SOAP, context information is passed as SOAP headers.

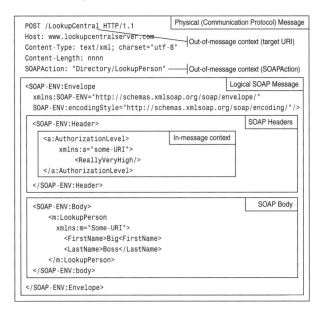

FIGURE 3.18

Logical versus physical messages.

Sometimes, SOAP messages have to be passed over protocols whose physical messages do not have any mechanism for storing context. Consider pure sockets-based exchanges. By default, in these cases the physical and the logical message are one and the same. In these cases, you have four options for passing context information:

- By convention, as in, "When listening on port 12345, I know that I have to invoke service X."

- By entirely using SOAP's header-based extensibility mechanism to pass all context information.

- By custom-building a very light physical protocol under SOAP messages, as in, "The first CRLF delimited line of message will be the target URI; the rest will be the SOAP message."

- By using a lightweight protocol that can be layered on top of the physical protocol and can be used to move SOAP messages. Examples of such protocols are Simple MIME Exchange Protocol (SMXP) or Blocks Extensible Exchange Protocol (BEEP).

As in most cases in the software industry, reinventing the wheel is a bad idea. Therefore, the second and fourth approaches listed here typically make the most sense. The first approach is not extensible and can leave you in a tight spot if requirements change. The third approach smells of reinventing the wheel. The cost of going with the second approach is that you have to make sure that all clients interacting with your Web service will be able to support the necessary extensions. The cost of going with the fourth approach is that it might require additional infrastructure for both requestors and providers.

Another consideration that comes into play is the interaction pattern supported by the transport protocol. For example, HTTP is a request-response protocol. It makes RPCs and request-response messaging interactions very simple. For other protocols, you might have to explicitly manage the association of requests and responses. As we mentioned in the previous section, Chapter 6 discusses this topic in more detail.

Contrary to popular belief, Web services do not have to involve stateless interactions. For example, Web services could be designed in a session-oriented manner. This is probably not the best design for a high-volume Web service, but it could work fine in many cases. HTTP sessions can be leveraged to provide context information related to the session. Otherwise, you will have to use a session ID of some kind, much in the same way a message conversation ID is used.

Finally, when choosing transport protocols for Web services, think carefully about external requirements. You may discover important factors entirely outside the needs of the Web service engine. For example, when considering Web services over sockets as a higher-performance alternative to Web services over HTTP (requests and responses don't have to go through the Web server), you might want to consider the following factors:

- If services have to be available over a public unsecured network, is it an acceptable risk to open a hole through the firewall for Web service traffic?

- Can clients support SSL to ensure the privacy of messages? Surprisingly, some clients can speak HTTPS but not straight SSL.

- What are the back-end load balancing and failover requirements? Straight sockets-based communication requires *sticky* load balancing. You establish a session with one server and you have to keep using this server. This approach potentially compromises scalability and failover, unless steps are taken to build request redirection and session persistence and failover capabilities into the system.

As with most things in the software industry, there is no single correct approach and no single right answer. Investigate your requirements carefully and do not be easily tempted by seemingly exciting, out-of-the-ordinary solutions. The rest of this section provides some more details about how certain protocols can be used with SOAP.

HTTP/S

This chapter has shown many examples of SOAP over HTTP. The SOAP specification defines a binding of SOAP over HTTP with the following set of rules:

- The MIME media type of both HTTP requests and responses (defined in the Content-Type HTTP header) must be text/xml.

- Requests must come as HTTP POST operations.

- The SOAPAction header is reserved as a hint to the SOAP processor as to which Web service is being invoked. The value of the header can be any URI; it is implementation-specific.

- Successful SOAP message processing must return an HTTP error code in the 200 range. Typically, this is 200 OK.

- In the case of an error generated while processing the SOAP message, the HTTP response code must be 500 Internal Server Error and it must include a SOAP message with a Fault element describing the error.

In addition to these simple rules, the SOAP specification defines how SOAP messages can be exchanged over HTTP using the HTTP Extension Framework (RFC 2774, http://www.normos.org/ietf/rfc/rfc2774.txt), but this information is not very relevant to us.

In short, HTTP is the most commonly used mechanism for exchanging SOAP messages. It is aided by the industry's experience building relatively secure, scalable, reliable networks to handle HTTP traffic and by the fact that traditional Web applications and application servers primarily use HTTP. HTTP is not perfect, but we are very good at working around its limitations.

For secure message exchanges, you can use HTTPS instead of HTTP. The most common extension on top of what the SOAP specification describes is the use of HTTP usernames and passwords to authenticate Web service clients. Combined with HTTPS, this approach offers a good-enough level of security for most e-commerce scenarios. Chapter 5 discusses the role of HTTPS in Web services.

SOAP Messages with Attachments

SOAP messages will often have attachments of various types. The prototypical example is an insurance claim form in XML format that has an accident picture associated with it and/or a scanned copy of the signed accident report form. The SOAP Messages with Attachments specification defines a simple mechanism for encoding a SOAP message in a MIME multipart structure and associating this message with any number of parts (attachments) in that structure. These attachments can be in their native format, which is typically binary.

Without going into too many details, the SOAP message becomes the root of the multipart/related MIME structure. The message refers to attachments using a URI with the cid: prefix, which stands for "content ID" and uniquely identifies the parts of the MIME structure. Here is how this is done. Note that some long lines (such as the Content-Type header) have been broken in two for better readability:

```
MIME-Version: 1.0
Content-Type: Multipart/Related; boundary=MIME_boundary; type=text/xml;
        start="<claim061400a.xml@claiming-it.com>"
Content-Description: This is the optional message description.

--MIME_boundary
Content-Type: text/xml; charset=UTF-8
Content-Transfer-Encoding: 8bit
Content-ID: <claim061400a.xml@claiming-it.com>

<?xml version='1.0' ?>
<SOAP-ENV:Envelope
xmlns:SOAP-ENV="http://schemas.xmlsoap.org/soap/envelope/">
<SOAP-ENV:Body>
..
<theSignedForm href="cid:claim061400a.tiff@claiming-it.com"/>
..
</SOAP-ENV:Body>
</SOAP-ENV:Envelope>

--MIME_boundary
Content-Type: image/tiff
```

```
Content-Transfer-Encoding: binary
Content-ID: <claim061400a.tiff@claiming-it.com>

...binary TIFF image...
--MIME_boundary--
```

One excellent thing about encapsulating SOAP messages in a MIME structure is that the packaging is independent of an actual transport protocol. In a sense, the MIME package is another logical message on top of the SOAP message. This type of MIME structure can then be bound to any number of other protocols. The specification defines a binding to HTTP, an example of which is shown here:

```
POST /insuranceClaims HTTP/1.1
Host: www.risky-stuff.com
Content-Type: Multipart/Related; boundary=MIME_boundary; type=text/xml;
        start="<claim061400a.xml@claiming-it.com>"
Content-Length: XXXX
SOAPAction: http://schemas.risky-stuff.com/Auto-Claim
...
```

SOAP over SMTP

E-mail is pervasive on the Internet. The important e-mail-related protocols are Simple Mail Transfer Protocol (SMTP), Post Office Protocol (POP), and Internet Message Access Protocol (IMAP). E-mail is a great way to exchange SOAP messages when synchronicity is not required because:

- E-mail messages can easily carry SOAP messages.

- E-mail messages have extensible headers that can be used to transmit context information outside the SOAP message body.

- Both sending and receiving of e-mail messages can be configured to require authentication. Further, using S/MIME with e-mail provides additional security for a range of applications.

- E-mail can support one-to-one and one-to-many participant configurations.

- E-mail messaging is buffered and queued with reliable dispatch that automatically includes multiple retries and failed delivery notification.

- The Internet e-mail server infrastructure is highly scalable.

Together, these factors make e-mail a very suitable alternative to HTTP for asynchronous Web service messaging applications.

Other Protocols

Despite its low-tech nature, FTP can be very useful for simple one-way messaging using Web services. Access to FTP servers can be authenticated. Further, roles-based restrictions can be applied to particular directories on the FTP server. When using FTP, SOAP messages are mapped onto the files that are being transferred. Typically, the file names indicate the target of the SOAP message.

In addition, with companies such as Microsoft backing SMXP for their Hailstorm initiatives, the protocol is emerging as a potential candidate to layer on top of straight socket-based communications for transmission of SOAP messages.

Finally, sophisticated messaging infrastructures such as IBM's MQSeries, Microsoft's Message Queue (MSMQ), and the Java Messaging Service (JMS) are well-suited for the transport of SOAP messages. Chapter 5 shows an example of SOAP messaging using JMS.

The key constraint limiting the wide deployment of SOAP bindings to protocols other than HTTP and e-mail is the requirement of Web service interoperability. HTTP and e-mail are so pervasive that they are likely to remain the preferred choices for SOAP message transport for the foreseeable future.

Summary

This chapter addressed the fourth level of the Web services interoperability stack—XML messaging. It focused on explaining some of the core features of XML protocols and SOAP 1.1 as the *de facto* standard for Web service messaging and invocation. The goal was to give you a solid understanding of SOAP and a first-hand experience building and consuming Web services using the Apache Axis engine. To this end, we covered, in some detail:

- The evolution of XML protocols from first-generation technologies based on pure XML 1.0 (WDDX and XML-RPC) to XML Schema- and Namespace-powered second-generation protocols, of which SOAP is a prime example. The chapter also discussed the motivation and history behind SOAP's creation.

- The simple yet flexible design of the SOAP envelope framework, including versioning and vertical extensibility using SOAP headers. In SOAP, all context information orthogonal to what is in the SOAP body is carried via headers. SOAP's envelope framework allows you to design higher-level protocols on top of SOAP in a decentralized manner.

- SOAP intermediaries as the key innovation enabling horizontal extensibility. Because of intermediaries, Web services can be organized into very flexible system and network architectures and value-added services can be provided on top of basic Web service messaging.

- SOAP error handling using SOAP faults. Any robust messaging protocol needs a well-designed exception-handling model. With their ability to communicate error information targeted at both software and humans, as well as clearly identifying the source of the error condition, SOAP faults make it possible to integrate SOAP as part of robust, mission-critical systems.

- Encoding data using SOAP. The chapter covered both SOAP's abstract data model encoding and a number of other heuristics for determining an appropriate data representation model for SOAP messages.

- Using SOAP for both messaging and RPC applications. By design, SOAP is independent of all traditional aspects of messaging: participant organization, interaction pattern, synchronicity, and so on. As a result, SOAP can be used for just about any distributed system. This chapter provided some guidelines that help narrow the space of what is possible to the space of what makes sense in the real-world solutions.

- Using SOAP over multiple protocols. The SOAP specification mentions an HTTP binding for SOAP, but Web services can be meaningfully bound to many other packaging and protocol schemes: MIME packages to support attachments, SMTP for scalable asynchronous messaging without the need for special middleware, and many others.

During the course of the chapter, we developed two meaningful e-commerce Web services for SkatesTown: an inventory check RPC service (with or without e-mail confirmations) and a purchase order submission messaging service. Our implementation on both the server and the client used design best practices for separating data and business logic from the details of SOAP and XML processing.

The Road Ahead

This chapter focused on the *de facto* standard protocol for Web service invocation as of the time of this writing—SOAP 1.1. (SOAP 1.2 is still in early draft stage.) However, many more pieces to the puzzle are required to bring meaningful Web services-enabled business solutions online. The rest of the book will complete the Web services puzzle. Chapter 5 focuses on building secure, robust, scalable enterprise-grade Web services. Chapter 6 introduces the concept of service descriptions and the Web Services Description Language (WSDL). Chapter 7 discusses service registries and the Universal Description, Discovery and Integration (UDDI) effort. Chapter 8 reviews the state of the currently available Web services tooling. Chapter 9 looks at the exciting world of Web service futures. This said, the next chapter offers a short detour for those who are truly excited about building and consuming extensible, high-performance Web services—it is about building Web services using the advanced features of Apache Axis.

Resources

- *BEEP*—RFC 3080: "The Blocks Extensible Exchange Protocol Core" (IETF, March 2001). Available at `http://www.ietf.org/rfc/rfc3080.txt`.

- *DOM Level 2 Core*—W3C (World Wide Web Consortium) Document Object Model Level 2 Core (W3C, November 2000). Available at `http://www.w3.org/TR/2000/REC-DOM-Level-2-Core-20001113`.

- *HTTP extensions*—RFC 2774: "An HTTP Extension Framework" (IETF, February 2000). Available at `http://www.ietf.org/rfc/rfc2774.txt`.

- *HTTP/1.1*—RFC 2616: "Hypertext Transfer Protocol—HTTP/1.1" (IETF, January 1997). Available at `http://www.ietf.org/rfc/rfc2616.txt`.

- *JAXP*—Java API for XML Processing 1.1 (Sun Microsystems, Inc., February 2001). Available at `http://java.sun.com/xml/xml_jaxp.html`.

- *MIME*—RFC 2045: "Multipurpose Internet Mail Extensions (MIME) Part One: Format of Internet Message Bodies" (IETF, November 1996). Available at `http://www.ietf.org/rfc/rfc2045.txt`.

- *SMXP*—Simple MIME eXchange Protocol (SMXP) (First Virtual, May 1995). Available at `http://wuarchive.wustl.edu/packages/first-virtual/docs/smxp-spec.txt`.

- *XML*—Extensible Markup Language (XML) 1.0, Second Edition (W3C, August 2000). Available at `http://www.w3.org/TR/2000/WD-xml-2e-20000814`.

- *XML Namespaces*—"Namespaces in XML" (W3C, January 1999). Available at `http://www.w3.org/TR/1999/REC-xml-names-19990114`.

- *XML Schema Part 1: Structures*—"XML Schema Part 1: Structures" (W3C, May 2001). Available at `http://www.w3.org/TR/2001/REC-xmlschema-1-20010502`.

- *XML Schema Part 2: Datatypes*—"XML Schema Part 2: Datatypes" (W3C, May 2001). Available at `http://www.w3.org/TR/2001/REC-xmlschema-1-20010502`.

Creating Web Services

IN THIS CHAPTER

So far, we've seen some very simple examples of Web services without going into any detail about the environment in which these Web services are running. Obviously, the SOAP implementation that comes with this book is the *Axis* 📖 project from the Apache Software Foundation, but we've skimmed over the details. This chapter will focus on giving a detailed overview of Axis ranging from how to configure Axis itself to how to install, configure, and write Web services. In this chapter, we review the primary or common APIs and tasks associated with using Axis, in the context of complete working examples. However, Axis has many rich features that continue to evolve. (For a complete reference to the features in Axis, see `http://xml.apache.org/axis`.)

While there will always be a need for new Web services that satisfy new requirements, typically Web services will be deployed to allow access to existing business logic through additional channels. By reusing the core business logic that has already been deployed and tested, a brand-new opportunity for business collaborations can be exploited by simply building a bridge between a SOAP processor and the existing business logic. This chapter will explore how to build these bridges between Axis and existing applications.

Why and What Is Axis?

Axis is the latest version of the Apache SOAP project. The acronym Axis means Apache Extensible Interaction System, a fancy way of saying it's a SOAP processor that allows for an assortment of pluggable components to be configured in a variety of ways. We chose this SOAP processor for a few reasons. First, most of the authors of this book are (or have been) involved in the development of Axis from its inception. Second, we believe that Axis's flexibility and overall design will allow it to become one of the leading SOAP processors very quickly. And third, because it is an Apache open source project, we believe it will gain the benefits of having contributors from a wide range of backgrounds and companies, giving it a technological edge over other SOAP implementations. But, only time will tell.

Apache SOAP v2 (`http://xml.apache.org/soap`), the predecessor to Axis, is a fairly good implementation of the SOAP specification, but it has its limitations. Although it can be used for deploying Web services, the performance and pluggability of SOAP v2 leave a lot to be desired. At the time of this writing, Axis is already quite a bit faster than SOAP v2; and although SOAP v2 provides some level of pluggability for components like different kinds of Web services or for different *transports* 📖, these features were added as an afterthought—the design deficiencies of these features shows through in their usability (or lack thereof). SOAP v2 also isn't fully compliant with the SOAP 1.1 specification.

It is important to note that at the time of this writing Axis has not yet released its first version. It has, however, released an alpha version. This alpha version is not complete (or fully SOAP 1.1 spec compliant), but it is functional enough for people to start kicking the tires and getting a feel for whether the architecture is good. By the time the first release does come out (before the end of 2001, we hope) it will be fully spec compliant. As with any project, customer feedback is an important step in the development process, so releasing an alpha version is a key milestone in Axis' development cycle. This chapter will focus mainly on the current functionality of Axis—when appropriate, however, it will give insight into the possible future features of Axis (the design could change).

The Axis Architecture

From the start, Axis was designed with a completely open and pluggable architecture. In its simplest form, Axis can be viewed as a thin layer that sits between the business logic and the network transport carrying your data.

As depicted in Figure 4.1, Axis is simply the means by which the SOAP message is taken from a transport (such as HTTP) and handed to the Web service and the means by which any response is formatted as a SOAP message to then be sent back to the requestor. Although this might seem like an oversimplification, Axis is designed to be used in a wide range of environments and by deployment engineers with varying skill levels. When you're first experimenting with Web services, or if you don't need complex configurations, Axis by default will make the deployment of Web services very easy. The "Simple Web Services" section will describe this further by showing you how to quickly take Java code and deploy it as a Web service in Axis. However, if you need a more complex processing model, Axis can be configured to support that, too.

FIGURE 4.1
Basic overview of Axis.

Axis Components

Next, we're going to focus on the various components of Axis. Each item in the following list will be discussed in more detail, but here's brief summary of the key components:

- *Axis Engine* 📖—The main entry point into the SOAP processor
- *Handlers* 📖—The basic building blocks inside Axis that link Axis to existing back-end systems

- *Chain* 📖—An ordered collection of handlers (and a handler itself)
- *Transports*—Mechanisms by which SOAP messages flow into and out of Axis
- *Deployment/Configuration*—Means through which Web services are made available through Axis
- *Serializers/Deserializers*—Code that will convert native (for example, Java) datatypes into XML and back

Axis Engine

As you could probably guess, the Axis engine is the focal point of the Axis SOAP processor. The engine's job is to act as the main entry point into Axis' message processing model as well as to coordinate the SOAP message's flow through the various components. The engine is also responsible for ensuring that the SOAP semantics are followed—for example, it will verify that the mustUnderstand checks are properly performed. In the following sections, we'll discuss the other components that make up the processing model, but it is important to know that the engine is the piece responsible for coordinating the order in which those other components are invoked. As we discuss each of these components, we'll describe their interaction with the engine in more detail.

During the design process of Axis, it was realized that it would be impossible to design a SOAP message processor in such a way that it could work for the wide-ranging uses we wanted for Axis unless it was flexible enough to allow deployment engineers (configuration administrations) to control the message flow itself. Allowing people to tell Axis which message processing logic to perform, in what order, and when, became a clear requirement. It also became apparent that there would be no way of knowing how people would want to process the SOAP messages. For example, many people see SOAP as simply another Remote Procedure Call (RPC) mechanism—which is a valid use. However, there is no reason the exact same SOAP message that might be treated as an RPC message by one SOAP processor could not be treated as an XML document and simply run through an XSLT processor by another. As long they both adhere to the SOAP specification, and of course follow the semantic rules defined by the Web service definition, exactly how the SOAP message is processed is wide open. So, how does Axis handle these challenges? Handlers and chains.

Handlers and Chains

At its most basic level, Axis is all about chaining together pieces of message processing logic. Figure 4.1 shows just one piece: the Web service itself. Often, you'll need to perform additional processing on the message either before or after the Web service itself is invoked. For example, some logging might need to take place, or SOAP headers might need to be processed. You can accomplish this two ways: Place this additional logic in the Web service itself or allow for additional pieces of code to be executed outside of, but before and after, the Web service.

For this purpose, Axis has the notion of *chains*. Chains are simply ordered collections of components (code) that Axis will invoke sequentially and in the order specified.

The components that are used to build these chains are called *handlers*. Each handler has the opportunity to examine or modify the SOAP message in order to complete its job. For example, it is possible to have a handler in the chain that will look for any encrypted data in the message and decrypt it before the Web service itself is invoked (SOAP encryption is explained in more detail in Chapter 5, "Using SOAP for e-Business"). By modularizing the work in this way, each handler is free to focus on its core job and not worry about any possible auxiliary work that might need to be done, thereby eliminating code duplication. Also, if new pre- or post-processing is needed in the future, it becomes a simple matter of plugging new handlers into the chain through configuration changes to Axis rather than having to make code changes to the Web service. This also allows third-party vendors to produce Axis handlers that can be snapped into any configuration without prior knowledge of the exact environment, configuration, or Web service being invoked.

Handlers are the basic building blocks inside Axis. Everything, even the Axis engine and the chains themselves, is a handler. As a result, the deployment engineer is free to configure Axis in an unlimited number of ways. It is possible for a preprocessing handler shown in Figure 4.2 to be a chain that itself contains a collection of handlers (or even more chains). Aside from each handler having access to the SOAP message, each handler can also be involved in the production of any possible SOAP response message. We'll give more details in the "Building Handlers" section, but it is worth reiterating that each handler does have access to (and can change) the *request message* and any possible *response message* that might exist during the processing flow through the Axis processor.

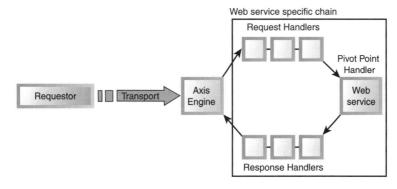

FIGURE 4.2
Pre- and post-processing is done by defining a chain.

Chains are the mechanisms by which handlers are grouped together. The concept is simple; a chain is an ordered collection of handlers that together can be viewed as a single unit of processing. As with any good rule, there is a slight complication—certain types of chains have the notion of a *pivot point* 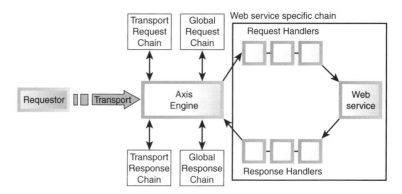 handler, which is the point at which the chain notes that it has switched from processing the request SOAP message (request processing) and is now processing the response SOAP message (response processing). The need for this logical split between request, pivot point, and response handlers in a chain will be made clearer later. This pivot point handler also serves as the one handler in these types of chains that is the real reason the chain exists—to dispatch the message to the target Web service (the other handlers are there for request and response processing of the message). The most common use of this type of chain (also called *targeted-chain* because it is viewed as pointing to the pivot point handler) is the Web service–specific chain. In Figure 4.2, a Web service chain has request and response processing handlers defined, but the pivot point handler invokes the Web service. Even though Axis has, for programmer convenience, defined a particular kind of chain encapsulating these three pieces, when a chain is defined there is no reason that all three pieces need to be used. For example, it is possible to define a chain that is just a collection of handlers without a specific pivot point—it is there merely as a configuration option.

Figure 4.2 shows that it is possible to define a chain of handlers that are invoked for a particular Web service. However, what if chains need to be invoked for *all* Web service invocations flowing through Axis? Or, what if certain chains need to be invoked only if the message came in on HTTP, whereas if the message was delivered via SMTP those chains should not be invoked? To support these configurations, Axis has the notion of *transport specific chains* and *global chains*.

As shown in Figure 4.3, Axis allows the definition of chains that are invoked based on the type of transport used in the delivery of the SOAP message (transport specific chains) and chains that should be invoked for all Web services (global chains).

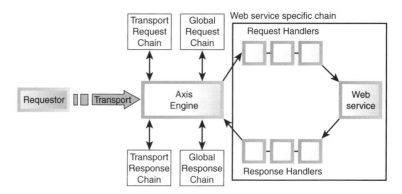

FIGURE 4.3
Axis includes three different levels of chaining.

Transport-specific chains might be defined to process such things as transport-specific compression, or authentication. The "Configuration Methods" section will discuss the way to deploy chains, but it is important to note that transport specific chains are targeted-chains. The request and response sides are clearly separated so that the Axis engine knows exactly which subset of handlers to invoke at the start of the message flow and which set to invoke at the end of the message flow. Although it was possible to design Axis so that there were two completely separate chains defined (rather than one with a request and a response side), it was decided that because they would always be used in conjunction with each other, and because it is expected that there will be a large number of transport specific chains, it would be easier from a usability point of view to define them as one chain with two sides.

Global chains come in handy in cases when all Web services require the same processing regardless of how the message was delivered or what the specific Web service itself is—for example, SkatesTown might want to keep a log of all Web service requests, and placing a logging handler in the global chain becomes a cleaner way of deploying it than placing it in each Web service–specific chain. Unlike transport chains that use targeted-chains, the global chain is split into two separate chains. Because, conceptually, there is only one global chain, it was decided that it would be easier for deployment engineers to define two separately named chains (`global.request` and `global.response`) rather than one chain with two sides. We'll discuss the details of how to name chains in the "Configuring Axis" section.

Within the Axis server-side engine, the order of chain processing is as follows:

1. If a transport-specific chain is defined, then the handlers labeled as the request handlers defined for that chain are invoked.
2. If a chain named `global.request` is defined, then it is invoked.
3. The Web service–specific chain is invoked. Exactly how the Web service–specific chain is identified is discussed later. As noted before, this chain is a targeted-chain and has three groupings of handlers: the request handlers, the Web service itself (at the pivot point), and the response handlers. They are invoked in that order.
4. If a chain named `global.response` is defined, it is invoked.
5. If a transport specific chain is defined, then the handlers labeled as the response handlers defined for that chain are invoked.

This processing model should allow a deployment engineer to have the complete flexibility of placing any handler at any point in the flow of messages through the server Axis engine.

In Figure 4.3, the Web service is shown as a handler at the pivot point in the Web service–specific chain. One layer of code is not shown: the *dispatcher* 📖.

Figure 4.4 shows a dispatcher as the pivot point handler in the Web service–specific chain.

Like all handlers, this dispatcher is responsible for acting as the bridge between Axis and your business logic. It is the job of the dispatcher to locate and invoke the appropriate piece of code associated with the desired Web service. For example, Axis comes with an *RPCDispatcher* 📖 whose job is to convert the SOAP message from XML into Java objects, locate the appropriate Java method to invoke, invoke it, and convert any possible response data back into XML and place it in the response SOAP message. By having a dispatch handler do this work, it can be used for any Java Web service invoked. Likewise, the Web service itself does not need to be concerned with the details of how the data was delivered or how to convert XML into Java objects; it can concentrate on doing its real job.

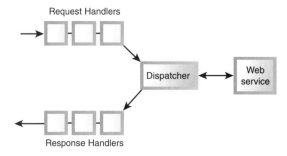

FIGURE 4.4
Handlers, acting as dispatchers, are the bridges between Axis and application logic.

Although dispatchers have been presented in the context of invoking the Web service, any of the handlers in any of the chains could be dispatchers. In other words, there is no reason why any of the request/response processing handlers need to have the business logic directly inside them. Those handlers could be dispatchers that extract the necessary data from the SOAP message and pass it along to external code in the proper format.

Transports

In order to complete the overall picture of the Axis architecture, one more piece of the puzzle needs to be brought in: transports. All the figures show a single Axis engine with a single transport delivering the SOAP message; however, this need not be the case.

Figure 4.5 shows that Axis can support a variety of transports, not just HTTP. Actually, Axis itself doesn't support multiple transports. Axis is designed such that the Axis engine can be viewed simply as a chunk of code that is called with an incoming message and returns an outgoing message. *Transport listeners* 📖 (such as servlets that wait for a SOAP message), although key in the overall picture of how Axis is used, are themselves not part of the Axis engine. It is assumed that the mechanism by which the Axis engine is created (a new one on each request or shared instance) will be managed by the transport listeners. Axis comes with a set of transport listeners (such as the `AxisServlet`) that you can use, but if you require special processing, it is assumed that you will modify the shipped transport listener to suit your needs or write a new one.

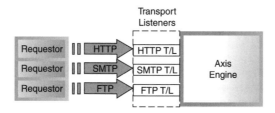

FIGURE 4.5
Multiple transports.

The role of the transport listener is to deliver the SOAP message to the Axis engine. This could mean listening on port 80 for an HTTP request or waiting for a file to be FTPed to a certain directory and then handing that message to the Axis engine. Aside from invoking the Axis engine, the transport listener must also tell the Axis engine which transport was used—this allows Axis to invoke any transport-specific chain that might have been configured.

The delineation between whether certain processing should be in the transport listener or in the transport specific chain is an issue left up to the deployment engineer. For example, in the HTTP case, the servlet waiting for SOAP requests can also perform any basic HTTP authentication checks before invoking the Axis engine. It is also perfectly acceptable for the servlet to not perform that check and leave it up to a handler on the transport specific chain to do it. The choice is left open.

Listing 4.1 shows a sample transport listener that does nothing more than look for a file called `inMsg` in the current directory. If the file is found, the transport listener uses it as the requesting SOAP message, calls Axis on it, and then places any response back into a file called `outMsg`.

LISTING 4.1 FileListener.java

```
import java.io.File;
import java.io.FileInputStream;
import java.io.FileOutputStream;
import java.io.FileNotFoundException;
import org.apache.axis.AxisFault;
import org.apache.axis.AxisEngine;
import org.apache.axis.server.AxisServer;
import org.apache.axis.Message;
```

LISTING 4.1   Continued

```
import org.apache.axis.MessageContext;
import org.apache.axis.message.SOAPEnvelope;
import org.apache.axis.message.SOAPFaultElement;

public class FileListener {
    public void run() {
      while (true) {
        try {
          // Look for an incoming msg, create a new Message object
          FileInputStream input = new FileInputStream("inMsg");
          AxisEngine engine = AxisServer.getSingleton();
          MessageContext msgContext = new MessageContext(engine);
          Message msg = new Message(input);

          try {
            //Set it as the "request" message
            msgContext.setRequestMessage(msg);

            // Set the Transport
            msgContext.setTransportName("file");

            // Invoke the Axis engine
            engine.invoke(msgContext);
          }
          catch(Exception e) {
            // Catch any error and stick it in the response
            if (!(e instanceof AxisFault))
              e = new AxisFault(e);
            AxisFault af = (AxisFault)e;
            msg = msgContext.getResponseMessage();
            if (msg == null) {
                msgContext.setResponseMessage(new Message(af));
            } else {
                SOAPEnvelope env = msg.getAsSOAPEnvelope();
                env.clearBody();
                env.addBodyElement(new SOAPFaultElement(af));
            }
          }

          // Close and delete the incoming message
          input.close();
          (new File("inMsg")).delete();

          // Place the response message in a file called "outMsg"
```

LISTING 4.1 Continued

```
        msg = msgContext.getResponseMessage();
        FileOutputStream output = new FileOutputStream("outMsg");
        String result = (String)msg.getAsString();
        output.write(result.getBytes());
        output.close();

        System.out.println("Processed a request");
      } catch(Exception exp) {
        if (!(exp instanceof FileNotFoundException))
          exp.printStackTrace();
      }
      // Sleep for a sec and then loop
      try {
        Thread.sleep( 1000 );
      } catch(Exception e) {
      }
    }
  }

  static public void main(String[] args) {
    (new FileListener()).run();
  }
}
```

Let's walk through this example. The `FileListener`'s `run()` method will loop forever while waiting for a new message to arrive. Once there, an `InputStream` is created for it. The listener will then ask Axis for an instance of an `AxisServer`—the `getSingleton()` method will return the same instance each time. Next we create a *MessageContext* 📖 object. This will be discussed more in the "Building Handlers" section, but for now it is simply an object that will contain all the data (request and response messages, meta-data, and so on) about this current SOAP message flow; it is passed to each handler as it is invoked. Inside this object we place a new `Message` object that is created by passing in the file's `InputStream`. This will be the request message. There's only one more thing to do before we invoke the engine, and that's to tell Axis the name of the transport that was used to retrieve the message—in this case, `file`. When the engine wants to invoke the transport-specific chain, it will look for one named `file` and, if found, invoke it.

The rest of the code processes any result from the engine. We must, of course, handle any error conditions. The Axis engine can throw an *AxisFault* 📖 (see the "Fault" section) that must be caught and used to create a response message. The `catch` block will also check to see if a response message already exists and clear any XML from the `Body` section if there is one.

In either the successful case or the faulting case, the code will then get the response message as a `String`, write it out to a file called `outMsg`, and then go look for more messages.

Completing the overall picture of what the Axis engine's architecture looks like, we have Figure 4.6.

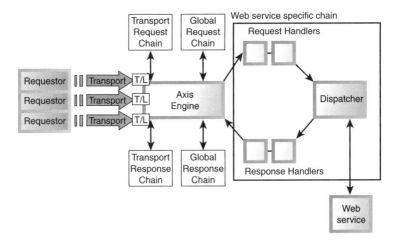

FIGURE 4.6

Complete Axis architecture.

Although the final picture of the Axis engine's processing model might seem a bit complex, it really is nothing more than defining handlers and chains. Of course, we've overlooked one very important issue; up to this point, the focus has been on what an Axis engine does when it is on the receiving side of the SOAP message path (the server). Axis can be used on the client side, as well. With just a few slight changes, all the concepts we've mentioned up to now apply on the client as shown in Figure 4.7.

It should be clear that almost all the same components that appeared on the server are on the client as well; they are just invoked in a slightly different order:

1. The request handlers of the Web service–specific request chain are invoked.

2. The `global.request` chain is invoked.

3. The transport chain is invoked. Notice that here the entire chain is invoked, not just the request side. There is no need to split the request and response invocations because they would be called one right after the other anyway. Also note that at the pivot point of the transport specific chain is a *transport sender* 📖; more on this later.

4. The `global.response` chain is invoked.

5. The response handlers of the Web service–specific response chain are invoked.

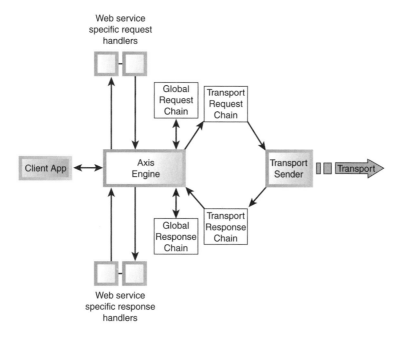

FIGURE 4.7

Axis client architecture.

As mentioned in Step 3, there is something new here: a *transport sender*. A transport sender is a handler that is responsible for taking the request SOAP message and sending it to a SOAP server. For example, one of the transport senders that is shipped with Axis is an HTTP transport sender that will take the request SOAP message, open an HTTP socket connection to the specified HTTP server, do a POST of the SOAP message, and wait for a response. The response is then placed in the response message portion of the `MessageContext` object.

Because transport senders are just handlers, they can be placed in any chain in any configuration. So, it is technically possible that the transport chain shown in Figure 4.7 could have multiple transport senders if you desire a multicast scenario. It is also possible that a transport sender could be placed in one of the chains on the server such that the response message could be sent over a different transport than it was received on (for example, the transport listener could be an HTTP servlet, but the SOAP response message could be sent back via SMTP).

Locating the Service Chain

We've talked about how there are service-specific chains, but we haven't yet touched on how the service chain is selected by the Axis engine. An interesting aspect of SOAP is that it doesn't mandate how to determine the exact Web service to invoke. This might seem odd—but it is accurate. Many different common practices have been established, and each one is valid. Here are just three of the more common ones:

- SOAPAction—The value of the SOAPAction HTTP header is used to match the service name.

- *URL*—The URL of the incoming HTTP request is used to match the service name. For example, if the URL used to access Axis was `http://localhost:8080/axis/servlet/AxisServlet/MyService`, then the SOAP engine would look for a service chain called `myService`.

- *Namespace*—Perhaps the most used method. It takes the namespace of the first XML element in the SOAP Body block and tries to find a service chain that matches.

Axis could have chosen one method, most likely the namespace approach, but doing so would have limited the options available to its users. Instead, Axis lets you choose how services are determined. A handler can be written and placed in the transport chain or global chain that can determine which service chain to choose. This handler is free to use any algorithm it wants to make this determination. However, if a service chain has not been selected by the time the Axis engine gets to the point in its processing that it wants to invoke the service specific chain, it will default to the namespace selection method.

XML Parsing

Axis has been designed and coded with a watchful eye towards performance. For this reason, when tackling the problem of how to parse an XML stream efficiently, a SAX-based approach was chosen over a DOM-based one. As we discussed in Chapter 2, "XML Primer," SAX XML parsing does not read the entire XML stream into memory; rather, it triggers callbacks based on the types of XML tokens that are encountered. It then becomes the responsibility of those callback routines to do any buffering of data or saving of state that is needed so that subsequent callbacks still have access to any previously seen data. Even though SAX is used for parsing, a DOM-based representation of XML sometimes is used when passing around XML blocks—as will be seen in the "Document-Centric Services" section. In various discussions and examples in this chapter, we'll need to talk about concepts and features in terms of using a SAX parser or writing SAX callback routines. We assume that you are familiar with these concepts, and we will not explain the specific details of how to write code utilizing a SAX parser in great detail.

With that overview of what Axis is and how it works, now we can move on to actually using it.

Installing Axis

Installing an Axis server is relatively simple. In the servlet engine's directory structure is a `webapps` directory. This directory contains the various Web applications that are deployed. The Axis distribution includes a `webapps` directory as well, and contains a directory named `axis`. Copy the `axis` directory into the servlet engine's `webapps` directory. In this new `axis` directory should be a WEB-INF/lib directory. There, you should place all the JAR files Axis will need to run. You should already see axis.jar. Currently, Axis will need one only additional JAR file: xerces.jar (available from the Apache Xerces distribution at http://xml.apache.org) or any other JAXP-compliant parser. Copy the parser's JAR file into the WEB-INF/lib directory.

When services are deployed, the Java class files should be placed in the axis/WEB-INF/classes directory; or if there are JAR files, they should be placed in the axis/WEB-INF/lib directory. If you plan to use the *JWS* 📖 feature of Axis (see the "Simple Web Services" section), you will also need to make sure that the Java tools.jar file is either in the axis/WEB-INF/lib directory or in your servlet engine's classpath.

Installing the client is simply a matter of making sure the axis.jar and xerces.jar files are in your classpath.

Configuring Axis

There are four different types of configuration files. Each will contain the same type of data, but the outermost XML element will vary:

- *client-config.xml* 📖—This is the configuration information for the Axis engine when it is invoked on the client. This file needs to be in the current working directory of the client application. This file has the format

```
<engineConfig>
  ...configuration XML...
</engineConfig>
```

- *server-config.xml* 📖—This is the configuration information for the Axis engine when it is invoked on the server. This file needs to be in the servlet engine's axis/WEB-INF directory in the HTTP case, or in the current working directory for other transports. This file has the format

```
<engineConfig>
  ...configuration XML...
</engineConfig>
```

- *deploy.xml* 📖—This is the file used by the *AdminClient* 📖 to deploy new handlers, chains, and services. The AdminClient is an administrative tool used for deploying and undeploying Axis resources (such as handlers and chains). The AdminClient uses a document-centric Web service—it takes the XML file passed to it and sends it to the Axis server for processing (more later). Unlike the first two configuration files, the name of this file can be anything. This file has the format

```
<m:deploy xmlns:m="AdminService">
  ...configuration XML...
</m:deploy>
```

- *undeploy.xml* 📖—This is the file used by the `AdminClient` to undeploy resources. The `AdminClient` will remove any named resources listed as immediate child elements of the `undeploy` XML element. Unlike the first two configuration files, the name of this file can be anything. This file has the format

```
<m:undeploy xmlns:m="AdminService">
   ...resources to be removed...
</m:undeploy>
```

In the first three cases, ...*configuration XML*... section will contain one of the following XML elements:

- handler

```
<handler name="handler_name" class="class_name">
  [<option name="option_name" value="option_value"/>]...
</handler>
```

```
Example:
<!-- Define an EMail handler -->
<handler name="EMail" class="com.skatestown.services.EMailHandler" />
```

Defines a single handler named *handler_name* whose class is given by *class_name*. The optional name/value pairs are defined by each specific handler and will be available to the handler at runtime.

- chain

```
<chain name="chain_name" {flow="list_of_handlers" |
      request="list_of_handlers" pivot="handler_name"
      response="list_of_handlers"}>
  [<option name="option_name" value="option_value"/>]...
</chain>
```

```
Example:
<!--Define a chain consisting of 2 handlers, a Java RPC Dispatcher
   and the Email handler from chapter 3 -->
<chain name="myChain" flow="RPCDispatcher, Email" />
```

Defines a chain called *chain_name* that consists of either the list of handlers specified in the `flow` attribute or the handlers specified by the `request`, `pivot` and `response` attributes combined. The optional name/value pairs will be available to the chain at runtime. There are two reserved chain names: `global.request` and `global.response`. These names should be used when defining the global chains.

- service

```
<service name="service_name" [request="list_of_handlers"]
      [pivot="handler_name"]
      [response="list_of_handlers"]>
```

```
[<option name="option_name" value="option_value"/>]...
</service>
```

Example:

```
<!-- Define a service chain with the "RPCDispatcher" at the pivot-point
     and Email handler to mail the response. The class and method name
     that the RPCDispatcher will use are passed in as options -->
<service name="InventoryCheck" pivot="RPCDispatcher" response="Email">
  <option name="className"
   value="com.skatestown.services.InventoryCheck"/>
  <option name="methodName" value="doCheck"/>
</service>
```

Defines a service chain consisting of the list of handlers specified in the request, pivot, and response attributes combined. The optional name/value pairs will be available to the service at runtime. The name specified here should match the namespace URI of the first body entry of the incoming SOAP request message.

- transport

```
<transport name="transport_name" [request="list_of_handlers"]
          [pivot="handler_name"]
          [response="list_of_handlers"]>
  [<option name="option_name" value="option_value"/>]...
</transport>
```

Example:

```
<!-- Define a transport specific chain that will invoke a "uudecode"
     handler on the request message and the "uuencode" handler on the
     response message - these will only be invoked for those messages
     that come in using the "file" transport -->
<transport name="file" request="uudecode" response="uuencode"/>
```

Defines a transport chain consisting of the list of handlers specified in the request, pivot, and response attributes combined. The optional name/value pairs will be available to the transport chain at runtime. The name specified on this definition must match the name of the transport specified by the transport listener on the setTransportName() method.

- beanMappings

```
<beanMappings>
  <x:name xmlns:x="namespace_uri" classname="class_name" />
</beanMappings>
```

4

Example:

```
<beanMappings>
  <x:po xmlns:x="http://www.skatestown.com/ns/po"
        classname="www.skatestown.com.data.PO" />
</beanMappings>
```

Defines the bean serializer/deserializer class (*class_name*) to be used for the bean named *name* in the namespace *namespace_uri*. This is a convenient way of using the default Java bean serializer and deserializer for your Java beans. We'll give more details about serializers and deserializers in the "Data Encoding/Decoding" section.

- typeMappings

```
<typeMappings>
  <x:name xmlns:x="namespace_uri" type="soap_type" serializer="class_name"
            deserializerFactory="class_name" />
</typeMappings>
```

```
Example:
<typeMappings>
  <x:PO xmlns:x="http://www.skatestown.com/ns/po" type="po"
        serializer="serializePO"
        deserializerFactory="deserializePOFactory" />
</typeMappings>
```

Defines a mapping between the type found in the SOAP message (*soap_type*) in the specified namespace *namespace_uri* with the specified serializer and deserializer. We'll give more details about serializers and deserializers in the "Data Encoding/Decoding" section.

The fourth configuration file, undeploy.xml, has a slightly different format. In this file, you just list the types of resources to be undeployed and their names. For example:

```
<m:undeploy xmlns:m="AdminService">
  <handler name="logger" />
  <service name="DoCheck" />
  <transport name="file" />
</m:undeploy>
```

In this example, three resources will be undeployed: a handler named logger, a service chain named DoCheck, and a transport chain named file.

Configuration Methods

You can configure the Axis server two ways: You can modify the server-config.xml file directly by adding or removing the XML configuration data, or you can use the AdminClient tool. This tool lets you remotely modify the server's configuration. By default, Axis will only allow the AdminClient to be run from the same machine as the server (for security reasons), but this is easily changed (see the "Security" section).

To run the AdminClient, you must first create an XML file with the list of changes to be made. Inside this XML file should be just the list of resources (handlers, chains, services, and so on) that should be deployed or undeployed. As previously shown, the XML's root element should be named deploy in the case where new resources are being added and undeploy when they are being removed. Once all the deployment information is placed in an XML file, you can invoke AdminClient:

```
> java org.apache.axis.client.AdminClient
   -l http://localhost:8080/axis/servlet/AxisServlet deploy.xml
```

Note that this assumes an HTTP transport and that the Axis servlet is available and waiting for requests on the specified URL (http://localhost:8080/axis/servlet/AxisServlet). This invocation will work for deploying new resources to an Axis engine running as a server. To add new resources to an Axis client engine, you'll need to modify the client-config.xml file used by the client Axis engine. This file will reside in the current working directory. Following is one of the sample XML files from Chapter 3 that is used as input to the AdminClient:

```
<m:deploy xmlns:m="AdminService">
  <handler name="URLMapper" class="org.apache.axis.handlers.http.URLMapper"/>
  <handler name="ActionHandler"
           class="org.apache.axis.handlers.http.HTTPActionHandler"/>

  <transport name="http" request="URLMapper"/>

  <!-- Chapter 3 example 3 services -->
  <handler name="EMail" class="com.skatestown.services.EMailHandler"/>
  <service name="InventoryCheck" pivot="RPCDispatcher" response="EMail">
    <option name="className" value="com.skatestown.services.InventoryCheck"/>
    <option name="methodName" value="doCheck"/>
  </service>

  <!-- Chapter 3 example 4 services -->
  <service name="POSubmission" pivot="MsgDispatcher">
    <option name="className" value="com.skatestown.services.POSubmission"/>
    <option name="methodName" value="doSubmission"/>
  </service>

</m:deploy>
```

Although it is possible to run the AdminClient tool to change the configuration information of the Axis client engine, it is easier to simply modify the client-config.xml file that resides in the current working directory.

4

CREATING WEB
SERVICES

Once a Web resource is deployed, either to the client or the server, it will be available until it is undeployed—even across servlet engine restarts.

At the time of publication, Axis' deployment XML files use a very simple XML definition format. Although this format works for now, it doesn't quite support the full features that Axis is planning to have. Eventually, Axis will switch to a new XML format called *Web Services Deployment Descriptor* (*WSDD*) 📖. Although WSDD is still under development, it should be more robust than the current XML deployment file. One other advantage is that WSDD will have a WSDL flavor that should allow for Web services that are defined in WSDL to be deployed by having the WSDD point to their WSDL file. But all of this is still being designed.

By default, Axis will have several handlers, chains, and services automatically deployed. If a `server-config.xml` file is not found in the *appRoot*/WEB-INF directory by the Axis server, Axis will default to have the following pre-deployed:

- *JWSProcessor service*—Looks for and processes JWS files (JWS was briefly discussed in Chapter 3, and will be discussed in more detail later in this chapter).
- *RPCProvider handler*—Locates and invokes a Java class method.
- *AdminService service*—Takes as input an XML document that will be interpreted as a deployment data XML file containing the list of new handlers, chains, and services to deploy (or undeploy).
- *HTTPSender handler*—Is used by an Axis client to send a SOAP request to a SOAP server. It can also be used on the server side when a message should be sent to another SOAP server using HTTP (for example, an intermediary).

If a `client-config.xml` file is not found, then Axis will default to having just one handler pre-deployed: the `HTTPSender`, for use in sending a SOAP request over HTTP.

Security

Currently, Axis includes only one minor security feature. By default, the AdminService will only allow deployment of new resources from the same machine running the Axis server. By using the `enableRemoteAdmin` option on the AdminService, resources can be deployed from any other machine as well. The `server-config.xml` file should be changed as follows:

```
<service name="AdminService" pivot="RPCDispatcher">
 <option name="className" value="org.apache.axis.util.Admin"/>
 <option name="methodName" value="AdminService"/>
 <option name="enableRemoteAdmin" value="true"/>
</service>
```

Note, however, that security can be added to Axis through the development of handlers that perform the desired security checks. This addition is being planned for development in time for Axis' first release.

Simple Web Services

By far the easiest and quickest way to deploy a Java Web service is through Axis' Java Web Service (JWS) facility. JWS lets you place a Java file in your Web application directory structure, and Axis will automatically find it, compile it, and deploy the methods automatically. Using the example from Chapter 3, we have the JWS (or Java) file shown in Listing 4.2.

LISTING 4.2   InventoryCheck.jws

```java
import org.apache.axis.MessageContext;
import bws.BookUtil;
import com.skatestown.data.Product;
import com.skatestown.backend.ProductDB;

/**
 * Inventory check Web service
 */
public class InventoryCheck
{
    /**
     * Checks inventory availability given a product SKU and
     * a desired product quantity.
     *
     * @param msgContext    This is the Axis message processing context
     *                      BookUtil needs this to extract deployment
     *                      information to load the product database.
     * @param sku           product SKU
     * @param quantity      quantity desired
     * @return              true|false based on product availability
     * @exception Exception most likely a problem accessing the DB
     */
    public static boolean doCheck(MessageContext msgContext,
                                  String sku, int quantity)
    throws Exception
    {
        ProductDB db = BookUtil.getProductDB(msgContext);
        Product prod = db.getBySKU(sku);
        return (prod != null && prod.getNumInStock() >= quantity);
    }
}
```

All you need to do is place this file in the Axis webapps directory structure with a `.jws` extension instead of `.java`. So, to access this example on the CD, because it is in the `ch3/ex2` directory, the URL for this Web service would be `http://localhost:8080/bws/ch3/ex2/InventoryCheck.jws`. It's as easy as that.

One important thing to remember is that all public methods will be available as Web services. So, use JWS files with care.

Client-Side Programming

Accessing a Web service from the client can be (almost) as easy. In the simplest case of wanting to access an RPC SOAP service, let's take a closer look at the example from Chapter 3, shown in Listing 4.3.

LISTING 4.3   InventoryCheckClient.java

```java
package ch3.ex2;

import org.apache.axis.client.ServiceClient;

/*
 * Inventory check web service client
 */
public class InventoryCheckClient {
    /**
     * Service URL
     */
    String url;

    /**
     * Point a client at a given service URL
     */
    public InventoryCheckClient(String url) {
        this.url = url;
    }

    /**
     * Invoke the inventory check web service
     */
    public boolean doCheck(String sku, int quantity) throws Exception {
        ServiceClient call = new ServiceClient(url);
        Object[] params = new Object[]{ sku, new Integer(quantity), };
        Boolean result = (Boolean)call.invoke("", "doCheck", params);
        return result.booleanValue();
    }

}
```

As shown here, a *ServiceClient* 📖 object is needed. This object is used as the portal through which the client application connects with the Web service. The constructor takes the URL of the target SOAP server. Once the ServiceClient object knows where to find the service, all that is left is to invoke the Web service itself. Notice that the client.invoke() method call takes three parameters: the value of the HTTP SOAPAction header, which in this call is just an empty string; the name of the Web service's method to invoke (doCheck); and an array containing the Java objects representing the parameters for the method. The return value of the invoke() method is a Java object of type Object, so it will need to be cast to the proper return type before it is used.

Sometimes each parameter passed to the method needs to have a specific name associated with it. For example, some SOAP servers will use the parameter names in the method-matching algorithm. In these cases, a slight change to the way invoke() is called is required:

```
Boolean result = (Boolean) call.invoke(
            " ",
            "doCheck",
            new Object[] { new RPCParam("skuName", sku),
                        new RPCParam("quantity", new Integer(quantity))});
```

Notice that now instead of passing in an array of Java objects, an array of RPCParams is passed in, where each RPCParam consists of the name of the parameter (skuName and quantity in this example) and the value of the parameter (sku and quantity).

When talking with an Axis server or any other SOAP server that does explicit typing of the XML stream (this means the datatype of the parameters and return value of the RPC call is placed in the SOAP message), the Axis client can use that typing information to know how to deserialize the return value. However, some SOAP servers do not do this; in this instance, they are expecting the client to know the datatype through some other means (perhaps WSDL). When this occurs, it becomes the responsibility of the client application to tell the Axis client what type the return value is—which just requires a couple lines of code. The complete client application looks like Listing 4.4

4

CREATING WEB
SERVICES

LISTING 4.4   InventoryCheckClient.java

```
package ch3.ex2;

import org.apache.axis.client.ServiceClient;

/*
 * Inventory check web service client
 */
```

LISTING 4.4   Continued

```
public class InventoryCheckClient
{
    /**
     * Service URL
     */
    private String url;

    /**
     * Point a client at a given service URL
     */
    public InventoryCheckClient(String targetUrl)
    {
        url = targetUrl;
    }

    /**
     * Invoke the inventory check web service
     */
    public boolean doCheck(String sku, int quantity) throws Exception
    {
        ServiceClient call = new ServiceClient(url);
        ServiceDecription sd = new ServiceDescription("return", true);
        sd.setOutputType(new QName(Constants.URI_2001_SCHEMA_XSD, "boolean"));
        call.setServiceDescription(sd);
        Boolean result = (Boolean) call.invoke(
            "",
            "doCheck",
            new Object[] { sku, new Integer(quantity) } );
        return result.booleanValue();
    }
}
```

In this example we've added the definition of a `ServiceDescription` object. This object is used by the client to notify the Axis client of various pieces of metadata about the Web service being invoked. In this instance we're defining the `OutputType` (return type) of the method as a `boolean` using the 2001 W3C XML Schema definition. The `ServiceDescription` constructor takes two parameters: a name assigned to this object (return parameter names aren't used very much as they are basically ignored) and an indication of whether this service is an RPC service (true indicates that it is). The only other code change associates this `ServiceDescription` object with the `ServiceClient`, and this is done through the `setServiceDescription()` method call.

Advanced Web Service Deployment

Although JWS files are convenient, sometimes you'll need more complex Web service configurations. For example, some pre- or post-processing might be needed for a particular Web service, or perhaps the Web service isn't a Java program and a special dispatcher is needed (more on these later). In these cases, you can't use JWS files, and you need a more robust deployment mechanism. This is when you'll use the `server-config.xml` file and the `AdminClient` (mentioned previously).

For example, let's say we want to deploy the same `InventoryCheck` service in the JWS scenario, but this time we also want to have a handler email a copy of each response message. To do this, we must first create a deployment XML file for the `AdminClient`:

```
<m:deploy xmlns:m="AdminService">
  <handler name="email" class="com.skatestown.services.EMailHandler" />
  <service name="InvetoryCheck" pivot="RPCDispatcher" response="email">
    <option name="className" value="com.skatestown.services.InventoryCheck" />
    <option name="methodName" value="doCheck" />
  </service>
</m:deploy>
```

Notice that we added a handler called `email`, whose class name is `com.skatestown.services.EMailHandler`. In addition, a new service chain is defined that invokes the `RPCDispatcher` and this new email handler. The `RPCDispatcher` is the handler that will locate and invoke the Java method for the Web service. Notice that in the definition of the service, we provide some options—`className` and `methodName`. These options will be used in the `RPCDispatchhandler`—it will create a new instance of `com.skatestown.service.InventoryCheck` class and then invoke the `doCheck` method (of course passing in the parameters from the SOAP request message). To deploy these new resources, the `AdminClient` is used:

```
> java org.apache.axis.client.AdminClient deploy.xml
```

Once deployed, we need to copy the `InventoryCheck.class` file into the `axis/WEB-INF/classes` directory. We should then be set to run the client.

Document-Centric Services

Up to this point, our focus has been on the simple RPC case where the Web service being invoked is a Java method. This is just one way to use SOAP and Axis. As discussed in previous chapters, there is also document-centric SOAP processing. In this scenario, rather than the SOAP processor converting the XML into Java objects and then calling a method, the XML is left untouched and is simply handed to a method for processing. This method is then free to do whatever it wants with the XML. Supporting this approach in Axis is a simple matter of changing the dispatcher that is used. In the RPC case, an RPCDispatcher handler was used; now a MsgDispatcher handler must be used. This handler will locate the appropriate method (as specified by the deployment information) and then call it, passing in the request XML SOAP message as a parameter. The deployment of a document-centric service will look like this:

```
<service name="POSubmission" pivot="MsgDispatcher">
 <option name="className" value="POSubmission"/>
 <option name="methodName" value="doSubmission"/>
</service>
```

This code shows the deployment information for a service chain called POSubmission. Notice that it uses MsgDispatcher at the pivot point, and as options it passes in the className and the actual method that should be located and invoked. Unlike the RPC case, where the parameters to the method can be determined by the needs of the service, MsgDispatcher assumes that all document-centric methods have the same method signature, as follows:

```
public Document doSubmission(MessageContext msgContext, Document xml)
    throws AxisFault;
```

Notice that the service takes two parameters, a MessageContext and a Document (more on MessageContext later in the "Building Handlers" section; for now, just know that it is Axis-specific data that is made available to the service if it needs it). The service also returns a Document object, which is used as the body of the response SOAP message. Notice that the input and output messages are W3C Document objects, and not SAX events—this is done as a matter of convenience for the handler writer. However, by the time Axis is released, the handler might have the option of processing the SAX events directly. If an error occurs during processing, the service should throw an AxisFault (see the "Faults" section). Listing 4.5 shows a sample service (from Chapter 3).

LISTING 4.5   POSubmission.java

```
package com.skatestown.services;

import org.w3c.dom.Document;
import org.apache.axis.MessageContext;
import javax.xml.parsers.DocumentBuilder;
import javax.xml.parsers.DocumentBuilderFactory;
import com.skatestown.data.PO;
import com.skatestown.data.Invoice;
import com.skatestown.backend.ProductDB;
import com.skatestown.backend.POProcessor;
import com.skatestown.xml.Serializer;
import com.skatestown.xml.Deserializer;
import bws.BookUtil;
```

LISTING 4.5 Continued

```
/**
 * Purchase order submission service
 */
public class POSubmission {
    /**
     * Submit a purchase order and generate an invoice
     */
    public Document doSubmission(MessageContext msgContext, Document inDoc)
        throws Exception
    {
        // Create a PO from the XML document
        DocumentBuilderFactory factory = DocumentBuilderFactory.newInstance();
        DocumentBuilder builder = factory.newDocumentBuilder();
        PO po = Deserializer.createPO(inDoc.getDocumentElement());

        // Get the product database
        ProductDB db = BookUtil.getProductDB(msgContext);

        // Create an invoice from the PO
        POProcessor processor = new POProcessor(db);
        Invoice invoice = processor.processPO(po);

        // Serialize the invoice to XML
        Document newDoc = Serializer.writeInvoice(builder, invoice);

        return newDoc;
    }

}
```

To deploy it, we use the `AdminClient`:

```
java org.apache.axis.client.AdminClient po_deploy.xml
```

The `po_deploy.xml` file looks like this:

```
<m:deploy xmlns:m="AdminService">
  <service name="http://www.skatestown.com/ns/po" pivot="MsgDispatcher">
   <option name="className" value="com.skatestown.services.POSubmission"/>
   <option name="methodName" value="doSubmission"/>
  </service>
</m:deploy>
```

Although invoking an RPC Web service is relative easy, invoking a document-centric Web service requires a little more work, but not much. A corresponding client would look like Listing 4.6.

4

LISTING 4.6   POSubmissionClient.java

```java
package ch3.ex4;

import java.io.InputStream;
import java.io.StringWriter;
import org.apache.axis.encoding.SerializationContext;
import org.apache.axis.message.SOAPEnvelope;
import org.apache.axis.message.SOAPBodyElement;
import org.apache.axis.client.ServiceClient;
import org.apache.axis.Message;
import org.apache.axis.MessageContext;

/**
 * Purchase order submission client
 */
public class POSubmissionClient {
    /**
     * Target service URL
     */
    String url;

    /**
     * Create a client with a target URL
     */
    public POSubmissionClient(String url) {
        this.url = url;
    }

    /**
     * Invoke the PO submission web service
     *
     * @param po Purchase order document
     * @return Invoice document
     * @exception Exception I/O error or Axis error
     */
    public String invoke(InputStream po) throws Exception {
        // Send the message
        ServiceClient client = new ServiceClient(url);
        client.setRequestMessage(new Message(po, true));
        client.getMessageContext().
                setTargetService("http://www.skatestown.com/ns/po");
        client.invoke();

        // Retrieve the response body
        MessageContext ctx = client.getMessageContext();
```

LISTING 4.6   Continued

```
        Message outMsg = ctx.getResponseMessage();
        SOAPEnvelope envelope = outMsg.getAsSOAPEnvelope();
        SOAPBodyElement body = envelope.getFirstBody();

        // Get the XML from the body
        StringWriter w = new StringWriter();
        SerializationContext sc = new SerializationContext(w, ctx);
        body.output(sc);
        return w.toString();
    }
}
```

The example starts by creating a `ServiceClient` object and gives it the location of the SOAP server. Next, it creates an Axis `Message` object. This object will contain the actual XML of the SOAP message. As input to the constructor, it takes an input stream (the XML for the body of the SOAP envelope) and a `boolean` indicating whether this XML input stream is the entire SOAP envelope or just the body—`true` indicates that it is just the body. The `ServiceClient` object is then told of the request message through the `setRequestMessage()` method call, and then the Web service itself is invoked. Once the service is invoked, the response message is obtained. This allows for the client to access any part of the response and not just the body. However, in this case, we ask for the first body element to convert it to a `String` and return it.

Data Encoding/Decoding

Switching back to RPC, so far we've deferred the entire notion of how the data is converted between Java objects and the XML. This section will go into the steps involved in creating customized serializers and deserializers that can be used in Axis. Although the concept of what serializers and deserializers do is not terribly complex, writing one for Axis requires a good working knowledge of how to use a SAX parser. Chapter 2 had a good, but brief, discussion of how SAX parsers work and how to use them—this section will assume that you are well versed enough with SAX that usage of SAX terms, without the details behind them, will be appropriate.

As we discussed in Chapter 2, the concepts of serializers and deserializers are really quite simple—they are just pieces of code that will convert data (in its native state, such as a Java object) into XML in the serializing case, and from XML back into the data's native state in the deserializing case. If your classes are Java beans, then you can use the Bean serializer and deserializer that comes with Axis. To do this, all you have to do is tell Axis to use the Bean serializer/deserializer when it encounters your class. For example, on the client side the code might look like the following:

```
// register the PurchaseOrder class
String  URL = "http://localhost:8080/axis/servlet/AxisServlet";
ServiceClient client = new ServiceClient(URL);
QName qn = new QName("http://www.skatestown.com/ns/po", "po");
Class cls = com.skatestown.data.PO.class;
client.addSerializer(cls, qn, new BeanSerializer(cls));
client.addDeserializerFactory(qn, cls, BeanSerializer.getFactory());
```

In this code, the addSerializer() method will create a serializer association between the class PO and its namespace, http://www.skatestown.com/ns/po, and the BeanSerializer. Then we do the same thing for the deserializing side.

While on the server, a beanMapping would need to be deployed (for example, in the XML file passed to the AdminClient):

```
<beanMappings xmlns:bid=" http://www.skatestown.com/ns/po">
  <bid:po classname="com.skatestown.data.PO"/>
</beanMappings>
```

However, sometimes the BeanSerializer isn't enough, and you'll need an even more customized serializer/deserializer and specialized code that manually examines or creates the XML. In this case, it is just a matter of writing a few Java classes.

You need a serializing class that should implement the Serializer interface. This interface has just one method:

```
public interface Serializer extends java.io.Serializable {
    public void serialize(QName name, Attributes attributes,
                          Object value, SerializationContext context)
        throws IOException;
}
```

This method should, construct a block of XML with a root element with the given name and attributes, and the body should be the serialized version of value. This method assumes that SAX events will be generated against the SerializationContext passed to it. The SerializationContext object is a utility class that provides functions necessary for writing XML to a Writer, including maintaining namespace mappings, serialization of data objects, and automatic handling of multi-ref encoding of object graphs.

Next, you need a class that implements the DeserializationFactory interface. This interface has just one method, as well:

```
public interface DeserializerFactory extends java.io.Serializable
{
    public Deserializer getDeserializer(Class cls);
}
```

This method should return an instance of the `Deserializer` class. Whether it returns the same instance or a new instance each time is an implementation choice—you use a factory because the deserializers are processing SAX events, so they will need to maintain some state information between each SAX event callback. If a single deserializer existed and multiple threads were deserializing objects at the same time, they would override each other's work.

The final class you need to write is the `deserializer` class (the class the `deserializer` factory returns). This class should extend the `Deserializer` class. Inside this class should be any of the SAX callback methods needed to deserialize the incoming SAX event stream. The exact implementation of these methods is left completely up to you. The only requirement is that when it is done, the methods set a field in the base `Deserializer` class called `value` to the Java object represented by the XML. As a quick example, Axis comes with a Base64 serializer and deserializer. The deserializer is very small, and simply implements the SAX `characters()` method:

```
static class Base64Deser extends Deserializer {
    public void characters(char[] chars, int start, int end) throws
                        SAXException {
        setValue(Base64.decode(chars, start, end));
    }
}
```

The `Base64.decode`, method does the actual decoding and just returns a Java object.

Building Handlers

Handlers are the key building blocks of Axis. As previously described, configuring Axis simply requires defining the types of handlers deployed and the order in which handlers are placed in the chains. A handler is nothing more than a piece of code that examines some (or all) of a SOAP message and then acts on it. Axis makes no assumptions about what each handler does; each one is free to do as little or as much work as needed. The specific details of how to write a handler are outside the scope of this book; however, we'll give a brief overview here. If you want to write a handler, you should consult the Axis documentation.

As each handler is invoked, it is passed a `MessageContext` object that contains all the information about the current state of the processing of the SOAP message. In particular, some of the key pieces of data in the `MessageContext` are as follows:

- `requestMessage`—The SOAP message that is the incoming or requesting message. Typically this is the message that handlers *before* the pivot point use as input.

- `responseMessage`—The SOAP message that is the outgoing or response message. Typically this is the message into which handlers *after* the pivot point will place their response message (if any).

- `targetService`—The name of the service-specific chain that will be invoked by the Axis engine. If a handler's job is to determine which Web service is being called, it needs to set this field by calling the `setTargetService()` method, passing it the name of the service-specific chain.
- `bag`—A Hashtable that can be used to store any metadata about the processing of the current message. Handlers can use this Hashtable to share information. For example, one handler can place in it information that another handler, later in the chain, can then retrieve and use in its own processing. This process requires some out-of-band knowledge between handlers so they know what key to use to store and retrieve the data.

The logic inside a handler is relatively straightforward. Each handler, whether it is on the request chain, on the response chain, or the pivot point handler, can access any of the data in the `MessageContext`. As a result, both the request and any possible response message that might exist are available and can be modified. Sometimes a handler can be placed on the request or the response side of a chain—in this case, requesting the request or response message explicitly could result in the wrong message being returned. For this reason, a `getCurrentMessage()` method on the `MessageContext` object will return either the request or response message, depending on whether the handler appears before or after the pivot point.

Once a message has been obtained, the handler is free to examine or process any part of the message. The handler can ask for the entire message, the body of the message, or any specific header. Because the SOAP specification has very specific rules for the processing of `mustUnderstand` headers, it is important than any handler that does process a header set the `processed` flag on that header by calling `setProcessed(true)` on that `SOAPHeader` object. Axis will use this information to determine whether to throw a `mustUnderstand` fault if all the `mustUnderstand` headers have not been processed.

Specialized Pivot Point Handlers, a.k.a. Providers

New technology like Web services can be viewed as simply a new means of accessing existing IT assets. When you're looking at the wide variety of ways in which data can be accessed (servlets, Web services, Java RMI, and so on), you can see that each of them uses a different mechanism for transferring the data from one source to another; however, the business logic that is executed should not change based on the means of data transport. In keeping with this separation of roles, Axis' handlers will typically be written in such a way that they are simply the bridge between Axis and your existing business logic. Of course, it is possible to write handlers such that all of the code is contained within the handler itself, but when the next big thing comes along, chances are it would require more work than if a clean delineation had been kept between the means of transporting the data and the business logic. This concept is very similar to how many people write their servlets or JSPs; the HTML presentation logic is in the JSP, whereas the real work is done through accessing beans or some external Java code.

In keeping with this separation, the pivot point handlers should be written such that their job is to interpret the incoming SOAP message, locate the business resources needed to perform the desired task, execute the task, and then place any response data into the response SOAP message. Although we discuss this subject in terms of a pivot point handler, this same design pattern can (and should) be used for any of the handlers written no matter where in the chains they appear.

There is no limit to the types of resources that handlers can access. By the time Axis ships its first release, it should contain handlers that will enable access to resources such as:

- Enterprise Java Beans
- Scripting languages through the Bean Scripting Framework
- COM objects
- J2EE connectors
- Code fragments in non-Java languages

However, currently, Axis is only at an alpha state, and only two types of handlers come with it: a Java RPC handler and a Java Message handler. The Java RPC handler will examine the body of the request message and convert it into a procedure call. In other words, it will deserialize the XML elements in the body into individual Java objects (the method parameters) and, based on the method name (also in the body element), call that specified method with those Java objects as parameters. If there is a return value from the procedure call, it will be serialized and placed into the body of the response SOAP message. (It might be useful to examine the code for this handler—you can find it in the Axis source in a file called `org/apache/axis/providers/java/RPCProvider.java`.)

The other handler that comes with Axis is the Java Message handler. This handler is similar to the Java RPC handler in that it will examine the body of the request SOAP message to determine which Java method to call. However, unlike the RPC handler, which will deserialize the XML into Java objects, the Message handler will take the XML as is and simply pass it along to the desired method untouched. This approach is useful in a document-centric processing model—one in which the business logic wishes to receive the data in raw XML rather than to have Axis try to do any conversions.

As long as it is possible to write Java code to access the desired resource, there is no reason why a handler cannot be written to access it—thus making Axis an incredibly flexible and powerful SOAP processor. Of course, sometimes a handler's role is to perform a task that is SOAP specific, and in that case placing the logic inside the handler itself might make sense. For example, a handler that determines which Web service to invoke would probably not need to access any back-end systems, but instead would use just the data in the SOAP message.

4

Ultimately, the choice of how to design and write a handler is not mandated by Axis, but rather is left up to the handler writer. Axis does not place any restrictions on your design choices in hopes that the system remains flexible and pluggable enough that it can be used in a limitless number of configurations.

Faults

Currently, Axis has a very simple mechanism for dealing with error conditions. The code (whether it is the Web service or some pluggable component such as a handler) can throw an exception, which will then be caught by the Axis engine and propagated back to the transport listener. The transport listener will then typically return it to the client (in the HTTP case)—but that is an implementation choice. If the exception that is thrown is a Java exception, it will be converted into a specialized Axis class, `AxisFault`. This class is defined to contain all the information that would go into a SOAP fault response message. The `faultcode` is set to `Server.generalException`, and the `detail` part of the fault will contain the stack trace.

If you require more specialized detail, the code that throws the exception can throw an `AxisFault` directly. The `AxisFault` class has two constructors:

```
public AxisFault(String code, String str, String actor, Element[] details);
public AxisFault(QFault code, String str, String actor, Element[] details);
```

Like the SOAP fault definition, `AxisFaults` contain `faultcode`, `faultstring`, `faultactor`, and `faultdetails` fields. The `QFault` class is a utility class that contains the fully qualified name of the fault code (namespace and local name). The `faultdetails` field is an array of DOM elements so that the specific XML that is contained in the fault can be tailored to any specific needs.

When Axis is completed, it is expected to include a more robust system for handling faults. In particular, some of the ideas being discussed include:

- The ability to define a mapping between Java exceptions and `AxisFaults`
- The ability to define fault chains where specific chains will be invoked based on the type of `AxisFault` thrown
- The ability for handlers to have an undo mechanism so that some type of rollback can be performed in the event of an error

These ideas are not guaranteed to be implemented in the first release of Axis; they are just the current list of ideas being considered.

Message Patterns

It should be obvious that Axis is nicely designed to handle a request/response message processing pattern. However, it is not limited to this single message-flow pattern. As we stated earlier, each handler and service has available to it a `MessageContext` object that will contain both the request and response message; however, you don't have to use both of these messages. It is possible to configure chains of handlers that process the request message but produce no response message. In the HTTP transport environment, doing so might seem strange; but in a non-request/response transport (such as SMTP), this is a much more likely scenario. In this one-way message pattern, the Axis engine can be configured to use only handlers that examine the request message and do not use the response message at all. Note that if a handler is invoked that does generate a response SOAP message, but the transport listener chooses not to do anything with the response SOAP message inside the `MessageContext` object, then the response will be ignored. Axis assumes that the transport listener knows how to deal with the response message, and if it ignores any response, then that must be the correct behavior.

At the time of this writing, Axis does not yet support the notion of asynchronous message processing, but it should by the time of its first release. In this model, Axis will allow the client to asynchronously invoke a Web service and at some later point in time request the response, thus allowing the client to perform other actions while the Web service is doing its job.

Building and Deploying an Intermediary

Although Axis can support the notion of a SOAP intermediary, Axis itself needs to do very little to support it. An *intermediary* is a SOAP processing node that does some work based on the requesting SOAP message, but is not the final destination of the message; so, it is responsible for forwarding the message to the next SOAP processing node in the message path. From an Axis configuration point of view, this is a simple matter of defining a chain that has as its pivot point a Transport Sender handler. This handler will determine the next SOAP processing node in the message path and send the SOAP message to it. In this way, the handler is acting like a SOAP client, so the same client APIs normally used in writing an Axis client application can (and should) be used in this handler in conjunction with any server-side APIs needed to process or interpret the incoming SOAP message.

The SOAP specification requires that two things must take place in a SOAP intermediary: All message headers targeted for this intermediary (for example, the actor attribute on the header pointing to a certain URI) are removed before the message is sent to the next SOAP processing node, and if any of those message headers are marked with the `mustUnderstand=1` attribute, they must be understood by this SOAP node or a fault must be thrown. In order to locate all the SOAP headers targeted for this actor, a handler can use the following method on the `SOAPEnvelope` object:

```
public Enumeration getHeadersByName(String namespace, String localPart);
```

This method will return an enumeration of SOAPHeader objects. Once each header is processed, it is very important that the handler notify the Axis engine that this header has been processed by calling the setProcessed() method:

```
Enumeration enum = soapEnv.getHeadersByName(http://www.skatestown.com/, "foo");
while (enum.hasMoreElements()) {
  SOAPHeader header = (SOAPHeader) enum.nextElement();
  // process header here
  header.setProcessed(true);
}
```

Setting the Processed flag on this header indicates to Axis that the header has been successfully processed. The Axis engine will then use this information to determine if any headers in the message marked with a mustUnderstand=1 attribute are unprocessed, and if so throw a mustUnderstand fault.

Currently, in the alpha release of Axis, intermediary support is not complete. In particular, support is not yet included for indicating which headers should be removed before the message should be sent to the next SOAP processing node.

SOAP V1.2

Axis is written to support the SOAP 1.1 specification. In the alpha release, it supports/implements almost all of the specification, and by the time the first release is done, the entire specification will be supported. The W3C XML Protocol working group is currently working on the next version of the SOAP specification (v1.2), and members of the Axis development team are constantly watching the group's activity to ensure that they will fully support that version of the specification.

As of now, the changes proposed to the SOAP specification are not so sweeping that they will dramatically change the definition of SOAP. The group's main focus is fixing any ambiguities or bugs in the v1.1 specification. However, a few changes will make a SOAP v1.2 message incompatible with a SOAP 1.1 message, so those interested in watching (or being involved in) the working group's activities should join its mailing list. The group's Web site is at http://www.w3.org/2000/xp/Group/.

Monitoring

Axis comes with a tool that can be useful in monitoring the TCP/IP traffic between your SOAP client and SOAP server. The tool is called *tcpmon* and can be executed by running

```
java org.apache.axis.utils.tcpmon
```

or

```
java org.apache.axis.utils.tcpmon 81 localhost 8080
```

The first command will bring up the tool and take you to an Admin page that allows you to enter a port number on which `tcpmon` will listen, a target host, and a target port number to which the incoming request should be routed. By simply routing your SOAP client's requests through `tcpmon`, you will be able to see the request and response SOAP messages. The second command will let you start `tcpmon` by specifying the listening port number (81 in the previous example), the target host name, and the port number (localhost and 8080 in this case) on the command line—thus bypassing the Admin page. Figure 4.8 shows what `tcpmon` looks like.

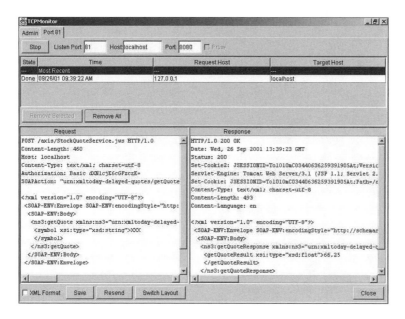

FIGURE 4.8
TCPMonitor can be used to examine the request and response messages.

You'll notice that each request/response pair is given its own entry table at the top of the window, allowing you to select which specific flow to examine. Below the table is the request and response data. You can save the data to a file, ask `tcpmon` to try to make the XML look nice (add linefeeds and spaces), switch between a side-by-side layout and a top-bottom layout, or even ask it to resend the request data. When resending the data, you are free to modify the data in the request side of the window before resending; thus, you can make a change to test a server with new XML without having to change any client code.

Summary

Because Axis is still under development and only at an alpha stage, you should consult the Axis Web site and documentation for the latest features and APIs. We hope this chapter has provided you with a basic understanding of what Axis is, how it works, and how you can use it for new Web services as well as leverage it to access existing IT assets and resources with minimal work. In Chapter 5, we'll focus on how to use SOAP (and in particular Axis) in some scenarios that go beyond simply invoking a Web service; these scenarios are more like the real world and deal with the issues that companies face every day.

Using SOAP for e-Business

IN THIS CHAPTER

In Chapter 3, "Simple Object Access Protocol (SOAP)," you saw how SOAP enables applications to interact with each other, and in Chapter 4, "Creating Web Services," you saw that Axis is an example SOAP infrastructure. With SOAP, applications can be coupled loosely—more importantly, in a decentralized manner. On the basis of such an advantage, in this chapter we review a collection of topics that are required for starting a *serious* e-Business with Web services.

First, we consider security, assuming that business-to-business (B2B) collaboration is performed in terms of SOAP messaging. We will begin by discussing familiar technologies such as *HTTP Basic Authentication (BASIC-AUTH)* and *Secure Socket Layer (SSL)* , then move to SOAP-specific security, such as *SOAP Digital Signature* and encryption. We'll also discuss *Public Key Infrastructure(PKI)* as a basis for many security technologies.

Then, we shift our focus to intranet applications that are configured to process incoming SOAP messages, which might potentially produce response messages. This approach is called *Enterprise Application Integration* (EAI) because typical enterprises have a portfolio of existing applications that should be integrated properly to achieve additional business goals. We will take *Enterprise JavaBeans* (EJBs) , *Java Message Service* (JMS) and *Java 2 Platform Enterprise Edition* (J2EE) as a basis for integrating applications.

Finally, we discuss technologies required for high-volume SOAP servers in terms of *Quality of Service (QoS)* . Performance, scalability, and availability are important issues whenever you're developing real applications. We will consider how existing technologies in that area are adopted for developing scalable SOAP servers.

Web Services Security

e-Business relies on information exchange between trading partners over networks, often the Internet. Therefore, there are always security risks, because messages could be stolen, lost, or modified. Four security requirements must be addressed to ensure the safety of information exchange among trading partners:

- *Confidentiality* guarantees that exchanged information is protected against eavesdroppers.
- *Authentication* guarantees that access to e-Business applications and data is restricted to only those who can provide the appropriate proof of identity.
- *Integrity* refers to assurance that the message was not modified accidentally or deliberately in transit.
- *Non-repudiation* guarantees that the sender of the message cannot deny that he/she sent it.

Note that these requirements are related to cryptography because they concern how to protect communicated data. Apart from cryptography, we must also consider protection of resources such as data and applications in such a way that only appropriate entities are allowed to access the particular resources. A fifth requirement is summarized as follows:

- *Authorization* is a process to decide whether the identity can access the particular resource.

In this section, we review a collection of security technologies that specifically address information exchange among trading partners via SOAP messaging. Figure 5.1 depicts a security architecture that you should keep in mind throughout this section.

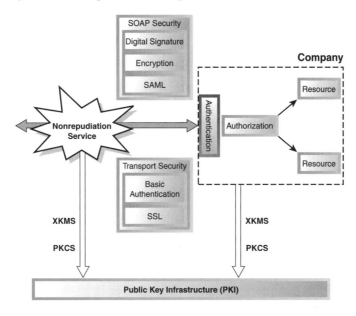

FIGURE 5.1
Security architecture for SOAP messaging.

We begin by reviewing well-known security technologies: BASIC-AUTH and SSL. They are considered to be transport security, as shown in the figure.

Transport security is useful to some extent, but it fails to ensure non-repudiation and is not enough when you have to include third-party intermediaries. SOAP security provides transport-agnostic security measures. We will discuss digital signatures and encryption for SOAP messages.

We will introduce a non-repudiation service that ensures the delivery of the message with a timestamp. This notary third party is a good practical example of a *SOAP intermediary* 📖.

Focusing on the internal process within our example company, we will describe authorization to protect resources by giving appropriate permissions to the accessing entity. We will mainly discuss *role-based access control* 📖 and briefly show how it can be implemented.

Finally, we will discuss Public Key Infrastructure (PKI), which provides a foundation to a solution for the four risks: confidentiality, authentication, integrity, and non-repudiation. Although PKI is a solid technology basis, it is fairly difficult to implement and use through Public Key Cryptography Standards (PKCS). We will see an emerging standard, called *XML Key Management Services* (XKMS) 📖, which enables key management via XML. Let's begin by establishing the example scenario we'll use in our code samples throughout the chapter.

Example Scenario

In our discussion of security, we'll continue our SkatesTown example. SkatesTown's CTO, Dean Caroll, is beginning to become concerned with security now that the business is expanding. SkatesTown is doing business with a large number of companies, and most of them are not Fortune-500 companies. Currently, SkatesTown's Web services are secured only with SSL and BASIC-AUTH. Although Dean notices that the combination of the two is not enough, he cannot think of a better mechanism in terms of security.

To ease Dean's concern, Al Rosen of Silver Bullet Consulting was asked to advise Dean about what kind of security features to address in the next development phase. This was not an easy task for Al either, because there are numerous security technologies and specifications. It is not possible and not meaningful to cover all of them. Therefore, he selected a fairly small number of security features and applied them to SkatesTown's SOAP-based transactions, as we'll present throughout this chapter.

SSL and HTTP Basic Authentication

The most popular security method on the Internet is a combination of BASIC-AUTH and SSL. This method is widely adopted in many B2C shopping sites such as Amazon.com (http://www.amazon.com) because its configuration is fairly simple, but it still provides a necessary security level for a small amount of transactions. Here, we review BASIC-AUTH and SSL with examples of how to use them with Axis.

HTTP Basic Authentication

You probably have experienced being required to enter a user ID and password while visiting a Web site. BASIC-AUTH is often called password authentication; its specification is defined in RFC 2617 (BASIC-AUTH). The typical BASIC-AUTH interaction between a Web browser and a Web server is illustrated in Figure 5.2.

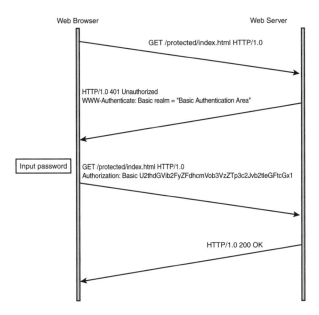

Web Browser   Web Server

GET /protected/index.html HTTP/1.0

HTTP/1.0 401 Unauthorized
WWW-Authenticate: Basic realm = "Basic Authentication Area"

Input password

GET /protected/index.html HTTP/1.0
Authorization: Basic U2thdGVib2FyZFdhcmVVob3VzTp3c2Jvb2tleGFtcGx1

HTTP/1.0 200 OK

FIGURE 5.2

Interaction protocol for basic authentication.

When the Web browser sends an HTTP request to access a protected Web resource, the Web server returns an HTTP response, which includes the error code "401 Unauthorized" and the following HTTP header:

`WWW-Authenticate: Basic realm="Realm Name"`

Realm 📖 is a name given to a set of Web resources, and it is a unit to be protected. *Basic* in front of *realm* indicates a type of authentication—in this case, BASIC-AUTH. Based on this information, the Web browser shows a login dialog to the user. Then, the Web browser sends an HTTP request again including the following HTTP header:

`Authorization: Basic credential`

Although the credential looks like encrypted text, it is logically plain text because its format is simply UserName:Password encoded with *Base64* 📖—for example, U2thdGVib... in Figure 5.2 can be decoded to SkateboardWarehouse:wsbookexample.

The Web server authenticates the user with the user ID and password included in the credential. If the given user ID and password are wrong, "401 Unauthorized" is returned. Moreover, the Web server has an *access control list* (ACL) 📖 that specifies who can access what and checks whether the authenticated user can access the Web resource. If the check succeeds, then "200 OK" is returned; otherwise, "401 Unauthorized" is returned.

BASIC-AUTH in Axis

In this section, we review how to use BASIC-AUTH in Axis. On the server side, BASIC-AUTH is performed by middleware such as a Web server or servlet container. We do not have to modify the server programs at all, but change the server configuration. For Tomcat, we only modify its web.xml configuration file, as shown in Listing 5.1.

LISTING 5.1   Configuration for Basic Authentication in Tomcat

```
<web-app>
    <display-name>Basic Authentication Sample</display-name>

  <servlet>
    <servlet-name>AxisServletProtected</servlet-name>
    <display-name>Apache-Axis Servlet</display-name>
    <servlet-class>org.apache.axis.transport.http.AxisServlet</servlet-class>
  </servlet>
  <servlet-mapping>
    <servlet-name>AxisServletProtected</servlet-name>
    <url-pattern>services/protected</url-pattern>
  </servlet-mapping>
  <security-constraint>
    <web-resource-collection>
       <web-resource-name>Protected Area</web-resource-name>
       <!-- Define the context-relative URL(s) to be protected -->
       <url-pattern>/services/protected</url-pattern>
       <!-- If you list http methods, only those methods are protected -->
       <http-method>GET</http-method>
       <http-method>POST</http-method>
    </web-resource-collection>
    <auth-constraint>
       <!-- Anyone with one of the listed roles may access this area -->
       <role-name>MyCustomer</role-name>
```

Listing 5.1 Continued

```
    </auth-constraint>
  </security-constraint>
  <login-config>
    <auth-method>BASIC</auth-method>
    <realm-name>Protected Area</realm-name>
  </login-config>
</web-app>
```

The `security-constraint` element defines a realm and ACL. `web-resource-collection` specifies a collection of Web resources, each located at `url-pattern`, accessed by an HTTP method like `POST`. `auth-constraint` specifies who can access the realm. `login-config` specifies authentication method on the realm—for example, BASIC-AUTH (indicated by BASIC).

On the client side, we have to make sure that the user ID and password are properly embedded in the HTTP request. Axis provides a basic function for performing BASIC-AUTH, so the development of the client is fairly easy. Listing 5.2 shows a `POSubmission` program that can access servers via BASIC-AUTH.

Listing 5.2 `POSubmission` that Performs Basic Authentication

```java
package ch5.ex1;

import java.io.*;
import org.apache.axis.encoding.SerializationContext;
import org.apache.axis.message.SOAPEnvelope;
import org.apache.axis.message.SOAPBodyElement;
import org.apache.axis.client.ServiceClient;
import org.apache.axis.Message;
import org.apache.axis.MessageContext;

/**
 * Purchase order submission client
 */
public class POSubmission
{
    /**
     * Target service URL
     */
    private String url;
    private String userid;
    private String password;
```

LISTING 5.2   Continued

```
/**
 * Create a client with a target URL
 */
public POSubmission(String targetUrl, String userid, String password)
{
    this.url = targetUrl;
    this.userid = userid;
    this.password = password;
}

/**
 * Invoke the PO submission web service
 *
 * @param po Purchase order document
 * @return Invoice document
 * @exception Exception I/O error or Axis error
 */
public String invoke(InputStream po) throws Exception
{
    // Send the message
    ServiceClient client = new ServiceClient(url);
    client.setRequestMessage(new Message(po, true));
    call.set(Transport.USER, userid);
    call.set(Transport.PASSWORD, password);
    client.invoke();

    // Retrieve the response body
    MessageContext ctx = client.getMessageContext();
    Message outMsg = ctx.getResponseMessage();
    SOAPEnvelope envelope = outMsg.getAsSOAPEnvelope();
    SOAPBodyElement body = envelope.getFirstBody();

    // Get the XML from the body
    StringWriter w = new StringWriter();
    SerializationContext sc = new SerializationContext(w, ctx);
    body.output(sc);
    return w.toString();
}
}
```

The difference from the original POSubmission (Listing 3.12) is shown in bold. Member variables userid and password are added, and they are set to the ServiceClient object in the invoke() method. As you can imagine, these values are used to create an Authorization header, with the base64 encoding of SkateboardWarehouse:wsbookexample, which is included in HTTP request. Unlike the challenge-response protocol in Figure 5.2, the HTTP request here is accepted directly because the Authorization header is included.

The new POSubmission sample can be executed with our example navigator shipped with this book. Go to /ch5/ex1/basicauth.jsp, specify a user ID and password, and click the Submit PO button (see Figure 5.3). By entering the values **SkateboardWarehouse** and **wsbookexample**, you can successfully submit the purchase order. Otherwise, you will receive an error message.

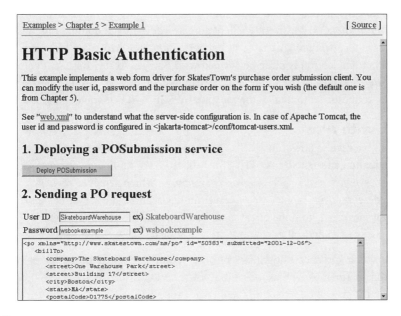

FIGURE 5.3

Example navigator GUI for basic authentication.

Secure Socket Layer (SSL)

BASIC-AUTH is useful, but on its own, it is not secure enough because the user ID and password are virtually unprotected. That is, an attacker can easily eavesdrop on the wire and either take the password to impersonate the user or tamper with the transmitted data.

SSL is a protocol for transmitting data in a secure way using encryption methods. With SSL, you can fulfill three of the five security requirements mentioned earlier: confidentiality, authentication, and integrity. You are probably familiar which *HTTPS* , which is HTTP over SSL. However, other application layer protocols such as *TELNET* and *FTP* can be performed over SSL because SSL is located between the application layer and the transport layer (TCP).

In order to establish a secure communication channel, the server and client have to authenticate each other. With SSL, the client can authenticate the server (*server authentication*) and vice versa (*client authentication*). Currently, client authentication is not common because it requires the client to have a *certificate* issued by a *certificate authority* (*CA*) such as VeriSign. Instead, client authentication is often performed with BASIC-AUTH for client convenience. However, in Web services of the future, not only human clients but also business applications will also make requests, so mutual authentication by SSL will become common.

Using SSL with Axis

In this section, we review how to use SSL with Axis and address the combination of SSL server authentication and BASIC-AUTH. SSL is based on a public key cryptography system, also called an *asymmetrical key cryptography system*, in which separate keys are used for encryption and decryption. In the case of server authentication, the server has a *private key* to decrypt messages from the client, and the client has the server's *public key* for encrypting messages it sends after the session is established.

In the case of secret key encryption, more effort is required: Storage of the secret key by each communications partner, as well as the (initial) distribution of the secret key to those partners, must be secured. This can be a daunting and error-prone task.

You can create private and public keys using the keytool program provided with the JDK. If you add the -genkey option, the keytool command generates a private key and its public key (the command is broken here because of printing constraints, but it actually appears on a single line):

```
keytool -genkey -keyalg RSA -sigalg MD5withRSA -keysize 1024 -alias SkatesTown
➥-dname "CN=Purchase Order Service, OU=Purchase Order Department, O=SkatesTown,
➥L=..., S=NY, C=US" -keypass wsbookexample -storepass wsbookexample -keystore
➥ SkatesTown.ks -storetype JKS
```

The options are summarized in Table 5.1. The generated private key and related information are stored in a *keystore* 📖 file, and keystore file information can also be specified in the command (for example, -keystore and -storetype).

The -keyalg and -keysize options specify the specification of the private key. -dname specifies an identification (X.500 *Distinguished Name* 📖) for the key, and -alias indicates an alias for the key (unique within the keystore). In addition, a password for accessing the key can be specified with -keypass (by default, it is the same as the keystore password).

A public key corresponding to the private key is also generated with this command, and is included in a certificate, which will be published to the client. Note that the certificate itself is described in more detail in PKI section. The certificate must be signed in order to demonstrate integrity. The signature algorithm is specified by the -sigalg option. Although we would like to specify *who* signed (or will sign) the certificate, that information cannot be specified with keytool. In this case, the certificate is signed by the private key that is generated, making it a *self-signed certificate*. A self-signed certificate is not practical for real use, but is sufficiently useful for the purpose of experimenting with SSL.

TABLE 5.1   Options for the keytool Command

Option	Value	Meaning
-keyalg	RSA	Format of the private key is *RSA* 📖
-keysize	1024	Key size is 1024 bits
-alias	SkatesTown	Key alias is *SkatesTown*
-dname	CN=Purchase Order Service,...	Identification of the key is *CN=Purchase Order Service, ...*
-keypass	wsbookexample	Password for the private key is *wsbookexample*
-sigalg	MD5withRSA	Method for signing certificate is *MD5* 📖 with RSA
-storepass	wsbookexample	Password for the keystore file is *wsbookexample*
-keystore	SkatesTown.ks	Keystore file name is SkatesTown.ks
-keystoretype	JKS	Keystore file type is *Java Key Store (JKS)* 📖

The generated certificate can be extracted with the following `keytool` command:

```
keytool -export -alias SkatesTown -file SkatesTown.cer -keystore SkatesTown.ks
➥ -storepass wsbookexample
```

The extracted certificate is stored in `SkatesTown.cer`. Next, we import the server certificate to a client keystore using the following command:

```
keytool -import -trustcacerts -alias SkatesTown -file SkatesTown.cer -keystore
➥ SkateboardWarehouse.ks -storepass wsbookexample -storetype JKS
```

The client uses the imported certificate to trust the server that owns that certificate. When a client establishes a session, the server sends a server certificate to the client. If the certificate is a member of the certificates included in the client keystore, the client trusts the server and so proceeds to the session.

We provide a browser interface for `keytool` within our example navigator. Visit `/ch5/ex2/index.jsp`. If you specify some parameters, `keytool` commands are automatically generated and executed (see Figure 5.4). You can create keystore files, export certificates, and import them to other keystore files.

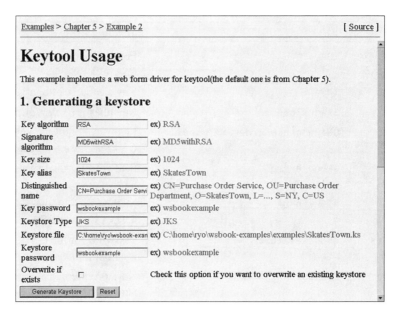

FIGURE 5.4

Example navigator GUI for `keytool`*.*

Let's examine the SSL configuration for a Web server (Tomcat in this case). In the `<tomcat-home>/conf/server.xml` file, you need to add the `Connector` section shown in Listing 5.3.

LISTING 5.3   Tomcat Configuration for SSL

```
<Connector className="org.apache.tomcat.service.PoolTcpConnector">
   <Parameter name="handler"
      value="org.apache.tomcat.service.http.HttpConnectionHandler"/>
   <Parameter name="port" value="8443"/>
   <Parameter name="socketFactory"
      value="org.apache.tomcat.net.SSLSocketFactory"/>
   <Parameter name="keystore"
      value="c:\ws-book\SkatesTown.ks" />
   <Parameter name="keypass" value="wsbookexample"/>
   <Parameter name="clientAuth" value="false"/>
</Connector>
```

HTTPS settings are specified in the `Parameter` elements. The `port` parameter indicates a port number for SSL connections. `socketFactory` specifies the Java factory class that will create SSL socket objects. With `keystore` and `keypass`, Tomcat can get a private key for SSL session. Note that Tomcat assumes (and hence requires) that the server's keystore password is identical to the private key password. Finally, `clientAuth` specifies whether client authentication is performed. Note that you have to modify `<java_home>/jre/security/java.security` to run Tomcat with SSL. Refer to the section "Java Secure Socket Extension" later in this chapter to learn how to modify this file and then execute Tomcat.

For the client, you must set up Java system properties that are required when invoking SSL. Listing 5.4 shows a modified `POSubmission` program. As you can see, the keystore type (`storetype`), keystore file name (`keystore`), and keystore password (`storepass`) are fed to the constructor, and the parameters are set for system properties. We will review these properties in the section "Java Secure Socket Extension." Although we specify the system parameters programmatically, you can specify them with the `-D` option of the `java` command. In that case, you do not have to change the Listing 5.2 program at all. The section "Java Secure Socket Extension" will show such an alternative example.

LISTING 5.4   POSubmission that Performs Basic Authentication and SSL

```java
package ch5.ex3;

import java.io.StringBufferInputStream;
import java.io.StringWriter;
import org.apache.axis.encoding.SerializationContext;
import org.apache.axis.message.SOAPEnvelope;
import org.apache.axis.message.SOAPBodyElement;
import org.apache.axis.client.ServiceClient;
import org.apache.axis.client.Transport;
import org.apache.axis.transport.http.HTTPTransport;
import org.apache.axis.Message;
import org.apache.axis.MessageContext;
import org.apache.axis.encoding.ServiceDescription;

final public class DoOrder {
    final String url;
    final Strint storetype;
    final Strint keystore;
    final String storepass;
    final String uid;
    final String password;

    public DoOrder(String url,
                   Strint storetype,
                   Strint keystore,
                   String storepass,
                   String uid,
                   String password)
    {
        this.url = url;
        this.storetype = storetype;
        this.keystore = keystore;
        this.storepass = storepass;
        this.uid = uid;
        this.password = password;
    }
```

LISTING 5.4 Continued

```
        public synchronized static String invoke(String xml) throws Exception {
          String[][] props = {
              { "javax.net.ssl.trustStore", keystore, },
              { "javax.net.ssl.keyStore", keystore, },
              { "javax.net.ssl.keyStorePassword", storepass, },
              { "javax.net.ssl.keyStoreType", storetype, },
          };
          for (int i = 0; i < props.length; i++)
              System.getProperties().setProperty(props[i][0], props[i][1]);

              ServiceClient client =
➥new ServiceClient(new HTTPTransport(url, "PO"));
          client.set(MessageContext.USERID, uid);
          client.set(MessageContext.PASSWORD, password);
              client.setRequestMessage(new Message(new
➥StringBufferInputStream(xml), true));
              client.invoke();

              Message outMsg = client.getMessageContext().getResponseMessage();
              ServiceDescription svc = new ServiceDescription("doOrder",
false);
              client.getMessageContext().setServiceDescription(svc);

              SOAPEnvelope envelope = outMsg.getAsSOAPEnvelope();
              SOAPBodyElement body = envelope.getFirstBody();
              StringWriter writer = new StringWriter();
              SerializationContext ctx = new SerializationContext(writer,
➥client.getMessageContext());
              body.output(ctx);
              return writer.toString();
        }
}
```

You can execute POSubmission with BASIC-AUTH and SSL via /ch5/ex3/index.jsp in the example navigator. Specify some values in the page, such as the keystore file, keystore password, and so on, if you want, and then click the Submit PO button (see Figure 5.5).

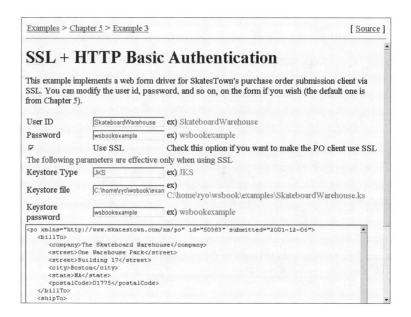

FIGURE 5.5

Example navigator GUI for basic authentication and SSL.

Java Secure Socket Extension

There is a standard API for SSL, called the *Java Secure Socket Extension* (JSSE) ▭. Tomcat also uses Sun JSSE in its SSL implementation, but no additional Tomcat configuration is required. However, you do have to configure any Java Runtime Environment (JRE) that will run programs using JSSE, including Tomcat with SSL enabled. So, in the case of a Tomcat Web server, the following JSSE setup applies to the server- and client-side.

In order to use JSSE, you must first set up a *security provider* ▭. The concept of a security provider is defined in the *Java Cryptographic Architecture* (JCA) ▭. Because we describe JCA later, this section only explains how to configure it.

The easiest way to set up a security provider is to modify `<java-home>\jre\lib\security\java.security`. The file contains a list of at least one provider in the form `security.provider.<n>`. Add the JSSE security provider as follows:

```
security.provider.1=sun.security.provider.Sun
security.provider.2=com.sun.rsajca.Provider
security.provider.3=com.sun.net.ssl.internal.ssl.Provider
```

Next, add the three JSSE JAR files to the classpath: `jsse.jar`, `jnet.jar`, and `jcert.jar`. Alternatively, the files might be directly copied to the `<java-home>\jre\lib\ext` directory.

After JSSE configuration is finished, the client program can be executed using the following command:

```
java -Djava.protocol.handler.pkgs=com.sun.net.ssl.internal.www.protocol
➥-Djavax.net.ssl.trustStore=SkateboardWarehouse.ks
➥-Djavax.net.ssl.keyStore=SkateboardWarehouse.ks
➥-Djavax.net.ssl.keyStorePassword=wsbookexample
➥-Djavax.net.ssl.keyStoreType=jks ExamplePOClient
➥-l https://localhost:8443/axis/servlet/AxisServlet
```

You might notice that the target protocol is changed from HTTP to HTTPS. The system property `java.protocol.handler.pkgs` enables programs to handle HTTPS in the URL class. Other system properties specify information to access a client keystore. Trusted certificates in the client keystore are examined when a server sends its certificate to determine whether the server is trusted.

The SSL Protocol

SSL was proposed by Netscape Communications and has been widely used since the explosion of the World Wide Web, because it is supported by Netscape Navigator and Microsoft Internet Explorer. The latest version of SSL, 3.0, has been presented to the *Internet Engineering Task Force* (IETF) 📖 for standardization. Another closely related protocol called *Transport Layer Security protocol* (TLS) 📖 is currently on version 1.0, published as RFC 2246. There are no major differences between SSL and TLS. TLS has not yet become widely used, so SSL 3.0 is still dominant.

Let's review the SSL protocol in more detail. Figure 5.6 illustrates how a security *handshake* establishes a secure connection between the client and server. Once the handshake completes, the server and client have a common secret key with which data is encrypted and decrypted. In other words, SSL uses the public key(s) to encrypt exchanges for the sole purpose of generating the shared secret key.

Despite the advantages of using public key encryption alone, SSL combines them. It does so because the public key encryption system takes more time to encrypt and decrypt messages than the secret key encryption system. Thus, the combination used by SSL takes advantage of both the easy maintenance of public key encryption and the quicker operating speed of secret key encryption.

Let's take a closer look at the SSL handshake protocol, again referring to Figure 5.6. At phase I, the client starts the handshake, and then sends a random number, a list of supported ciphers, and compression algorithms. At phase II, the server selects a cipher and a compression algorithm and notifies the client. Then it sends another random number and a server certificate (which includes a public key). At phase III, the client sends a pre-master secret to the server, encrypting it with the server public key. Finally, the client might send a client certificate. Now the handshake is completed.

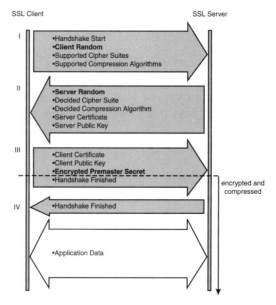

FIGURE 5.6

SSL security handshake protocol.

The server and the client each generate a *master secret* by combining the random number that the server sent, the random number that the client sent, and the pre-master secret. Several secret keys are created from the master secret. For example, one is used for encrypting transmitted data, and another is used for calculating digest value of the date for integrity.

SSL ensures authentication (by verifying the certificates), confidentiality (by encrypting the data with a secret key), and integrity (by digesting the data). However, non-repudiation is not ensured with SSL because the *Message Authentication Code* (*MAC*) value of transmitted data is calculated with a common secret key.

Digital Signature

Returning to our example scenario, Dean Caroll now understands that the combination of BASIC-AUTH and SSL is a good starting point to secure SOAP-based communication with trading partner. He also understands an immediate problem with non-repudiation. Without non-repudiation, a company can repudiate its purchase order even if the company actually sent the order request, or the company can claim that the number of products is wrong. With respect to exchange of XML messages between two parties, a digital signature provides a means to prove that the sending party created the message. Al Rosen emphasized that there is already a stable version of the *XML Digital Signature* 📖 specification, which will become a *W3C* 📖 /IETF standard. Furthermore, Digital Signature for SOAP, based on the XML Digital Signature, is published as a *W3C Note* 📖.

SOAP Signature Example

Currently, the Axis platform does not include signature functions, but the IBM Web Services Toolkit (WSTK) 2.4 includes signature and verification handlers for Axis. These handlers can be embedded in Axis handler chains, as shown in Figure 5.7.

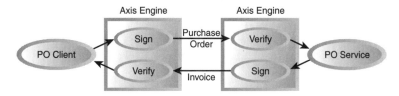

FIGURE 5.7
Signature and verifier handlers for purchase order processing service.

In our purchase order example, the client sends a purchase order document and receives an invoice document. In practice, these two documents should be signed; otherwise, one of the parties can repudiate that it sent the document.

Figure 5.7 illustrates a handler configuration that causes both documents to be signed and verified. The signature handler at the service requestor's side signs the purchase order. On the service provider's side, the verifier handler verifies the signature of the purchase order document. The invoice is signed by the service provider and verified by the service requestor.

Listing 5.5 shows a digitally signed purchase order document. `SOAP-SEC:Signature` includes a signature on the purchase order and specifies a collection of parameters to create the signature. The details of this digitally signed SOAP message are described in the following section.

LISTING 5.5   Purchase Order with a SOAP Digital Signature

```
<SOAP-ENV:Envelope
    xmlns:SOAP-ENV="http://schemas.xmlsoap.org/soap/envelope/">
    <SOAP-ENV:Header>
      <SOAP-SEC:Signature
         SOAP-ENV:actor=""
         SOAP-ENV:mustUnderstand="1"
         xmlns:SOAP-ENV="http://schemas.xmlsoap.org/soap/envelope/"
         xmlns:SOAP-SEC="http://schemas.xmlsoap.org/soap/security/2000-12">
         <dsig:Signature xmlns:dsig="http://www.w3.org/2000/09/xmldsig#">
            <dsig:SignedInfo>
               <dsig:CanonicalizationMethod
           Algorithm="http://www.w3.org/TR/2001/REC-xml-c14n-20010315"/>
        <dsig:SignatureMethod
           Algorithm="http://www.w3.org/2000/09/xmldsig#rsa-sha1"/>
               <dsig:Reference URI="#43871">
                  <dsig:Transforms>
                     <dsig:Transform
             Algorithm=
                "http://www.w3.org/TR/2000/CR-xml-c14n-20001026"/>
                  </dsig:Transforms>
                  <dsig:DigestMethod
           Algorithm="http://www.w3.org/2000/09/xmldsig#sha1"/>
         <dsig:DigestValue>... Base64-encoded Digest Value...
         </dsig:DigestValue>
               </dsig:Reference>
            </dsig:SignedInfo>
            <dsig:SignatureValue>
               ... Base64-encoded Signature Value
            </dsig:SignatureValue>
            <KeyInfo xmlns="http://www.w3.org/2000/09/xmldsig#">
               <KeyValue>
                  <RSAKeyValue>
                     <Modulus>... Base64-encoded Modulus...</Modulus>
                     <Exponent>AQAB</Exponent>
                  </RSAKeyValue>
               </KeyValue>
               <X509Data>
                  <X509IssuerSerial>
```

LISTING 5.5   Continued

```
                        <X509IssuerName>
➡                   CN=Purchase Order Service
➡                   OU=Purchase Order Department, O=SkatesTown, L=...,
➡                   S=NY, C=US ....Formatted for printing
➡                </X509IssuerName>
                        <X509SerialNumber>993353832</X509SerialNumber>
                    </X509IssuerSerial>
                    <X509SubjectName>
➡                   CN=Purchase Order Service,
➡                   OU=Purchase Order Department, O=SkatesTown, L=...,
➡                   S=NY, C=US ....Formatted for printing
➡                </X509SubjectName>
                    <X509Certificate>
                        ... Base64-encoded X.509 Certificate
                    </X509Certificate>
                </X509Data>
            </KeyInfo>
          </dsig:Signature>
        </SOAP-SEC:Signature>
      </SOAP-ENV:Header>
      <SOAP-ENV:Body>
        <po xmlns="http://www.skatestown.com/ns/po"
          id="43871" submitted="2001-12-06">
          ...
        </po>
      </SOAP-ENV:Body>
</SOAP-ENV:Envelope>
```

The digital signature scenario can be executed with the example navigator. Go to
/ch5/ex4/index.jsp, specify parameters if you want, and click the Submit PO button (see
Figure 5.8).

Deployment descriptors for the example are shown in Listings 5.6 and 5.7. At the client side,
request messages are signed via the sign handler, response messages are verified and logged
via verify and log handlers (see Listing 5.6). At the server side, request messages are verified
and logged, and response messages are signed (see Listing 5.7). As you can see in the listings,
you need to specify some parameters for sign handlers, such as a keystore file, key alias, store
password, and key password. On the other hand, the verify handler does not require as much
information.

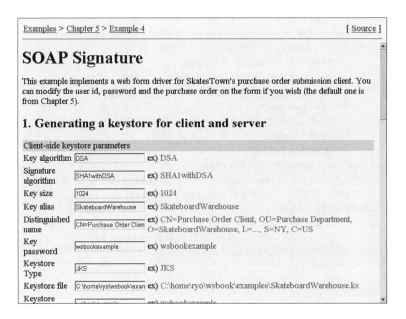

FIGURE 5.8

Example navigator GUI for a digital signature.

LISTING 5.6   Deployment Descriptor for a Digital Signature at the Client

```
<deploy>
   <handler name="log" class="org.apache.axis.handlers.LogHandler"/>
   <handler name="sign" class="com.ibm.wstk.axis.handlers.Signer">
      <option name="alias" value="SkateboardWarehouse"/>
      <option name="keyPassword" value="wsbookexample"/>
      <option name="keyStore"
➥     value="C:\home\ryo\wsbook\examples\SkateboardWarehouse.ks" />
      <option name="keyStorePassword" value="wsbookexample"/>
   </handler>
   <handler name="verify" class="com.ibm.wstk.axis.handlers.Verifier"/>
   <service name="http://www.skatestown.com/ns/po"
➥     request="sign,log" response="log,verify"/>
</deploy>
```

LISTING **5.7**   Deployment Descriptor for a Digital Signature at the Server

```
<deploy>
   <handler name="log" class="org.apache.axis.handlers.LogHandler"/>
   <handler name="verify" class="com.ibm.wstk.axis.handlers.Verifier"/>
   <handler name="sign" class="com.ibm.wstk.axis.handlers.Signer">
      <option name="alias" value="SkatesTown"/>
      <option name="keyPassword" value="wsbookexample"/>
      <option name="keyStore"
➥ value="C:\home\ryo\wsbook\examples\SkatesTown.ks" />
      <option name="keyStorePassword" value="wsbookexample"/>
   </handler>
   <service name="http://www.skatestown.com/ns/po"
➥request="log,verify" pivot="MsgDispatcher" response="sign,log">
      <option name="className" value="com.skatestown.services.POSubmission"/>
       <option name="methodName" value="doSubmission"/>
   </service>
</deploy>
```

SOAP Signature Details

In the XML Digital Signature specification (XML Signature), an element Signature is defined with its descendants under the *namespace* 📖 http://www.w3.org/2000/09/xmldsig#. The SOAP Signature specification defines how to embed the Signature element in SOAP messages as a header entry. You can sign all or part of the message. Furthermore, if a message has attachments, these too can be signed. In our example, the body entry for the purchase order is signed. Let's take a closer look at our signed PO example. In the example, the target element of the signature is po:po. Briefly, the digest value of the po:po sub-tree is calculated, and the value is signed and included in the Signature element.

Let's first review how to get the digest value of the target. The target is specified by Reference under the SignedInfo element. Its URI attribute indicates the target in such a way that the id attribute of the po element is referenced. The target is transformed by XML-C14N—that is, a *canonicalization* 📖 method for XML. (XML Canonicalization is a W3C Recommendation to generate a canonical form for physically different but logically equivalent XML documents.) With XML-C14N, we can check whether XML documents are *semantically* equivalent using a standardized code set, the order of attributes, tab processing, and so on. The following two documents are quite different at a glance:

```
<?xml version="1.0" encoding="us-ascii"?>
<foo
    b="b"
    a="a"
></foo>


<?xml version="1.0" encoding="us-ascii"?>
<foo a="a" b="b"/>
```

However, with XML-C14N, they are translated into the following identical document:

```
<?xml version="1.0" encoding="us-ascii"?>
<foo a="a" b="b"></foo>
```

After translation, a digest value is calculated with an algorithm specified by the `DigestMethod` element. Here *SHA1* 📖 is used. The calculated value is inserted in `DigestValue` element, represented in Base64 format.

The value of the target is not signed directly. Rather, the `SignedInfo` element is actually signed. An algorithm specified by the `CanonicalizationMethod` element—that is, XML-C14N—canonicalizes `SignedInfo`. The canonicalized `SignedInfo` is signed with an algorithm specified by `SignatureMethod`: RSA-SHA1. This algorithm calculates a digest value of the `SignedInfo` subtree, and then signs it with a RSA private key. The calculated value is inserted into the `SignatureValue` element, represented in Base64 format.

Optionally, the signer can include a `KeyInfo` element to attach key information. More specifically, the example includes an X.509 certificate, which contains a public key corresponding to the private key that signed the digest value. Because the certificate is *Abstract Syntax Notation One (ASN.1)* 📖 binary data, its Base64 representation is there.

So far, we have reviewed the XML Signature syntax in the signature processing process. Verification is carried out in the same manner. First, we check the value of the `DigestValue` element according to XML-C14N and SHA1. Next, we calculate a digest value for the `SignedInfo` subtree to compare it with the value in the `SignatureValue` element. More precisely, the signature value is decrypted with the public key, and then compared to the calculated value.

XML Encryption

SSL is useful for ensuring confidentiality. However, at least two problems exist in the context of SOAP messaging. By definition, SOAP messaging can include intermediaries, and any of them could be owned by organizations other than the service requestor or the service provider. The first problem is that any of these third parties might need to read the message. Inherently, transport-level security solutions like SSL assume that communication occurs only directly between two parties. The second problem is that SSL encrypts the whole message. In some cases, you might want to encrypt only parts of the message. SOAP Encryption can resolve these problems.

We now update our purchase order document to include card information, as shown in Listing 5.8. Instead of a `BillTo` element, we insert `CardInfo` so that the service requestor can pay with the card. When SkatesTown receives the document from the Skateboard Warehouse, it does not have to know the card information. Instead, it could just forward it to a credit company to determine if the Skateboard Warehouse is reliable in terms of the payment. SSL is not sufficient for this purpose, because SkatesTown can read the card information.

LISTING 5.8 Purchase Order that Includes Card Information

```
<po xmlns="http://www.skatestown.com/ns/po-with-card" id="43871"
➥submitted="2001-10-05">
    .   <cardInfo>
        <name>Purchase Order Client</name>
        <company>VISA</company>
        <expiration>02/2005</expiration>
        <number>1234123412341234</number>
    </cardInfo>
    <shipTo>
        <company>The Skateboard Warehouse</company>
        <street>One Warehouse Park</street>
        <street>Building 17</street>
        <city>Boston</city>
        <state>MA</state>
        <postalCode>01775</postalCode>
    </shipTo>
    <order>
        <item sku="318-BP" quantity="5">
            <description>Skateboard backpack; five pockets</description>
        </item>
        <item sku="947-TI" quantity="12">
            <description>Street-style titanium skateboard.</description>
        </item>
        <item sku="008-PR" quantity="1000"/>
    </order>
</po>
```

At present, there is no standard specification for SOAP Encryption. Even the *XML Encryption* specification was published only very recently as a *W3C Working Draft*, and so is subject to change. The discussion here is based on the preliminary draft of SOAP Encryption included in WSTK 2.4. After our SOAP Encryption review, we will review the *Java Cryptographic Architecture* (JCA), which provides a basis for implementing SOAP Encryption and SOAP Signature.

5

SOAP Encryption: Syntax and Processing

Let's look at an XML Encryption example first. Listing 5.9 is an encrypted version of the purchase order document.

LISTING 5.9   Encrypted Purchase Order Document

```
<po xmlns="http://www.skatestown.com/ns/po-with-card"
➥id="43871" submitted="2001-10-05">
   <enc:EncryptedData
      Type="http://www.w3.org/2001/04/xmlenc#Element">
      <enc:EncryptionMethod
         Algorithm="urn:nist-gov:aes-128-cbc"/>
      <ds:KeyInfo>
         <ds:KeyName>Shared key</ds:KeyName>
      </ds:KeyInfo>
      <enc:CipherData>abCdeF...</enc:CipherData>
   </enc:EncryptedData>
   ...
</po>
```

This shows the simplest case, where two parties share a common secret key. Note that namespace ds is a prefix for the XML Digital Signature namespace. The XML Encryption specification reuses elements from the XML Digital Signature namespace as much as possible.

The EncryptedData element is a root element for the encrypted part, and its Type attribute indicates that the encrypted data is an XML element. The EncryptionMethod element specifies an encryption algorithm, and KeyInfo specifies a secret key. Based on the secret key and the algorithm, the card information is encrypted and stored in the CipherData element.

Listing 5.10 shows encryption with a public key.

LISTING 5.10   Encryption with a Public Key

```
<po xmlns="http://www.skatestown.com/ns/po-with-card" id="43871"
➥submitted="2001-10-05">
   <enc:EncryptedData
      Type="http://www.w3.org/2001/04/xmlenc#Element">
      <enc:EncryptionMethod
         Algorithm="urn:nist-gov:aes-128-cbc"/>
      <ds:KeyInfo>
         <enc:EncryptedKey>
            <enc:EncryptionMethod
               Algorithm="urn:rsadsi-com:rsa-v2.0"/>
            <ds:KeyInfo>
```

LISTING 5.10   Continued

```
            <ds:KeyName>Receiver's key</ds:KeyName>
          </ds:KeyInfo>
          <enc:CipherData>ghIjkL...</enc:CipherData>
        </enc:EncryptedKey>
      </ds:KeyInfo>
      <enc:CipherData>abCdeF...</enc:CipherData>
    </enc:EncryptedData>
  ...
</po>
```

The idea here is that the sender generates a random secret key, encrypts the key with the receiver's public key, and encrypts the data with the secret key. Let's look at EncryptedKey first. EncryptionMethod specifies the encryption algorithm, and KeyInfo specifies the receiver's public key. Based on these elements, a secret key is encrypted to store in CipherData. Outer CipherData comes from an encryption based on the secret key and an encryption algorithm specified by the outer EncryptionAlgorithm.

Let's move on to SOAP Encryption. SOAP Encryption defines a SOAP-SEC:Encryption element, which includes a reference to the location of the encrypted data. Listing 5.11 is a sample that includes SOAP Encryption.

LISTING 5.11   SOAP Encryption Example

```
<SOAP-ENV:Envelope xmlns:SOAP-ENV="http://schemas.xmlsoap.org/soap/envelope/">
   <SOAP-ENV:Header>
      <SOAP-SEC:Encryption
         xmlns:SOAP-SEC="http://schemas.xmlsoap.org/soap/security/2000-12">
         <SOAP-SEC:Manifest>
            <SOAP-SEC:Reference URI="#id-0"/>
         </SOAP-SEC:Manifest>
      </SOAP-SEC:Encryption>
   </SOAP-ENV:Header>
   <SOAP-ENV:Body>
      <po xmlns="http://www.skatestown.com/ns/po-with-card" id="43871"
➥   submitted="2001-10-05">
         <enc:EncryptedData xmlns:enc="http://www.w3.org/2000/11/temp-xmlenc"
            Id="id-0" Type="http://www.w3.org/2001/04/xmlenc#Element">
            ...
         </enc:EncryptedData>
         ...
      </po>
   </SOAP-ENV:Body>
</SOAP-ENV:Envelope>
```

5

The encrypted po is included in the SOAP body, adding an Id attribute to the EncryptedData element. The Id attribute is referred to by SOAP-SEC:Reference within the SOAP-SEC:Encryption header entry.

The encryption header is intended to be a directive to SOAP intermediaries. With actorURI, you can specify a particular SOAP intermediary. Therefore, you can tell the intermediary to decrypt the data, specifying where the encrypted data is located. Thus, you can embed encryption and decryption methods into the SOAP messaging path in a flexible manner.

Java Cryptography Architecture and Java Cryptography Extension

In order to implement SOAP Signature and SOAP Encryption with Java, you need to understand *Java Cryptography Architecture* (JCA) and *Java Cryptography Extension* (JCE) 📖. JSSE is also developed on top of JCA/JCE. In this section, we review JCA/JCE in more detail to help you understand the cryptography architecture of Java.

JCA and JCE incorporate public key technologies. JCA provides a framework for accessing and developing core cryptographic functions. Implementation and algorithm independence is addressed so that applications are insulated from cryptographic details. In other words, cryptographic implementation and algorithms can be changed without modifying any application programs.

JCA provides an API for digital signature, message digest, key management, certificate management, and access control, as well as a basic security framework. The JCE API provides encryption and key exchange. The separation of the JCA and JCE APIs stems from export regulations by the United States Commerce Department.

In the section on SSL, we discussed how to configure the `<java-home>\jre\lib\security\java.security` file to use SSL. As we mentioned, each security provider is specified in the following format:

```
security.provider.<n>=<Security Provider Class>
```

The number indicates a priority, and the right side specifies a security provider class. Each provider class is a subclass of `java.security.Provider` and supports some or all parts of Java security algorithms, such as DSA, RSA, MD5, or SHA-1. For SSL, we added the third line, as follows:

```
security.provider.1=sun.security.provider.Sun
security.provider.2=com.sun.rsajca.Provider
security.provider.3=com.sun.net.ssl.internal.ssl.Provider
```

When a security algorithm is required, providers are asked whether they support the particular algorithm according to the priority. For example, if SHA1withRSA is required, the second provider is chosen. Although the second and third providers both support it, the second one has higher priority. If SSL is required, the third provider is chosen because only it supports SSL.

Combining SOAP and Transport Security

So far, we have reviewed transport-layer security (BASIC-AUTH and SSL) and SOAP-level security (SOAP Signature and SOAP Encryption). You might ask: Why do we need SOAP-level security in addition to transport-level security like SSL? The reason is related to the SOAP intermediary concept. As we reviewed in Chapter 3, SOAP messages can travel to multiple hosts, potentially relying on different transports such as HTTP and *SMTP* 📖. This indirect and transport-agnostic nature of SOAP implies that transport-layer security alone is insufficient.

On the other hand, you might ask: Is transport-layer security unnecessary? In theory, we could provide a complete set of SOAP security features with which transport-layer security would no longer be needed. However, this approach will discard existing security infrastructure to some extent, and is therefore not acceptable.

SOAP-level security should be considered complementary to transport-layer security. For example, suppose that you want to send a signed message to a destination, ensuring confidentiality. No intermediary exists, and no element-wise encryption is required. In this case, why not simply use a combination of SOAP Signature and SSL? We should combine SOAP-level and transport-layer security properly considering the environment and application requirements.

Notary Service

BASIC-AUTH/SSL, SOAP Signature, and SOAP Encryption are a proper set of technologies with which you can generally fulfill the four basic security requirements: confidentiality, authentication, integrity, and non-repudiation. However, there is a further requirement: *non-repudiation of message receipt*. At the client side, for example, if SkatesTown receives a purchase order document from Skateboard Warehouse, it should return an invoice document. Then, it starts processing the order—that is, shipping products in the order. However, Skateboard Warehouse might not receive the invoice because of network trouble, or it might claim that the invoice was not delivered. Or, if the invoice delivery takes more than 10 days, Skateboard Warehouse can, by policy, consider the order unplaced or misplaced.

We want to ensure that the message has been received at the destination, and to know when it was received. In the context of SOAP, it might be a good idea to include a notary service as a SOAP intermediary between the trading parties, as shown in Figure 5.9. The notary service provider is trusted by both SkatesTown and their customers. When there is a disagreement on message delivery between two parties, the notary service can arbitrate the problem on the basis of its log database.

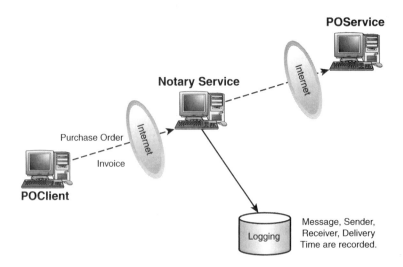

FIGURE 5.9
Notary service as SOAP intermediary.

From a business perspective, this structure is beneficial for three parties. Trading parties can perform business transactions safely simply by contracting with the notary service. The notary service can earn money according to the transaction volume. The only problem here is whether the notary service is a *real* trusted party. A number of notary services have emerged already, such as VeriSign. Most of them aim solely at trusted storage of data such as medical records. However, once they are trusted widely, they could play the role of a notary in our business structure.

What is the benefit of SOAP in Figure 5.9? We could develop the same business structure without SOAP. Flexibility is the main benefit. The Axis architecture allows trading partners to focus completely on building business-level service requestor and service provider applications, with the caveat that they must respectively produce and consume XML documents. At configuration time, handlers, potentially including handlers to invoke intermediaries, can be deployed at the requestor and/or provider side to enhance functionality or security of the message send and receipt. When these extra handlers are added, the requestor and provider applications do not have to change at all. This shows the flexibility of SOAP-based development using Axis.

Authorization

So far, we have examined security technologies with which Web services can authenticate users and protect transmitted data from eavesdropping or alteration by inappropriate parties. From a technology point of view, network security relies on cryptographic methods, such as message digests, digital signatures, and message encryption. Authorization, the security aspect covered in this section, is different from the others because it is not based on cryptography.

Authorization denotes granting authority, including granting access to resources based upon access rights. The purpose is to control access over resources, such as Web resources, databases, and so on. Perhaps the most basic implementation of this idea is the access control list (ACL), which defines a mapping from entities to resources that can be accessed by each entity. A slightly more sophisticated model is role-based access control (RBAC), which maps entities to roles and then roles to resources. This model simply adds one extra layer of abstraction to the ACL model.

Three types of authorization methods are relevant for our SOAP architecture. URL authorization controls access to Web resources such as HTML pages and servlets. Java class authorization can be implemented using the *Java Authentication and Authorization Services (JAAS)* 📖 package. Finally, an authenticated entity might be issued a standardized set of security assertions that describe access rights for that entity and can be shared among trading partners. These three methods are examined in detail in the remainder of this section.

URL Authorization

We have already reviewed some aspects of URL authorization in BASIC-AUTH in the Axis section. Tomcat provides a means to define user identities, user-role mapping, and role-resource mapping. The file <TOMCAT>/conf/tomcat-user.xml contains these mappings as shown in Listing 5.12.

LISTING 5.12 Tomcat User File Configuration

```
<tomcat-users>
  <user name="SkateboardWarehouse" password="wsbookexample"
➥roles="MyCustomer" />
  <user name="WeMakeIt" password="wsbookexample" roles="MySupplier" />
  <user name="Both" password="wsbookexample" roles="MyCustomer,MySupplier" />
```

The `tomcat-users` element includes a collection of users, and `user` defines a user identity, password, and any roles assigned to it. Listing 5.13 illustrates access control for servlets.

LISTING 5.13   Configuration of Access Control over Servlets

```
<web-app>
    <display-name>Basic Authentication Sample</display-name>
    <servlet>
        <servlet-name>PriceCheckServlet</servlet-name>
        <servlet-class>com.sams.xxxx.PriceCheckServlet</servlet-class>
    </servlet>
    <servlet>
        <servlet-name>POServlet</servlet-name>
        <servlet-class>com.sams.xxxx.POServlet</servlet-class>
    </servlet>
    <servlet-mapping>
        <servlet-name>POServlet</servlet-name>
        <url-pattern>/servlet/justsample/POServlet</url-pattern>
    </servlet-mapping>
    <servlet-mapping>
        <servlet-name>PriceCheckServlet</servlet-name>
        <url-pattern>/servlet/justsample/PriceCheckServlet</url-pattern>
    </servlet-mapping>
    <security-constraint>
        <web-resource-collection>
            <web-resource-name>Protected Area</web-resource-name>
            <url-pattern>/servlet/justsample/POServlet</url-pattern>
            <http-method>POST</http-method>
        </web-resource-collection>
        <auth-constraint>
            <role-name>MyCustomer</role-name >
        </auth-constraint>
    </security-constraint>
    <login-config>
        <auth-method>BASIC</auth-method>
        <realm-name>Protected Area</realm-name>
    </login-config>
</web-app>
```

The sample here is quite different from the one in the section "SSL and Basic Authentication" because we have different servlets for price checking and purchase order processing. Because Axis has a router servlet, all application classes are accessed through the router. However, if we prepare a servlet for each application class, controlling access to each of them is fairly simple, as the example demonstrates.

Access Control for Java Classes

How can we perform authorization of individual Web services within the router servlet in Axis? We have to control access to Java classes this time. Let's examine JAAS authorization over Java classes.

JAAS is an extension of the Java 2 Security Architecture (J2SA). Historically, Java security has focused on security for mobile code such as Applets. In J2SA terms, permissions are *granted* to a *codebase*, the origin of the code that is being executed. Listing 5.14 is an excerpt from `<TOMCAT>/conf/tomcat.policy`.

LISTING 5.14 Permission Declaration in a Tomcat Policy File

```
// Tomcat gets all permissions
grant codeBase "file:${tomcat.home}/lib/-" {
      permission java.security.AllPermission;
};

grant codeBase "file:${tomcat.home}/classes/-" {
      permission java.security.AllPermission;
};

// Example webapp policy
// By default we grant read access on webapp dir and
// write in workdir
grant codeBase "file:${tomcat.home}/webapps/examples" {
      permission java.net.SocketPermission "localhost:1024-", "listen";
      permission java.util.PropertyPermission "*", "read";
};
```

The first and second declarations show that Tomcat system classes are given all permissions. On the other hand, the third `grant` statement shows that the Tomcat example Web applications can only listen to localhost:1024 and read properties. In other words, they cannot listen to other hosts or ports, read or write files, or do any action other than those specified.

Code-based authorization is useful. But in the case of SOAP Messaging using Axis, we need authorization based on the entity that is the origin of the request, also called the (authenticated) requestor. Figure 5.10 illustrates how a JAAS-based authorization mechanism can be added to Apache Axis. Entities including bold lines are JAAS objects.

5

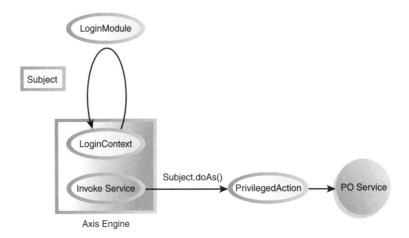

FIGURE 5.10

Authorization for Axis with JAAS.

The central data structure in JAAS is the *subject*. A subject is any entity (such as a person or company), and it is represented by a collection of security-related properties such as user ID, group, roles, employee number, and so on. These properties are called *principals* in J2SA. JAAS performs two major tasks: authentication and authorization. The subject is discovered and a subject with associated principals is *produced* at the authentication phase, and then the subject is retrieved and examined, or *consumed*, at the authorization phase to decide whether the subject can perform the requested action.

Let's review Figure 5.10 more closely. In Axis Engine, we first create a LoginContext and perform login to start authentication. It starts processing the order—that is, shipping products in the order. The following is a sample code:

```
LoginContext lc = null;
try {
  Subject subject = new Subject();
  Hashtable hash = new Hashtable();
  hash.put("http.username", userid);
  //this value should be taken from the Axis MessageContext
  hash.put("http.password", password);
  // this value is also from the message context
  subject.getPublicCredentials().add(hash);
  lc = new LoginContext("AxisLogin", subject);
  lc.login();
} catch (Exception le) {}
```

The idea here is that an initial subject is created including BASIC-AUTH information. The user ID might be mapped to another ID for the preceding steps. When you invoke `LoginContext.login()`, a `LoginModule` is created and invoked, at which time it creates and attaches principals to the subject (in the case of the `AxisLogin` login module, these are Axis-specific principals). But these login modules are pluggable, so we can assume that, given our previous scenario, the `MyCustomer` role will be added to the subject if the HTTP username was *Skateboard Warehouse*.

When invoking the service, we call `Subject.doAs()` so that only authorized subjects will be able to perform the operation. The actual invocation looks like this:

```
Subject.doAs(subject,
             new AxisPrivilegedAction(uri,method));
```

This invocation leads us to the invocation of the `run()` method in `AxisPrivilegedAction`. Within the `run()` method, access permission on the associated resource (specified by a URI and method in the previous program) is checked, and the target method is invoked only if no `AccessControlException` is thrown. You can implement `PrivilegedAction` classes in any way. For example, we could have a role-action mapping database containing triples like `<role, uri, method>`, and our action class could check the database to authorize the given request. If the database has a triple of the form `<MyCustomers,supplier:po,processpo>`, a request to perform a purchase order by *Skateboard Warehouse* should be allowed.

We have now explored how to create an Axis authorization mechanism using JAAS. As we address enterprise application integration, we also need to consider authorization in the EJB security model. This topic will be covered in the section, "J2EE Security Model".

Security Assertions

So far, we have reviewed how to perform authorization on a single party. However, in an open e-Business world, many unfamiliar business entities might need to access our Web services. In this case, it is not desirable to set up usernames and passwords in the Web server configuration for every possible entity. In order to address authorization in this case, the idea of a *security assertion* is being discussed and standardized. In this section, we review the concept of a security assertion, referring to the architecture mode of the *Security Assertion Markup Language* (*SAML*) 📖. We won't review SAML syntax because the current syntax is subject to change.

SAML defines an XML document layout specifying the following security assertions:

- Authentication assertion
- Attribute assertion
- Decision assertion

These assertions are produced by their respective *authorities*. In some cases, the authorities are located within the same company that hosts the Web service, but they could be located anywhere on the Internet. Especially in the latter case, interoperability is important, and thus SAML is defined in the XML format.

Figure 5.11 illustrates how two parties can interact with each other via a security assertion authority. First, POClient sends a request to the authority with a user ID and password. The authority authenticates the requestor, and issues a document that contains authentication and attribute assertions. For example, the document says the requestor is the Skateboard Warehouse, and the company is ranked AA (very good). POClient sends a purchase order attaching the security assertion to POService as a SOAP header. Then, POService performs authorization, completely relying on the received assertion.

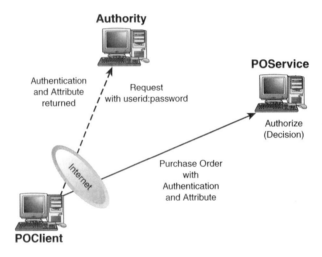

FIGURE 5.11
Interaction with security assertion authority.

A security assertion document is a kind of ticket. The identity of the carrier is not authenticated by the receiver. This implies the possibility of a *single sign-on* 📖 for distributed, multiparty Internet services. Furthermore, the ticket idea also ensures the anonymity of the requestor, because the requestor does not have to show its identity to the target service.

We can expect that standardized security assertions will have a big impact on business because with them, companies no longer have to manage authentication information on all companies they trade information with. The current world of e-Business consists solely of transactions among familiar companies. Given trusted third parties to play the role of assertion authorities, an open-ended, more flexible, and more scaleable e-Business infrastructure is possible. Standardized security assertions via conventions like SAML provides a technology basis to accomplish such a business structure.

Public Key Infrastructure and Key Management

To complete the security discussion, this section covers Public Key Infrastructure (PKI). So far, we have assumed that we can obtain the public key representing a given entity for purposes of encryption and digital signature. However, how can we know the public key is authentic and really represents the entity whose name is on it? PKI provides a basis to ensure the authenticity of all retrieved public keys.

The process that ensures key authenticity is key management, which breaks down into registration and retrieval. Recently, the XML Key Management Specification (XKMS) has been published. Directly accessing PKI requires users to do secure key generation and exchange on their own, but key management is much simpler with XKMS.

In the rest of this section, we give an overview of PKI, reviewing its key constructs, and present the XKMS standard for key management.

Public Key Infrastructure

PKI seems complicated because it combines a large number of technologies and concepts. But you only need to know that its main goal is to provide a mechanism to ensure proof of identity. The thing used to prove an identity is called a *certificate*. In order to manage certificates, there needs to be an issuer(s) of certificates, called a *certificate authority*, and a stored collection of certificates, called a *certificate repository*. These three constructs are central in PKI.

A *certificate* is a proof of identity. With a certificate, you can relate an entity to its public key. Because the certificate itself is digitally signed, you can trust its contents as long as you can trust the issuer. The X509 Certificate, which is the most popular certificate format, will be described in more detail later.

A *certificate authority* (*CA*) is an entity that issues certificates. If you can trust the CA, you can trust certificates issued by the CA. PKI assumes a fairly small number of CAs (such as VeriSign) and allows a CA to issue certificates for other CAs. As a result, certificates are organized into a hierarchy, as shown in Figure 5.12. The root is called a *root CA*, intermediary nodes are called *subordinate CAs*, and terminal nodes are called *end entities*. The path for an end entity to a root CA is called a *certificate path* 📖. If two end entities have a common CA, they can establish trust with each other.

A *certificate repository* (CR) is a public database from which end entities can get certificates. Although CRs are often developed on top of a *Lightweight Directory Access Protocol* (LDAP) server, they can be developed in any way (for example, based on an HTTP server). Furthermore, it is still very common to omit the CR in real cases, such as when certificates are exchanged via floppy disks.

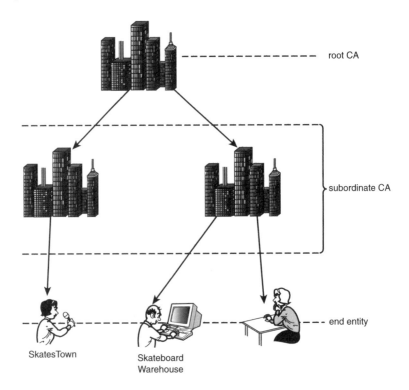

FIGURE 5.12
PKI trust model.

In addition, certificates can be revoked for various reasons. For example, private keys can be stolen or lost. A CA must distribute a *Certificate Revocation List* (CRL) to warn everyone not to accept the associated certificate as proof of identity in such cases. End entities must check the CRL as well as the certificate path.

Let's take a closer look at X.509 Certificate Version 3. Its main constructs are summarized as follows:

- *Version*—Version of X.509 Certificate, such as version 3.
- *Serial Number*—A unique identifier for the issuer.
- *Signature*—Algorithm for digital signature, such as Sha1WithRSAEncryption.
- *Issuer*—ID of the issuer specified by Distinguished Name (DN), such as "C=JP, ST=Kanagawa, L=Yamato, O=IBM, OU=TRL, CN=CA Admin/Email=caadmin@jp.ibm.com"
- *Validity*—Duration of validity, specified by start and end dates.
- *Subject*—ID of the owner, specified by DN.
- *Subject Public Key Info*—Public key and its algorithm. A typical example of an algorithm is RSAEncryption.

You might notice that an X.509 Certificate defines only the technical details of the certificate concept—for example, that the owner (subject) and the public key are related, and the relationship is digitally signed.

XML Key Management Specification (XKMS)

From an application point of view, our immediate concern should be how to manage certificates and public keys. PKI defines a collection of operations on certificates, such as retrieval, registration, backup, revocation, recovery, and so on. With XKMS, applications can interact using PKI without focusing on the myriad of fine details in PKI such as ASN.1.

XKMS was published as a W3C Note in March 2001 by VeriSign, Microsoft, and WebMethods. XKMS has two major components: XML Key Information Service Specification (X-KISS), and XML Key Registration Service Specification (X-KRSS). One of the main goals of XKMS is to complement the emerging W3C standards, such as XML Digital Signature and XML Encryption. Actually, key information is represented by the ds:KeyInfo element defined by XML Digital Signature.

Let's examine X-KISS with a digital signature example. Listing 5.15 is a modified SOAP message including a digital signature.

LISTING 5.15 SOAP Digital Signature with a Distinguished Name

```
<SOAP-ENV:Envelope
   xmlns:SOAP-ENV="http://schemas.xmlsoap.org/soap/envelope/">
   <SOAP-ENV:Header>
      <SOAP-SEC:Signature
         SOAP-ENV:actor=""
         SOAP-ENV:mustUnderstand="1"
         xmlns:SOAP-ENV="http://schemas.xmlsoap.org/soap/envelope/"
         xmlns:SOAP-SEC="http://schemas.xmlsoap.org/soap/security/2000-12">
         <dsig:Signature xmlns:dsig="http://www.w3.org/2000/09/xmldsig#">
            <dsig:SignedInfo>
               ...
            </dsig:SignedInfo>
            <dsig:SignatureValue>
               ... Base64-encoded Signature Value...
            </dsig:SignatureValue>
            <dsig:KeyInfo xmlns="http://www.w3.org/2000/09/xmldsig#">
               <dsig:KeyName>
➡              CN=Purchase Order Client,
➡              OU=Purchase Department, O=SkateboardWarehouse,
➡              L=..., S=NY, C=US
➡           </dsig:KeyName>
            </dsig:KeyInfo>
         </dsig:Signature>
      </SOAP-SEC:Signature>
   </SOAP-ENV:Header>
   <SOAP-ENV:Body>
      <t:po id="43871" submitted="2001-10-05">
         <t:nonce>2001-10-05T12:13:14Z</t:nonce>
.        ...
      </t:po>
   </SOAP-ENV:Body>
</SOAP-ENV:Envelope>
```

The KeyName element under KeyInfo specifies only the DN of the certificate owner, and there is no longer any detailed certificate information. For signature verification, we need the public key. The key value of the public key can be retrieved via X-KISS, as in Listing 5.16.

LISTING 5.16   Query for Retrieving a Key Value

```
<SOAP-ENV:Envelope xmlns:SOAP-ENV="http://schemas.xmlso ap.org/soap/envelope/">
  <SOAP-ENV:Body>
    <Locate xmlns="http://www.xkms.org/schema/xkms-2001-01-20">
      <Query>
        <KeyInfo xmlns="http://www.w3.org/2000/09/xmldsig#">
          <KeyName>
➥         CN=Purchase Order Client, OU=Purchase Department,
➥         O=SkateboardWarehouse, L=..., S=NY, C=US</KeyName>
        </KeyInfo>
      </Query>
      <Respond>
        <string>KeyValue</string>
      </Respond>
    </Locate>
  </SOAP-ENV:Body>
</SOAP-ENV:Envelope>
```

The Locate element includes a query on KeyInfo, and a format of the response. This message
requests a public key for the DN specified by the KeyName element. Listing 5.17 shows its
response.

LISTING 5.17   Response for the Key Value Query

```
<SOAP-ENV:Envelope xmlns:SOAP-ENV="http://schemas.xmlsoap.org/soap/envelope/" >
  <SOAP-ENV:Body>
    <LocateResult xmlns="http://www.xkms.org/schema/xkms-2001-01-20">
      <Result>Success</Result>
      <Answer>
        <KeyInfo xmlns="http://www.w3.org/2000/09/xmldsig#">
          <KeyValue>
            <DSAKeyValue>
              <P>
                  /X9TgR11EilS30qcLuzk5/YRt1I870QAwx4/gLZRJmlFXUAiUftZPY1
➥             Y+r/F9bow9sbVWzXgTuAHTRv8mZgt2uZUKWkn5/oBHsQIsJPu6nX/rf
➥             GG/g7V+fGqKYVDwT7g/bTxR7DAjVUE1oWkTL2dfOuK2HXKu/yIgMZnd
➥             FIAcc=
              </P>
              <Q>12BQjxUjC8yykrmCouuEC/BYHPU=</Q>
```

LISTING 5.17   Continued

```
                    <G>
                        9+GghdabPd7LvKtcNrhXuXmUr7v6OuqC+VdMCz0HgmdRWVeOutRZT+Z
➥       xBxCBgLRJFn
                        Ej6EwoFhO3zwkyjMim4TwWeotUfI0o4KOuHiuzpnWRbqN/C/ohNWLx+
➥       2J6ASQ7zKTx
                        vqhRkImog9/hWuWfBpKLZ16Ae1UlZAFMO/7PSSo=

                    </G>
                    <Y>
                        Q9N/x1cj2LSaV9ZdKPl0Sl9HhqbBdloc/AvxvY41sQREau9s/HmPwFd
➥       Tgn6iRCdXrg
                        Y2HaiQYOlBdt09UW+q2XjvY1vdrWhXlxy8VdSFEdMCla926o38igZjF
➥       qXF0LOlBKTK
                        LQTsCzWWxDB6sK8LkvaUikUFpudYa/rWP562GUI=
                    </Y>
                </DSAKeyValue>
            </KeyValue>
        </KeyInfo>
      </Answer>
    </LocateResult>
  </SOAP-ENV:Body>
</SOAP-ENV:Envelope>
```

The value of the public key is included in KeyValue element. With this value, we can verify the signature of the initial SOAP message.

As shown in the example, X-KISS helps applications obtain cryptographic key information. In addition to key value retrieval, it can be used to validate a binding between a key name and key value. It is also useful for getting key information from an X.509 certificate. In a complementary way, X-KRSS provides key registration, revocation, and recovery services.

Although we reviewed interactions between applications and XKMS servers, how do XKMS servers interact with PKI entities such as CAs and CRs? Unfortunately, XKMS is just an interface, and therefore it does not prescribe how XKMS servers should behave. XKMS could be used to support certificate-less keys when full-featured PKI is not required. However, XKMS is most valuable if XKMS servers provide a lightweight interface to PKI. In that case, a XKMS server could cache the certificate path and CRL when it receives a key registration or retrieval request, and then periodically check the CRL to keep its database up-to-date.

One of the important aspects of XKMS is that key management functions are provided in terms of Web services. In this way, complex certificate processing logic is abstracted away from applications and into server-side components. Furthermore, key management could be administered at a single point within an entire enterprise. This is advantageous for simplifying enterprise management.

How to Get Started with Security

So far, Dean Caroll of SkatesTown has a pretty good understanding of the security architecture for SOAP and the technologies available in this area. The acceptance and maturation of each technology is quite different, however. For example, BASIC-AUTH and SSL are widely accepted, and adopting them is not a problem. On the other hand, the new SAML proposal does not even have an initial specification.

Al Rosen suggests that SkatesTown should begin with digital signatures in addition to BASIC-AUTH and SSL. A signature is immediately required for non-repudiation, and XML Signature is now a proposed recommendation. Al also recommends adding encryption and authorization once digital signatures are in place.

A working group has just been formed for XML Encryption, so its specification can still change drastically. As for authorization, we are not sure whether JAAS will be broadly accepted. We need to see how it converges with the EJB authorization model, as we described in the "EJB Security" section. SAML and non-repudiation services are under discussion, and they are worth keeping an eye on. Finally, although there are few XKMS products, you should try one of them; WSTK 2.4 includes a demonstration. XKMS can drastically decrease the workload to integrate your systems with PKI.

Enterprise Application Integration

In real business situations, it is not sufficient to develop Web applications with servlets alone. Integration of existing applications and business processes is more important. SkatesTown has a number of legacy applications such as order management, inventory management, and delivery systems, and is eager to integrate them. This process is called Enterprise Application Integration (EAI).

A basis for EAI must be interaction models that support synchronous and/or asynchronous interactions among applications. The interaction models should include coordination of transactions over applications and a secure execution environment. Robustness, flexibility, and scalability are also required to implement the models.

In this section, we describe Java 2 Enterprise Edition (J2EE) as a vehicle to perform EAI. Enterprise Java Beans (EJBs) provide a message-oriented and object-oriented component interaction model that supports both synchronous and asynchronous interactions. J2EE is a framework to integrate EJBs and other Web application components such as the servlet container. With J2EE, a request to a servlet can be performed within a transaction context in a secure manner.

The rest of this section is structured as follows: First, we review a typical SOAP server architecture for EAI on the basis of J2EE. Transactions and reliable messaging are respectively described in the context of the SOAP server architecture. Finally, we review the J2EE security model, referring to the previous section.

SOAP Server Based on J2EE

The J2EE specification addresses the development of new business services that combine many of the new, best-of-breed applications while leveraging previous investments in legacy systems. Because these services are architected as multitier applications including Web clients, Web servers, servlet containers, application servers, and databases, the main goal of J2EE is to reduce the cost and complexity of developing these multitier services, resulting in services that can be rapidly deployed and easily enhanced. Accordingly, J2EE is a meta-specification over a collection of existing Java standards as follows:

- *Servlet*—The HTTP server-side API to process HTTP requests and to return HTTP responses.
- *Java Server Page (JSP)*—A text-based solution to process a request to create a response. More specifically, you can include Java programs in HTML documents.
- *Enterprise Java Beans (EJB)*—A standard component architecture for building distributed object-oriented applications, especially strongly combined with database systems.
- *Java Database Connectivity (JDBC)*—The API for connectivity with database systems.
- *Java Message Service (JMS)*—A standard API for messaging that supports reliable point-to-point messaging, as well as the publish-subscribe model.
- *Java Naming and Directory Interface (JNDI)*—The standard API for naming and directory access.
- *JavaMail*—The standard API to send e-mail notifications.
- *JavaBeans Activation Framework (JAF)*—A framework to handle an arbitrary piece of data, such as MIME byte streams. The JavaMail API uses the JAF API, so it must be included as well.

We will not examine all these specifications. Rather, we'll consider how to architect a SOAP server on top of J2EE. Figure 5.13 shows an initial cut of the SOAP server architecture that takes into account EAI. In this architecture, the front-end is an HTTP server, and a servlet container sits next to it. The server hosts a SOAP engine (for example, Axis), which is the heart of a SOAP server. At the back end, we might have an application server—that is, an EJB container, database, or collection of business applications.

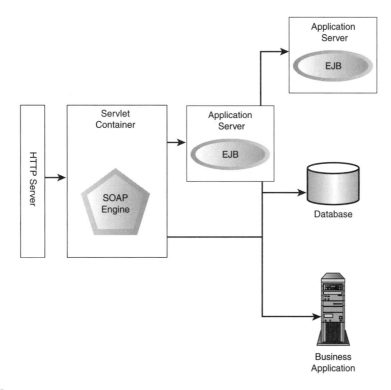

FIGURE 5.13
SOAP server on J2EE architecture.

In the simplest case, we only have a Java program within a servlet container as in most examples mentioned so far. The Java program can access a database via JDBC, or invoke a business application via JMS. An application can be provided as an EJB (hosted by the application server). The EJB can invoke a database, a business application, or even another EJB object hosted by another application server.

5

USING **SOAP** FOR
E-BUSINESS

One of key features of J2EE is transaction support. The next section describes transactions in terms of the path of SOAP engines, EJB objects, and databases. In addition, reliable messaging is discussed, especially taking JMS into account. J2EE provides a security model that includes authorization to EJB. The J2EE security model is also discussed, clarifying further requirements for the SOAP server.

Transaction Processing

So far, our purchase order example had been simplified so that we could focus on addressing SOAP features. However, in reality, the process is much more complicated because we might have to integrate multiple applications, data, and even business processes. In this section, we extend the purchase order example to include a *transaction* 📖, which is a widely used computational model for constructing reliable and available distributed applications.

We include two databases in our purchase order example: Product and Order. The Product database stores product information, such as name, type, and description. Furthermore, inventory management is performed with this database so that only products in stock are sold. The Order database records purchase orders that are accepted.

We have to extend our purchase order program to integrate the Product and Order databases. There are two operations in this new context:

1. Update the Product database to reduce the amount of inventory on hand based on how many of each product the customer orders.

2. Update the Order database to add a record of the purchase order.

However, simply executing these operations sequentially is not sufficient because the application might fail just after completing the first operation. In this case, the stock number in the Product database is decreased, but the order is not recorded. The result of the application should be *all or nothing*—that is, all of the operations must complete, or none of the operations should be allowed to complete. Such a requirement is called *atomicity* and is one of key properties of transaction processing. In addition to atomicity, transactions should have three other properties: *consistency*, *isolation*, and *durability*. These properties will be described more in detail after we review how our program can be implemented with EJB.

With EJB, data resources are represented as Java objects, and transaction processing over the objects is ensured. Figure 5.14 illustrates an overview of the purchase order program, which incorporates databases with EJB. A Product object in the EJB container corresponds to a record in the product table. In the same manner, an Order object corresponds to a record in the order table. These EJB objects are called *Entity Beans* 📖 because they represent entities in data resources.

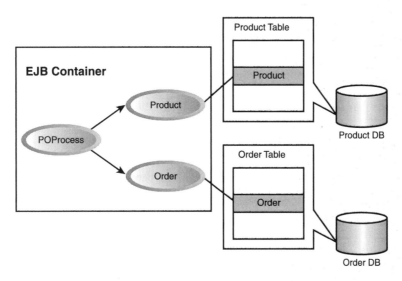

FIGURE 5.14
Purchase order processing with EJB.

On the other hand, the POProcess object reads and updates data in a database on behalf of the client. A *Session Bean* 📖 is an EJB object that performs business logic on behalf of a client in a distributed, transactional context. When the POProcess object receives a client request, it reads and updates databases via Product and Order objects. Although it is complicated to update the date on multiple resources during transaction processing, the EJB container provides a simple way to perform transactions.

Let's review our EJB objects. When providing EJB objects, we must implement a *home interface* 📖, remote interface, and component implementation. As a result, nine Java classes should be provided, as listed in Table 5.2. Note that *Container Managed Persistence* (*CMP*) 📖 will be described in more detail in the examples.

TABLE 5.2   EJB Classes for Purchase Order Program

EJB Type	Home Interface	Remote Interface	Component Implementation
CMP Entity Bean	ProductHome	Product	ProductBean
CMP Entity Bean	OrderHome	Order	OrderBean
Session Bean	POProcessHome	POProcess	POProcessBean

Let's take a closer look at some of these EJBs. Listing 5.18 is the definition of the Product EJB. Product is an interface for a product, so it defines a collection of methods to get and set data fields, such as SKU, Name, Type, and so on. POProcess uses this interface to look up and update the fields.

LISTING 5.18   Definition of the Product Interface

```
public interface Product extends javax.ejb.EJBObject {
    String getSKU() throws java.rmi.RemoteException;
    void setSKU(String newValue) throws java.rmi.RemoteException;
    String getName() throws java.rmi.RemoteException;
    void setName(String newValue) throws java.rmi.RemoteException;
    String getType() throws java.rmi.RemoteException;
    void setType(String newValue) throws java.rmi.RemoteException;
    String getDesc() throws java.rmi.RemoteException;
    void setDesc(String newValue) throws java.rmi.RemoteException;
    int getPrice() throws java.rmi.RemoteException;
    void setPrice(int newValue) throws java.rmi.RemoteException;
    int getInStock() throws java.rmi.RemoteException;
    void setInStock(int newValue) throws java.rmi.RemoteException;
}
```

ProductBean is the implementation of Product; therefore, it defines the set/get methods and data fields for them. In addition, it implements a collection of methods defined by the EntityBean interface, such as ejbCreate, ebjLoad, ejbActivate, and so on (see Listing 5.19). These methods are derived from an EJB object lifecycle model. The lifecycle model is beyond the scope of this book, so interested readers should refer to the EJB specification.

LISTING 5.19   ProductBean Class

```
public class ProductBean implements EntityBean {
    private javax.ejb.EntityContext entityContext = null;
    public String sku;
    public int price;
    public String name;
    public String type;
    public String desc;
    public int inStock;

    public void ejbActivate() throws java.rmi.RemoteException {}
    public String ejbCreate(java.lang.String sku)
        throws javax.ejb.CreateException, java.rmi.RemoteException
```

LISTING 5.19 Continued

```
{
    this.sku = sku;
    return sku;
}
public void ejbLoad() throws java.rmi.RemoteException {}
public void ejbPassivate() throws java.rmi.RemoteException {}
public void ejbPostCreate(java.lang.String argProductId)
    throws java.rmi.RemoteException {}
public void ejbRemove()
    throws java.rmi.RemoteException,
            javax.ejb.RemoveException {}
public void ejbStore() throws java.rmi.RemoteException {}
public javax.ejb.EntityContext getEntityContext() {
    return entityContext;
}
public void setEntityContext(javax.ejb.EntityContext ctx)
    throws java.rmi.RemoteException
{
    entityContext = ctx;
}
public void unsetEntityContext() throws java.rmi.RemoteException {
    entityContext = null;
}

public String getSKU() {
    return sku;
}
public void setSKU(String newValue) {
    this.sku = newValue;
}
public String getName() {
    return name;
}
public void setName(String newValue) {
    this.name = newValue;
}
public String getType() {
    return type;
}
public void setType(String newValue) {
    this.type = newValue;
}
```

LISTING 5.19   Continued

```
    public String getDesc() {
        return this.desc;
    }
    public void setDesc(String newValue) {
        this.desc = newValue;
    }
    public int getPrice() {
        return price;
    }
    public void setPrice(int newValue) {
        this.price = newValue;
    }
    public int getInStock() {
        return inStock;
    }
    public void setInStock(int newValue) {
        this.inStock = newValue;
    }
}
```

As you can see, defining `Product` and `ProductBean` is pretty easy, because doing so is almost the same as creating ordinary Java programs. Now, how do you relate `Product` to the database? You do not have to change the program at all; rather, you can define the mapping to database at deployment time. It is worthwhile to mention that EJB programs are deployed with *deployment descriptors*, each of which declares all the EJB's external dependencies (such as the names of resources that the EJB uses).

Listing 5.20 is a definition for `Product` excerpted from the deployment descriptor of our application. As you can see, it defines that `Product` is a CMP bean (see `persisence-type` element), specifying which fields of the CMP bean are managed by the EJB container. Note that how these fields are persisted is left to each vendor. It also must be noted that Listing 5.20 is an EJB 1.1 style deployment descriptor that is different from the format defined for EJB 2.0.

LISTING 5.20   Deployment Descriptor for the Product EJB

```
    <entity>
      <display-name>Product</display-name>
      <ejb-name>Product</ejb-name>
      <home>ProductHome</home>
      <remote>Product</remote>
      <ejb-class>ProductBean</ejb-class>
```

LISTING 5.20   Continued

```
      <persistence-type>Container</persistence-type>
      <prim-key-class>java.lang.String</prim-key-class>
      <reentrant>False</reentrant>
      <cmp-version>1.x</cmp-version>
      <cmp-field>
        <description>no description</description>
        <field-name>name</field-name>
      </cmp-field>
      <cmp-field>
        <description>no description</description>
        <field-name>type</field-name>
      </cmp-field>
      <cmp-field>
        <description>no description</description>
        <field-name>inStock</field-name>
      </cmp-field>
      <cmp-field>
        <description>no description</description>
        <field-name>price</field-name>
      </cmp-field>
      <cmp-field>
        <description>no description</description>
        <field-name>desc</field-name>
      </cmp-field>
      <cmp-field>
        <description>no description</description>
        <field-name>sku</field-name>
      </cmp-field>
      <primkey-field>sku</primkey-field>
      <security-identity>
        <description></description>
        <use-caller-identity></use-caller-identity>
      </security-identity>
    </entity>
```

Product, ProductHome, and ProductBeans are specified with home, remote, and ejb-class elements. persistence-type specifies a Container to indicate that this entity bean is CMP. The field-name element under cmp-field indicates a data field that is included in ProductBean and will appear as a column name in a database table.

Because the definition of Order is inherently the same as Product, we move on to the POProcess session bean. Its core portion can be found in POProcessBean.order(). Listing 5.21 is a portion of POProcessBean.

LISTING 5.21   POProcessBean Class

```
public class POProcessBean implements SessionBean {
    public Order order(String shipId, String billId, String sku, int quantity)
        throws POProcessException
    {
        try {
            Product product  = productHome.findByPrimaryKey(sku);
            if (quantity>product.getInStock()) {
                throw( new POProcessException("Stock is not enough"));
            }
            product.setInStock(product.getInStock()-quantity);
            Order order  = orderHome.create(""+System.currentTimeMillis());
            System.out.println("order class: " + order.getClass() );
            order.setBillTo(billId);
            order.setShipTo(shipId);
            order.setSKU(sku);
            order.setProductName(product.getName());
            order.setQuantity(quantity);
            int total=quantity*product.getPrice();
            order.setTotalPrice(total);
            if (total>MAX_TOTAL) {
                throw( new POProcessException("Exceed the max charge
                ("+MAX_TOTAL+")"));
            }
            return order;
        } catch(POProcessException e) {
            mySessionContext.setRollbackOnly();
            throw e;
        } catch(RemoteException e) {
            throw new EJBException("Fail in Order.order: " +e.getMessage());
        } catch(CreateException e) {
            throw new EJBException("Fail in Order.order: " +e.getMessage());
        } catch(FinderException e) {
            throw new EJBException("Fail in Order.order: " +e.getMessage());
        }
    }
}
```

In plain terms, the processes here are as follows:

1. Find a product based on a given SKU ID.

2. Update the inStock data field if the order quantity exceeds the stocked products.

3. Create an order based on the given request and the product information.

4. Place the order only if the total charge is less than a value (MAX_TOTAL).

The sequence of operations is performed within a transaction context although you see very few instructions related to transactions. If you use `UserTransaction` class, you invoke the `begin()` method to start a transaction, the `commit()` method to complete it, and the `rollback()` method to abort it. However, explicitly comitting and rolling back transactions is not a good practice. Rather, you are strongly advised to use container-managed transactions instead. If you take this approach, operations are performed automatically in a transactional context. Only if you want to allow rollback should you invoke `setRolebackOnly()` method of the `SessionContext` class as shown in the listing. For example, if the total charge is more than `MAX_TOTAL`, the update on `Product` and the creation of the `Order` object is undone.

ACID and Two-Phase Commit

So far, we have only mentioned atomicity. Now, we will review the four transaction properties known as *ACID (Atomicity, Consistency, Isolation*, and *Durability)* , and we will discuss the popular two-phase commit transaction protocol.

Atomicity ensures that a computation will either terminate normally, updating the involved data resources in the intended way, or abort, updating nothing. In other words, no intermediate situation can exist where data resources are partially updated. This property should be ensured even if there is a system failure. In our example without atomicity, if we encountered a system failure, we would have a situation in which the product database is updated, but the order database is not updated.

Consistency ensures that only consistent-state changes to data resources occur despite concurrent access and system failures. In our case, we have the following constraint over the product and order databases:

([initial stock]-[current stock])*price == [total charge in orders]

The consistency property relies on application programs to some extent, unlike other properties, because constraints on data are not explicitly represented. More specifically, such constraints are embedded in application logic; therefore, a transaction management system cannot monitor them.

Isolation ensures that concurrent computations do not interfere with each other. In other words, the result of concurrent execution of transactions should be equivalent to the case of sequential execution. In our example, the `inStock` field of `Product` is critical data, so it requires isolation. Assume that the stock is 10, and two transactions are executed, each of which requires 8 products. Without proper isolation, or a locking mechanism, both transactions would successfully terminate as long as they both satisfy the atomicity constraint.

Durability ensures that once the transaction terminates normally, its result is stored permanently. Generally speaking, termination of a transaction does not mean the completion of a database update; rather, it means that necessary information for updating is recorded. Therefore, this property is related to recovery from failure.

The *two-phase commit* *(TPC)*[gl] protocol is a broadly accepted solution for ensuring the ACID properties over distributed data resources. The TPC protocol defines two types of messages: "prepare" and "commit". To complete a transaction, these messages are sent to all data resources. However, the prepare and commit messages are never mixed; therefore, the completion phase is comprised of two phases: the prepare and commit phases. This simple principle is the basis for various transaction theories.

EJB wraps TPC protocols carefully so that application programmers can develop transaction processing easily and safely. Container-managed transaction is a typical example to simplify development. In summary, EJB lets you develop transaction processing properly without worrying about the details of transaction theories.

Executing EJB from Axis

In this section, we execute the EJB version of the purchase order with Axis. Go to `/ch5/ex5/index.jsp` in the example navigator. Through the page, you can specify the shipping ID, billing ID, SKU, and quantity, and issue a purchase order (see Figure 5.15). As long as the database indicates that sufficient quantity exists to fill the order, you receive an invoice. Otherwise, you receive an error message.

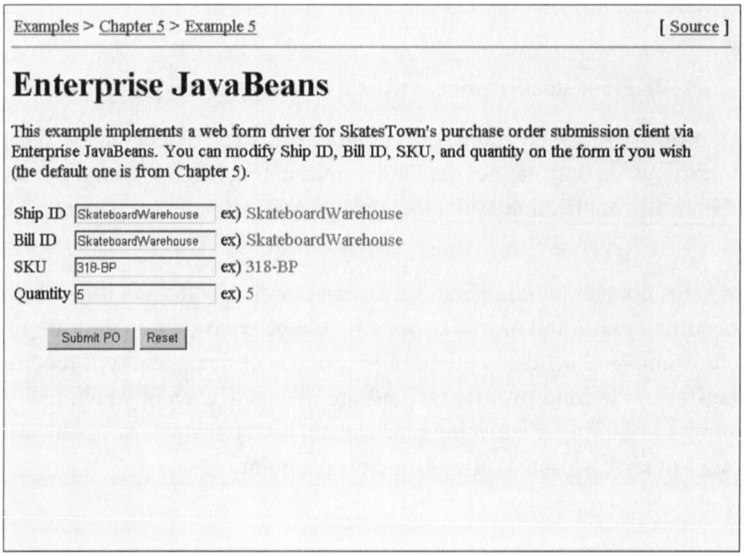

FIGURE 5.15

Example navigator GUI to invoke EJB purchase order.

Listing 5.22 shows a SOAP client program for the purchase order.

LISTING 5.22   Client Code for Invoking an EJB Service

```
public class POProcessClient {
    private String url;
    private String urn;
    public POProcessClient(String targetUrl, String serviceUrn)
    {
        url = targetUrl;
        urn = serviceUrn;
    }
    public OrderData order(String shipid, String billid,
                           String sku, int quantity)
        throws Exception
    {
        ServiceClient client = new ServiceClient(endpointURL);
        OrderData order =
            (OrderData)client.invoke(urn, "order",
                    new Object[] {shipid, billid, sku, new Integer(quantity)});
        return order;
    }
}
```

As you can see, there is no difference from ordinary *Remote Procedure Call* (*RPC*) 📖 invocations at the client side. At the server side, some Universal Resource Name (URN) such as urn:X-SkatesTown:EJBPOService is bound to an EJB object of the POProcess class instead of a Java object. If the member variable urn in POProcessClient is urn:X-SkatesTown:EJBPOService, the RPC request from the client is dispatched to the EJB object as in an ordinary RPC invocation.

Using EJB with SOAP Engines

Let's examine how we can use EJB with SOAP engines. Our motivation for introducing EJB was to carry out EAI. EJB objects can be published externally through a SOAP engine. The example in this section has demonstrated that you can integrate multiple databases even when they are distributed in a complicated configuration. However, you might also want to integrate other kinds of applications. For example, you might have an inventory management application instead of the product database in our example. In some cases, you can use a *Bean-Managed Persistence* (*BMP*) 📖 Entity Bean instead of a CMP Entity Bean.

Furthermore, the *J2EE Connector Architecture* 📖 Specification has been released and is much more sophisticated than the BMP Entity Bean for improving EAI. Although the J2EE Connector Architecture can be viewed as a generalization of JDBC connection pooling, it provides a good framework to integrate legacy applications, addressing connection pooling, transactions, and security. If you're going to perform EAI, you should check out J2EE Connector Architecture.

Once you understand EJB transaction processing capability, a question arises: Can the SOAP engine be improved with EJB? Axis currently provides a SOAP engine that works on top of the servlet container. Let's examine how to move the SOAP engine to an EJB container.

Figure 5.16 illustrates an architecture where a SOAP engine is located within an EJB container. Because requests are sent via various transports, there might be different types of listeners, such as SMTP Listeners, FTP Listeners, and HTTP Listeners. An HTTP Listener is developed as a servlet. Each listener delegates the incoming request to the EJB container via the *Remote Method Invocation over Internet Inter-ORB (RMI-IIOP) protocol* 📖. Once a request is received, the SOAP engine does not consult the transport listener again in the processing of that request.

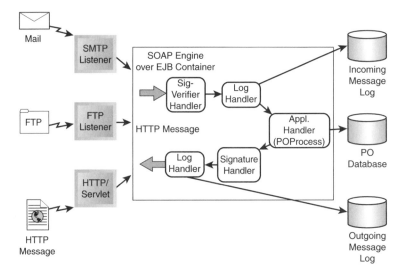

FIGURE 5.16
SOAP Engine within EJB Container

Within the SOAP engine, there are five handlers to process the request. First, the digital signature of the message is verified, then the message is logged, and the POProcess EJB is invoked to process the purchase order in the message. The response from POProcess, an invoice, is digitally signed and logged before being returned to the requestor.

In practice, the SOAP engine would be implemented as a *Stateless Session Bean* and would invoke the handler chain from the EJB. If you use container managed transactions, a transaction starts automatically when the SOAP engine is invoked. So, atomicity over the update of three databases is ensured within the transaction context. This architecture is especially useful in the case of a system failure. The system might fail during execution of the signature handler in Figure 5.16. In that case, we cannot return an invoice to the requestor, and we might want to roll back the previous operations. This architecture allows us to roll back the transaction automatically so that we do not have to worry about complicated recovery sequences.

A SOAP engine within a servlet can handle normal errors that are typically recognized by Java exceptions. However, it cannot handle system failures properly because such an engine does not record enough information for recovery. On the other hand, the EJB-based architecture is robust against system failure in the sense that a recovery sequence is automatically and properly carried out by the EJB container.

Transactions over the Internet

Dean Caroll of SkatesTown now realizes the advantages of using transactions to integrate legacy applications. Transactions ensure that application data is consistently updated and simplify error handling tremendously. However, he has one lingering concern: Can we use the transaction processing model for B2B collaboration over Internet?

There are some standardization efforts for modeling transaction processing onto B2B. *Transaction Internet Protocol* (TIP) 📖 provides a simplified two-phase commit protocol. TIP does not require a very large infrastructure, but it has not garnered broader support because of its complexity. *XML Transaction Authority Markup Language* (XAML) 📖 is another effort for representing transaction protocol in XML. It was announced in October 2000, but so far no specification has been published.

What is the key difficulty in managing transactions over the Internet? We need to keep the two-phase commitment (TPC) protocol in mind. According to the TPC protocol, a transaction manager sends prepare messages to resource managers, and eventually receives OK messages from them. Once a resource manager sends the OK message, it has to wait for a commit or abort message from the transaction manager. This suggests that the resource manager might have to wait a while for the message. Within an intranet, we can expect each system to be stable, and thus the network to be stable. However, we cannot expect the same level of stability when relying on other companies' systems using the Internet.

A more practical approach is to instead use *compensation transactions*, which have proper transaction models for the Internet. In our purchase order example, we can reconstruct the architecture to use compensation transactions by including two transactions (product and order databases updated with different transactions). Assume that the product database is successfully updated, but some problem occurs during the order creation. In that case, we issue a compensation transaction to cancel the update on the product database. Although ACID properties are not ensured here, many real cases can be covered with this protocol.

Reliable Messaging

The EJB architecture integrates object-oriented programming with transaction processing in an elegant way. Its distributed object architecture relies on a client-server model where the client sends a request and waits for a response from a server synchronously. This synchronous invocation model fits into transaction processing model we have thoroughly reviewed. However, the synchronous model has several limitations that are crucial for EAI.

Mainly, the problems are related to communication between the client and server. With a synchronous model, when a communication failure occurs, the client receives an error message. Accordingly, the client must send the identical request to the server later. In some cases, the client might not want to retry, but would prefer to have someone send the request when communication is restored.

This problem can be resolved by *message queuing* 📖, where the client puts a message on a queue, and the server gets a message from the queue. The message in the queue is often recorded in persistent storage; therefore, the message is sure to be sent to the server. Thus, message queuing is often called *reliable messaging* 📖 or *guaranteed message delivery* 📖. Furthermore, message queuing is closely related to transaction processing because the queue can be considered a transaction resource.

Let's examine Java Message Service (JMS), which is a standard API for message queuing systems. First, we will update our purchase order example to include JMS. Then, we will examine the EJB 2.0 *Message-driven Bean* 📖, which is asynchronously invoked to handle the processing of incoming JMS messages as in JMS applications. Finally, we consider how to adopt JMS as a SOAP transport.

Message Queuing with JMS

We could make our purchase order program more functional by assuming that there is an order management system instead of an order database. Figure 5.17 illustrates this extension including a message queue front-ending the order management system. POProcess puts order information in the queue, and proceeds to the next operation without blocking. On the other hand, the order management system asynchronously gets the information from the queue to record the order information.

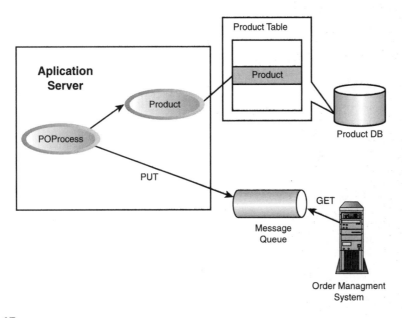

FIGURE 5.17

Application integration with message queue.

Let's rewrite our purchase order example using JMS. Listing 5.23 is a modification of
POProcessBean, namely, POProcessBeanJMS.

LISTING 5.23   POProcessBeanJMS Class

```
public class POProcessBeanJMS implements SessionBean {
    public OrderData order(String shipId, String billId, String sku, int
    quantity)
        throws POProcessException
    {
        try {
            Product product = productHome.findByPrimaryKey(sku);
            if (quantity > product.getInStock()) {
                throw new POProcessException("Stock is not enough");
            }
            product.setInStock(product.getInStock() - quantity);
            OrderData order = new OrderData("" + System.currentTimeMillis());
            order.setBillTo(billId);
            order.setShipTo(shipId);
```

LISTING 5.23 Continued

```
            order.setSKU(sku);
            order.setProductName(product.getName());
            order.setQuantity(quantity);
            int total = quantity * product.getPrice();
            order.setTotalPrice(total);
            queueConnectionFactory = (QueueConnectionFactory)
                jndiContext.lookup("QueueConnectionFactory");
            queue = (Queue)jndiContext.lookup(queueName);
            queueConnection =
                queueConnectionFactory.createQueueConnection();
            queueSession =
                queueConnection.createQueueSession(false,
                    Session.AUTO_ACKNOWLEDGE);
            queueSender = queueSession.createSender(queue);
            ObjectMessage message = queueSession.createObjectMessage();
            message.setObject(order);
            queueSender.send(message);
            if (total > MAX_TOTAL) {
                throw new POProcessException("Exceed the max charge (" +
                            MAX_TOTAL + ")");
            }
            return order;
        } catch(POProcessException e) {
            mySessionContext.setRollbackOnly();
            throw e;
        } catch(RemoteException e) {
            throw new EJBException("Fail in Order.order: " +e.getMessage());
        } catch(Exception e) {
            throw new EJBException("Fail in Order.order: " +e.getMessage());
        }
    }
}
```

Note that the entity bean Order is replaced by a Java class OrderData. The typical way of using JMS, as shown in bold in the program, is as follows:

1. Look up QueueConnectionFactory and a queue via JNDI.

2. Create a connection and a session object to access a queue manager.

3. Create a queue sender object.

4. Create a message object and send it.

Because queues can be transaction resources, they adhere to transaction management. More specifically, when the order() method is invoked in Listing 5.23, a transaction starts automatically. Then, only when the method successfully exits is a commit message sent to the queue manager. The message is then placed into the queue where the server can get it.

Let's look at the server side, namely `OrderManagementListener`, which is the front end of the order management system. Listing 5.24 is an `OrderManagementListener` class that gets order messages from the queue.

LISTING 5.24   `OrderManagementListener` Class

```java
public class OrderManagementListener implements MessageListener {
    public static void main(String[] args) {

        ...................
        try {
            jndiContext = new InitialContext();
            queueConnectionFactory = (QueueConnectionFactory)
                jndiContext.lookup("QueueConnectionFactory");
            queue = (Queue) jndiContext.lookup(queueName);
            queueConnection =
                queueConnectionFactory.createQueueConnection();
            queueSession =
                queueConnection.createQueueSession(false,
                    Session.AUTO_ACKNOWLEDGE);
            queueReceiver = queueSession.createReceiver(queue);
            queueConnection.start();
            queueReceiver.setMessageListener(this);


            ......

        } catch (Exception e) {
        } finally {
            if (queueConnection != null) {
                try {
                    queueConnection.close();
                } catch (JMSException e) {}
            }
        }
    }
    public void onMessage(javax.jms.Message msg) {
        if(msg instanceof ObjectMessage) {
            ObjectMessage message = (ObjectMessage)msg;
            OrderData order = (OrderData)message.getObject();
            // invoke order management system
        } else {
            // do something
        }
    }}
```

Unlike on the client side, a queue receiver object is created to get messages from the queue. We extract an `OrderData` object from a JMS message, then invoke the order management system with the order data. Again, the message is received only when a transaction is committed at the client side.

You can integrate applications in a loosely coupled and extensible manner with message queuing. First, the client does not have to know who receives the message. Second, even if the server is not available because of a server failure or communication problem, the client can still continue to send requests as long as the queue is available. In addition, load balancing is also possible by simply adding replications of the server.

Message-driven Bean

One of main improvements in EJB 2.0 is the introduction of the Message-driven Bean (MDB). MDB improves the programming of the server side although it does not affect the client side at all.

Let's look at `OrderManagementListener` again. It is a standalone Java program; therefore, transaction management is not provided at all. You might want to invoke your order management system within a transaction context. MDBs meet such a requirement.

Listing 5.25 is `OrderManagementMDB`. The functionality is the same as `OrderManagementListener`, but there is no code to set up a queue connection and session. In other words, basic operations for getting a message from the queue are performed by an EJB platform; accordingly, MDB just receives the dispatched messages. More importantly, the `onMessage()` method is executed in a transactional context. Note that if transaction rolls back, the message receipt is also rolled back (in other words, the message is put back on the queue).

LISTING 5.25   `OrderManagementMDB` Class

```
public class OrderManagementMDB implements MessageDrivenBean {

    public void onMessage(Message inMessage) {
        ObjectMessage msg = null;
        try {
            if (inMessage instanceof ObjectMessage) {
                msg = (ObjectMessage)inMessage;
                OrderData order = (OrderData)msg.getObject();
                // Invoke order management system
            } else {
            }
        } catch (Exception e) {}
    }

}
```

Although OrderManagementMDB defines four methods, only `onMessage()` is shown here. In contrast to `OrderManagementListener`, a procedure for receiving messages from the queue is not necessary. So, this class can focus on extracting the `OrderData` object and invoking the order management system.

MDB is convenient; however, we need an EJB container for performing it. On the other hand, the JMS client can be a standalone Java program like `OrderManagementListener`. In some cases, you might use JMS directly (you might not have a proper EJB container in your platform).

JMS As a SOAP Transport

Because SOAP is transport-agnostic, you can use JMS for its transport instead of HTTP. Furthermore, the concept of an intermediary suggests that SOAP messages can be routed to multiple nodes via different transports. Figure 5.18 illustrates a possible configuration that contains both concepts. Inter-company communication is performed via HTTP(S). The receiver company has a SOAP intermediary that receives SOAP messages via HTTP and forwards them to backend applications via JMS. The key idea here is that the external firewall allows HTTP to pass, whereas the internal firewall allows only JMS.

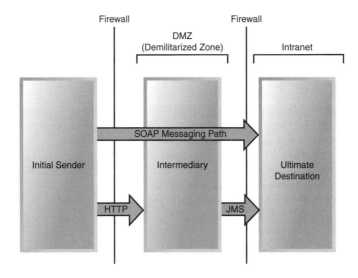

FIGURE 5.18
SOAP messaging that includes both HTTP and JMS.

This configuration is typical for several reasons. First, you can augment message processing by adding functions to an intermediary without changing the backend applications. For example, you might add digital signature verification and logging functions there. Even in that case, you do not have to change the backend applications. In addition, some companies do not want to accept HTTP through their internal firewall for security reasons. However, strictly speaking, simply eliminating HTTP does not necessarily improve the security level. The intermediary also plays a role of security domain boundary; for example, credential mapping from external IDs to internal IDs is performed.

SOAP JMS transport is necessary especially for enterprise customers. Although Axis does not currently support JMS transport, a prototype implementation is provided in our examples. Listing 5.26 is an excerpt from the JMSSender class for the requestor side.

LISTING 5.26   JMSSender Class

```
public class JMSSender extends BasicHandler {
    private void sendMessage(MessageContext msgContext, String messageTxt)
        throws AxisFault {
        BytesMessage msg;
        try {
            queueConnection = queueFactory.createQueueConnection();
            queueSession =
              queueConnection.createQueueSession(false,
                                            Session.AUTO_ACKNOWLEDGE);
            queueSender = queueSession.createSender(queue);
            msg = queueSession.createBytesMessage();
            msg.writeUTF(messageTxt);
            TemporaryQueue replyTo = queueSession.createTemporaryQueue();
            msg.setJMSReplyTo(replyTo);
            queueSender.send(msg);
            queueConnection.start();
            QueueReceiver receiver = queueSession.createReceiver(replyTo);
            javax.jms.Message replyMsg = receiver.receive();
            if (replyMsg instanceof BytesMessage) {
                String replyTxt = ((BytesMessage)replyMsg).readUTF();
                org.apache.axis.Message respMsg =
                  new org.apache.axis.Message(replyTxt);
                msgContext.setResponseMessage(respMsg);
            }
            closeConnection();
        } catch (JMSException e) {
            throw new AxisFault("JMSSender.sendMessage",
                        "JMSException: " + e, null, null);
        }
    }
    ......
}
```

The sendMessage() method in the class implements a synchronous request/response by combining two JMS messages. It creates a temporary queue for a response, sets it as the reply-to queue in the request message, and sends the message to a request queue. Then, it waits until a response message is delivered to the temporary queue.

Listing 5.27 is a portion of the JMSListener class for the service provider side.

LISTING 5.27   JMSListener Class

```
public class JMSListener implements MessageListener {
    public void onMessage(javax.jms.Message msg) {
        BytesMessage bytesMsg = null;
        org.apache.axis.Message respMessage = null;
        MessageContext msgContext = null;
        String msgTxt = null;
        AxisEngine engine = AxisServer.getSingleton();
        msgContext = new MessageContext(engine);
        try {
            if (!msg instanceof BytesMessage) {
                // do error handling ......
            }
            bytesMsg = (BytesMessage) msg;
            replyQueue = (Queue)(bytesMsg.getJMSReplyTo());
            sender = session.createSender(replyQueue);
            msgTxt = bytesMsg.readUTF();
            org.apache.axis.Message soapMessage =
                new org.apache.axis.Message(msgTxt);
            msgContext.setRequestMessage(soapMessage);
            msgContext.setTransportName(transportName);
            engine.invoke(msgContext);
            respMessage = msgContext.getResponseMessage();
            String respString = respMessage.getAsString();
            BytesMessage reply = session.createBytesMessage();
            reply.writeUTF(respString);
            sender.send(reply);
        } catch (Exception e) {
            // do error handling
        }
    }
}
```

The central method in this class is onMessage(). Here, we get the reply queue from the incoming message and create a queue sender for returning the response. Main processing is invoked with engine.invoke(). Finally, we respond via the temporary queue created by the sender.

To execute SOAP over JMS, visit /ch5/ex6/index.jsp in the example navigator (see Figure 5.19). Like other pages, specify some parameters and click the Submit PO button.

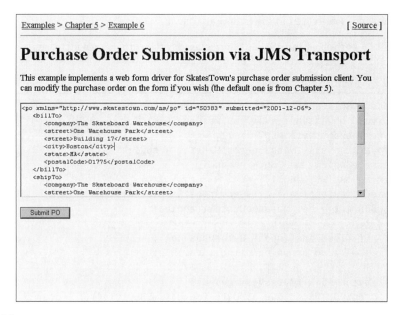

FIGURE 5.19
Example navigator GUI for SOAP over JMS.

Reliable Messaging on the Internet

In addition to transactions, SkatesTown's Dean Caroll wants to use other means to reliably transmit messages over the Internet. Unfortunately, despite some ongoing efforts, there is still no broadly accepted standard in reliable messaging. As in our previous analysis of security technologies, we can approach this issue at the two levels: messaging and transport.

An example of a messaging-level approach can be found in the *ebXML* 📖 *Transport, Routing and Packaging* (ebXML TRP) specification. It defines the MessageHeader element, which is present as a child of the SOAP header element; this element can contain a collection of parameters to perform reliable messaging in a transport-agnostic manner. Although this specification is well described, it is unfortunately not broadly accepted at this moment.

JMS, as described in this section, is an approach for reliable messaging. However, it requires transport products other than HTTP, such as IBM MQ Series. Recently, IBM announced *HTTPR* 📖 to provide HTTP with reliability and asynchronicity features. There is some commonality between TRP and HTTPR models; for example, they both assume message handlers are present at the sender and receiver sides. Accordingly, their protocols are similar. The big difference is whether their parameters are defined as a SOAP header entry or HTTP headers. HTTPR is IBM proprietary, so whether it will be widely accepted is not certain.

J2EE Security Model

So far, we have reviewed transaction processing aspects of J2EE, focusing particularly on EJB and JMS. In addition to transaction processing, J2EE especially addresses security. We have already reviewed security technologies such as SSL, digital signatures, and encryption. In this section, we review an end-to-end security model provided in J2EE.

Figure 5.20 depicts J2EE security architecture, which is based on a role-based access control (RBAC). The HTTP server or servlet container authenticates a requestor, assigning roles to it. Within the servlet container, access to Web resources is authorized based on a URL permission list (not shown in the figure). Within the EJB container, access to EJB objects is authorized based on a method permission list. Permission lists are mappings between roles and target objects: Web resources and EJB objects.

RBAC is flexible because role assignment rules and permission lists can be independently defined. There is a trick here: A credential containing a user ID travels along the method invocation path, which can span multiple EJB containers, and roles are assigned to the requestor at each container for authorization. This concept is especially useful when the system configuration is extremely complex.

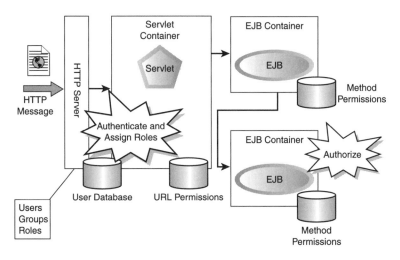

FIGURE 5.20
J2EE security architecture.

J2EE requires compliant platforms to support the following three authentication methods:

- HTTP basic authentication
- SSL client authentication
- Form-based authentication

Note that we will not discuss the third method because the client is not a browser, but a stand-alone application.

Authorization in J2EE

Using BASIC-AUTH, let's review how user IDs and roles are defined in J2EE. The following is an excerpt from application.xml, which is a deployment descriptor for the overall J2EE application:

```
<application>
    ...
    <security-role>
        <role-name>GoodCustomer</role-name>
    </security-role>
</application>
```

The GoodCustomer role is used in the J2EE application. J2EE does not prescribe any particular means for user definition and user-role mapping. The following is a platform-dependent format extracted from Sun's J2EE Reference Implementation:

```
<j2ee-ri-specific-information>
    <server-name></server-name>
    <rolemapping>
        <role name="GoodCustomer">
            <principals>
                <principal>
                    <name>ABCRetailer</name>
                </principal>
            </principals>
        </role>
    </rolemapping>
    ......
</j2ee-ri-specific-information>
```

With this format, you can enumerate user IDs within the role element. A principal indicates a user or a user group. In this example, user ABCRetailer can have a role GoodCustomer.

Let's take a look at method permission definition for EJB objects. The following is an excerpt from ejb.xml, which is a deployment descriptor for EJBs:

```
<ejb-jar>
   <display-name>OrderEjb</display-name>
   <enterprise-beans>
   </enterprise-beans>
   <assembly-descriptor>
    <security-role>
      <role-name>GoodCustomer</role-name>
    </security-role>
    <method-permission>
      <role-name>GoodCustomer</role-name>
      <method>
        <ejb-name>POProcess</ejb-name>
        <method-intf>Remote</method-intf>
        <method-name>order</method-name>
        <method-params>
          <method-param>java.lang.String</method-param>
          <method-param>java.lang.String</method-param>
          <method-param>java.lang.String</method-param>
          <method-param>int</method-param>
        </method-params>
      </method>
    </method-permission>
   </assembly-descriptor>
</ejb-jar>
```

The security-role element includes a collection of roles that are referenced somewhere in this file. method-permission indicates who can access the target method with role. role-name specifies the role name for this method permission, in this case, GoodCustomer.

Relation to JAAS

You might notice that there is some commonality between J2EE RBAC and JAAS, which we reviewed in Section "Access Control for Java Classes." A J2EE credential contains a user ID and roles. On the other hand, a JAAS subject contains a user ID and principals. So, we can provide a mapping between roles in J2EE credential and principals in a JAAS subject. Thus, the J2EE credential and the JAAS subject converge in theory.

A potential scenario for using JAAS in J2EE is described as follows (http://www.research.ibm.com/journal/sj/401/koved.html):

> "The EJB container issues a Subject.doAs( ) call to establish the credentials before invoking the EJB object. Through the EJB object's internal actions (e.g., through the ORB), AccessController.checkPermission( ) is called to determine whether the caller is authorized for the method."

This indicates that EJB authorization could be implemented with JAAS. Although there is no standard for this purpose, JSR 115 might resolve this J2EE and JAAS migration issue.

Once the issue is resolved, we could provide a security framework that accepts credentials (such as BASIC-AUTH, SSL client authentication, or digital signatures) and authorizes access to Web resources, Java classes, and EJB.

Quality of Service

Sophisticated e-Business Web services should be able to provide various levels of quality according to customer requirements and choices. The Quality of Service (QoS) concept originated in the communications industry, based on the portion of sent packets that is received at the target without corruption. There is a similar concept in e-Business, although applications involving banking or air ticket reservation are still not allowed to perform erroneous operations or stop operations. This section describes an architecture for enterprise SOAP servers, paying special attention to QoS for e-Business applications. We provide an overview of the architecture for the enterprise SOAP server, followed by a detailed treatment of the various aspects of QoS.

Enterprise SOAP Server

In the section "Enterprise Application Integration," we reviewed how to integrate existing applications with the J2EE architecture. The typical configuration is comprised of a Web server, a servlet container, some EJB Containers, Databases, and backend applications. The Web server, Servlet container and EJB Containers portion of this configuration is related to integration. This portion is termed *Web Service Container* (WSC) for the sake of discussion in this section.

What happens if a WSC receives a large number of requests, beyond its capacity to process them? It is likely that the WSC will take itself offline or, worse yet, one component (such as the Web server) will crash the computer that it is running on. A known technique to avoid such a situation is to prepare clones of the original WSC for load-balancing. Once you introduce clones, the configuration becomes fairly complicated. Therefore, you need a solid architecture to manage various aspects of the whole system, such as the status of each component and security.

Figure 5.21 illustrates an architectural overview of an enterprise SOAP server. At the heart of this architecture is a collection of Web Services Containers (WSCs). Each WSC invokes backend systems, such as the order management system, and databases. For the sake of simplification, assume that the backend systems and databases are at least as scalable as the WSCs. For example, databases are configured into a Data Area Network in which data replication is automatically performed in preparation for a possible fail-over.

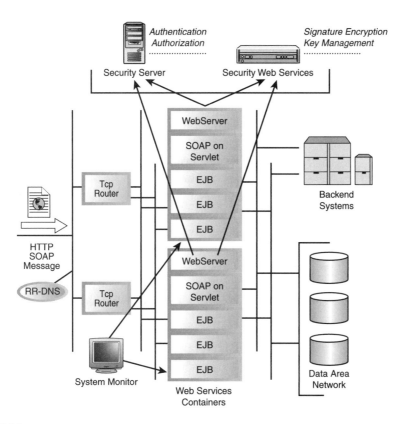

FIGURE 5.21

An architecture for an enterprise SOAP server.

Load-balancing, for instance, would be performed by a *Round-Robin Domain Name Service* (*RR-DNS*) 📖 and a *TCP Router* 📖, which dispatches an incoming SOAP message to one of the WSCs. A system monitor checks the status of each component in each WSC and might start up another WSC clone when the load becomes too high, for example. In this complex configuration, managing end-to-end security is a difficult task. In the enterprise SOAP server architecture, there is a single secure domain where all security information is managed; this information is the basis for all security decisions.

Note that the architecture for the enterprise SOAP server shown in Figure 5.21 is not necessarily the best architecture. To come up with the best architecture, the business and system requirements must be considered. However, the architecture in Figure 5.21 does clearly show what aspects should be considered for the purpose of developing an e-Business QoS. Each aspect is discussed in detail in the following sections.

High Availability

Availability is an obvious QoS requirement because users generally expect that services are always, or very nearly always, available. If a service is frequently unavailable, users stop relying on its service provider. An airline ticket reservation system, for example, requires 99% availability; the service can be unavailable for only two hours per week.

Load-balancing is a means to achieving high availability, especially in terms of increasing the scalability of the system. As shown in Figure 5.21, it combines two techniques: RR-DNS and the TCP Router. A Domain Name Service (DNS) maps domain names (hostnames) to IP addresses, and the round-robin variety of DNS allows a hostname to be mapped to one of several IP addresses. An IP address is chosen in round-robin manner, meaning that consecutive requests are assigned to the available IP addresses in a pre-determined sequence, repeating itself at the end of the sequence. HTTP redirect is often used instead of RR-DNS for the same purpose. When a client accesses a server, the server responds with a redirect instruction to one of the available hosts. One disadvantage of this approach is that URLs of the target hosts are visible and then are potentially stored on the client side (such as in a browser's recent URL list or a bookmark), and the client might directly access this URL in subsequent requests. Thus, the purpose of load-balancing might be defeated.

Using TCP routers, you can configure clusters to scale up processing power. A TCP router forwards incoming requests to WSCs. Although the router's name and IP address are public, the addresses of WSCs are hidden from the client. The TCP router could use a load-based algorithm to select a target WSC, or simply adopt the round-robin process. There are many commercially available TCP routers, such as IBM Network Dispatcher (ND). ND can run on several operating systems, such as Windows, AIX, and Solaris, and can forward up to 10,000 messages per second when it runs on an embedded OS. In addition to the TCP router approach, you can use a technique called *Network Address Translation* (*NAT*) 📖. NAT dynamically edits a particular IP packet header to change the destination address, and edits the return packet in the same manner. Cisco Local Director is an example of a commercial product for NAT.

Scaling up the system with load-balancing techniques might decrease the risk of system failure, but system failure can still occur. But WSC clones, in addition to being used to increase scalability, can also serve as a backup of the original WSC, taking over the processing when the WSC fails. This introduces the system properties of *redundancy* (using clones for possible backup) and *fault tolerance* (performing an automated procedure in case of fail-over).

Another issue related to system failure is *recovery*. Generally speaking, recovery requires the system to perform a complicated recovery sequence. For example, some kind of status indicator might be recorded at certain checkpoints, and the recovery process might rely on the status history. However, because the SOAP server uses transaction processing, there need not be such a complicated recovery sequence in the enterprise server architecture. By definition, operations within a transaction context are committed or aborted. Therefore, in the event of a system failure, the EJB containers will perform most of the recovery sequence on behalf of applications.

System Management

In order to completely fulfill the requirement for high availability, system management must also be considered. Because the configuration of real e-Business systems is fairly complex, as shown in Figure 5.21, there needs to be a systematic means to manage the whole system. Ideally, there would be a single point of management, from which even system resources at other sites can be managed. System management might include the following tasks:

- Monitoring the status of system resources
- Sending alert information to system administrators
- Remotely configuring, deploying, and controlling system resources
- Automatically resolving system resource issues if possible

Typically, system management requires agents, each of which monitors one or more system resources and continuously sends information to the system monitor. Because sending too much information unduly consumes network bandwidth, a proper filtering mechanism is also required.

The system monitor in Figure 5.21 is a central controller to perform system management. On the basis of the information sent by agents, the system monitor controls system resources: It starts/stops a resource, adds a resource, or changes the configuration of a resource. Generally, system administrators interact with the system monitor to remotely control system resources. Optionally, the system monitor could adjust automatically without consulting the system administrator when certain known problems are detected. Of course, this is possible only when you provide the system monitor with a remedy procedure in advance.

Several types of system resources need to be monitored: network devices, operating systems, databases, application servers, applications, and so on. Network device management is easy to implement in the sense that there is a standard specification of network management, called *Simple Network Management Protocol (SNMP)* 📖, and a large number of devices support SNMP.

On the other hand, system software and middleware packages each have their own management tools. For example, operating systems might collect values of key system parameters, such as application statuses, number of users logged in, jobs in a print queue, system load,

5

USING **SOAP** FOR
E-BUSINESS

free disk space, and other properties. In this case, total system management vendors should provide an agent to retrieve these OS parameters and report them to their system monitor.

The application monitor is the hardest task because application-specific agents have to be developed. In the case of the enterprise SOAP server, a system monitor agent must be placed in the Axis engine. WSTK 2.4 provides a beta implementation of system management for Apache SOAP. It can collect the following information:

- Total number of SOAP services deployed
- Total number of RPC calls to all services combined
- Total number of successful invocations of each service
- Average response/transaction time for successful requests

The implementation of this SOAP system management is based on the *Java Management Extension* (*JMX*) ▢. With JMX, you can construct and maintain resource objects that contain key parameters, and embed agents to monitor the values of those parameters. WSTK 2.4 will be extended to include additional features, such as operations to change the behavior of a service and system administrator notification when certain criteria are met.

In summary, system management is a complex task because different types of system resources, located at potentially many different sites, need to be monitored and controlled from one point. Although some aspects, such as network management, already have well-developed solutions, emerging areas have not been organized for system management. One immediate problem is that there is no standard way to manage J2EE platforms. However, there is ongoing discussion toward the goal of standardizing J2EE Management in JSR 77.

Enterprise Security

A complex system configuration requires an integrated security architecture. Middleware applications, such as Web servers, application servers, and databases, provide their own respective security functions. However, the security functions should be integrated in a centralized manner, as shown in the previous section. In addition, highly confidential information, such as private keys, must be protected. This centralized approach also contributes to the protection of the single secure domain.

The security server in Figure 5.21 is an aggregation of commercial security products. It has a user registry in an LDAP server that manages user IDs, passwords, certificates, security attributes, roles, and so on. In this architecture, the Web server neither stores nor checks user IDs and passwords, but rather delegates user authentication to the security server. In addition to the user registry, the security server can manage access control rules for authorization and a table for mapping user IDs between different security domains. For example, when users need to access a backend legacy system, their Internet IDs might be mapped to IDs for the legacy system.

On the other hand, the security Web services shown in Figure 5.21 address XML- and SOAP-level security issues. As described earlier, SOAP digital signature and encryption handlers are provided in the form of Java classes and embedded in the Axis engine. However, this configuration requires private keys to be distributed to the original and all clone nodes.

XKMS suggests managing public and private keys in a single repository and accessing that repository via SOAP messages. You can apply this Web services approach to the signature and encryption handlers. First, manageability of security handlers is improved because they are simply invoked from various Axis nodes. Second, manageability of security information is improved because it is protected in a secure domain. In future development, a more comprehensive collection of security services, such as timer and authorization handlers, might be specified and provided in addition to signature and encryption. Thus, some of the functions in the security server could become security Web services.

Summary

This chapter discussed how you can perform serious e-Business functions with Web services. After reading this chapter, you know that there are many emerging standards in this area, with which you can bring Web services to the real world. Of course, it's important to keep your eyes on standardization activities in W3C, *OASIS* 📖, and the *Java Community Processes* 📖 known as Java Specification Requests (JSR). However, it is extremely hard to follow all the activities. One reasonable approach is to clarify first what you want in your business and systems in order to narrow down the activities and standards you must monitor.

You should now have a fairly solid picture of security standards. Although some technologies are under development, you can make your Web services secure to some extent with SSL, BASIC-AUTH, and digital signatures. Other technologies should be chosen after paying particular attention to how they have matured and how much you need them in your business.

Standards in Enterprise Application Integration (EAI) are in some sense mature because they are based on a long history of system integration evolution including transactions, reliable messaging, distributed objects, security, and so on. However, you must also know that important concepts like transactions and reliable messaging cannot be applied to B2B easily on the Internet. We are eagerly awaiting standardization efforts in this area.

Another issue addressed here was how to fit Web services technologies and standards into EAI environments. For example, BASIC-AUTH has been integrated into the J2EE architecture, so authorization on EJB objects can be performed based on it. However, how do we perform authorization on ordinary Java objects? Can we perform authorization if we authenticate a requestor with a digital signature? When adopting a Web services technology, you also have to consider how it can be integrated into your existing EAI environment.

We also reviewed examples of *core Web services*. XKMS is the best example here. Because it is difficult to access PKI, Web services for PKI must be appreciated. As we envisioned in Figure 5.21, other security functions would be provided as Web services, such as signature and encryption services. In the same manner, work is underway on publishing system management functions as Web services. Once such Web services are provided, customers can understand the system status of the service provider. This could be a good basis for QoS improvement in a decentralized manner.

Resources

- *ASN.1*—"Information Technology—Abstract Syntax Notation One (ASN.1): Specification of Basic Notation" (ITU-T Recommendation X.680, 1997). ISO/IEC 8824-1:1998.

- *Base64*—"Multipurpose Internet Mail Extensions (MIME) Part One: Format of Internet Message Bodies" (IETF, November 1996). Available at `http://www.ietf.org/rfc/rfc2045.txt`.

- *BASIC-AUTH*—RFC 2617: "HTTP Authentication: Basic and Digest Access Authentication" (IETF, June 1999). Available at `http://www.ietf.org/rfc/rfc2617.txt`.

- *Canonical XML*—"Canonical XML Version 1.0" (W3C, March 2001). Available at `http://www.w3.org/TR/2001/REC-xml-c14n-20010315`.

- *CRL*—"Internet X.509 Public Key Infrastructure Certificate and CRL Profile" (IETF, January 1999). Available at `http://www.ietf.org/rfc/rfc2459.txt`.

- *ebXML TRP*—Message Service Specification ebXML Transport, Routing & Packaging Version 1.0 (UN/CEFACT and OASIS, May 2001). Available at `http://www.ebxml.org/specs/`.

- *EJB*—Enterprise JavaBeans Specification, Version 2.0 (Sun Microsystems, August 2001). Available at `http://java.sun.com/products/ejb/`.

- *HTTPR*—"A Primer for HTTPR: An overview of the Reliable HTTP Protocol" (IBM, July 2001). Available at `http://www-106.ibm.com/developerworks/webservices/library/ws-phtt/`.

- *IETF*—The Internet Engineering Task Force. Available at `http://www.ietf.org/`.

- *J2EE*—Java 2 Platform Enterprise Edition Specification, v1.3 (Sun Microsystems, August 2001). Available at `http://java.sun.com/j2ee/`.

- *J2EE Connector*—J2EE Connector Architecture Specification, Version 1.0. (Sun Microsystems, August 2001). J2EE Connector Specification (Sun Microsystems). Available at `http://java.sun.com/j2ee/`.

- *J2EE MGMT*—"JSR 77: J2EE Management" (JCP, September 2001). Available at `http://jcp.org/jsr/detail/77.jsp`.

- *JAAS*—Java Authentication and Authorization Service (Sun Microsystems). Available at `http://java.sun.com/products/jaas/`.

- *JAF*—JavaBeans Activation Framework Specification, Version 1.0a (Sun Microsystems, May 1999). Available at `http://java.sun.com/products/javabeans/glasgow/jaf.html`.

- *JASPCFC*—JSR 115: Java Authorization Service Provider Contract for Containers (JCP, April 2001). Available at `http://jcp.org/jsr/detail/115.jsp`.

- *JavaMail*—JavaMail 1.2 (Sun Microsystems, December 2000). Available at `http://java.sun.com/products/javamail/`.

- *JCE*—Java Cryptography Extension (JCE) (Sun Microsystems). Available at `http://java.sun.com/products/jce/`.

- *JMX*—Java Management Extensions Instrumentation and Agent Specification, v1.0 (Sun Microsystems, July 2000). Available at `http://java.sun.com/products/JavaManagement/`.

- *JNDI*—Java Naming and Directory Interface 1.2 (Sun Microsystems). Available at `http://java.sun.com/products/jndi/`.

- *JSP*—JavaServer Pages Specification Version 1.2 (Sun Microsystems, September 2001). Available at `http://java.sun.com/products/jsp/`.

- *JSSE*—Java Secure Socket Extension (Sun Microsystems). Available at `http://java.sun.com/products/jsse/`.

- *OASIS*—Organization for the Advancement of Structured Information Standards. Available at `http://www.oasis-open.org/`.

- *PKCS*—"Public-Key Cryptography Standards" (RSA Laboratories). Available at `http://www.rsalabs.com/pkcs/`.

- *PKI*—Internet X.509 Public Key Infrastructure Certificate Management Protocols (IETF, March 1999). Available at `http://www.ietf.org/rfc/rfc2510.txt`.

- *RMI-IIOP*—"Remote Method Invocation (RMI) over Internet Inter-Orb Protocol (IIOP)" (Sun Microsystems). Available at `http://java.sun.com/products/rmi-iiop/`.

- *SAML*—"Security Assertion Markup Language" (OASIS). Available at `http://www.oasis-open.org/committees/security/`.

- *Servlet*—Java Servlet Specification Version 2.3 (Sun Microsystems, September 2001). Available at `http://java.sun.com/products/servlet/`.

5

USING **SOAP** FOR
E-BUSINESS

- *SNMP*—"Introduction to Version 3 of the Internet-standard Network Management Framework" (IETF, April 1999). Available at `http://www.ietf.org/rfc/rfc2570.txt`.

- *SOAP Signature*—"SOAP Security Extensions: Digital Signature" (W3C, February 2001). Available at `http://www.w3.org/TR/SOAP-dsig/`.

- *SSL*—The SSL Protocol Version 3.0 (Netscape Communications, November 1996). Available at `http://home.netscape.com/eng/ssl3/draft302.txt`.

- *TIP*—Transaction Internet Protocol Version 3.0 (W3C, July 1998). Available at `http://www.ietf.org/rfc/rfc2371.txt`.

- *TLS*—RFC 2246: "The TLS Protocol Version 1.0" (IETF, January 1999). Available at `http://www.ietf.org/rfc/rfc2246.txt`.

- *VeriSign*—VeriSign, Inc. Available at `http://www.verisign.com/`.

- *WSTK*—IBM Web Services Toolkit 2.4 (IBM, September 2001). Available at `http://www.alphaworks.ibm.com/tech/webservicestoolkit`.

- *X.500 Distinguished Name*—"Information technology—Open Systems Interconnection—The Directory: Overview of Concepts, Models and Services" (ITU-T Recommendation X.500, 1997). ISO/IEC 9594-1:1998.

- *XAML*—Transaction Authority Markup Language. Available at `http://www.xaml.org/`.

- *XKMS*—XML Key Management Specification (W3C, March 2001). Available at `http://www.w3.org/TR/xkms/`.

- *XML Encryption*—"XML Encryption Syntax and Processing WG Working Draft" (W3C, June 2001). Available at `http://www.w3.org/TR/2001/WD-xmlenc-core-20010626/`.

- *XML Signature*—"XML-Signature Syntax and Processing" (W3C, August 2001). Available at `http://www.w3.org/TR/2001/PR-xmldsig-core-20010820/`.

Describing Web Services

IN THIS CHAPTER

To this point, we have described XML and positioned it as the underpinnings of the SOAP messaging protocol. Given that XML is a self-describing, human-readable representation of data, isn't that enough to make a SOAP message also self-describing? If so, then why do we need an approach for service descriptions? We'll answer this question in this chapter.

Why Service Descriptions?

Let's look at this problem from the service requestor's perspective. A customer of SkatesTown wants to invoke the POSubmission service. How does the customer know what kind of message to send? Sure, they know to use SOAP, but SOAP is the format of the envelope; SOAP itself does not clarify what message to actually put into the envelope. The customer needs to understand what XML to put into the body of the SOAP envelope, what format the response message might come in, and whether a response is to be expected. The customer also needs to know what messaging protocol to use to send the message and what network address to send the message to.

One way for the customer to determine what XML to send is to examine a textual description of the service published on the SkatesTown Web site. Although doing so is simple, it does allow some potential problems. The textual description might not be terribly precise and can allow the customer's developers to misinterpret the specification. This results in too much trial and error on the customer's part to get the message format right.

Another approach is to include sample message formats in the documentation. The developer can then observe the samples and modify them to suit his/her company's needs. This approach is slightly better in that the developer can get the message format correct with fewer iterations, but the customer still must do too much hand-crafted code development. If each Web service required analysis, design, and coding to invoke, the Web services approach would quickly pass into the dustbin of technology history.

To make the job of invoking Web services easier for the service requestor, we need a formal mechanism to describe the service. This formal approach provides unambiguous specification of what the service requestor needs to do in order to invoke the Web service. As a result of the formality of the service description, software tool developers can provide tooling to automate the development of code to invoke Web services.

Role of Service Description in a Service-Oriented Architecture

Service description is key within a service-oriented architecture (SOA). A service description is involved in each of the three operations of SOA: publish, find, and bind.

Recall the SOA approach, depicted in Figure 6.1. The service provider publishes a service description to one or more service registries. The description of the service is published in service registries, not the actual code for the Web service itself. The service provider uses a service description to tell the service requestor everything it needs to know in order to properly understand how to invoke the Web service.

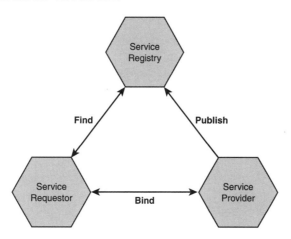

FIGURE 6.1
Service-oriented architecture.

Similarly, the service description is central to the find operation. The service requestor uses aspects of the service description; for example, you might be looking for a Web service that implements a particular purchase order standard, as the basis for the find query to a service registry. (In Chapter 7, "Discovering Web Services," we discuss service registries at length and describe the find and publish operations in more detail.) The result of the find operation is ultimately a service description made available to the service requestor.

Why does the service provider publish a service description? To communicate to service requestors how to invoke a Web service. Why does a service requestor want to get hold of a service description? Because it describes exactly what needs to happen at the bind operation. Service description is key to the bind operation, describing exactly what message format needs to be delivered to what network address in order to invoke a Web service.

Well Defined Service

What makes a good service description? What aspects of the Web service must be described in order for the Web service to be considered sufficiently defined?

Submissions to the W3C (http://www.w3.org/2001/03/WSWS-popa/paper51) have described a *stack* of Web services description standards that describe various aspects of a Web service. Details based on this stack are depicted in Figure 6.2.

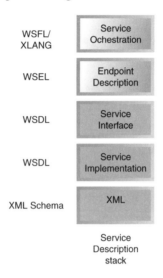

WSFL/XLANG	Service Ochestration
WSEL	Endpoint Description
WSDL	Service Interface
WSDL	Service Implementation
XML Schema	XML

Service
Description
stack

FIGURE 6.2

The service description stack.

The layers of the service description stack can be divided into two broad groups: functional layers and non-functional layers. The bottom three layers are functional in nature, in that they describe details of how the Web service is invoked, where it is invoked, and so on. The upper layers are non-functional, or non-operational in nature, in that they do not directly inform the mechanisms of invocation, but rather provide other details that influence whether a service requestor would choose to invoke the Web service.

Functional Description

The bottom, functional layers of the service description stack define the *interface definition language (IDL)* equivalent of the service description. The interface description language layers for Web service description serve the same function as IDLs in other distributed computing approaches (see the section "History of IDLs"). Let's examine the relationships between these layers. Fundamentally, it is the functional description of the Web service that determines what the service requestor needs to do in order to invoke a Web service.

Like most things in Web services, XML is at the basis of service description. XML is the type definition that is exploited, by default, in the service implementation and service interface definition layers of the stack. As we saw in Chapter 3, "Simple Object Access Protocol (SOAP)," XML describes the datatypes for the elements that flow within the SOAP message, and in particular, within the SOAP payload, which need to be formatted by the service requestor and interpreted by the service provider. Much of the effort within a Web services infrastructure goes into properly encoding and decoding XML elements to/from native programming language objects.

The *service implementation definition* and the *service interface definition* both use the Web Services Description Language (WSDL) standard. We will describe the WSDL language in more detail later in this chapter in the "Web Services Definition Language (WSDL)" section.

The service implementation definition describes *where* the service is located, or more precisely, to which network address the message must be sent in order to invoke the Web service.

The service interface definition describes exactly *what* message needs to be sent and *how* to use the various Internet standard messaging protocols and encoding schemes in order to format the message in a manner acceptable to the service provider.

Non-Functional Description

The IDL level description embodied by the functional description layers of the service description stack is very important, but there is more that should be described about a Web service.

What do we mean by the term *non-functional description*? Basically, these layers can be characterized in contrast to the functional layers. Whereas the functional layers describe where to send the message, what the message syntax needs to look like, and how to use the protocols and encoding schemes, the non-functional description addresses *why* a service requestor should invoke the Web service—for example, what business function the Web service addresses and how it fits into a broader business process. A non-functional description also gives more details about *who* the service provider is. For example, does the service provider provide auditing and ensure privacy?

You can use the Web Services Endpoint Language (WSEL) to describe the environment or endpoint which hosts the Web service. Characteristics of the hosting environment could include the security policy in place at the service provider, what levels of quality of service are available to support Web service invocation, what kind of privacy policy is enforced by the service provider, and so on. At one level, you can think of the non-functional description layers as descriptions of the Web service that do not affect the shape of the SOAP message body. Non-functional descriptions might have some influence on the syntax of the message, related to orthogonal extensions of the message (for example, parameters related to a required security protocol), but the core shape of the payload of the message is derived from the functional description. At this point, WSEL is not a concrete proposal, but rather a vague notion of requirement expressed within the Web services community.

As we will examine in Chapter 7, the UDDI service registry also has impact on the certain non-functional aspects of the service description. In particular, the taxonomy scheme supported by UDDI is another mechanism by which a service provider can describe what kind of service is being provided and what business function it supports.

Aggregation/Orchestration Description

The Web Services Flow Language (WSFL) is one technique to describe how a collection of Web services can be arranged or orchestrated into a higher level business process. WSFL addresses items like the proper order in which to invoke a set of Web services. Essentially, WSFL describes how these individual Web services fit into a bigger picture, such as a business process or a multi-party, multi-operation long running transaction.

Another approach, developed by Microsoft, is the XLANG language, part of the .NET initiative (`http://www.gotdotnet.com/team/xml_wsspecs/xlang-c/default.htm`). A third approach, Business Process Markup, sponsored by a consortium (BPMI, `http://www.bpmi.org/bpml-spec.esp`) also exists in the marketplace. To date, none of these approaches has emerged as a dominant standard in this space.

Stack Summary

Currently, most of the work has been devoted to establishing and evolving the IDL-level of the service description stack. The WSDL approach has only recently been established, and it continues to gain adoption with better runtime support and tooling support from multiple vendors and use by developers.

The standards related to the non-functional description are still in their infancy. WSEL is only briefly mentioned as part of the WSFL specification. There is no other publicly available information on WSEL. The same is true for aggregation/orchestration; WSFL itself remains as a proposal in the area, and has yet to undergo the rigors of submission and modification through an open standards body such as the W3C. We expect that standards in these layers of the service description stack will continue to evolve and mature.

To summarize, a Web service is described using a combination of techniques. A Web service's description is used to unambiguously answer several questions about the Web service. These questions and how they are addressed are summarized in Table 6.1.

TABLE 6.1 Roles of Each Layer of the Service Description Stack

Question	Where Addressed
Who	Non-functional description
What	Service interface
Where	Service implementation
Why	Non-functional description
How	Service interface

For the remainder of this chapter, let's focus on the use of the WSDL standard as the functional description of a Web service. Toward the end of the chapter, in the "Web Services Endpoint Language (WSEL)" section, we will briefly revisit the non-functional layers of the service description stack.

History of IDLs

Before we dive into the WSDL discussion, a little background might be helpful. Every distributed computing approach has a mechanism for describing components. Let's examine a brief history of IDLs.

Interface definition languages (IDLs) have a long history in distributed computing. The major use of IDL came as part of the Open Software Foundation's Distributed Computing Environment (DCE) in its specification on RPC in 1994. DCE IDL was a breakthrough concept that quickly spread to other distributed computing initiatives, such as Object Management Group's (OMG) CORBA IDL and Microsoft's COM IDL and COM ODL (Object Definition Language). As with most such technologies, the various flavors of IDL are slightly different and, therefore, more or less incompatible. All hopes are now on WSDL to bring unity back to this crucial area of distributed computing, at least in the area of Web services.

Most people used to developing simple software frown when they first hear about IDL. They say, "Why bother defining the interfaces of any software operations? Just get a pointer/reference to an object or a function and make the call." The reason is that, if a software system has even the slightest amount of heterogeneity, this simple approach won't work. Let's consider some possibilities:

- It can be difficult to obtain a reference to the target that implements the operation you want to call. For example, the target could be in another executable on the same machine or on another machine.

- The function/method calling convention varies significantly between programming languages or even based on compilation parameters, such as the level of optimization. If even the slightest difference exists between the invoker's and the target's environments, it is likely that the call will fail.

- Data encoding rules vary considerably between programming languages (strings in Pascal are length-prefixed while they are null-terminated in C/C++) and platforms (numbers can be represented in little- vs. big-endian format).

The best way to approach these problems, given that software implementations and deployments are, and will forever be, highly heterogeneous, is to agree on a bridging strategy. This strategy establishes common ground in the middle (the bridge) without worrying about how the roads at the endpoints are constructed. In distributed computing, a bridging strategy involves two parts:

1. Agreeing on *how* to make an invocation: the mechanics of naming, activation, data encoding, error handling, and so on. This is what distributed computing standards such as DCE, CORBA, and COM do.

2. Specifying *what* to call: the operation names, their signatures, return types, and any exceptions that they might generate. This is the job of IDL.

In a typical distributed computing architecture, a tool called an IDL compiler combines the information in an IDL file together with the conventions on how to make invocations to code-generate the pieces that make the bridge work. The client that wants to invoke operations will use a *client proxy* 📖 (sometimes called a *client stub*). The proxy has the same interface as the operation provider. It can be used as a local object on the client. The proxy implementation knows how to encode and marshal the invocation data to the operation provider and how to capture the operation result and return it to the client. The operation provider will wrap its implementation inside a *skeleton* 📖 (sometimes called a *server stub*) implementation that is code-generated by the IDL compiler. The skeleton knows how to capture the data sent by the proxy and pass it to the actual implementation. It also knows how to package the result of operations and send it back to the client. Proxies and skeletons are helped by a lot of sophisticated distributed computing middleware. A key part of the story is that proxies and skeletons need not be generated by the same IDL compilers, as long as these compilers are following the same distributed computing conventions. This is the power of IDL—it describes everything that is necessary to make invocation possible in a distributed environment.

DCE IDL specified flat function interfaces. There was no notion of object instance context when making calls. CORBA IDL changed that by adding many important extensions to IDL. CORBA IDL is the *de facto* IDL standard on non-Microsoft environments. It is also standardized internationally as ISO/IEC 14750.

CORBA IDL is purely declarative; it provides no implementation details. It defines a remote object API concisely (the spec is less than 40 pages long) and covers key issues such as naming, complex type definition, in/out/in-out parameters and exceptions. The syntax is reminiscent of C++ with some additional keywords to cover additional concepts. The following is a brief example of a CORBA IDL specification for an account and an interest account:

```
module Accounts
{
    interface Account
    {
        readonly attribute string number;
        readonly attribute float balance;

        exception InsuffucientFunds (string detail);

        float debit(in float amount) raises (InsufficientFunds);
        float credit(in float amount);
    }

    interface InterestAccount : Account
    {
        readonly attribute float rate;
    }
}
```

The information in the IDL file is self-describing and very readable. You can also see that IDL supports the notion of inheritance, which makes it convenient to describe object-oriented distributed systems. In fact, CORBA IDL even supports the notion of multiple interface inheritance as in `MyPetTurtle` deriving from both `Pet` and `Animal`.

In a CORBA-enabled environment, the previous IDL above can be used to invoke the CORBA object via dynamic invocation from a scripting language, generate proxies for client access to the object, generate skeletons for the actual account implementation to be plugged into the CORBA middleware, regardless of its actual implementation language, and store information about the implementation in an *interface repository* (a central store of metadata about CORBA components' interfaces).

For various historical reasons, Microsoft used to have two versions of IDL. COM IDL was closely based on DCE IDL, although it lacked some of the advanced features supported by

COM. COM ODL had support for these features but was incompatible with COM IDL. Clearly, that was an odd state of affairs, and Microsoft fixed things a few years ago when it merged the two IDL languages. The following example shows a somewhat simplified version of the Account and InterestAccount interfaces in Microsoft's IDL:

```
[
   object, uuid(E9FF28F4-B79F-469A-B2D9-477FF19873A0), dual
]
interface IAccount : IDispatch
{
[propget, id(1)] HRESULT balance([out, retval] float *pVal);
[id(2)] HRESULT debit(in float amount, [out, retval] float *pVal);
[id(3)] HRESULT credit(in float amount, [out, retval] float *pVal);
};


[
   object, uuid(5B93E296-4FF5-4A6C-A64E-51A7B6C20B6C), dual
]
interface IInterestAccount : IAccount
{
   [propget, id(1)] HRESULT rate([out, retval] float *pVal);
};


[
   uuid(22AE9E3F-DC3C-478E-BC00-13A735D57167), version(1.0)
]
library AccountLib
{
   [
      uuid(0D1630F9-C4E0-46A6-BCDF-A9B752DBDD94)
   ]
   coclass Account
   {
      [default] interface IAccount;
   };

   [
      uuid(F949F2A1-18C1-4010-A062-6B8DF49D4BCE)
   ]
   coclass InterestAccount
   {
      [default] interface IInterestAccount;
   };
};
```

Needless to say, Microsoft's ODL is not syntax-compatible, or even concept-compatible, with CORBA IDL. For example, metadata about elements is provided via *attributes*. Attributes prefix elements using the format [name(value), ...]. The convention is to prefix interface names with a capital *I*. To support dynamic invocation from scripting languages, interfaces must inherit from IDispatch and methods need to identify their location in dynamic dispatch tables with the id attribute. COM does not support exceptions. Error information is communicated via the return value of a method, which must be an HRESULT (an integer with well-defined error codes). Therefore, the *real* return value of a method is identified as [out, retval] in the IDL. Finally, COM supports a true separation of interfaces (IAccount and IInterestAccount) from implementations (Account and InterestAccount). The latter are identified by the coclass keyword in the account library. COM uses UUIDs exclusively to register interfaces and implementation classes under unique names. Apart from these differences, COM objects can be used exactly like CORBA objects.

Programmers working with modern languages, such as Java, C#, and any other .NET Common Language Runtime (CLR) languages have the luxury of being able to engage in distributed computing applications typically without having to worry much about IDL. Has IDL become irrelevant in these cases? Not at all! IDL is not present on the surface, but IDL concepts are working behind the scenes.

Both Java and the CLR languages are fully introspectable. This means that a compiled language component carries complete metadata about itself, such as information about its parent class, properties, methods, and any supported interfaces. This information is sufficient to replace the need for an explicit IDL description of the component. That is why, for example, Java developers can invoke the RMI compiler directly on their object without having to generate IDL first.

However, in the cases where these languages need to interoperate with components built using other programming languages, there is no substitute for IDL. In short, separating interfaces from implementations is the only guaranteed mechanism for ensuring the potential for interoperability across programming languages, platforms, machines, address spaces, memory models and object versions. On the Web, where heterogeneity is the rule, this is more important than ever.

Web Services Definition Language (WSDL)

The Web Services Definition Language (WSDL) is a proposed standard to describe the technical invocation syntax of a Web service. WSDL was submitted to the W3C for standardization by IBM, Microsoft, and others in September 2000. The current version of the specification, WSDL 1.1, is available at http://www.w3.org/TR/wsdl.

A WSDL service description is an XML document conformant to the WSDL schema definition. As we asserted earlier, a WSDL document is not a complete service description, but rather it covers the lower levels of the service description stack—the raw technical description of the service's interface. WSDL is the IDL for Web services. Essentially, a WSDL description describes three fundamental properties of a Web service:

- *What* a service does—the operations (methods) the service provides
- *How* a service is accessed—details of the data formats and protocols necessary to access the service's operations
- *Where* a service is located—details of the protocol-specific network address, such as a URL

WSDL Information Model

The WSDL information model takes full advantage of the separation between abstract specifications and concrete implementations of these specifications. This reflects the split between service interface definition (abstract interface) and service implementation definition (concrete endpoint) discussed previously in the context of the service description stack.

The description of the endpoint's capabilities is the abstract interface specification represented in WSDL by a *portType* 📖. A *binding mechanism* 📖, represented in WSDL by a `binding` element, is used to map the abstract definition of the Web service to a specific implementation using a particular messaging protocol, data encoding model, and underlying communication protocol. When the binding is combined with an address where the implementation can be accessed, the abstract endpoint has become a *concrete endpoint* 📖 that service requestors can invoke. This combination is represented by a WSDL `port` element.

An abstract interface can support any number of *operations* 📖. An operation is defined by the set of *messages* 📖 that define its interaction pattern.

For the abstract concepts of message and operation, concrete counterparts are specified in the `binding` element.

Like all good applications of XML, the WSDL schema defines several high level or major elements in the language. Let's take a look at Web service description in terms of the major elements in WSDL:

- `portType`—A Web service's abstract interface definition (think Java interface definition) where each child `operation` element defines an abstract *method* signature.
- `message`—Defines a set of parameters referred to by the method signatures or operations. A message can be further decomposed into `parts` (think detailed method parameter format definitions).

- `types`—Defines the collection of all the data types used in the Web service as referenced by various message part elements (think base data types; think XML).

- `binding`—Contains details of how the elements in an abstract interface (`portType`) are converted into a concrete representation in a particular combination of data formats and protocols (think encoding schemes; think SOAP over HTTP).

- `port` 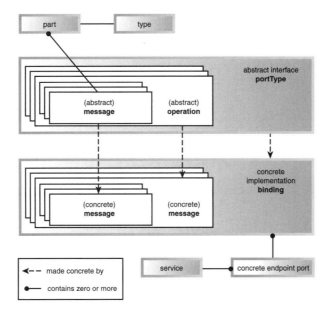—Expresses how a binding is deployed at a particular network endpoint (think details about a particular server on a particular network location; think place where you specify HTTP URL).

- `service`—A poorly named element. A named collection of ports (think arbitrary bag of Web services, for example, the ports associated with steps in a multistep business transaction).

So the `portType` (with details from the `message` and `type` elements) describes the *what* of the Web service. The `binding` element describes the *how*, and the `port` and `service` elements describe the *where* of the Web service.

Figure 6.3 shows the relationship between these elements in WSDL.

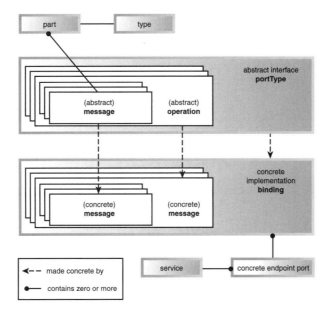

FIGURE 6.3
The WSDL information model.

The figure shows one possible view of the organization of the WSDL information model. You can see a clear relationship between the abstract and concrete notions of message and operation as contained in the `portType` and `binding` elements. The words in bold on the diagram signify the terms from the WSDL specification. The element names used in WSDL are somewhat confusing because no consistent naming convention allows you to distinguish between abstract and concrete concepts. You simply have to memorize which elements represent abstract concepts and which elements represent concrete concepts.

At first glance, WSDL seems to be quite complicated. Part of this appearance is due to the factoring chosen by the WSDL authors. This complexity feels a lot like the complexity observed with a highly normalized relational data model. Although the same information can be more succinctly expressed, the flexibility that results from the factoring in WSDL is occasionally quite necessary. So, just as you might have learned to cope with understanding highly normalized relational models, practice with reading WSDL documents will help you to focus on the important aspects of a Web service description.

Origin of WSDL

WSDL was not the first IDL language for Web services. IBM had developed a language called Network Accessible Service Specification Language (NASSL) to further early internal adoption of SOAP. Meanwhile, Microsoft had developed SOAP Contract Language (SCL), which itself was an evolution of Microsoft's earlier attempt at a SOAP IDL called Service Definition Language.

IBM and Microsoft realized that having competing IDLs in the SOAP space would hinder rapid adoption of Web services. WSDL is the result of hard work and compromise in merging NASSL and SCL. As a result of this merger, a single ubiquitous mechanism describes the interface definition of Web services: WSDL. To make WSDL a standard, IBM, Microsoft, and several other companies brought it forward to the W3C for standardization.

Elements of the WSDL Language

Let's take a closer look at the elements of a WSDL description. Although we examine these elements in detail, the good news is that you don't have to become an expert in WSDL. The software industry continues to churn out tools to generate WSDL from existing IT assets like COM objects and Enterprise Java Beans (EJBs) and to generate client-side stubs or proxies (access mechanism helper classes) from WSDL on the service requestor side to ease the burden of invoking Web services. Later in this chapter, we will take a closer look at the WSDL tooling available in Axis. However, by reviewing WSDL, you will get a good background in case the tools don't generate exactly the WSDL or Java to fit your particular circumstances.

None of the tools to date support the entire breadth of WSDL features. For some time to come, WSDL descriptions will need to be hand crafted, and client and Web service implementation code will have to be manually developed.

The best way to learn WSDL is to examine a collection of WSDL documents. An excellent registry of WSDL documents can be found at the salcentral Web services brokerage (http://www.salcentral.com) or the xmethods Web site (www.xmethods.net). Go to either of these sites and browse the collection of WSDL documents found there. After a little practice, reading a WSDL document will become as familiar as reading Java code.

So, what does a WSDL description look like? Let's discuss the WSDL language in the context of two WSDL examples. In the following sections, we will discuss how the various elements of the WSDL language are used to describe two of SkatesTown's Web services.

Example WSDL Documents

We will examine the WSDL description for the (relatively simple) priceCheck service provided by SkatesTown. The priceCheck service was added by Al Rosen in response to growing demand from customers to extend the inventoryCheck Web service to include price information as well as availability. You will see in Chapter 7 how this service prepares SkatesTown to participate in dynamic e-marketplaces.

The priceCheck Web service is an extension of the inventoryCheck Web service, allowing a requestor to determine the price of one of SkatesTown's products. The response is a price and the number of units of that item currently available from inventory.

The entire priceCheck WSDL document is shown in Listing 6.1.

LISTING 6.1   The priceCheck WSDL Document

```xml
<?xml version="1.0"?>
<definitions name="PriceCheck"
   targetNamespace="http://www.skatestown.com/services/PriceCheck"
   xmlns:pc="http://www.skatestown.com/services/PriceCheck"
   xmlns:avail="http://www.skatestown.com/ns/availability"
   xmlns:xsd="http://www.w3.org/2001/XMLSchema"
   xmlns:soap="http://schemas.xmlsoap.org/wsdl/soap/"
   xmlns="http://schemas.xmlsoap.org/wsdl/">

   <!-- Type definitions -->
   <types>
      <xsd:schema targetNamespace="http://www.skatestown.com/ns/availability"
         xmlns:xsd="http://www.w3.org/2001/XMLSchema">
         <xsd:complexType name="availabilityType">
```

LISTING 6.1   Continued

```
            <xsd:sequence>
               <xsd:element name="sku" type="xsd:string"/>
               <xsd:element name="price" type="xsd:double"/>
               <xsd:element name="quantityAvailable" type="xsd:integer"/>
            </xsd:sequence>
         </xsd:complexType>
      </xsd:schema>
   </types>

   <!-- Message definitions -->
   <!-- A PriceCheckRequest is simply an item code (sku)  -->
   <message name="PriceCheckRequest">
      <part name="sku" type="xsd:string"/>
   </message>

   <!-- A PriceCheckResponse consists of an availability structure,   -->
   <!-- defined above.                                                -->
   <message name="PriceCheckResponse">
      <part name="result" type="avail:availabilityType"/>
   </message>

   <!-- Port type definitions -->
   <portType name="PriceCheckPortType">
      <operation name="checkPrice">
        <input message="pc:PriceCheckRequest"/>
        <output message="pc:PriceCheckResponse"/>
      </operation>
   </portType>

   <!-- Binding definitions -->
   <binding name="PriceCheckSOAPBinding" type="pc:PriceCheckPortType">
      <soap:binding style="rpc"
         transport="http://schemas.xmlsoap.org/soap/http"/>
      <operation name="checkPrice">
        <soap:operation soapAction=""/>
        <input>
           <soap:body use="encoded"
                      namespace=
                         "http://www.skatestown.com/services/PriceCheck"
                      encodingStyle=
                         "http://schemas.xmlsoap.org/soap/encoding/"/>
        </input>
        <output>
           <soap:body use="encoded"
                      namespace=
                         "http://www.skatestown.com/services/PriceCheck"
```

LISTING 6.1   Continued

```
                        encodingStyle=
                          "http://schemas.xmlsoap.org/soap/encoding/"/>
        </output>
      </operation>
    </binding>

    <!-- Service definition -->
    <service name="PriceCheckService">
      <port name="PriceCheck" binding="pc:PriceCheckSOAPBinding">
        <soap:address
          location=
            "http://localhost:8080/axis/services/PriceCheck"/>
      </port>
    </service>
</definitions>
```

This WSDL document will come up again in Chapter 7 when we discuss how WSDL documents are published and found in a UDDI registry.

The second example woven into the next sections illustrates more sophisticated uses of WSDL (but by no means is it the most complicated use). We have included the entire WSDL file in Listing 6.2, but don't panic; we explain the business purpose of this Web service and each part of the WSDL in subsequent paragraphs. For now, just take a quick glance at it, and let the explanations clarify any questions. Refer back to this listing frequently.

LISTING 6.2   The StockAvailableNotification WSDL Document

```
<?xml version="1.0" ?>
<definitions name="StockAvailableNotification"
        targetNamespace=
          "http://www.skatestown.com/services/StockAvailableNotification"
        xmlns:xsd="http://www.w3.org/2000/10/XMLSchema"
        xmlns:reg="http://www.skatestown.com/ns/registrationRequest"
        xmlns:soap="http://schemas.xmlsoap.org/wsdl/soap/"
        xmlns:soapenc="http://schemas.xmlsoap.org/soap/encoding/"
        xmlns="http://schemas.xmlsoap.org/wsdl/">

    <!-- Type definitions from the registration schema-->
    <types>
      <xsd:schema targetNamespace=
                    "http://www.skatestown.com/ns/registrationRequest"
        xmlns:xsd="http://www.w3.org/2000/10/XMLSchema"
        xmlns="http://www.skatestown.com/schemas/ns/registrationRequest">

        <xsd:complexType name="registrationRequest">
```

LISTING 6.2   Continued

```
                  <xsd:sequence>
                     <xsd:element name="items">
                        <xsd:complexType name="ArrayOfItem">
                           <complexContent>
                              <restriction base="soapenc:Array">
                                 <attribute ref="soapenc:arrayType"
                                     wsdl:arrayType="xsd:string[]"/>
                              </restriction>
                           </complexContent>
                        </complexType>
                     </xsd:element>

                     <xsd:element name="address" type="xsd:uriReference"/>

                     <xsd:element name="transport"
                                  default="http://schemas.xmlsoap.org/soap/smtp"
                                  minOccurs="0">
                        <xsd:simpleType>
                           <xsd:restriction base="xsd:uriReference">
                              <xsd:enumeration
                                 value="http://schemas.xmlsoap.org/soap/http"/>
                              <xsd:enumeration
                                 value="http://schemas.xmlsoap.org/soap/smtp"/>
                           </xsd:restriction>
                        </xsd:simpleType>
                     </xsd:element>

                     <xsd:element name="clientArg" type="xsd:string" minOccurs="0"/>
                  </xsd:sequence>
               </xsd:complexType>

            <xsd:simpleType name="correlationID">
               <xsd:restriction base="xsd:string">
               <!-- some appropriate restriction -->
               </xsd:restriction>
            </xsd:simpleType>
         </xsd:schema>
      </types>

      <!-- Message definitions -->
      <message name="StockAvailableRegistrationRequest">
         <part name="registration" element="reg:registrationRequest"/>
         <part name="expiration" type="xsd:timeInstant"/>
      </message>
```

LISTING 6.2   Continued

```xml
<message name="StockAvailableRegistrationResponse">
   <part name="correlationID" type="reg:correlationID"/>
</message>

<message name="StockAvailableRegistrationError">
   <part name="errorString" type="xsd:string"/>
</message>

<message name="StockAvailableExpirationError">
   <part name="errorString" type="xsd:string"/>
</message>

<message name="StockAvailableNotification">
   <part name="timeStamp" type="xsd:timeInstant"/>
   <part name="correlationID" type="reg:correlationID"/>
   <part name="items" type="reg:items"/>
   <part name="clientArg" type="xsd:string"/>
</message>

<message name="StockAvailableExpirationNotification">
   <part name="timeStamp" type="xsd:timeInstant"/>
   <part name="correlationID" type="reg:correlationID"/>
   <part name="items" type="reg:ArrayOfItem"/>
   <part name="clientArg" type="xsd:string"/>
</message>

<message name="StockAvailableCancellation">
   <part name="correlationID" type="reg:correlationID"/>
</message>

<!-- Port type definitions -->
<portType name="StockAvailableNotificationPortType">
   <!--Registration Operation -->
   <operation name="registration">
      <input message="StockAvailableRegistrationRequest"/>
      <output message="StockAvailableRegistrationResponse"/>
      <fault message="StockAvailableRegistrationError"
         name="StockAvailableNotificationErrorMessage"/>
      <fault message="StockAvailableExpirationError"
         name="StockAvailableExpirationError"/>
   </operation>

   <!--Notification Operation -->
   <operation name="notification">
```

LISTING 6.2   Continued

```xml
            <output message="StockAvailableNotification"/>
        </operation>

        <!--Expiration Notification Operation -->
        <operation name="expirationNotification">
            <output message="StockAvailableExpirationNotification"/>
        </operation>

        <!--Cancellation Operation -->
        <operation name="cancellation">
            <input message=" StockAvailableCancellation"/>
        </operation>
    </portType>

    <!-- Binding definitions -->
    <binding name="StockAvailableNotificationSOAPBinding"
        type="StockAvailableNotificationPortType">
        <soap:binding style="rpc"
                transport="http://schemas.xmlsoap.org/soap/http"/>

        <documentation>
            Note: the requestor must invoke the registration operation first.
        </documentation>

        <operation name="registration">
            <soap:operation soapAction=
                "http://www.skatestown.com/StockAvailableNotification/registration">
            <input>
                <soap:header message="StockAvailableRegistrationRequest"
                        part="expiration" use="encoded"
                        namespace="http://www.skatestown.com/ns/registrationRequest"
                        encodingStyle="http://schemas.xmlsoap.org/soap/encoding/"/>
                    <soap:headerfault message="StockAvailableExpirationError"
                        part="errorString" use="encoded"
                        namespace="http://www.skatestown.com/ns/registrationRequest"
                        encodingStyle="http://schemas.xmlsoap.org/soap/encoding/"/>
                </soap:header>
                <soap:body parts="registration" use="literal" style="document"/>
            </input>
            <output>
                <soap:body use="encoded"
                    namespace="http://www.skatestown.com/ns/registrationRequest"
                    encodingStyle="http://schemas.xmlsoap.org/soap/encoding/"/>
```

LISTING 6.2 Continued

```
      </output>
      <fault name="StockAvailableNotificationErrorMessage">
         <soap:fault name="StockAvailableNotificationErrorMessage"
             namespace="http://www.skatestown.com/ns/registrationRequest"
             encodingStyle="http://schemas.xmlsoap.org/soap/encoding/"/>
      </fault>
   </operation>

   <operation name="notification">
      <output>
         <soap:body use="encoded"
             namespace="http://www.skatestown.com/ns/registrationRequest"
             encodingStyle="http://schemas.xmlsoap.org/soap/encoding/"/>
      </output>
   </operation>

   <operation name="cancellation">
      <soap:operation soapAction=
        "http://www.skatestown.com/StockAvailableNotification/cancellation">
      <input>
         <soap:body use="encoded"
             namespace="http://www.skatestown.com/ns/registrationRequest"
             encodingStyle="http://schemas.xmlsoap.org/soap/encoding/"/>
      </input>
   </operation>
</binding>

<!-- Service definition -->
<service name="StockAvailableNotificationService">
   <port name="StockAvailableNotificationPort" binding="
        StockAvailableNotificationSOAPBinding ">
      <soap:address location=
        "http://www.skatestown.com/axis/services/StockNotification"/>
   </port>
</service>

</definitions>
```

The StockAvailableNotification Web service is provided by SkatesTown to support product ordering. The RegistrationRequest schema defines the data types. In particular, this Web service is used when a customer places an order with SkatesTown, but one or more of the items is not currently available from SkatesTown's inventory. The purpose of this service is to allow customers of SkatesTown to register to be notified when all the products in their order are once again available for sale from inventory. This Web service has four operations.

The first operation allows the customer to register for a notification. This is a request/response operation. The customer invokes this service, passing in a collection of item numbers (for out of stock product numbers), network address, (default is an e-mail address) an optional transport type (valid values are `"http://schemas.xmlsoap.org/soap/http"` and `"http://schemas.xmlsoap.org/soap/smtp"`), and a `client` argument token of type `string`. The `client` argument token is opaque to the service; it is a requestor-specific correlation identifier. The `client` argument is returned by the notification operation.

This operation also includes an expiration time to be included in the message (as a `soap:header`, as we will discover).

The *normal* response of this operation is a provider-side *correlation id* 📖 (a string).

The possible fault messages include:

- Invalid product number (one of the product numbers does not correspond to a product in SkatesTown's product catalog)
- Invalid transport (some value other than `smtp` or `http` was specified)
- Invalid expiration (this appears as a `soap:headerfault` 📖 if the original expiration time header was invalid in some way; we will describe `soap:headerfault` elements in more detail in the section "SOAP Fault and HeaderFault Formatting").

The second operation, `notification`, uses the `notification` *transmission primitive* 📖 in WSDL (we'll talk about transmission primitives in more detail later). This message is sent from SkatesTown to the requestor's address indicated in the registration operation. This message indicates a timestamp, the provider-side correlation ID established in the registration message, the item numbers from the registration message, and the requestor-specific correlation ID.

The third operation, `expirationNotification`, also uses the `notification` transmission primitive in WSDL. This message is sent from SkatesTown to the requestor's address when the expiration period indicated on the original registration operation expires. This message indicates a timestamp, the provider-side correlation ID established in the registration message, the item numbers from the registration message, and the requestor-specific correlation ID.

The fourth operation is a one-way operation for cancellation of the notification. It allows the requestor to abandon its interest in the notification. The cancellation message is simply the provider-side correlation ID.

Now, let's examine the WSDL language element by element, using the `priceCheck` WSDL to show the simple, typical use and the `StockAvailableNotification` example to show more sophisticated WSDL use.

PortType

The best starting point to understanding a Web service using a WSDL document is the portType element. The portType element describes the interface to a Web service. This is the most succinct description of what the service does; understand the portType, and you understand what the Web service does. The rest of the elements in the WSDL definition are essentially details that the portType depends upon; we will examine them in later sections.

The portType in the priceCheck service description looks like this:

```
<!-- Port type definitions -->
<portType name="PriceCheckPortType">
   <operation name="checkPrice">
      <input message="PriceCheckRequest"/>
      <output message="PriceCheckResponse"/>
   </operation>
</portType>
```

A WSDL document can contain zero or more portType definitions. Typically, most WSDL documents contain a single portType. This convention separates out different Web service interface definitions into different documents. This granularity of separation is good for reasons of reuse, and when we discuss how UDDI can be used to register WSDL documents, this best practice will become apparent.

A portType element has a single name attribute. In our case, the priceCheck Web service contains a portType of name PriceCheckPortType. Often, you will see the name of the portType follow this pattern: *nameOfWebService*PortType. If there are multiple portTypes in a WSDL file, each portType must have a different name.

Pretty simple so far, but simple, well-factored Web services often result in a simple looking portType. Much of the detail is in the rest of the elements in the WSDL definition, and as far as the portType element is concerned, the detail is in the collection of operation child elements. Just as a Java interface definition is comprised mainly of method signatures, the interesting part of a portType definition is the collection of operation elements it contains.

Operation

An operation element in WSDL is the equivalent of a method signature in Java. An operation defines a method on a Web service, including the name of the method and the input parameters and the output or return type of the method.

The PriceCheck portType describes one operation, named (cleverly) checkPrice. The portType for the StockAvailableNotification service defines four operations: registration, notification, expirationNotification, and cancellation.

The `checkPrice` operation defines an input message and output message. If we invoke the `checkPrice` operation with a `priceCheckRequestMessage` (we'll see what exactly these messages look like in the next section), the Web service will return a `priceCheckResponseMessage`.

That is all there is to an `operation` element. The `operation` elements define a combination of input, output, and fault messages. The WSDL specification defines four different combinations of input, output, and fault messages. WSDL uses the term *transmission primitive* to describe these combinations. Chapter 3 introduced these concepts as interaction patterns. We now revisit these concepts in the context of how to use WSDL to describe these patterns.

Request-Response Style of Operation

This is the most common form of operation. The request-response operation defines an input message, output message, and an optional collection of fault messages. Because many Web services are deployed using SOAP over HTTP, request-response is the most common form of operation type found in WSDL documents. The `checkPrice` operation is a request-response operation as is the registration operation from the `StockAvailableNotification` service. Request-response messages can be informational, retrieving information about some object represented by a Web service; or a request-response operation can be behavioral, where the message changes the state of the service provider and information about the new state is included in the response. The `checkPrice` operation is an informational style message. The registration operation is a behavior service, because it updates the provider's server with new information about a requestor waiting on a `stockAvailable` event to fire.

Although `checkPrice` does not use it, the request-response transmission primitive allows the service provider to list the possible fault messages that can appear in response to a Web service invocation. The `fault message` element is used within the `StockAvailableNotificationPortType` as part of the registration operation's definition:

```
<portType name="StockAvailableNotificationPortType">
   <!--Registration Operation -->
   <operation name="registration">
      <input message="StockAvailableRegistrationRequest"/>
      <output message="StockAvailableRegistrationResponse"/>
      <fault message="StockAvailableRegistrationError"
         name="StockAvailableNotificationErrorMessage"/>
      <fault message="StockAvailableExpirationError"
         name="StockAvailableExpirationError"/>
   </operation>
```

`Fault` elements must be named, and the name must be unique among all the fault elements defined for the operation. Like the input and output elements, the `fault` element uses a message element to describe the data contents of the fault.

One-way Style of Operation

A one-way operation does not have an `output` element (or a `fault` element for that matter). A one-way operation is like a data sink. A one-way message would be used to change state of the service provider. Clearly a one-way message is useless for informational purposes (no response is sent back to the requestor).

The cancellation operation from the `StockAvailableNotification` service is a one-way operation:

```
<!--Cancellation Operation -->
<operation name="cancellation">
   <input message=" StockAvailableCancellation"/>
</operation>
```

Because many Web services are accessed through SOAP over HTTP, many one-way messages end up being request-response messages, with the response being a simple HTTP-level acknowledgement of the message. The operation does not model the acknowledgement or transport-level message flow for a couple of reasons. First, the details of the transport protocol is a detail of the binding element, not the operation element. Second, no application-level semantic is transmitted in response to the Web service invocation.

Notification Style of Operation

A notification operation is like a one-way push from the service provider. Output messages are pushed to the service requestor as the result of some event on the service provider side, such as a time-out or operation completion. The notification operation in the `StockAvailableNotification` Web service is a notification type of operation; SkatesTown pushes a message to the requestor when a particular item is once again in stock. The notification style of interaction is commonly used in systems built around asynchronous messaging. Although systems with asynchronous messaging might be a little harder to conceptualize and implement, they are much more loosely coupled, and, therefore, are easier to maintain; often this flexibility adds robustness to the system.

Given the notification operation is a one-way push message, how does SkatesTown know where to push the output messages to? Nothing in the WSDL specification describes this directly. This correlation semantic must be described by other means. One mechanism used to address this problem is to have a network address (a URL or e-mail address) as a parameter in another message.

In the case of the `StockAvailableNotification` Web service, SkatesTown has created the registration operation shown in Listing 6.2 for just the purpose of determining where to send a notification message. The service requestor must invoke the registration operation first, and then the notification operation will be able to send a message to the requestor. The ordering requirement of these operations—that is, the fact that the registration operation must be invoked in order to receive notification messages—cannot be described in WSDL. Potentially, this ordering semantic might be represented in the WSEL language (described briefly later in this chapter). At this point, SkatesTown must describe this semantic using prose. The following documentation element appears with this portType:

```
<documentation>
    Note: the requestor must invoke the registration operation first.
</documentation>
```

Solicit-Response Style of Operation

A solicit-response operation models a push operation similar to a notification operation. However, unlike the notification style of operation, the solicit-response operation expects an input (response) from the service requestor in response to the solicit-response output flow. A solicit-response operation could look like this:

```
<portType name="someName">
   <operation name="exampleSolicitResponse">
      <output message="pushThis"/>
      <input message="responseToPush"/>
      <fault name="someFaultName" message="faultPushedToRequestor"/>
   </operation>
</portType>
```

Output and fault flows are pushed to the service requestor as the result of some event on the service provider side, such as a time out or operation completion. The solicit-response style of operation has the same problem as the notification style of operation: where to push the output/fault messages. Again, the solution is the same as we discussed with the notification style of operation.

The only way to tell the difference between a request-response operation and a solicit-response operation is the ordering of the input and output elements. In request-response, the input child element comes first. In solicit-response, the output child element comes first.

Rounding Out the Operation Element

The current state of the WSDL tooling really emphasizes request-response and one-way messages. Because solicit-response messages require some sort of correlation or registration to associate the message with something meaningful to the requestor, they require a level of association that is beyond the simple semantics represented by WSDL. The operation-ordering semantic could not be enforced in generated code. Similarly, a notification message requires a preceding registration message from the service requestor. Again, this correlation semantic cannot be directly represented in WSDL. Most tools do not support solicit-response or notification. For that matter, most tools support only request-response.

Let's consider a couple of final details related to the `operation` element. The WSDL specification allows the input, output, and fault messages to have a `name` attribute. Typically, this `name` attribute is not specified by the designer on `input` and `output` elements. This detail is often too much clutter in the WSDL document (as if a WSDL document is not already too cluttered!). And besides, WSDL provides default values for these names based on the operation name. For example, we repeat our `priceCheck` example, this time filling in the default values that WSDL would have supplied:

```
<!-- Port type definitions -->
<portType name="PriceCheckPortType">
   <operation name="checkPrice">
      <input name="checkPriceRequest" message="PriceCheckRequest"/>
      <output name="checkPriceResponse" message="PriceCheckResponse"/>
   </operation>
</portType>
```

Typically, the `name` attribute of the `input` and `output` element doesn't add much. Further, you will find that many WSDL designers already encode this information into the names of the message elements they define. If you do add a name to an `input` or `output` element, this name must be unique among all the `input` and `output` elements within the `portType`. Table 6.2 describes the default names for `input` and `output` elements, for an operation named XXX.

TABLE 6.2 Defaults for `Input` and `Output` Elements for Operation XXX

	Input	*Output*
Request-Response	XXXRequest	XXXResponse
One-Way	XXX	Not applicable
Solicit-Response	XXXSolicit	XXXResponse
Notification	Not applicable	XXX

`Fault` elements, of course, require a name, because several `fault` elements can be associated with any operation and the fault name is used to distinguish between the collection of possible faults. This is particularly important in the `binding` element, which describes the mapping between the `fault` element and the way the fault is presented in a protocol-specific fashion.

WSDL also lets you specify a `parameterOrder` attribute on an operation. The `parameterOrder` operation is used only for RPC-style operations. This is a bit of a layering violation in the specification, because the `portType` is abstract, and its nature as an RPC or document-centric message is revealed in the binding element. Further, this element is informational only, and is completely optional, even for operations that are described as RPC within the `binding` element. The only purpose of this attribute is to provide a mechanism to describe the original parameter ordering of the RPC function as a list of part names (we will see part names discussed in the following "Message" section) separated by spaces.

So far, we have not defined what we mean by a `priceCheckRequest` message, or any of the messages for that matter. These are simply abstract messages. The composition of an abstract message is detailed in a `message` element, described next.

Message

A message is a very simple concept. A message is a collection of parts. A WSDL document can contain zero or more `message` elements. Each `message` element can be used as an input message, output message, or fault message within an operation.

What is a message? Let's take a look at the messages defined in the `priceCheck` WSDL:

```
<!-- Message definitions -->
<!-- A PriceCheckRequest is simply an item code (sku)  -->
<message name="PriceCheckRequest">
   <part name="sku" type="xsd:string"/>
</message>

<!-- A PriceCheckResponse consists of an availability structure,   -->
<!-- defined above.                                                -->
<message name="PriceCheckResponse">
   <part name="result" type="avail:availabilityType"/>
</message>
```

The first message, `PriceCheckRequest`, is a simple `message` element. Recall that `PriceCheckRequest` is used as the input message to the `checkPrice` operation. All `message` elements must have a name, and that name must be unique among all the `message` elements defined in the WSDL document.

The `PriceCheckRequest` message defines one `part` element named `item`. A `part` element is made up of two properties: the name of the part and the type of the part. The `name` attribute must be unique among all the `part` child elements of the `message` element. The `type` property of the part is defined as either a `type` attribute (a `simpleType`, `complexType` from the XSD schema type system) or an `element` attribute (also defined using the XSD schema type system). We will examine types in more detail in the next section. Often, the name of the part says it all, and you need not dive into the details of how the types associated with the part are modeled. As we will see later, the item part will turn into a `method` parameter in the service invocation.

In the `PriceCheckRequest` example, the type of the part named item is a simple string. The XML comment above the element definition (we could have used a WSDL `documentation` element) indicates that the string is to be interpreted as an item code. Of course, a better model might have been to define a complex type giving a pattern or range that an item code should be constrained to. However, we didn't make that choice here.

The only other message element defined in the priceCheck WSDL is PriceCheckResponse. The PriceCheckResponse message describes the format of the output message of the checkPrice operation. Like its companion message, PriceCheckResponse defines a single part. The result part is slightly more interesting because its type is a complex type defined in the namespace corresponding to the avail: prefix.

That's it for simple messages. You can see that the separation of messages from the operation is extremely well factored, but somewhat overkill for this kind of simple example. Many WSDL documents do not require the full power achieved by factoring messages from operations and decomposing messages into parts.

The parts mechanism in WSDL is used to allow a message to be decomposed into smaller units or parts. Each part can be manifested in different ways in the various network protocols. This mapping between parts and protocol-specific components is described in the binding element. Some parts of the messages can appear as SOAP header elements. Some parts can be mapped to HTTP headers. Some parts can be used as individual parameters in an RPC message. You really cannot understand the true use of a part until you look at how the abstract notion of the part is mapped into a concrete data representation. This mapping is the responsibility of the binding element.

StockAvailableNotification is an example of a complex, multipart message:

```
<message name="StockAvailableNotification">
    <part name="timeStamp" type="xsd:timeInstant"/>
    <part name="correlationID" type="reg:correlationID"/>
    <part name="items" type="reg:items"/>
    <part name="clientArg" type="xsd:string"/>
</message>
```

We will examine how different parts are modeled as different components of a message in the "SOAP Header Formatting" section.

Type

We have seen the message element in WSDL, and the part elements that are contained within it. However, some of the types used in these example WSDL documents need further discussion.

The default type system in WSDL is XML Schema (XSD). This approach is useful to describe most of the type used in the messages to invoke a Web service. The types element in the priceCheck WSDL is pretty typical of the use of this element:

```
<!-- Type definitions -->
<types>
   <xsd:schema targetNamespace="http://www.skatestown.com/ns/availability"
      xmlns:xsd="http://www.w3.org/2001/XMLSchema">
      <xsd:complexType name="availabilityType">
         <xsd:sequence>
            <xsd:element name="sku" type="xsd:string"/>
            <xsd:element name="price" type="xsd:double"/>
            <xsd:element name="quantityAvailable" type="xsd:integer"/>
         </xsd:sequence>
      </xsd:complexType>
   </xsd:schema>
</types>
```

The contents of the `types` element look very much like a schema definition using XSD. Many organizations already have XML schemas defined. Because the `types` element in WSDL is defined to contain one or more schema definition elements, WSDL repurposes work already done in XML. Business objects already modeled in XML can be used as parts of the message elements and, therefore, used to define the input and output elements for the Web services' operations.

For the `priceCheck` WSDL, the availability type is defined using a `types` element from WSDL. Recall that the availability type was used as part of the `PriceCheckResponse` message. This is all standard XML schema work that we covered in Chapter 2, "XML Primer."

WSDL is quite flexible in the type system used. Although XML Schema is the predominant type system used, the `types` element allows you the flexibility to describe a completely different type system. The `types` element has an `extensibility` element that lets you describe another type system, say the Java type system, and define all the messages in terms of this type system. Consider, however, that deviating from the XML Schema type system increases the chances that more service requestors will be unable to invoke your Web service.

There are several variants of XML Schema; schema has been under development by the W3C for several years. The XML Schema version referenced in the listings is `http://www.w3.org/2001/XMLSchema`. You might also encounter other versions of schema used in `types` elements (and as we will see later in the `definitions` element, too): `http://www.w3.org/2000/10/XMLSchema` and often `http://www.w3.org/1999/XMLSchema`. These declarations have subtle implications on some sophisticated use of the XML Schema language. Consult advanced resources on XML schema for more detail.

The `types` element is essentially a place for the WSDL document to define some user-defined XML types for later use in the `message` elements. A WSDL document can have at most one `types` element in a document. When a `types` element appears in a WSDL document, it typically contains a single schema definition element, although it is legal to have more than one schema definition element. You will typically see multiple schema definition elements if the Web service is using datatypes defined elsewhere in multiple schemas.

Let's take a closer look at the way the items type is defined within SkatesTown's registrationRequest schema. Normally, to define a type that contains a repeating group of elements, you would use the following style of XML schema:

```
<xsd:complexType name="registrationRequest">
    <xsd:sequence>
        <xsd:element name="items"
            type="xsd:string" maxOccurs="unbounded" />
```

However, in WSDL, repeating groups such as this must be modeled using the array data type from the SOAP encoding namespace (xmlns:soapenc="http://schemas.xmlsoap.org/soap/encoding/"). This is another jarring example where an aspect of the message encoding (really the domain of the binding element, as we will see in the next section) imposes itself on the base datatyping mechanism in WSDL. This is an artifact of the common use of WSDL to model SOAP messages. So, regardless of whether your Web service uses SOAP, you need to use the array datatype from the SOAP encoding namespace to model repeating groups. The following snippet shows the registrationRequest type:

```
<xsd:complexType name="registrationRequest">
    <xsd:sequence>
        <xsd:element name="items">
            <xsd:complexType name="ArrayOfItem">
                <complexContent>
                    <restriction base="soapenc:Array">
                        <attribute ref="soapenc:arrayType"
                            wsdl:arrayType="xsd:string[]"/>
                    </restriction>
                </complexContent>
            </complexType>
        </xsd:element>
```

By convention, the name of the type is ArrayOfXXX, where XXX is the base type of the elements that are to appear in the repeating group. The type itself is an extension of the base Array type in the SOAP encoding namespace. WSDL adds an arrayType attribute to let you formally declare the exact base type of the repeating group (in this case, it is simply the string base type from XML schema). Note that the [] characters also specify the array has a single dimension.

That's it for types. Essentially, the complexity is in modeling XML, not in modeling WSDL.

Binding

We have seen that the `PriceCheck` and `StockAvailableNotification` services define several operations, and we have some idea about the sorts of XML elements that these operations need as input and produce for output. However, to this point, we still do not know how to format the message to invoke these operations. We haven't seen anything in the WSDL description that relates to SOAP headers, SOAP bodies, SOAP encoding, and so on. The `portType`, `message`, and `type` elements define the *abstract* or *reusable* portion of the WSDL definition. Is this service invoked by a SOAP message, or a simple HTTP POST of an XML payload? Is this an RPC invocation or a document-centric message invocation? These details are given by one or more `binding` elements associated with the `portType`.

The `binding` element in WSDL tells the service requestor how to format the message in a protocol-*specific* manner. Each `portType` can have one or more `binding` elements associated with it. For a given `portType`, a `binding` element can describe how to invoke operations using a single messaging/transport protocol, like SOAP over HTTP, SOAP over SMTP, a simple HTTP POST operation, or any other valid combination of networking and messaging protocol standards.

Let's take a look at the `binding` element in the `priceCheck` WSDL:

```
<!-- Binding definitions -->
<binding name="PriceCheckSOAPBinding" type="pc:PriceCheckPortType">
  <soap:binding style="rpc"
     transport=
     "http://schemas.xmlsoap.org/soap/http"/>
  <operation name="checkPrice">
     <soap:operation soapAction=""/>
     <input>
        <soap:body use="encoded"
        namespace="http://www.skatestown.com/services/PriceCheck"
        encodingStyle="http://schemas.xmlsoap.org/soap/encoding/"/>
     </input>
     <output>
        <soap:body use="encoded"
        namespace="http://www.skatestown.com/services/PriceCheck"
        encodingStyle="http://schemas.xmlsoap.org/soap/encoding/"/>
     </output>
  </operation>
</binding>
```

The name of this `binding` element is `PriceCheckSOAPBinding`. The name must be unique among all the `binding` elements defined in the WSDL document. Conventionally, the name of the binding combines the `portType` name with the name(s) of the protocol(s) to which the binding maps. The `type` attribute identifies which `portType` this binding describes. Because WSDL uses name referencing to link the `binding` element to a `portType`, you can now see why `portType` name uniqueness is so important. We will see the same is true for binding name uniqueness when we discuss how the `port` element references a `binding` element.

Typically, most WSDL documents contain only a single binding. The reason is similar to why conventional WSDL documents contain a single `portType` element: convenience of reuse.

Now, which protocol is this `binding` element mapping the `priceCheck` `portType` to? We need to look for clues inside the `binding` element (besides the naming convention, of course). The first clue is the prefix of the first child element, `soap:binding`. This is a pretty strong hint that this binding is related to the SOAP messaging protocol. So, the `PriceCheckSOAPBinding` element describes how the `priceCheck` `portType` (remember, `priceCheck` is an abstract service interface definition) is expressed using SOAP.

How are the *SOAP* aspects of the `priceCheck` service invocation described in this `binding` element? WSDL defines a very clever extensibility convention that allows the `binding` element to be extended, with elements from different XML namespaces, to describe bindings to any number of messaging and transport protocols. Pick a messaging/transport protocol set, find the WSDL convention that corresponds to that pair, and fill in the details. The WSDL spec defines three standard binding extensions for SOAP/HTTP, HTTP GET/POST, and SOAP with MIME attachments. All sorts of activities are underway to define additional binding conventions.

The `PriceCheckSOAPBinding` element shown earlier decorates the elements from the `priceCheck` `portType` in four ways (invocation style, SOAPAction, input message appearance, and output message appearance), as explained in the following sections. This is a pretty straightforward use of the SOAP binding extension convention described in the WSDL specification. The SOAP binding style also specifies the way SOAP headers, SOAP faults, and SOAP headerfaults should be formatted. These additional aspects of the SOAP binding convention are illustrated in the `StockAvailableNotificationSOAPBinding`.

Invocation Style

The first use of the SOAP binding extension indicates the style of invocation:

```
<soap:binding style="rpc"
              transport="http://schemas.xmlsoap.org/soap/http"/>
```

This declaration applies to the entire binding. It indicates that all operations for the `priceCheck` `portType` are defined in this binding as SOAP messages. Further, the `style` attribute indicates that operations will follow the remote procedure call (RPC) conventions on the SOAP body as defined in the SOAP specification. This default can be explicitly overridden by a style declaration in a child `operation` element. The other alternative value for the `style` attribute is `document`, meaning the body of the SOAP message is to be interpreted as straight XML, more of a document-centric message send than a remote procedure call. The default value of this attribute is `document`. The registration operation from the `StockAvailableNotification` service uses a `document` style for the input flow.

The `transport` attribute tells you that the requestor must send the SOAP message using HTTP. Other possible values for this attribute could include `http://schemas.xmlsoap.org/soap/SMTP/`, `http://schemas.xmlsoap.org/soap/ftp/`, and so on.

SOAPAction

The second use of the SOAP binding extension is:

```
<operation name="checkPrice">
   <soap:operation SOAPAction=""/>
```

This declaration indicates the value that should be placed in the `SOAPAction` HTTP header as part of the HTTP message carrying the `priceCheck` service invocation message. As we discussed in Chapter 3, the purpose of the `SOAPAction` header is to describe the intent of the message. In the case of the `checkPrice` operation, the WSDL tells the service requestor to put an empty string as the value for the `SOAPAction` header. Although an empty string is a valid value for `SOAPAction`, it is not terribly helpful for the SOAP router. Note that a `SOAPAction` header with value of empty string indicates that the URI of the request is the place where the intent of the message is to be found. If the `SOAPAction` value is completely empty, no intent of the message is to be found. Better conventions with SOAP would require the requestor to put an interesting value as the `SOAPAction` to help some SOAP routers dispatch the message to the appropriate Web service. The operations in the `StockAvailableNotification` service use this convention:

```
<operation name="registration">
   <soap:operation
      soapAction=
      "http://www.skatestown.com/StockAvailableNotification/registration">
```

and

```
<operation name="cancellation">
   <soap:operation
      soapAction=
      "http://www.skatestown.com/StockAvailableNotification/cancellation">
```

This shows that different operations in the same `portType` can be assigned different `SOAPAction` headers by the `binding` element. Note that the `notification` and `expirationNotification` operation elements do not have `soap:operation` child elements. These operations are not invoked using SOAP over HTTP by the requestor.

Note, however, that the semantics of the `SOAPAction` header are quite controversial. As of this writing, the XML Protocol Working Group of the W3C is considering removing the `SOAPAction` HTTP header concept from the XML Protocol (the follow-up to SOAP). This is another reason why the URL dispatch is very popular, especially with things like Axis JWS files. This technique is demonstrated in all the examples in Chapter 3. We recommend using the URL of the message to express the intent of the message.

This `soap:operation` element can also be used to override the default style specified in the `soap:binding` element's `style` attribute. In the case of the `StockAvailableNotificationSOAPBinding`, the default style is `rpc`. However, the `registration` operation overrides this default to use the document style for its input message:

```
<operation name="registration">
  <soap:operation
    soapAction=
    "http://www.skatestown.com/StockAvailableNotification/registration">
. . .
    <soap:body parts="registration" use="literal" style="document"/>
```

Input Message Appearance

The third use of the SOAP binding extension in the `priceCheck` WSDL document describes exactly how the input message to the `checkPrice` appears in the parts of the SOAP message:

```
<input>
  <soap:body use="encoded"
        namespace="http://www.skatestown.com/services/PriceCheck"
    encodingStyle="http://schemas.xmlsoap.org/soap/encoding/"/>
</input>
```

In this case, it is a pretty simple mapping. The entire input message, `PriceCheckRequest` (remember, from the `portType` declaration for the `checkPrice` operation) is declared to be abstract in this case (`use="encoded"`). This means that the XML defining the input message and its parts are in fact abstract, and the real, concrete representation of the data is to be derived by applying the encoding scheme indicated in the `encodingStyle` attribute. This is a long-winded way to say that the message should appear as part of the SOAP `body` element and that the SOAP engine on the service provider's network will deserialize the information from XML to another format (such as Java types) using the encoding style defined in the SOAP specification.

The `soap:body` declaration also interacts with the style of the operation. Because the `checkPrice` operation was declared as RPC style, the parts of the `checkPrice` input message will appear as child elements of the `SOAP:body` element in the SOAP message. Further, these parts will appear as parameters in the style of the RPC convention defined by the SOAP specification. Here is an example SOAP message that conforms to the pattern this binding element describes for the input of the `checkPrice` operation:

```
<?xml version="1.0" encoding="UTF-8"?>
<SOAP-ENV:Envelope xmlns:SOAP-ENV="http://schemas.xmlsoap.org/soap/envelope/"
  xmlns:xsd="http://www.w3.org/2001/XMLSchema"
```

```
      xmlns:xsi="http://www.w3.org/2001/XMLSchema-instance">
  <SOAP-ENV:Body>
   <ns3:checkPrice xmlns:ns3="http://www.skatestown.com/services/PriceCheck">
    <sku xsi:type="xsd:string">947-TI
    </sku>
   </ns3:checkPrice>
  </SOAP-ENV:Body>
 </SOAP-ENV:Envelope>
```

Output Message Appearance

The fourth use of the SOAP binding extension in our example describes exactly how the output message of checkPrice should appear. Nothing new is introduced with this example. For completeness, here is an example response that corresponds to the pattern described in the binding element for the output of the checkPrice operation:

```
<?xml version="1.0" encoding="UTF-8"?>
<SOAP-ENV:Envelope
   SOAP-ENV:encodingStyle="http://schemas.xmlsoap.org/soap/encoding/"
   xmlns:SOAP-ENV="http://schemas.xmlsoap.org/soap/envelope/"
   xmlns:xsd="http://www.w3.org/2001/XMLSchema"
   xmlns:xsi="http://www.w3.org/2001/XMLSchema-instance">
  <SOAP-ENV:Body>
   <ns3:checkPriceResponse
   xmlns:ns3="http://www.skatestown.com/services/PriceCheck">
    <checkPriceResult href="#id0"/>
   </ns3:checkPriceResponse>
   <multiRef id="id0" xsi:type="ns5:AvailabilityType"
   xmlns:ns5="http://www.skatestown.com/ns/availability">
    <quantityAvailable xsi:type="xsd:int">36
    </quantityAvailable>
    <price xsi:type="xsd:double">129.0
    </price>
    <sku xsi:type="xsd:string">947-TI
    </sku>
   </multiRef>
  </SOAP-ENV:Body>
 </SOAP-ENV:Envelope>
```

SOAP Header Formatting

The SOAP extension also defines the way SOAP headers are described in WSDL. The notification operation within the StockAvailableNotification Web service allows an expiration to be carried in the input message as a SOAP header. This is described in terms of SOAP within the binding element's operation child element:

```
<operation name="registration">
   <soap:operation
      soapAction=
      "http://www.skatestown.com/StockAvailableNotification/registration">
   <input>
      <soap:header message="StockAvailableRegistrationRequest"
            part="expiration" use="encoded"
            namespace="http://www.skatestown.com/ns/registrationRequest"
            encodingStyle="http://schemas.xmlsoap.org/soap/encoding/"/>
```

The soap:header element indicates that the expiration part of the
StockAvailableRegistrationRequest message appears as a SOAP header. The attributes of
the soap:header element are similar to the soap:body element. Note that only the "expiration"
part of the message appears in the header. The rest of the message appears in the body of the
SOAP message.

SOAP Fault and HeaderFault Formatting

The soap:fault extension is an additional facility described by the SOAP binding extension
that does not appear in the priceCheck WSDL, but does appear in the
StockAvailableNotification WSDL. The soap:fault extension describes how a fault element (like the one described in the registration operation in the
StockAvailableNotificationPortType) is mapped into SOAP. A use of this extension is
shown here:

```
<operation name="registration">

. . .

   <fault name="StockAvailableNotificationErrorMessage">
      <soap:fault name="StockAvailableNotificationErrorMessage"
            namespace="http://www.skatestown.com/ns/registrationRequest"
            encodingStyle="http://schemas.xmlsoap.org/soap/encoding/"/>
   </fault>
```

The soap:fault extension has the same attributes as the soap:body extension. The fault message must have a single part.

SOAP requires that any errors generated by the SOAP engine when processing a SOAP header
must be communicated back to the requestor in the form of a header, not in the body of a fault
message. MustUnderstand faults are communicated this way, for example. The SOAP
extension in WSDL defines the soap:headerfault element for just this purpose. A
soap:headerfault element is used to describe how the StockAvailableExpirationError is
expressed in SOAP, as a fault header that could potentially flow to communicate errors related
to how the requestor formats the expiration header. The following example shows how WSDL
models this situation:

```
    <operation name="registration">
      <soap:operation
        soapAction=
        "http://www.skatestown.com/StockAvailableNotification/registration">
      <input>
        <soap:header message="StockAvailableRegistrationRequest"
. . .
            <soap:headerfault message="StockAvailableExpirationError"
                part="errorString" use="encoded"
                namespace="http://www.skatestown.com/ns/registrationRequest"
                encodingStyle="http://schemas.xmlsoap.org/soap/encoding/"/>
. . .
```

The `soap:headerfault` element is associated with the `soap:header` definition that might be in error, not as part of a fault or output message part of the operation.

Example `SMTPBinding`

As a slight variant on the SOAP binding theme, consider the possibility of sending a `priceCheck` request using e-mail. SkatesTown could provide an additional SMTP binding to the `priceCheck portType`, allowing a customer to e-mail a `priceCheck` request and receive as a reply e-mail the `priceCheck` response message.

Not much changes with this new binding. Of course, the `priceCheck portType` and the messages and types it references do not change. What does change is additional `binding`, `port`, and `service` elements (we will discuss `port` and `service` elements in separate sections later). The biggest changes include use of a different URI for the `transport` attribute of the `soap:binding` element to indicate SMTP is the transport mechanism. Also, the format of the `location` attribute in the `soap:address` child element of the port is different, reflecting an e-mail address format of the location. Another change is the use of literal form for the input and output message. It is a natural exchange to have an XML document itself as the e-mail message and response going between SkatesTown and its customer. Nothing precludes using RPC over SMTP; this is a matter of your choice:

```
<!-- Binding definitions -->
<binding name="PriceCheckSMTPBinding" type="pc:PriceCheckPortType">
    <soap:binding style="document"
        transport="http://schemas.xmlsoap.org/soap/smtp"/>
    <operation name="checkPrice">
        <input>
            <soap:body use="literal"/>
        </input>
        <output>
            <soap:body use="literal"/>
```

```
            </output>
         </operation>
    </binding>

    <!-- Service definition -->
    <service name="PriceCheckSMTPService">
       <port name="PriceCheckSMTP" binding="PriceCheckSMTPBinding">
          <soap:address location="mailto:priceCheck@skatestown.com"/>
       </port>
    </service>
```

And that is pretty much it for the WSDL binding element and the SOAP extensions to the WSDL binding element.

So, we now know that the only format supported for the priceCheck and StockAvailableNotification services is SOAP, and we know how the abstract types should be mapped into concrete objects. We now have (almost) all the details needed to invoke these Web services. At this point, we know we must use a SOAP message something like the following to invoke the checkPrice operation:

```
HTTP/1.0 200 OK
Content-Type: text/xml; charset=utf-8
Content-Length: 719
Set-Cookie2: JSESSIONID=6321fmkki1;Version=1;Discard;Path="/axis"
Set-Cookie: JSESSIONID=6321fmkki1;Path=/axis
Servlet-Engine: Tomcat Web Server/3.2.3 (JSP 1.1; Servlet 2.2; Java 1.3.0;
Windows 2000 5.0 x86; java.vendor=IBM Corporation)


<?xml version="1.0" encoding="UTF-8"?>

 <SOAP-ENV:Envelope
    SOAP-ENV:encodingStyle="http://schemas.xmlsoap.org/soap/encoding/"
    xmlns:SOAP-ENV="http://schemas.xmlsoap.org/soap/envelope/"
    xmlns:xsd="http://www.w3.org/2001/XMLSchema"
    xmlns:xsi="http://www.w3.org/2001/XMLSchema-instance">
  <SOAP-ENV:Body>
   <ns3:checkPriceResponse
    xmlns:ns3="http://www.skatestown.com/services/PriceCheck">
    <checkPriceResult href="#id0"/>
   </ns3:checkPriceResponse>
   <multiRef id="id0" xsi:type="ns5:AvailabilityType"
    xmlns:ns5="http://www.skatestown.com/ns/availability">
    <quantityAvailable xsi:type="xsd:int">36
```

```
      </quantityAvailable>
      <price xsi:type="xsd:double">129.0
      </price>
      <sku xsi:type="xsd:string">947-TI
      </sku>
     </multiRef>
   </SOAP-ENV:Body>
 </SOAP-ENV:Envelope>
```

The only missing piece is the network address; what URL do we send the message to? These details are given in the `port` and `service` elements.

Port

The `port` element in WSDL is very simple. Its only purpose is to specify the network address of the endpoint hosting the Web service. More precisely, the `port` element associates a single protocol-specific address to an individual `binding` element. `Port` elements are named, and the name must be unique among all the ports within a WSDL document. The `port` element for the `priceCheckSOAPBinding` is:

```
<port name="PriceCheck" binding="pc:PriceCheckSOAPBinding">
    <soap:address location=
          "http://localhost:8080/axis/servlet/AxisServlet/PriceCheck"/>
</port>
```

This binding indicates the URL to which SOAP messages should be sent in order to invoke the `priceCheck` operations over SOAP. Note the `soap:address` element; this is another aspect of the SOAP extension to WSDL. Most of the extension is in the `binding` element, and this is the only part of the extension outside the `binding` element.

That's it for the `port` element. We would be all done with our examination of the WSDL elements except that the `port` element does not stand alone. `Port` elements are children of the `service` element.

Service

The purpose of the `service` element is to contain a set of related `port` elements. Nothing more. Although a WSDL document can contain a collection of `service` elements, conventionally a WSDL document contains a single `service` element. Each `service` element is named, and each name must be unique among all the services in the WSDL document. The following shows the entire `service` element for the `priceCheck` Web service:

```
<!-- Service definition -->
<service name="PriceCheckService">
```

```
<port name="PriceCheck" binding="PriceCheckSOAPBinding">
   <soap:address location=
      "http://www.skatestown.com/axis/services/PriceCheck "/>
</port>
</service>
```

That's it. It seems like quite a lot of bother to waste all these elements to express a group of ports. Why would a designer group several ports together into a service element?

One reason is to group the ports related to the same service interface (portType) but expressed by different protocols (bindings). For example, if the priceCheck portType was implemented in two ways, one using SOAP over HTTP and another using SOAP over SMTP, a single service element could contain the port describing the URL for the SOAP/HTTP network endpoint and the port describing the e-mail address for the SOAP/SMTP network endpoint.

Another reason might be to group related but different portTypes together. For example, if the designer of the StockAvailabilityNotification Web service had chosen to split out the notification operation into a separate portType (certainly justifiable), then it would be advantageous to relate the port for the registration service together with the port describing the network endpoint for the binding for the notification operation.

That is the bulk of the important elements in a WSDL definition. We now examine a few other miscellaneous elements that appear in a WSDL document.

Definitions

The root element of a WSDL document is a definitions element. A definitions element contains all of the other WSDL elements. A definitions element can contain:

- Optionally, one types element
- Zero or more message elements
- Zero or more portType elements (conventionally just one)
- Zero or more binding elements (conventionally just one, for the portType element)
- Zero or more service elements (again, usually just one)

The definitions element might also contain a documentation element (we'll talk about this in the next section) and zero or more import elements (we'll talk about the import element after the documentation element).

The definitions element itself contains a name attribute (the name usually corresponds to the name of the Web service itself) and the usual XML namespace declarations. The following is the definitions element from the priceCheck WSDL:

```
<?xml version="1.0"?>
<definitions name="PriceCheck"
    targetNamespace="http://www.skatestown.com/services/PriceCheck"
    xmlns:pc="http://www.skatestown.com/services/PriceCheck"
    xmlns:avail="http://www.skatestown.com/ns/availability"
    xmlns:xsd="http://www.w3.org/2001/XMLSchema"
    xmlns:soap="http://schemas.xmlsoap.org/wsdl/soap/"
    xmlns="http://schemas.xmlsoap.org/wsdl/">
. . .
</definitions>
```

Except for the value of the `name` attribute and the `xmlns:pc` and `xmlns:avail` declarations, you will see this pattern at the beginning of every WSDL document. For WSDL documents that declare types with repeating groups (arrays), you will also see the SOAP encoding namespace declaration here.

Documentation

You have seen the `documentation` element before. It was used to communicate the relationship between the registration operation and the notification operation in the `StockAvailabilityNotification` Web service. The `documentation` element can contain any combination of text or other child elements. Any other WSDL element can contain a `documentation` element, usually as the first child element.

Conventional Use of the Import Element

WSDL defines an additional `import` element that allows WSDL documents to be linked together. The `import` element lets you reuse WSDL documents. Really, an `import` element binds a network location to an XML namespace. The following line shows the definition of an `import` element in WSDL:

```
<import namespace="uri" location="uri"/>
```

As described previously, many developers split their WSDL designs into two parts, each placed in a separate document. The service interface definition, containing the `types`, `message`, `portType`, and `binding` elements, appears in one file. The service interface definition encapsulates the reusable components of a service description. You can then place this file, for example, on a well-known Web site (on an e-marketplace, for example) for everyone to view. Each organization that wants to implement a Web service conformant to that well-known service interface definition would describe a service implementation definition, containing the `port` and `service` elements, describing how that common, reusable, service interface definition was, in fact, implemented at the network endpoint hosted by that organization. (You will see in Chapter 7 that this split is very important for registering WSDL Web service definitions in

UDDI.) Figure 6.4 outlines how the major elements in WSDL are divided between the service interface definition and the service implementation definition.

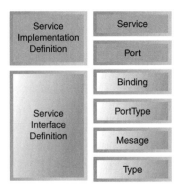

FIGURE 6.4

Service implementation definition, service interface definition, and WSDL elements.

The designers at SkatesTown used this technique for the poSubmission WSDL. The poSubmission WSDL is a service description for the poSubmission SOAP service you saw in Chapter 3. It uses schema definitions from Chapter 2. The service interface definition for the poSubmission service interface definition file appears as follows:

```
<?xml version="1.0" ?>
<definitions name="poSubmission"
        targetNamespace=
           "http://www.skatestown.com/services/interfaces/poSubmission.wsdl"
        xmlns:xsd="http://www.w3.org/2001/XMLSchema"
        xmlns:po="http://www.skatestown.com/ns/po"
        xmlns:inv="http://www.skatestown.com/ns/invoice"
        xmlns:soap="http://schemas.xmlsoap.org/wsdl/soap/"
        xmlns="http://schemas.xmlsoap.org/wsdl/">

    <!-- Type definitions -->
    <types>
       <xsd:schema targetNamespace="http://www.skatestown.com/ns/invoice" ...>
       <!-- rest of invoice schema definition from chapter 2 -->
       <include schemaLocation="http://www.skatestown.com/ns/invoice.xsd"/>
       </xsd:schema>

       <xsd:schema targetNamespace="http://www.skatestown.com/ns/po" ...>
       <!-- rest of purchaseOrder schema definition from chapter 2 -->
       <include schemaLocation="http://www.skatestown.com/ns/po.xsd"/>
       </xsd:schema>
    </types>
```

```
<!-- Message definitions -->
<message name="poSubmissionRequest">
   <part name="purchaseOrder" element="po:po"/>
</message>

<message name="poSubmissionResponse">
   <part name="invoice" element="inv:invoice"/>
</message>

<!-- Port type definitions -->
<portType name="poSubmissionPortType">
   <operation name="doSubmission">
      <input message="poSubmissionRequest"/>
      <output message="poSubmissionResponse"/>
   </operation>
</portType>

<!-- Binding definitions -->
<binding name="poSubmissionSOAPBinding"
   type="poSubmissionPortType">
   <soap:binding style="document"
            transport="http://schemas.xmlsoap.org/soap/http"/>
   <operation name="placePO">
      <soap:operation soapAction=
         "http://www.skatestown.com/services/poSubmission/submitPO"/>
      <input>
         <soap:body parts="purchaseOrder" use="literal"/>
      </input>
      <output>
         <soap:body parts="invoice" use="literal"/>
      </output>
   </operation>
</binding>
</definitions>
```

Note the use of the XML Schema include tag, importing the elements defined in the po and invoice schema definitions.

This WSDL file is a typical pattern for a simple document-centric SOAP service. The messages are simple document instances; the SOAP binding indicates the use of literal encoding—no deserialization of the XML message into programming language–specific objects will occur.

This service interface definition can be reused by many organizations. This is especially true if the data formats (the purchase order and invoice schemas) are industry standard.

The information specific to how SkatesTown implements the poSubmission service interface is contained in the poSubmissionService service implementation definition file:

```
<?xml version="1.0" ?>
<definitions name="poSubmissionService"
        targetNamespace=
            "http://www.skatestown.com/services/POSubmissionService.wsdl"
        xmlns:xsd="http://www.w3.org/2001/XMLSchema"
        xmlns:pop=
            "http://www.skatestown.com/services/interfaces/poSubmission.wsdl"
        xmlns:soap="http://schemas.xmlsoap.org/wsdl/soap/"
        xmlns="http://schemas.xmlsoap.org/wsdl/">
  <import
    namespace=
        "http://www.skatestown.com/services/interfaces/poSubmission.wsdl"
    location=
        "http://www.skatestown.com/services/interfaces/poSubmission.wsdl"/>

  <!-- Service definition -->
  <service name="poSubmissionService">
    <port name="poSubmissionSOAPPort" binding="pop:poSubmissionSOAPBinding">
      <soap:address
          location=
              "http://www.skatestown.com/axis/services/submitPO"/>
    </port>
  </service>

</definitions>
```

This technique is a nice separation of concerns. The service implementation document is quite succinct and contains information that is truly specific to the implementation of this type of service by SkatesTown.

Another convention, sometimes followed by WSDL designers, is to separate the binding from the service interface definition. It remains quite controversial that the service interface definition includes, by convention, the binding element. After all, the binding element, when used with the SOAP extensions to WSDL, includes the SOAPAction attribute in the operation element. This really has more to do with implementation than reusable description. As you will see in Chapter 7, part of the argument to keep the binding element in with the other reusable elements was due to the convention of registering WSDL documents within UDDI.

WSDL Extension Mechanism

The WSDL language allows each of the WSDL elements to be extended with elements from other namespaces. The language specification further defines standard extensions for SOAP, HTTP GET/POST operations, and MIME attachments. You have seen the use of the SOAP extension extensively in the previous sections of this chapter. We will briefly describe the other two extension frameworks here.

WSDL Descriptions of HTTP GET/POST Web Services

Imagine a variant on the priceCheck Web service that was tuned to support Web browsers. This variant on the priceCheck Web service would use URL encoding to include the item number as part of the service request using HTTP GET. An invocation of this service could look like an HTTP GET message sent to the following URL:

http://www.skatestown.com/checkPrice?item=xxx1234.

The priceCheck WSDL definition would be extended to include a new binding element:

```
<!-- Binding definitions -->
. . .
  <binding name="PriceCheckHTTPGetBinding" type="PriceCheckPortType">
    <http:binding verb="GET"/>
    <operation name="checkPrice">
      <http:operation location="checkPrice"/>
      <input>
        <http:urlEncoded/>
      </input>
      <output>
        <mime:content type="text/xml"/>
      </output>
    </operation>
  </binding>
```

The first HTTP extension is shown as the first child of the binding element. This element indicates that the GET verb is used (the other option was the POST verb).

The second HTTP extension is shown as the first child of the operation element. This element indicates that the service is to be invoked at the relative URI location. This is to be combined with the absolute URI location indicated in the port element (we'll review that shortly).

The third HTTP extension is shown as the first child of the input element. This element indicates that the parts of the input message are encoded in the request URI as name/value pairs, where the HTTP GET parameter names correspond to the WSDL message part names. Recall that the input message to the checkPrice operation is the PriceCheckRequest message, and it has only one part: a string named item. This means that the value of the input will appear in the URI, following the string ?item=.

The fourth HTTP extension is shown as the first child of the output element. This element indicates that the priceCheckResponse message will appear as XML text.

The last thing required is to update the service element of the priceCheck WSDL to include a port describing the http:address of the priceCheckHTTPGetBinding. This update is shown in the following listing:

```
<!-- Service definition -->
<service name="PriceCheckService">
. . .
    <port name="PriceCheckBrowserPort" binding="PriceCheckHTTPGetBinding">
        <http:address location="http://www.skatestown.com/"/>
    </port>
. . .
```

Here the URL of the priceCheck service is given using the http:address WSDL extension. Just like the SOAP extension, most of the HTTP extension is in the binding element (where you would expect it), and the only remaining piece is an extension to the port element expressing the endpoint network address in a protocol-specific manner.

The HTTP extension also specifies how to express the input message as HTTP POST using FORM-POST and how to express the input using urlReplacement. Refer to the WSDL specification for more detail.

WSDL Descriptions of Web Services Incorporating MIME

WSDL also supports a standard extension to describe message parts as MIME. We covered SOAP with MIME attachments in Chapter 3. This extension would be used if the designers at SkatesTown decided to include (in addition to the normal SOAP response) a GIF or JPEG image of the part queried in a priceCheck service invocation. To support this addition, the following changes would be necessary in the priceCheck WSDL. First, the response message would be updated to include the new part:

```
<message name="PriceCheckResponse">
    <part name="result" type="avail:availability"/>
    <part name="picture" type="xsd:binary"/>
</message>
```

This change does not exercise the MIME extension standard, because the MIME extensions are only within the binding element. However, the only change necessary in the binding element is to indicate that the output is modeled as multipart MIME, with the result part appearing as one MIME part, the SOAP body; the picture appears in another MIME part as GIF or JPEG. The following listing shows the binding element with these changes:

```
<!-- Binding definitions -->
<binding name="PriceCheckSOAPBinding" type="PriceCheckPortType">
    <soap:binding style="rpc"
            transport="http://schemas.xmlsoap.org/soap/http"/>
    <operation name="checkPrice">
        <soap:operation SOAPAction=""/>
        <input>
            <soap:body use="encoded"
                namespace="http://www.skatestown.com/ns/availability"
```

```
                encodingStyle="http://schemas.xmlsoap.org/soap/encoding/"/>
        </input>
        <output>
           <mime:multipartRelated>
              <mime:part>
                    <soap:body use="encoded"
                 namespace="http://www.skatestown.com/services/PriceCheck"
                 encodingStyle="http://schemas.xmlsoap.org/soap/encoding/"/>
              </mime:part>
              <mime:part>
                 <mime:content part="picture" type="image/gif"/>
                 <mime:content part="picture" type="image/jpeg"/>
              </mime:part>
           </mime:multipartRelated>
        </output>
     </operation>
   </binding>
```

Really, the only thing that has changed is within the output element (added definitions are in bold). Note the duplicate mime:content elements with the part named picture. When you see them, you are to interpret them as alternative formats, one of which might appear.

We have examined the WSDL standard for service description, but how does it address automating the invocation of Web services by the service requestor? The next section examines one approach: using WSDL to create Java interfaces or proxies to invoke Web services. We will also talk about how to generate WSDL from existing Java code.

WSDL and Java

In this section, we review the relationship between Java and WSDL. As you will see in Chapter 8, "Interoperability, Tools, and Middleware Products," many Web services development and/or runtime environments include WSDL tooling support. We review the tooling support in Axis (alpha 2 release) for generating service implementation code based on a WSDL, and the tooling support for generating a WSDL document from a Java implementation of a service.

Deriving Code from WSDL

Because WSDL is an IDL-level service description language, it is a good idea to make sure that it accurately represents the service it describes. You have two choices: Either you can manually design and code the service based on your understanding of a WSDL document, or you can use a tool to generate as much of the code for the service as possible.

Al Rosen used the WSDL2java program in Axis to generate the code implementing the priceCheck service. Al entered the following in his command line:

```
java org.apache.axis.wsdl.Wsdl2java --verbose --skeleton --messageContext  --
package ch6.ex1
   --output c:\book\ch6\ex1 c:\book\ch6\ex1\pricecheck.wsdl
```

The output of the command was:

```
Parsing XML File: c:\book\ch6\ex1\pricecheck.wsdl

Using package name: ch6.ex1
Generating portType interface: PriceCheckPortType.java
Generating server-side PortType interface: PriceCheckPortTypeAxis.java
Generating client-side stub: PriceCheckSOAPBindingStub.java
Generating server-side skeleton: PriceCheckSOAPBindingSkeleton.java
Generating type implementation: AvailabilityType.java
Generating type implementation holder: AvailabilityTypeHolder.java
Generating service class: PriceCheckService.java
Generating deployment document: deploy.xml
Generating deployment document: undeploy.xml
```

Let's take a look at each one of these files generated by the WSDL tooling in Axis and discuss how these files were generated from the WSDL definition of the priceCheck service. We will also discuss the steps Al Rosen took to quickly get the priceCheck service running and tested.

Overview of the Files Generated by WSDL2Java

The Axis WSDL tooling generates files for use on the client and the server. For the client, Axis generates three files:

- An interface definition for each portType element (PriceCheckPortType.java in our case)

- A client-side stub class for each binding element (PriceCheckSOAPBindingStub.java in our case)

- A factory-pattern style class for each service (PriceCheckService.java in our case)

The intention of the portType-based interface is to specify the interface the client application should use to interact with the Web service via the client-side stub. The binding-based client-side stub is a proxy for the Web service in the client's programming language and runtime environment. The service-based factory class returns a client-side stub instance complete with a network endpoint address.

For the server, Axis generates three files:

- A modified interface file for each portType, specific for use by the Axis engine (PriceCheckPortTypeAxis.java in our case)

- A server-side skeleton based on each binding element (PriceCheckSOAPBindingSkeleton.java in our case)

- A server-side "empty" service implementation file for each `binding` element
  (`PriceCheckSOAPBindingImpl.java` in our case)

The server-side interface is generated only if the `--messageContext` option is used (we'll talk about this option a little later). Otherwise, the server-side interface is the same as the client-side interface. This interface specifies the interface the server expects the target Web service to implement. The server-side skeleton is invoked by the Axis engine and is responsible for invoking the target Web service. The extra level of indirection is not needed in many cases; however, when there are in/out and multiple out parameters, the server-side skeleton comes into play.

For each complex type defined, two encoding classes are generated: one defining a basic Java implementation of the structure defined by the complex type (`AvailabilityType.java` in our case) and a class to implement RPC in, in/out, and out parameter semantics (`AvailabilityTypeHolder.java` in our case).

Finally, the Axis tooling generates a deployment descriptor file called `deploy.xml` that can be used to deploy the service to an Axis server. A symmetric `undeploy.xml` is generated to undeploy the service from the Axis server.

Let's take a look at the details of the files generated by the Axis WSDL tooling from the `priceCheck.wsdl` example.

Generating Classes for Serialization/Deserialization

The `priceCheck.wsdl` file defined one complex type structure:

```
<!-- Type definitions -->
<types>
   <xsd:schema targetNamespace="http://www.skatestown.com/ns/availability"
       xmlns:xsd="http://www.w3.org/2001/XMLSchema">
      <xsd:complexType name="availabilityType">
        <xsd:sequence>
           <xsd:element name="sku" type="xsd:string"/>
           <xsd:element name="price" type="xsd:double"/>
           <xsd:element name="quantityAvailable" type="xsd:integer"/>
        </xsd:sequence>
      </xsd:complexType>
   </xsd:schema>
</types>
```

From the `availabilityType` complex type, the `AvailabilityType.java` encoding class is generated. Because only one complex type element is defined in `priceCheck.wsdl`, only one encoding class is generated.

The `AvailabilityType.java` class defines a straightforward Java representation of the `availabilityType` complex type. The name of the class is derived from the value of the `name` attribute of the `complexType` element. The class itself defines one public instance variable for each of the child elements in the type:

```
public class AvailabilityType implements java.io.Serializable {
    private String sku;
    private double price;
    private int quantityAvailable;
```

The names of the instance variables are from the names of the child elements of the `availabilityType` complex type.

The Axis WSDL tooling also generates a public no-arg constructor

```
public AvailabilityType() {
}
```

and a public constructor containing parameters for each of the instance variables generated:

```
public AvailabilityType(String sku, double price, int quantityAvailable) {
    this.sku = sku;
    this.price = price;
    this.quantityAvailable = quantityAvailable;
}
```

Finally, the Axis WSDL tooling generates a pair of accessor methods (one get method and one set method) for each instance variable. For example, the accessor methods for the `sku` instance variable are as follows:

```
public String getSku() {
    return sku;
}

public void setSku(String sku) {
    this.sku = sku;
}
```

That's it for the encoding class for `AvailabilityType`. The other Java classes generated by the Axis WSDL tooling use this class to manipulate `availabilityType` elements. This class is also used as part of the *BeanMapping* 📖 deployed with this service. We will discuss this a little later in the section on generating the deployment XML.

Another file was generated for the `availabilityType` complex type: `AvailabilityTypeHolder.java`. This file is used to implement the behavior of in/out and multiple out parameters in an RPC-style Web service. We'll examine the role of *holder* 📖 classes when we examine the in/out and multiple out parameters in more detail. As it turns out,

priceCheck does not have any in/out parameters and only has one out parameter, so the
AvailabilityTypeHolder.java file is not used.

As of the Axis alpha-2 release, the Axis WSDL tooling is at a very early stage. The Axis
WSDL tooling will generate encoding classes for complex types and even handle elements referencing other complex types. Axis supports the common simple types from XML Schema
(but not all of the simple types) and does not support the use of the XML Schema extension
mechanism to base new types from existing types. Axis WSDL tooling also does not support
nesting of complex types.

Generating the Client Stub Factory, Stub, and Interface

The client stub is a class that encapsulates the details of the SOAP and networking protocol
layers from the application. The client stub presents an interface based on the portType to the
application. The application does not need to know anything about SOAP, HTTP, or any of
those lower-level details. The application invokes the interface and retrieves a response in
terms of Java method invocation and Java data types.

The interface generated for the priceCheck portType is shown here:

```
public interface PriceCheckPortType extends java.rmi.Remote {
    public AvailabilityType checkPrice(String sku)
        throws java.rmi.RemoteException;
}
```

The interface closely reflects the portType definition:

```
<!-- Port type definitions -->
<portType name="PriceCheckPortType">
    <operation name="checkPrice">
        <input message="pc:PriceCheckRequest"/>
        <output message="pc:PriceCheckResponse"/>
    </operation>
</portType>
```

The name of the interface class is derived from the name of the portType. The only method
signature, checkPrice, reflects the fact that only one operation, checkPrice, was defined for
the portType. The signature of the method reflects the input, output, and fault elements of
the operation. The input parameter, a String parameter named sku, reflects the message definition for the PriceCheckRequest:

```
<message name="PriceCheckRequest">
    <part name="sku" type="xsd:string"/>
</message>
```

The return type of the method, AvailabilityType, reflects the message definition for
PriceCheckResponse:

6

```
<message name="PriceCheckResponse">
  <part name="result" type="avail:availabilityType"/>
</message>
```

This is the first use for the `AvailabilityType` encoding type we discussed earlier.

The client application, then, can be coded to that interface. In the simple `PriceCheckTest` class, we see the invocation lines

```
PriceCheckService pcs = new PriceCheckService();
PriceCheckPortType pcpt = pcs.getPriceCheck();
AvailabilityType at = pcpt.checkPrice(args[0]);
```

where `args[0]` is a string (that should correspond to a valid stock keeping unit [SKU]) taken from the command line. In this case, the application uses the `PriceCheckService` to create an instance of the client stub populated with the endpoint address of the `priceCheck` Web service. (We'll discuss the client stub in more detail shortly.) The `PriceCheckService` factory could be used in many other ways—for example, to determine the endpoint address of the Web service implementation from a UDDI lookup. Regardless of the method used to derive a client stub, the `portType` remains the same, allowing the client application to rely on coding to that interface. The bindings might be different, either pointing to different Web services at different endpoint addresses, or perhaps even using different network transports, such as e-mail. Perhaps the Web service is a local method call within the same JVM. The client application is insulated from these changes because it is coding to an interface defined by a `portType`. This level of loose coupling between the requestor's application and the service provider makes Web services really great!

The complete `PriceCheckTest` class is presented in Listing 6.3.

LISTING 6.3 The `PriceCheckTest` Class

```
package ch6.ex1;
import java.text.NumberFormat;

public class PriceCheckTest {
  public static void main(String[] args){
    if(args.length != 1){
      System.err.println("Usage: PriceCheckTest sku");
      System.exit(1);
    }
    try{
      PriceCheckService pcs = new PriceCheckService();
      PriceCheckPortType pcpt = pcs.getPriceCheck();
      AvailabilityType at = pcpt.checkPrice(args[0]);
```

LISTING 6.3   Continued

```
        NumberFormat df = NumberFormat.getCurrencyInstance();

        System.out.println("One " + args[0] + " costs: " +
            df.format(at.getPrice()) + ".");
        System.out.println("There are " + at.getQuantityAvailable() + "
            available.");
    }catch (Exception e){
        System.err.println("Something wrong with the PriceCheck request");
        e.printStackTrace();
    }
  }
}
```

The `PriceCheckService` class, generated from the service element in the `PriceCheck` WSDL,
is straightforward. The complete class is shown in Listing 6.4.

LISTING 6.4   The `PriceCheckService` Class

```
package ch6.ex1;
public class PriceCheckService{

    // Use to get a proxy class for PriceCheck
    private final java.lang.String PriceCheck_address =
  "http://localhost:8080/axis/services/PriceCheck";
    public PriceCheckPortType getPriceCheck() {
        java.net.URL endpoint;
        try {
            endpoint = new java.net.URL(PriceCheck_address);
        }
        catch (java.net.MalformedURLException e) {
            return null; // unlikely as URL was validated in wsdl2java
        }
        return getPriceCheck(endpoint);
    }

    public PriceCheckPortType getPriceCheck(java.net.URL portAddress) {
        try {
            return new PriceCheckSOAPBindingStub(portAddress);
        }
        catch (org.apache.axis.SerializationException e) {
            return null; // ???
        }
    }
}
```

The name of the class is derived from the name of the service found in the `priceCheck` WSDL. The network address used

```
private final java.lang.String PriceCheck_address =
"http://localhost:8080/axis/services/PriceCheck";
```

is derived from the `soap:address` element of the port:

```
<port name="PriceCheck" binding="pc:PriceCheckSOAPBinding">
    <soap:address
        location="http://localhost:8080/axis/services/PriceCheck"/>
</port>
```

The client application uses the client stub generated by Axis to invoke a Web service using a particular binding mechanism. The Axis WSDL tooling generates a client stub for each binding element found in the WSDL document. The client stub class has the same name as the `binding` element and implements the interface defined for the `portType` named in the `binding` element. A complete listing for the `PriceCheckSOAPBindingStub` appears in Listing 6.5.

LISTING 6.5   The `PriceCheckSOAPBindingStub` Class

```
package ch6.ex1;
public class PriceCheckSOAPBindingStub extends org.apache.axis.wsdl.Stub
        implements PriceCheckPortType{
    private org.apache.axis.client.ServiceClient call =
        new org.apache.axis.client.ServiceClient(
            new org.apache.axis.transport.http.HTTPTransport());
    private java.util.Hashtable properties = new java.util.Hashtable();

    public PriceCheckSOAPBindingStub(java.net.URL endpointURL)
    throws org.apache.axis.SerializationException {
        this();
        call.set(org.apache.axis.transport.http.HTTPTransport.URL,
            endpointURL.toString());
    }
    public PriceCheckSOAPBindingStub()
        throws org.apache.axis.SerializationException {
        try {

            org.apache.axis.utils.QName qn1 =
                new org.apache.axis.utils.QName(
                    "http://www.skatestown.com/ns/availability",
                "AvailabilityType");
            Class cls = AvailabilityType.class;
            call.addSerializer(cls, qn1,
                new org.apache.axis.encoding.BeanSerializer(cls));
```

LISTING 6.5 Continued

```
            call.addDeserializerFactory(qn1, cls,
         org.apache.axis.encoding.BeanSerializer.getFactory());
        }
        catch (Throwable t) {
            throw new org.apache.axis.SerializationException
                ("AvailabilityType", t);
        }


    }

    public void _setProperty(String name, Object value) {
        properties.put(name, value);
    }

    // From org.apache.axis.wsdl.Stub
    public Object _getProperty(String name) {
        return properties.get(name);
    }

    // From org.apache.axis.wsdl.Stub
    public void _setTargetEndpoint(java.net.URL address) {
        call.set(org.apache.axis.transport.http.HTTPTransport.URL,
            address.toString());
    }

    // From org.apache.axis.wsdl.Stub
    public java.net.URL _getTargetEndpoint() {
        try {
            return new java.net.URL((String)
         call.get(org.apache.axis.transport.http.HTTPTransport.URL));
        }
        catch (java.net.MalformedURLException mue) {
            return null; // ???
        }
    }

    // From org.apache.axis.wsdl.Stub
    public synchronized void setMaintainSession(boolean session) {
        call.setMaintainSession(session);
    }

    // From javax.naming.Referenceable
    public javax.naming.Reference getReference() {
        return null; // ???
```

LISTING 6.5   Continued

```
    }

    public AvailabilityType checkPrice(String sku)
        throws java.rmi.RemoteException{
        if (call.get(org.apache.axis.transport.http.HTTPTransport.URL)
    == null){
            throw new org.apache.axis.NoEndPointException();
        }
        call.set(org.apache.axis.transport.http.HTTPTransport.ACTION, "");
        Object resp =
call.invoke("http://www.skatestown.com/services/PriceCheck",
            "checkPrice", new Object[]
                {new org.apache.axis.message.RPCParam("sku", sku)});

        if (resp instanceof java.rmi.RemoteException) {
            throw (java.rmi.RemoteException)resp;
        }
        else {
            return (AvailabilityType) resp;
        }
    }
}

}
```

Most of the client stub code is generated to manipulate the `ServiceClient`, which, as you saw in Chapter 4, is the major interface between client applications and the Axis engine on the requestor side. Properties that are set include the transport and the network address of the service (given as a parameter, from the client application or the stub factory class). The client stub also configures the `ServiceClient` with serializers and deserializers for each `complexType` involved in the binding (that is, derived from the `portType`) using the encoding classes discussed earlier:

```
            org.apache.axis.utils.QName qn1 = new org.apache.axis.utils.QName
                ("http://www.skatestown.com/ns/availability", "AvailabilityType");
            Class cls = AvailabilityType.class;
            call.addSerializer (cls, qn1,
                new org.apache.axis.encoding.BeanSerializer (cls));
            call.addDeserializerFactory (qn1, cls,
                org.apache.axis.encoding.BeanSerializer.getFactory ());
```

These serializers and deserializers are very important because they are the part of the Axis engine that is responsible for converting something that looks like this

```
    <ns3:checkPriceResponse
xmlns:ns3="http://www.skatestown.com/services/PriceCheck">
    <checkPriceResult href="#id0"/>
```

```
    </ns3:checkPriceResponse>
    <multiRef id="id0" xsi:type="ns5:AvailabilityType"
        xmlns:ns5="http://www.skatestown.com/ns/availability">
     <quantityAvailable xsi:type="xsd:int">36
     </quantityAvailable>
     <price xsi:type="xsd:double">129.0
     </price>
     <sku xsi:type="xsd:string">947-TI
     </sku>
    </multiRef>
```

into an instance of AvailabilityType, with the quantityAvailable, price, and sku instance variables properly set.

Finally, the core purpose of the client stub is to provide an implementation of each operation defined in the interface generated from the portType. In the PriceCheckSOAPBindingStub, there is one method implementation: checkPrice. This method is responsible for gathering the parameters, using the ServiceClient to invoke the Web service, and return the marshaled result back to the client application:

```
    public AvailabilityType checkPrice(String sku)
        throws java.rmi.RemoteException{
        if (call.get(org.apache.axis.transport.http.HTTPTransport.URL) == null){
            throw new org.apache.axis.NoEndPointException();
        }
        call.set(org.apache.axis.transport.http.HTTPTransport.ACTION, "");
        Object resp = call.invoke("http://www.skatestown.com/services/
            PriceCheck", "checkPrice", new Object[]
                {new org.apache.axis.message.RPCParam("sku", sku)});

        if (resp instanceof java.rmi.RemoteException) {
            throw (java.rmi.RemoteException)resp;
        }
        else {
            return (AvailabilityType) resp;
        }
    }
```

And that is it for the Java code generated for use on the client side.

Generating the Server Skeleton and Interface

Generated code is also useful on the server side to insulate the implementation of the Web service from the details of SOAP, the network transport, and even Axis itself.

The server-side interface can take one of two forms, depending on whether the Web service implementation needs context information to be passed to it. Many Web service implementations are standalone; they need no information from the Axis engine relating to the context of the request (information about the requestor, transport specific information like the servlet context, other environment properties, and so on). In this case, the client-side interface based on portType is sufficient. However, for cases where context is required from the Axis engine, you should use the --messageContext option on the Wsdl2java, generating a server-side interface. The server-side interface generated from the priceCheck WSDL appears in Listing 6.6.

LISTING 6.6   The PriceCheckPortTypeAxis Interface

```
package ch6.ex1;
public interface PriceCheckPortTypeAxis extends java.rmi.Remote {
    public AvailabilityType checkPrice(org.apache.axis.MessageContext ctx,
        String sku) throws java.rmi.RemoteException;
}
```

The server-side interface has the name of the portType appended with the string *Axis*; for example, PriceCheckPortTypeAxis.java. This interface is similar to the client-side interface, except that each method signature includes as its first parameter a MessageContext parameter, allowing the Web service implementation access to the environment through this object. Using MessageContext is a good way to encapsulate access to information such as the transport. The downside of doing this is that your Web service implementation is tied very closely to Axis. Al Rosen chose this approach for the priceCheck Web service because he used the same method to get at the ProductDatabase as the InventoryCheck Web service, and that method uses MessageContext.

The server-side skeleton is quite simple. One such class is defined for each binding element in the WSDL document, as shown in Listing 6.7.

LISTING 6.7   The PriceCheckSOAPBindingSkeleton Interface

```
package ch6.ex1;
public class PriceCheckSOAPBindingSkeleton{
    private PriceCheckPortTypeAxis impl;

    public PriceCheckSOAPBindingSkeleton() {
        this.impl = new PriceCheckSOAPBindingImpl();
    }

    public PriceCheckSOAPBindingSkeleton(PriceCheckPortTypeAxis impl) {
        this.impl = impl;
    }
```

LISTING 6.7   Continued

```
public Object checkPrice(org.apache.axis.MessageContext ctx, String sku)
   throws java.rmi.RemoteException
{
   Object ret = impl.checkPrice(ctx, sku);
   return ret;
}


}
```

The skeleton defines a couple of simple constructors, allowing it to be associated with an implementation of the server-side interface—that is, an implementation of the Web service. In fact, the code is generated to look for one particular implementation class, named PriceCheckSOAPBindingImpl by default. A sample PriceCheckSOAPBindingImpl.java file is also generated, with trivial contents:

```
package ch6.ex1;

public class PriceCheckSOAPBindingImpl implements PriceCheckPortTypeAxis {
    public AvailabilityType checkPrice(org.apache.axis.MessageContext ctx,
  String sku)
        throws java.rmi.RemoteException {
        throw new java.rmi.RemoteException ("Not Yet Implemented");
    }
}
```

The skeleton generates an implementation method for each operation in the portType. Each operation is the same, invoking the corresponding method in the actual Web service implementation class.

The checkPrice implementation in the PriceCheckSOAPBindingSkeleton is quite simple:

```
public Object checkPrice(org.apache.axis.MessageContext ctx, String sku)
   throws java.rmi.RemoteException
{
   Object ret = impl.checkPrice(ctx, sku);
   return ret;
}
```

However, for Web services that involve in/out and out parameters, the implementation of the skeleton operation becomes much trickier.

In/out and Multiple Out Parameters

In certain RPC situations, WSDL can specify message parts that appear on both the input message and output message; these translate to in/out parameters. Further, WSDL can specify an output message with more than one part. In/out and multipart output messages pose an interesting problem for translating WSDL to Java.

Consider the following example WSDL:

```
<wsdl:message name="inmsg">
   <wsdl:part name="in1" type="in"/>
   <wsdl:part name="inout1" type="inout"/>
</wsdl:message>

<wsdl:message name="outmsg">
   <wsdl:part name="inout1" type="inout"/>
   <wsdl:part name="out1" type="out"/>
   <wsdl:part name="out2" type="out"/>
</wsdl:message>

<wsdl:portType name="pt1">
   <wsdl:operation name="op1">
      <wsdl:input message="inmsg"/>
      <wsdl:output message="outmsg"/>
   </wsdl:operation>
</wsdl:portType>
```

The operation named op1 has a message part named inout1 appearing in both the input message and output message. Further, you will notice that the output message of the operation has three output parts: the inout1 part, and two parts that appear only in the output message, out1 and out2.

How is it possible in Java to have a parameter that is both on the input and the output, or to have multiple output values? This is where the holder classes come in.

As we have seen, Axis WSDL tooling generates holder classes for each of the input, output, and in/out parameters. The classes generated when this WSDL file was processed included InHolder.Java, InOutHolder.Java, and OutHolder.Java. These holder classes are simple: They contain a value of the given underlying type and provide a simple constructor.

Now, the skeleton generated for the following binding

```
<wsdl:binding name="pt1SOAPBinding1" type="pt1">
   <soap:binding style="rpc"
transport="http://schemas.xmlsoap.org/soap/http"/>
   <wsdl:operation name="op1">
      <soap:operation soapAction="op1"/>
```

```
            <wsdl:input>
              <soap:body use="encoded"
                    namespace="someNamespace"
              encodingStyle="http://schemas.xmlsoap.org/soap/encoding/"/>
              </wsdl:input>
            <wsdl:output>
              <soap:body use="encoded"
                    namespace="someNamespace"
              encodingStyle="http://schemas.xmlsoap.org/soap/encoding/"/>
              </wsdl:output>
          </wsdl:operation>
      </wsdl:binding>
```

looks like this:

```
public Object op1(org.apache.axis.MessageContext ctx, In in1, Inout inout1)
    throws java.rmi.RemoteException
    {
        InoutHolder inout1Holder = new InoutHolder(inout1);
        OutHolder out2Holder = new OutHolder();
        Object ret = impl.op1(ctx, in1, inout1Holder, out2Holder);
        org.apache.axis.server.ParamList list =
            new org.apache.axis.server.ParamList();
        list.add(new org.apache.axis.message.RPCParam("out1", ret));
        list.add(new org.apache.axis.message.RPCParam
            ("inout1", inout1Holder._value));
        list.add(new org.apache.axis.message.RPCParam
            ("out2", out2Holder._value));
        return list;
    }
```

Note the way the target Web service is dispatched. Holder objects are created for the in/out and the second out parameter and passed to the implementation. The implementation then puts a value in the Out2Holder object passed and potentially modifies the value in the InoutHolder that is passed. All three values are passed back to the requestor as RPCParams.

Consider the test program shown in Listing 6.8.

LISTING 6.8   The In/Out and Out Parameter Test Program

```
package ch6.ex5;
public class Test {
   public static void main(String[] args){
       if(args.length != 2){
          System.err.println("Usage: Test int1 int2");
          System.err.println
             ("Multiplies int1 by int2 and returns that as out parm,");
```

LISTING 6.8   Continued

```
        System.err.println("Adds value of int1 to int2 (as inout parm)");
        System.err.println
           ("Adds new value of inout parm with the result of the
  multiplication"
              + "to produce return value.");


        System.exit(1);
     }
     try{
        int int1 = Integer.valueOf(args[0]).intValue();
        int int2 = Integer.valueOf(args[1]).intValue();

        pt1 stub = new In_Out_Parm().getIn_Out_Test_Port();
        In in1 = new In(int1);
        InoutHolder inout1 = new InoutHolder(new Inout(int2));
        OutHolder out2 = new OutHolder();

           Out res = stub.op1 (in1, inout1, out2);

        System.out.println(int1 + "*" + int2 + " = " + out2._value.getE3());
        System.out.println(int1 + "+" + int2 + " = " + inout1._value.getE2());
        System.out.println(int1 + "*" + int2 + " + " + int1 + "+"
              + int2 + " = " + res.getE3());
     }catch (Exception e){
        System.err.println("Something wrong with the Test service");
        e.printStackTrace();
     }
   }
}
```

When this is run with the command

```
java ch6.ex5.Test 2 3
```

The following SOAP message is generated:

```
POST /axis/servlet/AxisServlet/In_Out_Test_Port HTTP/1.0
. . .
<?xml version="1.0" encoding="UTF-8"?>
<SOAP-ENV:Envelope
   xmlns:SOAP-ENV="http://schemas.xmlsoap.org/soap/envelope/"
   xmlns:xsd="http://www.w3.org/2001/XMLSchema"
   xmlns:xsi="http://www.w3.org/2001/XMLSchema-instance">

   <SOAP-ENV:Body>
```

```
      <ns3:op1 xmlns:ns3="someNamespace">
         <in1 href="#id0"/>
         <inout1 href="#id1"/>
      </ns3:op1>
      <multiRef id="id1" xsi:type="ns6:Inout"
         xmlns:ns6="anotherNamespace">
         <e2 xsi:type="xsd:int">3
         </e2>
      </multiRef>
      <multiRef id="id0" xsi:type="ns10:In" xmlns:ns10="anotherNamespace">
         <e1 xsi:type="xsd:int">2
         </e1>
      </multiRef>
   </SOAP-ENV:Body>
</SOAP-ENV:Envelope>
```

A sample Web service implementation of this service looks like Listing 6.9.

LISTING 6.9   Example In/Out and Out Parameter Web Service Implementation

```
package ch6.ex5;

import java.rmi.RemoteException;

import org.apache.axis.MessageContext;

public class pt1SOAPBinding1Impl implements pt1Axis {

   /**
    * @see pt1Axis#op1(MessageContext, In, InoutHolder, OutHolder)
    * multiply the value of inout by in and toss it into out2
    * add in to inout and toss that into inout
    * return the total of inout and out2
    */
   public Out op1(MessageContext ctx, In in1, InoutHolder inout1,
                  OutHolder out2)
      throws RemoteException {
         out2._value = new Out();
         out2._value.setE3(in1.getE1()*inout1._value.getE2());
         inout1._value.setE2(inout1._value.getE2() + in1.getE1());
         return new Out(inout1._value.getE2() + out2._value.getE3());
   }

   /**
    * in case the messageContext parm was not used
    */
```

Listing 6.9 Continued

```
    public Out op1(In in1, InoutHolder inout1, OutHolder out2)
        throws RemoteException {
            out2._value = new Out();
            out2._value.setE3(in1.getE1()*inout1._value.getE2());
            inout1._value.setE2(inout1._value.getE2() + in1.getE1());
            return new Out(inout1._value.getE2() + out2._value.getE3());
    }

}
```

This is a simple program that takes the input value and increments the in/out value by that amount. Further, it returns in one output parameter the product of the in and the original in/out value, and in the "real" output of the message, returns the sum of the newly incremented in/out value and the other output parameter. It is a useless function, but it illustrates the in/out and multiple out situations in a simple fashion.

This program produces the following output SOAP response:

```
HTTP/1.0 200 OK. . .
<?xml version="1.0" encoding="UTF-8"?>
<SOAP-ENV:Envelope
    SOAP-ENV:encodingStyle=http://schemas.xmlsoap.org/soap/encoding/
    xmlns:SOAP-ENV=http://schemas.xmlsoap.org/soap/envelope/
    xmlns:xsd=http://www.w3.org/2001/XMLSchema
    xmlns:xsi="http://www.w3.org/2001/XMLSchema-instance">
    <SOAP-ENV:Body>
        <ns3:op1Response xmlns:ns3="someNamespace">
            <out1 href="#id0"/>
            <inout1 href="#id1"/>
            <out2 href="#id2"/>
        </ns3:op1Response>
        <multiRef id="id2" xsi:type="ns7:Out"
            xmlns:ns7="anotherNamespace">
            <e3 xsi:type="xsd:int">6
            </e3>
        </multiRef>
        <multiRef id="id1" xsi:type="ns11:Inout"
            xmlns:ns11="anotherNamespace">
            <e2 xsi:type="xsd:int">5
            </e2>
        </multiRef>
        <multiRef id="id0" xsi:type="ns15:Out"
            xmlns:ns15="anotherNamespace">
            <e3 xsi:type="xsd:int">11
```

```
        </e3>
      </multiRef>
   </SOAP-ENV:Body>
</SOAP-ENV:Envelope>
```

Note the way the `multiref` element is used to contain the holder values back to the requestor. The test program shown in Listing 6.8 then takes these values from the returned holder classes and prints the following out on the screen:

```
2*3 = 6
2+3 = 5
2*3 + 2+3 = 11
```

This would have been extremely tricky to do manually, but it was nothing for the Axis WSDL tooling.

Now, back to our `priceCheck` example.

Generating the Deployment XML

In order for the Axis engine to know about a service, the service needs to be deployed. The current mechanism of deploying services in Axis is through a deployment descriptor, a `deploy.xml` file. Instructions on how to deploy a Web service are included in generated comments at the beginning of the `deploy.xml` file.

A `deploy.xml` file is generated to deploy all the Web services defined in a WSDL document. A `service` element is generated for each `port` element in the WSDL file. The `deploy.xml` file generated from `priceCheck.wsdl` is shown in Listing 6.10.

LISTING 6.10   The `deploy.xml` File Generated from `priceCheck.wsdl`

```
<!--                                                     -->
<!--Use this file to deploy some handlers/chains and services  -->
<!--Two ways to do this:                                 -->
<!--   java org.apache.axis.utils.Admin deploy.xml       -->
<!--      from the same dir that the Axis engine runs    -->
<!--or                                                   -->
<!--   java org.apache.axis.client.AdminClient deploy.xml   -->
<!--      after the axis server is running               -->
<!--This file will be replaced by WSDD once it's ready   -->

<m:deploy xmlns:m="AdminService">

   <!-- Services from PriceCheckService WSDL service -->

   <service name="PriceCheck" pivot="RPCDispatcher">
     <option name="className" value="PriceCheckSOAPBindingSkeleton"/>
```

LISTING 6.10 Continued

```
        <option name="methodName" value=" checkPrice"/>
    </service>

    <beanMappings xmlns:avail="http://www.skatestown.com/ns/availability">
        <avail:AvailabilityType classname= "AvailabilityType"/>
    </beanMappings>
</m:deploy>
```

The value of the pivot handler is determined by the value of the `style` element of the
`soap:operation` element; RPC generates RPCDispatcher, and document generates
MsgDispatcher. An `option` element with the name `className` is generated for the binding referenced by the port. The actual value is set to the name of the skeleton Java file. The
`methodName` option element contains a list of methods, one for each operation in the binding,
each separated by a space. This deployment tells the Axis engine to invoke the
`PriceCheckSOAPBindingSkeleton` class using the `checkPrice` operation. (Note that the
deployment file has been modified to reflect the package names where the actual class files
have been placed.)

The `deploy.xml` file also contains a collection of serializers associated with the Web service,
associating an encoding class, in this case `AvailabilityType.Java`, with the corresponding
type and namespace:

```
<beanMappings xmlns:avail="http://www.skatestown.com/ns/availability">
    <avail:AvailabilityType classname="AvailabilityType"/>
</beanMappings>
```

The Axis WSDL tooling also generates a document to undeploy the Web service. This document
is called `undeploy.xml`. The undeploy contains a `service` element for each port in the
WSDL document; this corresponds to the `service` elements generated in the `deploy.xml` file.
The `undeploy.xml` file generated from `priceCheck.wsdl` is shown in Listing 6.11.

LISTING 6.11 The undeploy.xml File Generated from priceCheck.wsdl

```
<!--                                                        -->
<!--Use this file to undeploy some handlers/chains and services  -->
<!--Two ways to do this:                                    -->
<!--    java org.apache.axis.utils.Admin undeploy.xml       -->
<!--       from the same dir that the Axis engine runs      -->
<!--or                                                      -->
<!--    java org.apache.axis.client.AdminClient undeploy.xml -->
<!--       after the axis server is running                 -->
<!--This file will be replaced by WSDD once it's ready      -->
```

LISTING 6.11   Continued

```
<m:undeploy xmlns:m="AdminService">

    <!-- Services from PriceCheckService WSDL service -->

    <service name="PriceCheck" pivot="RPCDispatcher">
    </service>
</m:undeploy>
```

Putting It All Together: A Running PriceCheck Service

The previous sections described the WSDL tooling in Axis, but what steps must Al Rosen take to get the priceCheck service running?

The first step, of course, is to acquire WSDL. Al Rosen created the priceCheck.wsdl file by hand. In the next section, we will discuss ways to generate WDSL from existing code, and in Chapter 7, we will see how to get a WSDL description from a services registry like UDDI.

Al then issued the Wsdl2java command shown previously to invoke the Axis WSDL tooling. This step generated the files we discussed earlier. Note that Al used the following options:

- --skeleton, telling WSDL2java to generate server-side files (skeleton, deploy.xml, and undeploy.xml)
- --messageContext, because Al knew the actual priceCheck Web service would use code from the InventoryCheck Web service that needed this parameter
- --package, to add package declarations to each file
- --output, to put the generated files in the proper directory

Next, Al created an implementation of a priceCheck service, PriceCheckSOAPBindingImpl, shown in Listing 6.12. This file completely replaces the generated PriceCheckSOAPBindingImpl.java file. This is the name of the class the PriceCheckSOAPBindingSkeleton is coded to invoke.

LISTING 6.12   An Implementation of the PriceCheck Web Service

```
package ch6.ex1;
import org.apache.axis.MessageContext;
import bws.BookUtil;
import com.skatestown.data.Product;
import com.skatestown.backend.ProductDB;

/**
 * PriceCheck Web service, based on Inventory Web Service
 * Created by implementing a PriceCheckSOAPBindingImpl
 */
```

Listing 6.12   Continued

```
public class PriceCheckSOAPBindingImpl implements PriceCheckPortTypeAxis,
   PriceCheckPortType {
  /**
   * Checks price and quantity available given a product SKU
   *
   * @param msgContext  This is the Axis message processing context
   *                    BookUtil needs this to extract deployment
   *                    information to load the product database.
   * @param sku         product SKU
   * @return            A structure indicating price and quantity for the sku
   * @exception Exception most likely a problem accessing the DB
   */
  public AvailabilityType checkPrice (MessageContext msgContext,String sku)
       throws java.rmi.RemoteException{
    ProductDB db = null;
    try{
       db = BookUtil.getProductDB(msgContext);
    }catch (Exception e){
       throw new java.rmi.RemoteException(e.getMessage());
    }
    Product prod = db.getBySKU(sku);
    if(prod == null){
       throw new
          java.rmi.RemoteException("Product sku: " + sku + " not found.");
    }

    AvailabilityType at = new AvailabilityType();
    at.setSku(sku);
    at.setQuantityAvailable(prod.getNumInStock());
    at.setPrice(prod.getUnitPrice());
    return at;
  }

  public AvailabilityType checkPrice (String sku)
       throws java.rmi.RemoteException{
     throw new java.rmi.RemoteException(
       "Need to generate WSDL with -messageContext option!");
  }
}
```

This implementation is based on the InventoryCheck Web service you saw in Chapter 3. The input parameter sku is used to retrieve the product record from the product database. From this information, an Availability object is created, filled in with values, and returned to the requestor.

The next step is to deploy the Web service to a server. In this case, Al moved the .class files to a webApps directory under his Web application server and started the server. Al then updated the deploy.xml file to make sure the proper path structure was reflected in the className option element and the beanMappings elements. (Note that this step was required even though Al used the --package option.) Al then invoked the AdminClient, following the instructions in the comments found in the deploy.xml file, deploying the Web service to Axis. The priceCheck Web service is now available to requestors.

The PriceCheckTest client application (shown in Listing 6.3) simply takes a sku from the command line and uses the generated client-side stub to invoke for the priceCheck Web service. The results of the priceCheck are then printed to the console.

For example, if Al ran the command

```
java ch6.ex1.PriceCheckTest 947-TI
```

the output could look like this:

```
One 947-TI costs: $129.00.
There are 36 available.
```

That's it for generating Java and XML from WSDL. The point here is that tooling allowed Al Rosen to focus on the business application and not worry about the intricacies of SOAP and Axis. Al focused on creating the WSDL description for the Web service, the actual business logic implementing the Web service, and a simple test client. The Axis WSDL tooling generated the rest based on the WSDL description of the Web service.

Summarizing WSDL to Java

Table 6.3 summarizes the parts of a WSDL document that map to different pieces of the generated Java and deployment XML.

TABLE 6.3 How WSDL Elements Map to Generated Java and Deployment XML

WSDL Elements	Generated Java/XML	Example
<types>		
each complexType	• Generate a serializer/deserializer class	• **AvailabilityType**.java
	• Generate a holder class • Configure the serviceClient in the client stub with serializers/deserializers	• **AvailabilityType** Holder.java

TABLE 6.3 Continued

WSDL Elements	Generated Java/XML	Example
`<portType>`	• Generate a `BeanMapping` in the `deploy.xml` file	
	• Generate a client-side interface class	• **`PriceCheckPortType`**.`java`
	• Generate a server-side interface class	• **`PriceCheckPortTypeAxis`.** `java`
each operation	• Becomes a method signature in the interface	• `AvailabilityType` **`checkPrice`**(String sku)…
each input part	• Becomes an input parameter to the interface method	• `AvailabilityType` checkPrice(**`String sku`**)…
each output part	• First part becomes the return type of the method	
	• Subsequent parts become method parameters represented by holder classes for the type defined by the part	• **`AvailabilityType`** checkPrice(String sku)…
each `fault` element	• Generates a class defining a Java exception of the same name	• Does not appear in `PriceCheck`
	• Generates a Java exception added to the method signature	
`<binding>`	• Generates a client-side stub • Generates a server-side skeleton	• PriceCheckSOAPBinding Stub.java
	• Generates a pair of option elements (`className` and `methodName`) in the `deploy.xml` file	• PriceCheckSOAPBinding Skeleton.java • PriceCheckSOAPBinding Impl.java
each `soap:operation`	• Sets the SOAPAction property of the `ServiceClient` in the client stub from the value of the soapAction attribute	• `call.set (HTTPTransport. ACTION, " ");`
	• Sets the handler in `deploy.xml` based on the value of `soap:style`	

Table 6.3   Continued

WSDL Elements	Generated Java/XML	Example
	• Generates an implementation method in the client-side stub	
	• Generates a skeleton method in the server-side skeleton	
	• Generates an entry in the deploy.xml methodList	
`<port>`	• Sets the endpointURL in the service class from the soap:address element	• endpointURL = "http://localhost:8080/ axis/servlet/
	• Generates one service element in deploy.xml	AxisServlet/ PriceCheck";
	• Generates one service element in undeploy.xml	
`<service>`	• Generates one service class	• PriceCheckService.java
	• Generates one deploy.xml file	
	• Generates one undeploy.xml file	

Deriving WSDL from Code

We mentioned in the previous section that Al Rosen needed to manually create the priceCheck WSDL definition. For applications that already exist, there are alternative approaches to coming up with the WSDL definition. Axis WSDL tooling can generate a WSDL document from a Java class.

Axis makes available the WSDL for any deployed service. You can examine the WSDL by invoking the service using HTTP get (from a Web browser) with the ?WSDL parameter. Figure 6.5 shows the WSDL generated by Axis for the InventoryCheck service.

The WSDL for the service is generated by visiting all the chains and handlers deployed for the service, including service-specific chains, transport-specific chains, and global chains. Doing so ensures that each component of the deployment is incorporated into the WSDL for the Web service.

The core WSDL is generated based on the Java class definition, defining the operations and messages that are core to any WSDL description. Other details, such as the SOAPAction value, are also determined by the deployment.

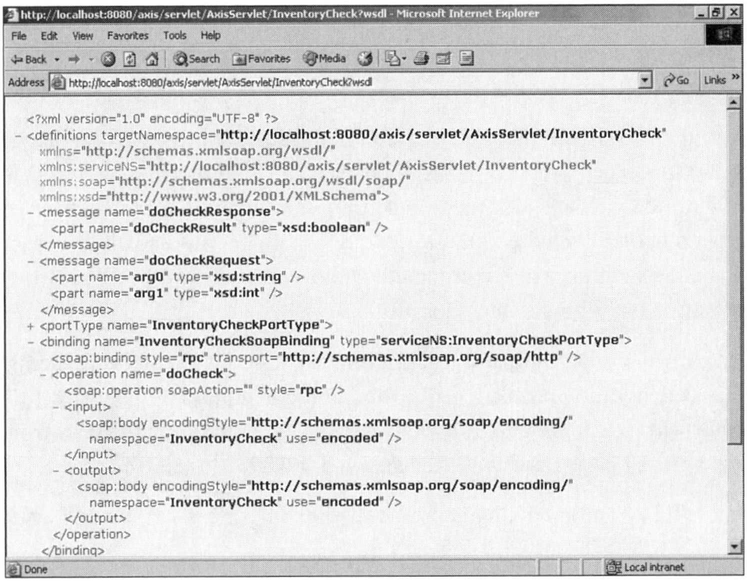

FIGURE 6.5
Generating the WSDL for the InventoryCheck *Web service.*

Much work continues in the area of generating WSDL from Java and other programming language artifacts, such as EJBs, database schemas, and so on. This is another area of Web services that is seeing a lot of effort in standardization and tooling. We will see some examples of other Web services environments and tooling in Chapter 8.

Future Service Description Efforts

WSDL is the basis for service description, but it is not the only component. WSDL describes details of invocation syntax. There is more to describe about a Web service than just the IDL-level details. At this point, higher level description mechanisms layered on top of WSDL are still emerging; no standards exist in this space.

Web Services Endpoint Language (WSEL)

As part of the Web Services Flow Language (WSFL) specification
(http://www.ibm.com/software/solutions/webservices/pdf/WSFL.pdf), IBM hinted at a new language, based on WSDL, to describe non-functional characteristics of a Web service. IBM calls this language Web Services End-point Language (WSEL).

The purpose of WSEL is to formally model non-functional characteristics of a Web service—things like quality of service (QoS) statements, privacy policy, auditing policy, and so on.

These items do not directly affect the syntax of the message (certainly not the core part of the message), but they can affect whether the service requestor chooses to collaborate with a particular service provider.

This level of service description is especially important for asynchronous message flows. For example, a WSEL-specified property of the Web service could include the expected response time, possible duration estimates for the interaction, or number of acceptable retries. This would be the basis upon which the requestor could establish time-out behavior and safely assume that the collaboration will not complete and execute whatever rollback or compensation mechanism is associated with the interaction.

Other standards are emerging in this space, not directly based on WSDL, including work done surrounding the collaboration protocol profile and agreement markup language (cppML) from the ebXML effort (http://www.ebxml.org/specs/ebCCP.pdf), and DAML-S from the daml.org group (http://www.daml.org/services/daml-s/2001/05/).

Watch this space. End-point modeling is one of the next big areas for standardization within Web services.

Web Services Flow Language (WSFL)

The final layer of the service description stack is the flow layer or orchestration layer. It is this layer of specification that the WSFL addresses.

WSDL is used to describe the detailed information necessary to invoke a Web service; a single Web service, WSDL has no notion of sequencing several Web service invocations or ordering the operation invocations within a single Web service.

The Web Services Flow Language (WSFL) builds upon the work in WSDL, describing how to organize and orchestrate a series of Web services invocations into an overall business process or workflow. You would use WSFL to model long-running multistep business collaborations between multiple business partners.

IBM published the WSFL specification in May 2001. It is IBM's intention to partner with other organizations to standardize WSFL. There are other mechanisms to organize and orchestrate Web services. Microsoft, for example, defines a similar language called XLANG. It is difficult to predict how the industry will address these two approaches to Web services orchestration or whether they ultimately will converge to one standard. This book, however, will briefly describe how WSFL can be used as part of the overall service description stack.

WSFL is an XML language somewhat similar to WSDL. WSFL is used to orchestrate, or organize, the sequencing of Web services invocations. With WSFL, you can:

- Describe a business process that is composed of a sequence of activities, some or all of which might be Web services
- Describe the business process itself as a Web service, specifying the relationships between various role players in the workflow

The exciting aspect of WSFL is that it allows new, higher-level Web services to be created by combining or orchestrating other Web services. So, the more Web services that are created, the more possibilities there exist for orchestrating them into more powerful Web services. This enables a *network effect* to occur, making Web services a very powerful concept for business process integration.

WSFL leverages the `portType` element from WSDL to define the basic component or activity interface in the workflow system. The business process is then modeled as a state machine, where activities are modeled as Web service invocations and the invocations are sequenced by state transition events (control flow). Eventually, as more organizations adopt Web services and publish Web services for partner consumption over the Internet, we will see standard `portType` or service interface definitions emerge, thereby allowing organizations to incorporate and integrate their partners' business processes into their own workflows. Until these standard service interface definitions begin emerging, we will see WSFL used predominantly for orchestrating internal business processes and activities.

So, watch the Web services orchestration space, too. The final piece of the Web services puzzle will appear when it is possible to model a business process, including sequencing, compensation mechanisms, branching, and so on, using a standard supported by a variety of third-party tooling. Furthermore, because Web services technology fosters process integration between business partners, Web services orchestration standards will allow an organization to formalize how it collaborates with its business partners.

Completion Criteria for Web Services Standardization Efforts

With the advent of WSEL and WSFL augmenting WSDL, we observe a very important pattern emerging. Given the assertion that all Web services technologies must follow the naming pattern WS*L, we can conclude that when 26 specifications are standardized, one for each letter of the alphabet, then Web services will be "done" ☺.

Summary

We began this chapter with a question: How does the requestor know what message format should be used to invoke a Web service? We motivated the role of service description within a service-oriented architecture and explained how service description was the basis for the publish, find, and bind operations. We reviewed the characteristics of a well-defined service and outlined a service description *stack*. The basis of a well-defined service is an IDL-level description of its interface, described using the Web Services Definition Language (WSDL). We reviewed the WSDL language in great detail, using Web service descriptions for several of SkatesTown's services. We also reviewed how WSDL relates to Java programming language artifacts, including building Java client-side proxies and server-side skeletons from a WSDL definition and generating WSDL definitions from existing Java program assets. We concluded this chapter by discussing the future direction of the Web service description stack, in particular the standardization efforts around the Web Services Endpoint Language (WSEL) and the Web Services Flow Language (WSFL).

In the next chapter, we will review the role of service registries in a service oriented architecture, and in particular, outline the role of the Universal Description Discovery and Integration (UDDI) standard.

Discovering Web Services

IN THIS CHAPTER

This chapter introduces the topic of discovering Web services and, in particular, the role of a services registry in a service-oriented architecture. We discuss several alternatives to service registries, and in particular focus on the Universal Description, Discovery and Integration (UDDI) standard. After explaining the core APIs in UDDI Version 1.0 and highlighting the important APIs in UDDI Version 2.0, we discuss the role of UDDI as a private services registry, including the convention of storing WSDL service descriptions in a UDDI registry.

We also introduce some business partners of SkatesTown and discuss how a service registry such as UDDI can be used to help integrate their Web services. In the last section, we'll introduce sample Java code that gives an example of how these partners can be pulled together in a sample supply chain.

The Role of Service Discovery

In previous chapters, we have examined SOAP and service description mechanisms. But, how does the requestor know where to send the SOAP message? What kind of message should the requestor send to properly invoke the Web service? These questions can be addressed by the Web service's description. In a service-oriented architecture, Web services metadata (especially its service description) is key to maintaining loose coupling between service requestors and service providers.

In Chapter 6, "Describing Web Services," we discussed Web Services Description Language (WSDL), the most popular mechanism of service description for Web services. But in order for a Web service to be invoked, it must be discovered somehow. How was the business partner discovered, establishing the potential relationship between service requestor and service provider? How did the service requestor find out about the services provided by a service provider? How did the requestor obtain the WSDL service description from the service provider? Addressing these questions is the role of the service registry within a service-oriented architecture.

The Role of Registries

As we look at the evolution of object programming and component programming models, it is clear that the concept of an object or component registry is an essential element in the framework, facilitating the discovery and the use of components. Imagine trying to write Java code without having access to a browsable set of JavaDocs, or working in Smalltalk without having access to a class browser. If you consider the Web services concept as an evolution of component programming, it follows that for the purpose of service discovery, you need to have access to registries of business and service descriptions that can be browsed and queried.

Recall the service-oriented architecture from Chapter 1, repeated here in Figure 7.1.

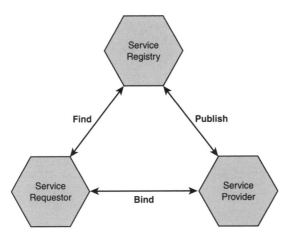

FIGURE 7.1
Service-oriented architecture.

In a service-oriented architecture, the service provider publishes the service description of a Web service to a service registry. The service requestor queries the service registry (through a find operation) to retrieve one or more service descriptions that meet certain criteria, fulfilling a step within the application's business processes. The service description contains sufficient information to allow a service requestor to bind to and invoke the Web service.

Service Discovery at Design Time and Runtime

It is important to note that service discovery can happen at application design time or at runtime. At application design time, a human designer, through a browser or other user interface, performs a find operation on a service registry, examines the result of the find, and incorporates the service description returned by the find into application logic. We discussed in Chapter 6 some of the tooling that can consume WSDL service descriptions and generate code for integration with the application.

In many cases, the service interface definition is used to build a proxy that the application logic uses to invoke the Web service and consume its response. The actual service implementation, including network location and other properties, such as which network protocol to use, is left unbound at design time, to be determined at runtime. At runtime, then, the application itself issues a find operation against the service registry to locate one or more service implementation definitions that match the service interface definition used by the application. Based on application logic such as best price, best terms, and so on, the application chooses which Web service from among the results of the find operation to invoke, extracts network location and other information from the service implementation definition, and invokes the Web service.

Multiple Mechanisms of Service Discovery

The role of the service registry in a service-oriented architecture can be fulfilled by several different mechanisms. Recall that the purpose of the registry is to provide mechanisms by which the service provider can deliver service description(s) to service requestors.

Figure 7.2 illustrates a continuum of service description techniques.

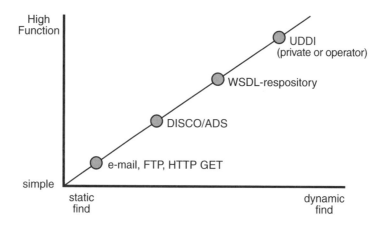

FIGURE 7.2
Kinds of service registries.

There is a trade-off here between simplicity of the registry mechanism and the sophistication of the publishing/searching techniques. Let's briefly discuss each of these points on the continuum.

The simplest approach is for the service provider to directly send the service description to the service requestor. This approach uses tried-and-true techniques such as e-mail, FTP, or even "sneaker-net" to file-transfer the service description to the service requestor. This approach is useful, particularly if the service requestor already has a business relationship with the service provider.

This approach is very simple—in fact, there really is no registry per se; manual techniques using network protocols implement the publish and find operations. However, the approach is not very dynamic and certainly provides little opportunity for anonymity. If for some reason the description of the service changes, it becomes more difficult for the service provider to communicate this to any and all service requestors that use that service. This approach does not yield very loosely coupled systems; the application must be reworked in order to change which business partner's Web service is invoked. Of course, the service requestor could cache the service descriptions in some sort of repository, but that technique then begins to look a lot less simple.

Many Web services runtimes, including Axis, provide a mechanism by which the Web Service description can be retrieved using a simple HTTP GET operation. In Chapter 6, we showed how the ?WSDL parameter can be used to return the WSDL for any Web service deployed to Axis.

The second approach uses basic Web techniques to publish and advertise Web service descriptions to a Web site. In this case, the Web site acts as a service registry, and the publish operation is simply an act of Web publication. A simple browser can retrieve a list of service descriptions and the find operation is complete. Simple techniques such as these provide the basics of a find operation, and in many cases this basic approach is sufficient for the requestor to obtain the service description.

Techniques such as IBM's *ADS* 📖 or Microsoft's .NET *DISCO* 📖 provide improvements on the simple HTTP GET. With this technique, the service provider publishes service descriptions to one or more Web sites, using one of the ADS or DISCO conventional file formats. The service provider then communicates the URL of one of these Web sites to potential service requestors. In fact, even that step is not necessary, because DISCO and ADS have been built with Web crawlers in mind. So, just as Web crawling built up directories of the World Wide Web, so could Web crawlers build up directories for the "Web service" Web.

With ADS or DISCO, the service requestor uses HTTP GET to do a find operation. The result of the find operation is a list of service descriptions. It is now up to the service requestor to determine which of the Web services is pertinent to the business task at hand and invoke that Web service. Although this approach does remove some of the update concerns for the service provider, it still doesn't give the service requestor much extra information about the purpose of the Web service, nor does it give much additional information about the service provider.

The third approach is a repository of WSDL documents. This is similar in spirit to the previous kind of service registry in that it uses HTTP GET as the primary means by which the service requestor retrieves the service description. However, a WSDL repository, such as SalCentral (www.salcentral.com), additionally offers improved facilities for the service requestor, such as notification when a service description has changed. SalCentral also offers good searching tools, including a rudimentary categorization technique. XMethods (www.xmethods.com) is another example of a public registry of WSDL documents.

The most sophisticated approach to service registries is *Universal Description Discovery and Integration (UDDI)* 📖 (http://www.uddi.org). UDDI provides very sophisticated publish and find capabilities. UDDI includes much more information than just the service description, including business metadata and taxonomies of businesses and services. UDDI not only answers the question, "Where is the Web service located?" UDDI also addresses questions such as, "How does the requestor know what business is providing the service?" Unlike the other techniques, UDDI does not depend on any one particular mechanism of service description.

As we saw in Chapter 1, "Web Services Overview," the Web services community in the W3C has described two layers in the service discovery stack: an inspection layer and a discovery (UDDI) layer. So far, no standard has been proposed or emerged at the inspection layer. We expect that something in this space will emerge to augment UDDI at the simpler end of the spectrum.

Because there is only one standard for service discovery, this chapter will focus on the UDDI specification for service registry and how it is used. We will examine UDDI by reviewing its API and major data structures found in Version 1.0 of the UDDI specification. Throughout the chapter, we discuss the important role of the *UDDI Business Registry* 📖 (www.uddi.org). We also examine the role of privately hosted UDDI registries as different implementations of the UDDI specification, addressing different service discovery needs. Having covered these roles, we can discuss the new features introduced in UDDI Version 2.0. We will conclude this chapter with an explanation of the best practices for registering WSDL-based Web service descriptions in UDDI.

Scenario Updates

As SkatesTown sells more skateboards, its network of suppliers expands. Let's examine some of the new partners SkatesTown now deals with:

- The Sports Equipment Manufacturing Consortium (SEMC) is a self-funded consortium of the major manufacturers of sports equipment, whose mission is to establish a set of e-Business standards for this industry. SkatesTown belongs to the consortium and has started implementing and using the SEMC standards.

- WeMakeIt Inc. is a large manufacturer of industrial components. Its business is to be a components supplier to a wide variety of different finished goods manufacturers. WeMakeIt Inc. manufactures a large range of components in its manufacturing sites in the USA, Europe, and Asia. Of particular interest to SkatesTown, WeMakeIt Inc. manufactures a line of small nylon wheels and wheel bearings ideal for skateboards. Joanna Pravard is the lead Web services developer for WeMakeIt Inc. Joanna is responsible for all of WeMakeIt Inc.'s Web services technologies, including its UDDI registries and its entry in the UDDI Business Registry.

- A recently created e-marketplace, called e-Torus, has formed to provide efficient buying and selling of wheels and wheel bearings components to finished goods manufacturers.

As part of the e-marketplace, e-Torus runs a private UDDI registry listing all the manufacturers of wheels, bearings, and related components. This private UDDI is also a place where service interface standards are established for the marketplace, making B2B buying and selling of these components more efficient and less error prone.

- Al Rosen of Silver Bullet Consulting "discovered" e-Torus and got SkatesTown to use their e-marketplace services. It is through e-Torus that SkatesTown established its business relationship with WeMakeIt Inc.

- Some smaller manufacturers, competing with WeMakeIt Inc. in the small wheels and related components e-marketplace, are also briefly introduced to illustrate the benefits of dynamic bind operations. This list includes wheel manufacturers, MakeCircles Inc. and WheelsMadeHere.

UDDI

In early 2000, as the idea of Web services began gaining momentum within the community, it became clear that Web services registries were going to be essential for the concept to become practical. Furthermore, in view of the movement towards open standards in the community, anything but a standard interface and search mechanism for these registries would be unacceptable. Such a registry standard would have to be endorsed by several, if not all, of the large software providers, and adopted by the various industries. Thus, the UDDI initiative, the result of several months of collaboration between representatives from Ariba, IBM, and Microsoft starting in the spring of 2000, was born and formally announced on September 6, 2000. Support for UDDI has expanded beyond the original three companies. Currently, the UDDI project (http://www.uddi.org) involves a community of more than 310 companies.

The purpose of UDDI is to facilitate service discovery both at design time and dynamically at runtime. Consequently, the UDDI project runs a public online business (and corresponding services) registry, which first went live on May 2, 2001. This registry is referred to as the UDDI Business Registry. The UDDI Business Registry actually consists of two replicated registries currently hosted by two companies (IBM and Microsoft) called the *UDDI Operators* 📖. Hewlett-Packard has joined the Operators group but has not released its registry as of this writing. More registry Operators are expected to join the Operators group.

Becoming a UDDI registry Operator involves some strict agreements about data replication, data privacy, and policies. From a registered business perspective and from a user perspective, the requirement is that different Operator registries should be theoretically indistinguishable. Businesses can register with any UDDI Operator, and their information will be replicated to the other Operators' registries. As a result, users can search *any* Operator site and find businesses *regardless* of which Operator these businesses used to register. There are, however, some subtle issues involved with the decision as to which Operator to use to register your business. For example, some Operators might ask for additional optional information that is not required by UDDI (such as surveys or marketing information). *This information is not replicated to other Operators.* Another fact to keep in mind is that once you register with an Operator, all updates to your information must be performed through that Operator. This is the case because different Operators implement different security and authentication policies, so authentication information cannot be easily replicated.

UDDI is more than a business and services registry, however. It also defines a set of data structures and an API specification for programmatically registering and finding businesses, services, bindings, and service types. In typical Web services scenarios, Web service providers will want to publish their business and service descriptions to a registry, and service requestors, whether at design time or runtime, will want to query the registry for service descriptions. The UDDI API specification, therefore, provides a set of *publication APIs* 📖 to register services and *inquiry APIs* 📖 to find services. These will be explored in the following sections, as SkatesTown decides to start using UDDI to register itself and find business partners.

In addition to providing a programmatic API, UDDI registry Operators each provide a Web-based user interface for registering, managing, and finding businesses and services in the registry. These Web sites provide a subset of the programmatic API and are relatively self-explanatory, once you have mastered the concepts introduced in this chapter. Their use will be covered in the section "Using the UDDI Web Browser Interface." As of this writing, IBM had its UDDI Web site at `http://www.ibm.com/services/uddi` and Microsoft at `http://uddi.microsoft.com`. Of course, all the operator nodes are accessible from `http://www.uddi.org`.

The UDDI Usage Model

In this section, we'll first examine some typical requirements for a registry of metadata, defining some typical data elements and operations. We will then provide an overview of the UDDI data structures and API, relating them to the original requirements. We will also explore some common UDDI operations that can be performed through the Web browser-based interface to UDDI, as provided by the main UDDI Operators. In doing so, we will introduce the main theme of the SkatesTown scenario that will be used throughout this chapter.

The UDDI Registry Requirements: Overview

Registries in general, whether for software components, services, or otherwise, have some basic requirements:

- A set of data structure specifications for the metadata to be stored in the registry
- A set of Create, Read, Update, Delete (CRUD) operation specifications for storing, deleting, and querying the data in the registry

Common registry requirements for the metadata are:

- Ownership and containment (I usually own the data I publish, and all the subdata that is contained within, unless I reassign ownership.)

- Categorization (Data can be classified in one or more categories, mainly to facilitate searching and organization.)

- A logical referencing mechanism (I can use references as pointers to other parts of the registry.)

Common registry requirements for the operations are:

- Authentication for operations that change information and for public registries

- Open access for read and query operations

The registry part of UDDI is no different: It has an information model that represents the data structure specifications and an API for the operation specifications. The UDDI information model was designed to be flexible and extensible to allow for any user defined service description models.

Because the UDDI specification is an ongoing process of refinement and extension, the bulk of this chapter will describe UDDI Version 1.0 (V1), available at the UDDI Web site. Future versions will only extend the current version with more functionality, while taking care of issues such as replication, versioning, and security. The section "What's New in V2" will describe the UDDI extensions proposed in V2.

The UDDI Data Structures: Overview

Version 1.0 of the UDDI specification allows entities such as businesses and organizations to register public information about themselves and details of the services they offer. It also allows entities such as businesses, standards bodies, and industry groups to register information about the types of services they have defined, about standards and abstractions, and to refer to them by their assigned identifiers. In effect, it is as if UDDI is offering two different registries: a business registry and a reference type registry. Correspondingly, UDDI has at its core two fundamental root data structures: businessEntity and *tModel* 📖.

The businessEntity Data Structure

Business entity information is conceptually divided into what's commonly known as White, Yellow, and Green pages:

- *White pages* contain general contact information about the entity. The SkatesTown entry would contain its name, address, and contact information such as phone, fax, and e-mail.

- *Yellow pages* contain classification information about the types and location of the services the entity offers. Again, for SkatesTown, this could be their classification as a sports equipment manufacturer and retailer, and as a skateboard manufacturer and retailer.

- *Green pages* contain information about the details of how to invoke the offered services. If SkatesTown were to offer its catalog online, its Green pages entry would have a reference to its catalog URL.

It is important to note that this is a conceptual model only, and that UDDI does not specify any particular storage model. Conceptually, however, an entity's White pages entry will contain classification information that points to its place in the various Yellow pages, and an entity's business service entries will contain implementation information that points to entries in the Green pages. This is reflected in the details of the businessEntity structure (see Figure 7.3). The businessEntity element, in addition to various contact, identifier, and taxonomy information, contains a businessServices element, which is a container for businessService elements. A businessService element in turn contains a bindingTemplates element, which is a container for bindingTemplate elements. Finally, bindingTemplate entries point to tModel entries. The details of these structures will be explored in the next sections.

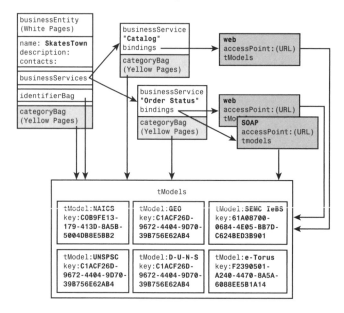

FIGURE 7.3
UDDI information model.

The tModel Data Structure

The other important structure in the UDDI information model is the tModel element. Entries in the Green pages, where invocation details are described, are actually business-specific binding details for service types and other abstractions defined elsewhere. These reusable abstractions are referred to as *technology models*, and their corresponding UDDI data structure is the tModel element. This element allows industry groups, standards bodies, and individual businesses to specify reusable abstract definitions of service types that others can use and combine, creating, in effect, a signature for a service.

In the UDDI identification scheme, each instance of the four types of entries is assigned a unique identifier by the UDDI node upon initial registration. In addition, according to the UDDI containment scheme, each instance of a contained structure (businessService and bindingTemplate) holds a key reference to its containing entity (in this case, businessEntity and businessService, respectively) in a strict parent-child relationship. These identifiers are Universal Unique Identifiers (UUIDs) that follow the OSF Distributed Computing Environment (DCE) conventions (http://www.osf.org/onlinepubs/9629399/apdxa.htm). They follow the familiar 8-4-4-4-12 pattern (such as F775A3A6-FF3E-4B85-B1DE-F0F99D0E2C6D). In addition, tModel references are given the uuid: URN qualifier.

Finally, it was deemed important that private (that is, non-Operator but otherwise UDDI compatible) UDDI registries be able to extend the businessEntity structure to include data for their own purposes. To this end, the businessEntityExt structure was specified. UDDI registry Operators, however, will not provide extensions in their publicly online available business entity data.

The UDDI API: Overview

In addition to defining the data structures to be stored in the registry, the UDDI specification provides two main types of API operations: the Publication API and the Inquiry API. These APIs define a set of 20 SOAP messages over HTTP or HTTPS that must be understood by any UDDI-conformant registry. The SOAP body of the API messages and responses are XML structures defined in the UDDI specification.

The Publication API is an authenticated set of operations that allows organizations to publish information, whether business, service, implementation, or service type specification, to the UDDI registry. Aside from requiring an *authentication token* 📖 and the use of the HTTPS protocol in the authenticated operations, UDDI does not specify an authentication method. Instead, each Operator must provide their own authentication mechanism.

The Inquiry API is a non-authenticated public set of operations that allows users to extract information out of the UDDI registry. Inquiries can follow two different patterns: a browsing pattern to find general information (the find operations), usually followed by a drill-down pattern to find specific detail information (the get_Detail operations).

Corresponding to the four structure types (businessEntity, businessService, bindingTemplate, and tModel), UDDI provides four save operations (save_business, save_service, save_binding, and save_tModel), four delete operations (delete_business, delete_service, delete_binding, and delete_tModel), four find operations (find_business, find_service, find_binding, and find_tModel) and four get_Detail operations (get_businessDetail, get_serviceDetail, get_bindingDetail, and get_tModelDetail); see Table 7.1.

TABLE 7.1   The CRUD API messages Defined by the UDDI Spec

	Business	*Service*	*Binding*	*tModel*
Save/Update	save_business	save_service	save_binding	save_tModel
Delete	delete_business	delete_service	delete_binding	delete_tModel
Find	find_business	find_service	find_binding	find_tModel
GetDetail	get_businessDetail	get_serviceDetail	get_bindingDetail	get_tModelDetail

You can use the save operations to create a new entry or to update an existing one. When creating a new entry, the entry identification key parameter is not supplied in the call, but instead is assigned by the Operator and returned in the Operator's response. To update an existing entry, this Operator-assigned key is supplied in the call. The delete operations take the Operator assigned keys as parameters and remove the corresponding entries from the registry. The delete_tModel operation is an exception that will be discussed in the section "The Delete Operations."

The find operations are passed a set of search criteria and generally return a (possibly empty) list structure containing information about entries that match the search criteria. The get_detail operations are passed a list of identifiers and return detailed information about the entries referred to by the supplied keys. The API provides one additional get_detail operation, get_businessDetailExt, to allow the retrieval of extended business information from non-Operator nodes that implement these extensions.

In addition, because the Publication API is a set of authenticated operations, where authentication is token-based, the API provides two authentication operations, get_authToken and discard_authToken.

Finally, getRegisteredInfo is an authenticated operation that returns all the businessEntity and tModel keys registered by an accredited user.

In the next sections, we will cover in detail the UDDI data structures and API and go through examples as SkatesTown registers its information so that potential clients can locate it, and so that it can locate potential suppliers.

It is important to note that it is possible to perform most of the Publication and Inquiry API functions (such as some `find` and `get_Details` operations) through the individual Operators' Web sites. The next section will go through such an example while introducing one of the main scenarios that will be used throughout the chapter. In addition to being more complete and powerful than what's available through the browser interface, however, the API is intended to allow businesses to perform all the operations programmatically, in order to facilitate dynamic (runtime) service discovery. Keep that in mind as we go through the next examples.

Using the UDDI Web Browser Interface

Before we examine the API in detail, it will be useful to briefly explore the browser interface to UDDI. UDDI Operators, as part of their responsibility to the UDDI consortium, have each provided a free public Web-based interface to their UDDI business registries. This interface allows organizations to register their businesses, along with contact information and services provided. Service type definitions can also be entered (these will be covered in more detail later in the section "The UDDI `tModel` Concept").

In this next example, SkatesTown will register its business and the contact information of Dean Carroll, the company's chief technology officer. It will also register its online catalog as an HTTP-based Web service, and classify it under the North American Industry Classification System (NAICS) taxonomy (we will discuss taxonomies in more detail in the section "More on Classification and Categorization"). Although this basic example will be explored in more detail and expanded significantly throughout our discussion of the UDDI API, it provides the main theme for the UDDI usage model.

The first step in using the UDDI registries is to register an ID and obtain an authentication token. Both IBM (`https://www-3.ibm.com/services/uddi/protect/registry.html`) and Microsoft (`http://uddi.microsoft.com/register.aspx`) registries require a username and password as a method of authentication. In the following example Dean Carroll, SkatesTown CTO, will use the IBM Test registry.

Figure 7.4 shows the registration page. Dean enters **skatestown** as the user ID and fills out the rest of the required information. Once registered, Dean can start the process of adding a new business entry. Having entered the business name, he then has the option of entering a business description, business contact information, and business locator information, which allows other users to find SkatesTown through a variety of keyword searches on the Add New Business Web page.

FIGURE 7.4

The UDDI Registration Web page.

A variety of contact information can be entered, including descriptions, phone numbers, e-mail addresses, and mailing addresses. Finally, the business is categorized by entering locator information. The UDDI Version 1.0 specification provides a set of pre-determined taxonomies to be used for this purpose (see the section "More on Classification and Categorization"). For this instance, Dean will use the NAICS taxonomy and drill down to the 33992 category, "Sporting and Athletic Goods Manufacturing" (see Figure 7.5).

The next step is to enter a Web service registration. In this case, Dean will register the online Check Order Status Web service provided by SkatesTown. The service registration page allows for a variety of information to be entered about the service, including a description (what is this service?), access point information (how do I invoke it?) and locator information (what kind of service is it?).

Figures 7.6 and 7.7 show a high-level view of all the SkatesTown business and service information that was entered, respectively.

FIGURE 7.5

The NAICS Category 33992 Selection Web page.

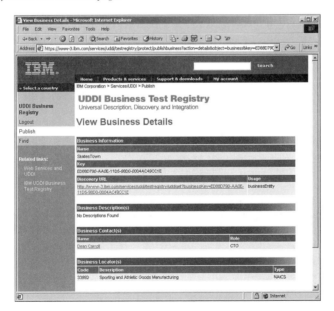

FIGURE 7.6

The UDDI Business Details Web page.

7

DISCOVERING
WEB SERVICES

FIGURE 7.7

The UDDI Service Details Web page.

It is interesting to notice that in both cases, the UDDI registry has generated unique keys for the business entry and the service entry. In addition, it has generated a URL for the business description (under the title Discovery URL) that returns the following XML document, describing the SkatesTown UDDI business entry:

```xml
<?xml version="1.0" encoding="utf-8" ?>
<businessDetail generic="1.0" xmlns="urn:uddi-org:api"
   operator="www.ibm.com/services/uddi" truncated="false">
   <businessEntity authorizedName="0100003BG0"
      operator="www.ibm.com/services/uddi"
      businessKey="ED88D790-AA0E-11D5-98D0-0004AC49CC1E">
      <discoveryURLs>
         <discoveryURL useType="businessEntity">
http://www-3.ibm.com/services/uddi/testregistry/uddiget?
businessKey=ED88D790-AA0E-11D5-98D0-0004AC49CC1E
      </discoveryURL>
      </discoveryURLs>
      <name>SkatesTown</name>
      <contacts>
         <contact useType="CTO">
            <personName>Dean Carroll</personName>
         </contact>
      </contacts>
```

```
<businessServices>
    <businessService serviceKey="C8013A60-AA10-11D5-98D0-0004AC49CC1E"
        businessKey="ED88D790-AA0E-11D5-98D0-0004AC49CC1E">
    <name>Check Order Status</name>
    <description xml:lang="en">Check your order status online
    </description>
    <bindingTemplates>
        <bindingTemplate
            bindingKey="C8061C60-AA10-11D5-98D0-0004AC49CC1E"
            serviceKey="C8013A60-AA10-11D5-98D0-0004AC49CC1E">
        <description xml:lang="en">
            This is a web based (http) order status service
        </description>
        <accessPoint URLType="http">
         http://www.skatestown.com/services/orderStatus</accessPoint>
        <tModelInstanceDetails>
            <tModelInstanceInfo
                tModelKey="UUID:68DE9E80-AD09-469D-8A37-088422BFBC36">
            </tModelInstanceInfo>
        </tModelInstanceDetails>
        </bindingTemplate>
    </bindingTemplates>
    <categoryBag>
        <keyedReference
            tModelKey="UUID:C0B9FE13-179F-413D-8A5B-5004DB8E5BB2"
            keyName="Sporting and Athletic Goods Manufacturing"
            keyValue="33992">
        </keyedReference>
    </categoryBag>
    </businessService>
</businessServices>
<categoryBag>
    <keyedReference tModelKey="UUID:C0B9FE13-179F-413D-8A5B-5004DB8E5BB2"
        keyName="Sporting and Athletic Goods Manufacturing"
        keyValue="33992">
    </keyedReference>
</categoryBag>
    </businessEntity>
</businessDetail>
```

We will be seeing more of this type of XML document as we expand on the example in the next sections, by exploring the UDDI data structure and API.

The UDDI tModel Concept

Before we begin publishing more services to UDDI, we need to explore the concept of a tModel in detail, because it is essential to how services are described.

What Is a `tModel`?

In order to invoke a service, you sometimes need to know a large amount of detail in terms of document formats, transport protocols, input and output parameters, URNs, business process, and so on. These details in general could be supplied in the description of the service implementation. In Chapter 6, Listing 6.1, you saw an example of a WSDL definition for the `PriceCheck` service for SkatesTown. That definition contained both abstract reusable information (the service interface definition) and concrete implementation information (the service implementation definition). If software engineering has taught us one thing in the last decade, it is the power of abstraction and re-use. Suppose that another company belonging to the same SEMC consortium were to implement an identical service. It would have to repeat the same bulk of information in its WSDL document, with the only difference being the endpoint address for the implementation of its SOAP service. Suppose, however, that the SEMC consortium were to abstract out the service interface definition of the WSDL document and publish it as a consortium standard. This would enable both companies (and any other company in the consortium) to reference that abstract definition and only have to supply their concrete implementation endpoint. That abstract service interface definition is, in essence, a perfect example of a `tModel`.

In general, these types of service specifications could be applicable in several different places for different services, or for different bindings for the same service. They can also be specified by an industry consortium as we saw in the examples, a standards body, or a large corporation for the use by its suppliers. Thus conformance to a known and predefined set of specifications becomes very important. The `tModel` concept is the mechanism for such abstractions. It allows various entities (businesses, standards bodies, industry groups, and so on) to publish abstract specifications to be used by other entities in implementing services. In our previous examples, the SEMC would register its `http://www.semc-consortium.org/BP/PriceCheck` specification as a `tModel`, which would be assigned a unique identifier key and be referenced by all businesses in the consortium, such as `SkatesTown`. In addition, clients wanting to find businesses that conform to that SEMC specification can query the registry for businesses referencing that `tModel`.

How to Use `tModels`

It is important to stress that based on the UDDI specification, a `tModel` could define just about anything: It consists of a key, a name, a description, and a URL. This simplicity is a powerful concept, but it can also be a double-edged sword. On the one hand, because of the simplicity in defining a `tModel`, you can define anything you want, even if it's not useful to or reusable by anyone else. On the other hand, if used properly, you can use `tModels` to specify the standards and templates that will be used in the next generation of e-Business on the Web.

Throughout the UDDI data structures, `tModels` are used as references. By convention, the UDDI specification suggests two main uses for them. The primary use is in defining what is called a *technical fingerprint*. This refers to any technical specifications or pre-arranged agreements on how to conduct business. For example, `tModels` can be created by industry groups such as RosettaNet (`http://www.rosettanet.org`), or by companies wishing to standardize the way they deal with suppliers. Our examples illustrate how SkatesTown and MyTurningWheels are using a specification defined by another entity, namely SEMC.

The other main use for `tModels` is in defining namespaces to be used in the `identifierBag` and `categoryBag` structures. This will be covered in more detail in the section "More on Classification and Categorization."

The `tModel` Structure

As we already discussed, the `tModel` structure is very simple. In general, an entity that acts as a reference needs a name, a description, some reference material that describes the details of its use, and a resolvable, unique identifier. This is true of a UDDI `tModel`. It has a key, a name, a description, an optional descriptive overview document, and some categorization and identification information (see Figure 7.8).

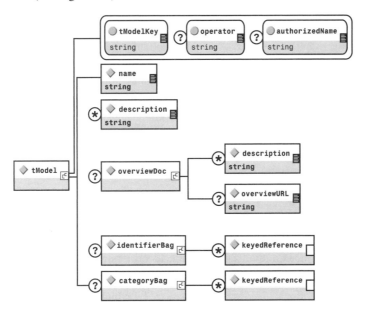

FIGURE 7.8

The `tModel` structure.

`tModel` attributes are as follows:

- `tModelKey`—The unique identifier for the `tModel`. It is assigned by the UDDI Operator and cannot be edited or modified. For this reason, it should not be supplied in the original `tModel` registration. When a new `tModel` is registered, the UDDI Operator assigns a unique `tModelKey` in the form of a UUID and returns that key in the response. This key can then be used in subsequent queries and updates.

- `operator`—The certified name of the Operator that owns the UDDI node to which the `tModel` is registered. It is originally assigned by the UDDI Operator and cannot be edited or modified by the entity. For this reason, it should not be supplied in the original registration.

- `authorizedName`—The name provided by the Operator to the authenticated user who registered the `tModel`. It is originally assigned by the UDDI Operator and cannot be edited or modified by the entity. For this reason, it should not be supplied in the original registration.

`tModel` elements are as follows:

- `name`—Required. The `tModel`'s name.

- `description`—Optional repeating. Textual description of the `tModel`.

- `overviewDoc`—Optional. In addition to its basic information, a `tModel` structure might contain an optional `overviewDoc` element. The `overviewDoc` structure is used to provide an overview description of the `tModel` and its intended use. It has an optional repeating string description element and an optional `overviewURL` that should be used to point to a document that provides a description and a technical specification of the `tModel`. It is suggested that this document be HTML based and suitable for retrieval in a browser through the HTTP GET operation.

- `identifierBag`—Optional. This element allows `tModels` to be identified by associating them with a predefined identification namespace, such as defined by an industry group, or provided by UDDI (such as the Dun & Bradstreet Data Universal Numbering System D-U-N-S®). This is done through a set of `keyedReference` elements, each of which is a key/value pair. The identification information can be very useful when you're searching for a particular `tModel` in the UDDI registry. Identifiers will be discussed in more detail in the section "More on Classification and Categorization."

- `categoryBag`—Optional. This is the mechanism by which `tModels` can be categorized within various taxonomies, either provided by industry groups, or provided by UDDI. UDDI Operators will initially support three taxonomies. Categorization will be discussed in more detail in the section "More on Classification and Categorization."

More on Classification and Categorization

As we previously stated, one of the main objectives of the UDDI registries is the discovery of services, whether statically (design time) or dynamically (runtime). This entails a form of search through a large space of entries. In a reasonably populated registry, depending on the search mechanism, this could return a very large set of hits. An early requirement for UDDI, therefore, was a way to perform intelligent searches. Until the semantic problem (see Chapter 9, "Future Concepts") is addressed in a satisfactory manner, the best current mechanism to facilitate such searches is through taxonomic categorization and classification.

Categorization is the process of creating categories, whereas *classification* is the process of assigning objects to these predefined categories (or classes). There are several types of classification schemes (such as the Library of Congress Classification used in most libraries), but for a large space such as businesses and services, the most useful ones are hierarchical in nature. In general, hierarchies are very powerful for organizing data (consider XML!). One of the most powerful examples of the importance of hierarchical classification in the age of the Web is Yahoo! In addition to a search engine, Yahoo! offers an extensive classification scheme. For example, to find manufacturers of skateboards, you would naturally traverse the Yahoo! classification tree to get to `Business_and_Economy/Shopping_and_Services/Sports/Skateboarding/Deck_and_Truck_Manufacturers/`.

It can be argued that the first-generation Web (the information Web of HTML and CGI pages) did not attain its potential until the Yahoo! classification scheme became available. Similarly, a registry such as UDDI would be very difficult to use without some classification schemes.

The first version of UDDI includes in its core specifications three predefined classification schemes: the North American Industry Classification System (NAICS) for classifying businesses by industry (`http://www.ntis.gov/product/naics.htm`), the Universal Standard Products and Services Classification (UNSPSC) for product and service classifications (`http://eccma.org/unspsc`), and the ISO 3166 standard for geographic location classifications (`http://www.din.de/gremien/nas/nabd/iso3166ma`). In order to take advantage of these schemes, businesses need to provide the relevant classification information as they register their entries. This is done through the `categoryBag` element. This element contains a set of `keyedReference` elements (see Figure 7.9), each of which has attributes forming a name/value pair and an optional `tModelKey`. The `tModelKey` is a simple but powerful extension mechanism that acts as a namespace qualifier for the values specified in the name/value pair. For example, if SkatesTown wanted to classify its business using the Yahoo! classification scheme, (assuming that Yahoo has registered the scheme as a `tModel` with an assigned key of 3D4EC875-E54F-4D8D-9CBF-346D48BCAD9C), the company could add the following `keyedReference` to its categoryBag, using the reference to the Yahoo! classification tModel as a namespace for its category:

```
<keyedReference
    keyName="Yahoo Business Taxonomy"
    keyValue="Business_and_Economy/Shopping_and_Services/Sports/
Skateboarding/Deck_and_Truck_Manufacturers"
    tModelKey="UUID:3D4EC875-E54F-4D8D-9CBF-346D48BCAD9C"/>
```

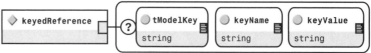

FIGURE 7.9

The keyedReference *structure.*

Another important use for the keyedReference element is in the identifierBag structure. The identifierBag is very similar to the categoryBag construct in structure in that it is a container for a set of keyedReference elements. Instead of *categorization* information, however, the identifierBag (as its name implies) is used to provide *identification* information. This mechanism allows registered entities, whether businesses or tModels, to be associated with some declared identification scheme, such as a tax ID or an industry group ID, in a consistent manner. This, in turn, provides a richer context and an additional mechanism for searching across UDDI entries.

As an example, consider that the D-U-N-S number is defined as a tModel in the UDDI Taxonomy namespace (see the section "UDDI Core tModel"). In a similar manner, e-Torus can define its own business registry under this model. Businesses in the e-Torus marketplace can identify themselves using that tModel as a namespace. The details of the e-Torus Registry Number tModel would look like this (it is of type identifier in the UDDI Type taxonomy):

```
<tModel tModelKey="uuid:F2390501-A240-4470-8A5A-6088EE5B1A14">
    <name>et:e-Torus-registry</name>
    <description xml:lang="en">e-Torus Registry Number</description>
    <categoryBag>
        <keyedReference
            keyName=" Unique identifiers for member companies"
            keyValue="identifier"
            tModelKey="uuid:C1ACF26D-9672-4404-9D70-39B756E62AB4"/>
    </categoryBag>
</tModel>
```

This means that businesses that want to provide their e-Torus Registry Number as identification for search purposes can do so by adding keyed reference pointing to this tModel in their categoryBag. You will see such examples in the section "The Business Entity Structure."

The `save_tModel` Structure

Organizations or businesses can define, create, and publish their own `tModels` using the `save_tModel` operation. A `save_tModel` message needs to be constructed with a `save_tModel` structure in the `body` element of the SOAP envelope, and the `tModel` structure contained within (see Figure 7.10).

`save_tModel` has this message signature:

```
<save_tModel generic="1.0" xmlns="urn:uddi-org:api" >
    <authInfo/>
    <tModel/> [<tModel/>...] | <uploadRegister/> [<uploadRegister/>...]
</save_tModel>
```

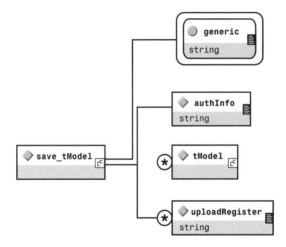

FIGURE 7.10
The `save_tModel` message structure.

`save_tModel` has a single attribute: `generic`, which is required. This attribute is present on all the UDDI API operations. As the UDDI specification grows and is modified, Operator sites will have to manage versions of the API, and will be required to support all current versions. The generic attribute specifies the version of the API to which a particular operation belongs. In UDDI V1 operations, this is the string `"1.0"`.

`save_tModel` has the following elements:

- `authInfo`—Required. All Publication API operations are authenticated because they create or modify business information. Supplying an authentication token in this element provides authentication. The token is obtained from the UDDI node Operator either by an Operator-specific mechanism or through the `get_authToken` operation where there is no other Operator-specific mechanism.

- tModel—Optional repeating. tModel information as described in the section "The tModel Data Structure." One or more structures can be registered in this manner in the same call.

- uploadRegister—Optional repeating. This is a URL that points to an XML document containing a valid tModel structure, resolvable through an HTTP GET operation. The uploadRegister and tModel elements should not both be included in the same save_tModel operation.

Authentication

As you have already seen, all Publication API operations need to be authenticated. Privacy, security, and authentication are crucial for the UDDI Operators to build a trusted relationship with UDDI users. However, because there is still no one clearly universal and widely accepted standard for authentication, various Operators have different authentication policies. As a result, the UDDI authentication mechanism involves getting an opaque authentication token by means specified by the UDDI Operator, using it in the authInfo attribute, and then, optionally, discarding it. In addition, all Publication API messages are SSL encrypted. UDDI Operator nodes can specify their own specific mechanism for getting a token. In case no Operator-specific mechanism is provided, Operators are required to implement the get_authToken API. Authentication in this case is performed by first getting an opaque authentication token from the UDDI registry through the get_authToken call (see Figure 7.11), supplying that token in the authInfo element in the subsequent calls, and finally discarding the token through the discard_authToken call (see Figure 7.12). This process is described in the next examples.

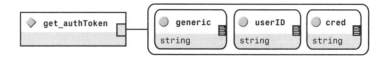

FIGURE 7.11
The get_authToken message structure.

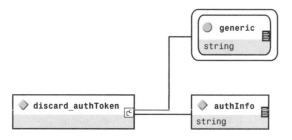

FIGURE 7.12
The discard_authToken message structure.

Before being allowed to publish information to an Operator node, a prospective user will need to establish some credentials through an initial pre-registration step, which is Operator dependent. As a result of this initial step, each registering entity is either issued an authentication token (such as a certificate) or a user ID and password. These values are passed in the `authInfo` element of the Publishing API calls, or the `userID` and `cred` elements of the `get_authToken` call, respectively.

The following is an example of the `get_authToken` message where the sender has pre-registered with the UDDI Operator site and been assigned a user ID and password:

```
<get_authToken generic="1.0" xmlns="urn:uddi-org:api"
   userID="{userID assigned by Operator}"
   cred="{password chosen at registration}"/>
```

The result of the `get_authToken` operation is an `authToken` structure (see Figure 7.13) identifying the Operator and providing a token, usually in the form of a UUID.

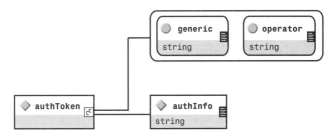

FIGURE 7.13

The authToken structure.

The response to the previous message, assuming the correct password was supplied and the user is pre-registered, is shown:

```
<authToken generic="1.0"
   xmlns="urn:uddi-org:api"
   operator="UDDIOperator">
   <authInfo>5BA16322-B5ED-4300-8F2F-420DA3A212D2</authInfo>
</authToken>
```

The `discard_authToken` operation is used to inform the token issuer that the token is no longer valid and can be discarded. Subsequent Publishing API calls using the same token should be rejected. It passes as parameter the token received in the `get_authToken` operation:

```
<discard_authToken generic="1.0" xmlns="urn:uddi-org:api">
   <authInfo>5BA16322-B5ED-4300-8F2F-420DA3A212D2</authInfo>
</discard_authToken>
```

Publishing `tModel` Information in UDDI

SkatesTown belongs to an industry consortium, the Sports Equipment Manufacturing Consortium (SEMC), which has published a set of specifications for conducting business on the Internet, including specifications for order management, and in particular order status processing. When implemented by manufacturers, these specifications are intended to facilitate the process of customers' checking the status of their orders. The SEMC published its specifications under several `tModels`. The root specification that covers the overall SEMC set of specifications is registered in this section.

As discussed in the previous section on authentication, it is assumed here that the SEMC has already registered with a UDDI Operator, and that the Operator uses a user ID and password authentication scheme. In order to use the Publication API, we need to get an authentication token:

```
<get_authToken generic="1.0" xmlns="urn:uddi-org:api"
      userID="SEMC" cred="thisbetterbeareallygoodpassword:wemakestuff"/>
```

The Operator UDDI node then would send a response:

```
<authToken generic="1.0" xmlns="urn:uddi-org:api"
   operator="UDDIOperator">
      <authInfo>50D1FEBF-4D47-4D8F-A9A5-56403DF080AB</authInfo>
</authToken>
```

The `authInfo` token is then used in the `save_tModel` call. The following shows what a new `tModel` registration document would look like:

```
<save_tModel generic="1.0" xmlns="urn:uddi-org:api">
   <authInfo>50D1FEBF-4D47-4D8F-A9A5-56403DF080AB</authInfo>
   <tModel tModelKey="">
      <name>Sports Equipment Manufacturing Consortium
         e-business Specification V1.2</name>
      <description xml:lang="en">Root tModel for the SEMC set of
         specifications for e-business on the Internet</description>
      <overviewDoc>
      <description xml:lang="en">This document describes the structure,
         sections and requirements for the SEMC IeBS specification V1.2
      </description>
         <overviewURL>http://www.semc-consortium.org/SEMC-IeBS.html
         </overviewURL>
      </overviewDoc>
      <identifierBag>
         <keyedReference
            keyName="DUNS" keyValue="00-222-2222"
            tModelKey="uuid:D9392AEE-9A13-4B6E-B528-5A0D08BD4BF9"/>
      </identifierBag>
      <categoryBag>
```

```
        <keyedReference
            keyName="types" keyValue="specification"
            tModelKey="uuid:C1ACF26D-9672-4404-9D70-39B756E62AB4"/>
      </categoryBag>
   </tModel>
</save_tModel>
```

In this example, the SEMC is using the authentication token that it received in the previous get_authToken call. Registering the information is very straightforward. In addition to a name and brief description, an overviewURL is given, pointing to the SEMC Web pages that describe the set of specifications. identifierBag and categoryBag information is included. The identifierBag information lists the D-U-N-S number for the consortium, which will facilitate searching for the tModels registered by SEMC (the number shown is fictitious and only used for illustration). The categoryBag information uses the canonical UDDI tModel supertype for specification, indicating that this tModel is a *specification* type of tModel. Canonical UDDI tModels are described in the section "UDDI Core tModels."

The UDDI registry would then assign a key to the tModel, register it, and send the following acknowledgement response. Notice that the Operator has assigned a unique tModelKey to the tModel, along with an authorizedName (SEMC.org) and an Operator (UDDIOperator).

The following is a response to the SEMC save_tModel Message:

```
<tModelDetail generic="1.0" operator="UDDIOperator"
   truncated="false" xmlns="urn:uddi-org:api">
<tModel authorizedName="SEMC.org"
   operator="UDDIOperator"
   tModelKey="uuid:61A08700-0684-4E05-BB7D-C624BED3B901">
   <name>Sports Equipment Manufacturing Consortium
      eBusiness Specification V1.2</name>
   <description xml:lang="en">Root tModel for the SEMC set of
      specifications for eBusiness on the Internet</description>
   <overviewDoc>
   <description xml:lang="en">This document describes the structure,
      sections and requirements for the SEMC IeBS specification V1.2
      </description>
      <overviewURL>http://www. semc.org/SEMC-IeBS.html</overviewURL>
   </overviewDoc>
   <identifierBag>
      <keyedReference
         keyName="DUNS" keyValue="00-222-2222"
         tModelKey="uuid:D9392AEE-9A13-4B6E-B528-5A0D08BD4BF9"/>
   </identifierBag>
   <categoryBag>
      <keyedReference
         keyName="types" keyValue="specification"
```

7

DISCOVERING
WEB SERVICES

```
            tModelKey="uuid:C1ACF26D-9672-4404-9D70-39B756E62AB4"/>
      </categoryBag>
   </tModel>
</tModelDetail>
```

Next, the SEMC registers an Order Management specification V1.5 using the following message. Notice that one of the keyed references in the `categoryBag` element points to the root SEMC IeBS specification V1.2, indicating that this `tModel` is part of that hierarchy, again facilitating searches. Here is what that `tModel` looks like:

```
<save_tModel generic="1.0" xmlns="urn:uddi-org:api">
   <authInfo>50D1FEBF-4D47-4D8F-A9A5-56403DF080AB</authInfo>
   <tModel tModelKey="">
      <name>Sports Equipment Manifacturing Consortium
         Order Management V1.5</name>
      <description xml:lang="en">tModel for the SEMC Order Management set of
         specifications V1.5</description>
      <overviewDoc>
      <description xml:lang="en">This document describes the details and
         conformance requirements for the SEMC IeBS Order Management V1.5
         specification
      </description>
         <overviewURL>http://www.semc-consortium.org/SEMC-IeBS/OrderMgmt.html
            </overviewURL>
      </overviewDoc>
      <identifierBag>
         <keyedReference
            keyName="DUNS" keyValue="00-222-2222"
            tModelKey="uuid:D9392AEE-9A13-4B6E-B528-5A0D08BD4BF9"/>
      </identifierBag>
      <categoryBag>
         <keyedReference
            keyName="types" keyValue="specification"
            tModelKey="uuid:C1ACF26D-9672-4404-9D70-39B756E62AB4"/>
         <keyedReference
            keyName="types" keyValue="specification"
            tModelKey="uuid:61A08700-0684-4E05-BB7D-C624BED3B901"/>
      </categoryBag>
   </tModel>
</save_tModel>
```

The UDDI registry again registers the `tModel` and assigns it a `tModel` key (for future examples, let's assume this key has a value of 6E986185-3937-442F-8916-209DA01DF837).

UDDI Core `tModels`

As we saw in the previous example, SEMC declared its specifications to be of the *specification* type, using a types namespace provided by UDDI. The first release of the UDDI specification registered several tModels for use as a starting set. UDDI defines a root or *supertype* tModel for all types, used to establish a hierarchical taxonomy of types. Then, all other type tModels are defined in this tModel's namespace (including the UDDI Type itself, which is self-referential, as seen from its definition).

The UDDI type taxonomy tModel has the following definition:

```
<tModel tModelKey="UUID:C1ACF26D-9672-4404-9D70-39B756E62AB4">
   <name>uddi-org:types</name>
   <description xml:lang="en">UDDI Type Taxonomy</description>
   <overviewDoc>
      <description xml:lang="en">Taxonomy used to categorize Service
Descriptions</description>
      <overviewURL>http://www.uddi.org/specification.html</overviewURL>
   </overviewDoc>
   <categoryBag>
      <keyedReference keyName="types" keyValue="categorization"
         tModelKey="UUID:C1ACF26D-9672-4404-9D70-39B756E62AB4"/>
   </categoryBag>
</tModel>
```

Figure 7.14 lists all the UDDI types belonging to this taxonomy. These types can be used to categorize other tModels.

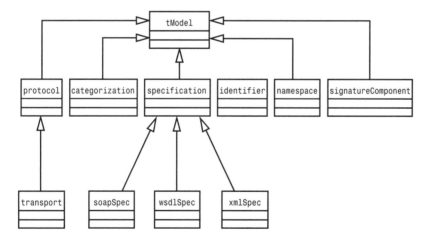

FIGURE 7.14
The core tModel taxonomy hierarchy.

Let's look at how this works. For example, the Dun & Bradstreet D-U-N-S® number is defined as follows:

```
<tModel tModelKey="UUID:8609C81E-EE1F-4D5A-B202-3EB13AD01823">
   <name>dnb-com:D-U-N-S</name>
   <description xml:lang="en">Dun &amp; Bradstreet D-U-N-S®
Number</description>
   <overviewDoc>
      <description xml:lang="en">This tModel is used for the Dun
         &amp; Bradstreet  D-U-N-S(r) Number identifier.</description>
      <overviewURL>http://www.uddi.org/specification.html</overviewURL>
   </overviewDoc>
   <categoryBag>
      <keyedReference keyName="types" keyValue="identifier"
         tModelKey="UUID:C1ACF26D-9672-4404-9D70-39B756E62AB4"/>
   </categoryBag>
</tModel>
```

In the keyedReference element in the categoryBag, the tModelKey value of C1ACF26D-9672-4404-9D70-39B756E62AB4 is the key for the UDDI Type Taxonomy tModel, which is the namespace for all UDDI Types. Of all the possible values in the taxonomy of this core namespace, this tModel is categorized as an identifier type (through the *keyValue* attribute). (The authorizedName and operator attributes of the tModel element will be omitted in all the examples in this section because they are irrelevant to the point being illustrated.)

Next, UDDI defines some core tModels for the three main API services. These tModels are all classified in the UDDI Type tModel namespace as being of types specification, xmlSpec, and soapSpec:

```
<tModel tModelKey="UUID:4CD7E4BC-648B-426D-9936-443EAAC8AE23">
   <name>uddi-org:inquiry</name>
   <description xml:lang="en">UDDI Inquiry API - Core Specification
   </description>
   <overviewDoc>
      <description xml:lang="en">This tModel defines the inquiry API
         calls for interacting with the UDDI registry.</description>
      <overviewURL>http://www.uddi.org/specification.html</overviewURL>
   </overviewDoc>
   <categoryBag>
      <keyedReference keyName="types" keyValue="specification"
         tModelKey="UUID:C1ACF26D-9672-4404-9D70-39B756E62AB4"/>
      <keyedReference keyName="types" keyValue="xmlSpec"
         tModelKey="UUID:C1ACF26D-9672-4404-9D70-39B756E62AB4"/>
      <keyedReference keyName="types" keyValue="soapSpec"
         tModelKey="UUID:C1ACF26D-9672-4404-9D70-39B756E62AB4"/>
   </categoryBag>
</tModel>
```

The UDDI Publication API core specification tModel has the following definition:

```
<tModel tModelKey="UUID:64C756D1-3374-4E00-AE83-EE12E38FAE63">
    <name>uddi-org:publication</name>
    <description xml:lang="en">UDDI Publication API - Core Specification
    </description>
    <overviewDoc>
        <description xml:lang="en">This tModel defines the publication
            API calls for interacting with the UDDI registry.</description>
        <overviewURL>http://www.uddi.org/specification.html</overviewURL>
    </overviewDoc>
    <categoryBag>
        <keyedReference keyName="types" keyValue="specification"
            tModelKey="UUID:C1ACF26D-9672-4404-9D70-39B756E62AB4"/>
        <keyedReference keyName="types" keyValue="xmlSpec"
            tModelKey="UUID:C1ACF26D-9672-4404-9D70-39B756E62AB4"/>
        <keyedReference keyName="types" keyValue="soapSpec"
            tModelKey="UUID:C1ACF26D-9672-4404-9D70-39B756E62AB4"/>
    </categoryBag>
</tModel>
```

The UDDI Taxonomy API core specification tModel has the following definition:

```
<tModel tModelKey="UUID:3FB66FB7-5FC3-462F-A351-C140D9BD8304">
    <name>uddi-org:taxonomy</name>
    <description xml:lang="en">UDDI Taxonomy API</description>
    <overviewDoc>
        <description xml:lang="en">This tModel defines the taxonomy
            maintenance API calls for interacting with the UDDI registry
        </description>
        <overviewURL>http://www.uddi.org/specification.html</overviewURL>
    </overviewDoc>
    <categoryBag>
        <keyedReference keyName="types" keyValue="specification"
            tModelKey="UUID:C1ACF26D-9672-4404-9D70-39B756E62AB4"/>
        <keyedReference keyName="types" keyValue="xmlSpec"
            tModelKey="UUID:C1ACF26D-9672-4404-9D70-39B756E62AB4"/>
        <keyedReference keyName="types" keyValue="soapSpec"
            tModelKey="UUID:C1ACF26D-9672-4404-9D70-39B756E62AB4"/>
    </categoryBag>
</tModel>
```

The different taxonomies are also defined in the spec. The NAICS taxonomy is as follows:

```
<tModel tModelKey="UUID:C0B9FE13-179F-413D-8A5B-5004DB8E5BB2">
    <name>ntis-gov:naics:1997</name>
    <description xml:lang="en">Business Taxonomy: NAICS (1997 Release)
    </description>
```

7

DISCOVERING
WEB SERVICES

```
<overviewDoc>
   <description xml:lang="en">This tModel defines the NAICS
      industry taxonomy.</description>
   <overviewURL>http://www.uddi.org/specification.html</overviewURL>
</overviewDoc>
<categoryBag>
   <keyedReference keyName="types" keyValue="categorization"
      tModelKey="UUID:C1ACF26D-9672-4404-9D70-39B756E62AB4"/>
</categoryBag>
</tModel>
```

The UNSPSC taxonomy is as follows:

```
<tModel tModelKey="UUID:DB77450D-9FA8-45D4-A7BC-04411D14E384">
   <name>unspsc-org:unspsc:3-1</name>
   <description xml:lang="en">Product Taxonomy: UNSPSC (Version 3.1)
   </description>
   <overviewDoc>
      <description xml:lang="en">This tModel defines the UNSPSC
         product taxonomy.</description>
      <overviewURL>http://www.uddi.org/specification.html</overviewURL>
   </overviewDoc>
   <categoryBag>
      <keyedReference keyName="types" keyValue="categorization"
         tModelKey="UUID:C1ACF26D-9672-4404-9D70-39B756E62AB4"/>
   </categoryBag>
</tModel>
```

The ISO 3166-1:1997 and 3166-2:1998 geographic taxonomy is as follows:

```
<tModel tModelKey="UUID:4E49A8D6-D5A2-4FC2-93A0-0411D8D19E88">
   <name>iso-ch:3166:1999</name>
   <description xml:lang="en">ISO 3166-1:1997 and 3166-2:1998. Codes
      for names of countries and their subdivisions. Part 1: Country
      codes. Part 2:Country subdivision codes. Update newsletters
      include ISO 3166-1 V-1 (1998-02-05), V-2 (1999-10-01), ISO
      3166-2 I-1 (1998)</description>
   <overviewDoc>
      <description xml:lang="en">Taxonomy used to categorize entries
         by geographic location.</description>
      <overviewURL>http://www.uddi.org/iso-ch-3166-1999.html</overviewURL>
   </overviewDoc>
   <categoryBag>
      <keyedReference keyName="types" keyValue="categorization"
         tModelKey="UUID:C1ACF26D-9672-4404-9D70-39B756E62AB4"/>
   </categoryBag>
</tModel>
```

Finally, a miscellaneous taxonomy for entries that do not validate in the other taxonomies is as follows:

```
<tModel tModelKey="UUID:A035A07C-F362-44DD-8F95-E2B134BF43B4">
   <name>uddi-org:misc-taxonomy</name>
   <description xml:lang="en">Other Taxonomy</description>
   <overviewDoc>
      <description xml:lang="en">This tModel defines an unidentified taxonomy
      </description>
      <overviewURL>http://www.uddi.org/specification.html</overviewURL>
   </overviewDoc>
   <categoryBag>
      <keyedReference keyName="types" keyValue="categorization"
         tModelKey="UUID:C1ACF26D-9672-4404-9D70-39B756E62AB4"/>
   </categoryBag>
</tModel>
```

The last `tModel` is the Dun and Bradstreet D-U-N-S number, which we've already seen.

Publishing Business Information to a UDDI Registry

Let's now go through some detailed examples of businesses using the UDDI registry. SkatesTown has decided to start using UDDI to publish its information and find business partners. To publish its business information, SkatesTown needs to construct a `businessEntity` structure and send it in a SOAP message using the `save_business` call. Let's look in more detail at the `businessEntity` structure.

The `businessEntity` Structure

The `businessEntity` element is the top-level element in the UDDI information data structure (see Figure 7.15). The structure is used to represent information about an entity or a business. It is also used as a container for the business services element and indirectly for the corresponding implementation and binding details of all the services that an entity provides. Its top structure is relatively similar to the other top structure in the UDDI information model, the `tModel`, in that it has for attributes a unique key, an Operator, and an authorized name. Again, just like a `tModel` structure, its elements include `name`, `description`, `categoryBag`, and `identifierBag` information. In addition, it has contact information, and it acts as the container for the business services.

`businessEntity` has the following attributes:

- `businessKey`—The unique identifier for the business entity. It is assigned by the UDDI Operator and cannot be edited or modified by the entity. For this reason, it should not be supplied in the original business entity registration. When a new entity is registered, the UDDI Operator assigns a unique `businessKey` in the form of a UUID and returns that key in the response. This key can then be used in subsequent queries and updates.

- operator—The certified name of the Operator that owns the UDDI node to which the entity is registered. It is originally assigned by the UDDI Operator and cannot be edited or modified by the entity. For this reason, it should not be supplied in the original registration.

- authorizedName—The name provided by the Operator. It is originally assigned by the UDDI Operator and cannot be edited or modified by the entity. For this reason, it should not be supplied in the original registration.

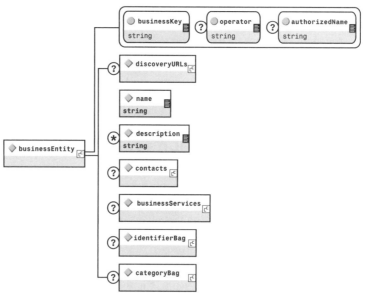

FIGURE 7.15
The businessEntity structure.

businessEntity has the following elements:

- discoveryURLs—Optional. A container for discoveryURL elements, which provide alternate means for discovering the services. For example, businesses can provide a Web site to their services, or use a convention such as the eCo Framework (http://www.oasis-open.org/cover/ecoFramework.html) service description convention. A UDDI Operator will automatically assign a URL for every registered business entity. The discoveryURL element has a useType attribute, which can be used to describe the corresponding URL. (See the example under "conacts" on the next page.) UDDI reserves two useType strings, businessEntity and businessEntityExt, which will be described later.

- name—Required. The entity's name.

- description—Optional repeating. Textual description of the business or organization.

- contacts—Optional. A container for contact elements, which provide contact information for the entity. As seen from Figure 7.16, contact information includes required information such as a person's name, and optional information such as a description, phone, e-mail, and address. The various use_type attributes are used for text entries describing the type of information entered, such as product manager, technical support, and cell phone. The following is an example of SkatesTown contact information:

```
<contact useType="Technical Information">
    <description>CTO for technical information</description>
    <personName>Dean Carroll</personName>
    <phone useType="Main Office">1.212.555.0001</phone>
    <email useType="CTO">dean.carroll@SkatesTown.com</email>
    <email useType="General Information">info@SkatesTown.com</email>
    <address useType="Main Office" sortCode="10001">
        <addressLine>2001 Skate Services Ln</addressLine>
        <addressLine>New York, NY 10001</addressLine>
        <addressLine>USA</addressLine>
    </address>
</contact>
```

- businessServices—Optional repeating. A container for businessService elements, which are used to describe logical groupings of services. The businessService structure will be described in detail in the section "The businessService Structure."

- identifierBag—Optional. Identical in use to the identifierBag element in the tModel Structure (see the section "The tModel Structure").

- categoryBag—Optional. The mechanism by which businesses can enter Yellow Pages classification information. Its use is identical to the categoryBag element in the tModel structure (see the section "The tModel Structure").

The save_business Operation

In order to publish the business information to the UDDI registry, you need to construct a save_business message with a save_business structure in the body element of the SOAP envelope, and the businessEntity structure contained within (see Figure 7.17). This structure is very similar to the save_tModel structure, the only difference being that it contains a businessEntity element, and that the uploadRegister information should point to valid businessEntity information:

```
<save_business generic="1.0" xmlns="urn:uddi-org:api">
   <authInfo/>
   <businessEntity/> [<businessEntity/>...] | <uploadRegister/>
[<uploadRegister/>...]
</save_business>
```

7

DISCOVERING
WEB SERVICES

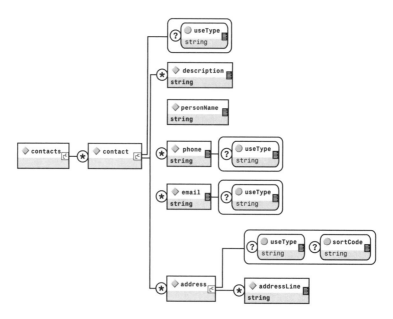

FIGURE 7.16

The contacts structure.

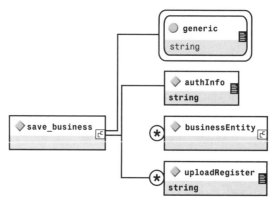

FIGURE 7.17

The save_business *message structure.*

The response to a save_business SOAP message is a businessDetail structure reflecting the final results of the save_business operation.

Putting It Together: `save_business` Example

First, as we saw, SkatesTown needs to get an authentication token. Although it is important to keep in mind that all Publication API calls are authenticated, this step will be omitted from now on for brevity. The `authInfo` token is then used in the `save_business` call. The following shows what a new business entity registration document would look like:

```
<save_business generic="1.0" xmlns="urn:uddi-org:api">
   <authInfo>65EC92F4-21C4-4EA6-B438-9994C4BD24CB</authInfo>
   <businessEntity>
      <name>SkatesTown</name>
      <description xml:lang="en">Provides the best skate products in the world
      </description>
      <contacts>
         <contact useType="Technical Information">
            <description xml:lang="en">CTO for technical information
            </description>
            <personName>Dean Carroll</personName>
            <phone useType="Main Office">1.212.555.0001</phone>
            <email useType="CTO">dean.carroll@SkatesTown.com</email>
            <email useType="General Information">info@SkatesTown.com</email>
            <address useType="Main Office" sortCode="10001">
               <addressLine>2001 Skate Services Ln</addressLine>
               <addressLine>New York, NY 10001</addressLine>
               <addressLine>USA</addressLine>
            </address>
         </contact>
      </contacts>
      <categoryBag>
         <keyedReference
            keyName="Sporting and Athletic Goods Manufacturing"
            keyValue="33992"
            tModelKey="UUID:C0B9FE13-179F-413D-8A5B-5004DB8E5BB2" />
         <keyedReference
            keyName="New York" keyValue="US-NY"
               tModelKey="UUID:4E49A8D6-D5A2-4FC2-93A0-0411D8D19E88" />
      </categoryBag>
      <identifierBag>
         <keyedReference keyName="DUNS" keyValue="00-111-1111"
            tModelKey="UUID:8609C81E-EE1F-4D5A-B202-3EB13AD01823" />
      </identifierBag>
   </businessEntity>
</save_business>
```

In this example, SkatesTown has used the authentication token that it received in the previous `get_authToken` call, and registered information about itself. In addition to its business name, description, and technical contact information (CTO), it has categorized itself under code

33992 (Sporting and Athletic Goods Manufacturing) of the NAICS classification and in the US-NY value of the geographic location classification and provided its Dun & Bradstreet D-U-N-S number as identifier. Note that the `businessKey` element is not supplied, because this is a new registration.

In response, the Operator UDDI node would send this confirmation:

```
<businessDetail
    generic="1.0" operator="UDDIOperator" truncated="false">
    <businessEntity
        businessKey="uuid:D7B8D630-59E7-11D5-9675-95373BEF0080"
        operator="UDDIOperator"
        authorizedName="Dean Carroll">
        <discoveryURLs>
            <discoveryURL useType="businessEntity">
                http://www.UDDIOperator.com?
businessKey=55BB30D8-565A-4EF9-BA2E-83118AED644D
            </discoveryURL>
        <discoveryURLs>
        <name>SkatesTown</name>
        <description xml:lang="en">Provides the best skate products in the world
        </description>
        <contacts>
            <contact useType="Technical Information">
                <description xml:lang="en">CTO for technical information
                </description>
                <personName>Dean Carroll</personName>
                <phone useType="Main Office">1.212.555.0001</phone>
                <email useType="CTO">
                    dean.carroll@SkatesTown.com</email>
                <email useType="General Information">
                    info@SkatesTown.com</email>
                <address useType="Main Office" sortCode="10001">
                    <addressLine>2001 Skate Services Ln</addressLine>
                    <addressLine>New York, NY 10001</addressLine>
                    <addressLine>USA</addressLine>
                </address>
            </contact>
        </contacts>
        <categoryBag>
            <keyedReference
                keyName="Sporting and Athletic Goods Manufacturing"
                keyValue="33992"
                tModelKey="UUID:C0B9FE13-179F-413D-8A5B-5004DB8E5BB2" />
            <keyedReference
                keyName="New York" keyValue="US-NY"
```

```
            tModelKey="UUID:4E49A8D6-D5A2-4FC2-93A0-0411D8D19E88"/>
        </categoryBag>
        <identifierBag>
            <keyedReference keyName="DUNS" keyValue="00-111-1111"
                tModelKey="UUID:8609C81E-EE1F-4D5A-B202-3EB13AD01823"/>
        </identifierBag>
    </businessEntity>
</businessDetail>
```

Notice that in its response, the UDDI Operator has assigned a unique identifier to the entity and filled out the businessKey, operator, and authorizedName attributes for the businessEntity element. It also assigned a discoveryURL address for the business in the Operator's domain space. This URL returns an XML document containing the businessEntity structure for SkatesTown.

This example showed how a business would register its entry for the first time. Having been assigned a businessKey, it can now use the businessKey to update its information, such as adding a new contact for sales when a VP of Sales is hired, (assuming the company has obtained an authentication token). The example message is as follows:

```
<save_business generic="1.0" xmlns="urn:uddi-org:api">
    <authInfo>87CD1C7F-2D23-4324-A927-82B557134DF8</authInfo>
    <businessEntity
        businessKey="uuid:D7B8D630-59E7-11D5-9675-95373BEF0080">
        <name>SkatesTown</name>
        <description xml:lang="en">Provides the best skate products in the world
        </description>
        <contacts>
            <contact useType="Technical Information">
                <description xml:lang="en">CTO for technical
                    information</description>
                <personName>Dean Carroll</personName>
                <phone useType="Main Office">1.212.555.0001</phone>
                <email useType="CTO">
                    dean.carroll@SkatesTown.com</email>
                <email useType="General Information">
                    info@SkatesTown.com</email>
                <address useType="Main Office" sortCode="10001">
                    <addressLine>2001 Skate Services Ln</addressLine>
                    <addressLine>New York, NY 10001</addressLine>
                    <addressLine>USA</addressLine>
                </address>
            </contact>
            <contact useType="Sales Information">
                <description xml:lang="en">VP Sales</description>
                <personName>Sandy Smith</personName>
```

```
          <phone useType="Main Office">1.212.555.0001</phone>
          <phone useType="Mobile">1.212.555.8888</phone>
          <email useType="VP Sales">
              sandy.smith@SkatesTown.com</email>
          <email useType="Sales Information">
              sales@SkatesTown.com</email>
          <address useType="Main Office" sortCode="10001">
              <addressLine>2001 Skate Services Ln</addressLine>
              <addressLine>New York, NY 10001</addressLine>
              <addressLine>USA</addressLine>
          </address>
      </contact>
  </contacts>
  <categoryBag>
     <keyedReference
        keyName="Sporting and Athletic Goods Manufacturing"
        keyValue="33992"
        tModelKey="UUID:C0B9FE13-179F-413D-8A5B-5004DB8E5BB2"/>
     <keyedReference
        keyName="New York" keyValue="US-NY"
            tModelKey="UUID:4E49A8D6-D5A2-4FC2-93A0-0411D8D19E88"/>
  </categoryBag>
  <identifierBag>
     <keyedReference keyName="DUNS" keyValue="00-111-1111"
        tModelKey="UUID:8609C81E-EE1F-4D5A-B202-3EB13AD01823"/>
  </identifierBag>
  </businessEntity>
</save_business>
```

Publishing Service Information to a UDDI Registry

SkatesTown next decides to publish its product catalog online as a service, and to publish another service that will enable its customers to check the status of their orders. This last service follows the SEMC specification V1.5 in the required documents and process. UDDI service information consists of two main types—logical (abstract) reusable service description and specific (concrete) implementation details—for the different bindings for the same logical service. In the case of the order status service, for instance, the abstract service description for order status has already been specified by SEMC and will be used by SkatesTown through a reference to its tModel.

Furthermore, SkatesTown decides to offer two interfaces for this service: one Web (browser) based and another SOAP based. Both Web-based and SOAP-based services are pre-defined logical service descriptions. However, they require two different concrete implementations, and their binding details are different (for example, specifying different URLs for sending the requests). The next sections will go through the details of defining and registering an online catalog service with one binding (Web-based), and an order status service with two bindings (Web and SOAP-based).

To publish service information, SkatesTown first needs to construct a businessService structure. This structure can then be published in one of two ways: by including it in the initial businessEntity structure and publishing it through the initial save_business message, or by sending it independently in a save_service message. This is analogous to the mechanisms used to publish businessEntity information with the save_business message. Let's look in more detail at the businessService structure.

The businessService Structure

The businessService structure is the root element for describing a logical business service, such as a stock quote service, or a securities buying service (see Figure 7.18). Different implementation details and bindings for the same logical service, if offered, are grouped under the same businessService element, through the bindingTemplates element. Obviously, one or more businessService elements can be contained in a businessServices element.

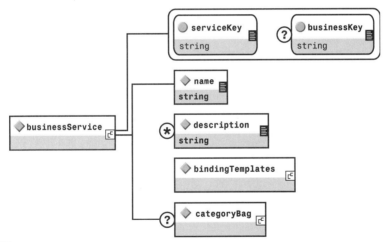

FIGURE 7.18
The businessService *structure.*

businessService has the following attributes:

- serviceKey—The unique identifier for the service. It is assigned by the UDDI Operator and cannot be edited or modified by the entity. For this reason, it should not be supplied in the original registration. When a new entity is registered, the UDDI Operator assigns a unique serviceKey and returns that key in the response. This key is then used in subsequent queries and updates.

7

- businessKey—The key of the containing businessEntity. If the businessService is being registered in a separate call through the save_service operation, this element should contain the Operator-assigned businessKey generated in the save_business call. Otherwise, the key should be left blank and will be filled in by the Operator in the response.

businessService has the following elements:

- name—Required. Name of the service, as provided by the business.
- description—Optional, repeating. Description of the service, as provided by the business.
- bindingTemplates—Required. The containing root element for bindingTemplate structures that provide the technical information on the various implementations of the service. We will explore binding templates in more detail in the section "The bindingTemplate Structure."
- categoryBag—Optional. Similar in function to the businessEntity category bag. Services can be categorized under various taxonomies.

Let's see how SkatesTown can register its Web-based service to offer its catalog to customers. We'll begin composing the businessService entry for this service:

```
<businessService businessKey="uuid:55BB30D8-565A-4EF9-BA2E-83118AED644D"
   serviceKey="">
   <name>Online Catalog</name>
   <description>This is the SkatesTown online retail catalog.
You can use it to buy equipment from us</description>
   <bindingTemplates>
      ...
   </bindingTemplates>
   <categoryBag>
      <keyedReference
         keyName="Sporting and Athletic Goods Manufacturing" keyValue="33992"
         tModelKey="UUID:C0B9FE13-179F-413D-8A5B-5004DB8E5BB2"/>
   </categoryBag>
</businessService>
```

The next step involves specifying what the bindings will be for that service. Let's look more closely at the bindingTemplate structure.

The bindingTemplate Structure

In a certain sense, the bindingTemplate structure is the end goal of UDDI. Other structures allow you to get information about businesses, their descriptions, contact information, categorization and taxonomy information, and what kind of services they offer. After a decision is made on using a particular service from a particular provider, however, the bindingTemplate subtree holds the necessary technical information for the service to actually be invoked. The same logical service can have more than one binding (such as a SOAP-based HTTP binding, an HTTP browser-based binding, and an e-mail SMTP binding). Each of these bindings is described in its own bindingTemplate structure. This is generally a combination of access point information and tModel references and their specific parameters (see Figure 7.19).

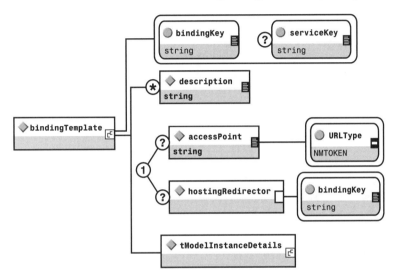

FIGURE 7.19

The bindingTemplate *structure.*

bindingTemplate has the following attributes:

- bindingKey—By now, you are familiar with the key referencing scheme used in UDDI. Like other keys, the bindingKey is the unique identifier for the binding. It is assigned by the UDDI Operator and cannot be edited or modified. When a new binding is registered, the UDDI Operator assigns a unique bindingKey and returns that key in the response. This key is then used in subsequent queries and updates.
- serviceKey—The key of the containing businessService. If the bindingTemplate is being registered in a separate call through the save_binding operation, this element should contain the Operator-assigned serviceKey generated in the save_service call. Otherwise, the key should be left blank and will be filled in by the Operator in the response.

`bindingTemplate` has the following elements:

- `description`—Optional repeated. Textual description of the binding template for this service.

- `accessPoint`—One of either `accessPoint` or `hostingRedirector` is required. This is a string that conveys the network address of the service to be invoked. The string value can convey many different types of addresses and can only be processed in the context of the whole `bindingTemplate` data. The type of address being conveyed is specified in the `URLType` attribute. For example, the same service can have two different bindings, one for HTTP and one for HTTPS. This would be conveyed as two different `bindingTemplate` elements within the same `businessService` entry. The access points for the two `bindingTemplates` would have the two URLs, one with a `URLType` of `http` and the other with a `URLType` of `https`. The allowed `URLType` values are `mailto`, `http`, `https`, `ftp`, `fax`, `phone`, and `other`.

- `hostingRedirector`—One of either `accessPoint` or `hostingRedirector` is required. The `hostingRedirector` element is generally used in cases where an entity is exposing a service hosted by another entity, such as an ASP, or in cases where different services have the same description and bindings and need to re-use the same binding template. In these cases, the `bindingKey` attribute in the `hostingRedirector` element points to the actual binding details for the service. If, during a `get_bindingDetails` operation, a `hostingRedirector` element is found, the calling application should go to the specified binding for details.

- `tModelInstanceDetails`—Simple container for `tModelInstanceDetail` structures (see the section "The `tModelInstanceDetail` Structure").

Let us now continue with the previous example of defining the Web-based catalog service for SkatesTown. The only relevant information is the access point, which is a URL to be used in a Web browser. Its `URLType` is `http`:

```
<bindingTemplates>
  <bindingTemplate bindingKey="" serviceKey=""
    <description xml:lang="en">This is a web based (http) online catalog
    </description>
    <accessPoint URLType="http">
       http://www.skatestown.com/services/catalog</accessPoint>
    <tModelInstanceDetails>
...
    </tModelInstanceDetails>
  </bindingTemplate>
</bindingTemplates>
```

The only thing left to specify is the tModelInstanceDetail structure. Let's examine that in more detail.

The tModelInstanceDetail Structure

The tModelInstanceDetail structure is a container for tModelInstanceInfo structures (see Figure 7.20) and is where the final invocation details of the service are defined. As we've already discussed, each registered business service can have one or more bindings, each of which usually refers to one or more tModels. For example, when SkatesTown registers a service that conforms to the SEMC IeBS 1.2 specification, it might decide to provide the service using two bindings, one SOAP/HTTP-based and another e-mail/SMTP-based. In this case, both bindings will have at least two tModelInstanceInfo structures, one of which will reference the SEMC tModel. The SOAP service will also reference the SOAP specification tModel in a separate tModelInstanceInfo structure, whereas the SMTP service will reference the SMTP specification tModel. This effectively provides several benefits: For example, the service will re-use existing abstractions for the specifications while allowing other businesses to locate it based on its technical fingerprint of using both SEMC and SOAP.

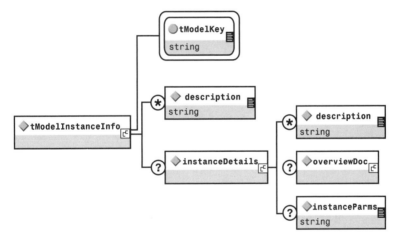

FIGURE 7.20
The tModelInstanceInfo *structure.*

The tModelInstanceInfo structure has one important required attribute, tModelKey. This is the UUID reference to the tModel associated with this structure. Its presence indicates that the binding for the containing business service implements, conforms to, or is somehow associated with this tModel. In our example, this would be a reference to the IeBS tModel or the SOAP or SMTP tModels. In addition, it has two optional elements: a repeating description element and the InstanceDetails element.

The `InstanceDetails` element is a container that is used when parameters specific to the `tModel` being referenced need to be set. An example of this could be a specific port number that is left unspecified in the `tModel` but that needs to be set at invocation time. There are two mechanisms to set parameters through the `instanceParms` element. In the first mechanism, the parameter values could be specified inside the element. In this case, it is suggested that these be a namespace-qualified XML string (from outside the UDDI namespaces). In the other mechanism, a URL to the location of the parameters is supplied.

In the simple case of the SkatesTown online catalog, all we need to supply is the `tModel` reference to the `uddi-org:http` tModel (68DE9E80-AD09-469D-8A37-088422BFBC36), which is for HTTP- or browser-based services.

The following code finishes the `bindingTemplates` definition for SkatesTown:

```
<bindingTemplates>
   <bindingTemplate bindingKey="" serviceKey=""
      <description xml:lang="en">This is a web based (http) online catalog
      </description>
      <accessPoint URLType="http">
         http://www.skatestown.com/services/catalog</accessPoint>
      <tModelInstanceDetails>
         <tModelInstanceInfo
            tModelKey="UUID:68DE9E80-AD09-469D-8A37-088422BFBC36D">
            <description xml:lang="en">HTTP Address</description>
         </tModelInstanceInfo>
      </tModelInstanceDetails>
   </bindingTemplate>
</bindingTemplates>
```

The `save_service` Operation

Similar to publishing a business entity structure with the `save_business` message, a business service can be published along with its binding templates using the `save_service` message. In this instance, we need to construct a `save_service` SOAP message containing a `save_service` structure in the body element of the SOAP envelope, and the `businessService` structure contained within (see Figure 7.21).

`save_service` has this message signature:

```
<save_service generic="1.0" xmlns="urn:uddi-org:api">
   <authInfo/>
   <businessService/> [<businessService/>...]
</save_service>
```

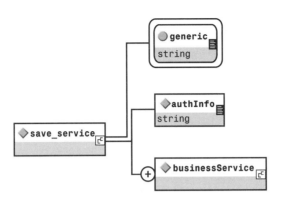

FIGURE 7.21
The save_service *message structure.*

Putting It Together: save_service Example

We will now register the simple online catalog service for SkatesTown using the save_service message. Notice that we supply the businessKey for SkatesTown but leave the serviceKey and bindingKey attributes empty to indicate these are new entries. Again, we have omitted the required step of getting an authentication token.

Here is the save_service message for the SkatesTown online catalog (example: business).

```
<save_service generic="1.0">
   <authInfo>5BA16322-B5ED-D300-8F2F-420DA3A212D2</authInfo>
   <businessService serviceKey=""
      businessKey="55BB30D8-565A-4EF9-BA2E-83118AED644D">
      <name>Online Catalog</name>
      <description>This is the SkatesTown online retail catalog.
You can use it to buy equipment from us</description>
      <bindingTemplates>
         <bindingTemplate bindingKey="">
            <description>This is a web based (http) online
               catalog</description>
            <accessPoint URLType="http">
               http://www.skatestown.com/services/catalog</accessPoint>
            <tModelInstanceDetails>
               <tModelInstanceInfo
                  tModelKey="UUID:68DE9E80-AD09-469D-8A37-088422BFBC36D">
                  <description>HTTP Address</description>
               </tModelInstanceInfo>
            </tModelInstanceDetails>
         </bindingTemplate>
      </bindingTemplates>
```

```
      <categoryBag>
        <keyedReference
          keyName="Sporting and Athletic Goods Manufacturing"
          keyValue="33992"
          tModelKey="UUID:C0B9FE13-179F-413D-8A5B-5004DB8E5BB2"/>
      </categoryBag>
    </businessService>
</save_service>
```

The registry returns a businessService structure with the serviceKey and bindingKey assigned to the new service and binding, respectively.

Next, we will construct and register a service to allow customers to check the status of their orders, as defined by the SEMC IeBS Order Management specification. This service will have two bindings, one browser-based, and another SOAP-based. First, we will register the new service with just the browser-based binding. Here is the SkatesTown checkOrderStatus save_service message:

```
<save_service generic="1.0">
    <authInfo>5BA16322-B5ED-D300-8F2F-420DA3A212D2</authInfo>
    <businessService serviceKey=""
        businessKey="55BB30D8-565A-4EF9-BA2E-83118AED644D">
        <name>Check Order Status</name>
        <description>Check your order status online. You can use a browser
          or SOAP messages</description>
        <bindingTemplates>
            <bindingTemplate bindingKey="" serviceKey="">
                <description>This is a web based (http) order status service
                </description>
                <accessPoint URLType="http">
                    http://www.skatestown.com/services/orderStatus</accessPoint>
                <tModelInstanceDetails>
                    <tModelInstanceInfo
                        tModelKey="UUID:68DE9E80-AD09-469D-8A37-088422BFBC36D">
                        <description>HTTP Address</description>
                    </tModelInstanceInfo>
                </tModelInstanceDetails>
            </bindingTemplate>
        </bindingTemplates>
        <categoryBag>
          <keyedReference
            keyName="Sporting and Athletic Goods Manufacturing"
            keyValue="33992"
            tModelKey="UUID:C0B9FE13-179F-413D-8A5B-5004DB8E5BB2"/>
          <keyedReference
            keyName="SEMC: IeBS V1.2"
```

```
            keyValue="OM1.5"
            tModelKey="6E986185-3937-442F-8916-209DA01DF837"/>
        </categoryBag>
    </businessService>
</save_service>
```

The UDDI registry returns a businessService structure business with the appropriate newly
assigned serviceKey and bindingKey:

```
<businessService serviceKey="4C379407-3E1E-DC97-B1C7-F68597DA4ABB"
    businessKey="55BB30D8-565A-4EF9-BA2E-83118AED644D">
    <name>Check Order Status</name>
    <description>Check your order status online.
        You can use a browser or SOAP messages</description>
    <bindingTemplates>
        <bindingTemplate bindingKey="C2BC244D-B4DD-A779-8CD8-45753760D055"
            serviceKey="4C379407-3E1E-DC97-B1C7-F68597DA4ABB">
...
        </bindingTemplate>
    </bindingTemplates>
    <categoryBag>
...
    </categoryBag>
</businessService>
```

The next step illustrates the need for a separate save_binding message. It involves registering
a new binding to an existing service, in this case a new SOAP binding to the Check Order
Status service.

Publishing a Binding Using the save_binding Operation

The save_binding message can be used to add a new binding to an existing service by passing
business a non-blank serviceKey, or to update an existing binding by passing a non-blank
bindingKey. It can also be used to move an existing binding from one service to another by
passing non-blank serviceKeys and bindingKeys. Being part of the authenticated Publishing
API, it requires an authInfo element, and it takes one or more bindingTemplate elements as
the new bindings to be added to existing services (see Figure 7.22):

```
<save_binding generic="1.0" xmlns="urn:uddi-org:api">
    <authInfo/>
    <bindingTemplate/> [<bindingTemplate/>...]
</save_binding>
```

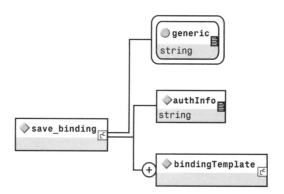

FIGURE 7.22
The save_binding *message structure.*

In the next step of the example, SBC has convinced SkatesTown to implement a programmatic method for customers to check their order status through a SOAP interface. This is a new binding to the existing Check Order Status service, and can be added to the existing businessService entry with the save_binding message. By passing the serviceKey, this message indicates to the registry that this binding should be contained within the existing Check Order Status businessService for SkatesTown. The tModel for the SEMC Order Management specification can be used as a reference to the necessary data formats, parameters, authentication, and all other invocation details for customers who want to use this service.

Here is the SkatesTown SOAP Check Order Status save_binding message:

```
<save_binding generic="1.0">
    <authInfo>2E6BAE12-04E3-DBC2-90DB-A96E21406F79</authInfo>
    <bindingTemplate bindingKey=""
        serviceKey="4C379407-3E1E-DC97-B1C7-F68597DA4ABB">
        <description>This is a SOAP based order status service</description>
        <accessPoint URLType="https">
           https://www.skatestown.com:7000/SEMC/getOrderStatus
        </accessPoint>
        <tModelInstanceDetails>
           <tModelInstanceInfo
              tModelKey="UUID:68DE9E80-AD09-469D-8A37-088422BFBC36D">
              <description>SOAP Order Status service</description>
           </tModelInstanceInfo>
           <tModelInstanceInfo
              tModelKey="UUID:6E986185-3937-442F-8916-209DA01DF837">
              <description>SEMC Order Management V1.5</description>
           </tModelInstanceInfo>
        </tModelInstanceDetails>
    </bindingTemplate>
</save_binding>
```

The Delete Operations

The API provides four delete operations, one for each of the core data structures. The delete operations are fairly straightforward. They all require an authentication token for the authInfo element and are passed the keys to the structures to be deleted. The only exception to the pattern has to do with deleting a tModel: It is important to note that if a registered owner uses the delete_tModel operation to delete a tModel, the tModel will not actually be removed from the registry, but will only be marked as hidden. It would still be available to the registered user but will not be returned by any find operation. The registered owner can reinstate the tModel by using the save_tModel call and passing the original tModel key.

delete_tModel has this message signature:

```
<delete_tModel generic="1.0" xmlns="urn:uddi-org:api">
    <authInfo/>
    <tModelKey/>
    [ <tModelKey/> ...]
</delete_tModel>
```

delete_business has this message signature:

```
<delete_business generic="1.0" xmlns="urn:uddi-org:api">
    <authInfo/>
    <businessKey/>
    [ <businessKey/> ...]
</delete_ business>
```

delete_service has this message signature:

```
<delete_service generic="1.0" xmlns="urn:uddi-org:api">
    <authInfo/>
    <serviceKey/>
    [ <serviceKey/> ...]
</delete_service>
```

delete_binding has this message signature:

```
<delete_binding generic="1.0" xmlns="urn:uddi-org:api">
    <authInfo/>
    <bindingKey/>
    [ <bindingKey/> ...]
</delete_binding>
```

What would happen if SkatesTown were to attempt to delete an entry that it does not control? Let's try to send the following message:

```
<delete_tModel generic="1.0">
    <authInfo>D2BD49A6-1A1F-B8C9-8F4B-CDCE210AE072</authInfo>
    <tModelKey>UUID:68DE9E80-AD09-469D-8A37-088422BFBC36</tModelKey>
</delete_tModel>
```

This message attempts to delete the `uddi-org:http` tModel, one of the core UDDI tModels used to categorize HTTP-based Web services. Because SkatesTown does not own or control that tModel, this is obviously a bad thing to do. The next section explores some of the details of error handling in UDDI.

Error Handling in the UDDI API

As you'd expect, the UDDI API only specifies application-level error handling, leaving the SOAP errors to be handled by the SOAP messaging infrastructure. The main container structure for UDDI application level errors is the `dispositionReport` structure, which is returned within a SOAP Fault response message (see Figure 7.23).

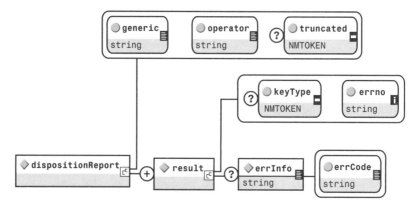

FIGURE 7.23

The dispositionReport structure.

If SkatesTown tried to delete a core UDDI, as we started doing in the previous section, or any tModel that it does not control, the following message would be returned:

```
<Fault>
    <faultcode>Client</faultcode>
    <faultstring>Client Error</faultstring>
    <detail>
        <dispositionReport generic="1.0"
            operator="UDDIOperator" xmlns="urn:uddi-org:api">
            <result errno="10130">
                <errInfo errCode="E_operatorMismatch">E_operatorMismatch
                    (10130) Cannot change data that was mastered at another
                    Operator site. tModel=UUID:68DE9E80-AD09-469D-8A37-088422BFBC36
                </errInfo>
            </result>
        </dispositionReport>
    </detail>
</Fault>
```

The UDDI API V1 specification lists 19 different error codes, listed in the specification available at the UDDI site. It is the calling application's responsibility to intercept and interpret these codes.

Finding Information in a UDDI Registry

As we saw in the section "The UDDI Usage Model," in addition to the Publication API, the UDDI specification provides for an Inquiry API. The Inquiry API has two types of operations that are associated with the core UDDI data types: `find` operations and `get_Details` operations. The `find` operations, in general, are used in what is considered browsing or searching mode, and their purpose is similar to database search operations that can return several hits based on a set of search criteria.

All `find` operations can take an optional `maxRows` attribute whose value is used to instruct the UDDI Operator to limit the number of results returned. All `find` operations can also include an optional `findQualifiers` element as a container for `findQualifier` elements that can be used to modify the search behavior. The current specification lists six qualifiers, with self-evident names: `exactNameMatch`, `caseSensitiveMatch`, `sortByNameAsc`, `sortByNameDesc`, `sortByDateAsc`, and `sortByDateDesc`.

The following sections will give some examples of search qualifiers, but the complete description of the qualifiers and their rules of precedence can be found in the UDDI Programmer's API 1.0 document available from the UDDI site. `find` operations, except for the `find_binding` operation, return `List` structures. `List` structures contain `Info` elements, which can contain a set of references if the search is successful, or are empty otherwise. We will explore the results in more detail in the next sections.

The `find_business` Operation

In a typical scenario, you might be looking for a business entry, if you know its name, in order to get information about the services they provide, or you might be looking for a business based on a combination of products or services you need and a geographic location, or you might be looking for a business that conforms to a certain industry standard set of `tModels`. The `find_business` operation allows you to find business entities that match a set of search criteria (see Figure 7.24):

```
<find_business generic="1.0" [ maxRows="nn" ] xmlns="urn:uddi-org:api">
   [<findQualifiers/>]
   <name/> | <identifierBag/> | <categoryBag/> | <tModelBag/> | <discoveryURLs>
</find_business>
```

FIGURE 7.24

The find_business *message structure.*

In addition to the findQualifiers element, the find_business structure might contain only one of the following elements:

- name—String of partial name of the business, for leftmost matching. The names of the businesses in the returned businessList all start with this string.

- identifierBag—A set of keyedReferences to be matched on a logical OR basis. All the businesses in the returned businessList have at least one keyedReference in their identifierBag registry entry that matches one of these.

- categoryBag—A set of keyedReferences to be matched on a logical AND basis. All the businesses in the returned businessList have all these matching keyedReferences in their categoryBag registry entry.

- tModelBag—A set of tModelKeys to be matched on a logical AND basis. All the businesses in the returned businessList have all these matching tModelKeys in their various binding templates.

- discoveryURLs—A set of discoveryURLs to be matched on a logical OR basis. If the useType attributes are passed as empty strings, then they are not taken into account in the matching operation.

The find_business operation returns a businessList structure (see Figure 7.25) that contains a set of businessInfo elements if the search is successful. Otherwise, it is empty. If the Operator site deems the number of hits too large, the businessList set is truncated and the truncated attribute is set to true. Note that the businessInfo structure also contains the serviceInfos element, which will be covered in the next section.

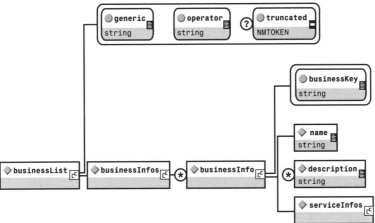

FIGURE 7.25
The businessList *structure.*

The following example shows one of the most basic searches in UDDI. We are searching for the latest (sortByDateDesc) two (maxRows=2) businesses that registered, and whose name starts with the letter *S*. Note that the businessInfo elements contain serviceInfos elements (we'll ignore them for now; they will be covered in the next section):

```
<find_business generic="1.0" maxRows="2" xmlns="urn:uddi-org:api">
    <findQualifiers>
        <findQualifier>sortByDateDesc</findQualifier>
    </findQualifiers>
    <name>S</name>
</find_business>
```

```
<businessList generic="1.0" operator="UDDIOperator"
    truncated="false" xmlns="urn:uddi-org:api">
    <businessInfos>
        <businessInfo businessKey="0B345610-57A4-11D5-A554-AB7D0DF538B6">
            <name>SEMC</name>
            <description xml:lang="en">Sports Equipment Manufacturing Consortium
            </description>
```

```
            <serviceInfos>
...
            </serviceInfos>
        </businessInfo>
        <businessInfo businessKey="D7B8D630-59E7-11D5-9675-95373BEF0080">
            <name>SkatesTown</name>
            <description xml:lang="en">Provides the best skate products
                in the world</description>
            <serviceInfos>
...
            <serviceInfos>
        </businessInfo>
    </businessInfos>
</businessList>
```

Another search method is to query for businesses that belong to a certain category, using the categoryBag parameter. In the next example, potential SkatesTown customers are looking for the latest business to register under code 33992 in the NAICS taxonomy (Sporting and Athletic Goods Manufacturing). This is done by passing the keyValue (33992) and the NAICS tModel as namespace (uuid:C0B9FE13-179F-413D-8A5B-5004DB8E5BB2). Here is an example find_business message using a categoryBag:

```
<find_business generic="1.0" maxRows="1" xmlns="urn:uddi-org:api">
    <findQualifiers>
        <findQualifier>sortByDateDesc</findQualifier>
    </findQualifiers>
    <categoryBag>
        <keyedReference keyName="Sporting and Athletic Goods Manufacturing"
            keyValue="33992"
            tModelKey="uuid:C0B9FE13-179F-413D-8A5B-5004DB8E5BB2"/>
    </categoryBag>
</find_business>

<businessList generic="1.0" operator="UDDIOperator"
    truncated="false" xmlns="urn:uddi-org:api">
    <businessInfos>
        <businessInfo businessKey="D7B8D630-59E7-11D5-9675-95373BEF0080">
            <name>SkatesTown</name>
            <description xml:lang="en">Provides the best skate products
                in the world</description>
            <serviceInfos>
...
            <serviceInfos>
        </businessInfo>
    </businessInfos>
</businessList>
```

In this last example, a potential SkatesTown customer has been given SkatesTown's D-U-N-S number, and is searching for the company's UDDI entry by supplying that value in a keyedReference, with the D-U-N-S tModel key as namespace. Here is a find_business message using identifierBag:

```
<find_business generic="1.0" maxRows="2" xmlns="urn:uddi-org:api">
    <identifierBag>
        <keyedReference keyName="" keyValue="00-111-1111"
        tModelKey="UUID:8609C81E-EE1F-4D5A-B202-3EB13AD01823"/>
    </identifierBag>
</find_business>

<businessList generic="1.0" operator="UDDIOperator"
    truncated="false" xmlns="urn:uddi-org:api">
    <businessInfos>
        <businessInfo businessKey="D7B8D630-59E7-11D5-9675-95373BEF0080">
            <name>SkatesTown</name>
            <description xml:lang="en">Provides the best skate products
                in the world</description>
            <serviceInfos>
...
            <serviceInfos>
        </businessInfo>
    </businessInfos>
</businessList>
```

The find_service Operation

The find_service operation is somewhat different in spirit from the find_business operation. It assumes that you have already found a business and have its businessKey either through the find_business operation or by outside means. Having found a potential business partner, you might be looking for any services they offer within a certain category of products and services using one of the standard taxonomies, or you might be looking for services that conform to a set of industry tModels. Given a businessKey value as an attribute, this operation will retrieve all the services provided by that business that meet the given search criteria. The find_service parameters passed in the contained elements are similar in intent to the ones found in the find_business call (see Figure 7.26):

```
<find_service businessKey="uuid_key" generic="1.0"  [ maxRows="nn" ]
    xmlns="urn:uddi-org:api">
    [<findQualifiers/>]
    <name/> | <categoryBag/> | <tModelBag/>
</find_service>
```

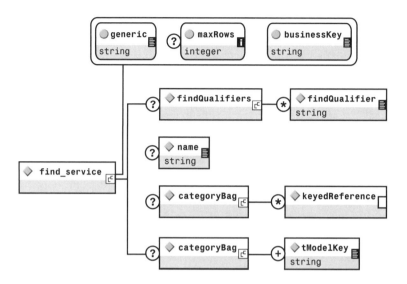

FIGURE 7.26

The find_service *message structure.*

This operation will return a serviceList structure (see Figure 7.27) that contains a set of serviceInfo elements if the search is successful. Otherwise, it is empty. If the Operator site deems the number of hits too large, the serviceList set is truncated and the truncated attribute is set to true.

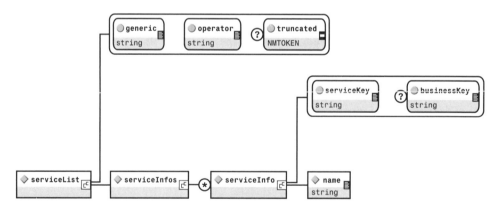

FIGURE 7.27

The serviceList *structure.*

As a potential customer, we now have the businessKey for SkatesTown (obtained through any one of the example find_business messages we saw in the previous section). We are next looking to see if they offer a service to check order status online, according to the SEMC specification. To perform a strict name query (querying for a service with a known name), a simple call would be:

```
<find_service businessKey="D7B8D630-59E7-11D5-9675-95373BEF0080"
   generic="1.0" xmlns="urn:uddi-org:api">
   <name>Check Order Status</name>
</find_service>

<serviceList generic="1.0" operator="UDDIOperator"
   truncated="false" xmlns="urn:uddi-org:api">
   <serviceInfos>
      <serviceInfo businessKey="D7B8D630-59E7-11D5-9675-95373BEF0080"
         serviceKey="BFEF1360-5A1F-11D5-8DC6-B0C1144E197E">
         <name>Check Order Status</name>
      </serviceInfo>
   </serviceInfos>
</serviceList>
```

The next listing shows the message to send if we were looking for SkatesTown services that conform to the SEMC Order Management V1.5 (in this case, it turns out, there is just one, the Check Order Status service):

```
<find_service businessKey="D7B8D630-59E7-11D5-9675-95373BEF0080"
   generic="1.0" xmlns="urn:uddi-org:api">
   <categoryBag>
      <keyedReference
         keyName="SEMC: IeBS V1.2"
         keyValue="OM1.5"
         tModelKey="6E986185-3937-442F-8916-209DA01DF837"/>
   </categoryBag>
</find_business>

<serviceList generic="1.0" operator="UDDIOperator"
   truncated="false" xmlns="urn:uddi-org:api">
   <serviceInfos>
      <serviceInfo businessKey="D7B8D630-59E7-11D5-9675-95373BEF0080"
         serviceKey="BFEF1360-5A1F-11D5-8DC6-B0C1144E197E">
         <name>Check Order Status</name>
      </serviceInfo>
   </serviceInfos>
</serviceList>
```

The `find_binding` Operation

Usually the last step in the browsing activity, the `find_binding` operation, is used to find binding templates within a business service (see Figure 7.28). The root service key, presumably found with a previous `find_service` call, is passed as an attribute. The `tModelBag` element, as in the other find calls, is a container for one or more `tModelKey` elements, and is used to pass a set of `tModel` references to be matched by the binding templates. Here is the `find_binding` message structure:

```
<find_binding serviceKey="uuid_key" generic="1.0"  [ maxRows="nn" ]
   xmlns="urn:uddi-org:api">
   [<findQualifiers/>]
   <tModelBag/>
</find_binding>
```

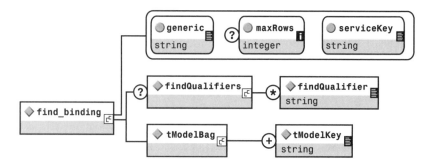

FIGURE 7.28
The find_binding *message structure.*

The `find_binding` operation returns a `bindingDetail` structure (see Figure 7.29) that contains a set of `bindingTemplate` elements if the search is successful. Otherwise, it is empty. This operation is slightly different in spirit from the other find operations in that its end result is a set of detailed information about the bindings, and not just references to the bindings. In other words, it returns a `Detail` structure and not a `List` structure. Another important consideration is that, because of the effect of the `hostingRedirector` element, the operation might return bindings that are not part of the business service that was passed as a parameter. This will happen if there are bindings that match the `tModelBag` references and that are not owned by the root business entity, because they are part of services being redirected to another hosting organization (maybe an aggregator or an ASP) using the `hostingRedirector` element.

By drilling down, we have now found the service we are looking for (Check Order Status). We next need to know if SkatesTown has an HTTP binding for that service. We know the HTTP service `tModel` key because it's one of the core `tModel`s. We can supply that `tModel` key as parameter to the `find_binding` message:

```
<find_binding generic="1.0"
   serviceKey="BFEF1360-5A1F-11D5-8DC6-B0C1144E197E"
   maxRows="2" xmlns="urn:uddi-org:api">>
   <tModelBag>
      <tModelKey>uuid:68DE9E80-AD09-469D-8A37-088422BFBC36</tModelKey>
   </tModelBag>
</find_binding>
```

This will return the (at most two) bindingDetail structure containing the bindingTemplate for the Web-based binding of the Check Order Status service.

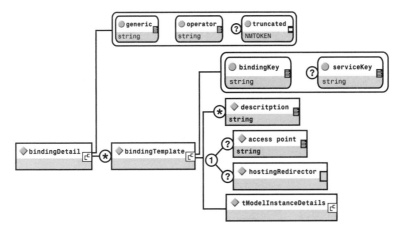

FIGURE 7.29
The bindingDetail structure.

The find_tModel Operation

The find_tModel operation is almost identical in all aspects to the find_business and find_service operations, both in terms of the parameters that it takes and the type of results it returns (see Figure 7.30):

```
<find_tModel generic="1.0" [ maxRows="nn" ] xmlns="urn:uddi-org:api">
   [<findQualifiers/>]
   <name/> | <identifierBag/> | <categoryBag/>
</find_tModel>
```

The operation returns a tModelList structure (see Figure 7.31), which follows the same principle as the other List structures. Consequently, the tModelInfos structure contains a set of tModelInfo elements if the search is successful, or is empty otherwise. If the Operator site deems the number of hits too large, the serviceList set is truncated and the truncated attribute is set to true.

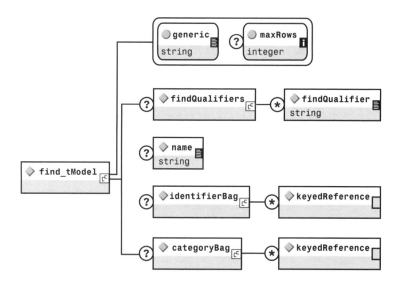

FIGURE 7.30

The find_tModel *message structure.*

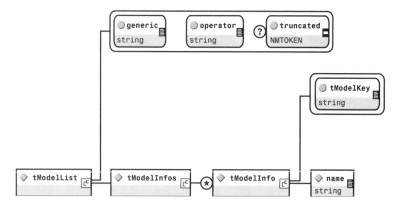

FIGURE 7.31

The tModelList *structure.*

Getting Business and Service Details from a UDDI Registry

As opposed to the find operations, the get_Details operations are generally used, as their name suggests, to retrieve detail information about specific entities, usually ones found after using the find operations. They are passed one or more unique reference keys as parameters and return the details of the corresponding entries in a Detail structure.

The `get_businessDetail` Operation

The `get_businessDetail` operation takes a set of `businessKey` references and returns a `businessDetail` structure, which contains a set of `businessEntity` elements that correspond to the passed keys:

```
<get_businessDetail generic="1.0" xmlns="urn:uddi-org:api">
   <businessKey/>
   [ <businessKey/> ...]
</get_businessDetail>
```

For example, the following message

```
<get_businessDetail generic="1.0" xmlns="urn:uddi-org:api">
   <businessKey>D7B8D630-59E7-11D5-9675-95373BEF0080</businessKey>
</get_businessDetail>
```

returns the same `businessDetail` message shown previously.

The `get_serviceDetail` Operation

The `get_serviceDetail` operation takes a set of `serviceKey` references and returns a `serviceDetail` structure, which contains a set of `businessService` elements that correspond to the passed keys:

```
<get_serviceDetail generic="1.0" xmlns="urn:uddi-org:api">
   <serviceKey/>
   [ <serviceKey/> ...]
</get_serviceDetail>
```

The `get_bindingDetail` Operation

The `get_bindingDetail` operation takes a set of `bindingKey` references and returns the same `bindingDetail` structure returned by the `find_binding` operation described earlier, which contains a set of `bindingTemplate` elements that correspond to the passed keys:

```
<get_bindingDetail generic="1.0" xmlns="urn:uddi-org:api">
   <bindingKey/>
   [ <bindingKey/> ...]
</get_bindingDetail>
```

The `get_tModelDetail` Operation

The `get_tModelDetail` operation takes a set of `tModelKey` references and returns a `tModelDetail` structure, which contains a set of `tModel` elements that correspond to the passed keys:

```
<get_tModelDetail generic="1.0" xmlns="urn:uddi-org:api">
   <tModelKey/>
   [ <tModelKey/> ...]
</get_tModelDetail>
```

Summarizing UDDI Version 1.0

In this section, we have explored in detail the UDDI information model and the UDDI API from the perspective of SkatesTown and some of its customers or potential customers. So far, an implicit assumption has been that all operations have been performed on a public UDDI registry. This obviously need not be the case. The next section explores the concept and applications of private UDDI registries.

Private UDDI Registries

In this section, we talk about implementations of the UDDI specification outside the context of the UDDI Business Registry. We use the term *private UDDI* 📖 to refer to these UDDI registries that are not operator nodes within the UDDI Business Registry. Many organizations host their own, private implementations of UDDI for various reasons. We will examine several categories of private UDDI and discuss how SkatesTown, WeMakeIt Inc., and e-Torus use private UDDI registries.

This section is based on a series of articles published on the IBM developerWorks Web site (`http://www.ibm.com/developerWorks`) titled "Role of Private UDDI."

Why Would a Company Host a Private UDDI Registry?

There are several reasons a company would want to host a private UDDI registry. To address this question, we need to look at why a company would use a UDDI registry at all, and then examine the circumstances that would encourage them to choose private UDDI registries.

In the beginning of this chapter, we discussed the role of a service discovery in a service-oriented architecture (see "The Role of Service Discovery"). The central idea was to provide a mechanism by which a service provider can communicate the Web service description to service requestors. A service registry, based on UDDI, is one important mechanism to publish and search for service descriptions.

UDDI provides a standard message API to publish and find service descriptions from a repository. This standard is supported and used by many organizations; there are multiple UDDI registry implementations to choose from.

Some organizations will choose to advertise all of their Web services descriptions in the UDDI Business Registry. These companies will also use the UDDI Business Registry to search for any business partner's Web service descriptions. The UDDI Business Registry is in a well-known location (`www.uddi.org`) and therefore highly visible on the Web. Everyone in the Web services community knows about UDDI and knows how to use the UDDI Business Registry for find and publish. Being advertised in the UDDI Business Registry maximizes the visibility of the business and the services it makes available to potential business partners.

The UDDI Business Registry is not the only place to register business and service descriptions in a UDDI format. Many organizations are choosing to host their own, private UDDI registries. These companies make this choice for several reasons: control of access to the information, control over updating the information, and reliability of the content of the registry. As we discuss later, choosing to host a private UDDI registry does not preclude also using the UDDI Business Registry. Far from it, many organizations coordinate the use of their private UDDI registries with occasional access to the UDDI Business Registry.

The broad visibility of the UDDI Business Registry has a downside for some organizations. Some organizations want to restrict who is allowed to view sensitive service description information and the network address at which their Web services are accessible. For this reason, many organizations choose to advertise just their company in the UDDI Business Registry; the only Web service they advertise is the UDDI Inquiry API Web service to one of their private UDDI registries. In this way, potential partners who are interested in learning more about a business's Web services capabilities are encouraged to contact the business's private UDDI registry. The business hosting the private UDDI gains control over access to Web services information through a registration and authentication scheme. Because it controls its private UDDI registry, access can be tracked and monitored and, if necessary, follow-up can be initiated with a potential partner showing interest in the business by executing a find operation.

Some organizations will use a private UDDI registry to control the visibility of service description information. Some organizations are simply not comfortable with having this information managed by some other organization, including an open consortium such as UDDI.org.

For Web services with network location that changes with some frequency, direct control over changes to the service description entries in UDDI is necessary.

Many organizations will choose to host a private UDDI to ensure consistency of service description information to support runtime discovery of Web services. This consistency is at the business level (who is the partner) and how the service is described (use of service interface definition standards). We illustrate an example of how private UDDI registries support dynamic find in the "Putting It All Together: WSDL-based UDDI and Dynamic Find" section of this chapter.

The UDDI Business Registry contains business and service information about companies from a broad range of industries. Very few of these entries are of interest to any given businessperson searching for a particular partner or Web service implementation. For those businesses categorized within a particular industry (using the NAICS taxonomy, for example), not all of these businesses are desired partners. Worse, there is no guarantee that a company classified in a particular way does, in fact, do business in that industry. Some organizations will use a private UDDI to ensure that only services from approved business partners appear in the services registry. As new partners are approved, their UDDI entries are added to the private UDDI registry. As business relationships dissolve, the UDDI entries for those partners are removed.

The flexibility provided by UDDI to register services regardless of how they are described is both a benefit and drawback for users. Many organizations, such as SkatesTown, have standardized on WSDL as the mechanism for IDL-level service description. These companies have adopted tooling to enable their applications to bind to Web services described using WSDL. Web services registered in UDDI that use some other service description technique, such as an ASCII text document, are not useful to these applications. Organizations that have standardized on a common service description mechanism, such as WSDL, will use a private UDDI to make sure that the entries in their service registry also use WSDL as the mechanism of service description. We discuss the convention for using UDDI to register Web services using WSDL in a later section, "Using WSDL with UDDI." Further, most organizations have enabled their applications to consume Web services of a given type. If a Web service is not based on one of a pre-selected set of Web service types, then it is not useful to the business's applications and, therefore, should not be registered in their private UDDI registry.

A private UDDI registry, therefore, offers a target-rich environment so that an application, at runtime, can do a find against the registry. A business policy, defined by human developers at design time, is used as the search pattern in the find operation. The search pattern describes desired Web service type and other characteristics, such as non-functional requirements such specific to the business policy. The Web services discovered by this search criteria will fit the business need of the application, be in a format that is directly consumable by the application, and be hosted by a known and approved business partner.

Supporting dynamic runtime discovery and binding to Web services at runtime is one of the key points of flexibility in a service-oriented architecture. This flexibility is important to the characteristic of loosely coupled application integration, either within an organization or between business partners.

Let's take a look at five types of private UDDI node and examine how SkatesTown, WeMakeIt Inc., and e-Torus use them.

Five Types of Private UDDI

The UDDI specification was defined to allow the possibility of private UDDI registries. A private UDDI registry can implement some or all of the UDDI APIs. A private UDDI is certainly not bound to any restrictions articulated by the UDDI Operator's agreement, and in particular, does not participate in the replication mechanism within the UDDI Business Registry. A private UDDI registry might alter the behavior of the common UDDI operations, for example, requiring an authentication SOAP header on the find operations. A private UDDI registry can offer additional APIs over and above those defined by the UDDI specification.

There are five broad categories of private UDDI use, summarized here and described in more detail in the following sections:

- E-marketplace UDDI
- Portal UDDI
- Partner catalog UDDI (also known as Vetted partners or rolodex-like UDDI)
- Internal Enterprise Application Integration UDDI
- Test Bed UDDI

E-Marketplace UDDI

This type of private UDDI node would be hosted by an e-marketplace, an industry standards organization, or some other consortium of organizations that compete/participate in an industry. All publish and find (inquiry) APIs are typically deployed for Internet access.

The e-Torus organization hosts an e-marketplace private UDDI on its Web site. All buyers and sellers of small wheels, nylon, steel and aluminum, and related components such as wheel bearings, come to this site and use this private UDDI registry.

The entries in the e-marketplace type of private UDDI are all related to businesses within a particular industry or narrow range of related industries. Further, the membership process allows the entries in this UDDI to be pre-filtered to include only legitimate businesses participating in the industry. The membership process can also restrict who is allowed to invoke find operations against the UDDI node.

The e-Torus organization provides a mechanism for registration at its Web site. Each user from each participating member organization must register with the e-Torus Web site to receive an authentication token. This registration and the corresponding authentication token is associated with the e-Torus business registry example of `identifierBags` discussed in "More on Classification and Categorization." This authentication token can be stored as a cookie on a Web browser. The authentication token must be included as a SOAP header on any find operation and is required by the UDDI API specification to be part of any publish operation issued against e-Torus's private e-marketplace UDDI. This authentication token allows e-Torus to track which members are doing publish and find operations, and support a small subscription fee for the size and number of publish operations done by each company, as well as the number of find operations and the size of the result sets.

An e-marketplace UDDI is a target-rich environment for finding Web services metadata for doing business within a particular e-marketplace or industry. The e-marketplace hosted by e-Torus is clearly the place to be seen in the small wheel and bearing world. The e-marketplace UDDI is also the logical place to find industry-specific custom taxonomies (standard product coding hierarchies, specializations of NAICS categories, etc.) as well as standard Web service interface definition `tModels` for common business processes in the industry.

As detailed in the section "Using WSDL With UDDI," e-Torus hosts a set of standard `tModels` for Web services used in this e-marketplace. This set of `tModels` includes standards for synchronous `priceCheck` (based on work donated to e-Torus by SkatesTown), formal asynchronous RFQ, and purchase order placement. These standard Web service types are all based on a common orders suite WSDL document managed by e-Torus.

This type of private UDDI allows an e-marketplace organization to provide value-add to Web services advertisement and searching, such as: providing Quality of Service (QoS) monitoring on the partner's Web services response times, doing better business bureau–style industry self monitoring of business practices of its member's Web services, and so on.

An e-marketplace type of private UDDI registry is where finds in serious machine-to-machine B2B can happen. Because e-Torus monitors the participants in the e-marketplace, SkatesTown can trust that the entries in the e-Torus UDDI registry are all legitimate suppliers. As we detail in the section "Using WSDL with UDDI," SkatesTown can do a find against the e-Torus e-marketplace UDDI node to discover all the suppliers of nylon wheels for skateboards as part of the dynamic bind implementation of the `priceCheck` feature of its reorder application. The e-Torus organization is considering a value-add feature that sorts the result set of a particular kind of find operation for RFQ service, by price value returned by invoking the business's `priceCheck` Web service.

Portal UDDI

Web services technology is defining the standard way to use the Internet for machine-to-machine B2B. This use of the Internet can be contrasted with the current browser-based or HTML-based World Wide Web by calling it the *semantic Web* or the *transactional Web*. (See Chapter 9, "Future Concepts.") Just as a company has a Web presence on the browser-based World Wide Web (`http://www.WeMakeIt.com`), so too might it have presence on the semantic web (such as `http://www.WeMakeIt.com/services/uddi/servlet/uddi`). The private UDDI representing the organization's semantic Web presence is called a portal UDDI.

The portal UDDI hosted by WeMakeIt Inc. resides within the company's demilitarized zone (DMZ), part of WeMakeIt Inc.'s edge of the network architecture. The entries in WeMakeIt Inc.'s private portal UDDI registry contain descriptions for those Web services that WeMakeIt Inc. wishes to provide to external partners. Clearly, it is in the company's interests to keep the find APIs available from the Internet; however, WeMakeIt Inc. does not allow access to the publish APIs from the Internet, restricting publish to internal processes only. WeMakeIt Inc. also hosts its product code taxonomy in its private Portal UDDI registry. Partners that wish to do business with WeMakeIt Inc. examine its private Portal UDDI registry to determine what formats the company accepts for purchase orders and the WSDL description of the purchase order placement service, including its network address.

When WeMakeIt Inc. wants to deploy a new Web service, it publishes the Web service's description to its portal UDDI.

As part of WeMakeIt Inc.'s businessEntity registration in the UDDI Business Registry, the URL for its private Portal UDDI registry is used as a discoveryURL element, with the useType attribute set to urn:uddi-inquiry-api. A segment of WeMakeIt Inc.'s businessEntity entry is shown here:

```
<businessEntity authorizedName="..."
    businessKey="DCD2B450-A4C0-11D5-AF98-BD95162D3AC9" ...>
  <discoveryURLs>
    <discoveryURL useType="businessEntity">
      http://www.someoperator.com/uddiget?businessKey=EF433600...
    </discoveryURL>
    <discoveryURL useType="urn:uddi-inquiry-api">
      http://www.WeMakeIt.com/services/uddi/servlet/uddi
    </discoveryURL>
  </discoveryURLs>
  <name>WeMakeIt Inc.</name>
...
</businessEntity>
```

The portal type of private UDDI registry gives a company ultimate control over how metadata describing its Web services is used. For example, companies are free to restrict find access to the registry. Companies are free to tailor the response to find and get operations based on some property associated with the requestor (such as gold member status). Companies are able to monitor and manage the number of find operations being made against their data and potentially derive information about the interested parties.

Partner Catalog UDDI

This type of private UDDI node sits behind the firewall. It provides a very target-rich environment against which Web services finds and binds can be made. A partner catalog UDDI registry contains only Web service description metadata published by trusted business partners. WeMakeIt Inc. has a partner catalog UDDI registry containing entries for those organizations with which it has formal business relationships. In most cases, neither the publish nor find APIs to the partner catalog UDDI registry are available over the Internet; restricting access to all APIs to internal applications only.

Businesses today do business with organizations they know. The use of this mechanism allows an organization to build applications in a service-oriented way, taking advantage of dynamic binding against Web services at runtime based on a Web service interface built into the application at design time. This style of programming is described in a later section, "Putting It All Together: WSDL-Based UDDI and Dynamic Find." Because the partner catalog UDDI registry contains only approved business partners, this style of dynamic binding does not imply the risk of dealing with an unknown service provider. No matter which Web service is returned by the find operation, we know it is provided by a validated business partner.

WeMakeIt Inc. uses its partner catalog private UDDI to help in its own supply chain automation systems. Web services technology allows WeMakeIt Inc. to do process integration with their suppliers. Using Web services, WeMakeIt Inc. can reduce transaction costs for supply chain tasks, such as supply reordering, in a way that does not lock them into any particular supplier. The management at WeMakeIt Inc. agrees to do business with some supplier. Joanna Pravard examines the UDDI entries for that partner (either from the UDDI Business Registry, an e-marketplace UDDI like e-Torus, or the supplier's portal UDDI). Joanna copies these entries into WeMakeIt Inc.'s partner catalog UDDI. This process is repeated for each supplier, as new suppliers are found and business terms are negotiated. The set of suppliers change over time as business relationships are formed and dissolved. Changes to this set are reflected by changes in the entries within WeMakeIt Inc.'s partner catalog UDDI registry.

Proxies are generated from WSDL service interface definitions by WeMakeIt Inc.'s developers. WeMakeIt Inc.'s applications are coded to use these proxies and to do finds against its partner catalog private UDDI registry. The applications do not need to be recoded to cope with the changing list of approved partners. The application uses the UDDI entries to determine the set of available Web services and chooses one or more of the best Web services from this set to invoke. This choice is based upon WeMakeIt Inc.'s business policies, such as choosing the best price, best delivery terms, and so on. The Web service of the supplier is then invoked by the application and business is done.

To make this dynamic binding application support complete, Joanna Pravard places restrictions on the kinds of entries that can be published into the partner catalog UDDI registry. Joanna works with each supplier to make sure the supplier's businessServices are properly categorized according to WeMakeIt Inc.'s product code taxonomy. Joanna makes sure that each businessService follows the standard convention for publishing WSDL using UDDI (see "Using WSDL with UDDI"). And further, Joanna makes sure that each tModel referenced by these businessServices is from a set of approved, standard tModels supported by WeMakeIt Inc.'s applications. This allows Joanna to guarantee the shape of entries that are placed within the UDDI node and, therefore, what applications can expect in response to find operations.

Internal Enterprise Application Integration UDDI

The Internal Enterprise Application Integration (EAI) type of UDDI registry is similar to the partner catalog type, except it contains entries for Web services provided by other departments or groups within an organization. Many organizations treat their partner catalog UDDI and Internal Enterprise Application Integration UDDI as logical views on the same physical registry.

The major difference that separates the Internal EAI type of private UDDI from the partner catalog type is the potential for common administrative domain that can dictate standards (which tModels are used, common use of WSDL portTypes, and so on). This allows the Internal EAI type of UDDI registry to operate with different publish restrictions than those suggested for the partner catalog type. For example, the Internal EAI UDDI registry could restrict the publication of new tModels and thereby restrict publishing of businessService entries and bindingTemplate entries to accept only entries associated with a fixed set of tModels. The fixed set of tModels corresponds to the technology standards chosen by the decision makers controlling the common administrative domain.

Of course, this kind of UDDI registry exists completely hidden behind the organization's firewall. Publish and find operations are restricted to applications within the organization.

Test UDDI

Programmers use this type of private UDDI registry to test applications. The testing can be for both requestor applications and provider Web services.

SkatesTown uses this type of private UDDI registry to test that the UDDI entries describing its purchase order placement Web service were accurate and that UDDI-aware tools can generate proxies from the UDDI entries to access its purchase order placement Web service.

WeMakeIt Inc. also uses a test UDDI to test its applications' ability to cope with external services. For example, Joanna Pravard uses a test UDDI to make sure that different variants of the RFQ Web service provided by various suppliers all run correctly with WeMakeIt Inc.'s reorder application. Joanna runs trials against any new UDDI entry discovered from the UDDI Business Registry, any e-marketplace such as e-Torus' e-marketplace private UDDI, or a supplier's private portal UDDI. Joanna copies a UDDI entry from the source UDDI registry to the test UDDI first, then runs a battery of tests to make sure WeMakeIt Inc.'s applications can use the information found in the entry and then, only after testing, she promotes the entry to the WeMakeIt Inc.'s partner catalog UDDI. The notion of promote is used here to describe copying a UDDI entry from one UDDI registry to another. A UDDI entry can be promoted from one registry to another using a variety of techniques including: manual re-publication of the UDDI entry (destroying the correspondence between the UUID keys of each entry), or using a modified API that allows a record to be created in a UDDI repository with UUID keys already assigned. Techniques to facilitate promotion are being considered as part of the UDDI Version 3.0 specification.

What's New in UDDI Version 2.0?

A lot has happened in the UDDI community since Version 1.0 of the UDDI specification was released on September 6, 2000. The UDDI community has broadened from the three charter members (Ariba, IBM, and Microsoft) to include over 280 advisory group members! As a result of this influx of additional contributors (and hence their requirements), UDDI has increased in scope and functionality. Let's briefly highlight the new functionality covered in UDDI v2.0 and then detail how these features can be used by SkatesTown or WeMakeIt Inc.

These changes are documented in the Version 2.0 UDDI specification documentation set available at www.uddi.org (copyright © 2001 by Accenture, Ariba, Inc., Commerce One, Inc., Compaq Computer Corporation, Equifax, Inc., Fujitsu Limited, Hewlett-Packard Company, 12 Technologies, Inc., Intel Corporation, International Business Machines Corporation, Microsoft Corporation, Oracle Corporation, SAP AG, Sun Microsystems, Inc., and Verisign, Inc. All Rights Reserved). This specification was released on June 8, 2001.

Overview of Changes in UDDI V2.0

We can categorize the changes from Version 1.0 to Version 2.0 of the UDDI specification into these broad areas:

- Third-party taxonomy support
- Modeling business relationships with assertions
- Changes to the Inquiry API
- Changes to the Publication API
- Other minor, miscellaneous changes

Overall, none of these changes have a dramatic impact on SkatesTown or WeMakeIt Inc., but some of the changes are useful for WeMakeIt Inc. The changes are incremental in nature, and outside of the assertions and perhaps the third-party taxonomy feature described next, the changes are not likely to be dramatically exploited by SkatesTown, WeMakeIt Inc., or organizations like them.

Third-Party Taxonomies

Taxonomies are the primary means in UDDI of organizing and, therefore, searching for entries. UDDI Version 2.0 added a feature by which third parties could specify new taxonomies and provide a service by which UDDI registries, in particular operator nodes within the UDDI Business Registry, could validate categorizations asserted against a taxonomy developed by a third party. Most of the new findQualifiers (see the section "New Find Qualifiers") added in UDDI Version 2.0 are suited for referencing these third-party taxonomies in find messages.

Why would anyone want to define a new taxonomy? UDDI provides, by default, three canonical taxonomies: NAICS, for industry classifications; UN/SPSC, for product/service classifications; and ISO 3166, for geographic classifications. These general-purpose taxonomies are quite useful for broadly classifying businesses or services. However, a particular industry might want to define a new taxonomy to detail product classifications according to a scheme commonly used in their industry. A third-party QoS guarantor might wish to define an identifier scheme, classifying businesses and their services according to some new QoS metric for Web services. Organizations can choose to convert their product codes into a taxonomy and categorize which businessService entries are associated with requesting, purchasing, and getting post-sales support on each of their products.

WeMakeIt Inc. decides to create a canonical parts code scheme for all the parts WeMakeIt Inc. uses in its manufacturing lines. Because WeMakeIt Inc. is a manufacturer of a wide and frequently changing variety of goods, this list of product codes is constantly updated. By creating this taxonomy, WeMakeIt Inc. can make its private UDDI partner catalog registry extremely useful. WeMakeIt Inc. requires all its suppliers to use Web services to interact with WeMakeIt Inc.'s automated supply reordering system. All the partners are required to categorize their UDDI businessService entries using WeMakeIt Inc.'s custom parts code taxonomy. In this way, the businessService entries in WeMakeIt Inc.'s partner catalog UDDI are all classified according to its parts code. When WeMakeIt Inc. needs to reorder a part, it can issue a taxonomy-based find operation and retrieve all the business partners that deal in that part. WeMakeIt Inc. can then issue RFQs, purchase orders, and so on, to resupply a manufacturing line, or to just-in-time prepare for an upcoming manufacturing run.

Let's examine the steps WeMakeIt Inc. used to set up its third-party taxonomy.

First, WeMakeIt Inc. used their existing product code scheme as the basis of the taxonomy. It created a relational database containing product codes for the 10,000 or so supplies that it has ever ordered in the past. WeMakeIt Inc. built a small Web-based application to browse the database, displaying code to product name mappings.

Next, WeMakeIt Inc. created a tModel to describe its product code taxonomy and register it in the UDDI Business Registry. Alternatively, WeMakeIt Inc. could have created the tModel in its own portal private UDDI registry and promoted it to the UDDI Business Registry. Regardless, the save_tModel message looks like this:

```
<save_tModel generic="2.0" xmlns="urn:uddi-org:api_v2" >
   <authInfo>...</authInfo>
   <tModel tModelKey="">
      <name>WeMakeIt Product Code Taxonomy</name>
      <description xml:lang="en">WeMakeIt Inc. classfies all its supplies...
      </description>
      <overviewDoc>
         <overviewURL>
            http://www.wemakeit.com/supplies/browseReorderCatalog
         </overviewURL>
```

```
    </overviewDoc>
    <categoryBag>
       <keyedReference
            keyName="TModel categorization type"
            keyValue="categorization"
            tModelKey="UUID:C1ACF26D-9672-4404-9D70-39B756E62AB4"/>
                        <!-- UDDI Types tModelKey -->
    </categoryBag>
  </tModel>
</save_tModel>
```

The `tModelKey` assigned by the UDDI registry (say, UUID:E0AC1230-4CC1-11D5-B353-B4D70FD31643) is remembered and documented in the Web pages associated with the reorder catalog browser WeMakeIt Inc. hosts at `http://www.wemakeit.com/supplies/browseReorderCatalog`. This entry categorizes WeMakeIt Inc.'s product code scheme as a categorization `tModel`. WeMakeIt Inc. tells all its suppliers to get this `tModel` and use it to classify their `businessEntity` and `businessServices` according to which of these product codes the supplier provides.

Because WeMakeIt Inc. wants their suppliers properly categorized, it provides a validation mechanism for its taxonomy. WeMakeIt Inc. sets up a Web service to validate any UDDI entry that is categorized using its custom taxonomy. This Web service is conformant to the `validate_values` requirements specified in the UDDI Version 2.0 programmer's API. WeMakeIt Inc. registers this service with the UDDI Business Registry using the mechanism specified by the operator node that controls WeMakeIt Inc.'s entries. It tells all its suppliers to reference this `validate_values` Web service with their private portal UDDI registries.

Without this effort, WeMakeIt Inc.'s custom taxonomy will remained unchecked. The difference between a checked and an unchecked taxonomy is fairly important. With a checked taxonomy, any `save_business`, `save_service`, or `save_tModel` (although `save_tModel` is unlikely to use WeMakeIt Inc.'s taxonomy) that references this taxonomy will use the `validate_values` service published by WeMakeIt Inc. If an entry specifies an invalid category, or WeMakeIt Inc.'s `validate_values` service returns an error for some reason, the save operation for the entry fails.

If WeMakeIt Inc. developed an unchecked taxonomy, there would be no way that its suppliers could ensure that their classifications accurately reflected WeMakeIt Inc.'s supplies coding scheme.

Let's examine WeMakeIt Inc.'s `validate_values` Web service in a little more detail.

The UDDI registry that is attempting to validate the use of WeMakeIt Inc.'s taxonomy would send a `validate_values` message to the service registered by WeMakeIt Inc. with that registry. Details of the taxonomy validation service are specific to each UDDI registry implementation.

The `validate_values` message syntax looks like this:

```
<validate_values generic="2.0" xmlns="urn:uddi-org:api_v2">
   <businessEntity/>... | <businessService/>... | <tModel/>...
<validate_values>
```

In the case of WeMakeIt Inc., its `validate_values` service would receive this message, extract the key values used in any `keyedReference` element referencing its taxonomy `tModelKey`, and do a simple lookup of this `keyValue` against its product code database to make sure the `keyValue` used by the entry's categorization is a valid value. Its `validate_values` service ignores all other details of the entry being categorized.

The `validate_values` service must return a `dispositionReport` as specified in the UDDI Version 2.0 API specification with `errorCode` set to `E_success` and `errno` set to the value `0`. If an error occurs (for example, if one of the `keyValues` is not within the product code set), the service must return a SOAP fault containing a `dispositionReport` containing the error details. In this case, the only error that would be returned from WeMakeIt Inc.'s `validate_values` service is `E_invalidValue`. The error text, of course, indicates which `keyedReference` element caused the error. Only the first error is reported.

Modeling Relationships between `businessEntity` Entries

In UDDI Version 1.0, each company is represented by a single `businessEntity`. So, small organizations like SkatesTown were modeled with the same technique as larger, more complicated organizations like WeMakeIt Inc. Prior to UDDI Version 2.0, UDDI provided no formal mechanism to model the relationship between individual business units within a large organization.

The feature of *publication assertions* was introduced in UDDI Version 2.0 to address the publication needs of large, complex organizations. Any pair of `businessEntity` entries can be associated in some fashion, reflecting their business relationship. Using this feature, the relationship between WeMakeIt Inc. and its subsidiaries in Asia and Europe can be formally modeled.

A new find message, `find_relatedBusinesses`, was added to allow requestors to view these relationships. This new find message is described in more detail in the section "Added `find_relatedBusiness` Message". The only relationships visible through the `find_relatedBusinesses` message are those that have been validated by the owners of both `businessEntity` entries. The `businessEntity` relationship feature was built this way to avoid false and misleading claims about the relationships between one business and another. Unless both parties assert the relationship exists, it is not visible from UDDI.

Let's review how WeMakeIt Inc. would create the relationships between the `businessEntity` representing the corporate holding company WeMakeIt Inc. and its two subsidiaries, WeMakeIt Asia Inc. and WeMakeIt Europe PLC.

First, WeMakeIt Inc. would create `businessEntity` entries for all three business units, using the `save_business` message. Let's assume these entries are created in WeMakeIt Inc.'s private portal UDDI node and later promoted to the UDDI Business Registry. The example would be the same if WeMakeIt Inc. did all this registration in the UDDI Business Registry. In the case of WeMakeIt Inc., Joanna Pravard manages the UDDI entries in WeMakeIt Inc.'s private UDDI registries, as well as the UDDI Business Registry. For other, more complicated organizations, different people might manage each `businessEntity` separately.

Joanna must now make several publisher assertions to describe the relationships between WeMakeIt Inc. and its two subsidiaries:

- Assert that WeMakeIt Inc. is the parent of WeMakeIt Asia Inc.
- Assert that WeMakeIt Asia Inc. is a child of WeMakeIt Inc.
- Assert that WeMakeIt Inc. is the parent of WeMakeIt Europe PLC.
- Assert that WeMakeIt Europe PLC. is a child of WeMakeIt Inc.

After the first two assertions are made, using the `add_publisherAssertions` message (described later), the relationship between WeMakeIt Inc. and WeMakeIt Asia Inc. would be visible through the `find_relatedBusinesses` message. After the last two assertions are made, the relationship between WeMakeIt Inc. and WeMakeIt Europe PLC would be visible. Note that Joanna could make all four assertions at once using a single invocation of `add_publisherAssertions` like this:

```
<add_publisherAssertions generic="2.0" xmlns="urn:uddi-org:api_v2" >
    <authInfo>...</authInfo>
    <publisherAssertion>
        <!-- BusinessKey for WeMakeIt Inc.-->
        <fromKey>DCD2B450-A4C0-11D5-AF98-BD95162D3AC9</fromKey>
        <!-- BusinessKey for WeMakeIt Inc. Asia -->
        <toKey>DCD5C190-A4C0-11D5-AF98-BD95162D3AC9</fromKey>
        <keyedReference
            tModelKey="uuid:807A2C6A-EE22-470d-ADC7-E0424A337C03"
            keyValue="parent-child"/>
    </publisherAssertion>

    <publisherAssertion>
        <!-- BusinessKey for WeMakeIt Inc.-->
        <fromKey>DCD2B450-A4C0-11D5-AF98-BD95162D3AC9</fromKey>
        <!-- BusinessKey for WeMakeIt Inc. Europe -->
```

```
    <toKey>DCD5C191-A4C0-11D5-AF98-BD95162D3AC9</fromKey>
    <keyedReference
        tModelKey="uuid:807A2C6A-EE22-470d-ADC7-E0424A337C03"
        keyValue="parent-child"/>
</publisherAssertion>

<!-- etc. for the other two assertions -->

</add_publisherAssertions>
```

Note the use of `keyedReference` in the `add_publisherAssertions` message. The business relationships feature of UDDI makes use of a special, canonical `tModel` to specify the different kinds of relationships. There are three possible key values for the relationships `tModel` in UDDI Version 2.0:

- *parent-child*—The `businessEntity` represented by the `fromKey` is the parent of the `businessEntity` represented by the `toKey`. This value is used in the previous example.

- *peer-peer*—The `businessEntities` represented by the `toKey` and `fromKey` are peers. It is not likely this form will be used very frequently outside of private UDDI registries.

- *identity*—The two `businessEntities` are the same organization.

As a result of issuing this `add_publisherAssertions` message, the assertions that appear in the `find_relatedBusinesses` example would be visible.

After Joanna registers this information with the UDDI Business Registry, she should occasionally issue a `get_assertionStatusReport`, which will tell her if any other individual has attempted to assert a relationship with any of Joanna's `businessEntity` entries. Joanna will, of course, reject each of these assertions, simply by not acting. If the relationship is not mutually asserted, it is not visible.

To summarize the components described in this section, UDDI has defined a business relationship facility based on pair-wise assertions of the relationship between two `businessEntity` elements. To support this, UDDI Version 2.0 added the following:

- The `find_relatedBusiness` message to the inquiry API

- Five new messages to the publisher's API: `add_publisherAssertions`, `set_publisherAssertions`, `delete_publisherAssertions`, `get_assertionStatusReport`, and `get_publisherAssertions` (see the section "Changes to the Publication API")

- One additional canonical `tModel`, to represent UDDI `businessEntity` relationship descriptions

7

DISCOVERING WEB SERVICES

Changes to the Inquiry API

The find operation in UDDI has increased in sophistication. Version 2.0 of UDDI has introduced changes in the following find-related areas:

- Added a `find_relatedBusinesses` message
- Multiple language support for business and service names
- Less restrictive `find_business`
- New find qualifiers

Added `find_relatedBusinesses` Message

This new message was added to the UDDI Version 2.0 Inquiry API as part of the new facility to model relationships between `businessEntities` (see "Modeling Relationships between `businessEntity` Entries"). The `find_relatedBusinesses` message is used to return a list of `businessEntities` related in some specified way with a target `businessEntity`.

The structure of the `find_relatedBusinesses` message looks like this:

```
<find_relatedBusinesses generic="2.0" xmlns="urn:uddi-org:api_v2" >
      [<findQualifiers/>]
      <businessKey/>
      [<keyedReference/>]
</find_relatedBusinesses>
```

The target of the search is specified by the required `businessKey` argument. This argument is the UUID of the `businessEntity`. The `businessEntity` must be present within the UDDI registry.

Like all the other find messages in the Inquiry API, the results found in the response message are subject to the values of the `findQualifiers` arguments. A discussion on the use of `findQualifiers` argument in find messages can be found in the section "Finding Information in a UDDI Registry."

The `keyedReference` argument can be used to restrict which related `businessEntities` are returned in the response message. This argument is optional and can appear at most once in the message. The value of the `keyedReference` should reference the `uddi-org:relationships` `tModel`, and `keyValues` should be taken from the small set of values associated with this `tModel`.

For example, if a potential client wished to determine what subsidiaries WeMakeIt Inc. had registered with its entry in the UDDI Business Registry, it would use the following find message:

```
<find_relatedBusinesses generic="2.0" xmlns="urn:uddi-org:api_v2" >
      <businessKey>DCD2B450-A4C0-11D5-AF98-BD95162D3AC9</businessKey>
```

```
    <keyedReference
        tModelKey= "uuid:807A2C6A-EE22-470d-ADC7-E0424A337C03"
        keyValue="parent-child"/>
</find_relatedBusinesses>
```

Of course, the client would use a `find_business` message to locate the UUID `businessKey` for WeMakeIt Inc. The `keyValue` attribute in the `keyedReference` element was set to `"parent-child"`, reflecting that the client is looking for "child" `businessEntities` (subsidiaries) of WeMakeIt Inc.

The result of this message is a list of `businessEntities` that WeMakeIt Inc. asserted were its child or subsidiary `businessEntities`. The following would be the response to the `find_relatedBusinesses` example message:

```
<relatedBusinessList generic="2.0" operator="uddi.anOperator"
        xmlns="urn:uddi-org:api_v2.0">
    <businessKey>DCD2B450-A4C0-11D5-AF98-BD95162D3AC9</businessKey>
    <relatedBusinessInfos>
        <relatedBusinessInfo>
            <businessKey>DCD5C190-A4C0-11D5-AF98-BD95162D3AC9</businessKey>
            <name>WeMakeIt Asia Inc.</name>
            <description>WeMakeIt Asia provides outsourced man...</description>
            <sharedRelationships>
                <keyedReference
                    tModelKey=""uuid:807A2C6A..."
                    keyValue="parent-child"/>
            </sharedRelationships>
        </relatedBusinessInfo>
        <relatedBusinessInfo>
            <businessKey>DCD5C191-A4C0-11D5-AF98-BD95162D3AC9</businessKey>
            <name>WeMakeIt Europe Plc.</name>
            <description>WeMakeIt Europe provides outsourced m...</description>
            <sharedRelationships>
                <keyedReference
                    tModelKey=""uuid:807A2C6A..."
                    keyValue="parent-child"/>
            </sharedRelationships>
        </relatedBusinessInfo>
        ...
    </relatedBusinessInfos>
</relatedBusinessList>
```

Of course, if there are no related businesses to the target `businessEntity`, then the response message would contain an empty `relatedBusinessInfos` element. An error message will be returned if the `businessKey` argument does not correspond to a target `businessEntity` in the registry or (like any other find message) if one of the `findQualifiers` arguments is invalid.

Multiple Language Support for Business and Service Names

One extremely useful enhancement in Version 2.0 of UDDI is its support for multiple names for businessEntity and multiple names for businessService. The primary purpose of this change is to support multiple language translations of the business or service name.

WeMakeIt Inc. intends to exploit this feature in its businessEntity entry in the UDDI Business Registry. Whereas previously the company included only the English version of its name, WeMakeIt Inc. intends to include a Spanish and French translation of the name to serve the entire North American Free Trade Zone market and to assist in winning contracts with clients in the European Union.

Here is the new businessEntity entry for WeMakeIt Inc.:

```
<businessEntity
      businessKey="DCD2B450-A4C0-11D5-AF98-BD95162D3AC9"
      authorizedName="JPavard"
      operator=...>
   <name>WeMakeIt Inc.</name>
   <name xml:lang="fr">Nous Faisons Tout Inc.</name>
   <name xml:lang="sp">Carbarundo Inc.</name>
   ...
</businessEntity>
```

Although WeMakeIt Inc. can save its businessEntity elements with any number of child name elements, at most one of the names (which must be the first name element) can appear without an xml:lang attribute qualifier. (This is also true for description elements.) Any additional name element must have a unique xml:lang attribute qualifier. Note that the first name element (the one without xml:lang attribute) is assigned the code for US English, because that is the default language Joanna specified when she registered WeMakeIt Inc. with the UDDI Business Registry.

The impact of the businessEntity name change was great for WeMakeIt Inc., because it allowed the company to advertise in international markets. However, this name change facility is also supported the businessService element. This application of the multiple names facility is perhaps more useful. WeMakeIt Inc. has one businessService advertised in the UDDI Business Registry, that being its private portal UDDI (see the earlier discussion of portal UDDI nodes as part of the private UDDI discussion). The additional language translations available on the name element of businessService make it easier to find WeMakeIt Inc. The additional service name translations make a great accompaniment to the language translations of its service descriptions.

Here is the new businessService entry for WeMakeIt Inc., advertising its private portal UDDI:

```
<businessService
      businessKey="DCD2B450-A4C0-11D5-AF98-BD95162D3AC9"
```

```
        serviceKey="... />
    <name>Private Portal UDDI Inquiry API.</name>
    <name xml:lang="fr">Prive Portal UDDI Inquirer</name>
    ...
</businessService>
```

UDDI Version 2.0 also makes it easier to find businesses using multiple names (again, each name element in the query must be in a separate language). Although this feature is nice in theory, the majority of businesses will use a single name in their UDDI businessEntity entries. For the record, the new find_business API in Version 2.0 allows up to five names to appear in the query. If any of the name elements in the query match on both the value of the name element and the language attribute, then the businessEntity is returned in the result set of the find operation. This feature has also been defined for the find_service API. WeMakeIt Inc. expects that many international clients browsing its private portal UDDI node will use this facility.

Less Restrictive find_business

UDDI Version 2.0 reduced some restrictions on the parameters in the find_business query. In Version 1.0 of UDDI, the find_business service was defined by the UDDI Programmer's API specification with the following syntax:

```
<find_business generic="1.0" [ maxRows="nn" ] xmlns="urn:uddi-org:api" >
    [<findQualifiers/>]
    <name/> | <identifierBag/> | <categoryBag/> | <tModelBag/> |
        <discoveryURLs>
</find_business>
```

The major consequence of this is that the name, identifierBag, categoryBag, tModelBag, and discoveryURLs find arguments were all mutually exclusive. If a find_business had more than one of these arguments specified, the result of the inquiry would be an error message, of type E_tooManyOptions.

The Version 2.0 find_business removes this restriction. With UDDI Version 2.0, a programmer at WeMakeIt Inc. can search a UDDI registry for businesses offering Wheel Bearings (according to the UNSPSC code) that have services based on the e-Torus standard order suite POPlacement service interface and whose name starts with the letter *A*. A rough sketch of the find_business with these parameters is as follows:

```
<find_business generic="1.0" xmlns="urn:uddi-org:api_v2" >
    <name>A%</name>
    <categoryBag>
        <keyedReference
            <!-- UNSPSC 3.1 -->
            tModelKey="uuid:DB77450D-9FA8-45D4-A7BC-04411D14E384"
            keyName="Wheel bearings"
            keyValue="31171503"/>
```

```
    </categoryBag>
    <tModelBag>
        <tModelKey>UUID:D16D8A40-4F07-11D5-B842-87383803123D</tModelKey>
    </tModelBag>
</find_business>
```

In Version 2.0, the `E_tooManyOptions` error occurs only when more than five name arguments are included in the `find_business` invocation.

New Find Qualifiers

UDDI Version 2.0 added six new values to the permitted set of valid `findQualifiers` in find messages. The use of `findQualifier` arguments in find messages is described previously in the section "Finding Information in a UDDI Registry."

The new `findQualifiers` add more flexibility to the find messages. Most of the new `findQualifiers` extend the sophistication of `categoryBag` (for example, taxonomy-based) or `identifierBag` find operations. Let's take a brief look at each of the new `findQualifiers`.

orLikeKeys

This `findQualifier` is used on find messages involving `categoryBag` or `identifierBag` arguments. The find behavior specified by the use of this `findQualifier` is to OR together any `keyedReference` elements associated with the same `tModelKey` (such as references to the same taxonomy, identifier system, or other namespacing mechanism). Of course, `keyedReference` elements from separate `tModelKeys` are still ANDed together.

For example, if SkatesTown wanted to find all businesses that are:

- In UNSPSC category 311715 (bearings) or in subcategory 31171503 (wheel bearings), 31171505 (roller bearings), or 31171515 (plain bearings)

- And also are located in the United States or Canada (Geo taxonomy codes US and CA)

then the following `find_business` message would be used:

```
<find_business generic="2.0" xmlns="urn:uddi-org:api_v2" >
    <findQualifiers>
        <findQualifier>orLikeKeys</findQualifier>
    </findQualifiers>
    <categoryBag>
        <!-- UNSPSC 3.1 patterns -->
        <keyedReference
            tModelKey="uuid:DB77450D-9FA8-45D4-A7BC-04411D14E384"
            keyValue="311715"
            keyName="Bearings"/>
        <keyedReference
            tModelKey="uuid:DB77450D-9FA8-45D4-A7BC-04411D14E384"
```

```
                keyValue="31171503"
                keyName="Wheel Bearings"/>
        <keyedReference
                tModelKey="uuid:DB77450D-9FA8-45D4-A7BC-04411D14E384"
                keyValue="31171505"
                keyName="Roller Bearings"/>
        <keyedReference
                tModelKey="uuid:DB77450D-9FA8-45D4-A7BC-04411D14E384"
                keyValue="31171515"
                keyName="Plain Bearings"/>
        <!-- GEO Taxonomy patterns ISO 3166-1 -->
        <keyedReference
                tModelKey="uuid:61668105-B6B6-425c-914B-409FB252C36D"
                keyValue="UA"
                keyName="United States"/>
        <keyedReference
                tModelKey="uuid:61668105-B6B6-425c-914B-409FB252C36D"
                keyValue="CA"
                keyName="Canada"/>
    </categoryBag>
</find_business>
```

This facility is very important to support sophisticated searches of hierarchical taxonomies (such as UNSPSC) by specifying a `categoryBag` of all the `keyValues` associated with a particular branch of the taxonomy.

orAllKeys

By default, any `categoryBag` or `identifierBag` based search uses a logical AND of all `keyedReference` elements when matching. The affect of this `findQualifier` is that all of this default logical AND behavior is reversed to be logical OR. So if any entry matches any of the `keyedReference` elements in any of the `categoryBag` or `identifierBag` arguments, then it is included in the result set of the message.

This `findQualifier` would be used if SkatesTown wanted to find any business that was categorized according to UNSPSC code 31171503 (wheel bearings) or 31171515 (plain bearings) or categorized in NAICS code 33992 (sporting and athletic goods). The following `find_business` message illustrates the use of this `findQualifier`:

```
<find_business generic="2.0" xmlns="urn:uddi-org:api_v2" >
    <findQualifiers>
        <findQualifier>orAllKeys</findQualifier>
    </findQualifiers>
    <categoryBag>
        <!-- UN/SPSC patterns -->
        <keyedReference
```

```
        tModelKey="uuid:DB77450D-9FA8-45D4-A7BC-04411D14E384"
        keyValue="31171503"
        keyName="Wheel Bearings"/>
    <keyedReference
        tModelKey="uuid:DB77450D-9FA8-45D4-A7BC-04411D14E384"
        keyValue="31171515"
        keyName="Plain Bearings"/>
    <!-- NAICS patterns -->
    <keyedReference
        tModelKey="uuid:C0B9FE13-179F-413D-8A5B-5004DB8E5BB2"
        keyValue="33992"
        keyName="Sporting and Athletic Goods"/>
  </categoryBag>
</find_business>
```

combineCategoryBags

This is an interesting new wrinkle on the find_business message only. The use of this findQualifier modifies the behavior of categoryBag-based searches. The idea is that with this qualifier, the categoryBag of the businessEntity and all contained or referenced businessService elements are treated as a single, logical, aggregated categoryBag for purposes of matching. The response message will contain a businessList containing businessInfo elements for each businessEntity entry whose logical, aggregated categoryBag matched with any of the keyedReference elements contained in the categoryBag argument of the find_business message.

SkatesTown would use this feature in the case where some business partners categorized their businessEntity entries according to NAICS and their businessServices according to UN/SPSC, whereas other business partners might use both taxonomies for businessEntity only.

serviceSubset

This is a handy new feature for the find_business message only. This findQualifier combines with other find arguments to restrict the response set to include only those businessEntity entries that include businessService elements that are categorized according to the categoryBag element (the find_business message must include a categoryBag argument). The categoryBag argument is applied to businessService elements, not businessEntity elements. The response of this message is a businessList containing businessEntity entries that contain or reference those businessServices whose categoryBag element matches the technical fingerprint specified in the categoryBag argument of the find operation. The serviceInfo elements contained within the businessService elements in the response will contain only those businessService entries matched by the categoryBag comparison (and not all the other businessServices that businessEntity has registered with the UDDI registry).

So if you are looking for all businesses that implement a service categorized in a particular way, this is the findQualifier to use. Consider an example find_business message using the serviceSubset findQualifier. If you wanted to find all businesses that advertise a businessService for a product within a given UNSPSC code, say 31171503 (wheel bearings), use serviceSubset and the categoryBag identifying the UNSPSC taxonomy with the key value for the given category. The following is an example of this kind of find:

```
<find_business generic="2.0" xmlns="urn:uddi-org:api_v2" >
    <findQualifiers>
        <findQualifier>serviceSubset</findQualifier>
    </findQualifiers>
    <categoryBag>
        <keyedReference
            tModelKey="uuid:DB77450D-9FA8-45D4-A7BC-04411D14E384"
            keyValue="31171503"
            keyName="Wheel Bearings"/>
    </categoryBag>
</find_business>
```

The result of this message is a list of businessEntities that have services categorized under the given UNSPSC category, and serviceInfo elements for each of the services so categorized.

andAllKeys

This findQualifier specifies the default behavior of doing logical AND of any keyedReference as part of indentifierBag or categoryBag arguments in the find message. This is the default behavior inherited from UDDI Version 1.0 find messages. Because the findQualifier orLikeKeys (discussed earlier) was introduced, andAllKeys was added to the list of valid findQualifier arguments for completeness sake.

Soundex

Soundex is a term used to describe name-based searches for entity names that sound alike.

This findQualifier can be used on the find_business and find_service messages to locate businesses or services with similar sounding names. This is the only new findQualifier not associated with categoryBag- or identifierBag-based find messages.

A find message that looks like

```
<find_business generic="2.0" xmlns="urn:uddi-org:api_v2" >
    <findQualifiers>
        <findQualifier>soundex</findQualifier>
    </findQualifiers>
    <name>Wee May Kit</name>
</find_business>
```

will return a response message with a `businessList` containing a `businessInfo` element for WeMakeIt Inc. and any other `businessEntity` that sounds like "Wee May Kit." If multiple name parameters were in the find message (recall in UDDI `find_xxx` you can now specify up to five name arguments), the `businessList` would return entries that matched *any* of the names.

Changes to the Publication API

The changes made to the Publication API in UDDI Version 2.0 are all related to the publication assertions feature supporting the modeling of business relationships in UDDI. First, a set of five additional messages—`add_publisherAssertions`, `set_publisherAssertions`, `delete_publisherAssertions`, `get_assertionStatusReport`, and `get_publisherAssertions`—directly manage the business relationship assertions. Second, a related modification of the `save_business` behavior allows a `businessService` to be shared between `businessEntities`. The mechanism of modeling business relationships using the publication assertion feature is described in the section "Modeling Relationships between `businessEntity` Entries."

The `add_publisherAssertions` and `delete_publisherAssertions` messages are used to insert, update, and delete individual or small sets of publisher assertions. The `set_publisherAssertions` message manages an entire set of assertions as a single set. The `get_publisherAssertions` message is used to retrieve the entire set of assertions; it often will be used in conjunction with the `set_publisherAssertions` message. Finally, the set of new messages includes the administrative `get_assertionStatusReport` message, which is used to determine which assertions have been made referencing owned `businessEntity` entries that have yet to be acknowledged by reciprocal assertion of the business relationship.

Let's take a closer look at the five new publication messages and discuss how WeMakeIt Inc. would use these facilities.

add_publisherAssertions

This message is used to add one or more additional publisher assertions associated with `businessEntities` owned by the publisher. Like all the publication messages, entries acted upon must be owned by the user sending the message (the publisher, or technically the user associated with the `authInfo` element of the message). We saw in a previous example that Joanna Pravard would use this message to model the relationship between WeMakeIt Inc. and its subsidiaries. The benefit of this approach over the `set_publisherAssertions` is that assertions can be added incrementally, without having to refer to the entire set of assertions currently associated with the `businessEntity`.

delete_publisherAssertions

This message is used to delete one or more publisher assertions associated with businessEntity entries owned by the publisher. Joanna Pravard would use this message to remove assertions in case one of the subsidiaries is sold to another company, or one of the subsidiaries goes out of business.

Of course, another way to delete assertions is to delete one of the businessEntity entries referred to in the relationship. When the delete_business message executes, any assertion associated with that businessEntity is also deleted.

set_publisherAssertions

This message is similar to the add_publisherAssertions message, except that it acts on the entire set of publisher assertions associated with any businessEntity owned by the user who sends the message (the publisher, or technically the user associated with the authInfo element of the message). Note that unlike most of the other publication messages, this affects entries associated with the publisher, not an individual element or set of elements identified by UUID keys. The result of the message is to replace whatever set of assertions existed before the message was sent with the assertions contained within the message. Essentially any existing assertion that is not in the message is deleted, and any new assertion that is in the message is added.

This message can act as an analog to a delete_publisherAssertions message by passing an empty set of publisher assertions, deleting the entire set of existing assertions associated with any businessEntity owned by the publisher.

get_publisherAssertions

This message is used to retrieve the entire set of publisher assertions associated with a publisher. Joanna Pravard would use this message in preparation to use the set_publisherAssertions message. Joanna would issue the get_publisherAssertions message, examine the set of publisher assertions, add a few, remove a few, and then use this modified set of publisher assertions as the argument in a set_publisherAssertions message.

get_assertionStatusReport

This message is used to help publishers examine the set of assertions that reference any of their owned businessEntity entries. Joanna Pravard would use this message to see if any other publisher attempted to assert a relationship between one of his/her businessEntity entry and WeMakeIt Inc. Joanna, of course, would ignore these assertions. Until Joanna acknowledges these assertions by reciprocating with an assertion of her own, the relationship between WeMakeIt Inc. and the other businessEntity is not visible.

Sharing Services between `businessEntity` Entries

Different business units in a company might share Web services. For WeMakeIt Inc., in the case of their `POPlacement` Web service, a single instance of this Web service supports all three operating units. Although it is possible to duplicate `businessService` entries for this single Web service and place them separately into each separate `businessEntity`, this can become a maintenance headache for Joanna.

As a result of UDDI Version 2.0 modeling relationships between `businessEntity` entries, the facility has been added to share `businessService` entries between `businessEntity` entries. The behavior of the `save_business` message has been modified to allow a `businessService` contained by one `businessEntity` to be *shared* or *referenced by* a different `businessEntity`.

The `save_business` message takes one or more entire `businessEntity` elements as arguments. A `businessEntity` element can contain child `businessService` elements. If the `businessKey` child element of `businessService` has a value that is different from the `businessKey` of the `businessEntity` being saved, the `save_business` operation will add a reference from the `businessEntity` being saved to the `businessService`. The referenced `businessService` itself will not be changed as a result of the `save_business` operation.

A reference to a `businessService` can be removed from a `businessEntity` by sending a `save_business` message for that `businessEntity` without including a reference to the `businessService` in the `businessEntity` argument passed in the message.

Miscellaneous Changes

Several other smaller changes were made in UDDI Version 2.0, but none of them impact SkatesTown or WeMakeIt Inc. For the sake of completeness, here is a list of several other miscellaneous changes that appeared in UDDI Version 2.0.

Generic and Default XML Namespace Updated

Recall that messages in UDDI require the use of the oddly named `generic` attribute, as well as the conventional definition of the default XML namespace. Messages intended for UDDI Version 2.0 compatible registries should include these attributes in the `message` element as shown here:

```
<API_MESSAGE_NAME generic="2.0" xmlns="urn:uddi-org:api_v2" >
```

These attributes appear to be redundant. The value of having the `generic` attribute to distinguish specification version intention seems to be already covered by specifying the default namespace of the message. The danger of this redundancy is now illustrated as the first version change in UDDI has been made. This problem is described by the following passage from the UDDI Version 2.0 API specification:

"The use of generic value 1.0 with the UDDI Version 2.0 namespace, or generic value 2.0 with the UDDI Version 1.0 namespace is not considered to be a normal use of the versioning mechanism. Individual operators are permitted to interpret mixed versioning information as an error condition."

The specification does not explicitly dictate the legal combinations of values of these attributes. The client of the UDDI registry cannot determine what the outcome will be if the message mixes values for generic and the default namespace. It would have been better if the specification clearly required this to be an error condition or, better yet, removed the generic attribute altogether and relied solely on the value of the default namespace to indicate the version expectation of the message.

Miscellaneous Error Codes Changes

Table 7.2 summarizes the changes made to the expected error codes from Version 1.0 to Version 2.0.

TABLE 7.2   Changes in Error Codes for UDDI Version 2.0

Error	Code	Change	Comments
E_categorizationNotAllowed	20100	Retired	Version 2.0 uses E_valueNotAllowed.
E_invalidCategory	20000	Retired	Version 2.0 uses E_invalidValue when a keyValue of a category bag does not correspond to a valid category.
E_invalidURLPassed	10220	Do Not Use	Not used in Version 1.0 or Version 2.0.
E_keyRetired	10310	Do Not Use	Not used in Version 1.0 or Version 2.0; error in the V1.0 specification.
E_operatorMismatch	10130	Retired	Caused precedence problems with E_unknownUser; error in the V1.0 specification.

SOAPAction Header Use Updated

The role of the SOAPAction HTTP header was described in Chapter 3. Version 1.0 of the UDDI specification required that this header be left as an empty string. This recommendation is contrary to how many SOAP engines use SOAPAction as a processing hint. UDDI Version 2.0 now allows this header to have as a value the name of the API message contained within the SOAP body element. To support backward compatibility with UDDI Version 1.0, the SOAPAction header is still permitted to be an empty string.

New Canonical tModels Added

UDDI Version 1.0 established a convention to describe certain UDDI-specific, core tModels as canonical tModels. This set of canonical tModels described various technical specifications used in UDDI itself, including:

- Core UDDI API tModels describing the Inquiry API, the Publication API, and a taxonomy maintenance tModel

- Core tModels representing tModel type system (for categorizing tModels)

- Core categorization tModels supported by the UDDI Business Registry (NAICS, UNSPSC, and ISO 3166 Geographic taxonomy), the DUNS identifier system, and the Thomas Registry

- Protocol-specific tModels representing network protocols, such as SMTP, FTP, and so on

Version 2.0 augmented the core UDDI API tModels by adding version-specific tModels for the updated Inquiry, Publication, and taxonomy maintenance APIs:

tModel *Name*	*UUID*
UDDI Inquiry API v2.0	uuid:AC104DCC-D623-452f-88A7-F8ACD94D9B2B
UDDI Publication API v2.0	uuid:A2F36B65-2D66-4088-ABC7-914D0E05EB9E
UDDI Taxonomy API v2.0	uuid:1E3E9CBC-F8CE-41ab-8F99-88326BAD324A

The uddi-org:types tModel was extended to include two new types. First, a relationship type was added to support the publication assertions model of representing relationships between businessEntity entries. Second, an unvalidatable type was added to model Version 2.0 to categorize tModels representing third party taxonomies that are not externally validated.

The uddi-org:relationships canonical tModel was also added to support the publication assertions feature which is new in UDDI Version 2.0. This tModel is, of course, categorized in the uddi-org:types categorization under the relationship type category. The use of this tModel to support publication assertions is described in the section "Modeling Relationships between businessEntity Entries."

Replication Specification Published

Public description of the replication mechanism between operator nodes in the UDDI Business Registry appeared for the first time with the documentation set for UDDI Version 2.0. This specification is available at www.uddi.org.

Details of the mechanism used to share changes in UDDI entries between the operator nodes are interesting, but not of immediate concern to most UDDI users. This level of detail is, of course, very important to any organization building an implementation of UDDI that would be used as an operator node within the UDDI Business Registry.

This information might also be important for an organization considering using existing UDDI implementations to set up a private federation of UDDI registries within an organization. Large organizations, such as WeMakeIt Inc., might consider creating a private UDDI Business Registry. WeMakeIt Inc. could deploy a UDDI registry for each major division, or separate business unit. The replication mechanism could be used to keep Web service descriptions properly up-to-date between all registries within WeMakeIt Inc. As it turns out, WeMakeIt Inc. chose to implement a federation of private UDDI registries without the replication mechanism. The operating units felt that the volume of changes did not warrant the extra complication of setting up the replication mechanism. Besides, more targeted facilities, such as copy/paste and publish/subscribe, allowed each operating unit more fine grained control on which updates were communicated to other UDDI registries within WeMakeIt Inc.

Clearly, SkatesTown is too small an organization to consider hosting more than one private UDDI implementation, let alone building a private replication-based federation of UDDI registries.

Operators Manual Published

Also new in the UDDI Version 2.0 documentation set is a set of details outlining required behavior of operator nodes within the UDDI Business Registry. This specification is also available at `www.uddi.org`. The operators manual is important to WeMakeIt Inc. Although WeMakeIt Inc. has no intention of becoming an operator within the UDDI Business Registry, it does need to make sure its `validate_values` service is properly registered with the UDDI Business Registry, and, therefore, available to UDDI Business Registry nodes (and private UDDI registries) to validate the use of WeMakeIt Inc.'s product code taxonomy.

Using WSDL with UDDI

UDDI was designed to accommodate the registration of `businessService` entries regardless of the kind of service description mechanism used. A Web service, registered in UDDI as a `businessService`, can be described using WSDL, a plain ASCII text document, a RosettaNet pip, RDF, or any number of other description mechanisms. This is one of the aspects of UDDI that makes it generally applicable.

This section is for those developers who use WSDL to describe your Web services and wish to register them in UDDI. `UDDI.org` has published a best practices document that outlines the convention you should use for WSDL-described Web services. UDDI.org publishes best practices documents at `http://www.uddi.org/bestpractices.html`. Al Rosen uses this convention to format the UDDI entries for SkatesTown. Let's examine the steps that Al needs to do in order to properly register SkatesTown's `PriceCheck` service.

Saving a UDDI `businessService` Based on WSDL

In Chapter 6, we reviewed the major elements in WSDL and outlined the Web services convention of separating service interface definition from service implementation definition. Figure 7.32 outlines how the major elements of WSDL map into UDDI elements.

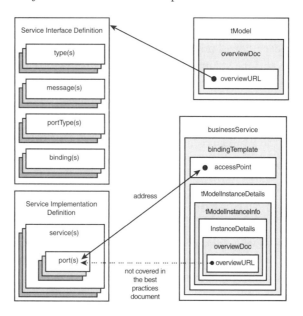

FIGURE 7.32
Mapping from WSDL to UDDI.

The best practices document for using WSDL in UDDI discusses how to represent the service interface definition as a `tModel`. Al Rosen followed an extended convention that defined how to reference the service implementation definition file from the `bindingTemplate` element.

Al starts with the WSDL file for SkatesTown's `priceCheck` service. We saw this file in Chapter 6. Al further updates the file from Chapter 6, preparing to save it in UDDI by decomposing the `priceCheck` service description into two files. The service interface definition is available at `www.skatestown.com/services//interfaces/priceCheckInterface.wsdl`. The service implementation definition is available at `http://www.skatestown.com/services/priceCheck.wsdl`.

The first thing Al must do is create a tModel to reference the service interface definition. Al chooses to create this tModel in the UDDI Business Registry itself for maximum exposure. Al could also have chosen to create this tModel in any private UDDI registry, but SkatesTown hoped to make this approach to priceCheck a standard among its supply chain partners, and therefore wanted maximum exposure. The save_service message looks like this:

```
<save_tModel generic="1.0" xmlns="urn:uddi-org:api">
    <authInfo>...</authInfo>
    <tModel>
        <name>SkatesTown PriceCheck Service Interface Definition</name>
        <description>This tModel defines the service interface definition
            for priceCheck services.
        </description>
        <overviewDoc>
            <overviewURL>
    http://www.skatesTown.com/services/interfaces/priceCheckInterface.wsdl
            </overviewURL>
        </overviewDoc>
        <categoryBag>
            <keyedReference
                keyName="uddi-org:types"
                keyValue="wsdlSpec"
                tModelKey="UUID:C1ACF26D-9672-4404-9D70-39B756E62AB4"/>
                <!-- UDDI Types tModelKey -->
        </categoryBag>
    </tModel>
</save_tModel>
```

The key points are:

- The overviewURL element gives the URL to where the service interface definition WSDL file can be found. This allows humans and UDDI/WSDL-aware tooling to locate the service interface definition. As we mentioned in Chapter 6, the goal of acquiring the service interface definition is to generate a client proxy for the requestor application.

- The purpose of the keyedReference element in the categoryBag is to make sure that this tModel is categorized as a WSDL specification document. UDDI/WSDL-aware tooling relies on consistent categorization as a guarantee of the contents of the resource referenced by the overviewURL.

- Remember those tModelKeys! The tModelKey assigned to SkatesTown's priceCheck tModel must be used in any subsequent businessService element. In this case, the tModelKey returned assigned by the UDDI operator was UUID:75F83600-4D6E-11D5-83B9-AFF41F112FA2.

No tModelKey is passed in the message; this signals to UDDI that the tModel is a new tModel.

Now that a tModel for SkatesTown's priceCheck service interface is generally available, it is possible to create a businessService element that models a Web service based on this interface. WeMakeIt Inc. can build a Web service based on this price Check standard. Therefore, WeMakeIt Inc.'s Joanna Pravard can define a businessService entry for WeMakeIt Inc.'s priceCheck Web service. The save_service message looks like:

```
<save_service generic="1.0" xmlns="urn:uddi-org:api">
    <authInfo>...</authInfo>
    <businessService businessKey="...">
        <name>WeMakeIt Inc.&apos;s Price Check Service</name>
        <description>This service is based on the Price Check service
            interface definition...
        </description>
        <bindingTemplates>
            <bindingTemplate>
                <description>See the PriceCheck service interface standard
                    Use the address in the svc impl. definition if the
                    accessPoint URL doesn&apos;t work.
            </description>
                <accessPointURLType="http">
                     www.wemakeit.com/axis/services/priceCheck
                </accessPoint>
                <tModelInstanceDetails>
                    <tModelInstanceInfo
                        tModelKey="UUID:75F83600-4D6E-11D5-83B9-AFF41F112FA2">
                        <instanceDetails>
                            <overviewDoc>
                                <description>Points to WeMakeIt Inc.&apos;s service
                                    implementation WSDL ...
                                </description>
                                <overviewURL>
                            www.wemakeit.com/webservices/descriptions/priceCheck.wsdl
                                </overviewURL>
                            </overviewDoc>
                        </instanceDetails>
                    </tModelInstanceInfo>
                </tModelInstanceDetails>
            </bindingTemplate>
        </bindingTemplates>
    </businessService>
</save_service>
```

The key points are:

- The accessPoint element is the URL at which the Web service can be invoked, although the ultimate source of truth for the Web service's location is in the service implementation file.

- The `tModelKey` element refers to the `tModel` representing the `priceCheck` service interface definition.

- The tModelInstance element follows an extended convention for locating the service implementation definition file. Joanna uses this additional convention because it allows WeMakeIt Inc. the flexibility of moving the location of this service without having to immediately update the UDDI entry. All WeMakeIt Inc. would have to do is update the service implementation definition (which it controls) and eventually update the accessPoint element of the UDDI entry. The advantage to this approach is that the change of location is made immediately in the local WSDL file and WeMakeIt Inc. does not have to wait until the UDDI entry change is replicated to all the UDDI Business Registry operator nodes.

More Complex WSDL and Corresponding UDDI Entries

For more sophisticated WSDL descriptions, the UDDI entries are slightly more tricky. Let's take a look at some of the entries for the e-Torus marketplace.

The e-Torus marketplace has established a standard, industry-wide service interface definition suite for supply reordering of small wheels and bearings. This suite has built upon the `priceCheck` service interface definition developed by SkatesTown and adding request for quote and purchase order placement. This resulted in a minor inconvenience to existing service implementations that referenced SkatesTown's `tModel`. The `businessService` entries for these services needed to be updated to reference the new `tModel` defined by e-Torus. Because e-Torus has incorporated SkatesTown's `priceCheck and POSubmission` service interface definitions into the order suite WSDL, this was a minor inconvenience in UDDI registration only; the programs continued to work.

The details of the e-Torus orderSuite WSDL are not relevant here, but we do include important portions of the WSDL as follows:

```xml
<?xml version="1.0"?>
<definitions name="e-Torus Order Suite"
   targetNamespace=
      "http://www.etorus.com/serviceInterfaces/orderSuiteInterface"
   xmlns:tns=
      "http://www.etorus.com/serviceInterfaces/orderSuiteInterface"
   xmlns:orderSchema="http://www.etorus.com/schemas/order.xsd"
   xmlns:soap="http://schemas.xmlsoap.org/wsdl/soap/"
   xmlns="http://schemas.xmlsoap.org/wsdl/">

   <types>
      <schema targetNamespace="http://www.e-Torus.com/schemas/order.xsd"
      <!-- incorporates priceCheck schema elements from SkatesTown -->
```

```
      ...
    </types>

<!-- Message definitions -->

    <message name="PriceCheckRequest">
        <part name="item" type="xsd:string"/>
    </message>
    <message name="PriceCheckResponse">
        <part name="result" type="orderSchema:availability"/>
    </message>

    <message name="RequestForQuotes">
        <part name="body" element="orderSchema:RFQ"/>
    </message>
    <message name="RFQResponse">
        <part name="body" element="orderSchema:RFQResponse"/>
    </message>

    <message name="poSubmissionRequest">
        <part name="purchaseOrder" element="orderSchema:po"/>
    </message>

    <message name="poSubmissionResponse">
        <part name="invoice" element="orderSchema:invoice"/>
    </message>
...

    <!-- Port type definitions -->

    <portType name="PriceCheckPortType">
        <operation name="checkPrice">
          <input message="tns:PriceCheckRequest"/>
          <output message="tns:PriceCheckResponse"/>
        </operation>
    </portType>

    <portType name="RFQPortType">
        <operation name="PlaceRFQ">
          <input message="tns:RequestForQuotes"/>
          <output message="tns:RFQResponse"/>
        </operation>
    </portType>

    <portType name="poSubmissionPortType">
        <operation name="doSubmission">
```

```
            <input message="tns:poSubmissionRequest"/>
            <output message="tns:poSubmissionResponse"/>
        </operation>
    </portType>
    ...

    <!-- Binding definitions -->
    <binding name="PriceCheckSOAPBinding" type="tns:PriceCheckPortType">
        <soap:binding style="rpc"
            transport="http://schemas.xmlsoap.org/soap/http"/>
        <operation name="checkPrice">
        ...
        </operation>
    </binding>

    <binding name="RFQSOAPBinding" type="tns:RFQPortType">
        <soap:binding style="document"
            transport="http://schemas.xmlsoap.org/soap/http"/>
        <operation name="PlaceRFQ">
        ...
        </operation>
    </binding>

    <binding name="poSubmissionSOAPBinding" type="tns:poSubmissionPortType">
        <soap:binding style="document"
            transport="http://schemas.xmlsoap.org/soap/http"/>
        <operation name="doSubmission">
        ...
        </operation>
    </binding>
</definitions>
```

This WSDL file is made available at the e-Torus Web site: `http://www.etorus.com/`
`webservices/interfaces/orderInterfaces.wsdl`.

Note that each business process has a separate `portType` (`PriceCheckPortType`, `RFQPortType`,
and `POSubmissionPortType` are shown). This allows each business process to have separate
binding definitions, providing for significant implementation flexibility for different security,
reliability, transport mechanism, and so on.

Because this service interface definition has different bindings, the UDDI entries, particularly
the `businessService` elements referencing this service interface definition, look slightly different.

So, e-Torus registers a `tModel` in its portal private UDDI for each of the bindings. This creates
a separate `tModel` for each binding in the service interface definition file. The technique for

7

DISCOVERING
WEB SERVICES

registering these tModels is slightly different from what Joanna Pravard used. Because the overviewURL references to the entire document, the developer at e-Torus followed the recommendation in the best practices document and used a URL fragment identifier (http://www.ietf.org/rfc/rfc2396.txt) to indicate exactly which binding in the service interface file each tModel references. The tModel record for the priceCheck binding looks like this:

```
<tModel
        tModelKey="UUID:72E5F9F0-A4C3-11D5-AF98-BD95162D3AC9" ...>
    <name>e-Torus order Service PriceCheck Interface Definition</name>
    <description xml:lang="en">
        This tModel defines the service interface definition for
        priceCheck within the e-Torus order suite of services.
    </description>
    <overviewDoc>
        <overviewURL>
            http://www.etorus.com/services/interfaces/
                orderInterfaces.wsdl#PriceCheckSOAPBinding
        </overviewURL>
    </overviewDoc>
    <categoryBag>
        <keyedReference
            keyName="uddi-org:types"
            keyValue="wsdlSpec"
            tModelKey="UUID:C1ACF26D-9672-4404-9D70-39B756E62AB4"/>
    </categoryBag>
</tModel>
```

Now, consider a businessService element for a Web service provided by one of the sellers in the e-Torus marketplace that implements the priceCheck binding tModel. A wheel manufacturer, MakeCircles Inc., is a member of the e-Torus e-marketplace. MakeCircles Inc. defines a service implementation definition file at http://www.makecircles.com/services/priceCheck.wsdl. This file contains ports for the entire set of order suite bindings as follows:

```
<?xml version="1.0"?>
<definitions name="orderSuite"
    targetNamespace="http://www.makecircles.com/wsdl/orderSuite"
    xmlns:tns="http://www.makecircles.com/wsdl/orderSuite"
    xmlns:order=
        "http://http://www.etorus.com/serviceInterfaces/orderSuiteInterface"
    xmlns:xsd="http://www.w3.org/2000/10/XMLSchema"
    xmlns:soap="http://schemas.xmlsoap.org/wsdl/soap/"
    xmlns="http://schemas.xmlsoap.org/wsdl/">
```

```
<import
   namespace=
   "http://www.etorus.com/serviceInterfaces/orderSuiteInterface"
   location=
   "http://www.etorus.com/services/interfaces/orderInterfaces.wsdl"
 />

 <service name="OrderServices">
    <documentation>
       PriceCheck service according to the e-Torus order standard
    </documentation>
    <port name="PriceCheckPort" binding="order:PriceCheckSOAPBinding">
       <soap:address
          location=http://www.makecircles.com/services/priceCheck/>
    </port>

    <port name="RFQPort" binding="order:RFQSOAPBinding">
       <soap:address
          location=http://www.makecircles.com/services/placeRFQ/>
    </port>

    <port name="POSubmissionPort" binding="order: poSubmissionSOAPBinding">
       <soap:address
          location=http://www.makecircles.com/services/submitPO/>
    </port>
 </service>
</definitions>
```

Let's take a look at a businessService entry for this service. Like Joanna Pravard, the developer at MakeCircles Inc. preferred to have control over where the network address of the services are actually kept, and chose to have the tModelInstanceDetails of the bindingTemplate reference the service implementation file as the ultimate source of truth for the Web service's network address. Note that the service has two ports. The bindingTemplate uses the same fragment identifier mechanism on the overviewURL to reference the particular priceCheck port:

```
<businessService
     businessKey="..."
     serviceKey="...">
  <name>MakeCircle&apos;s priceCheck Web service</name>
  <description>This service is based on the e-Torus PriceCheck orderSuite
service
     interface definition...
  </description>
  <bindingTemplates>
     <bindingTemplate
```

```
            bindingKey="BEF9B260-A4C7-11D5-AF98-BD95162D3AC9"
            serviceKey="BEF9B260-A4C7-11D5-AF98-BD95162D3AC9">
            <description>
                See the e-Torus order suite priceCheck service interface
                standard. Use the address in the svc impl. definition if the
                accessPoint URL does not work.
            </description>
                <accessPoint URLType="http">
                    http://www.makecircles.com/services/priceCheck
                </accessPoint>
                <tModelInstanceDetails>
                    <tModelInstanceInfo
                        tModelKey="UUID:B04E3710-4D86-11D5-83B9-AFF41F112FA2">
                        <description>
                            Points to MakeCircle&apos;s service
                            implementation WSDL ...
                        </description>
                        <instanceDetails>
                            <overviewDoc>
                                <overviewURL>
                        http://www.makecircles.com/webservices/descriptions/
                            rfq.wsdl#PriceCheckPort
                                </overviewURL>
                            </overviewDoc>
                        </instanceDetails>
                    </tModelInstanceInfo>
                </tModelInstanceDetails>
            </bindingTemplate>
        </bindingTemplates>
    </businessService>
```

Note the tModelKey refers to the RFQ binding as defined by e-Torus order standard service interface definition for order-based Web services.

Putting It All Together: WSDL-Based UDDI and Dynamic Find

By this point, SkatesTown is selling a lot of skateboards. Some of the company's partner retailers are now selling direct to customers via the Web, and those customers get real-time availability and pricing information from SkatesTown via Web services. Retailers use SkatesTown's Web services to order boards, and SkatesTown has committed to giving them real-time availability information for their big orders. In order for SkatesTown to meet this commitment in a cost-effective fashion, SkatesTown needs to verify components supply by orchestrating back-end queries to the e-Torus e-marketplace. For example, if a retailer orders 100 of SkatesTown's

MAXX skateboards, to be delivered in two weeks, the system can check the inventory of finished boards and parts, and then query the e-marketplace to make sure enough wheels, bearings, and so on will be available to SkatesTown in order to meet the commitment.

SkatesTown has all the pieces to do dynamic runtime bind of Web services. SkatesTown wants to use the power of the e-Torus marketplace to get the best supplier for any single reorder of wheels or bearings at any given point in time. For wheels and bearings, SkatesTown trusts the vendors active in the e-Torus marketplace. The reorder application that Al Rosen has put together uses dynamic bind to do `priceChecks` within the e-Marketplace to all vendors that follow the e-Torus order standard suite of service interfaces.

These are the steps Al Rosen used to develop SkatesTown's e-marketplace `priceCheck` application.

First, Al uses the Java generated from the `priceCheck` WSDL. You saw this done back in Chapter 6. Others, like Joanna Pravard would generate their company's proxy by retrieving the `tModel` associated with the e-Torus `priceCheck` service interface definition standard.

Al uses dynamic binding to fill in the URL to the proxy. Al codes the client application, using the *UDDI4J* 📖 API. UDDI4J is an open source project sponsored by IBM; source is available under the IBM Public License. Originally part of the WebServices Toolkit, UDDI4J source is now also available at
`http://oss.software.ibm.com/developerworks/projects/uddi4j`. UDDI4J defines a very straightforward and convenient mapping between the UDDI operations and data structures and Java methods and classes. UDDI4J makes it simple to incorporate UDDI operations as part of any Java program—exactly what Al needs to do.

Al's code does a find operation that retrieves all the vendors from the e-Torus e-marketplace private UDDI that implement the `priceCheck` binding `tModel` and also the `POSubmission` `tModel`. The find message appears as follows:

```
<find_business generic="1.0" xmlns="urn:uddi-org:api">
   <tModelBag>
      <tModelKey>UUID:5FE30870-A4C3-11D5-AF98-BD95162D3AC9</tModelKey>
      <tModelKey>UUID:72E5F9F0-A4C3-11D5-AF98-BD95162D3AC9</tModelKey>
   </tModelBag>
</find_business>
```

The first `tModel` key corresponds to the `POSubmission` `tModel`, and the second one refers to a `priceCheck` `tModel` (not shown in any listings).

The UDDI4J code fragment would look like this:

```
UDDIProxy proxy=new UDDIProxy();

String userid="...";
```

7

```
String password="...";

//set up the TModelBag to refer to both the priceCheck and PoSubmission
//suppliers must support both standards in order to be invoked by the
//application
TModelBag bag=new TModelBag();
Vector v=new Vector();

//UUID of POSubmission tModel
v.addElement("UUID:5FE30870-A4C3-11D5-AF98-BD95162D3AC");
//UUID of PriceCheck tModel
v.addElement("UUID:72E5F9F0-A4C3-11D5-AF98-BD95162D3AC");
bag.setTModelKeyStrings(v);

//finds all businesses that have a service implementing the priceCheck  and
POSubmission tModelsBusinessList bl=proxy.find_business(bag, null, 0);
```

A sample set of return values from execution of the find operation would look like this:

```
<businessList generic="1.0" ...
   <businessInfos>
      <businessInfo businessKey="DCD2B450-A4C0-11D5-AF98-BD95162D3AC9">
         <name>WeMakeIt Inc.</name>
         <serviceInfos>
            <serviceInfo
               businessKey="DCD2B450-A4C0-11D5-AF98-BD95162D3AC9"
               serviceKey="9732C900-A4C8-11D5-AF98-BD95162D3AC9">
               <name>WeMakeIt Inc.&apos;s POSubmission Service</name>
            </serviceInfo>
            <serviceInfo
               businessKey="DCD2B450-A4C0-11D5-AF98-BD95162D3AC9"
               serviceKey="ACE9DE00-A4C8-11D5-AF98-BD95162D3AC9">
               <name>WeMakeIt Inc.&apos;s POSubmission Service</name>
            </serviceInfo>
            <serviceInfo
               businessKey="DCD2B450-A4C0-11D5-AF98-BD95162D3AC9"
               serviceKey="D66199C0-A4C9-11D5-AF98-BD95162D3AC9">
               <name>WeMakeIt Inc.&apos;s RFQ Service</name>
            </serviceInfo>
            <serviceInfo
               businessKey="DCD2B450-A4C0-11D5-AF98-BD95162D3AC9"
               serviceKey="CEC8E160-A4CD-11D5-AF98-BD95162D3AC9">
               <name>WeMakeIt Inc.&apos;s Price Check Service</name>
            </serviceInfo>
         </serviceInfos>
      </businessInfo>
      <businessInfo businessKey="05064CC0-A4C1-11D5-AF98-BD95162D3AC9">
```

```
            <name>Wheels Made Here</name>
            <serviceInfos>
               <serviceInfo
                  businessKey="05064CC0-A4C1-11D5-AF98-BD95162D3AC9"
                  serviceKey="2065CFF0-A4CA-11D5-AF98-BD95162D3AC9">
               <name>Wheels Made Here&apos;s PO Submission Web service</name>
               </serviceInfo>
               <serviceInfo
                  businessKey="05064CC0-A4C1-11D5-AF98-BD95162D3AC9"
                  serviceKey="80DFFE50-A4CA-11D5-AF98-BD95162D3AC9">
                  <name>Wheels Made Here&apos;s priceCheck Placement Web
                     service</name>
               </serviceInfo>
               <serviceInfo
                  businessKey="05064CC0-A4C1-11D5-AF98-BD95162D3AC9"
                  serviceKey="BA661920-A4CA-11D5-AF98-BD95162D3AC9">
                  <name>Wheels Made Here&apos;s RFQ Web service</name>
               </serviceInfo>
            </serviceInfos>
         </businessInfo>
      </businessInfos>
</businessList>
```

For each serviceInfo found in the businessList object returned from the find operation, the code needs to locate the priceCheck service (remember we asked for all businesses that supported both priceCheck and POSubmission, so we need to isolate the priceCheck service). The location of the priceCheck service is found in a bindingTemplate. The priceCheck bindingTemplate is identified by the tModel within one of the bindingTemplate's tModelInstanceInfo elements. The algorithm proceeds as follows. Issue a find_binding for the service, given the tModel bag with the priceCheck tModel. The bindingDetail element returned from this call will contain the bindingTemplate referring to the priceCheck. Other bindingTemplates for other technologies might also be in the bindingDetail structure. Examine each bindingTemplate, looking for a tModelInstanceInfo element that refers to the priceCheck model. When that tModelInstanceInfo element is found, the algorithm has found the right bindingTemplate. The search is complete. This is demonstrated in the following listing, continuing from the previous code example:

```
//Find the binding that matches the TModel for priceCheck
TModelBag bag2=new TModelBag();
Vector v2=new Vector();
//UUID of priceCheck tModel
v2.addElement("UUID:72E5F9F0-A4C3-11D5-AF98-BD95162D3AC9");
bag2.setTModelKeyStrings(v2);
```

7

```
Vector biv=bl.getBusinessInfos().getBusinessInfoVector();
Enumeration e=biv.elements();
while(e.hasMoreElements()){
   BusinessInfo bi=(BusinessInfo)e.nextElement();
   ServiceInfos sis=bi.getServiceInfos();
   Vector siv=sis.getServiceInfoVector();
   Enumeration e2=siv.elements();

   //loop through the binding templates until a bt is found
   BindingTemplate bt=null;
   while(e2.hasMoreElements() && bt == null){
      ServiceInfo si=(ServiceInfo)e2.nextElement();

      //find the service's bindingDetail that corresponds to the
      //priceCheck tModel
      BindingDetail bd=proxy.find_binding(null, si.getServiceKey(), bag2,0);
      Vector btv=bd.getBindingTemplateVector();
      Enumeration e3=btv.elements();

      //the tModel is hidden in the TModelInstanceDetails
      while(e3.hasMoreElements() && bt == null){
         bt=(BindingTemplate)e3.nextElement();
         Vector tmidv=
            bt.getTModelInstanceDetails().getTModelInstanceInfoVector();
         Enumeration e4=tmidv.elements();

         TModelInstanceInfo tmii=null;
         while(e4.hasMoreElements() && tmii==null){
            tmii=(TModelInstanceInfo)e4.nextElement();
            if(! tmii.getTModelKey().equals
               ("UUID:B04E3710-4D86-11D5-83B9-AFF41F112FA2")){
               tmii=null;//continue
            }
         }
         if(tmii == null){
            bt=null; //continue
         }
      }
   }
}
```

The code then extracts the accessPoint element and invokes the priceCheck Web service. Sample code follows, continuing from the previous code sample:

```
//invoke the priceCheck WSDL proxy, passing access point, item
PriceCheckService pcs = new PriceCheckService();
PriceCheckPortType pcpt =
```

```
              pcs.getPriceCheck(new java.net.URL(bt.getAccessPoint().getText()));
         AvailabilityType at = pcpt.checkPrice(sku); //some SKU
         double price = at.getPrice();
         //cache the price in a data structure that associates the businessKey
with the price
  . . .
```

If the Web service invocation fails, the code should check to see if the InstanceDetails element includes a URL to a service implementation definition. If it does, the code should retrieve the service implementation definition and generate a proxy for that service. The Web service is invoked again, this time using the network address generated in the proxy.

All the responses from the invocations of all the Web services are aggregated, and the list of businessEntities is sorted by the response price of the priceCheck. The company with the best bid price is the winning supplier. Other policies, such as fastest delivery, can also be used to determine the winning supplier.

The final stage of the reorder process is to send a PO to the winning supplier. The actual order placement portion of the application has been built with a proxy generated from the POSubmission service interface standard defined by the e-Torus orderSuite standard WSDL. Like the priceCheck proxy, all the POSubmission proxy needs is a network address to send the purchase order. This information is supplied by the UDDI entries of the supplier that won the priceCheck bid. This is done by issuing a find_service message, passing the businessKey of the winner of the priceCheck bid and a tModelBag containing the UUID of the POPlacement TModel.

UDDI4J code to find the POSubmission service of the best price from priceCheck is as follows:

```
String winnerBusKey=...

//set up a TModel bag referencing the POSubmission TModel
TModelBag bag=new TModelBag();
Vector v=new Vector();
//UUID of POPlacement tModel
v.addElement("UUID:5FE30870-A4C3-11D5-AF98-BD95162D3AC9");
bag.setTModelKeyStrings(v);

//find the po submission service for the winning business
ServiceList sl=proxy.find_service(winnerBusKey, bag2, null, 0);
```

Once the POSubmission service of the winning bidder is found, the remainder of the code identifies the bindingTemplate in a fashion similar to the priceCheck portion of the code. Finally, the accessPoint information is extracted from the bindingTemplate element and given to the Web service proxy to invoke the POSubmission Web service of the supplier that won the priceCheck bid. Of course, if the invocation of the Web service fails, with an error that indicates a network failure, the application tries to extract a service implementation definition from the bindingTemplate, and if successful, uses the information in the service implementation definition to invoke the Web service.

UDDI4J code to find the POSubmission bindingTemplate of the best price from priceCheck and then invoke the Web service is as follows:

```
//traverse the bindingTemplates structure looking for the binding template for
//the POSubmission TModel
BindingTemplate bt=null;
Vector btv= bs.getBindingTemplates().getBindingTemplateVector();
Enumeration e2=btv.elements();

//the tModel is hidden in the TModelInstanceDetails
while(e2.hasMoreElements() && bt == null){
   bt=(BindingTemplate)e2.nextElement();
   Vector tmidv=bt.getTModelInstanceDetails().getTModelInstanceInfoVector();
   Enumeration e3=tmidv.elements();

   TModelInstanceInfo tmii=null;
   while(e3.hasMoreElements() && tmii==null){
      tmii=(TModelInstanceInfo)e3.nextElement();
      if(! tmii.getTModelKey().equals
         ("UUID:5FE30870-A4C3-11D5-AF98-BD95162D3AC9")){
         tmii=null;//continue
      }
   }
   if(tmii == null){
      bt=null; //continue
   }
}

//invoke the POSubmission WSDL proxy, passing access point, purchase Order
. . .
```

With that algorithm, SkatesTown can find the best supplier for a given part at a given moment in time and place a purchase order with that supplier by invoking a Web service.

The complete program listing for the dynamic find appears in Listing 7.1. Note that some of the program uses utilities to find the tModelKey and other features. Further, the code does not actually invoke the Web services, but rather prints out the access points of the Web services it would have invoked.

LISTING 7.1   The Dynamic Find Program

```java
package ch7.ex2;

import java.util.Vector;
import java.util.Enumeration;
import java.util.Hashtable;

import com.ibm.uddi.UDDIException;
import com.ibm.uddi.client.UDDIProxy;
import com.ibm.uddi.response.*;
import com.ibm.uddi.datatype.binding.*;
import com.ibm.uddi.datatype.service.BusinessService;
import com.ibm.uddi.datatype.binding.TModelInstanceDetails;
import com.ibm.uddi.util.TModelBag;

import ch7.UDDIExamples;
import ch7.Util;

import ch6.ex1.*;

/**
 * Chapter 7 - UDDI examples
 *
 * The final example of dynamic find.
 * SkatesTown does a find for all businesses that
 * implement PriceCheck and POSubmission.
 * Based on best priceCheck, a PO is placed with the
 * supplier with the best price.
 *
 */
public class DynamicFindSkatesTown extends UDDIExamples{

/**
 * Place a PO with the supplier that has best priceCheck price.
 * Use the supplier's POSubmission service to place the PO.
 */
public static void main (String args[]) {
    try {

        if(args.length != 1){
            System.err.println("Usage: DynamicFindSkatesTown SKU");
            System.exit(1);
        }

        String sku = args[0];
```

LISTING 7.1   Continued

```
    //set up the UDDIProxy
    setSecurity();

    UDDIProxy proxy = new UDDIProxy();
    proxy.setInquiryURL(inquiryAPI);
    proxy.setPublishURL(publishAPI);

    String priceCheckTModelKey =
        Util.getTModelKey("E-Torus order suite PriceCheck Service Interface
➥Definition");
    String POSubmissionTModelKey =
        Util.getTModelKey("E-Torus order PO Submission Service Interface
➥Definition");

    //set up the TModelBag to refer to both the priceCheck and POSubmission
    //suppliers must support both standards in order to be invoked by the
    //application
    TModelBag bag = new TModelBag();
    Vector v = new Vector();

    //UUID of priceCheck tModel
    v.addElement(priceCheckTModelKey);
    //UUID of POSubmission tModel
    v.addElement(POSubmissionTModelKey);
    bag.setTModelKeyStrings(v);

    //finds all businesses that have a service implementing the priceCheck
➥tModel
    BusinessList bl = proxy.find_business(bag, null, 0);

    //print it
    System.out.println("List the businesses that support priceCheck and
➥POSubmission");
    Util.printElement(bl);

    //loop through the BusinessList, invoking the priceCheck web service
    //Find the binding that matches the TModel for priceCheck
    TModelBag bag2 = new TModelBag();
    Vector v2 = new Vector();
    //UUID of priceCheck tModel
    v2.addElement(priceCheckTModelKey);
    bag2.setTModelKeyStrings(v2);
```

LISTING 7.1   Continued

```
        Vector biv = bl.getBusinessInfos().getBusinessInfoVector();
        Enumeration e = biv.elements();
        while(e.hasMoreElements()){
            BusinessInfo bi = (BusinessInfo)e.nextElement();
            ServiceInfos sis = bi.getServiceInfos();
            Vector siv = sis.getServiceInfoVector();
            Enumeration e2 = siv.elements();

            //loop through the binding templates until a bt is found
            BindingTemplate bt = null;
            while(e2.hasMoreElements() && bt == null){
                ServiceInfo si = (ServiceInfo)e2.nextElement();

                //find the service's bindingDetail that corresponds to the
➥priceCheck tModel
                BindingDetail bd = proxy.find_binding(null, si.getServiceKey(),
➥bag2,0);
                Vector btv = bd.getBindingTemplateVector();
                Enumeration e3 = btv.elements();

                //the tModel is hidden in the TModelInstanceDetails
                while(e3.hasMoreElements() && bt == null){
                    bt = (BindingTemplate)e3.nextElement();
                    Vector tmidv =
➥bt.getTModelInstanceDetails().getTModelInstanceInfoVector();
                    Enumeration e4 = tmidv.elements();

                    TModelInstanceInfo tmii = null;
                    while(e4.hasMoreElements() && tmii==null){
                        tmii = (TModelInstanceInfo)e4.nextElement();
                        if(! tmii.getTModelKey().equals(priceCheckTModelKey)){
                            tmii = null;//continue
                        }
                    }
                    if(tmii == null){
                        bt = null; //continue
                    }
                }
            }

        //invoke the priceCheck WSDL proxy, passing access point, item
        PriceCheckService pcs = new PriceCheckService();
        PriceCheckPortType pcpt = pcs.getPriceCheck(new
➥java.net.URL(bt.getAccessPoint().getText()));
```

LISTING 7.1   Continued

```
        //for now, avoid the invocation as the various company's services are
➥not set up
        //AvailabilityType at = pcpt.checkPrice(sku); //some SKU
        //double price = at.getPrice();

        //cache the price in a data structure that associates the businessKey
➥with the price

        //instead of invoking, print
        System.out.println("Business: " + bi.getNameString() + " priceCheck
➥service accessPoint: " + bt.getAccessPoint().getText());
    }

    //use the cache to determine the winning supplier's business Key based on
➥best price
    //force the issue by choosing We Make It Inc.
    String winnerBusKey = Util.getBusinessKey("WeMakeIt Inc.");

    TModelBag bag3 = new TModelBag();
    v = new Vector();
    v.addElement(POSubmissionTModelKey);
    bag3.setTModelKeyStrings(v);
    ServiceList sl = proxy.find_service(winnerBusKey, bag3, null, 0);
    ServiceInfos sis = sl.getServiceInfos();

    //take first matching service, normally one would check for multiples and
➥choose best
    ServiceInfo si = (ServiceInfo)sis.getServiceInfoVector().firstElement();
    ServiceDetail sd = proxy.get_serviceDetail(si.getServiceKey());
    BusinessService bs =
➥(BusinessService)sd.getBusinessServiceVector().firstElement();

    //traverse the bindingTemplates structure looking for the binding
➥template for
    //the POSubmission TModel
    BindingTemplate bt = null;
    Vector btv =  bs.getBindingTemplates().getBindingTemplateVector();
    Enumeration e2 = btv.elements();

    //the tModel is hidden in the TModelInstanceDetails
    while(e2.hasMoreElements() && bt == null){
        bt = (BindingTemplate)e2.nextElement();
```

LISTING 7.1 Continued

```
        Vector tmidv =
➥bt.getTModelInstanceDetails().getTModelInstanceInfoVector();
        Enumeration e3 = tmidv.elements();

        TModelInstanceInfo tmii = null;
        while(e3.hasMoreElements() && tmii==null){
            tmii = (TModelInstanceInfo)e3.nextElement();
            if(! tmii.getTModelKey().equals(POSubmissionTModelKey)){
                tmii = null;//continue
            }
        }
        if(tmii == null){
            bt = null; //continue
        }
    }

    //invoke the POSubmission WSDL proxy, passing access point, purchase
➥Order
    System.out.println(" PO service accessPoint: " +
➥bt.getAccessPoint().getText());

        // Handle possible errors
  } catch (UDDIException e) {
    DispositionReport dr = e.getDispositionReport();
    if (dr!=null) {
        System.out.println("UDDIException faultCode:" + e.getFaultCode() +
            "\n operator:" + dr.getOperator() +
            "\n generic:"  + dr.getGeneric() +
            "\n errno:"    + dr.getErrno() +
            "\n errCode:"  + dr.getErrCode() +
            "\n errInfoText:" + dr.getErrInfoText());
    }
    e.printStackTrace();

    // Catch any other exception that may occur
  } catch (Exception e) {
      e.printStackTrace();
  }

  System.exit(0);
  }
}
```

Summary

In this chapter, you have seen the role of service registries such as UDDI within a service-oriented architecture. We examined UDDI in some depth, reviewing its core data structures and APIs. We examined the use of UDDI for private service registries and how Version 2.0 enhances UDDI. Finally, we examined the convention of registering WSDL-based Web services in UDDI and how that convention can make UDDI effective for doing dynamic location of Web services at runtime.

To this point, we have covered the fundamental concepts of Web services: XML, SOAP (including the Axis implementation of the SOAP specification), various additional aspects of Web services such as security, Web services description using WSDL, and Web services registries focusing on UDDI.

In the next chapter, we survey the current set of tools and middleware supporting Web services.

Interoperability, Tools, and Middleware Products

IN THIS CHAPTER

We've learned, and watched SkatesTown learn, an awful lot about Web services so far. The last couple of chapters in particular dealt with getting Web service clients and servers talking to each other in a world where you don't necessarily have *a priori* knowledge of the systems you connect with. This chapter will dig a bit deeper into the subject of interoperability, especially the issues which arise when you're tying together systems that use completely different platforms and/or programming languages. We'll begin by discussing interoperability in general, and then move on to explore using some of the other available toolkits to integrate with SkatesTown's services.

Interoperability: The "Holy Grail" of Web Services

The promise of Web services lies in the ability to exchange data and functionality among partners using standards-based messages—and arbitrary technological infrastructures. This not only buys you the ability to talk to many new partners, but it also allows both you and your partners to avoid "lock in" to a particular development platform. If you've defined your outward-facing interface to the world in terms of XML, SOAP, WSDL, and UDDI, you can feel free to switch from Java to .NET and back again (not that you would be likely to really do so!) without ever disturbing your ongoing Web service–enabled partner relationships. Ideally, you should also be cleanly insulated from worrying about achieving interoperability with different implementations of these protocols. Sounds great, doesn't it? Well, in reality, things aren't always quite so easy—but they are getting there.

The SOAP 1.1 specification is somewhat vague about several issues and provides a lot of flexibility (too much, many say) in the way you choose to do things. For instance:

- Section 5 of the spec (which, if you'll recall from Chapter 3, "Simple Object Access Protocol (SOAP)," is the data encoding section) states that null values can be represented *either* by the omission of the XML element representing that value, *or* by an XML element with the xsi:nil attribute present and set to true (this is the ninth rule in the "rules for encoding" list in section 5.1). This can be a problem in several ways—an example would be a toolkit that doesn't care about the names of method arguments, but uses ordinal positioning of the XML-encoded arguments to match them up with the real arguments. If this toolkit has published a service, and another toolkit decides to simply omit arguments whose values are nil when making a request, we have a potential problem.

- The spec is not clear (in section 7) about how to represent a Remote Procedure Call (RPC) response with a void return type and no output parameters. This could, for instance, be an empty SOAP envelope, an empty SOAP method response element, or even an HTTP 204 (No Response) with no SOAP envelope. If faults are generated when toolkits don't see the version they expect, this could cause some trouble.

- It's not apparent how to decide exactly which body entry in an RPC-encoded message is the main one that would be processed as an RPC method call. (There can be multiple body entries in the case of multi-ref serialization, for instance.)

- It is possible with SOAP to make messages self-describing, in which case metadata about the contents of the message (for example, the `xsi:type` attribute on RPC parameters) is embedded within the message itself. It is equally possible to assume that such metadata is conveyed out-of-band in a Web Services Description Language (WSDL) document or via some other means. The problem is that when you're talking to new parties, it might be hard to know what is appropriate, especially because some toolkits rely heavily on the `xsi:type` element's presence in messages on the wire.

- The `SOAPAction` HTTP header is somewhat vaguely defined in section 6.1.1 of the spec as representing the "intent" of the message. Some packages don't use this value at all, and others absolutely require it for dispatching to the correct service. `SOAPAction` has been a classic source of interoperability problems.

These issues, and others like them, can provide some serious challenges when you are trying to create a world where any SOAP implementation can talk to any other with a reasonable chance of success. If we decide to use `xsi:nil="true"` for nulls, and you decide to omit elements, there is a significant chance that we might encounter some problems communicating. How can we begin to resolve these issues and move towards a maximally interoperable world? Luckily, there are at least two different answers to that question—and both are making great progress in parallel.

The Soapbuilders Community

Clearly, two things need to occur if different implementations hope to truly interoperate. The first is that the developers of these implementations need to be able to talk to each other in order to iron out problems. The second is that there need to be some sort of compatibility tests that can be used to judge whether a particular implementation can successfully talk to another.

A solution to both of these issues appeared in the form of the soapbuilders list, a very active community of SOAP developers on Yahoo. The list was started in January 2001 by Tony Hong of Xmethods as a place for SOAP implementers to congregate and a forum in which to discuss interoperability issues.

Some of the particular areas that have been discussed fruitfully on soapbuilders include:

- The various ways to express arrays in WSDL (see Chapter 6, "Describing Web Services").

- Differences in dealing with `xsi:type` requirements in various engines.

8

INTEROPERABILITY

- Issues regarding encoding styles, and whether it's reasonable to assume a default `encodingStyle` in the absence of an explicit `encodingStyle` attribute.

- The purpose and structure of the `SOAPAction` HTTP header.

- Lots of others—you can read the soapbuilders archives (see the resources section at the end of the chapter) yourself to check it out, and join the list to follow it into the future.

The Interoperability Lab

As we mentioned, soapbuilders also provided the community with a testing ground for SOAP implementations, in the form of the Interop Lab. You can find the Web pages for the tests at `http://www.xmethods.net/ilab`.

The Interop Lab represented the coming together of a number of similar efforts—Dave Winer and the Userland software team had developed a SOAP Validator test suite, there was discussion of how to do conformance tests on the various mailing lists, and the Apache SOAP development team had also been sketching out a test suite with Microsoft's .NET group.

Essentially, the Interop Lab tests involve a set of services that everyone agrees to implement at their nodes. The first round of these services test basic SOAP compatibility and the ability to serialize and deserialize simple data types. Many of the tests are of the form "echo this [string, integer, float, etc]"—this tests basic SOAP connectivity (envelopes are parsed and understood), deserialization (I understood the data you passed), and serialization (I sent you back something which you recognize is the same as what you passed me).

Several notable benefits have arisen from the xmethods/soapbuilders Interop Lab:

- Many bugs in various implementations have been found and fixed—in most cases quite rapidly due to quick feedback from the community.

- There is a well-known place that developers and consumers can visit to get a snapshot of the current state of features and bugs in a variety of implementations.

- When a new package comes out, the developers can rapidly get feedback from many sources telling them how their implementation plays well (or doesn't) with others.

- In May 2001, an Interopathon event was held at NetWorld/Interop in Las Vegas. Many vendors, both small and large, showed up for a couple of days of interoperability demonstrations and conversation. More than 20 different implementations supplied implementations of a simple digital marketplace system, simulating bidding and buying items from each other.

We're still ironing out a lot of issues, but the progress towards interoperability that has been achieved in a very short time is remarkable. There are more than 50 SOAP 1.1 implementations as of August 2001, and they're all learning to play well together.

The soapbuilders community is now working on higher-level interop testing, which includes testing of SOAP header functionality and WSDL as well as core SOAP. The community is also integrating an automatic (SOAP-based, of course) registry service for new endpoints—so when an implementation changes, they can make a SOAP call to the Interop Lab hub that will cause all the other implementations to re-run their tests against that endpoint.

The W3C: The Emergence of a Standardized SOAP

In parallel with the grass-roots, developer-driven soapbuilders effort, the *World Wide Web consortium (W3C)* is in the midst of a standardization effort to give SOAP a good cleaning. The W3C are the standards-keepers for XML technologies—XML, XSL, X-Link, XSLT, and so on.

The W3C XML Protocol group has two interesting qualities; first, it's the largest group (more than 70 members) that the W3C has yet run, and second, unlike most other W3C activities, the group is doing almost all its work in the open—there is a public mailing list, `xml-dist-app` (for "XML distributed applications"), on which most of the group discussions take place. Both of these points serve to illustrate the high level of interest in SOAP and Web services across the Internet community.

As we mentioned in Chapter 3, the XML Protocol group has produced a working draft of the SOAP 1.2 spec, which attempts to address some of the issues that were somewhat unclear in SOAP 1.1. The new spec can be found at the URL listed at the end of the chapter. SOAP 1.2 is divided into two specifications: part 1, the "Messaging Framework," is really core SOAP. Part 2, "Adjuncts," describes all of the normative, but non-core, portions of the SOAP framework, such as the HTTP binding and the RPC convention.

The new spec includes:

- A more precise definition of the SOAP processing model, which clears up some ambiguities regarding `MustUnderstand` in particular. This is in section 2, specifically sections 2.4 and 2.5.

- A standardized way of providing information about exactly which headers were the cause of a `MustUnderstand` fault (section 4.4.2).

- A versioning model that should make it possible for processors to negotiate version conflicts, or at least be more clear about what specific versioning problems occur (section 4.1.2 and the referenced versioning fault).

- An Abstract Model (actually a separate document) of the SOAP processing system, which begins to clarify how SOAP systems work in general, and can be used as a design tool.

8

INTEROPERABILITY

The XML Protocol group keeps an up-to-date list of issues against the SOAP spec, which you can find linked from the group Web page. Many of these issues, due to the public nature of the group's work, have also benefited greatly from conversations on the soapbuilders list. The combination of a dedicated group within the W3C and a vibrant community of developers who are actually building SOAP software today will hopefully result in a standard that not only addresses the concerns raised by SOAP 1.1, but also makes migration and implementation easy.

Future work within W3C might include standardizing WSDL and clearing up the ambiguities and issues with that spec, as well. If the work in these areas is successful, the resulting recommendations would go a long way toward resolving many of the interoperability problems that have been experienced thus far.

The Larger Web Services Landscape

Throughout the book, we've been focusing on Apache Axis, which has made sense because SkatesTown is an Axis-based enterprise. Now it's time to take a brief spin through some of the other technologies and packages that are helping to shape the Web services landscape.

Who are all these vendors with SOAP implementations? The remainder of this chapter will cover a brief overview of the breadth of the space, and then we'll dive into a few of the more popular SOAP implementations and see if we can get them to interoperate with SkatesTown.

> **NOTE**
>
> We've mentioned it before, but one point deserves to be stressed again—Web services are an emerging technology, and things in the space are moving fast. The list of implementations we put forth here is incomplete and will be out of date a few days after it's been typed! One of the best ways to keep track of all the activity is to use the very medium in which the technology is growing—the Web. A large and vibrant community of developers, thinkers, and users are all working together to shape the evolution of the emerging Web service-enabled net. At the end of the chapter, you'll find a list of some of our recommended Internet resources for finding out more and getting involved in the evolution of Web services.

Who's Building SOAP Systems?

If you ask the current crop of pundits to predict the major forces in the enterprise computing space over the next few years, you will find a remarkable consistency to their answers. Pretty much all of them agree that the platforms to watch are J2EE and .NET. Both platforms provide a solid infrastructure for doing distributed application development. So, what's going on in these two worlds with Web services?

The J2EE World

More and more vendors in the J2EE space are integrating Web services into their application server offerings, including:

- *BEA*—WebLogic Server, BEA's J2EE offering, now integrates support for SOAP, WSDL, and UDDI as of version 6.1.
- *IBM*—WebSphere began including a SOAP toolkit based on Apache SOAP version 2.1 in May 2001. IBM's strong commitment to Web services hasn't flagged since then, and they are continually pushing the space further along.
- *Iona*—Iona's XMLBus technology looks extremely promising. It includes both the ability to integrate with their J2EE environment (iPortal) and also a standalone Web service container.
- *Macromedia*—JRun is a lean, fast, and inexpensive J2EE server that was distributed by Allaire and has, as of 2001, been brought into Macromedia's product suite. Macromedia has released a Web service technology preview that runs on top of JRun 3.1 and plans to fully integrate Web services into JRun in version 4.0.

Other Java packages don't strictly fall under the J2EE umbrella, such as:

- *GLUE*—Produced by The Mind Electric, GLUE is a neat little package. We'll delve into it a bit deeper later in the chapter.
- *SOAP-RMI*—A team at the University of Indiana built this slot-in RMI replacement which uses SOAP as its underlying transport for remote invocation. The work they've done on making things fast (with a custom pull-based XML parser) and transparent is quite impressive.

Got .NET?

No survey of the Web services landscape would be complete without mentioning Microsoft's .NET initiative, perhaps the most sweeping Web services story out there.

We'll go into a lot more detail a bit later in the chapter, when we demonstrate how to integrate .NET Web services with our running examples. For now, suffice it to say .NET is Microsoft's attempt to fully internet-enable application development on the Windows platform.

Other Languages and Environments

Of course, plenty of other SOAP implementations are out there as well, written in everything from straight C to high-level scripting environments.

C/C++

Several C/C++ implementations are available, including Scott Seely's SimpleSOAP, eSOAP by Rosimildo da Silva, and SOAP packages from SQLData and Idoox.

Perl

Developmentor, one of the original SOAP instigators, built an early package in Perl. ActiveState has another in their PerlEx product.

One of the more popular SOAP libraries is SOAP::Lite, a Perl package by Paul Kulchenko. We'll cover this comprehensive and easy-to-use package in some detail also.

Python

The popular scripting language Python has a few SOAP packages available—they include SOAP.py by Cayce Ullman, the Zolera Soap Infrastructure (ZSI) by Rich Salz, and Adam Elman's SOAPy.

And That Ain't All, Folks...

Frontier, a popular scripting environment developed by Userland software (one of the originators of SOAP), has a SOAP implementation built in, along with support for XML-RPC, a somewhat simpler XML-based RPC protocol.

There are a couple of PHP implementations (PHP is an HTML scripting environment similar in some ways to Active Server Pages), two in Smalltalk, and several JavaScript clients.

There are also SOAP implementations designed for the PocketPC, and even a couple written in XSLT!

As you can see, there's a lot of SOAP out there! Although we can't cover all these implementations in detail, let's take some time to dig a little deeper into just a few of the more popular Web service toolkits available at the time of this writing. We'll see how easy it is for SkatesTown to connect their services and clients to partners who use completely different platforms. Note that though we've only selected a few of the available packages due to space constraints, many of those mentioned here (and on the sites you'll find at the end of the chapter) are equally powerful and easy to use.

SOAP::Lite—Web Services in Perl

In case you are not familiar with Perl (the Practical Extraction and Report Language), it is a very popular interpreted language designed by Larry Wall back in the late 1980s. Perl is in some ways like a cross between a scripting language and a 3GL.

The Perl motto is "there's more than one way to do it," and in keeping with that idea the language is *extremely* flexible in terms of its syntax and semantics. We're not going to describe the language itself here, so you might not get much by looking at the examples unless you already speak Perl. If you don't, you might consider spending a little time to learn it from one of the many books or Web sites penned by Perl devotees—it's always good to learn new things, and Perl is almost guaranteed to get you thinking in new and interesting ways about programming. For now, we're going to focus on showing you some SOAP examples using SOAP::Lite, a Perl package written by Paul Kulchenko.

OK—let's dive right in and take a look at a simple client written with SOAP::Lite for the PriceCheck service we built back in Chapter 6. This is the kind of thing that an online store built with Perl might use to access SkatesTown's pricing information via SOAP:

```
use SOAP::Lite;

print SOAP::Lite ->
        uri('urn:X-SkatesTown') ->
        proxy('http://localhost:8080/axis/services/PriceCheckService') ->
        checkPrice('SKU-NUMBER') ->
        result;
```

Looks pretty simple, no? The first line is just like a Java import statement; it loads the SOAP::Lite package so we can use it. The rest of the code is one virtual line calling into SOAP::Lite to perform a SOAP call. The uri() sets the body URI on the resulting SOAP message—this is identical to setting the namespace argument in the Axis client API. The proxy() tells SOAP::Lite where to actually send the message—this is equivalent to Axis' concept of endpoint. Clearly, checkPrice() is the method we're calling, and result gets us the result value.

Using WSDL with SOAP::Lite

The previous example included knowledge of the network endpoint for the service, and the namespace URI of the SOAP RPC element. This is a fine, and very dynamic, way to access services, but you might not want to specify this stuff every time you make a SOAP request. As you know, WSDL can help us out by encapsulating all that sort of service metadata into one package. SOAP::Lite has a very simple syntax for using WSDL to access a service:

```
use SOAP::Lite;
print SOAP::Lite ->
        service('PriceCheck.wsdl') ->
        checkPrice('SKU-NUMBER') ->
        result;
```

SOAP::Lite will dynamically generate a virtual proxy object for your service by parsing the WSDL file, and then allow you to call any of the operations using the standard -> syntax. This demonstrates some of the flexibility of the Perl language—because of Perl's dynamic nature, you don't have to know the available method signatures of the service up front in order to write calls like this one, or the previous one. Whereas in Java, the compiler would have to confirm that checkPrice() is a valid method on the service object, and that it indeed takes a single string argument, you have no such restriction in Perl. At runtime, the language interpreter will look for a checkPrice() method in the service after the WSDL file has been parsed.

Autodispatch

Another way to use the library to make SOAP calls is to activate the autodispatch feature. To do this, you register a package as an `autodispatch` handler. Once you've done that, any time Perl encounters an unknown function call, it will attempt to resolve it using the `autodispatch` handler you defined. In this case, we set it up so that for any such function, we attempt to call a SOAP method on a designated server. Let's take a look:

```
use SOAP::Lite +autodispatch =>
  proxy => 'http://localhost:8100/axis/Calculator.jws';

print "2 + 7 = " . add(2, 7) . "\n";
```

Because there's no `add()` function defined in the Perl code, the SOAP::Lite `autodispatch` handler is called, which results in a SOAP call to our specified endpoint, invoking the Calculator service automatically.

We feel a lot of kudos are due to Paul, who built a very comprehensive and easy to use package that fits very cleanly with the Perl style. Not only does SOAP::Lite speak SOAP, but also XML-RPC and Jabber (two other simple XML protocols). It also works across multiple transports (including SMTP and raw TCP), handles MIME attachments, and can deal with basic security. If you're a Perl developer interested in Web services, you owe it to yourself to learn more about SOAP::Lite. (Incidentally, a copy of SOAP::Lite is included with every copy of the ActivePerl distribution of Perl for Windows.)

The .NET Web Service World: A Brief Primer

What is .NET, exactly? Well, for all the details, you'll have to go and get one of the many .NET books or surf to http://www.gotdotnet.com—it's a big package. But we can skim the surface, and in particular, show you a few examples of using .NET to build and consume Web services that work alongside SkatesTown.

The .NET framework consists of three major components: a common runtime environment for managed code, a set of core class libraries to provide common features, and a Web-oriented infrastructure called ASP.NET. These work together to provide a unified developer experience that Microsoft hopes will be compelling enough to make it the premier platform for application development. Let's explore what the package holds.

Common Language Runtime

Most of the code you'll deal with in .NET exists in something called the Common Language Runtime (CLR). The CLR is very much like Java's virtual machine—CLR components are implemented as bytecode that runs in a managed environment. This means that the runtime will automatically handle such tasks as garbage collection, threading, security, and loading classes. The really cool thing about the CLR in relation to Web services is that any CLR component can be exposed as a Web service. That means that classes/objects written in C++, Visual Basic, C#, or even COBOL can be easily exported for use across the intranet or the Internet.

C#, incidentally, is Microsoft's new C++-derived object oriented programming language. It has a lot in common with Java, as we'll see when looking at some sample code.

Core classes

The .NET framework class library is akin to the Java class libraries—the classes therein provide services related to the following:

- Data types, structures and collections
- I/O, including files, network access, and streams
- XML manipulation
- GUI programming
- Security

ASP.NET

The final major component of the .NET framework is ASP.NET, the .NET foundation for building Web applications. ASP.NET is both the natural evolution of Active Server Pages and also a new set of tools and infrastructure for building Web UI and Web services.

A PriceCheck Client in .NET

Let's take a look at building a simple Web service client in the .NET framework. Note that we're using the .NET framework beta 2, which is the current version as of August 2001. By the time this book is in your hands, a later .NET release will probably be available.

A lot of this process is even easier using Visual Studio .Net, but for the client examples, we'll use the command line tools; these are all you'll have available if you're a Windows 98 user, and we want to maximize the potential that you'll be able to run these examples on your machine.

Because the .NET Web service tools are all deeply integrated with WSDL, we'll start by building a client for the SkatesTown price check service that we built WSDL for back in Chapter 6.

To begin, we want to build a proxy class to access the service based on the WSDL file, so to do, so we'll use the `wsdl.exe` tool that is provided in the `Bin/` directory of the .NET framework SDK installation. (You should have this directory on your path as a result of the .NET SDK setup.) The command and its results are as follows:

```
C:\MyServices> wsdl PriceCheck.wsdl
```

```
Microsoft (R) Web services Description Language Utility
[Microsoft (R) .NET Framework, Version 1.0.2914.16]
Copyright (C) Microsoft Corp. 1998-2001. All rights reserved.

Writing file 'C:\MyServices\PriceCheckService.cs'.
```

Now you'll notice a `PriceCheckService.cs` file in the current directory. This is the C# source code which was generated by the tool—take a look at it if you're interested; it's pretty straightforward. You'll notice that this class has exactly the same methods we exposed in the Java backend class—it is a *proxy* for our Web service, and can now be used by any .NET application to get at our price check functionality. The file also contains a C# version of our `AvailabilityType` class.

We could have also chosen to generate the code in other languages, such as Visual Basic, but we'll stick with C# for our purposes, because it's very comprehensible to Java developers.

To invoke the service, we'll need to wrap the service proxy class in a small bit of user interface so that we can use it. We open our favorite text editor and build the following C# code:

```
using System;

class PriceCheckClient {
    public static void Main(string [] args)
    {
        PriceCheckService stub = new PriceCheckService();
        availabilityType avail = stub.checkPrice("947-TI");
        Console.WriteLine("There are " + avail.quantityAvailable +
                " items available, ");
        Console.WriteLine("at a price of $" + avail.price.ToString() +
                " each. ");
    }
}
```

Clearly, this is an extremely basic little demonstration, with a hard-coded SKU argument. The point is simply to show you how using stubs in C#/.NET is similar to the same activity in Java/Axis.

We compile the application like so:

```
C:\MyServices> csc /r:System.Web.Services.dll /r:System.Xml.dll /r:System.dll
➥PriceCheckClient.cs PriceCheckService.cs
Microsoft (R) Visual C# Compiler Version 7.00.9254 [CLR version v1.0.2914]
Copyright (C) Microsoft Corp 2000-2001. All rights reserved.
```

csc is the C# compiler/linker. The /r flag tells the compiler to reference the indicated assemblies (an *assembly* in .NET is a packaged set of components, in a DLL or an EXE) and make their contents available during the build process. This command should result in creating a PriceCheckClient.exe in your current directory. If you run that program, you'll be able to make priceCheck requests from our SkatesTown database (see Figure 8.1).

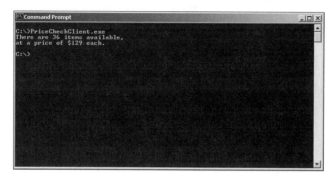

FIGURE 8.1
PriceCheck with a .NET client.

Exposing .NET Web Services: Package Tracking for SkatesTown

OK, so building clients in .NET is pretty simple. What about exposing services? Luckily, with ASP.NET, it's even easier. (For you Windows 98 folks out there, sorry; this section won't work for you. .NET's server-side components are strictly for Windows 2000 or later. If you want to try the example, please make sure you install the .NET server side components plus all prerequisites.)

Let's bring our attention back to SkatesTown for a minute for this example. For some months now, SkatesTown has been using ShipIt, Inc. to send their packages. All the shipping has happened behind the scenes, but some customers have (quite reasonably) been asking for the ability to get tracking numbers for their shipments. We'll walk you through a simple version of what ShipIt might do on its .NET-based system to provide this feature to SkatesTown.

We'll simulate the package-tracking application in .NET by building an .asmx file. As you'll see, ASMX files are a lot like JWS files—they allow you to drop source code into a regular old text file, and have the ASP.NET framework automatically compile and execute the code for you on demand. There are some differences, though.

For one thing, all ASMX files require a WebService directive at the beginning of the file, which tells the infrastructure what language the source code is expressed in and the name of the class which implements the actual service. ASMX files can use any of the supported .NET languages for Web services (right now that's C#, Visual Basic, and Jscript).

Another difference is that ASMX files automatically support an HTTP GET and POST binding as well as access via SOAP. This means you can call an ASMX-based Web service with just a browser, passing arguments as query string parameters or form fields. Of course, this doesn't allow for the kind of rich data mapping you can do with XML, but it is handy for services that only deal in simple types.

Let's take a look at a simple service implemented as an ASMX file; see Listing 8.1. This service does two things. First, it will generate new tracking numbers, which tie to instances of a PackageInfo class. Second, it will return a tracking report for an existing tracking number. (This example is not a real simulation of the situation—it has been vastly simplified to let us focus more on the Web service infrastructure and less on the application logic.)

LISTING 8.1   C# Package Tracking Service in .NET

```csharp
<%@ WebService Language="C#" Class="ShipIt.PackageService" %>

using System.Collections;
using System.Web.Services;
using System.Web.Services.Protocols;

namespace ShipIt {
    // Here's the "PackageInfo" class which represents
    // a package in transit.
    //
    public class PackageInfo {
        static int maxHops = 4;
        int hop = 1;

        int trackingNumber;

        string currentReport;

        public PackageInfo(int id)
        {
            trackingNumber = id;
            currentReport = "<h2>Tracking Report<h2> <ul>";
        }

         // Move a package one hop and update its
         // tracking log. Don't bother if it has
         // reached its destination.
        public void movePackage() {
            if (hop < maxHops) {
                currentReport += "<li>Arrived at hop #" + hop + "\n";
```

LISTING 8.1 Continued

```
                hop++;
        } else if (hop == maxHops) {
            currentReport += "<li>Delivered!\n";
            hop++;
        }
    }

    public string getTrackingReport() {
        return currentReport + "</ul>";
    }
}

[WebService(Namepace="http://BWS-ShipIt.com/")]
// This is a SOAP RPC service
[SoapRpcService]
public class PackageService : WebService {

    static int lastTrackingNumber = 1;
    static Hashtable trackedPackages = new Hashtable();

    [WebMethod]
    public int getTrackingNumber() {
        PackageInfo pi = new PackageInfo(lastTrackingNumber);
        trackedPackages.Add(lastTrackingNumber, pi);
        return lastTrackingNumber++;
    }

    [WebMethod]
    public string getTrackingReport(int trackingNumber) {
        PackageInfo pi =
            (PackageInfo)trackedPackages[trackingNumber];
        if (pi != null) {
            // For the sake of example, we move the package
            // one "step" each time this is called.
            pi.movePackage();
            return pi.getTrackingReport();
        }
        return "No such tracking number!";
    }
}
}
```

8

INTEROPERABILITY

We have a C# class; this is nothing new. But the text in the square brackets ([ ]) is different; these directives tell the runtime any meta-information we need to convey. In this case, we're marking each method that we would like to publish as a [WebMethod]. This tells the runtime that the marked methods are accessible via Web service interfaces from outside and should be included in a WSDL description of the service. There is also a [SoapRPCService] directive at the top of the class. It indicates that our class is a SOAP service that uses section-5 encoded payloads and the SOAP RPC style. By default, all .NET services are document-oriented and use literal encoding (see Chapter 3 for an explanation of the difference between literal and section-5 encoding). The [WebService] directive just above that one allows us to specify the namespace of the service (this will be the namespace of the body elements for the service requests and responses).

The getTrackingNumber() method creates a PackageInfo object and inserts that PackageInfo into a hashtable, indexed by an integer tracking number that we return to the user.

When generateTrackingReport() is called, we first look up the PackageInfo that was previously stored. Then, for the purposes of this simple example, we call movePackage() to move the package one hop along the path to its destination. Clearly, in the real world, getting a tracking report for a package does not actually move it closer to its destination (much as we might wish otherwise), but this is a quick and easy way for us to simulate movement. Once the PackageInfo has been moved, we simply return the tracking report generated by the PackageInfo class.

To deploy this service, just drop it into your Web hierarchy. For our purposes, we've put it in Inetpub\wwwroot\shipit\PackageService.asmx. Figure 8.2 shows what happens if we hit it with a browser.

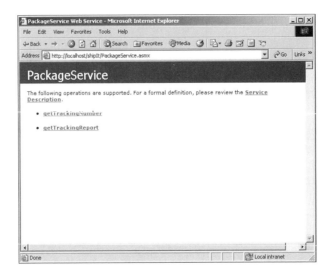

FIGURE 8.2

Browser view of .NET Package service URL.

This page is automatically generated for us by .NET, and it allows us to not only see what methods are available, but actually test the methods in the browser as well. You can try this out by clicking the method names to get a page that looks like Figure 8.3.

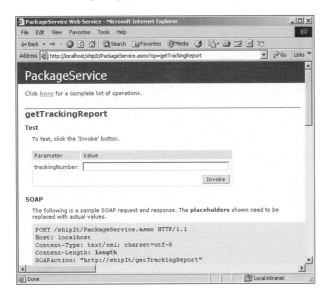

FIGURE 8.3
Expanded view of the getTrackingReport *method.*

You'll find the source code to this service in the dotnet/ directory of the examples. If you deploy this service to the location shipIt/PackageService.asmx on your machine (in other words, drop the file in IIS under wwwroot/shipIt/packageService.asmx), you'll be able to try an example that integrates this service into SkatesTown's order processing system. You'll find the example in Chapter 8 under the examples directory in the bws webapp. Just bring up the modified order page, submit the request, and you'll get a package tracking number along with your invoice (see Figure 8.4). Clicking the tracking link will get you a package tracking report.

We encourage you to examine the Java source for the tracking page (track.jsp) to see how this works; as usual, we've just got a JSP front end which calls a remote Web service. The only difference is that for this one, the service is provided by .NET—interoperability in action!

The modified POSubmissionClient class is also worth a look; it works exactly the same way as we've traditionally been writing this class for our examples—in particular, it doesn't expect the SOAP body (the returned invoice) to change in order to carry the tracking number. Rather, we do that by introducing a SOAP header that is plucked out by the client.

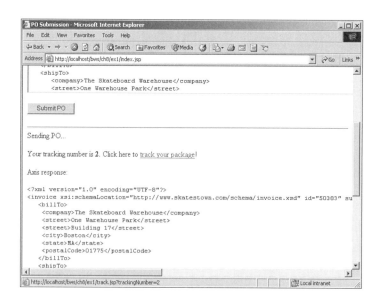

FIGURE 8.4

PO results with package tracking.

The header is produced by a modified version of the POSubmission service—
TrackingSubmission.java, which you'll find in com/skatestown/services alongside the
normal POSubmission class.

GLUE: Another Take on Java Web Services

GLUE, a commercial package put out by The Mind Electric, is another Java SOAP engine,
built to be small and fast. It includes its own custom XML parser, Electric XML, in addition to
the standard SOAP/WSDL functionality we know and love. GLUE is a very nice package, containing a lot of features that make Web service programming simple. Let's spin through a few
quick examples with this toolkit, too.

The GLUE Client for SkatesTown's `InventoryCheck` Service

Listing 8.2 shows how a client for our InventoryCheck service might appear in GLUE.

LISTING 8.2   GLUE Client for InventoryCheck Service

```
import electric.registry.Registry;

public class GlueCheck
  {
  public static void main( String[] args )
    throws Throwable
```

LISTING 8.2   Continued

```
  {
    if (args.length != 2) {
      System.out.println("usage: java GlueCheck <SKU> <quantity>");
      System.exit(-1);
    }

    // URL to WSDL of web service to invoke
    String url =
"http://localhost:8080/bws/services/InventoryCheck.jws?wsdl";

    // invoke using array of Objects
    Boolean result = (Boolean) Registry.invoke( url, "checkInventory",
                        new Object[]{ args[0], Integer.parseInt(args[1]) } );

    System.out.println( "result = " + result );
  }
}
```

This looks quite similar to the Axis client code we're used to looking at. GLUE uses the `Registry` class to dynamically invoke services (and also to publish them, as we'll soon see)—in this case, it's acting as the equivalent of Axis's `ServiceClient`. The `invoke()` method on GLUE's `Registry` class is static, so we pass the URL on each `invoke()` instead of embedding it within a `ServiceClient` instance as we would in Axis. Also, you'll note that the URL points to the `InventoryCheck` WSDL as opposed to the service endpoint itself. GLUE will dynamically parse the WSDL and invoke the service at the URL specified in the service description.

Exposing Services with GLUE : Package Tracking Take 2

GLUE also has a built-in HTTP server, similar to the `SimpleAxisServer` we talked about in Chapter 4, "Creating Web Services." Publishing a Java class as a Web service in GLUE is really simple—look at the `main()` method in Listing 8.3. (The rest of the code implements the same package tracking app we built in .NET earlier—and again, the Java version of the `PackageInfo` class is available in the `examples` directory.)

LISTING 8.3   Simple Web Service in GLUE (Using the Built-in HTTP Server)

```
import electric.registry.Registry;
import electric.server.http.HTTP;
import java.util.Hashtable;

public class TestService {
    private int lastTrackingNumber = 1;
    Hashtable trackingReports = new Hashtable();
```

8

INTEROPERABILITY

LISTING 8.3   Continued

```java
    // Synchronized just in case
    private synchronized int getNextTrackingNumber()
    {
      return lastTrackingNumber++;
    }

    // Move a package one hop and update its
    // tracking log. Don't bother if it has
    // reached its destination.
    public void movePackage(PackageInfo info)
    {
        if (!info.delivered())
            info.moveOneHop();
    }

    public int getTrackingNumber(String invoiceID) {
        PackageInfo info = new PackageInfo(invoiceID);
        int trackingNumber = getNextTrackingNumber();
        trackingReports.put(trackingNumber, info);
        return trackingNumber;
    }

    public String generateTrackingReport(int trackingNumber) {
        PackageInfo info = trackingReports.get(trackingNumber);

        // For the sake of example, we move the package
        // one "step" each time this is called.
        movePackage(info);

        // Now return the tracking report
        return info.getTrackingReport();
    }

    /**
     * The main() method is the actual meat of web service
     * publishing. First we start an HTTP server listening
     * on port 8081, then we publish the service, and
     * we're done!
     */
    public static void main(String [] args) {
        HTTP.startup("http://localhost:8081/glue");

        Registry.publish("urn:packageTracking", new TestService());
    }
}
```

Note that once you call the `publish()` API, the server creates background threads which listen for requests. Therefore, you won't be able to stop the server until you interrupt those threads (typically with Ctrl+C).

Other Features in GLUE

GLUE also provides some nice additional features, such as:

- Customization of serialization/deserialization via decorated XML Schema files. This feature lets you annotate a schema with metadata telling GLUE how to turn the XML into Java.
- A custom XML parser, ElectricXML, which is designed to be small and fast.
- A Java<->XML persistence engine.
- A built-in servlet engine.

It's definitely another package worth checking out.

Summary

Although SOAP on its own does not provide a complete interoperability framework, it does give you a foundation on which to build, and we expect that foundation to improve due to the efforts of both standard bodies such as the W3C and communities like soapbuilders. Higher-level standards such as WSDL help a lot, and luckily, Web service software is beginning to integrate WSDL support as a standard feature.

Clearly, you have many tools to choose from when you're dealing with SOAP, and more are becoming available every day. The momentum is huge, and we hope this chapter has given you a glimpse into the level of activity in the Web services arena, and a few specific examples of how easy it can be to make Java talk to C# talk to Perl.

As you'll see in Chapter 9, many people and organizations are contributing to that momentum and taking the service-enabled Web to the next level, in a variety of directions.

Resources

Specifications, groups, and communities:

- *SOAP version 1.2 specification*—http://www.w3.org/2000/xp/Group/#drafts
- *W3C XML Protocol group*—http://www.w3.org/2000/xp/Group/
- *The soapbuilders community*—http://groups.yahoo.com/groups/soapbuilders
- *WSDL group*—http://groups.yahoo.com/groups/wsdl
- *Xmethods Interoperability Lab*—http://xmethods.net/ilab

8

INTEROPERABILITY

- *SoapWare.org*—http://www.soapware.org/
- *IBM's DeveloperWorks Web service area*—http://ibm.com/developerworks/webservices/
- *The DevelopMentor SOAP mailing list*—http://discuss.develop.com/soap.html

These are the implementations we mentioned in the text. A much more comprehensive list of implementations is available on soapware.org:

- *SOAP::Lite (Perl)*—http://www.soaplite.com/
- *PerlEx (Perl)*—http://www.activestate.com/Products/Components/PerlEx/
- *.NET (C#, VB, C++)*—http://gotdotnet.com/
- *GLUE (Java)*—http://www.themindelectric.com/products/glue
- *WASP (Java)*—http://www.idoox.com/
- *Apache SOAP (Java)*—http://xml.apache.org/soap
- *SOAP RMI (Java)*—http://www.extreme.indiana.edu/soap/index.html
- *Iona's XMLBus (Java)*—http://www.xmlbus.com/
- *SOAPPy (Python)*—http://sourceforge.net/projects/pywebsvcs
- *SimpleSOAP (C++)*—http://scottseely.com/soap.htmeSOAP (C++), http://www.embedding.net/eSOAP
- *WASP for C++ (C++)*—http://www.idoox.com/products/waspc/index.html

Future Concepts

IN THIS CHAPTER

It is always difficult, especially where technology is concerned, to try to predict the future. This chapter, therefore, will only try to present some interesting concepts about where the authors see the future of computing taking us, as it relates to Web services. We will cover topics such as *ontologies* 📖 and the *Semantic Web* 📖, *software agents* 📖, *peer to peer* 📖 computing, *grid computing* 📖, and embedded Web services. Each of these topics can be the subject of a book on its own, so we clearly do not expect to cover them in detail. We will, however, try to give an indication of the relevance of these technologies to Web services. While doing so, we hope to generate enough interest in your mind to cause you to investigate these topics in more depth.

Computing as a Utility

Current trends seem to be pointing toward a future where computing will be viewed as a utility, in a model similar to electrical power or cable TV. The early indications came with the development of the *Application Service Provider* 📖 (ASP) model. ASP companies basically rent computing on their own platform to consumer companies who generally pay on a monthly subscription basis. Although it can be thought of as computing as a utility, the ASP model actually is somewhat restricted in the choice of platforms and in the choice of application functionality, among others.

For a better model of computing as a utility, the scenarios would look something like this:

- *Personal computing*—Dean Carroll, SkatesTown CTO, arrives at his hotel room. There is a plug in the wall, next to the electrical and phone outlets, labeled *Computing*. It takes a standard plug type. He plugs in his PDA (laptop, or any other computing platform). A network connection is automatically established. As he goes about doing his work, his local software agent (machine resident) finds the services that he is going to need, based on where he is and what he is about to do. (See the section "Software Agents" later in this chapter.) These could be software services if, for example, he is trying to collaborate with some colleagues in a different city (see the section "Peer-to-Peer Computing later in this chapter), or hardware services, if, for example, he needs to run a stress simulation on the latest board design. (See the section "Grid Computing" later in this chapter.)

- *Enterprise computing*—On the SkatesTown factory floor, a new manufacturing robot is brought in and plugged into the computing grid. After a short initialization period, it finds a controller, requests and receives a set of tasks, and starts working on them in coordination with all the other robots. On that same factory floor, as data from dealers, customers and suppliers comes in, it is processed and interpreted as requiring a change in the specs of the bearings being used in the wheels of the *MAXX* model (see Chapter 7, "Discovering Web Services") . The controller finds a design and simulation Web service, submits new requirements, and receives updated specs. As soon as these come in, the robot tasks are updated, and new bearings are ordered. This is done by finding supplier

Web services, in a process similar to the example described in Chapter 7's section "Putting It All Together: WSDL-Based UDDI and Dynamic Find," and combining them with shipping and insurance Web services, making sure that the ordered materials arrive at the shipping dock in time for the manufacturing run.

It can be argued that most of these tasks could be done by a combination of manual labor and custom applications and tools, using current technologies. Although this is true, the combination of system embedded intelligence, seamless integration of all the tasks, and lack of human involvement in the process of integration makes these scenarios remarkable. In the next sections, we will explore some of the technologies that will make this possible.

Web Services Everywhere: The Vision

As the previous examples illustrate, the manifestation of the global conceptual vision of Web services is relatively simple: A need is triggered in a system, whether through human intervention or through external automated triggers. This need is translated into one or more formalized requests through some intelligent interfaces. These requests make their way into the grid/ network and are routed intelligently to other entities that can act as possible fulfillers. The requestors and potential fulfillers negotiate a set of mutually satisfactory terms and the need is serviced. This simple cycle is shown in Figure 9.1.

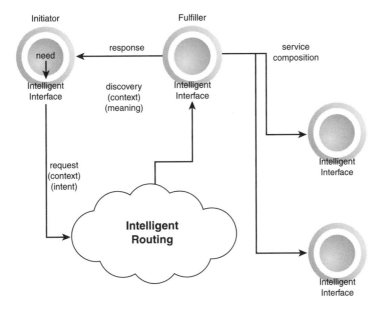

FIGURE 9.1

The Web services request-response cycle.

This general flow can be implemented using different architectural models, with two extremes being the ones we'll call the *centralized* and *peer* models.

The Centralized Model

In the centralized model (Figure 9.2), some relatively well-known public or private (also global or local) brokering services are central to the architecture. Entities wishing to provide services will make themselves known to these brokers, and entities seeking services will transmit their requests to the brokers. Brokers will have varying levels of intelligence built into them, allowing them to learn from experience, for example, in order to provide better matching capabilities to the incoming requests. Although the term *broker* implies an active role in putting requestor and provider together, with some possible benefit to the broker, we are including static services registries like UDDI (see Chapter 7) in this general category. A typical scenario would be for a requestor to discover one or more potential providers through the global broker, and maybe for one or more of these potential providers to discover and compose sub-services of their own through some private or local brokers in order to fulfill the request.

The current WSDL and UDDI technologies (discussed in Chapters 6, "Describing Web Services," and 7, "Discovering Web Services") are sufficient for design time (static) browsing, and some instances of runtime (dynamic) discovery of services. The next step in service description and discovery, however, will have to go beyond the level of syntactic *Interface Definition Languages* (such as WSDL) and taxonomies (such as used by UDDI) to incorporate a layer of intelligence and semantics that is required for true intervention-less interoperability.

The Peer Model

In the peer model (Figure 9.3), no central brokers or registries exist, but each node (or peer) in the network has its own forwarding list. This list can be based on results learned from previous experience, can be pre-built on initialization, can be a standalone external registry, such as the ones in the centralized model, or a combination of all these.

A typical scenario would be for a requestor to forward a request to a restricted set of peers, based on capabilities that these peers have declared or that the requestor has learned about them. Each of these peers in turn can either be a potential provider or intelligently forward the request to another set of their peers, based on experience or capability. This cycle is repeated until a provider is found or some kind of preset timeout or forwarding level (time to live) is reached. Again, current technologies such as SOAP Intermediaries, as discussed in Chapter 3, "Simple Object Access Protocol (SOAP)," and WSDL can be used to implement a basic level of this kind of architecture, but they lack the next level of intelligence and semantics to make them truly and seamlessly interoperable with no necessity for user intervention.

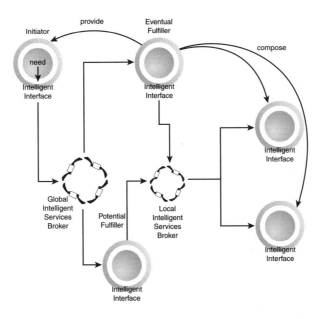

FIGURE 9.2

The Web services centralized model.

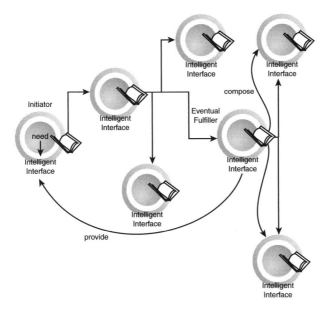

FIGURE 9.3

The Web services peer model.

Further Variation

Although, as mentioned, these two models might be extremes on the spectrum, Web services architectures will probably end up being a combination of the two, with independent peer nodes looking to some well-known brokers as needed.

In addition to the maturing of the Web services model, there will be increasing levels of complexity and variation in the different components of this vision, as current technologies mature and new technologies are created. For example, the process of expressing a need into some form of formal machine-understandable request can have various levels of automation and intelligence. The origin of the trigger itself can also be examined: Is it due to a user's action, an automated set of business rules, a networked device such as a cell phone, or an autonomous software agent's decision?

The process of routing that request to possible fulfillers is also a prime target for enhancement. In addition to the relatively static keyword searching provided by UDDI, for example, how can the meaning of the request be maintained and conveyed to different services, and how can the original intent of the requestor be maintained?

The same can be said about the process of negotiation between requestor and potential providers: What negotiation protocols will they follow, and how will they ensure that they are speaking the same language and that the terms they are using, although similar, actually mean the same thing? How will they prove their identities to each other and come to an enforceable agreement? Finally, in a recursive model of "Web services all the way down," how can these services in turn automatically find and compose other services to fulfill a particular goal? And, once the agreement is in place, how and where will the service be executed?

Although some of the mechanisms that answer these questions are already in place—and covered in this book, such as SOAP and SOAP Intermediaries (see Chapter 3), encryption and digital signatures (see Chapter 5, "Using SOAP for e-Business"), WSDL (see Chapter 6), and UDDI (see Chapter 7)—or are being developed, we are far from the full vision of automated Web services everywhere. The next few sections will introduce some of the current work on these topics.

Ontologies and the Semantic Web

Today's Web was originally designed for use by humans. It is now slowly being extended for use by machines. It can be argued, however, that all the current work in standards, protocols, interoperability stacks, and so on, are just facilitating the placement of bits on the wire, with little effort going to actually facilitate understanding the meaning of those bits and the content of the data being transmitted. If the eventual goal of the evolution of the Web is to facilitate integration between human tasks and machine tasks, meaning and context must be taken into account. At a minimum, it is clear that fundamental tasks, such as searching and task interoperability in general, would be greatly enhanced if the machines being used for the tasks had some semantic knowledge of the data.

Resource Description Framework

Of course, there have been numerous discussions as to what constitutes *understanding*. Leaving such discussions for the academic types, let us at least agree to require that Web content, and resources in general, be marked up with some structured metadata that can be processed by machines. Metadata is an essential component that facilitates tasks in everyday life and would be similarly beneficial if introduced into the framework of Web services. XML is the first installment that makes structured metadata possible, but XML is just a language, and another layer of meaning has to be built on top of it. This layer of meaning is increasingly being exposed through the *Resource Description Framework (RDF)* 📖, an application of XML developed under the auspices of the *W3C* 📖.

RDF, as the name implies, is a framework that enables you to describe resources as structured metadata, and to exchange and reuse these resources in various possibly unrelated applications. It is built on the three concepts (see Figure 9.4):

- *Resource*—A resource is anything that can be uniquely identified by a Uniform Resource Identifier (*URI*) 📖. Resources usually have a reference ID for cross-referencing. Resources also have properties.

- *Property*—A property is a resource that has a name and can be used to describe other resources. A property is defined as a property-type with a corresponding value. The value can either be an atomic value such as a string, or another resource. A collection of properties that refer to the same resource is called a *description*. RDF is essentially a mechanism to represent resources and their descriptions in a direct labeled graph (DLG). Property-types are namespace qualified, allowing different groups to use the same property-type name to mean different things.

- *Statement*—A statement is a combination of a resource, a property-type, and a value.

A simple RDF example that defines a small subset of the graph shown in the Figure 9.4 follows:

```
<?xml version="1.0"?>
<rdf:RDF xmlns:rdf="http://www.w3.org/1999/02/22-rdf-syntax-ns#"
   xmlns:books="urn:X-Skatestown.com/rdf/books/">
   xmlns:who="urn:X-Skatestown.com/rdf/who/">

   <rdf:Description rdf:ID="Book_012"
      rdf:about="http://skatestown.com/books/webservices">
```

9

```
        <books:title>Building Web Services</books:title>
        <books:author rdf:HREF="#Person_213"></books:author>
        <books:editor rdf:HREF="#Person_014"></books:editor>
    </rdf:Description>

    <rdf:Description rdf:ID="Person_213"
        rdf:about="http://skatestown.com/people/dean">
        <who:name>Dean Carroll</who:name>
        <who:email>dean@skatestown.com</who:email>
    </rdf:Description>

</rdf:RDF>
```

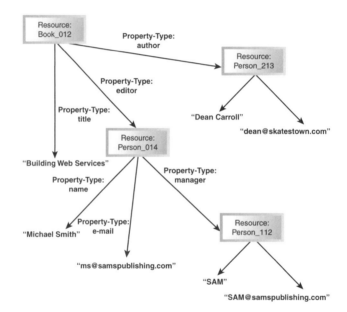

FIGURE 9.4

An example resource definition for a Web services book authored by Dean Carroll and published by Sams.

Ontologies

Having a framework to define resources and their relationship is only the first step. What if different applications use different identifiers from different RDF definitions to mean the same thing? In order for them to interoperate and exchange information, they must reconcile the two terms. This next layer of meaning on top of RDF is provided by ontologies. The term *ontology*, originally meaning "concerned with the nature and relations of being" (Merriam-Webster), has been abused by different communities. In general AI circles, it has come to mean a document containing a set of formal definitions of relations among terms. Common ontologies contain a taxonomy of terms and a set of inference rules to make sense of the terms, usually in machine readable form. This will allow a computer, for example, to know that the terms *author* and *creator*, found in two different schemas, actually mean the same thing when applied to a book.

Currently, the most comprehensive and widely accepted effort that extends XML and RDF for specifying and manipulating ontologies is DAML+OIL, a joint effort combining a DARPA sponsored language, DARPA Agent Markup Language (DAML), and a European Union Information Society Technologies sponsored language, Ontology Inference Layer or Ontology Interchange Language (OIL). DAML+OIL defines core resources and a large number of ontologies. For more information, see the "Resources" section at the end of this chapter.

Relating RDF to Web Services

Semantic Web technologies are clearly tightly related to Web services technologies and will eventually converge. For example, Web services providers can currently describe their services through WSDL and then register them on a UDDI registry, categorizing them according to some taxonomy in order to be discovered. Whereas current service descriptions and UDDI taxonomies are intended for human readers to browse, Web service descriptions and registries that are marked up using RDF and ontologies as a semantic enhancement to WSDL and UDDI can be machine readable, enabling dynamic discovery and invocation of services by software through common terminology and shared meaning. Several projects are underway to semantically enhance Web services by exploring the concept of marked up Web services. For example, the latest effort from DAML is DAML-S, a DAML-based Web service ontology to allow marking up Web services for automated discovery and invocation by software agents. Again, more references are provided in the "Resources" section.

Software Agents

The next requirement to facilitate integration between human tasks and machine tasks is for some intelligence to be injected at all levels into the overall system. This intelligence will probably take the form of intelligent software agents. Software agents will be able to process the resource definitions and ontologies being developed. The concept of software agents has been around for a few decades. Some might even consider it a failed experiment. However, as we examine the concepts, it will become clear that it was merely an idea that was ahead of its time, and that the infrastructure that makes it possible and useful is now available. The following is by no means intended to cover the topic. By last count, there are at least several dozen good books on the topic, and hundreds of articles. What we will attempt to do, however, is a quick introduction to the topic in the context of enabling the future of Web services.

We can categorize the concepts of intelligent software agents several ways. To add to the confusion, over the years, several definitions of *software agent* have evolved amidst the discussions of what constitutes intelligence. The two following definitions illustrate the wide spectrum of definitions:

> "Intelligent agents are software entities that carry out some set of operations on behalf of a user or another program with some degree of independence or autonomy, and in so doing, employ some knowledge or representation of the user's goals or desires."—IBM Intelligent Agent Definition (1996)

> "An agent is a computational process that implements the autonomous, communicating functionality of an application."—FIPA and OMG Architecture (1999)

As you can see, the first definition includes the concepts of a user and the user's goals and considers agents to be extensions of users. The second definition considers agents to be a pure functionality embedded within an application or computer program, with no mention or concept of users.

The software agent community has converged on a set of characteristics of autonomous software agents, some of which are considered to be important (autonomous, reactive, learning, goal-oriented, communicative), and others of which are still being debated (mobile, flexible, character):

- *Reactive*—Responds in a timely fashion to changes in the environment
- *Autonomous*—Exercises control over its own actions
- *Goal-oriented*—Does not simply act in response to the environment
- *Temporally continuous*—Is a continuously running process
- *Communicative*—Communicates with other agents, perhaps including people
- *Learning*—Changes its behavior based on its previous experience
- *Mobile*—Is able to transport itself from one machine to another
- *Flexible*—Actions are not scripted
- *Character*—Has a believable "personality" and emotional state

Relating Software Agents to Web Services

It becomes clear from the previous list of definitions that the concept of an autonomous intelligent software agent is closely aligned with that of a Web service, in that an agent can either be exposed as a Web service, or as the interface to a Web service, or can be part of the functionality of a Web service. Consider a functionality that is continuously running, communicative, goal-oriented, and that learns from its previous interactions, and then describe it in a WSDL document and publish it to UDDI; the result is a Web service, regardless of whether it's an intelligent airline booking service that uses a mainframe based process or a wine recommendation service based on a learning adaptive intelligent software agent.

An essential element of both the agent and Web services concepts is that of identity and integrity. In other words, how can agents prove who they are, and how can they prove the integrity of the information they are delivering? As in Web services, the use of digital signatures is starting to become more accepted in software agent applications, which leads us to another important topic: agent communications. Again, most of the standards that have emerged in agent communications have come out of DARPA funded efforts, in this case, the DARPA Knowledge Sharing Effort.

Notably, two specifications, one for knowledge representation and the other for knowledge exchange and message passing, have been established. The first specification is Knowledge Interchange Format (KIF), used to represent information to be exchanged between agents. KIF is an implementation-agnostic specification that is a prefix version of first order predicate logic supporting the definition of four types of expressions: terms (objects), sentences (facts), rules (inference), and definitions (constants). KIF knowledge bases are a set of sentences, rules, or definitions. The simple example shown here represents the information that SkatesTown is a company that sells skateboards:

```
(exists ((?x Sells) (?y Company) (?z Item))
        (and (Name ?y SkatesTown) (Name ?z SkateBoards)
             (Agent ?x ?y) (Object ?x ?z)))
```

The second specification is an Agent Communication Language, called Knowledge Query and Manipulation Language (KQML). Whereas KIF is used to represent knowledge, KQML is a message-format and message-handling protocol used for sharing information between agents at runtime. This is done through an extensible set of constructs called *performatives* because their intent is to cause an agent to perform a specific action. Expressing KIF and KQML in XML should be a relatively straightforward task, and efforts are underway to accomplish that ability. For example, the KQML message shown here, in which a user agent requests a registration for a SEMC-sponsored conference, illustrates the similarity of a KQML performative to a SOAP message:

```
(request
    :sender    (:name user_agent@tcp://skatestown.com:2020)
    :receiver (:name register_agent@tcp://semc-consortium.org:7070)
    :ontology semc
    :language SL
    :protocol semc-request
    :content
    ( action register_agent@tcp://semc-consortium.com:5001
       ( register
          (:venue conf#3434)
          (:arrival 10/02/2001)
          (:departure 10/15/2001)
          (:infos  ( ))
)))
```

Peer-to-Peer Computing

Peer-to-Peer (P2P) computing is a new name for a relatively old model of computing that is coming back into favor. Looking back at its history, the Internet started as a network of computers (peer nodes) communicating directly with each other. As computing models, software and network architectures grew and evolved, different models of computer networking were used, resulting in different architectures, most of them with the distinct notions of a client and a server, roles being performed by different machines. The pendulum seems to have swung back to the notion of a node on the network being both a client and a server at different times and in different contexts. This has been spurred by the availability of cheap computers, cheap bandwidth, cheap data storage, and idle processor cycles. We can then define P2P computing as computing through direct collaboration between nodes (without resorting to an intermediary such as a server), including the sharing of data, processing cycles, and resources, such as storage and printers. Within an organization, this has the advantage of relieving some of the load off the servers. Outside organizational boundaries, the P2P model will enable computing and sharing of resources in unstructured environments where it makes no sense to have servers.

P2P computing has been made famous by the Napster court battles and is mainly known as a model for file sharing. In fact, P2P is a full-fledged model of distributed computing that enables collaboration, intensive computation, resource sharing, and so on. Currently, however, most P2P applications provide only one type of service, and are usually limited to file sharing or instant messaging. Aside from the Napster example (which is not necessarily a true P2P model, because it requires the Napster servers as intermediaries, at least in the discovery phase), some common P2P applications include Gnutella and FreeNet, two information sharing applications; and Groove, a P2P collaboration platform that allows users to share a variety of tools in addition to files and documents.

Current P2P applications are also restricted in their deployment platform and differ significantly in their interfaces. There is, therefore, a definite need for an open platform for P2P application development to enable multiple kinds of device independent applications and services, and a common interface for interoperability. The JXTA project is the latest attempt to solve that problem, and it remains to be seen whether it succeeds. The core of the JXTA architecture is a set of three layers: the JXTA Core, which handles communications, peer establishment, and other low level services; the JXTA Services layer that handles common services, such as indexing, searching, and file sharing; and the JXTA Applications layer which is the deployment framework for applications such as e-mail, instant messaging, and file sharing. In addition, the JXTA architecture provides for a set of platform independent protocols for routing, discovery, binding, and other tasks.

Relating Peer Computing to Web Services

At its core, P2P computing is a kind of service-oriented architecture in that it enables distributed computing through the loose coupling of systems, with emphasis on resource (instead of service) description and dynamic discovery. The major differences are not technical, but in terms of maturity. Although Web service standards are maturing and their interoperability is being tested in open environments, P2P standards have been very slow to emerge, hindering their acceptance as a valid option for e-business. Eventually, however, both Web services and P2P standards will clearly converge, especially when it comes to service description (will P2P adopt WSDL?), dynamic discovery (will Web services adopt whatever mechanism the P2P community converges to?), and security.

Grid Computing

Whereas P2P computing emphasizes the concept of individual peers as collaborating computing entities and the concept of peer independence, grid computing is the latest movement in the field of distributed computing, distinguished from traditional distributed architectures by its emphasis on large-scale resource sharing that crosses organizational boundaries, and its emphasis on high performance computing. Grid computing is very closely related to traditional high-performance computing and cluster computing, topics that have been around for decades (it can be argued that the first clusters were developed by IBM in the 1960s to link mainframes and provide high performance computing). Grid computing, however, is different from clustering in that the concept tries to encapsulate clustered computing as a service (thus its relevance to Web services). The same trends that brought about P2P computing—cheap computers, bandwidth, and idle processors—also contributed to the emergence of Grid computing. An important additional contributing trend, however, has been the sharply increasing need for large-scale computation in scientific and military applications involving several different partnerships and virtual organizations.

According to one common definition, grid technologies have emerged in response to the "grid" problem, defined as: "coordinated resource sharing and problem solving in dynamic, multi-institutional virtual organizations." This concept of sharing computing resources across virtual organizations raises a large number of issues that traditional distributed computing does not address, but that are very close to some of the issues that Web services face: how to structure flexible just-in-time sharing relationships; how to structure fine grained access control over resources, taking care of local and global policies; and how to agree on quality of service, scheduling and co-allocation.

A well known, if relatively simple, example of shared computing resources through Grid computing, is the SETI@home project managed by the Space Sciences Laboratory of the University of California, Berkeley. SETI, the Search for Extraterrestrial Intelligence, is a scientific effort seeking to determine if there is intelligent life outside Earth. The SETI@home project is trying to detect signals of extra-terrestrial intelligence by scanning a 2.5MHz band of radio frequencies and processing them to look for narrowband signals. The computations involved would overwhelm the largest supercomputers in existence. In order to solve that problem, the project leverages idle processing power of millions of computers connected to the Internet, who contribute willingly to the project by downloading a client program that runs as a screensaver and processes data for the project when the computer is idle. On a periodic basis, the client connects to the SETI@home servers to upload results and download new data for the next computation. Although it can be considered a type of Grid computing, the SETI@home computations are well structured and involve all the computers asynchronously running the same client code.

More complex and technically significant examples of grid computing include the Grid Physics Network (GriPhyN), building a geographically distributed computational grid to perform some of the largest physics computations; the Data Grid project, a European project to build the infrastructure to handle large scale experiments with Petabyte-size datasets; and the Access Grid, another project aimed at building the infrastructure and software to enable highly distributed collaborations in conjunction with computational grids.

Relating Grid Computing to Web Services

Due to their critical interoperability requirements, grid architectures are moving toward standard protocols and a service-based architecture, although, again, Web service standards are at a more mature stage in their lifecycle. It is clear, however, that grid-type of computational power can be described and provided as a service, once all the issues with security, dynamic partnerships, access control and quality of service have been properly addressed.

Embedded Web Services

The final step in a "Web services everywhere" vision is the participation of devices in the Web services world. Devices in general can be either requestors or providers of Web services, if they are nodes on a network, or have access to nodes on a network. The concept of a URI is ideal for this, because URIs can point to any kind of resource, including devices. Traditional computing devices, such as laptops, desktops, and servers can obviously easily play those roles, but what about other (not necessarily computing) devices? On the next practical level, PDAs and cell phones can be considered as computing devices. It is easy to see how these smaller computing devices can be requestors of Web services. But they can also be providers of services. For example, my PDA might make available my calendar as a Web service for some restricted list of users. As we go down this chain of devices, even devices we think of as non-computing devices can participate in a Web services world. Think for example of your home entertainment center providing a list of Web services to be used by other devices on your home LAN.

In order to make this scenario a reality, we need to be able to embed Web services and Web services clients into these devices. In addition, it would be very useful if these devices could interact with registries such as UDDI. The computing power and capacity of devices has been growing in conjunction with the decreasing footprint of embedded Java and other computing platforms. These two lines have already crossed to the point where realistic Web services can be embedded in devices, devices can act as UDDI clients, as Web servers, and even UDDI registries can be embedded on some devices.

Pulling It All Together

As we mentioned in the introduction to this chapter, our intent was to quickly and briefly expose you to a variety of emerging and in some cases well-established technologies that are relevant to the future of Web services. Very soon, it will be technically possible to have an ecology of software and hardware Web services and a community of software agents living on various platforms, including small devices, monitoring users and systems needs, discovering and communicating with each other as peers, using ontologies to determine meaning and intent, discovering services as required by the issuing context, negotiating and generating just-in-time partnerships, composing services as needed, and fulfilling the initiating need (see Figure 9.5).

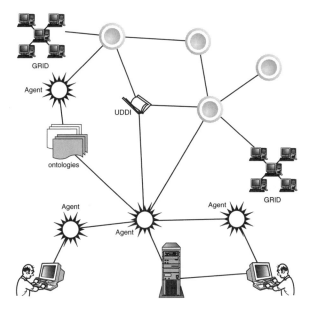

FIGURE 9.5
The possible future of interacting semantic Web services and agents.

Resources

Ontologies and the semantic Web:

- `http://www.semanticweb.org`
- `http://www.kr.org/top/projects.html`
- `http://www.w3.org/RDF`
- `http://www.daml.org`
- `http://www.daml.org/services`
- T. Berners-Lee, J. Hendler, O. Lassila, "The Semantic Web," *Scientific American* (May 2001). Available at `http://www.sciam.com/2001/0501issue/0501berners-lee.html`.
- E. Miller, "An Introduction to the Resource Description Framework." Available at `http://www.dlib.org/dlib/may98/miller/05miller.html`.
- R. Fikes and D.L. McGuinness, "An Axiomatic Semantics for RDF, RDF-S and DAML+OIL." Available at `http://www.daml.org/2001/03/axiomatic-semantics-030101.html`.

Software agents:

- `http://agents.umbc.edu`
- `http://www.cs.umbc.edu/kqml`
- `http://www.csee.umbc.edu/kif/`
- `http://www.fipa.org`
- S. Franklin and A. Graesser, "Is It an Agent, or Just a Program?: A Taxonomy for Autonomous Agents." Available at `http://www.msci.memphis.edu/~franklin/AgentProg.html`.
- D. Lange and M. Oshima, *Programming and Deploying Java Mobile Agents with Aglets* (Addison-Wesley, 1998).
- J. Bigus and J. Bigus, *Constructing Intelligent Agents with Java* (John Wiley & Sons, 1997).

P2P:

- `http://www.napster.com/`
- `http://setiathome.ssl.berkeley.edu/`
- `http://www.gnutellanews.com/`
- `http://freenet.sourceforge.net/`
- `http://www.groove.net`
- `http://www.jxta.org`

Grid computing:

- `http://www.gridforum.org/`
- `http://www.eu-datagrid.org`
- `http://www.griphyn.org/`
- `http://www-fp.mcs.anl.gov/fl/accessgrid/`
- `http://www.gridcomputing.com/`

Embedded Web services:

- `http://aladdin.grc.nasa.gov/`
- `http://www.csdmag.com/main/9803fe2.htm`
- `http://www.w3.org/Addressing/`
- `http://www.pocketsoap.com`

Glossary

Abstract Syntax Notation One (ASN.1)
A binary format for representing structured data.

Access Control List (ACL) The most common means by which a network security system decides to grant or deny access to network services. It is a list of the available services and the entities permitted to use each service.

accessor In the SOAP encoding, accessors are the link between a compound type and its constituent parts. The SOAP encoding uses XML elements to hold the parts of compound types. The accessors are either the element names (for structs) or the position of the elements (for arrays).

ACID The acronym for the four properties guaranteed by transactions: atomicity, consistency, isolation, and durability.

AdminClient A utility used to remotely deploy and undeploy Web resources to an Axis server.

AdminService A predeployed service in Axis that can be used to remotely deploy and undeploy Web resources such as services, handlers, and chains.

ADS IBM's Advertising and Discovery of Services, a simple, HTTP-based mechanism to advertise service descriptions on a Web page. For more information, see
`http://www.ibm.com/developerworks/library/ws-ads.html`. Compare with DISCO.

Application Service Providers (ASP)
Companies that host applications for other companies to use on a subscription basis, removing the need to buy software and allowing them to outsource part of their IT departments.

array   In the SOAP encoding, arrays are subclasses of the `SOAP-ENC:Array` schema type.

authentication token   A small packet of data, usually encrypted, that is passed between a client and a server, and that contains information establishing an identity.

Axis engine   The main entry point to the SOAP processor.

Axis (Apache Extensible Interaction System)   The Apache SOAP v3 project; see `http://xml.apache.org/axis`.

AxisFault   The Java object representing a fault (exception) generated during the processing of the SOAP message.

Base64   An encoding for binary data as described as a means of encoding email bodies in the IETF's MIME RFC. Base64 consists of only 64 of the 256 US-ASCII characters (A through Z, a through z, 0 through 9, +, /).

Bean-Managed Persistence (BMP)   Data transfer between an entity bean's variables and the resource manager managed by the entity bean.

BeanMapping   The mechanism in Axis used to serialize and deserialize XML elements into Java beans.

bind   An operation within a service-oriented architecture. The bind operation describes the set of tasks associated with a service requestor preparing to invoke and invoking a Web service provided by a service provider.

binding mechanism   The mechanism by which the abstract definition of a Web service (a `PortType`) is mapped into a concrete representation of the Web service within a given messaging protocol, network protocol, and encoding scheme. The WSDL binding element is the binding mechanism used for Web services.

body   The body of a SOAP message is contained within the `SOAP-ENV:Body` element.

business-to-business (B2B)   A characterization of interaction between businesses over the Internet. In a B2B interaction, applications between businesses communicate without human intervention being required during the interaction. Contrast with business-to-consumer (B2C)

business-to-consumer (B2C)   A characterization of interaction between a human being and a business over the Internet. In a B2C interaction, a human being, often using a Web browser, invokes applications provided by a business. Contrast with business-to-business (B2B).

canonicalization   A method for generating a physical representation, the canonical form, of an XML document that accounts for the permissible changes. For example, the order of attributes, tab processing, and a standardized code set are used to check the logical equivalence of two documents.

capabilities-based lookup   A type of SOA find operation in which the target of the search is described in terms of what operations, characteristics, and so on the target Web services need to fulfill. Contrast with a name-based lookup, where the target of the service is described in terms of a well-known name or other identifier such as an object ID.

CDATA section   CDATA sections are used to escape blocks of text containing characters that would otherwise be recognized as markup. CDATA sections begin with the string `<![CDATA[` and end with the string `]]>`. They can occur in all places where character data is allowed.

certificate authority (CA)   A trusted third party whose purpose is to sign certificates for network entities that it has authenticated. Other network entities can check the signature to verify that a CA has authenticated the bearer of a certificate.

certificate path   The line of ancestral CAs that signed a given PKI certificate. If a trusted signer is identified in the certificate path, that verifies the binding between the certificate's subject and the public key. The certificate path is also called the *certificate chain*.

Certificate Revocation List (CRL)   A list of certificates that have been revoked. This list is usually in a format specified by X.509.

certificate   A data record used for authenticating network entities such as a server or a client. A certificate contains standard information about its owner (called the *subject*) and the signing Certificate Authority (called the *issuer*), plus the owner's public key and the signature made by the CA. Network entities verify these signatures using CA certificates.

chain   An ordered collection of Axis handlers. A chain is also an Axis *handler*.

character reference   An escape sequence for characters in XML documents. The syntax for character references is an ampersand, followed by a pound/hash sign (#), followed by either a decimal character code or lowercase *x*, followed by a hexadecimal character code, followed by a semicolon. Example: the 8-bit character code 128 will be encoded in a UTF-8 XML document as `&#x80;`.

client proxy   A component on the client that acts as a substitute (or proxy) for the Web service. A client proxy presents a programming language–specific interface to be used by a client application to invoke the Web service and presents the response from the Web service in a programming language–specific manner back to the client. The term *client stub* is also used as a synonym.

client-config.xml   The Axis client-side configuration file.

compound type   In the SOAP encoding, compound types are composed of several parts, each of which has an accessor. These parts could be either simple or compound types.

concrete endpoint   An actual implementation of a Web service made available at a particular network address. A concrete endpoint is described using a WSDL `port` element.

connection-oriented messaging
Connection-oriented messaging requires that the sender and the recipient are both running and have a direct connection established between them. Also known as *direct messaging*.

Container Managed Persistence   Data transfer between an Entity Bean's variables and a resource manager managed by the Entity Bean's container.

control characters   Also known as non-whitespace control characters, these include the ASCII characters with codes 0 through 7, 9, 11, 12, or 14 through 31.

correlation ID   An identifier (usually a string) that is used to keep track of individual requests in a multistep series of Web services interactions.

declaration   The XML declaration is a processing instruction (PI) whose target is `xml`. It specifies the version of XML and, optionally, the character encoding in a document. Example: `<?xml version="1.0" encoding="UTF-8"?>`.

deploy.xml   A file used as input into the Axis `AdminClient` to deploy new Web resources such as handlers and chains.

deserialization   The process of generating a data structure from XML. Deserialization differs form parsing in that the data structure is typically focused on the logical structure of the document as opposed to its syntax.

direct messaging   See *connection-oriented messaging*.

DISCO   Microsoft's approach for using a simple, HTTP-based mechanism to advertise service descriptions on a Web page. For more information, see `http://msdn.microsoft.com/library/ default.asp?url=/library/en-us/ cpguidnf/html/cpconenablingdiscovery forwebservice.asp`. Compare with ADS.

dispatcher   An Axis handler that will locate and invoke the desired Web service.

document-centric   A document-centric view of processing a SOAP message occurs when the body of the SOAP envelope is viewed as an XML document rather than as an RPC call.

Document Object Model (DOM)   DOM provides an object-oriented view of XML documents by representing them as a hierarchy of objects mapped to XML markup (elements, attributes, text, comments, and so on).

ebXML   A standards body jointly initiated by The United Nations body for Trade Facilitation and Electronic Business (UN/CEFACT) and OASIS to standardize XML business specifications. ebXML intends to develop a technical framework that will enable XML to be utilized in a consistent manner for the exchange of all electronic business data.

element   A markup language term denoting the pairing of start and end tags.

embedded value   In the SOAP encoding, a value that is not independent; that is, a value embedded at the top level of the serialization.

Enterprise Application Integration (EAI)   A form of distributed computing where applications and business processes are combined to achieve higher goals. Although EAI can indicate integration both within and between organizations, we use EAI for intra-organizations in this book.

Enterprise Java Beans (EJB)   A component architecture for the development and deployment of object-oriented, distributed, enterprise-level applications. Applications written using the Enterprise Java Beans architecture are scalable, transactional, and secure.

entity   A named piece of information in an XML document. Internal entities are defined within the document. External entities have separate physical storage.

Entity Bean   An enterprise bean that represents persistent data maintained in a database. An Entity Bean can manage its own persistence or it can delegate this function to its container. An Entity Bean is identified by a primary key. If the container in which an Entity Bean is hosted crashes, the Entity Bean, its primary key, and any remote references survive the crash.

entity reference   Refers to the content of a named entity. The syntax for entity references is an ampersand (&), followed by the entity name, followed by a semicolon (;).

envelope   The SOAP envelope is the `SOAP-ENV:Envelope` element and its contents.

FTP (File Transmission Protocol)   A standard Internet protocol to exchange files on top of TCP/IP. FTP is often used to download programs and large files.

global chain   An Axis chain that is invoked for all Web services.

global.request   The name that should be used when defining the Axis *global chain* that is invoked to process the request message.

global.response   The name that should be used when defining the Axis *global chain* that is invoked to process the response message.

grid computing   A model of computation where clusters of machines at various locations on the network are harnessed to perform various high performance computations.

guaranteed message delivery   See *reliable messaging*.

handler   The basic building block inside Axis. It links Axis to existing back-end systems. Handlers are grouped into *chains*.

HeaderFault   An element of WSDL that describes how a SOAP fault message is communicated as a SOAP header.

headers   All SOAP headers are contained inside the `SOAP-ENV:Headers` element.

holder   The technique used to model in/out and multiple out parameters in Axis by wrapping the actual value in a class that can carry the modified value back to the requestor.

home interface   One of two interfaces for an enterprise bean. The home interface defines zero or more methods for managing an enterprise bean. The home interface of a Session Bean defines create and remove methods, whereas the home interface of an Entity Bean defines create, finder, and remove methods.

horizontal extensibility   Allows different parts of a SOAP message to be targeted toward different recipients along the message path. This is achieved through the use of SOAP intermediaries.

HTTP Basic Authentication (BASIC-AUTH)   An authentication mechanism in which a Web server authenticates an entity by extracting a user name and password from the HTTP request and comparing that data with existing user information stored in the web server.

HTTPR   A reliable messaging protocol using HTTP as a transport protocol, proposed by IBM; see `http://www.ibm.com/developerworks/webservices/library/ws-phtt/`.

HTTPS   Hypertext Transfer Protocol layered over the SSL protocol.

hybrid parsing   Combines push, pull, and one-step parsing to best serve particular scenarios.

independent value   In the SOAP encoding, all values that appear at the top level of the serialization are considered independent.

Inquiry API   A set of public non-authenticated operations that allows users to extract information from the UDDI Business Registry.

inspection   A level in the W3C discovery stack. Inspection is a technique of discovering the service description given that the details about the service, a service identifier or URL for example, is already known. Examples of inspection include ADS and DISCO.

instance   Also known as *XML instance* or *document instance*. Refers to an XML document as a specific instance from the set of possible documents allowed by a schema.

Interface Definition Language (IDL)   A language to describe function or object interfaces in a distributed computing environment, allowing compilers to generate proxy and stub code to marshal parameters between different computers. In Web services, the IDL of choice is WSDL.

interface repository   A central store of metadata about CORBA components' interfaces. This is a CORBA-specific implementation of the SOA services registry role.

intermediaries   Processing nodes on the SOAP message path that are different from the requestor and the final recipient of the message.

Internet Engineering Task Force (IETF)   The standards body that defines Internet operating protocols such as TCP/IP, URIs, and so on. The IETF's main documents are the RFCs.

J2EE Connector Architecture   An architecture for the integration of J2EE products with enterprise information systems. There are two parts to this architecture: a resource adapter provided by an enterprise information system vendor and the J2EE product that allows this resource adapter to be plugged in. This architecture defines a set of contracts that a resource adapter has to support to be plugged in to a J2EE product—transactions, security, and resource management.

Java 2 Platform Enterprise Edition(J2EE)   A meta-specification for developing and deploying enterprise applications with Java. J2EE platforms consist of a set of services, application programming interfaces (APIs), and protocols that provide the functionality for developing multitiered, Web-based applications.

Java Authentication and Authorization Services (JAAS)   A Java API that enables services to authenticate and enforce access controls on users. The reference implementation features a version of the standard Pluggable Authentication Module (PAM) framework and supports user-based authorization.

Java Community Processes   An open organization of international Java developers and licensees whose charter is to develop and revise Java technology specifications, reference implementations, and technology compatibility kits.

Java Cryptographic Architecture (JCA)   A framework for providing cryptographic capabilities to Java programs.

Java Cryptography Extension (JCE)   A Java framework and implementation of encryption, key generation, key agreement, and Message Authentication Code (MAC) algorithms. Support for encryption includes symmetric, asymmetric, block, and stream ciphers. The software also supports secure streams and sealed objects.

Java Management Extension (JMX)   A universal, open technology for system management, ready to be deployed across all industries, wherever management is or will be needed. By design, this new standard is suitable for adapting legacy systems, implementing new management solutions, and plugging in to those of the future.

Java Message Service (JMS)   An API for enterprise messaging systems. Implementations include IBM MQ Series and TIBCO Rendezvous.

Java Secure Socket Extension (JSSE)   A Java API that implements SSL and TLS protocols and supports data encryption, server authentication, message integrity, and client authentication.

Java Specification Requests (JSR)   A proposed or final specification for an addition or modification to the Java platform. At any one time numerous JSRs are moving through the review and approval process.

JAXP (Java API For XML Processing)   Defines a vendor-independent API for parsing and transforming XML documents.

JKS (Java Key Store)   A proprietary keystore format used by default in the Sun JDK's KeyStore API and `keytool` program.

JWS (Java Web Service)   A Java file that Axis will automatically compile and deploy as a Web service.

keystore   A repository of keys and certificates.

keytool   A tool for managing keys and certificates.

Lightweight Directory Access Protocol (LDAP)   A protocol for accessing online directory services.

logical structure   The logical structure of an XML document describes the organization of the concepts that define the meaning of the document.

MD5   A secure hash, or message digest, algorithm developed by Ron Rivest.

message   A WSDL element that describes a collection of parts of an input, output, or fault data flow associated with an operation. A message can be abstract or concrete, and the use is made clear only when the message is examined in the context of a binding mechanism.

Message Authentication Code (MAC)   A keyed-hash algorithm that is similar to secret-key digital signatures and is used to ensure data integrity. A hash value is calculated using a symmetric session key, which is included in the message itself, and then recalculated at the other end by the same key to verify that the data has not been altered in transit.

MessageContext   The object that is passed to each handler during the SOAP message flow through the Axis engine. The MessageContext object contains all the data needed to process the request or response SOAP message.

message-driven bean   An enterprise bean that receives and processes asynchronous messages. A message-driven bean has no

state for a specific client, but its instance variables can maintain state relating to the handling of client messages, including an open database connection and an object reference to an EJB object. A client accesses a message-driven bean by sending messages to the destination for which the message-driven bean is a message listener.

message queuing   A messaging system built around the concept of message queues. Each message is addressed to a specific queue; clients extract messages from the queue(s) established to hold their messages.

messaging   A model for distributed computing where systems interact through the passing of messages containing data.

meta-language   Can be used to define other languages. For example, XML Schema can be viewed as a language that describes the structure and datatypes of XML-based languages.

MsgDispatcher   An Axis handler that will locate and invoke a Java method. The entire body of the SOAP message is passed as a DOM object to the method.

multireference   In SOAP encoding, a value that is referred to by more than one accessor is considered multireference.

namespace   A standard that lets you specify a unique label for the set of element names defined by a particular Document Type Definition (DTD). A document using that DTD can be included in any other document without having a conflict between element names. The elements defined in your DTD are then uniquely identified so that, for example, the parser can tell when an element called <name> should be interpreted according to your DTD, rather than using the definition for an element called name in a different DTD.

Network Address Translation (NAT)   An address assignment system that allows an organization's IP network to appear from the outside to use a different IP address space than its component machines are actually using.

OASIS (Organization for the Advancement of Structured Information Standards)   See http://www.oasis-open.org/. OASIS sponsors a DTD repository at http://www.XML.org.

one-step parsing   Involves the parser generating a parse tree (typically, a DOM structure) from an XML document.

ontologies   Documents containing sets of formal definitions of relations among terms in machine readable format, usually in the form of a taxonomy of terms and a set of inference rules to make sense of the terms.

operation   A WSDL element that describes an individual method or function provided by a Web service. An operation is part of an abstract definition of a Web service interface (PortType).

peer-to-peer computing   A model of computation where nodes on the network are equal in status and can act as both clients to request information from other nodes and servers to provide that information to other nodes.

physical structure   The physical structure of an XML document describes the organization of syntax elements (elements, text, comments, and so on) in the document.

pivot point   The Axis handler in a targeted chain that is the point at which the Axis engine believes it has switched from processing the request SOAP message to processing the response SOAP message.

Port   A WSDL element indicating the endpoint address of a Web service in a communications protocol-specific fashion (for example, URL for HTTP, email address for SMTP, and so on).

PortType   A WSDL element that describes a collection of message signatures (operation elements) that define the abstract interface of the Web service.

principals   An identity assigned to a user as a result of authentication.

private key   The publicly unavailable key owned by an identity in a Public Key Cryptography system. It is used to decrypt incoming messages and sign outgoing ones.

Processing Instruction (PI)   A special directive to the applications processing XML documents. The syntax is <?PITarget ...?>. The PI target is a keyword meaningful to the processing application. Everything between the PI target and the ?> marker is considered the contents of the PI.

prolog   A section of XML documents that provides some metadata about the markup in the document such as information about the version of XML in use, information about the character encoding in use, information about the document's DTD, and any comments or processing instructions.

public key   The publicly available key in a Public Key Cryptography system, used to encrypt messages bound for its owner and to decrypt signatures made by its owner.

Public Key Infrastructure (PKI)   The architecture, organization, techniques, practices, and procedures that collectively support the implementation and operation of a certificate-based public key cryptographic system.

Publication API   A set of authenticated UDDI operations that allows organizations to publish information to the UDDI Business Registry.

publish   An operation within a service-oriented architecture, describing a contract between a service provider and a service registry. The publish operation describes the steps taken by a service provider to advertise a service description in a way that one or more service requestors can find that service description, and thereby be able understand what is required to invoke that service.

publish/subscribe messaging   A one-to-many model of messaging interaction where the sender sends a single message but copies it to multiple recipients. Also known as *topic-based messaging*.

pull parsing   Parsing mechanism in which the application always has to request the next piece of parsing information from the parser.

push parsing   Parsing mechanism in which the parser sends parsing events to the application processing an XML document.

Quality Of Service (QoS)   A general term encompassing a set of metrics relevant to a particular distributed computing scenario. Typically these include aspects of security, transaction-management, response times.

realm   A string, passed as part of an HTTP request during basic authentication, that defines a protected space. The protected resources on a server can be partitioned into a set of protected spaces, each with its own authentication scheme and/or authorization database.

reliable messaging   Process of delivering messages with various Quality of Service (QoS) options that guarantee the safe arrival of those messages at their destinations, even when machine failures occur. When reliable messaging is used, the following functionality is available: confirmation of receipt of messages, message logging and tracking, correlation of messages, retry attempts, and a choice of message delivery methods.

request message   The SOAP message that will be processed by the SOAP engine.

Resource Description Framework (RDF) An XML application that allows the description of resources as structured metadata in machine readable format, and the exchange and reuse of these resources in various and possibly unrelated applications.

response message   The response from a SOAP engine. Typically, this is generated as a result of processing a *request message*.

Remote Method Invocation over Internet Inter-ORB Protocol (RMI-IIOP) An implementation of RMI using the CORBA IIOP protocol. RMI over IIOP provides interoperability with CORBA objects implemented in any language if all the remote interfaces are originally defined as RMI interfaces.

role-based access control An access control mechanism based on *roles*: abstract logical groupings of users that are defined by a system administrator. When an application is deployed, roles are mapped to security identities, such as principals or groups, in the operational environment.

root element The first element in an XML document. The name derives from the fact that this element is the root of the element hierarchy.

Round-Robin Domain Name Service (RR-DNS) A DNS method of managing server congestion by distributing connection loads across multiple servers (containing identical content).

RPC (Remote Procedure Call) The concept of executing a function on another process or machine.

RPCDispatcher An Axis handler that will locate and invoke a Java method as a Web service. The body of the SOAP message is assumed to be an RPC call containing the method name and serialized versions of the parameters.

RSA The most widely known public key cryptographic algorithms. The security of RSA relies on the relative ease of finding large prime numbers and the comparative difficulty of factoring large integers.

SAX (Simple API For XML) Defines a simple event-based API for XML push parsing.

schema compilers Tools that analyze XML schemas and code-generate serialization and deserialization modules specific to the schemas.

Secure Socket Layer (SSL) A security protocol that ensures confidentiality and integrity of data exchanged over the Internet. The protocol allows client and server applications to communicate in such a way that third parties cannot eavesdrop or tamper with the content of the communication. Servers are always authenticated and clients are optionally authenticated.

Security Assertion Markup Language (SAML) A proposed standard that specifies a way of exchanging authentication and authorization information as an XML document.

semantic Web The evolution of the current Web, where Web information is augmented with machine-readable data about the semantics of the content, allowing automatic integration and interoperability between machines.

serialization The process of emitting XML markup from a data structure.

server-config.xml The Axis server-side configuration file.

ServiceClient An Axis Java class that is the portal through which clients will connect to the remote Web Service.

ServiceDescription   An Axis Java class that is used by the client to give the Axis engine metadata about the Web service being invoked.

service description   A unit of meta data describing the capabilities of a Web service. A service description is key to a service-oriented architecture in that it describes everything a service requestor needs to know in order to invoke a Web service. The most popular form of service description is WSDL. The W3C describes a service description stack, outlining all of the technologies associated with describing many facets of a Web service.

service implementation definition   A subset of WSDL elements focused on the actual endpoint definition of a Web service. This forms a conventional division of a WSDL document, separating the service implementation definition from service interface defintion.

service interface definition   A subset of WSDL elements focused on the reusable portions of a Web service; that is, elements that are likely to be shared between many actual Web service implementations hosted by different service providers. This forms a conventional division of a WSDL document, separating the service implementation definition from service interface defintion.

service orchestration   The act of combining two or more Web services to produce a higher level or more sophisticated Web service. Popular service orchestration techniques include IBM's WSFL and Microsoft's XLANG.

service oriented architecture (SOA)   An abstract pattern that applies to a wide variety of Web services situations. SOA defines an architecture consisting of three roles (service provider, service registry, and service requestor) that can be fulfilled or implemented by a variety of techniques. SOA also defines the contracts between these roles in terms of three operations: publish, find, and bind.

service provider   A role within a service-oriented architecture. A service provider is any business or entity that hosts one or more Web services for access by service requestors. Service providers publish service descriptions to one or more service registries and receive service invocations from one or more service requestors. Think of a service provider as a "server" in a client-server relationship with a service requestor.

service registry   A role within a service-oriented architecture. A service registry is any mechanism by which one or more service descriptions can be published by service providers and searched for or found by service requestors.

service requestor   A role within a service-oriented architecture. A service requestor is any business or entity that invokes a Web service provided by a service provider. Service requestors do find operations against one or more service registries to retrieve a service description for a Web service. Based on that service description, the service requestor invokes a Web service to fulfill some task within a business process. Think of a service requestor as a "client" in a client-server relationship with a service provider.

Session Bean   An enterprise bean that is created by a client and usually exists for the duration of a single client-server session. A Session Bean performs operations, such as calculations or accessing a database, for the client. Although a Session Bean might be transactional, it is not recoverable should a system crash occur. Session Bean objects can be either stateless or they can maintain conversational state across methods and transactions. If a Session Bean maintains state, the EJB container manages this state in any case where the object must be removed from memory. However, the Session Bean object itself must manage its own persistent data.

SGML/XML application   A term historically rooted in document-centric uses of SGML and XML. It describes the set of SGML/XML documents allowed by a schema.

SHA1 (Secure Hash Algorithm 1)   A message digest function designed by NIST and the NSA.

Simple Network Management Protocol (SNMP)   A network protocol used on the Internet to control devices. It is also used to monitor devices over a network.

Simple Object Access Protocol (SOAP) A lightweight protocol for exchange of information in a decentralized, distributed environment. It is an XML-based protocol that consists of three parts: an envelope that defines a framework for describing what is in a message and how to process it, a set of encoding rules for expressing instances of

application-defined datatypes, and a convention for representing remote procedure calls and responses. SOAP can potentially be used in combination with a variety of other protocols; however, the only bindings defined in this document describe how to use SOAP in combination with HTTP and HTTP Extension Framework (definition from `http://www.w3.org/TR/SOAP/`).

simple type   In the SOAP encoding, simple types map to the built-in XML Schema types, and types derived from them using schema extensibility.

single-reference   In the SOAP encoding, a value that is referred to by only one accessor is considered single-reference.

single sign-on   An authentication system set up such that the user has to sign-on only once to access multiple systems and applications. Possible benefits include easier access for the user and greater security (the user does not have to remember as many passwords).

skeleton   A server-side component that intermediates between the Web services middleware (such as the Axis engine) and the target Web service implementation. A skeleton will decode information sent from the service requestor and invoke the target Web service using a programming-language specific API. The skeleton also translates the response from the target Web service back into a format expected by the Web services middleware. The term *server stub* is also used as a synonym.

SMTP (Simple Message Transport Protocol)   A protocol for email.

SOAP Digital Signature   A specification describing the form and content of a SOAP 1.1 header entry carrying digital signature information.

SOAP Intermediary   A SOAP node that receives and forwards SOAP messages along the message path, acting on the messages.

software agent   For the purposes of this book, a program that assists people and acts on their behalf. Agents function by allowing people to delegate work to them.

struct   In the SOAP encoding, compound types whose parts are distinguished only by their name.

tags   Identify pieces of information in markup languages. They denote the beginning and end of elements. Elements begin with a start tag, such as <name>, and end with an end tag, such as </name>.

targeted-chain   An Axis chain that has a *pivot point* handler.

TCPMon   A proxy tool that comes with Apache Axis. It allows for the monitoring of SOAP messages over HTTP.

TCP router   A networked service that acts as a load balancing front-end to the clustered Web server. TCP request packets arrive at the public interface to the cluster where they are routed to an available processing node over the internal network connecting the router to the server nodes.

TELNET   An Internet protocol that allows you to log on to another computer on the Internet and interact with it as if you were physically present at that remote computer.

tModel   Refers to a *technology model,* a reusable abstract definition that is typically published by a standards body or an industry organization and referenced in the specification of a Web service that conforms to it.

topic-based messaging   See *publish/ subscribe messaging.*

transaction   An atomic unit of work that modifies data. A transaction encloses one or more program statements, all of which either complete or roll back. Transactions enable multiple users to access the same data concurrently.

Transaction Internet Protocol (TIP)   A simple two-phase commit protocol that specifies how different nodes agree on the outcome of a transaction; the content on which the nodes agree moves through other protocols like HTTP. TIP is currently a proposed IETF standard.

Transaction Manager   An object that provides the services and management functions required to support transaction demarcation, transactional resource management, synchronization, and transaction context propagation.

transmission primitive   A characterization of the message flow associated with an operation. There are four types of transmission primitives: request-response, one-way, solicit-response, and notification.

transport   The means through which a SOAP message is delivered to and from the SOAP processor; for example, HTTP.

Transport Layer Security protocol (TLS)   The latest version of the SSL protocol. It is an enhancement of SSL version 3.0, and is a proposed Internet Standard (see RFC2246).

transport listener   The piece of code that will wait for a SOAP request message, locate (or create) an Axis engine, and then invoke the engine with the request message.

transport sender   The piece of code that will take the response message generated by the Axis engine and send it to the appropriate target SOAP processor.

transport-specific chain   An Axis chain that is invoked based on the transport mechanism used.

Two-Phase Commit (TPC)   The process by which a relational database ensures that distributed transactions are performed in an orderly manner. In this system, transactions can be terminated by either committing them or rolling them back.

UDDI4J   A collection of Java interfaces and implementations for client access to a UDDI registry (`http://oss.software.ibm.com/developerworks/projects/uddi4j`).

UDDI Business Registry   An instance of the UDDI registry hosted at `www.uddi.org`.

UDDI Operators   Companies that run public instances of a UDDI Business Registry. Operators have signed an operator agreement that commits them, among other things, to support the UDDI API and to replicate registrations among themselves on a periodic basis.

undeploy.xml   A file used as input into the Axis AdminClient for undeploying Web resources such as handlers and chains.

Uniform Resource Identifier (URI)   The Web naming and addressing technology, consisting of strings that identify resources on the Web, such as documents, images and email addresses.

Universal Description, Discovery and Integration (UDDI)   A standards-based approach to very sophisticated service registry implementation. UDDI is also an implementation of a services registry located at `www.uddi.org`.

URL (Uniform Resource Locator)   A subset of URIs referring to Internet addresses (for example, `http://www.example.com/doc/`). URLs consist of an access protocol specifier (`http`), a host IP specifier (`www.example.com`), and optionally the path to a file or resource residing on that host (`/doc`).

URN (Uniform Resource Name)   URIs that are globally unique and persistent. They begin with the specifier `urn:`.

UUID (Universally Unique Identifier)   128-bit globally unique identifiers. They combine network card (Ethernet) addresses with a high-precision timestamp and an increment counter. For example: `2FAC1234-31F8-11B4-A222-08002B34C003`.

valid   A valid XML document is well-formed and follows the constraints of some schema.

vertical extensibility   Allows new pieces of information to be introduced in SOAP messages without breaking existing applications. This is achieved through the use of SOAP headers.

W3C (World Wide Web Consortium)
The international body that governs Internet standards. It was created in 1994 and is open to all interested organizations. Participation in the W3C allows member organizations to jointly develop protocols that promote the evolution of the Web while insuring its interoperability. The W3C holds the specifications for many of the Web technologies such as HTML, XML, and RDF.

W3C Note   A dated, public recognition of an idea, comment, or document by the W3C. Members wishing to have their ideas published at the W3C site as a Note must follow the Submission process.

W3C Working Draft   A W3C-published document that represents work in progress and a commitment by W3C to pursue work in the area focused on. A Working Draft does not imply consensus by a group or the W3C.

WDDX (Web Distributed Data Exchange)
A language- and platform-neutral XML technology for exchanging data between applications.

Web service   A platform- and implementation-independent software component that can be *described* using a service description language; *published* to a registry of services; *discovered* through a standard mechanism (at runtime or design time); *invoked* through a declared API, usually over a network; and *composed* with other services.

Web Services Deployment Descriptor (WSDD)   An XML-based file used that will be used (in future Axis releases) for deploying Web resources.

Web Services Description Language (WSDL)   A component of a service description that describes the interface definition of the Web service, details related to binding (network protocol and data encoding requirements), and the network location of the Web service. WSDL is published at `http://www.w3.org/TR/wsdl`.

Web Services Endpoint Language (WSEL)   A component of a service description that describes aspects of the Web service not directly addressed by the WSDL. These aspects are typically non-functional, not directly impacting the way the Web service invocation message must be formatted by the service requestor. Examples of non-functional properties include, privacy policy, quality of service (QoS) assertions, and so on. WSEL currently exists only as a high-level requirement as part of WSFL.

Web Services Flow Language (WSFL)   A mechanism for service orchestration based on flow composition. WSFL was published by IBM at `http://www.ibm.com/software/solutions/webservices/pdf/WSFL.pdf`.

well-formed   A well-formed XML document follows the rules of XML syntax.

X.500 distinguished name   A name by which an entity entered in an X.500 directory service is unambiguously identified.

XML digital signature   Addendum to an XML document containing information so that the authenticity of the signed document and also the identity of the signer can be verified.

XML encryption   A method for encrypting data and a specification for representing the resulting ciphertext in XML.

XML Key Management Services (XKMS)
A specification to access PKI in XML. XKMS uses the relative simplicity of XML to implement two key aspects of secure e-commerce, according to the specification's authors, Microsoft Corp. and VeriSign Inc. In the near future, the specification will be submitted to Web standards bodies for consideration as an open Internet standard. XKMS aims to simplify application building by moving digital signature handling and encryption out of the applications themselves.

XML protocol   Encompasses a set of rules and conventions for distributed computing using XML. XML protocols govern how communication happens and how data is represented in XML format on the wire. Examples of XML Protocols are WDDX, XML-RPC, and SOAP.

XML Transaction Authority Markup Language (XAML)   A set of XML-based message formats and interaction models that Web services can use to enable business transactions between multiple parties on the Internet. XAML is a vendor-neutral standard developed jointly by Bowstreet, Hewlett-Packard, IBM, Oracle, and Sun.

XML-RPC   A simple RPC mechanism that uses XML messages.

INDEX

SYMBOLS

A